PENGUIN BOOKS

THE MAKING OF MODERN RUSSIA

Lionel Kochan, who is married and has three children, was born in London in 1922 and educated at Haberdashers, Hampstead, at Corpus Christi College, Cambridge, where he was a scholar, and at the School of Slavonic and East European Studies. He took a Ph.D. at the London School of Economics. After lecturing in modern European history at the universities of Edinburgh and East Anglia, he was appointed to the Bearsted Readership in Jewish History at the University of Warwick. His works include *Russia and the Weimar Republic* (1954); *Acton on History* (1955); *The Struggle for Germany 1914–1945* (1963); *Russia in Revolution 1890–1918* (1966); *The Jew and his History* (1977); *Jews, Idols and Messiahs: The Challenge from History* (1990); and *The Jewish Renaissance and Some of its Discontents* (1992). Lionel Kochan completed his war service in the Intelligence Corps; he is very fond of chess.

John Keep was born near London in 1926 and studied Russian history at the University of London, where he took his Ph.D. in 1954. After a brief spell at the Foreign Office, he returned as Lecturer, then Reader, in Russian Studies; taught at the University of Washington; and in 1970 he was appointed Professor of Russian History at the University of Toronto, Canada. He retired in 1988 and now lives in Switzerland, where he enjoys hiking in the mountains. His works include *The Rise of Social Democracy in Russia* (1963), *The Russian Revolution: A Study in Mass Mobilization* (1976), *Soldiers of the Tsar: Army and Society in Russia, 1462–1874* (1985), *Last of the Empires: A History of the Soviet Union, 1945–91* (1995) and *Power and the People: Essays on Russian History* (1995).

The Making of Modern Russia

From Kiev Rus' to the Collapse of the Soviet Union

LIONEL KOCHAN AND JOHN KEEP

PENGUIN BOOKS

PENGUIN BOOKS

Published by the Penguin Group
Penguin Books Ltd, 27 Wrights Lane, London w8 5TZ, England
Penguin Books USA Inc., 375 Hudson Street, New York, New York 10014, USA
Penguin Books Australia Ltd, Ringwood, Victoria, Australia
Penguin Books Canada Ltd, 10 Alcorn Avenue, Toronto, Ontario, Canada M4V 3B2
Penguin Books (NZ) Ltd, 182–190 Wairau Road, Auckland 10, New Zealand

Penguin Books Ltd, Registered Offices: Harmondsworth, Middlesex, England

First published by Jonathan Cape 1962
Published in Pelican Books 1963
Second edition 1983
Reprinted in Penguin Books 1990
Third edition 1997
10 9 8 7 6 5 4 3 2 1

Set in 10/12pt Monotype Ehrhardt
Typeset by Rowland Phototypesetting Ltd, Bury St Edmunds, Suffolk
Printed in England by Clays Ltd, St Ives plc

To
JESSICA RACHEL
NATHANIEL HUGO
JULIUS MARTIN

CONTENTS

LIST OF MAPS   ix
FOREWORD TO THE THIRD EDITION   xi

1. *The Rise and Fall of Kiev Rus'*   1
2. *The Mongol Conquest and the Rise of Muscovy*   12
3. *The Formation of a National State*   20
4. *Ivan the Terrible and the Crisis of Russian Autocracy*   31
5. *The Time of Troubles*   42
6. *The Growth of Absolutism: The Early Romanovs*   55
7. *Expansion and Bureaucracy: The Age of Peter the Great*   79
8. *The Birth of Civil Society*   100
9. *Liberators and Gendarmes*   120
10. *From Reform to Assassination*   148
11. *Economic Development and Social Change in the Late Imperial Era*   176
12. *Towards the First Russian Revolution*   202
13. *Last Years of Empire*   228
14. *War and Revolution*   261
15. *Red Victory*   284
16. *Recovery and Consolidation*   313
17. *The Revolution and the World*   342
18. *Stalinism*   368
19. *The Great Patriotic War*   398
20. *Building an Empire, 1945–53*   427
21. *From Neo-Leninism to Stagnation*   453
22. *The Paradoxes of 'Mature Socialism'*   474

CONTENTS

23. *The USSR as a World Power*   494
24. *Gorbachev and After*   520

GLOSSARY   549
FURTHER READING   557
INDEX   583

LIST OF MAPS

1. Waterways of Eastern Europe   4
2. Kiev Rus' at its height, and its neighbours   13
3. The growth of Muscovy, 1300–1584   26
4. Russian westward and south-westward expansion in the reign of Catherine the Great   104
5. The Russian Empire in 1914   256
6. The Soviet Union   496

The first edition of this book, by Lionel Kochan, was published in 1962. Twenty-one years later a second revised edition appeared, with Richard Abraham as co-author. In 1994 Lionel Kochan invited John Keep, a friend and colleague, to write an up-to-date version that would take account of the considerable advances in knowledge and understanding that have taken place over the last quarter-century, while making use of the original so far as this had withstood the test of time. This new text has been vetted by the original author. The result is a cooperative endeavour that reflects the changed outlook of the mid 1990s.

The break-up of the USSR in 1991 has made it possible to view the Soviet era in historical perspective as a bygone era. In post-Soviet Russia, as in other states of the former Soviet Union, researchers have gained access to archives that were closed for many decades and have published their findings as monographs or, more usually, as articles in scholarly journals. *The Making of Modern Russia* attempts to incorporate the more important of these new facts and insights, and also to pay due heed to recent work by Western historians. In Britain and elsewhere 'sovietologists' have borrowed methodologies developed by practitioners of several disciplines, notably sociology, political science, and economics. A 'revisionist' school of interpretation has grown up which has greatly modified the earlier consensus on rural Russia under the tsarist regime, for example. Fresh light has also been cast on the phenomenon of Stalinism. There has been much progress in the study of inter-ethnic relations as well as of gender problems. Historians of foreign policy appreciate better than before the importance of Russia's relations with her Asian neighbours and are less 'Europocentric'. Much earlier writing was focused on Moscow or St Petersburg – understandable, no doubt, when dealing with a society structured on authoritarian lines, but such an approach does violence to developments in the provinces, especially those inhabited by national minority groups. On all these points we have tried to set the record straight, as well as to do justice, so far as space limitations allow, to the arts and to cultural life generally, not excluding popular culture.

Our story is brought up to the end of the Gorbachev era. Judgements on this must be provisional, and the same applies still more forcefully to the Yeltsin years, which are treated in outline here. The Russia of today has many features that were anticipated in earlier epochs of that country's tormented history. Knowledge of these parallels and continuities helps one to understand current dilemmas. There are, of course, many ways of looking at a nation's history. Our narrative is chronological, but rather like a tree with a slender trunk that gets bushier towards the top. This does not mean that we think earlier centuries any less significant than later ones: if anything, the reverse is the case. But the last two hundred years or so are better documented; they are probably of greater interest to the contemporary reader, and so deserve fuller treatment.

We would like to thank Peter Carson and Andrew Kidd, of Penguin UK, for their cooperation in making this book possible.

LK JK

CHAPTER I

The Rise and Fall of Kiev Rus'

The formative centuries of Russian history had their setting in a vast exposed plain, stretching from Eastern Europe to central Siberia. To the north and north-east, the White Sea and the Arctic Ocean formed the boundary. To the south lay the Black Sea, the Caspian, and the Caucasus mountains. The Urals are no kind of climatic or even physical barrier. Nowhere does their altitude exceed 6,000 feet. They rise from gradual foothills to a mean altitude of some 1,500 feet. Numerous valleys and passes make transit easy, both eastwards and westwards. Where does Europe end? Where does Asia begin? It is impossible to say. It is this geographical indeterminacy that helps to account for the perennial question: does Russia belong to Europe or to Asia, or does it form some complex world of its own?

The distinctive features of the plain are the uplands that form the watersheds of the area's river system. The Valdai hills, for example, some 200 miles north-west of Moscow, are nowhere more than a thousand feet above sea-level. Yet they are the source of such major rivers as the western Dvina, flowing into the Baltic; the Dnieper, flowing into the Black Sea; and the Volga, the greatest of all, which empties into the Caspian. These rivers and their tributaries linked the territory they watered to the countries beyond the seas. Portages connected one system with the next. It was at strategic points on these interlocking routes that the first Slav towns developed – Kiev, Novgorod, Polotsk, Chernigov, Smolensk. In the fifth century B.C., Herodotus already knew the Dnieper as 'the most productive river . . . in the whole world, excepting only the Nile . . . It has upon its banks the loveliest and most excellent pasturage for cattle; it contains abundance of the most delicious fish . . . the richest harvests spring up along its course and, where the ground is not sown, the heaviest crops of grass . . .'

This describes what was then 'Scythia', the fertile southern reaches of the Dnieper. Such vegetation was by no means uniform across the vast Eurasian plain through which the river slowly meandered. In the far north lay a belt of cold, barren tundra. Then comes a well-watered forest zone of enormous expanse, ill-suited to agriculture but nourishing well-nigh inexhaustible numbers of wild animals to provide food, clothing, and furs. To the south the forest gradually gives way to steppe or prairie, across which runs a belt of fertile 'black earth', which in a year with good rainfall can yield bumper crops. North and east of the Caspian, however, the soil is arid and sandy.

The ancestors of the eastern Slavs – the present-day Russians, Ukrainians, and Belarusians – inhabited an area east of the Carpathian mountains in what is now northern Ukraine. They were first stirred into movement by contact with nomadic or semi-nomadic hordes from Asia, notably the Huns in the late fourth and the Avars in the sixth century. Successive bands of warlike peoples poured westward across the steppe over the thousand years that followed the great Migration of Peoples (third to fifth centuries A.D.). Under this external pressure some Slav groups moved down into the Balkans. Meanwhile others, in less spectacular fashion, gradually spread eastward as far as the Don and northward to the rivers that flow into the eastern Baltic. By the ninth century they were settling in the Volga–Oka basin, the region where Moscow now stands. In this northern forest zone the newcomers intermingled with the aboriginal inhabitants, who were mostly of Finno-Ugrian or Baltic stock. The Slavs seem to have had a higher rate of reproduction, which would explain how they managed to assimilate their neighbours in an apparently peaceful manner. Throughout the Eurasian plain ethnic intermingling was the rule, not the exception.

The most dynamic eastern Slav groups were those living in the area of the middle Dnieper, on the border between forest and steppe, with its relatively rich soil. At first the principal crops were millet and barley; wheat and rye followed later. When clearing the virgin forest the settlers would work the land until it was exhausted and then move on, but the sowing of winter rye required a primitive form of crop rotation. Cattle, pigs, and sheep were raised. The rivers were a plentiful source of fish, while the woods yielded fruit, mushrooms, berries, nuts, and honey. People lived in small rectangular huts of wood and earth, dug deep into the soil as a protection against the long, cold winters. These huts were assembled to form hamlets, usually along the bank of a river. The inhabitants of these little communities were as often as not linked by kinship ties, but the basic social unit was the individual household, or *dvor*.

Apart from working the land, fishing and so on, members of the household, male and female, met their needs by engaging in a variety of handicrafts such as woodworking, potting or weaving. For many centuries the only specialized artisan was the smith, with his primitive forge. Ceramic ware was likewise simple – the potter's wheel was introduced only in the ninth century – and all but bereft of decoration. Trade at first took the form of tribute. It was largely in foreign hands: Khazars and Jews in the south, 'Varangian' Norsemen in the north.

The Khazars, a people of Turkic origin whose élite became converted to Judaism, controlled the southern steppe lands from the eighth to the mid tenth century. They imposed tribute on some of their Slavic neighbours, but their rule seems to have been relatively mild. Their merchants maintained contact with the wealthy Arab lands beyond the Caspian Sea and the Caucasus. Silver, textiles, and metals were imported in exchange for slaves, furs, and other products of the northern forests. Archaeologists have found hoards of Arab coins dating from the 780s onward at many sites along the Volga route, which extended from the Caspian all the way to the Baltic. As a channel of commerce and communication this river network was initially much more important than the better-known 'way from the Varangians to the Greeks'. The latter led from the Baltic shores via the western Dvina or the Volkhov to the Dnieper, and thence down to the Black Sea and along its western shore to Constantinople, capital of the mighty Byzantine empire.

This communication route was developed in the main by Norse warrior traders from eastern Scandinavia, who treated the inhabitants of the east European plain in much the same fashion as their Viking cousins treated the peoples of the British Isles, France, and the western Mediterranean. They set up forts at strategic points along the route, some of which eventually became important towns. They levied tribute on the natives, some of whom learned to join in this profitable activity. The proceeds could be exchanged or sold in the commercial centres situated at one end or the other of the water route. It was in this way that there came into being, in the ninth century, the Norse–Slav realm known to contemporaries as 'Rhos' or 'Rus''.

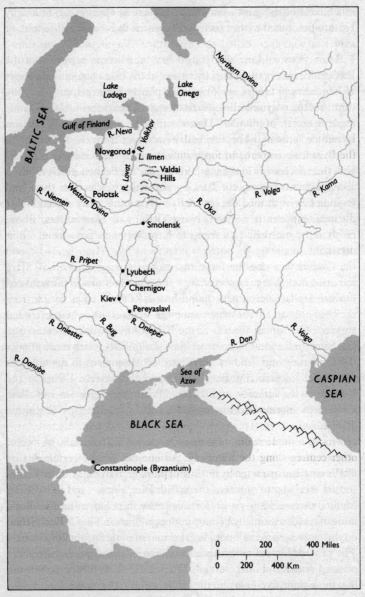

MAP 1. *Waterways of Eastern Europe*

The term Rus', first used of the Norsemen themselves, gradually came to be applied to the country over which they ruled and so to their subjects, who then called the Norsemen 'Varangians'. The future Russia first enters European history in 839, when some followers of a Rus' prince (*kagan*) appeared by chance at the court of Louis the Pious at Ingelheim in Germany. They were clearly Scandinavians. So, too, were the Rus' warriors who in 860 descended upon a terrified Constantinople in search of plunder. This was the first of several such raids on Byzantine territory. The new barbarian threat from the far north led the Byzantine emperor to forge alliances with the Khazars, and later with their successors in the southern steppe, the Pechenegs. Byzantium also sought to civilize the Rus' by regulating trade with them and sending Christian missionaries. A Rus'-Byzantine treaty signed in 911 distinguishes clearly between Norse (Rus') and Slav traders, whose rights and duties while wintering in Constantinople are spelled out in detail.

It was only a question of time before the more numerous Slavs absorbed their Varangian overlords. This gradual process is reflected in the legendary account of the origins of Rus' contained in *The Tale of Bygone Years*, a chronicle compiled in Kiev under ecclesiastical auspices early in the twelfth century. According to this story, in 862 the Slavs living near Novgorod invited the Varangians to rule over them because 'our land is great and rich but there is no order in it'. Actually Rurik (Hrørikr), a Varangian chieftain, had probably established his authority in the Lake Ilmen area earlier than the date given in the chronicle. This goes on to state that in 882 one of Rurik's descendants, Oleg (Helgi), conquered Kiev and so united the two centres in a single realm, placing members of his retinue in charge of other centres along the waterway. All one can say for certain is that the Varangians, attracted by the lure of plunder in Byzantium, gradually shifted their centre of interest from north to south – and in so doing exposed themselves to rapid assimilation by their Slav subjects. Oleg's immediate successors, Igor (Ingvair, d. 945/6) and his wife Olga (Helga, d. 969) were both Scandinavians, whereas their son Svyatoslav (r. 962–972/3) bore a Slav name. Still more important was the fact that members of the princely retinue, warriors who doubled as tribute collectors, became progressively slavicized.

Olga, who acted as regent after her husband's death until 962, when

5

Svyatoslav came of age, was evidently an energetic woman who did a lot to consolidate the Rurikid dynasty's power, notably by suppressing in cruel fashion a rebellious tribe in the interior, the Derevlyane, and regulating the Kievan realm's rudimentary administration. She visited Constantinople and was the first Rus' ruler to be baptized. Wisely, she refrained from forcing the new religion on her pagan subjects and sought to offset the influence of Orthodox Byzantium by inviting the Holy Roman Emperor to send Catholic missionaries to Rus' as well.

Under Svyatoslav a pagan reaction set in. Despite his Slavic name he behaved like a true Viking, engaging in continual warfare. He moved first against the Khazars, destroying their two main cities, Sarkel on the Don and Itil on the Volga, and mounted raids on the Crimea and areas in the northern Caucasus. This had the unintended result of bringing Rus' into confrontation with a more dangerous foe to the south, the Pechenegs. Svyatoslav then twice attacked the Bulgarian kingdom on the Danube. At first his advance met with Byzantine support, but a dispute over distribution of the booty led to a conflict that had fatal consequences for Svyatoslav. When returning to Kiev, his warriors were attacked at the Dnieper rapids by Pechenegs, who had evidently been tipped off by Constantinople, and overwhelmed. Svyatoslav's skull, it is said, was made into a drinking cup for a Pecheneg prince. More than seven centuries would pass before Russian soldiers again entered the Balkans.

The next half-century saw the emergence of Kiev Rus' as an acknowledged European power and the efflorescence of its culture. This was owed in large part to the adoption by Grand Prince Vladimir of Christianity, in its Eastern Orthodox form, as the country's official religion in 988/9. The population was baptized *en masse*, but conversion did not put a stop to animistic beliefs and traditions, which lived on surreptitiously for centuries. The choice of Orthodoxy, though favoured by Kiev's trade links with Byzantium, was not historically predetermined. The chronicle tale that emissaries were sent out from Kiev to report on the merits of Eastern and Western (Catholic) Christianity, Islam and Judaism reflects the historical reality that the country was exposed to diverse cultural influences from neighbouring lands. In return for accepting Orthodoxy, Vladimir secured political concessions from Byzantium, notably the hand in marriage of the emperor's sister, and Rus' never became a Byzantine dependency.

The Greek Orthodox clergy who came to propagate the gospel accepted the use of a language close to the vernacular, Church Slavonic, in the liturgy. This was something of a mixed blessing: it made the new faith more accessible, but prevented Rus' from sharing in the culture of lands to the west, based as this was on classical learning transmitted in Greek or Latin. For several centuries translations would be confined to ecclesiastical works. This was an activity carried on in the country's many monasteries, where local chronicles were also compiled. Monks and nuns engaged in charitable work and there was even some schooling. However, their achievements in the social and cultural fields were necessarily modest compared with those of the Catholic orders in medieval Western Europe, for they lacked the resources – and perhaps also the spiritual drive. For the Orthodox professed a faith that set greater store by piety than knowledge. Centred on the world beyond, on God's ineffable Holy Wisdom, it praised martyrdom and self-sacrifice in the divine cause but remained largely aloof from mundane secular concerns. The Church did, however, back the Kievan grand princes' efforts to build national unity and in return received the secular authorities' support in bolstering its own position. The relationship was somewhat equivocal, and eventually the balance would tip strongly towards paramountcy of the state.

The Church's influence was made manifest in ecclesiastical architecture, music (choral singing), and art: fine frescos and mosaics, iconostases abounding in representations of sacred figures, liturgical vessels, episcopal robes, and the like. Many of these artefacts were the work of Greek masters, who taught their skills to native artisans. The intellectual and moral impact of the conversion should not, however, be minimized. It gave believers an awareness that they were part of a vast Christian universe (*oikoumene*) and a sense of historical context that the old animistic religion had lacked. It helped to civilize people's conduct in the family and in society at large. Beyond that it shaped believers' self-identity. For centuries to come, until the age of modern nationalism, the common people of Rus' would define themselves as Orthodox.

Internationally, the country was little affected by the schism of 1054 between Byzantium and Rome, occasioned by the western (Latin) doctrine of papal supremacy. Nothing shows more clearly Kiev's high standing in Europe than the marriage alliances concluded by Vladimir's

7

successor, Yaroslav the Wise (r. 1019–54), and members of his family. He himself married a daughter of the Swedish king; his sons had German and Polish wives; and three daughters married the rulers of Hungary, Norway, and France. Anna, consort of the French king Henri I, was able to sign her name – whereas her husband was illiterate.

Population growth and political stabilization encouraged the development of agriculture, which was the source of most inhabitants' livelihood, especially in the southern parts of the realm. Yields remained low and uncertain. Because land was so plentiful, farmers lacked the incentive to improve their agricultural methods and to raise productivity. To the north, where the terrain was swampy and wooded, the cultivation of cereal crops was less important than livestock raising, and more particularly hunting and trapping fur-bearing animals: the sable, beaver, marten, red and black fox. Squirrel skins were dealt in by the tens of thousand and were used as small change; larger sums were exchanged in silver coins, some of them minted in Kiev.

This was the paramount town and the site of the grand prince's residence. Yaroslav sought to make it a Slav version of Constantinople, and it did indeed become a showpiece of the medieval world. In 1018 a Western writer claimed that the city had no fewer than 400 churches, a figure that probably included the little towers on the roofs of secular buildings. Kiev was surrounded by defensive walls, which were progressively extended as the city grew in size. It contained eight great market places attended by merchants from all the lands with which Rus' traded, from Scandinavia and Germany to Byzantium and the countries of the Orient. Other towns, like Novgorod or Smolensk, were less splendid, but in Novgorod archaeologists have discovered hundreds of birch-bark documents preserved in the muddy soil which show that literacy was more widespread than used to be thought. Many of them relate to commercial transactions or craft activities. Artisans were becoming more specialized: masons, bridge-builders, joiners, and the like, as well as metalworkers and those who processed leather or coarse textiles.

Many of these craftsmen worked for the local prince or members of his retinue, who needed arms, armour, and equipment for their almost continuous military service. Only slowly did the warrior élite turn to landowning as a source of revenue; they were either granted estates by the prince or else simply took what they wanted by force, imposing their will on the local population. There is evidence of such estates from the twelfth century onward. They were not dominant – more of them belonged to monasteries than to lay lords – and we should not make the common mistake of calling early Rus' society 'feudal'.

The bulk of the rural population consisted of *smerdi*: more or less free farmers with their own homestead, animals, and land, who might or might not belong to a rural community. They were their own masters to the extent of being able to bequeath property, almost without qualification, and in principle paid tax only to the prince according to the extent of their holdings. In practice matters might be more complex. Crop failure, warfare, or princely exactions might cause free home-steaders to fall into dependence on more prosperous or fortunate neighbours, who might well extend them a loan of seed to tide them over, which they would pledge themselves to work off within a given period. The *Russkaya pravda* ('Russian Justice'), the eleventh-century law code that is our chief source of information on social relations at this time, refers to several such groups of semi-dependent people. The *zakupi*, for instance, were landless peasants whose existence depended on the labour they performed for others. They had no tools of their own but used those of their masters. They did, however, possess independent households and theoretically their dependence ceased as soon as they had discharged their debt. Beneath them were the slaves, or *kholopy*, who generally performed menial jobs in an élite household.

With Yaroslav's death in 1054 the decay of Kiev Rus' set in at an increasing rate. Weaknesses in this first Russian state became all too obvious. Thus, its unity and integrity were endangered by the system of rule that Yaroslav enjoined on his deathbed. In principle, all his heirs – and he had five sons and a grandson – undertook to rule Russia collectively. The eldest heir ascended the throne of Kiev, receiving the title of grand prince. His brothers assumed rule over the lesser towns and adjacent territories, called apanages, depending on their position in the family hierarchy; the youngest brother, for example, received the smallest town. But this apportionment was in no wise final. When the grand prince of Kiev died, the throne was assumed by his next surviving brother, and this in turn led to a general 'moving up' among all the members of the ruling dynasty. This system inevitably became a source of dissension among the princes and their families. In 1097 a conference of princes at Lyubech attempted to give some order to the system of succession, but no lasting result was achieved. By about 1100 there were some twelve separate principalities on the territory of Kiev Rus', all virtually unconnected by any central power.

These internecine feuds naturally left the country less fitted than ever for self-defence against the latest wave of barbarian nomads from the East – the Cumans or Polovtsy. Their raids and depredations, not only on the trading routes but also against villages and homesteads, led to the increasing depopulation of the Dnieper basin. From the Smolensk region, for example, in 1160, Cuman raiders are said to have carried off into slavery some 10,000 Russians.

The Crusades were a second external factor tending to undermine Kiev's economic existence. The development of the Mediterranean as a trading highway to the Orient inevitably diminished the importance of Kiev and the Black Sea route to Byzantium and beyond. What Venice and Genoa won, Kiev lost. The capture of Constantinople during the fourth Crusade in 1203–4, expressly at Venetian instigation, was a powerful blow to Kiev's foreign trade.

In the meantime, other enemies were appearing in the north-west – the Teutonic Knights, the Lithuanians, and Swedes. From the south-west came the Hungarians, pressing eastwards. To the *smerd* threatened with enserfment, to the free population exposed to wholesale kidnapping, to the traders with their livelihood menaced, the response to deteriorating conditions was flight. One route led south-westwards to Galicia, but in the main the route led north-eastwards, from the Dnieper basin to the region of the upper Volga basin, and the Oka, where new centres of Russian life began to form, based on the natural economy of an environment hitherto peopled by the pagan Slavic and Finnish tribes of the northern forests.

The transfer of power to the north-east was dramatically illuminated in 1169. In that year a coalition of twelve princes under Andrey Bogolyubsky sacked Kiev; and Andrey removed the capital of Rus' to the township of Vladimir on the Klyazma river, in his native principality of Rostov-Suzdal'. But Vladimir was no more the capital of a united country than Kiev had been. When the Mongols and Tatars invaded Rus' in the last thrust westwards of the Eurasian nomads – successors to the Scythians, Huns, Avars, and Cumans – they found a dismembered country before them. Their conquest of 1237–40 decisively broke Slav contact with Europe, or at least Western Europe, and turned the country eastwards. The Dnieper basin was replaced by the more remote region of the Oka and the Volga as the dominant locale of Russian history. It was in this area under the aegis of the Tatars that the small principality of Moscow asserted its position as nucleus of the future Russia.

CHAPTER 2

The Mongol Conquest and the Rise of Muscovy

It was in 1223 that the Mongols first swept into Rus'. By 1240 they had conquered in two major invasions all the Slav principalities, and in 1242 they established their headquarters at Sarai, on the lower Volga. Here the Kipchak, or 'Golden' Horde, as it was called, held sway for two centuries or so over the steppe lands once occupied by the Khazars. Most of its subjects were nomadic cattle-raisers, but a minority of them settled down to agricultural and commercial pursuits. Clan rivalries encouraged retention of a warlike lifestyle, but this did not prevent the spread of an Islamic culture of considerable sophistication. The Horde won a measure of autonomy from the 'Great Khan' in distant Mongolia and the Mongol elements in its social élite were soon absorbed in the mainly Tatar local population.

All the eastern Slavs experienced Tatar domination, but in unequal measure. To the west, along the old waterway from the Dvina to the Dnieper, it lasted for no more than a century or so, as the local population came under the rule of Lithuanian (and eventually, in some cases, Polish) overlords. Although they remained Orthodox in religion, they were exposed to Catholic and other 'Latin' cultural influences. The social structure and institutional arrangements here became more complex, incorporating elements of Western feudalism. This encouraged the growth of a sense of separate ethnic identity, the basis of subsequent Ukrainian and Belarusian nationhood. Eastern Slavs consti tuted a majority of the population in the grand principality of Lithuania, whose territory for a time extended south as far as the steppes north of the Black Sea. Linked from 1382 onwards in a dynastic union with Poland, Lithuania was one of two major contenders for supremacy over all the eastern Slav lands.

Its chief rival was the grand principality of Muscovy, an inland realm centred on Moscow, whose influence was predominant in the forest zone from Novgorod in the north to Ryazan' in the south. Its base lay

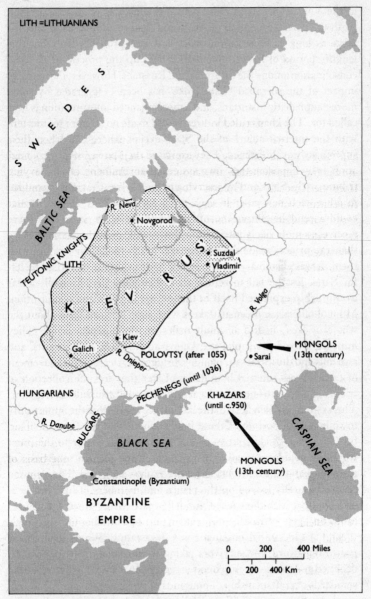

MAP 2. *Kiev Rus' at its height, and its neighbours*

in the Volga–Oka basin. The petty principalities of this vast region (with the partial exception of Novgorod) had to endure Tatar rule for twice as long as those to the west, and it is probably true that this lengthy period of foreign dominance held up the process of national consolidation among the future 'Great' Russians. However, the negative impact of the so-called 'Tatar yoke' has been exaggerated by some more nationalistic historians, and a more nuanced interpretation is now called for. The khans ruled indirectly and made no attempt to interfere with the internal affairs of the Slavs except where and when their supremacy was threatened. They exercised their power, not by colonization or by imposing their own system of government, but by levying tribute on the Slavs and by reserving to themselves the right to confirm in office each new ruler in each of the principalities. Before a ruler could ascend his throne he often had to travel to Sarai, and there receive, or more likely intrigue for, his *yarlyk*, or authorization. More than 130 princes made this pilgrimage. Many took their families with them. It was customary for the prince to draw up his will when he left for Sarai, lest he fail to return alive. Economically, Mongol–Tatar overlordship expressed itself in the levying of taxes and conscription. Mongol officials and census-takers were soon at work throughout the whole of Rus', listing all adult males on their paper scrolls. They imposed a fixed per capita tax, known to Russians as *dan'* (gift), and also tolls and duties on salt, ploughs, bridges, ferries, and the movement of cattle across internal boundaries. Later they left the collection of tribute and taxes to one of the local princes, usually the ruler of Moscow. This system was beneficial to the latter since it gave him the opportunity to siphon off a portion of these funds, whether in the form of silver, furs, or other goods, and so to build up his own power to the point where he could eventually challenge the hated foreign overlord. On the other hand, it led to tension between rulers and ruled. The common people naturally looked on the prince and members of his retinue as collaborators with the wicked 'infidel' – particularly when the princes called on Tatar warrior bands for aid in putting down popular uprisings.

The Tatars' initial onslaught was devastating. Whole towns were put to the sword, the survivors taking to the woods. The population declined and there was an economic regression, evident in deteriorating standards of craftsmanship. Thousands of artisans were carried off into captivity. Subsequently Tatar raiding parties launched many destructive attacks on principalities whose rulers they considered disobedient. Yet as well as warfare there was a certain amount of political interaction (and initially even intermarriage!) at the élite level. Moreover, the Orthodox Church benefited from the religious tolerance practised by the Mongols, a practice which the Tatar 'Golden Horde' continued even after it became Islamic. This protection allowed the monasteries to build up their economic power. It was now that the Church struck root in the consciousness of ordinary believers. Although clergy had to pray for the health of the khan, they managed to keep Christian traditions alive and on occasion stiffened the princes' resolve to cooperate with the aim of achieving emancipation from rule by the 'infidel'. Some principalities, notably Moscow, profited from the influx of refugees from more exposed areas, and by the mid fourteenth century, despite the ravages of the 'black death', the population is believed to have begun to recover. Russian merchants were able to ply the Volga route to eastern markets. Some transit trade was carried on with the Baltic lands through Novgorod, where the impact of Tatar rule was episodic.

A few Tatar words entered the Russian language. They mostly had to do with administrative or fiscal matters (e.g. 'treasury', 'toll'), where the overlords' influence was most marked. Likewise Russian cavalrymen wore Tatar garb and tried to emulate their famous tactical skills. But in general there was little direct borrowing, for the gulf between the two cultures was too wide. The Tatar impact on the history of the north-eastern Russian lands was chiefly indirect. Their rule caused Muscovy's leaders to look eastwards and weakened their links with the rest of Europe, and even with their cousins under Lithuanian rule. To the south, churchmen maintained contact with their superiors in Constantinople, and during the fourteenth century two Orthodox realms in the Balkans, Bulgaria and Serbia, were a source of fresh cultural influences with a faintly humanistic tinge, manifest in the striking icons of Andrey Rublev (c. 1360–1430). But the consolidation of Ottoman Turkish power in the Balkans, climaxing in the capture of Constantinople in 1453, diminished the volume of traffic along this channel to the outside world and enhanced Muscovy's relative isolation. Indeed, it created a new situation since Muscovite Russia was now the sole surviving Orthodox Christian realm.

By comparison with Renaissance Europe, the Russian lands were culturally backward; contemporaries in the West had barely heard of their existence. The 'Tatar yoke' was partly responsible for this situation, but there is no evidence that the Russian princes took from the Tatars their ideas on government. Autocracy and serfdom were autochthonous developments, which took place largely after Tatar rule had been cast off. They were necessitated basically by the problem of building a viable state order in highly unpropitious circumstances, in lands without clearly marked borders, where the needs of defence were paramount and the population was constantly tempted to escape the grasp of authority by fleeing into the wilderness. Muscovy's imperial ideology and spirit of exclusiveness owed far more to Byzantine precedents than they did to the Mongol–Tatar model.

It took more than two centuries before the insignificant principality of Moscow won undisputed supremacy over the other principalities of the north-east and could lay claim to have inherited the Mongol–Tatar legacy. The chronicles first mention Moscow in 1147. It was then nothing more than a village domain belonging to the prince of Rostov-Suzdal', and evidently a defence outpost against the south. In 1237 it was sacked by the Mongols and razed to the ground. In 1263 it re-enters history as the permanent capital of a minor principality ruled by Daniel, the youngest son of Alexander Nevsky, conqueror of the Swedes and Livonian Knights. ('Nevsky' is derived from 'Neva', the name of the river on which St Petersburg stands, the scene of Alexander's victory over the Swedes in 1240.)

What was it that made Moscow the nucleus of a national Russian state? There was the geographical factor, as in the case of Kiev. Moscow, situated on the river of the same name, enjoyed a sheltered position that was of inestimable advantage in the thirteenth and fourteenth centuries. At a time when the west and south-west were harassed by an expanding Lithuania which eventually reached the Black Sea, when the trans-Volgan territories were the prey of freebooters from Novgorod, barely distinguishable from pirates, and when the other outlying territories of Rus' to the south and east were the repeated victims of Tatar raids, the site of Moscow offered shelter and protection. No serious attack was made on it in the century and a quarter that separated Tatar conquest in 1238 from a Lithuanian foray of 1368.

Moscow also drew strength from its position in the Russian Mesopotamia, the area bounded by the upper Volga and the Oka. The axis of the future Muscovy was to be the Baltic–Volga–Caspian trade route. But before this stage was reached, Moscow already enjoyed a geo-commercial location on which, fundamentally, its expansion depended. Lying as it did on the Moskva river, flowing from north-west to south-east, and linking the system of the middle Oka with the system of the upper Volga, the principality, and later grand duchy, was thus connected with all the important river systems of northern and western Russia. Through a complex of portages and tributaries Moscow had access to the Volga on the north, east, and south, and to the Dnieper and western Dvina on the west. Farther afield, waterways led to the Baltic and the Black Sea. Moscow was thus situated at the centre of two supremely important trade routes and waterways crossing Rus' from north to south and from west to east – the Baltic–Caspian and the western Dvina–Volga.

Many of Moscow's geographical advantages were shared by Tver' to the north-west, and the fourteenth century opened with a bitter contest between the princes of the two lands. Moscow was favoured by political factors of crucial importance: both Tatar khans and Orthodox Church leaders supported Moscow as the lesser evil. As the increasingly desperate Tverians turned to the growing power of Lithuania for support, this motivation was reinforced. The Metropolitans of the Orthodox Church feared their Tatar overlords less than they feared the Catholics to the west, and from 1326 they began to reside in Moscow. The pious saw it as a divinely protected city and pilgrims came in droves. Thanks to the Church's support, the Muscovite rulers were able to reduce the debilitating effects of the apanage system and to adopt, alone in medieval Russia, something approaching primogeniture.

In seeking to extend their rule, a variety of methods was practised, few of them pretty. There was purchase, outright conquest, acquisition by diplomatic means, and the conclusion of treaties with petty prince-lings that left them masters in their domain but bound to Moscow by ties of service. Finally, there was colonization. The various processes were all in motion at the very beginning of the fourteenth century. When Daniel, the first ruler of Moscow, died in 1303 he was able to bequeath to his successor a principality that had doubled its area in a single reign. From that point, by and large, the history of Moscow shows a record of steady expansion. Among the earliest acquisitions were Mozhaisk and Kolomna. The first lay at the source of the Moskva river, the second at its junction with the Oka. The two towns thus gave control of the whole course of the river. Success here opened the way to further penetration northwards. Ivan Kalita (= 'money bags'), who ruled Moscow from 1325 to 1341, bought control of the important trans-Volgan territories of Uglich, Beloozero, and Galich. These were not immediately incorporated in his domains, but their rulers thereafter retained their positions by the grace of the prince of Moscow, who was invested by the Tatars with the dignity of grand prince of Vladimir.

Ivan strengthened this dependence by his policy of ransoming Slav prisoners from the Mongols and subsidizing their settlement on his newly dominated territory. In the second half of the fourteenth century and the first half of the fifteenth, Muscovy completed its most impressive phase of expansion. The seizure of Vladimir and Starodub gave command of the Klyazma river, and the gradual erosion of the independence of Nizhniy Novgorod and of other eastern principalities set Muscovy athwart the Volga itself. Nizhniy Novgorod, the gateway to the lower Volga, brought Moscow within striking distance of the road to Asia, with its particular prize the silk trade of the East.

The slow emergence of Muscovy as the paramount Slav principality was bound to influence the Slav–Mongol relationship. Concerned at the rise of Lithuania, the Mongols fostered the growth of the power destined to eclipse them. No Slav prince was more assiduous in courting the reigning khan, or more humble in his diplomacy, than the ruler of Muscovy. Lavish gifts could accomplish much at Sarai, and this weakness the relatively wealthy rulers of Moscow were well fitted to exploit. They also derived much of their influence at Sarai from the share they took in crushing movements hostile to the Mongols among the lesser Slav principalities.

It was through such devious methods that, as early as the reign of Ivan Kalita, Muscovy acquired the undignified but influential right of collecting the taxes imposed by the Mongols on the Slavs. This gave further pressure to Muscovy's financial squeeze. Moreover, in 1353 the principality became acknowledged by the Tatars as the judicial authority over the other princes of Rus'. This gradual accretion of strength and influence resulted, in 1380, in the first serious Slav attempt to cast off Mongol rule. At the field of Kulikovo near the Don a coalition of princes from northern Rus' led by Dmitriy Donskoy of Muscovy, fought and won a pitched battle against the overlord. But, though the victory was striking, it was in no way conclusive. Barely two years later the Mongols returned in force and utterly devastated Moscow. Vladimir, Mozhaisk, and other towns were similarly laid waste. In 1408 a renewed Tatar invasion led to further widespread ravages in Nizhniy Novgorod and elsewhere. In the second quarter of the fifteenth century a vicious civil war broke out within the ruling family. The feud was settled by Tatar intervention. But by this time, fortunately for Moscow, the Golden Horde was itself riven by disaffection. The leaders of powerful clans settled around Kazan', on the middle Volga, as well as those of the Crimea, began to assert their claims to autonomy. The balance of power was shifting decisively in Muscovy's favour. It was only a question of time before the grand prince of Moscow could take the decisive step of ceasing to pay the humiliating annual tribute to the khan, and so achieve independence.

CHAPTER 3

The Formation of a National State

Ivan III, also known as Ivan the Great, ruled Muscovy from 1462 to 1505. For the first time a clear personality emerges from the ruck of warring princes and grand dukes. Contarini, a Venetian traveller, describes Ivan in a report of 1476 as tall, lean, and handsome. Some forty years later another visitor to Moscow, Baron Herberstein, an envoy of the Holy Roman Emperor, was told that Ivan's mere appearance was enough to send into a swoon any woman who encountered him unprepared. If, writes Herberstein, drunkenness caused him to fall asleep during a banquet – and this was not infrequent – his guests would await in fear and trembling his return to consciousness, when he would resume his jocularity.

In political and military matters Ivan avoided frontal combats. His father had blinded one of his rivals for the throne and had been blinded in his turn. Ivan had learnt to achieve his aims through calculated and devious diplomacy. Force he used as a last resort.

As the creator of a centralized state, Ivan has been well compared with his contemporary, Louis XI of France. His reign was without doubt a watershed in the development of the future Russian state. For all the conquests of his forerunners, he found Muscovy flanked to the north by the great commercial republic of Novgorod, which dominated a vast area from the Gulf of Finland to the Urals. To the west stretched the Polish–Lithuanian realm, lying along the western Dvina and the Dnieper. South of Tula and Ryazan' lay a vast expanse of steppe-land, as far as the Black Sea and the Caspian, dominated by the Tatars of the Crimea and the 'Great Horde' on the lower Volga. To the east, the Tatar khanate of Kazan' stood athwart the middle Volga.

Apart from the absorption of the lesser Slav principalities such as Yaroslavl', Tver', Rostov, and Ryazan', it was no longer possible for Muscovy to advance farther without meeting head-on opposition from powerful empires. It is a measure of Ivan's success that by the end of his reign the Tatars were no longer a threat. They themselves, on the contrary, were now on the defensive. Novgorod and the other eastern Slav principalities had lost their independence to Muscovy, and battle had been joined with Lithuania and its ally, the Teutonic Order in the Baltic, for expansion to the west.

Internally also, the growth of absolutism with a pan-Russian ideology, and the emergence of a class of military serving landowners, mark the second half of the fifteenth century as a turning-point in Muscovy's political and economic development. When Ivan the Great came to power four main national tasks stretched before him: to elevate the power of the grand prince over his fraternal rivals and their apanages; to complete the 'ingathering' of the Slav lands, including Novgorod, under the standard of Muscovy; to win back from Lithuania the south-western lands that had once been part of Kiev Rus'; and to complete the emancipation from the Tatars.

Ivan was unremitting in his attacks on the power and privilege of his brothers and the other apanage princes. In 1472, he unceremoniously annexed the apanage of a brother who had died intestate. When his remaining brothers predictably objected he put them in their place, though he left them rope enough to hang themselves. In 1486, he annexed the largest of the apanages not owned by a brother. By the end of his reign, the capacity of the apanage system to disrupt the Russian state was radically reduced.

In dealing with the independent Russian principalities, Ivan strode ahead along the same path that had been marked out since the early years of the fourteenth century. In 1463 the princes of Yaroslavl' submitted to Muscovy, lost their independence, and accepted service with Ivan. In 1472 it was the turn of Perm', with its lands on both sides of the Kama river. Two years later the Rostov princes sold what remained of their territory to Moscow. Tver', at one time the most hostile to Moscow of all the Slav groupings, was undermined from within by the defection of its boyars to Moscow. An alliance between Tver' and Lithuania brought the conflict to a head, and in 1485 the town of Tver' fell without a blow to Ivan's encircling army. The ruler fled to Lithuania and Galicia, never to reappear on Muscovite soil. This same process was continued by Ivan's successor, with the absorption of Pskov and Ryazan'.

Of all the areas annexed by Ivan, the most important was Novgorod.

Novgorod was a thriving trading centre with access to the Baltic. It was also an ideological adversary: a commonwealth in which the conflicting interests of church, aristocracy, and artisans found expression in republican institutions. Its symbol was the bell that summoned its citizens to free discussion in their own assembly. Such a state was increasingly anomalous in a Russia torn between aristocratic Lithuania and the Muscovite grand princes obsessed with the 'patrimony of Yaroslav'. The struggle for Novgorod reached its culmination in Ivan III's reign. It had long been in the making. Repeated efforts to dominate Novgorod had been made over the past century and a half by the Muscovite princes. As far back as the days of Ivan Kalita, Novgorod had been forced to pay tribute to her south-eastern neighbour and to accept its princes as governors (with limited rights to intervene in the republic's internal affairs). But whereas the stakes had originally been river routes and furs, they were raised, when Lithuania emerged as Muscovy's principal rival, to nothing less than the orientation that all the Russian lands would take: to the west or to the east.

The fact is that the Novgorod policy of manoeuvring between her two powerful neighbours could succeed only as long as the latter were in relative equilibrium. This was threatened by the growing power of Muscovy and by a crisis in the Orthodox Church. The decline of Byzantium had reached such proportions by the early fifteenth century that the Emperor John VIII and many of the leading clergy, including the Metropolitan of Moscow, decided that only with the help of the West could the Orthodox world be saved from the Turks. At the Council of Florence in 1437–9, the Orthodox leaders submitted to the Pope. The Orthodox hierarchy in Lithuania accepted this union and aligned itself with the Catholic Church in Poland, but in Moscow the union was violently rejected. Metropolitan Isidore was ejected from his seat and the Russian Orthodox Church ceased to accept instruction from Byzantium. Both sides sought to obtain the adherence of Novgorod to their view of the split.

In the competition with Moscow, Novgorod was hopelessly handicapped by its vulnerability to economic blockade, its outmoded military system, and its open politics. From time to time power passed to an aristocratic faction that sought to use its ties with Lithuania to restore the republic's former freedom of action.

Early in 1471 the pro-Lithuanian party inside the city sought an agreement with Casimir IV, King of Poland and Grand Prince of Lithuania. Casimir was to respect the Orthodox Church and to support Novgorod against Moscow. The treaty would also entitle Casimir to install a Polish governor in Novgorod on condition that no change be made in the constitution. In May 1471 Ivan and his council of war decided to take up the challenge. Novgorod's new alliance enabled him to proclaim a religious war, a sort of crusade. The campaign took in not only Novgorod proper but also the far north. By August 1471 all resistance was over. An unexpectedly hot summer, which dried up the intervening swamps, helped to accelerate victory – as did the inefficient resistance put up by the Novgorodians. Demoralized by famine and inflation, many could see no point in fighting a hopeless war against the Grand Prince of Muscovy. In the battle along the river Shelon, for example, a Muscovite force of some 4,000 or 5,000 men overcame a Novgorod force many times stronger in number.

The peace that Ivan imposed was comparatively mild. He cancelled the treaty with Lithuania; an indemnity of 15,000 roubles was exacted; he forced Novgorod to yield up to Muscovy certain of its colonies and also to recognize his, Ivan's, sovereignty. This was not quite the end of Novgorod's independence, but there remained little left to lose. The end was a protracted affair and came after almost two decades of anti-Moscow riots and tumults inside the city and half-hearted attempts to reassert a claim to independence. Ivan fomented some of the disorder from outside in order to provide a pretext for intervention. He was also able to interfere with Novgorod's grain supply. By 1489 all was over, with the deportation of many thousands of Novgorod's boyars, merchants, and landowners. Their confiscated estates were bestowed on lesser nobles and other people from Muscovy who undertook, in return for the land, to render military service. As an independent political unit, Novgorod the Great no longer existed. It disappeared as a factor in European trade in 1494, when Ivan arrested all the Hanseatic merchants on Novgorod territory, closed their commercial offices and church, and confiscated all their goods. Not for the last time the rulers of Moscow showed that while trade might be desirable, the elimination of political contamination was even more important to them. Muscovy now enjoyed unchallenged sway over a vast fur-bearing empire that stretched from the Gulf of Finland to the Urals and beyond. The bell which had once called the citizens of Novgorod to their assembly would now praise autocrats in the Moscow Kremlin.

The subjugation of Novgorod left Ivan free to deal with his two other main opponents – Lithuania and the Tatars. This was a complex interdependent problem, with Ivan manoeuvring uneasily between the west and the south, endeavouring to prevent a union of the two fronts. His technique of exploiting his enemies' divisions could be used to better advantage than ever, now that the Tatars were split between several semi-independent khanates. In the 1460s Ivan had begun to withhold his due tribute from the 'Great Horde', as the Russians now called the former Golden Horde. Its leader, Khan Ahmed, was still a force to be reckoned with. Twice he summoned Ivan to his capital – without response. The climax came in 1480 when, in agreement with Lithuania, Ahmed launched a campaign against Muscovy. It ended in a strange anticlimax. The two forces came to face each other across the banks of the Ugra river, on Muscovy's south-western border. There was only one skirmish – and nothing more. The help that Ahmed was expecting from Lithuania never materialized. This made a full-scale campaign against Muscovy impossible, and he had no choice but to withdraw – as did Ivan, who for his part feared a Lithuanian attack.

This tragi-comic affair was, however, symbolic of the altered balance of forces. In 1502 the Great Horde ceased to exist as a cohesive body, and dwindled into the khanate of Astrakhan. Ivan could use his long-standing alliance with the Crimean khan, Mengli-girei, to keep Kazan' weak and also to threaten the Lithuanians. When this alliance collapsed under his successor, Vasiliy III, the Crimean Tatars launched a number of raids on Muscovite territory – forty-three in the first half of the sixteenth century alone. Muscovy responded to this continued threat from the south by constructing fortified defence lines along the steppe frontier and by modernizing its armed forces. Occasional 'gifts' were still paid to Tatar suzerains, but there could no longer be any question of their asserting a claim to overlordship. The 'yoke' was definitely a thing of the past.

To the west Ivan's successes were more modest. He persuaded or coerced several east Slavic princelings with land on the western side of the border with Lithuania to change their allegiance, and in 1494 seized Vyaz'ma. The Lithuanians were obliged to sign a treaty recognizing the Muscovite sovereign's title to rule *all* Russian lands, including those presently under their rule. Ivan also cleverly exploited alleged discrimination by Catholic prelates against Orthodox believers in west Russia. In 1500, after careful preparations, he launched a major offensive. His troops won a battle on the river Vedrosha, but the key strategic fortress-city of Smolensk eluded his grasp; it was not taken until 1514. Moreover, the pressure from Muscovy brought Lithuania and Poland closer together.

What sort of Muscovite state was it that emerged from the long struggle with the Tatars and the lesser Slav principalities? It can be seen in so many ways – as the victory of the forest over the steppe, as the transition from a society of independent principalities to an absolutist autocracy, or, economically, as an evolution from a system of diffused landholdings and power to a concentration of land and power in the hands of an autocrat backed by a dependent class of service-landholders. Muscovite society has been characterized as 'patrimonial'. In theory all land belonged to the grand prince, who could confiscate the holdings of unruly relatives or aristocrats and confer them on other servitors whom he deemed more reliable. We have seen examples of such practices in Ivan's policy towards Novgorod. Land was at that time the most important economic resource. Proprietors' rights to it, and to other possessions, were not firmly ensconced in law, for the legal system was embryonic.

Nevertheless one should not exaggerate the degree of arbitrariness that existed. Not only were such land grants by the sovereign made for purposes consonant with overall state interests – 'gentry' held their *pomest'ya* (equivalent to fiefs in the West; see further comment on page 68 on the term 'gentry') on condition that they and their children performed military service, and had to maintain themselves from the labour of their family and dependants – but a 'market' of sorts continued to exist in land, as it did in other commodities. Proprietors could buy, sell, or exchange their holdings, and on their death they would ordinarily be divided up among their heirs, a practice which inhibited noble families from accumulating landed wealth on a massive scale. The monasteries were far more successful than lay lords in doing so. Up to a point their economic activities benefited the community at large, since the Church continued to care for the poor, as well as giving security and employment to a large number of artisans and peasants. Neither ecclesiastical nor secular landowners took a modern managerial

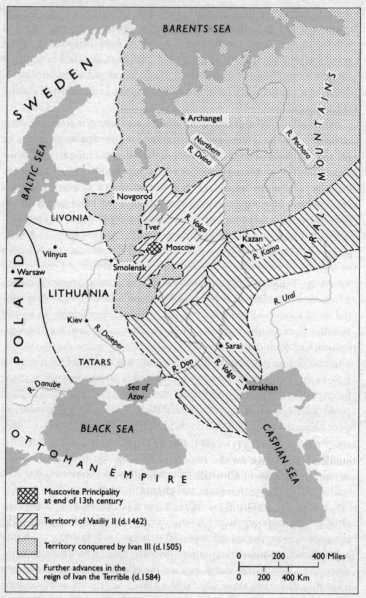

MAP 3. *The growth of Muscovy, 1300–1584*

approach to their properties. They were concerned not with profit but with sheer survival, living as they did in an environment where disaster might strike at any moment and reduce even the best endowed to beggary overnight.

Ivan III vastly extended the internal authority of the grand prince. He ruled as *samoderzhets*, or 'autocrat', a term that initially meant independence of external control but came to acquire the significance of a mighty power that none of his subjects might challenge with impunity, since the ruler was a semi-divine figure who owed account only to God. This new elevated concept of monarchy found expression in the adoption by Muscovy of the Byzantine double-eagle symbol of authority, occasional use of the appellation *tsar* (= Caesar), and the institution of elaborate coronation ceremonies. Ritual dominated life at the grand prince's court, which expanded in size and became hieratically stratified. There was something of an oriental flavour to all this, which foreigners, and later many historians, attributed to Tatar influence. Certainly the Muscovite monarchs did see themselves as heirs to the domains and dignity of the Chingisids, but the main source of inspiration was Byzantine. Churchmen elaborated several theories and legends to bolster the autocratic power ideologically. One of these, for example, claimed that the Rurikid dynasty was related genealogically to the Roman emperors. Another strained credulity to the limits by maintaining that the apostle St Andrew had visited Rus'.

Towards the end of Ivan's reign the so-called 'Judaizer' heresy entered the Muscovite realm by way of Novgorod and won some highly placed converts; even the ruler himself seems to have been attracted to it. Churchmen were divided in their response to this threat. The saintly monk Nilus (1433–1508), who on returning from Mount Athos founded a hermitage on the remote river Sora, stood for an ascetic, contemplative form of Christianity – his adherents were called 'non-possessors' – and held that the heresy should be combated by developing a higher form of spirituality. This view was defeated, at a church council held in 1504, by the followers of Joseph of Volokolamsk (1439/40–1515), known as 'Josephans'. They preached the need for more coercive means, to be applied by the secular power. The Josephan monastic foundation at Volokolamsk (1479) held large tracts of land, the income from which was used to train clergy and perform charitable deeds. Joseph argued that the grand prince had an obligation to protect

27

these possessions, and should resist the temptation to confiscate them for secular purposes, such as rewarding his servitors.

In return for such righteousness the Church exalted the autocrat for fulfilling God's purpose as embodied in 'Holy Rus'', the sole remaining Orthodox realm undefiled by Latin or other heresy. Quoting a Byzantine source, Joseph wrote that 'the tsar is in nature like unto all men, but in authority he is like unto God Himself'. According to this theory the Muscovite autocrat was the divinely ordained fountainhead of all authority, whether political, economic, military, or religious, although in the last respect his legitimacy depended on his zeal in defending the Orthodox cause. In Muscovy the association of Church and state was much closer than it was in the Latin West, where the strife between Papacy and Empire created a more pluralistic view of proper Christian government and a complex institutional structure developed that had no equivalent in the east Russian lands.

Churchmen further held that the fall of Byzantium to the Turks in 1453 was divine punishment for its apostasy in seeking closer relations with the Catholics. The logical consequence was to see Muscovy as God's chosen successor, the 'new Israel' or the 'third Rome'. This doctrine of the transference of sanctity from one centre to another, first elaborated in the south Slav lands, was most famously articulated by a monk from Pskov, Filofey (Philotheus). Referring to ancient Rome and to Byzantium (the 'second Rome'), he wrote to Vasiliy III that 'two Romes have fallen but the third stands and a fourth there shall not be'. The hopes of all Christianity, he concluded, were now focused on Muscovy. This was not intended as a justification for a militantly expansionist foreign policy, as some have thought. Rather it was designed to win for the Russian Church greater autonomy from the patriarchate of Constantinople. But later Russian rulers would indeed pervert its sense and use it in a way detrimental to the Church (which in 1667 would declare it heretical).

The boyar aristocracy also suffered a diminution of its rights at the hands of the autocracy. During the Kievan and Tatar periods they had been the princes' advisers and military-administrative agents. Their status was little different from that of the master they served. They were not his vassals in the Western sense, since the east Russian lands did not know feudalism, but independent freeholders. Their rights were enshrined in contracts with the princes which usually contained the formula 'and the boyars who dwell among us shall be at liberty to come and go'. A boyar might even have land in one principality yet serve the ruler of another. During the fifteenth century these rights were gradually whittled away along with those of the apanage princes. The rise of Muscovy to sole dominance meant that there were ever fewer rulers whom it was advantageous to serve. The grand prince had far more prestige and privileges to offer than anyone else. In this way the west Russian princelings, for example, were attracted from Lithuania to Muscovy, but when they tried to assert their ancient right to move in the reverse direction, they soon found that this was interpreted as treason! As a punishment they might lose some of their land, suffer relegation in the competition for scarce high-level jobs, and be barred from marrying into prestigious old Muscovite families. They dwindled into the category of 'serving princes', whose seniority was often lower than that of native Muscovite boyars.

The autocrats were careful not to offend the genealogical pride of these servitors, which they could manipulate in a way advantageous to their own power. Muscovite politics was the affair of a few families which had seats in the monarch's advisory council, or *duma*, according to their rank, where they monopolized the chief positions. Many of these aristocrats were granted land on service tenure (*pomest'ya*) which they held in addition to their patrimonial estates (*votchiny*). This was another way of binding them to the throne. Lower down the social scale were the junior servitors or 'gentry', who were more likely to depend wholly on their *pomest'ya*. They spent most of their lives on active service and seldom 'saw the sovereign's eyes' (as the phrase went), that is, they were remote from the royal court (*dvor*) that was the source of power and patronage. For such humble men even a brief visit to Moscow on some official errand was a mark of great favour.

Ivan's second marriage, in 1472, to Zoë (known in Russia as Sophia) Palaeologus, niece of the last Byzantine emperor and a ward of the Pope, was certainly a diplomatic *coup*, but it was less a major factor in promoting consolidation of the autocracy, as used to be thought, but rather one of its consequences. Its importance lay mainly in the cultural field. Although the Papacy backed the match, hoping to bring Muscovy into communion with Rome, this aim was frustrated: the prelates of the Orthodox Church, which had become autocephalous in 1448, were bitterly opposed to closer union. But a number of Italian artists and craftsmen were included in Sophia's entourage. Ivan, anxious to provide visual testimony to the international prestige that his marriage accorded him, launched a major building programme in the Moscow Kremlin. He summoned from Italy five architects, led by the famous Bolognese, Aristotle da Fioraventi. The latter was entrusted with the rebuilding of the Cathedral of the Dormition, originally built in the Kremlin in the days of Ivan Kalita. Its graceful, harmonious interior was splendidly decorated with icons, mosaics and frescos by a gifted Russian painter, Dionysius. Both here and in the city's other churches, there developed a blend of Byzantine plan, Russian onion-shaped domes, and minor Italianate architectural features. The tsar's residential and official quarters were also complemented by the construction of two stone buildings – the Palace of Facets, used for court ceremonies and the like, and the Terem Palace, for the royal family's private occupation. The walls of the Kremlin were strengthened and furnished with towers and gates. The Kremlin that visitors to Moscow see today, with its gilded cupolas and massive towers on a bluff overlooking the river, is very much Ivan III's handiwork, testifying to his desire to glorify the sacred capital of his newly independent realm.

Ivan the Great's outward panoply, his successes in foreign policy, and his establishment of autocracy were but the prelude to vast upheavals in the reign of his grandson, Ivan the Terrible. There was a spectacular political explosion; and the policy of creating pomest'ya wholesale rapidly brought on a land crisis – the immediate cause of so many of the convulsions affecting Russian history, in the sixteenth century no less than in the twentieth.

CHAPTER 4

Ivan the Terrible and the Crisis of Russian Autocracy

During his long reign (1533–84) Ivan IV, commonly known as 'the Dread' or 'the Terrible', instituted a radical transformation of Russian society. One of the great Renaissance princes, he combined superior intelligence and great strength of will with an obsessive attitude towards his autocratic prerogatives, which in later life degenerated into acute paranoia. Directly or indirectly, this cost the lives of many thousands of his subjects.

At Ivan's accession the north Russian forests were dotted with small villages and homesteads in which peasant families could generally hope to eke out a modest living. Some of them were dependent on monastic or lay landholders, but many more acknowledged no lord other than the grand prince himself. The population was on the rise. Along the major river systems a number of flourishing commercial centres developed where merchants grew rich and artisans plied their trade. To the south of Moscow, a region exposed to foreign attack, towns were little more than military outposts. This was where most of the ruler's noble servitors had their estates. Some of these lands, and the peasants who lived on them, were the hereditary possession of aristocrats who attended at court and held the great offices of the realm. But most land was held on conditional tenure by ordinary 'gentry': *dvoriane*, some of whom were called 'boyars' children' (i.e. junior boyars). They spent most of their lives on active service and so could not easily cultivate their fiefs (*pomest'ya*) or even look after them properly. If they were unlucky and became poor, they would quickly drop down to peasant level. This was still a relatively fluid society in which vertical divisions were more important than horizontal ones. Its chief characteristic was the key role played by the family or kinship group. The leading princely and boyar clans engaged in fierce rivalry over appointments and other honours, but this did not prevent them reaching compromises or forming coalitions. They also developed patronage networks which extended downward to embrace junior servitors.

By 1584, at Ivan's death, Muscovite society had become more rigid – but, paradoxically, less stable. War and terror overstrained the nation's resources, making life more precarious for everyone. In principle, the status of members of the élite now depended on decisions taken at the centre, by the ruler's officials and clerks. The bureaucracy expanded and the hierarchical ranking system became more complex. State service became an inescapable duty for all able-bodied nobles, but the mechanism for compensating them, mainly with land, had been badly disrupted. This had catastrophic economic consequences. Servitors were impelled to increase drastically the burden of taxes and dues imposed on their peasant dependants. Many succumbed to these exactions. Others reacted by fleeing *en masse* to the no man's land on the state's expanding eastern and southern borders, where they often joined bands of Cossacks. These hunters and warriors formed self-sustaining communities along the rivers that flowed through the southern steppe, and took pride in flouting the laws of the settled states whence they had fled. For Muscovy they represented an additional security threat. Meanwhile the drain of labour power from the centre and north-west undermined the state's fiscal and military viability. Whole regions lay desolate. Overall the picture was bleak indeed.

How far was the social crisis due to the disturbed personality of the Terrible Tsar himself? Why was there so much blood-letting during his reign? Some modern historians warn against exaggerating the ruler's role, pointing out that many decisions attributed to him will in fact have been taken by his advisers. A lot of the relevant documents have been destroyed or falsified – some of them at Ivan's command! – so that inevitably plenty of 'blank spots' remain. However, considerable progress has recently been made in clarifying the key issues, and today the trend is once again towards emphasizing the importance of Ivan's character traits as against anonymous 'objective' factors.

Ivan IV came to the throne at the age of three. In his early childhood, his mother, a Lithuanian princess, dominated the regency council. He was only eight when she died, perhaps a victim of poison. After that, aristocratic factions manoeuvred for the right to use Ivan as their pawn with no regard for his sensibility or any other considerations of propriety. Ivan was only thirteen when he intervened by having one of the leading aristocrats murdered. At the age of seventeen, Metropolitan Makariy had him crowned as tsar, a title hitherto used only in Muscovy's external relations. Theoretically, it implied superiority over all other political authorities on earth. Practically, it inflated Ivan's sense of self-importance and strengthened the Glinsky faction, to which his mother belonged. They arranged his marriage three weeks later to Anastasia Yur'eva-Zakharina, from an ancient boyar family later known as the Romanovs. She has been credited with moderating the tsar's violent behaviour until her death in 1560, and bore him six children, only two of whom survived her. Ivan was fond of his wife, but also helped to ruin her health by dragging her along on continual pilgrimages and hunting expeditions. The court was the scene of constant intrigue. In June 1547 fires broke out in Moscow, destroying much of the city. The Shuisky and Romanov families exploited the popular discontent against the Glinskys and in the ensuing tumult Ivan's maternal uncle was lynched by the mob. The young ruler was badly frightened and promptly set about righting the wrongs that afflicted his kingdom.

In this reforming activity he was assisted by several favourites, among them Alexei Adashev and the priest Silvester. Another associate, Prince A. M. Kurbsky, later called this group the 'Chosen Council', but it had no formal institutional status. Nor, indeed, did the traditional Boyar Duma, which for the time being played a lesser role. A new law code, the *Sudebnik*, was promulgated in 1550. Among other things it exempted the provincial gentry from the jurisdiction of the all-powerful governors (*namestniki*), whose corrupt ways were legendary, and confirmed earlier edicts giving them a leading role in locally elected bodies to fight banditry. In the north greater responsibility was also conferred on peasant community elders. But at the same time the central administrative offices (*prikazy*) were strengthened. Notable among them was the *Razryad*, which had charge of the noble cavalry. In connection with a series of campaigns launched against the Tatar khanate of Kazan', the reformers regularized the ranking of the top military posts and restricted the opportunities for aristocrats to make such appointments the object of precedence disputes.* Some one thousand select noble

---

* Known as *mestnichestvo*, a curious custom grew up whereby a nominee for high office would refuse to serve under someone whose service record (or that of his ancestors) was inferior to that of members of his own clan. Although clearly detrimental to efficiency, it could be manipulated by the ruler and his officials, who were called on to settle such disputes, and so survived until the late seventeenth century.

servitors were ordered to be given estates near the capital, where they could be mustered quickly. Furthermore, a corps of musketeers (*strel'tsy*) was established, consisting of trained soldiers armed with handguns, and the artillery was much improved. These measures marked the beginning of a regular standing army in Russia.

To ensure an adequate supply of land for *pomest'ya*, Ivan called on the Church to decline acceptance of property willed to monasteries by (mostly noble) laymen. This request met with a cool response by the Josephan clerics who dominated the 'council of One Hundred Chapters' (*Stoglav*), held in 1551. However, they did not have everything their own way and the assembly did take measures to bring the clergy under closer control, with the aim of stopping the immoral behaviour that was prevalent among churchmen and laymen alike.

The reforms led to a fragile domestic consensus which helped Muscovy win signal victories in the east. The conquest of Kazan' (1552) – its mighty citadel was blown up by German mercenary sappers – was followed by the brutal suppression of several rebellions led by Muslim loyalists. Possession of this strategic region turned Muscovy into a multinational empire which embraced various native peoples of the middle Volga (Chuvash, Cheremis) as well as Tatars. Four years later the khanate of Astrakhan' fell in turn. This gave Moscow control of the entire Volga waterway, bringing her borders to the shores of the Caspian and opening up the Urals and western Siberia to penetration by fur-trappers and Cossacks.

This last expansion was initially a private venture. The powerful Stroganov merchant dynasty, whose wealth was in salt mining in the north-east, hired a band of Cossack warrior adventurers led by one Yermak. Like the Spanish conquistadores in contemporary America, a small body of men in possession of firearms could accomplish much against poorly organized and ill-equipped tribesmen. In 1581/2 Yermak defeated Kuchum, khan of the Siberian Tatars, and installed himself in his capital (later Tobol'sk). He then had to withstand a long siege. Yermak was ambushed and slain, but by then regular troops were on their way to complete his work. Siberia provided the state with massive additional supplies of forest products, and there was nothing to stop pioneers going farther east until, in the 1630s, they reached the Pacific. But for many years to come there was very sparse settlement by Russians in this vast, inhospitable region. Its importance lay chiefly in providing a 'safety valve' that allowed the discontented to escape oppression. The state authorities had reason to look on its acquisition as something of a mixed blessing.

The subjugation of the Volga khanates strengthened Ivan's pride in his imperial majesty. He and his advisers now had to decide along which axis to continue the advance. Should Muscovy go on to tackle the Crimean Tatars in the southern steppe? Such a course was recommended by Adashev among others, but it presented serious logistical problems. It also risked antagonizing the Ottoman Turks, then at the height of their power, who were co-religionists and protectors of the Tatars. Wisely or not, Ivan chose to move west instead.

Livonia offered a tempting target. Its German rulers, who had gone over to Lutheranism, were weak and divided. A bold offensive seemed likely to give Muscovy control over its port cities, which had hitherto restricted Russian trade with the Baltic countries and beyond. Accordingly, in 1558, the tsar found a pretext and invaded. The attack was at first successful, but it alarmed Russia's neighbours, who had their own interests in the region: Sweden, Denmark, and above all Poland–Lithuania. In this way the Livonian war became generalized and dragged on for years. Its fortunes swayed to and fro, draining Muscovy's slender resources and exposing the government to internal strain. Moreover, the Polish and Lithuanian rulers, nervous at the loss of Polotsk and Muscovite appeals to the Orthodox in Lithuania, responded by cementing their alliance. The Union of Lublin (1569) converted the existing dynastic union of Poland and Lithuania into a Commonwealth: the two states were to have a single crown and certain joint institutions. This move blocked further Muscovite expansion westward for a century or so and shifted the balance of power to her disadvantage. The more civilized, aristocratic lifestyle in the west Russian lands had attractions for Muscovite nobles who resented their own rightless situation.

Ivan sought scapegoats at home for his foreign policy failures. Not entirely without reason, he suspected opposition among his boyars and the clergy, who had been half-hearted in endorsing his earlier reform programme. Already in 1553, before the war began, Ivan's advisers had aroused his displeasure by their behaviour when he suddenly fell ill. Instead of pledging allegiance to his infant son, as he demanded, they preferred his cousin, Prince Vladimir of Staritsa, as tsar or regent. Their motives were quite reasonable: they did not wish to repeat the internecine struggles that had marked Ivan's childhood. But factional politics were also involved, in that some clan leaders feared the ambitious Romanovs. When Ivan recovered, he seemed ready to overlook this 'treason', but suspicion rankled in his mind and he became more vengeful. He attributed Anastasia's death to conspiracy and alleged that his old adviser Silvester was implicated in it. 'If only you had not taken my young wife from me,' he wrote later, 'then there would have been no "sacrifices to Cronos" ' (i.e. massacres). Ivan went on to marry six more times – more often than the rules of the Church allowed – but none of these matches brought him happiness or dynastic reinforcement.

In 1562 the tsar disgraced several prominent aristocrats whom he distrusted. They lost their property and were deported to Kazan', or else had to take monastic vows. Later some were pardoned on the strength of written loyalty oaths, counter-signed by several sureties – kinsmen or neighbours who would be held responsible if the principal signatory made trouble again. The practice was not new, but Ivan made more extensive use of it. It helps to explain why the terror spread so widely in a fearful society where everyone was obliged to watch others and denounce them for any suspicious behaviour.

The first executions came in 1563. Next April, Kurbsky, Ivan's leading general in Livonia, fled across the front line and entered Polish service. Presumably he feared punishment for setbacks in the field. He then compounded his felony by writing letters criticizing the tsar for his arbitrary and cruel measures. The tsar responded with a lengthy epistle, full of biblical quotations, in which he sought to justify his God-given autocratic power. Angrily he denounced Kurbsky and other former advisers as treacherous self-seekers. 'Do you consider it [right] for ... overweening, cunning servants to rule and the tsar to be honoured only by virtue of his presidency, ... while in power he is in no way better than a servant?'* No longer able to rule by traditional means, Ivan adopted a dramatic stratagem. In December 1564 he withdrew, with his court and treasure, to a country residence,

---

* The authenticity of this correspondence has been questioned (E. L. Keenan 1971), but most scholars accept it as genuine. Even if it *were* composed later, it testifies to the importance of Kurbsky's defection. Otherwise why should a forger have chosen Kurbsky as a vehicle for his thoughts?

denounced alleged traitors in high places, and refused to return to Moscow unless given a free hand to rule as he wished. The ruse worked. The clergy and people readily agreed. Thereupon Ivan established his *oprichnina*, a separate court and administration, with its own territory, which he ruled through a 'security police' beholden only to himself. Nobles living there were screened and, if they failed to comply with their exactions, deported or killed. Clad in black, the dreaded *oprichniki* terrorized the rest of the kingdom, the *zemshchina*, where they uncovered one alleged plot after another. Among the victims were not just aristocrats but ordinary servitors, along with their kin and dependants, as well as clergy. The Moscow metropolitan, Philip, and Prince Vladimir of Staritsa were among the notables done to death. Ivan's sadistic associate, Fedor Basmanov, helped devise the most excruciating tortures. One unfortunate was boiled alive in public; others were hanged, impaled, crucified, or poisoned in their monastic retreats. The terror reached its climax in the winter of 1569/70, when Ivan mounted a surprise attack on Novgorod, where, on the strength of a denunciation, he suspected the authorities of treasonable contact with Poland. Establishing his court outside the city, he had some two to three thousand men and women murdered. Many victims were pushed through the ice on the frozen river Volkhov and drowned. A similar fate awaited Pskov, but at the last minute Ivan relented. Contemporaries attributed this to intercession by a 'holy fool', a naked simpleton named Nikola. Certainly the tsar took such 'divine' omens seriously, just as he believed in witchcraft.

In 1571 the Crimean Tatars launched a surprise attack on Moscow and burned the city. The *oprichnina* troops performed badly, which may have convinced Ivan that it was time to abandon this institution. It was restored briefly in 1575–6, but in later years the terror was on a less extensive scale. Recent researchers put the toll at about four thousand, but this figure excludes many thousands of anonymous dependants (e.g. household slaves) as well as countless peasants who died because their masters lost their means of livelihood. Some earlier historians sought to detect a rational element in the *oprichnina*, but it seems that it can best be explained by Ivan's paranoid delusions and the lack of any institutional restraints on his autocratic power.

Was there no resistance? The Moscow metropolitan, the highest religious dignitary, remonstrated with the tsar – and paid the penalty.

In 1566 the war forced Ivan to moderate his excesses and to call an Assembly of the Land to decide whether it should continue. The deputies, drawn from the nobility, clergy, and merchants in the *zemshch-ina*, agreed to back further hostilities, but added a complaint about the repression. This was misrepresented as treason and a number of delegates were beheaded or mutilated. In the circumstances, the tsar's subjects could scarcely do more. No one, even Kurbsky, questioned the principle of autocracy, only its 'tyrannical' distortion. The same moral dilemma would recur four centuries later, with Stalin's Great Terror, when the toll was incomparably higher and people had less opportunity to flee from its impact.

Many historians have noted the similarities between Russia and Spain at this time. Both states confronted feudal disunity and Islamic opponents, which they overcame by building strong military establishments and developing ideological justifications for assimilating their alien subjects. Neither shrank from terroristic methods in an effort to root out dangerous heretical ideas. But in the Russian case it was applied less systematically and for a shorter time, perhaps because the threat was less real. After all, apanages had been virtually eliminated before Ivan acceded to power. In so far as his actions were designed to avert their resurrection, he was tilting against windmills. Nor did the Orthodox Church undertake a serious missionary effort against the eastern infidels. On the contrary, Tatar nobles were readily accepted into the tsar's service and were even allowed to acquire Orthodox serfs! (The reverse did not apply.)

The enserfment of the Russian peasantry was a gradual process that owed as much to natural socio-economic factors as to actions by the state. In 1550 the judicial code called the *Sudebnik* confirmed an earlier statute that had fixed a two-week period after the harvest had been gathered in (around St George's Day, 26 November) as the time when a peasant who had paid his debts and met his other obligations could legally leave his lord's land. In practice, however, peasants probably moved whenever they chose without their masters being able to stop them, at least until the early 1580s, when, at the landowners' prompting, the government imposed a ban on movement in several successive years. Ivan's wars and domestic convulsions meant a vast increase in peasants' tax burdens (perhaps eightfold over the course of the century, allowing for devaluation of the coinage). After the 1560s, soaring grain prices made it easier for the more fortunately placed to meet their obligations. On top of these were the lord's dues, which mainly took the form of a share of the peasant's produce and his services.

In so far as cash entered into these dealings, it forced peasants to sell their goods on the market. But by and large the villages remained self-supporting, and there is little evidence to support those who have argued for the existence at this time of a capitalist nation-wide market. At the most one can speak of local (regional) trade networks in certain commodities, based on urban centres like Nizhniy Novgorod. Expansion to the east created new opportunities for Russian merchants and other pioneers to build up capital reserves and develop an entrepreneurial spirit. This was less feasible in trade with Russia's western neighbours, much of which was in foreign hands. During the Livonian war Muscovite merchants made good use of a major outlet at Narva on the Baltic coast, seized in 1558, but the greater prizes of Reval (Tallinn) and Riga eluded them, and when peace came even Narva passed into Swedish hands. The Polish-Lithuanian government likewise did its best to prevent arms and other warlike goods being shipped through the Baltic to Russia.

In this situation the arrival in 1553 of English merchant adventurers at the mouth of the northern Dvina was a godsend. Richard Chancellor's *Bona Fortuna* was the sole surviving vessel of three that had set sail from London in search of the fabled North-East Passage. Chancellor travelled on to Moscow, where he was warmly welcomed by the tsar. This contact led to the formation two years later of the Muscovy Company in London. Ivan granted it a charter allowing English merchants to engage in wholesale trade throughout his domains without payment of duty. These extensive privileges were sometimes abused, which led to friction, but even so, diplomatic contacts were maintained, and in 1567 the intrepid Anthony Jenkinson was able to journey to Persia by way of Muscovy. Yet Russia could not become the intermediary in east–west trade via the Volga route, as her leaders hoped, and the scale of Anglo-Russian commercial relations remained modest. The chief reason for this was geographic: the perilous voyage through Arctic waters to ports on the White Sea, frozen for much of the year, in sailing ships that could carry little freight. Another obstacle was that, whereas the English government put commercial interests first, for Ivan what counted most was the political aspect. In particular, he hoped to win

Queen Elizabeth I's support against the Catholic Poles, and at one point even sought her hand in marriage. Not surprisingly, the 'virgin queen' declined the offer, but later there was talk of another English bride for the ageing despot. Luckily for Lady Mary Hastings, a niece of the queen, Ivan died before anything came of the plan.

Despite the fear and contempt felt by many Western Europeans for 'barbarous' Muscovy, particularly in Germany, where pamphleteers made much of Russian atrocities in Livonia, a fair sprinkling of English, Scottish, Dutch, and north German merchants, artisans and mercenary soldiers – all Protestant by religion – arrived to serve the tsar. Among them was a Cambridge-educated astrologer and physician of German origin, Eleazar Bomelius, who is said to have prepared poisonous potions for Ivan's enemies. Arrested while trying to flee from Muscovy, he died under torture after implicating several prominent individuals, including the archbishop of Novgorod, who was deposed and likewise succumbed in mysterious circumstances. Heinrich von Staden, a German soldier of fortune, himself served in the *oprichnina* and compiled a graphic (if highly coloured) account of his experiences. Another Western traveller to Muscovy, after Ivan's death, was the Englishman Giles Fletcher, whose *Of the Russe Commonwealth* (1590) is still an indispensable source on conditions in the country, despite its obvious cultural bias.

As the Livonian war drifted to an inglorious end, the tsar became increasingly isolated, a recluse prey to nightmarish visions and fits of conscience-stricken guilt. His mental state was aggravated by a serious and painful bone disease, whose existence has been discovered by modern scientific study of his remains. In 1581, in a fit of rage, he killed his elder son and heir. His pregnant daughter-in-law, on whose behalf the son had intervened after Ivan insulted her, had a miscarriage and died. This thoughtless deed eventually put an end to the Rurikid dynasty, for Ivan's second son, Theodore (Fedor), was mentally and physically handicapped.

The tsar's own death three years later was appropriately dramatic. According to Sir Jerome Horsey, an agent of the Muscovy Company (but not always a reliable witness!), 'the Emperor began grievously to swell in his cods, with which he had most horribly offended above fifty years together, boasting of a thousand virgins he had deflowered.' Daily he would have himself carried into his treasure chamber, where he would fondle precious stones and discourse on their supposed curative powers. But none of the remedies suggested by the soothsayers could help him. The end came while Ivan was preparing to play a game of chess:

He sets his men* . . . the Emperor in his loose gown, shirt and linen hose, faints and falls backward. Great outcry and stir, one sent for aqua vita another to the apothecary for 'marigold and rose water' and to call his ghostly father and the physicians. In the mean he was strangled and stark dead.

Special guards were thrown round the Kremlin in case of disorder. But the succession passed easily enough to the tsarevich, Theodore Ioannovich. This was in fact wholly deceptive. Ivan's social convulsions and his last twenty-five years of war had brought Muscovy to the verge of anarchy. The true, prophetic verdict is that of Giles Fletcher, the English ambassador to the new tsar:

This desperate state of things at home maketh the people for the most part to wish for some foreign invasion, which they suppose to be the only means to rid them of the heavy yoke of his tyrannous government.

In a long-term perspective, however, the centralized service state which, in his earlier years, Ivan IV had done so much to improve would survive the ensuing crisis and, indeed, endure for centuries.

---

* 'All saving the King, which by no means he could not make stand in his place with all the rest upon the plain board.' (Horsey's note.)

CHAPTER 5

The Time of Troubles

With Theodore (1584–98) the Rurikid dynasty became extinct. The new ruler, crowned with full ceremony at the age of twenty-seven, was altogether unfitted for his lofty role. Although personally devout – bell-ringing was his favourite pastime – he was sick in body and mind. His accession meant that power shifted back to leaders of the boyar clans. It was they who in effect ran the exhausted country in his name for fourteen years during which it teetered on the brink of collapse. From 1598 to 1613 Russia suffered an age of upheaval greater than any experienced elsewhere in Europe during this generally turbulent era. As one ruler followed another to the Muscovite throne, most of them with dubious claims to legitimacy, the central administration collapsed. 'Foreign invaders and native brigands stalked the land, and desperate men and women fed on one another – figuratively and sometimes literally.'* As much as one third of the population may have perished from famine, disease, and other effects of civil strife. Psychologically, ordinary Russians were disoriented by the disappearance of a regime they had been taught to regard as sacrosanct, chosen by God to fulfil His divine purpose on earth. Unable to visualize any alternative to it, many people threw their support behind a succession of pretenders to the throne, each of whom claimed to be the rightful tsar, although their humble birth and mode of conduct made their lack of qualification to rule all too obvious. Only a handful of men in the highest reaches of society were driven by circumstances to think of introducing a constitutional order of sorts, in which power was to be shared between a foreign-born monarch and his counsellors, institutionalized in the Boyar Duma and an elected Assembly of the Land. But this novel idea of consensual or contractual rule, based as it was on Western (particularly Polish) models, was never set forth plainly. It was unpopu-

* Crummey, *The Formation of Muscovy, 1304–1613*, p. 205.

lar and did not – indeed, could not – take root in Muscovy, with its traditions of divine autocracy. Instead the so-called 'Time of Troubles' – the euphemism favoured by near-contemporary writers – ended with the restoration of autocracy under the first tsar of the Romanov dynasty, which was destined to reign for over three centuries until 1917. The ensuing revolutionary era (1917–21), and perhaps also the years that immediately followed the collapse of the Soviet regime in 1991, offer some intriguing parallels to the first inter-dynastic crisis. In each case the Russian people demonstrated qualities of fortitude and resilience that surprised foreign observers.

Since Theodore was so patently unfit to rule, recourse was had to a regent. Best placed for this role at court was his equerry, Boris Godunov, familiar to lovers of poetry and opera from the works of Pushkin and Mussorgsky. Of solid but undistinguished lineage – his family, like many, was of Tatar origin – he had served Ivan IV in the *oprichnina* and towards the end of Ivan's reign became one of the tsar's closest confidants. He achieved a master stroke by marrying his sister, Irina, to Theodore, thus making himself the new tsar's brother-in-law. Linked to the Romanov faction, he evoked envy and hatred among other old aristocratic families such as the Shuiskys and Mstislavskys. In 1587 these rivals stirred up a popular commotion in an effort to unseat Godunov. Spokesmen for the Moscow plebs demanded that Theodore divorce Irina, by whom he had as yet no children, and remarry. Godunov managed to turn the tables on the plotters, had several of them executed, and in the following year formally took the title of regent. A number of other prominent individuals shared the Shuiskys' disgrace, but Godunov wisely refrained from launching a new *oprichnina*. He was a masterly tactician who knew when to lie low, when to make alliances, and when to denounce erstwhile allies as 'traitors'. But he was also something of a statesman, and in any case much superior to his forerunner, Ivan IV, both in diplomacy and in coping with the Terrible Tsar's legacy of grave socio-economic problems.

In foreign affairs Godunov's policy was consistent and took due account of the country's straitened resources. His greatest success came in ecclesiastical politics, where he won the assent of the Patriarch of Constantinople to raise the undistinguished Job, Godunov's nominee as metropolitan of Moscow and All Russia, to the dignity of Patriarch

(1589). This astute move bolstered Moscow's claim to be the 'third Rome' and averted the danger that the Russian Church might come under the influence of the (Muslim) Ottoman Turks, who now controlled Constantinople. In the hope of furthering the Orthodox cause in Poland-Lithuania, Godunov put forward Tsar Theodore's candidature for the (elective) throne of the Commonwealth, and when this gambit failed concluded a lasting peace with the victor, Sigismund III. A war with Sweden allowed Russia to recover some of the territory on the Baltic shore lost during the previous reign. In the south the unmarked border advanced farther into the steppe with the construction of several fortress towns, such as Voronezh, Kursk, and Belgorod. Sensibly, some peasant fugitives in this frontier region were allowed to stay there to help buttress its defences, instead of being forcibly returned to their former masters.

This question became a prominent concern to landholders of all categories for the next half-century. In 1592/3 Theodore's government evidently issued a decree (the text of which has not survived) binding all peasants to their owners, so in effect abolishing the ancient right to depart in November each year. This was the logical conclusion which the tsar's officials drew from the completion of a cadaster over the previous decade. In 1597 came another decree, which gave nobles the right to reclaim any of their peasants who had fled during the previous five years. At the same time life was made harder for people in another category, those who had fallen into slavery because they could not repay debts to a landed proprietor. These measures are generally seen as designed to appeal to the poorer service 'gentry', although the officials probably thought primarily in terms of state interest. It seemed to them urgent to try to stabilize the tax-paying population by tying them down to residence in a particular locality, so forcing them to till the soil in order to survive. Whatever the motives, in practice the 1590s were relatively good years for the larger owners. They could offer potential peasant migrants greater security and better conditions. Some such magnates did not shrink from actually kidnapping peasants belonging to junior servitors. The five-year return period was probably an effort to reconcile both 'lobbies'. It was not very effective, since it could not be policed. In real life it was hard for the poorer owners, who were absent on service most of the time, to detect fugitives (at their own expense!) and to make good in the courts a claim for their return. Thus the legal imposition of bondage on the peasantry alienated some sections of the service élite as well as the mass of commoners.

Boris Godunov was widely distrusted because the power he wielded lacked legitimacy. He was also suspected of having engineered the assassination of the boy prince Dmitriy, the offspring of Ivan IV's last marriage to Maria Nagaya, at Uglich in 1591. This accusation had a long life, but most modern historians discount it, if only for lack of motive: Boris's sister, the tsar's consort, was pregnant at the time, so that there was an even chance of a male heir to the throne; in any case, Dmitriy was legally barred from the succession since his parents' marriage was uncanonical. On hearing of the boy's death, Boris sent his chief rival, Vasiliy Shuisky, with a commission to investigate. The verdict was that Dmitriy had accidentally stabbed himself during an epileptic fit. This explanation did not sound too convincing, and later Shuisky himself disowned it when it suited his purposes to do so. But even allowing that the investigation was unsatisfactory, there is no direct evidence to incriminate Godunov in Dmitriy's death – although, of course, the doubts on this score make fine dramatic material.

Whatever the truth, Theodore's expiry in 1598 further thickened the atmosphere. Power passed briefly to Tsarina Irina, but Muscovy was not yet ready for a woman ruler and she immediately took the veil. There was no choice but to tread the Polish path and *choose* a tsar – an unprecedented situation in Muscovite history. Godunov, by virtue of the power that he in fact exercised, was the favoured candidate. But before he would accept the throne, he insisted upon election by a *Zemsky sobor*. Godunov's agents were active among the Sobor so that its choice was eventually unanimous. Even so, he insisted on repeated pleas before he would accept the throne. The new tsar had to ensure that his election appear but a reluctant response to the demands of the Sobor.

In this Godunov succeeded, and, until famine nullified his efforts, his reign looked promising. He was, for example, the first tsar to take an interest in education, and sent a number of young Russians to study abroad in the West. Four came to England. For about twelve years Muscovy lost track of them. The only one who could then be traced was found to be earning his living as a minister of the Anglican Church. Godunov also tried to eliminate the more flagrant abuses in the workings of the judicial machinery.

Boris was a sick man at his election, oppressed by his fears for the future. As he felt his health and popularity wane, he reverted to repression. In 1600, the Romanovs, relatives of Ivan IV's first wife, were accused of plotting to bewitch the tsar and his family. The head of the clan, Fedor Nikitich, was forced to enter a monastery. He survived to found the next ruling dynasty, but his younger brothers died in exile.

A succession of disastrously poor harvests from 1601 to 1603 completed the social isolation of Godunov's regime. Especially in the central districts, millions of peasants were reduced to starvation. Desperate, they consumed their reserves of seed corn, then ate grass or birch bark, and collapsed in their huts. The market price of grain rose to a level that ordinary folk could not afford. To meet the crisis the authorities distributed money and grain from state stores, but this relief effort made matters worse by attracting thousands of famished people to Moscow, where they perished *en masse*. Godunov also temporarily restored the peasants' freedom to move, but by now the wealthier owners, unable to feed their dependants, simply drove them from their estates. Many serfs and slaves escaped to join the bands of fugitives that roamed the countryside, looting granaries and attacking anyone less destitute than themselves. In 1603 insurgents led by a bandit named Khlopko almost encircled Moscow, but were routed in a pitched battle near the capital. As yet the movement of popular rebellion lacked a clear ideological focus.

This was provided the next year by a former monk, Grigoriy Otrep'ev, who claimed that he was none other than the murdered prince Dmitriy: having miraculously escaped death, he had now decided to reveal his identity and, as the legitimate monarch, would lead his people to righteousness. This notion of a social utopia, to be realized by violent means under the guidance of a messiah, had enormous appeal for the naïve and the unscrupulous. There had been parallel movements in medieval Western Europe, but in Russia their resonance was far greater, and cases of 'pretenderism' would recur well into the eighteenth century.

The son of a provincial nobleman, Otrep'ev began his career in the service of the Romanovs and may have enjoyed their backing in his enterprise. He later became a deacon in a Moscow monastery, but in 1601 fled famine-stricken Muscovy for Poland. Assuming his false identity, he won the support of certain aristocrats eager to profit from

Russia's misfortune. Among them was Jerzy Mniszech, palatine of Sambor, who was in grave financial trouble. He hoped to recoup his family's fortune by backing the Pretender, whom he affianced to his own daughter, Marina, on condition that her suitor made himself tsar within a year. The papal nuncio in Poland was interested as well. He saw in the Pretender, who did in fact secretly leave the Orthodox Church for Catholicism, an instrument for the eventual conversion of Muscovy. At Jesuit instigation, Marina secured from her future consort the promise of the right to maintain Catholic priests at her court in Moscow, provision for the Catholic form of worship, and Catholic schools and churches in certain areas.

King Sigismund III was not taken in by the Pretender's claims when he first met him at Craców in 1604. But he gave him a pension, recognized him as the legitimate tsar, and announced, although he did not officially declare war on Muscovy, that Poles were free to engage themselves voluntarily in the small private army that the alleged tsarevich was forming. In the early autumn of 1604 this army of not more than some 4,000 men set out for Moscow.

Godunov, in the meantime, unsuccessfully sought to discredit the pretender and to whip up Orthodox sentiment against 'Latin and Lutheran heresy', but the demoralization of Godunov's regime was evident in the Pretender's easy advance along a general north-easterly route from Lviv to Moscow. His army rapidly grew, swollen by warring bands of malcontents, homeless peasants, and, at a later stage, the Cossacks of the Donets.

Like their fellows along the other southern rivers, the Cossacks were organized in rough-and-ready military-style communities. When not engaged in plundering travellers or raiding neighbouring settled states, they earned their livelihood by hunting and fishing. Formed largely of runaways from serfdom in Muscovy and Poland, they had no clearly defined political allegiance (although the ex-Muscovites were fiercely Orthodox) and valued above all their independent and anarchic lifestyle. Each group had its elected chief (*ataman*, *hetman*), but initially at least major questions were decided 'democratically' at an assembly of all able-bodied males (there were few women Cossacks). Gradually, however, policy came to be made by an élite who succeeded in acquiring landed property and power.

The Cossack recruits swiftly swelled the Pretender's forces. In

January 1605 government troops defeated them, but thereafter offered little resistance. Many men deserted, either because they believed that their enemy might indeed be Russia's lawful ruler or else for more mundane reasons. In April Godunov suddenly died, which further undercut army morale. His son, who succeeded him, failed to stop the rot and within two months had been overthrown in a plot orchestrated by one of the leading boyars, Vasiliy Shuisky. 'Dmitriy' entered Moscow in triumph. One of his first acts was to put to death his predecessor on the throne. Maria Nagaya was summoned from her convent. Delighted at the Godunovs' fall, and anxious to save her own neck, she publicly acknowledged that the pretender was her long-lost son. Few were deceived by the charade, but in July 1605 Grigory Otrep'ev was crowned tsar.

Assuredly he was one of the strangest rulers ever to occupy a throne. The French mercenary captain Jacques Margeret relates that he was small of stature, with an ugly, beardless face, a wart on his nose, and spiky red hair. He neither looked nor behaved like an Orthodox tsar. The Pretender consulted frequently with the boyars, displaying unusual quick-wittedness, but his decisions were often erratic. He lived in constant fear of exposure and tried to bolster his position by distributing largesse on a grand scale. Servitors of all ranks were given two years' salary. Members of old clans who had fallen into disfavour under Godunov were rehabilitated and given senior appointments. But these gestures were not enough to win them over. Boyars objected to the tsar's reliance on favourites from *oprichnina* families, or on Polish and other foreign mercenaries, to say nothing of the Jesuit priests in his entourage. He deposed the Patriarch and appointed an unsavoury Greek yes-man in his place, but was intelligent enough to resist pressure by his Catholic advisers to impose their faith on his subjects or to make territorial concessions to Poland. Instead he favoured an offensive to the south, and to this end organized war games in which his guards, ensconced in a mobile wooden fort, popularly nicknamed 'Hell', attacked another containing Russians. 'Snowballs served as weapons and the warriors left the battlefield covered with welts and bruises.' At night the Pretender

gave himself over to unrestrained debauchery with any who took his fancy – married women, pretty girls, and nuns ... The palace contained many secret doors. Women were brought there under cover of darkness and disappeared into unknown labyrinths.*

Among his trophies was Boris Godunov's daughter, Xenia. Reputedly he sired several dozen illegitimate children during his eleven months on the Muscovite throne.

More seriously, a force of rebellious Terek Cossacks marched up the Volga, demanding that their own leader, Peter, take over as ruler. To avert popular discontent the government made some concessions to the slaves and bonded peasants, or at least to their gentry masters (especially those in the south), and revived plans to take over monastic land in order to compensate them more generously. This affronted churchmen, already suspicious of the foreigners in the Pretender's midst.

The False Dmitriy's downfall was touched off by the arrival in Moscow of his Polish fiancée, Marina Mniszech. The prospective marriage scandalized the pious. At the wedding ceremony the bride refused to take communion in Orthodox fashion, yet was solemnly crowned queen in a Kremlin cathedral. The feasting continued the next day, a revered Orthodox holiday. Clashes broke out between Muscovites and foreigners who made no secret of their contempt for the tsar's subjects.

Vasiliy Shuisky and other boyars had long been plotting the Pretender's demise. An earlier conspiracy nearly cost Shuisky his life, for the secret leaked. He was arrested and his head was already on the block when the death sentence was commuted to one of exile. Later 'Dmitriy', under pressure from his counsellors, allowed Shuisky to return to Moscow. This was a fatal error. For the aristocratic clans had gone along with the impostor only in order to get rid of the Godunovs; their aim was a tsar drawn from their own ranks. For once their views coincided with those of the urban poor, infuriated by their ruler's misconduct while serfdom remained untouched. At dawn on 17 May 1606 200 armed 'gentry' entered the Kremlin, while a mob outside set upon the mercenaries and then poured into the sacred precincts. Otrep'ev jumped from a window, spraining his leg, but was seized and beaten to death. Some days later his much-abused body

* Skrynnikov, *Time of Troubles: Russia in Crisis, 1604–1618*, p. 19.

was burned and the ashes shot from a cannon to the four winds.

Shuisky succeeded him on the throne. He was not elected by a full *Zemsky sobor*, as Godunov had been, but acclaimed by a well-coached crowd of Muscovites. In the Boyar Duma his supporters were in a minority. To consolidate his position he signed a covenant promising not to disgrace or punish nobles without fair trial and not to repress their innocent relatives. This was hardly Magna Carta – the undertaking was not legally binding on his successors – but it did mark a departure from the strict autocracy of Ivan IV.

The desire of the possessing classes to make life more predictable owed a lot to the threat of social revolution. The Muscovite social order, based on serf bondage, was now gravely challenged by insurrectionary movements which, originating in the borderlands, won the support of broad segments of the population in the more stable central areas. For most of Shuisky's four-year reign the government's writ ran only in about half Muscovy's territory. Rebel bands multiplied and sometimes secured aid from abroad. The continuing civil strife encouraged neighbouring powers, Poland-Lithuania and Sweden, to intervene, so complicating the struggle still further. The non-Russian peoples were also drawn into the fray. The main advantage remaining to the central government was that its soldiers were generally better disciplined and equipped. Nor were its enemies united. On the contrary, the guerrilla chiefs frequently quarrelled with one another and found it hard to pursue policies acceptable both to their service-'gentry' followers and to their more plebeian ones, especially the militant Cossacks.

Shuisky's first serious challenger was Ivan Bolotnikov, a former provincial servitor whose family had been forced into slavery by the economic catastrophe of the 1570s. He escaped to join the Cossacks but was captured by a Tatar gang and sold to the Turks as a galley slave. A German ship captured him at sea and released him in Venice. He returned to Muscovy via Hungary and Poland at the head of 10,000 Cossacks. As an agitator and revolutionary, he was the first to put into political terms the land-hunger and despair of the peasantry. His 'excellent charters' called on peasants and slaves to rise against their masters, to seize the estates of the *pomeshchiki*, and to overthrow the existing social order. For a time, especially in the south, this heady call swelled Bolotnikov's following to a vast movement that carried him to the gates of Moscow. There it began to disintegrate when, through the accession of the lesser provincial nobility, the movement lost its homogeneous lower-class character. Bolotnikov's new recruits aimed only at unseating Shuisky – not at inaugurating a social revolution. Bolotnikov had to withdraw from Moscow to Tula. Then, although he had hitched his star to 'Tsarevich Peter', the soi-disant son of Tsar Theodore, the rebels eventually succumbed to Shuisky's siege in the autumn of 1607.

Hardly was the threat of a peasant revolution overcome than yet another centre of revolt arose. Under the leadership of a second False Dmitriy – like the first, a man of humble origin who gave out that he had escaped death not only at Uglich in 1591 but also at Moscow in 1606 – a mixed array, composed in the main of Polish plunderers and swashbucklers, marched on Moscow from Starodub, some 300 miles to the south-west of the capital.

Despite the support of Marina Mniszech, who bore him an heir, and of Philaret Romanov, promoted to metropolitan by the first False Dmitriy and to Patriarch by his reincarnation, the second False Dmitriy had less success than the first. Usually known as the 'Thief' or 'Scoundrel', the label applied by the Shuisky camp to discredit him, his forces never quite reached Moscow. He established himself at Tushino, a village some six miles to the west, and there he set up a sort of 'counter-government' with a separate court and appurtenances. Moscow and Tushino confronted each other. Many popular elements abandoned Shuisky for the Thief, for the latter was generous in his promises and bestowal of titles. This confrontation lasted about two years. Shuisky had lost the south, but the Thief was not strong enough to blockade the city and starve it into surrender. At the head of a force of more than 20,000 men, Jan Sapieha, a Polish noble and one of the powers behind the Thief, attempted to cut Moscow off from the north and the trading centre of the White Sea by seizing the strategic monastery of the Trinity and St Sergius. But its fortifications withstood the siege, to the enormous prestige of the Church as a national and centripetal force, and also helped to rally the pro-Shuisky forces in the north.

On the other hand, Shuisky came no nearer to overcoming the Thief, and in this extremity he called in Swedish aid. In return for the renunciation of Muscovy's claim to Livonia, Charles IX of Sweden placed at Shuisky's disposal a force of 6,000 French, German, Scottish, and English auxiliaries under General de la Gardie. This in its turn provoked Sigismund III, king of Poland, to declare open war on Shuisky, lest the whole of the Baltic coast fall into enemy hands. In 1609 Sigismund laid siege to Smolensk, the classic key to western Russia.

This precipitated the final phase of the Troubles. The Thief's camp first recovered but then disintegrated, its leader killed in a brawl; Shuisky was deposed by a popular assembly and obliged to become a monk; and a seven-man boyar council took over what remained of government in Moscow. These boyars hoped to master the crisis by inviting a Polish prince, King Sigismund's son Władysław, to rule the country on condition that he convert to Orthodoxy, abide by Muscovite customs, and confirm the nobles' privileges (notably, their powers over their serfs). In happier times such a contract might have been the starting-point for the development of constitutional government. But the scheme was wrecked by Sigismund, who after temporizing for years now wanted the Muscovite throne for himself, as well as possession of Smolensk. This prospect was unacceptable to Russians of all factions and led them to rally against the foreign intruders.

Before this happened Muscovy's fortunes touched their nadir: Polish troops not only took over a large area in the west of the country but also sent a detachment to garrison Moscow itself, while the Swedes advanced in the north-west, threatening Novgorod. This meant that the task of liberating the country had to be undertaken by popular levies (militias) raised on local initiative in provincial centres that had not yet been too badly affected by the troubles. Their organizers received moral backing from Patriarch Hermogen in Moscow. Incarcerated and eventually killed by the occupiers, the prelate became a symbol of patriotic resistance.

Socially, the levies consisted in the main of 'gentry' and townspeople, the latter's role being essentially to provide financial support. Institutionally, they were based on *ad hoc* assemblies of the land. Each urban community sent deputies to a representative council which exercised both military and political functions, but evidently saw its state-building role as temporary. The first response to Hermogen's appeals came from Ryazan', where Procopius Lyapunov, a serving nobleman, formed a socially disparate army that marched on Moscow early in 1611. On the way it was joined by another force under Prince

Dmitriy Trubetskoy and Cossack bands led by Ivan Zarutsky. But social tensions soon asserted themselves. In July Lyapunov was assassinated by Cossacks who objected to legislation passed by the council over landownership and fugitive serfs that was favourable to the gentry interest. Lyapunov's force withdrew; after a long siege the Poles captured Smolensk while the Swedes took Novgorod. In Pskov a new pretender appeared, sometimes referred to as the Third False Dmitriy, and another centre of disaffection appeared in the south under the nominal leadership of the 'Little Thief', the son of False Dmitriy II and Marina Mniszech (who had married in turn both the First and Second Pretender!).

The second national levy, formed in 1612, was rather more successful. Originating in Nizhniy Novgorod on the Volga, it found an inspiring leader in Kuz'ma Minin, a butcher by trade. Command of the force which he and his fellow-townsmen created was entrusted to an experienced soldier, Prince Dmitriy Pozharsky. The troops advanced cautiously, reaching Moscow by September. Again dissension broke out. Some of the Cossacks besieging the city, under Zarutsky, split off and went home. Trubetskoy's men, however, cooperated with Pozharsky. After bitter fighting the Polish garrison in the capital, which was in dire straits, capitulated.

Early in 1613 a freshly elected Assembly of the Land met to choose a new tsar. It was the most representative of all such gatherings, with perhaps as many as 500 members, who included a scattering of free peasants (from the north, where serfs were rare) as well as the groups traditionally present. Among the boyar deputies there were none from 'collaborationist' families, although Trubetskoy ensured that they could keep the large tracts of land they had recently acquired by dubious means. Cossacks were well represented, and it was they who, with help from the local garrison, forced on the assembly the choice of Mikhail Romanov.

Announced on 21 February, this decision came as a surprise. The successful candidate was only sixteen and had neither governmental experience nor strength of character. What chiefly told in his favour were the close ties between the Romanov family and the former ruling dynasty. Michael's father, Fedor Nikitich (Patriarch Philaret), had suffered under Godunov, then served in the Tushino camp (which made him acceptable to the Cossacks), and later had been treacherously taken captive by the Poles when negotiating with them on behalf of Russian interests. It was assumed that when he returned he would exercise real sovereign authority on his son's behalf. Such an arrangement seemed preferable to rule by someone from another (more compromised) boyar clan, a Cossack, or a foreigner. After the decision had been endorsed in the provinces, the first Romanov was duly crowned tsar in July 1613.

The Troubles were not quite over – it took several years before a peace of sorts was concluded with Poland and Sweden. Cossack banditry would long remain a problem and decades elapsed before Muscovy recovered from the devastation. It did so, remarkably, by restoring the previous political and socio-economic order, characterized by autocracy and serfdom, with as little change as possible. Continuity was the watchword. Rebellion brought no rewards for the mass of the population. Nor can it really be claimed that the 'gentry' (junior servitors) improved their relative position in the service hierarchy, for this was still dominated by members of the old boyar clans. The Church acquired additional prestige, but used it to buttress its traditionally exclusivist, even chauvinistic, world-view. Such an outlook found acceptance among the population at large, because, as it seemed, enforced exposure to foreign influences during the Troubles had led to nothing but harm. The spirit of rebelliousness, however, was kept alive by the victory of the conservative forces in society, and would reassert itself periodically whenever the state overtaxed the Russian people's proverbial patience.

CHAPTER 6

The Growth of Absolutism: The Early Romanovs

The first tsar of the new dynasty could scarcely rule like an autocrat of the old school. Apart from Michael Romanov's personal inadequacies – he grew up to become an amiable but passive individual who relied heavily on his counsellors – his treasury was empty. Yet the tasks facing the government were immense. Peace had to be made with the Poles and Swedes, who still occupied parts of Muscovy; bands of Cossacks and robbers roamed the countryside; vast tracts of abandoned land needed to be resettled and trade links revived. In this work of social reconstruction the leading role fell naturally to the more enterprising elements in the élite, with whom the central authorities had no choice but to cooperate. Within weeks of Michael's accession the wealthy Stroganov merchant family was prevailed upon to provide funds for current expenses. Later levies were imposed on all merchants, who on several occasions had to hand over one fifth of their capital to help replenish the government's coffers.

In the early years of Michael's reign important decisions were taken by a handful of notables drawn from various clan groupings, including those who had 'collaborated' with foreigners or social rebels during the Troubles; they were then put before the Assembly of the Land (*Zemsky sobor*) for endorsement. Historians used to ascribe to this body more institutional coherence than it actually possessed. It is by no means certain that it functioned in permanence, with periodical re-election of deputies, over several years. Nevertheless the assembly did enjoy popular prestige and its association, however nominal, with the government's actions gave the latter valuable extra credibility.

In 1619 Philaret, Michael's father, returned to Moscow from Polish captivity. He was at once made Patriarch and *de facto* assumed supreme power. Formally his title was 'Great Sovereign', which made him the equal of the tsar. The pair seem to have cooperated harmoniously; at least there is no hint of Michael objecting to the unusual arrangement.

Evidently he was overawed by his father's strong will and experience. Seen by some as a statesman of European dimensions, Philaret had demonstrated his political skills during the Troubles, when he had temporarily served the Second Pretender. His subsequent harsh fate made him fiercely anti-Polish and an advocate of firm government at home. For fourteen years he governed Muscovy as absolute ruler, dispensing so far as he could with the *Zemsky sobor* and relying instead on officials in the central chancelleries and, in the provinces, on military governors (*voyevody*) whom he invested with broad powers. Their activities were geared mainly to preparing a war of revenge against the Polish-Lithuanian Commonwealth. Philaret had two aims: first, to bring order into the state finances, notably by taking a new census of each household's resources; secondly, to rebuild the country's armed might.

These reforms (or, more properly, counter-reforms) were inspired by deeply held conservative principles. In his capacity as Patriarch, Philaret endeavoured to restrict foreign influences on Muscovite religious life. Likewise, his diplomacy was designed to enhance Russia's role in a Europe riven by the Thirty Years War, in particular by winning the support of the northern Protestant powers (Denmark, Sweden) – and even the Turks! – in any confrontation with the Catholic Poles. When he died, in October 1633, Russia found herself at a critical juncture in a conflict known to history as the 'War of Smolensk', which ended in stalemate.

This twenty-year span, as well as the rest of Michael's reign – he died in 1645 – is best regarded as a period of slow recovery and consolidation. It was followed, under his son Alexis (1645–76), by another era of internal turbulence and continuous warfare. That the central power withstood these pressures was largely owed to the fortitude of this remarkable ruler. A pious but courageous soldier, he had a curious mind and permitted members of his court to adopt an aristocratic lifestyle modelled on the contemporary West. His chief preoccupation, though, was to achieve domestic stability.

He perceived good order to be the necessary condition for the good life and for success in anything ... This simple principle lay at the very centre of his philosophy, side by side with his religious faith. It also encapsulated his primary political objectives: to command obedience; to impose conformity;

to counter provincialism and promote centralization; to achieve harmony. For this he had to be an effective autocrat.*

After a six-year interlude of weak government on Alexis's death, Russia came under the rule of a woman, the Regent Sophia (1682–9). She had a forceful character and was apparently well educated for her times – no mean feat when female members of the dynasty, as of other aristocratic families, lived in virtual seclusion. This background helps to explain her success in court politics. Although she was thwarted in her plans to have herself crowned as autocrat, and her tenure of power was not marked by any significant reforms at home, she patronized the arts and was relatively open-minded towards non-Orthodox believers. She knew Polish and helped to bring about a treaty with the Polish-Lithuanian Commonwealth (1686) that was highly advantageous to Muscovy. Her biographer concludes that she was 'the most determined and capable woman ever to rule Russia', apart from Catherine the Great.†

The exploits of Alexis and Sophia in many ways anticipated those of their illustrious successor, Peter I (1689–1725), known as 'the Great', who would cast Russian absolutism in a mould that endured throughout the imperial era: both forward-looking and repressive. Mesmerized by the cult of this monarch assiduously fostered by his adulators over several generations, historians were for long prone to underestimate his forerunners' achievements, but the balance has now been redressed. In fact the early Romanovs compare quite favourably with most of their European contemporaries.

Let us now consider in turn developments in the socio-economic field, foreign policy, and culture.

THE ONSET OF SERFDOM

Seventeenth-century Russians had a high natural fertility rate. Although there are no reliable demographic statistics for this era, study of the surviving cadastral survey books suggests that by mid century

* Longworth, *Alexis, Tsar of All the Russias* (1984), p. 229.
† Hughes, *Sophia, Regent of Russia, 1657–1704*, pp. 275–6.

the rural population had regained its level of the 1590s. In the towns this point was reached a little later. Demographic growth was apparently faster than it was in Western or Central Europe at this time. Agricultural output may have recovered at a similar pace. In any case, by the 1620s Muscovite Russia could export grain to Scandinavia in pursuit of her diplomatic ends. Gradually the 'waste lands' recorded by the surveyors were brought under the plough as fugitives returned and new settlers set up homesteads on vacant plots. On the domains of the Trinity and St Sergius monastery, which are comparatively well documented, arable land, which had formed 37 per cent of the total area in the late sixteenth century, stood at less than 2 per cent in 1614–16 but had climbed back to 23 per cent by 1640; thereafter recovery was swifter. (Here as elsewhere many households may have concealed their existence from the census-takers.) In the 1620s peasants categorized as landless cotters (*bobyli*) were far more numerous than before the Troubles (1578–94): 39 as against 13 per cent, but by the late 1670s their proportion had declined again to less than 8 per cent.

Many of the old land-registry books had either been destroyed in the Troubles or were no longer relevant. This gave ample scope to proprietors of all categories, but especially the wealthiest, to appropriate land that lay untilled or was sparsely settled. To some extent this practice had official sanction, for two reasons. First, it seemed the quickest way to bring land back into cultivation and so to raise revenue from it. Secondly, many magnates were related to the Romanovs by kinship ties or common interests. One of the most successful of these 'strong men' (to use a contemporary expression) was an uncle of the tsar, Ivan Nikitich Romanov. These great boyars generally tried to augment their hereditary estates in the central districts by acquiring more fertile land to the south and south-east, where they competed for resources with lesser proprietors: the *dvoriane* ('gentry') and various groups of non-privileged junior state servitors. The northern forested areas, by contrast, were largely left for the monasteries to acquire and settle.

They had already managed to expand their holdings during Ivan IV's reign, when many victims of his *oprichnina* had willed their property to the Church so that prayers might be said for the peace of their souls. Several decrees were issued to limit this practice, but they were ineffectual. During the Troubles the monastic estates suffered in the general ruin, but later peasants often found it convenient to seek ecclesiastical patronage, whether from monastic foundations or members of the episcopal establishment. They could hope that the administrators of such estates would conduct themselves in a less crudely exploitative fashion than secular lords, especially the provincial petty 'gentry'. The latter, having few resources themselves, were inclined to exert the heaviest pressure on their dependants. Magnates, who might own several estates run on their behalf by bailiffs (often slaves or former slaves), could afford to be more indulgent. As for the 'black' (tax-paying) or independent peasants, they were now found almost exclusively in the far north; elsewhere, in European Russia at least, they had fallen under the thumb of landed proprietors.

That such lords did indeed exploit their bondsmen need not be doubted, although the extant sources and historical literature give a one-sided picture of social relations in the countryside under what is sometimes misleadingly called 'feudalism'. In fact the seigniors and their serfs (or slaves) were mutually interdependent. As in a tug-of-war, each party was ever on the look-out for chances to assert itself to the other's disadvantage. In theory the masters held absolute power: they could discipline their dependants in harsh or cruel ways (but not kill them!), and fix as they pleased the amount of forced labour (*barshchina*) they had to perform and/or the amount of quitrent (*obrok*) they had to pay. The general tendency was for the former type of obligation, which was more onerous, to rise, although there were wide regional disparities. In practice it might not be easy to get away with gross abuses, for there was general respect for ancient local customs (*starina*) and a seignior who infringed them took a risk. Memories of recent insurgencies were still fresh and peasants who felt badly done by could flee – if not to distant parts, which required uncommon courage and skill, at least to the nearby woods or to another proprietor.

The usual direction of such flights, it appears, was from junior to senior servitors, i.e. from 'gentry' to magnates, which partly coincided with a geographical flow from the centre to the southern perimeter. The losers in this competition for scarce labour wanted the state to help them identify runaways and enforce their return. It will be recalled that in 1597 the legal term for return of fugitives had been set at five years. Ten years later Tsar Vasiliy Shuisky, anxious to meet the 'gentry's' wishes, had extended it to fifteen years, but in civil war conditions this ruling could not be implemented. With Michael's accession the old five-year term was reinstated. The Trinity monastery petitioned for an extension to nine years. This was granted and then made general. By 1642 the term had become ten years, or fifteen if the plaintiff could prove that his ex-serf had been abducted by another lord. The greedier, or more desperate, seigniors now became obsessed with this issue and agitated for a complete ban on peasant movement. In economic terms this amounted to eliminating the market in agricultural labour. It would have been more sensible for lords to improve rural conditions so that peasants had no incentive to flee. But it was of course too early to visualize an agrarian economy based on free-market principles in which there would be no place for serfdom. At the time its necessity was generally taken for granted – even by peasants who hated the system and yearned to escape it.

As it was, the 'gentry' got their way, at least formally. In 1649 Tsar Alexis, acting under the threat of rebellion, issued a law code (*Ulozhenie*) which provided that all fugitives, and members of their families, should be returned to their former masters, no matter how long ago they had fled. In this way all peasants became assigned in permanence to their proprietors. They were mere chattels, equivalent to physical objects, that could be moved about, bought or sold at their master's whim. The minimal value placed on their lives is clear from the provision that if a lord unintentionally killed another's peasant, he had to replace the dead man by one of his own dependants, together with his family.* A Muscovite serf even lost the right to own personal property, for this was deemed to belong ultimately to his seignior. He could also not take legal action to defend his interests, for in court he was 'represented' by his master. The relationship between lord and peasant was not regulated by law. It was considered to be a private matter. A distinction continued to be drawn between serf (*krepostnoy*) and slave (*kholop*), but in practice this was of little account. A slave paid no tax, since he was presumed to be propertyless, which was indeed normally the case, although those occupying positions of trust might be well rewarded; some slaves accompanied their masters on military campaigns as retainers. A serf's tax was paid on his behalf by his master, who

---

* *The Muscovite Law Code (Ulozhenie) of 1649*, pt. 1, ch. XIX, arts. 1–3, ch. XXI, art. 71.

expected to recoup his loss from the *obrok* he received. This might be in the form of cash or natural dues.

Although the law provided for near-universal bondage, in practice matters were not so cut and dried. During the later seventeenth century serfs continued to flee from their lords in such numbers that from time to time the authorities had to make concessions; for example, they allowed junior servitors on the exposed southern border to possess fugitives acquired illegally, so that they could render more effective service. There was also a fair number of itinerant peasants and artisans who earned their living by casual hired labour or else by begging. In the newly settled south-eastern districts, between the Oka and lower Volga, the rural population was far from reconciled to serfdom.

They demonstrated this by rising *en masse* in 1670, when the region was caught up in a great rebellion mounted by S. T. ('Stenka') Razin, a Don Cossack chieftain. The core of this insurrectionary movement comprised Cossacks discontented at non-payment of the government's annual subsidy and at the growth of a property-owning class in their once egalitarian communities. Like Bolotnikov earlier, Razin came from the élite, but for personal reasons – possibly the execution of a brother – threw in his lot with the poor. In 1667 he led a small force on a buccaneering expedition into the Caspian that brought much loot and fame. Three years later, at the head of 7,000 men, he marched up the Volga. His aim was to free the common people from the yoke of noble landlords and officials. He did not, like earlier pretenders, claim to be the rightful tsar, but cleverly appealed to the populace's monarchical sentiments by towing along a barge bearing a young man who was given out to be the tsar's recently deceased son. The towns on the lower Volga fell into his grasp with ease. Razin's men slaughtered loyalist officers or other representatives of officialdom and instituted a rudimentary form of self-rule on Cossack lines. Thousands responded eagerly to his message of liberation, not only townspeople but parish clergy and non-Russian tribesmen: Mordvinians, Mari, and Chuvash. (The Kalmyks, however, remained loyal to the government and the Bashkirs were too remote from the rebel-held zone to join in.)

When Razin's advance northwards was halted at Simbirsk, he sent out three large raiding parties to stir up the enserfed peasantry. A regular *jacquerie* resulted.

In such districts as Alatyr and Arzamas . . . manor houses were invaded by mobs of peasants and tribesmen on whose merest whim hung the lives of the owners and their families. Unpopular landlords were butchered on the spot, together with their wives and children. Others were spared if they surrendered their money and belongings. Many took to the woods . . . or fled to the nearest town, where if they were in luck government troops had arrived to protect them.*

Most of the killing was done by Cossacks or urban mobs rather than by peasants. Contrary to the impression fostered by some historians, this was less a manifestation of 'class struggle' than an expression of sectional grievances. Cossacks, townsmen, and natives each had their own axe to grind, and it was only Razin's charisma that held the movement together. When his furious but undisciplined forces went down to defeat at the hands of the tsar's better-equipped troops, his aura of invincibility dissipated and his military strength melted away. What remained was a utopian myth, expressed in tales and folk-songs whose popular appeal lasted for centuries. Razin, it was said, would one day arise from the dead and lead his people in another great campaign of vengeance that would bring about a state of bliss in which there would be neither poverty nor social injustice.

It was no coincidence that townspeople should have responded so eagerly to Razin's message of violent upheaval, for most urban residents had good grounds for discontent. Russian society was now becoming one of fixed estates (*sosloviya*) in which noble landowners held pride of place. Lower down the scale there were niches for merchants, divided into three categories, and for lesser urban folk (artisans, shopkeepers, etc.), known as *posadskiye lyudi*. Muscovite towns that were more than mere military strongholds had a *posad* or commercial quarter in which craftsmen with various specialities plied their trade. The most numerous group were the producers of foodstuffs: bakers, brewers, fishmongers, and so on. A second large group consisted of clothing workers: tailors, hatters, furriers, and the like, who worked mainly with wool and flax processed by rural spinners and weavers. Leather- and metal-workers made both military goods such as swords or axes and household utensils. The level of technique was still low. For instance, carpenters did not

* Avrich, *Russian Rebels, 1600–1800*, p. 102.

use saws. Yet we should not forget that the magical churches of Kizhi were built by skilled craftsmen using axes. Labour was poorly rewarded, and even a silversmith might sell his wares for not much more than the cost of the metal.

As late as 1683 there were but 2,367 artisans in Moscow and about 2,000 in Novgorod. In Kazan' the 318 registered artisans formed more than half the urban population, but elsewhere the proportion might be lower: in Kolomna only 22 per cent (159). The problem was that the *posadskiye lyudi* had to compete with other urban groups who engaged in much the same activities, as did peasants belonging to nearby landowners. There was little differentiation between town and country, and the division of labour had developed to a far lesser extent than in Western Europe. This helps to explain why Russian towns could not hope to win the same legal rights (except those under Polish rule) or play an equivalent role in promoting social and political progress. All urban artisanal and commercial pursuits were duplicated on the estates of lay and ecclesiastical lords, where there was probably a higher degree of specialization than in the towns.

The first large-scale production of salt, for instance, took place on monastic estates. These artisans might be either serfs or, less frequently, hired labourers. Much of their output went to meet the needs of other people living on the estate, which was an almost self-sufficient entity so far as most products were concerned, although some goods were produced for the market. Monasteries took the lead in arranging country fairs, whose dates coincided with church holidays. These fairs had a competitive advantage over those held in towns and also the regular trade carried on in their oriental-type bazaars.

Foreigners were struck by the number of shops in the capital. The Dutchman Kilburger, who visited Moscow in the late seventeenth century, wrote that there were more shops there 'than in Amsterdam or in some entire kingdoms'. Most were not much more than booths, stands, trestles or barrels with a few articles on top. They were grouped in rows according to the nature of their stock. Pedlars walked around hawking trinkets and miscellaneous objects. Not all the shopkeepers were Russians; some were from the West, many more from the Orient, notably from Armenia.

In the 1620s Tsar Michael and his advisers, anxious to rebuild the shattered economy quickly, exempted certain great lords from direct taxation on their estates. This encouraged them to set up suburban settlements where their dependants could compete on favourable terms with the townspeople who had to pay taxes. Wealthy nobles could also buy shops, houses and even whole urban districts for the same purpose. This naturally evoked protest. In 1619 Philaret set up a commission to investigate. It was ruled that the tax-exempt interlopers should vacate these premises after a given term – at first ten, then twenty-five years – and return to their owners' lands. But this policy was not carried through systematically, and what the government gave with one hand it took away with the other by extending tax exemption to some junior noble servitors as well. In consequence tax-exempt ('white') settlements multiplied and tension mounted.

In 1637 townspeople joined with gentry representatives in submitting a petition to the authorities for redress of grievances. This initiative was in a sense an expression of civic-mindedness. Cooperation between townspeople and 'gentry' continued for the next decade or so, and in 1648 even assumed a revolutionary hue. Just as the *Ulozhenie* of 1649 made concessions to 'gentry' interests over serfdom, so it did to the townspeople. Over the next three years all tax-exempt enclaves were confiscated without compensation and their residents integrated into the urban communities. Some 10,000 houses in all were affected. Henceforth only certain military groups were allowed to engage in trade or handicrafts. The logical result of this reform was that the townspeople became a closed hereditary caste, as firmly bound to their place of residence as were serfs. They could not leave their town even if they were willing to pay the same amount of tax elsewhere. They also did not gain any additional rights of self-government. Although they continued to elect certain local officials, these men's chief function was to further state interests as tax-collectors and the like, and their activities were closely supervised by the military governor.

This subordination of the towns to the state is the main reason why, although their number increased during the seventeenth century, there was only sluggish growth in the total number of registered *posadskiye lyudi*. To this must be added the impact of frequent fires, which spread rapidly, since the houses were of timber, periodic bouts of plague, and, last but not least, civil disturbances. The upheaval in Moscow in 1648 was followed by revolts in Pskov and Novgorod two years later, in protest at steeply rising food prices owing to grain exports; in 1662 there was also unrest in Moscow and several other towns over debasement of the coinage to pay for war expenses. In 1682 the capital was once more the scene of unrest, but this time, significantly, those responsible were not traders but members of a non-privileged military caste, the musketeers or *strel'tsy*. As for the privileged servitors, there was no longer any question of them cooperating with humble townsmen, whose status was now far inferior to theirs. In this way the consolidation of social divisions bolstered the pre-eminence of the absolutist state.

The early Romanovs' greatest success was to co-opt the merchants into serving their interests, so hindering emergence of an independent bourgeoisie. Officially, merchants were divided into three categories (four including the Stroganovs, who enjoyed exceptional status). The next most senior group, the *gosti*, enjoyed important privileges: to acquire landed estates and serfs, to travel abroad (impossible for other subjects of the tsar!), and to have their lawsuits heard in the ruler's court, not by corrupt local governors; on top of this, they were exempt from tax. In 1634 there were only seventeen *gosti*; by 1685 the figure had leaped to forty. Located in the capital, they performed commercial and revenue-raising tasks on behalf of the Crown. Merchants in the two lower categories were more scattered geographically and had fewer privileges. But all considered themselves superior to ordinary towns-people. Over the century the merchants' status also declined relative to that of the landowning nobility. They did not enjoy economic security and so one finds few stable, long-lasting mercantile dynasties.

This was because trade was fraught with such high risks. Any merchant who defaulted on a debt automatically brought ruin upon the individuals who had stood guarantee for him, but who hoped to share in the profits if his enterprise went well. If it did not, they might well be cudgelled in public. (There were as yet no banks to spread the risks more widely.) On the other hand, merchants who served as customs officials or operated taverns for the state, for instance, could accumulate vast illegal fortunes. To many these seemed more profitable activities than engaging in regular commerce. Moreover, state service enabled some men to achieve high rank. All in all, Muscovite merchants' situation bore more resemblance to that of traders in other parts of Eastern Europe than to that of their Western counterparts.

Foreigners continued to dominate Russia's international trade and even made inroads into the domestic market – a matter that led native merchants to complain frequently to the government. Alexis was sympathetic, and in 1667 the New Commercial Statute ordained that foreigners should trade only in border towns and pay duty in gold and silver bullion. The influx of bullion, largely in the form of coin (the so-called Joachimsthaler or, in Russian, *yefimki*) helps to explain why from 1638 onward Muscovy had a favourable balance of trade; the peak year in this respect was 1652. The volume of international commerce expanded considerably. As already mentioned, exports now included grain as well as such traditional forest products as furs, hemp and flax, wax, and so on. The chief imports, apart from bullion, were cloth, copper, and other metals. Gunpowder and weapons were also obtained from England, Sweden, and Holland. An increasingly large share comprised luxury articles such as French wines, items of personal adornment, or furnishings. In 1671 imports through Archangel included diamonds, gold and silver objects, 28,000 reams of paper, 10,000 'German' hats, and 837,000 pins and needles. Tsar Alexis was very taken by mechanical artefacts such as timepieces and clockwork toys.

Distant Archangel on the White Sea was now Russia's most important port, for as a result of the Troubles she had lost her direct access to the Baltic. The burghers of Reval (the modern Estonian capital of Tallinn) were particularly eager to impose heavy duties on goods in transit between Muscovy and such north German cities as Lübeck. There was, however, some direct trade overland with Sweden and Poland. Trade through Archangel is thought to have doubled or tripled in value in the first half of the seventeenth century. Each July, as a rule, a convoy of merchants would set out from the capital on the fourteen-day trip north, in time for the arrival of the foreign vessels – now mainly Dutch rather than English – and the annual fair, which lasted until September. The Volga route to Persia retained its importance, but commercial contact with the Black Sea region, once crucial, was now of little note. Towards the end of the century trade developed with China, and Muscovy was one of the first European countries where tea was drunk.

Links with Europe were facilitated by the creation of a postal service. Relay stations where fresh horses could be obtained were set up along major roads. There were two main routes: Moscow to Vilnius via Smolensk and Moscow to Riga via Novgorod. From Vilnius the post went on to the northern German cities. Letters from Moscow to Danzig took only a week, to Hamburg four weeks. Letters arriving in Moscow were first opened in the Ambassadors' Office (*Posolsky prikaz*), the rudimentary foreign ministry, so that no private individual should know what was happening, inside or outside the country, before the Court. This was one of the most frequent criticisms of the postal service. It was also accused of irregularity, and its officials of diverting to their own pockets any valuables or currency found in the opened packets. But it undeniably fulfilled a service. Within the country official messages might take months to reach their destination since distances were so immense. This was a major hindrance to administrative efficiency. Moreover, notions of geography were still hazy.

For the same reasons the vast industrial wealth of the Urals and Siberia was as yet scarcely tapped, although from the 1660s onward small amounts of copper and silver were mined. The beginnings of Russian industrial development can be traced to this period. They had much to do with military needs. Cannon and firearms were produced at state-owned plants in Moscow. In 1632 a Dutch entrepreneur, Andreas Vinius, and his brother were granted a patent to establish at Tula a plant to supply cannon, cannon balls, and musket barrels at agreed prices. In 1644 Vinius's rival, Peter Marselis, and a partner received permission to set up ironworks farther north, along the rivers Vaga and Kostroma; in return they were exempted from tax for twenty years. Far more important economically at the time was the production of salt and potash. One saltworks near Solikamsk produced one million puds* and earned 70,000 roubles a year. Potash manufacture near Nizhniy Novgorod yielded 10,000 and caviar production on the lower Volga 20,000 roubles a year. Elsewhere there were facilities for manufacturing rope, glass, leather, and silk articles. All these enterprises were small-scale and few lasted for long. Their labour force consisted mostly of serf bondsmen rather than hired hands. Some senior staff and foremen might be foreigners, who undertook to instruct Muscovite apprentices in their technical skills. We should remember that this was the age when, in another of Europe's peripheral regions, American plantations were worked by slave labour: Russia was not unique.

* One pud = 36 lb.

WARS IN THE WEST

The dominant group in Muscovite society consisted of 'the tsar's serving men', as they were then called, who ranged from the great boyars, 'Moscow nobles', and other groups (including the influential state secretaries or *d'yaki*) who served in the capital and were closely linked to the court, down to petty gentry who 'served from the provincial towns'. The latter comprised a part-time cavalry levy which was mobilized each spring to defend the southern frontier from Tatar or other raiders. Most of these privileged groups held and/or owned land, from which they were expected to support themselves; cash grants were made only rarely, in return for specific deeds of valour or endurance. In practice members of a junior servitor's family would work the land, alongside his bondsmen, while he was away on campaign – a situation that was not conducive to good husbandry. To call these men 'gentry' is thus misleading, although the Western term is too useful to discard.

As the century progressed, many such servitors found themselves enlisted in permanently functioning units and were to all intents and purposes regular officers (or even just soldiers). They received some military training, initially by foreign specialists, and their value in warfare was accordingly greater than that of the old levy. Socially their status was now not too different from the non-privileged servitors, who held land in collective tenure and had to pay tax. These latter were divided administratively into several categories: musketeers (*strel'tsy*), artillerymen (*pushkari*), fortress guards, and serving Cossacks.* Each group had features of a caste: sons were expected to take their fathers' places, any shortfall being made up by men freshly assigned by the government. These part-time soldiers tilled the soil or engaged in handicrafts when not needed for warfare. For this reason they were increasingly allocated to ceremonial or police duties. A posse of élite ('Moscow') musketeers, armed with halberds, would escort visiting foreign envoys from the frontier to the capital and back. Others, in the provinces, spent their duty hours chasing bandits or keeping order.

Much more significant militarily were the forces 'of the new forma-

---

* These *gorodovye kazaki* should not be confused with the members of the autonomous Cossack communities to the south, who served Muscovy from time to time as auxiliaries.

tion' with their foreign-sounding names: infantrymen (*soldaty*), cavalrymen (*reitary*), and dragoons (*draguny*). These came into being gradually from the 1630s onward. Initially they consisted of foreign mercenaries, but very soon came to be composed of Russians, who were drilled and officered first by foreigners and then, as they learned their job, natives. Each of these forces was administratively independent, but on campaign elements would be combined to form a composite armed force, commanded by a boyar who could call on foreign specialists for advice where necessary. This arrangement sounds clumsy, but actually it was flexible and corresponded well with Muscovy's needs and limited resources. An army could be mobilized and stood down quickly and without much trouble. The soldiers were less cut off from their civilian roots than in a modern standing army. Admittedly, the forces' fighting capacity left much to be desired. There were rivalries between commanders owing to the custom of 'place-seeking' (*mestnichestvo*, see page 33), and also between different units, which did not train together; on campaign supplies were intermittent and the military bureaucracy creaked badly. These defects would be attended to by Peter I; *mestnichestvo* was abolished in 1682, shortly before Sophia's accession. In the meantime the armed forces operated quite effectively in a series of strenuous conflicts.

Apart from the penetration of Siberia, these wars mainly served the purpose of reuniting the east Slavic lands, which meant a long duel with the Polish-Lithuanian Commonwealth and eventually brought confrontation with Turkey. During the century the balance of power gradually shifted in Muscovy's favour, anticipating Poland's eclipse a hundred years later in the partitions. Another strategic objective, in which economic factors played a greater role, was to break Swedish control of the eastern Baltic and win territory there.

The peace of Stolbovo (1617) cleared Novgorod of Swedish troops but also forced Russia to abandon Ingria, at the head of the Gulf of Finland, for the first time and to pay reparations. Poland proved a harder nut to crack. With Smolensk still in their possession the Poles could launch a fresh offensive that in 1618 brought them to the gates of Moscow. But this was the last time their troops would enter the Great Russian heartland. A fourteen-and-a-half-year armistice was concluded at Deulino. Poland retained Smolensk and Seversk, annexed during the Troubles, and still laid claim to the Muscovite throne. It was to avert this menace that Philaret, as we have seen, sought Swedish and even Turkish aid. This policy brought a decade of peace to the southern border. But the 'war of Smolensk' (1632–4) was a fiasco. The Turks proved inconstant allies and allowed the Crimean Tatars to attack, whereupon the gentry militiamen ran off home. After Gustavus Adolphus's death the Swedes lost interest in the Russian connection. Tsar Michael had to agree to peace terms that left the frontier unchanged. The sole gain was that Władysław, who had succeeded to the Polish throne, gave up his unrealistic claim to rule Muscovy as well.

Episodic skirmishing between Don Cossacks and Tatars on the southern steppes led in 1637 to the fall of the strategically placed Turkish fortress of Azov. The Cossacks offered it conditionally to Michael, but he was far from ready to face the Turks. In 1642 the prize had to be abandoned, and in consequence Tatar raiders again wrought havoc along the southern perimeter. Moscow continued to aid the Don Cossacks with arms and money, hoping to stabilize the area (a policy unpopular with the rank and file, as we have seen), but was unsure of their loyalty and so kept them on a short leash.

Indirect territorial expansion was harder towards the south-west, where it encountered Polish resistance. Warsaw was keen to bring its southern border provinces under closer control by extending settlement, establishing large estates, and offering the Dnieper Cossacks strictly limited opportunities to serve the king. Security considerations were complicated by religious differences and the rise of an embryonic national consciousness among the Ukrainians. In 1596, by the Union of Brest, some Orthodox bishops had accepted a deal whereby they recognized the Pope's authority but retained their traditional rites. The 'Uniate' Church was regarded as heretical by members of the lay Orthodox brotherhoods, which had strong popular roots, but was backed up to a point by the Polish government and Catholic clergy. The latter put pressure on the Orthodox, who saw themselves as victims of discrimination. The Cossacks strongly sympathized with their Orthodox fellow-believers and had grievances of their own which the Polish Crown could not afford to meet. Revolts broke out and were ruthlessly suppressed, so augmenting the tension between the Poles and their eastern Orthodox subjects in Ukraine, where an embryonic national consciousness was emerging.

In 1648 the Cossack chieftain Bohdan Hmelnyckyj led his people in a war of liberation in the course of which the Ukrainians, aided by the Crimean Tatars, seized control of a large swathe of territory, much of it inhabited by eastern Slavs. In their national-religious exaltation the rebels also slaughtered thousands of Ukrainian Jews: this was the first episode in Russia's tragic record of violent pogroms. When the tide of battle turned against the Cossacks and their supporters, Hmelnyckyj turned to Moscow. Alexis, nervous at the prospect of war with Poland, hesitated. But in 1653 an Assembly of the Land – the last such gathering held – endorsed the sovereign's decision to take the Cossack Host 'under his high hand'. What this meant was in doubt, even after an agreement was formally signed at Pereyaslavl' (January 1654). Did the Cossacks' oath of allegiance to the tsar confer a measure of autonomy on the Ukrainian lands, as their leaders thought, or did it signify unconditional acceptance of Moscow's authority, in accordance with autocratic norms? In the following years Muscovite governors and troops gradually established a strong presence in the territory and the Ukrainians' limited right to conduct their own foreign policy was curbed. After Hmelnyckyj's death in 1657 his successors reverted in disillusionment to a pro-Polish policy, but this caused divisions in Cossack opinion and soon Ukrainians were fighting each other, to the benefit of their more powerful neighbours.

Meanwhile the 'Northern War' between Muscovy and Poland (1654–67) began with victories for the former. Smolensk quickly fell, followed by Vilnius, Kovno, and large parts of Lithuania. The Muscovites had not only Cossack help but Swedish also, for Charles X, invading from the north, captured Warsaw and Cracow and proclaimed himself king of Poland. This was too much of a good thing for Alexis, who himself aspired to the Polish crown. He broke off his Polish campaign and turned on his ally, hoping to secure part of the Baltic coast. But his fight against Sweden brought him no success. Muscovy came to grief at Riga. Once again, the desire to reincorporate all the Russian lands took precedence over maritime commercial interests. Muscovy concluded with Sweden the peace of Kardis in 1661. All Livonia was returned to Sweden and the latter's possession of Estonia was confirmed.

Over the next few years the Poles recovered much lost ground, but by 1667 both sides had had enough. The armistice of Andrusovo partitioned the Ukraine. The territory on the left (eastern) bank of the

Dnieper fell to Muscovy, along with Smolensk and Seversk to the north. The tsar also acquired a small enclave on the right bank around the old capital of Kiev, which had been lost to Rus' some four centuries earlier. He was pledged to relinquish it after two years, but this promise was never kept.

Muscovy's hold over Kiev and the left-bank Ukraine was shaky until 1686, when an 'eternal peace' with Poland legitimized her acquisitions. This treaty was part of a grand coalition against Ottoman Turkey, formed under papal patronage, involving the Holy Roman Empire and Venice as well as the two signatories. It marked Muscovite Russia's definitive entry into the world of European diplomacy as well as her growing ascendancy over Poland. In 1687 and 1689 Russian troops twice advanced across the waterless southern steppes towards the Crimea, but failed to breach the Tatar defences. Another century would elapse before Russia could defeat her old foes and establish herself on the Black Sea littoral.

Meanwhile in Siberia bands of Cossacks and fur-trappers were pressing steadily eastwards. They met little organized resistance and soon a network of strong points was established from which the authorities levied tribute on the local tribes: the (Buddhist) Buryats, Tungus, and Yukagir among others. By 1631 one group of Cossacks had reached Lake Baikal. Soon afterwards another arrived on the shores of the Sea of Okhotsk. The adventurous Semen Dezhnev then sailed from the mouth of the river Kolyma around the Chukotka peninsula, the northeastern tip of Asia, landing on the coast of what later became known as the Bering Sea (1648–9). After another fifty years Muscovy added the remote Kamchatka peninsula to her domains. More important were the lands of Dauria, along the river Amur to the south. Settlement here provoked the Chinese, who in 1685 took the fort of Albazin. Some forty Cossacks in its little garrison surrendered and entered the service of the Emperor K'ang-hsi as his guards. The skirmishing on the border between the two empires was halted by the treaty of Nerchinsk (1689), which two Jesuit priests helped to mediate. This fixed the frontier for the next 150 years and laid the basis for a mutually profitable commercial relationship.

CULTURAL CHANGE AND THE WEST

In the wake of foreign technicians came a slow seepage into Muscovy of Western ideas. Ecclesiastical control had hitherto stultified such little speculative or scientific thought as existed. The Renaissance and Reformation had scarcely any impact on Russian culture, which developed independently from the West. The Church succeeded in neutralizing the influence of the Judaizer heresy (see Chapter 3), whose adherents questioned the doctrine of the Trinity and the divinity of Christ. Orthodox teaching circumscribed the minds of Russians at all levels of society. Recent scholarship has emphasized the role of personal faith in the lives of the common people. This often took the form of a belief in miracle healing cults associated with local saints. These were frowned on as superstitious by some senior churchmen. They made efforts to systematize religious worship throughout the land, but such rationalistic thinking was rejected by ordinary believers. The Troubles led to the growth of a moralistic tendency among the parish clergy, who began to preach sermons, hitherto generally absent from Orthodox church services. This mood spread to the social élite. The Zealots of Piety movement in the 1630s sought to extirpate 'pagan' entertainments, put down drunkenness, and discipline the clergy. It attracted support in high places, notably from the tsarevich Alexis, who inaugurated his reign with an attempt to impose these reformist ideas. It backfired badly.

The main reason for this was that the parish clergy, along with their flocks, continued to see 'holy Russia' as uniquely blessed with divine favour. Adherence to traditional rites and liturgical practices held out the promise of eternal salvation, and therefore the slightest change, however trivial, smacked of the devil. Their outlook was primitive and Manichean. They thought it mattered greatly whether one crossed oneself with two fingers, not three, and recited a double, not triple, Hallelujah. Behind this was a chauvinistic reaction against reformist clerics from the Ukraine, whose teachings were considered tainted by foreign influences, either Latin or Greek. For Kiev (and other 'west Russian' bishoprics) came under the authority of the Patriarch of Constantinople, not of Moscow. Ukraine was culturally ahead of Muscovy. In 1632 Petro Mohyla, a nobleman who had been educated in

Lviv (Poland) and Paris before he took monastic vows, set up a theological academy in Kiev patterned on Jesuit schools, with Latin as the medium of instruction. His aim was to utilize Catholic learning in order to provide Orthodox clergy with the intellectual equipment needed for effective confrontation with Catholics or Uniates. But his college – the first higher-educational institution anywhere in the east Slavic lands – was accused by non-Orthodox of spreading Prot-estantism, while for conservative-minded Orthodox, especially in Mus-covy, the college seemed a source of 'Latin heresy'. There were indeed grounds for their suspicions, since many of the corrections to the liturgy which the reformers insisted on were based on Latin sources. Ironically, however, the ancient texts used by the traditionalists were also defective.

The 'Old Believers', as the opponents of reform came to be called, were more justified in objecting to the high-handed methods used by Patriarch Nikon and his Ukrainian colleagues from 1652 onward to press their cause. Holy icons were trampled underfoot, dissenters exiled and even burnt at the stake. This was the fate of the archpriest Avvakum, the most outspoken opponent of the reforms, in 1682. His autobiography, a tale of courageous non-violent resistance to physical deprivation, torture, and humiliation, is a classic of early Russian literature. The 'Old Belief' gained support among the populace in several regions of the country and even won adherents in the aristocracy. Notable among them was Feodosia Morozova, who took the veil, was incarcerated in a monastic dungeon, and died of starvation in November 1675. Two months later the monks of the Solovetsky monastery in the White Sea, who sympathized with the Old Belief, were overwhelmed after an eight-year siege. Sophia's regency was marked by a wave of mass suicides as whole communities of alleged 'schismatics', believing that the kingdom of Antichrist was at hand, chose death rather than surrender to posses of troops sent against them. All this anticipated the fierce opposition that Peter I's Western-inspired reforms would provoke a few decades later.

The schism crippled the official Church by weakening its popular base. Nikon, who had an imperious temperament, quarrelled with Alexis's boyars and refused to exercise his duties as Patriarch (1658). Efforts to solve the crisis by negotiation failed and in 1667 he was unseated by decision of an Orthodox ecumenical council. In theological terms his offence was the 'Latin' error of preaching the supremacy of Church over state. In fact Nikon wanted a partnership of equals – the traditional Byzantine doctrine of 'symphony' between the two powers – but what ensued after his fall, tragically, was the Church's further subjection to secular authority. Nikon himself was treated with comparative leniency and died in 1681. His successors on the patriarchal throne had little genuine religious spirit and distinguished themselves mainly by their intolerant, repressive attitude. In this way the schism prepared the ground for the Patriarchate's abolition in 1721.

The arrival of clerics from Ukraine and, to a lesser extent, other Orthodox lands in Eastern Europe was the source of the 'Moscow Baroque' culture that flourished from the 1670s onward. Most evident in architecture, painting, and literature, 'it heralded not only the death of Old Russian culture but also the beginning of a prolonged stylistic era that ended only with the turn to Classicism in the 1760s'.* The number of stone buildings in Moscow proliferated. Their façades were articulated with engaged columns and pilasters; window surrounds were capped with pediments; scallop shells, volutes, and festoons were all part of the architects' repertoire. The Palace of Facets in the Kremlin accepted features of this style when refurbished by Osip Startsev (1684–5). Among the splendid ecclesiastical buildings erected at this time were the Cathedral of the Resurrection at Nikon's palatial 'New Jerusalem' monastery near Voskresenk, west of Moscow, and additions to the Novodevichy convent just outside the city. Commissioned by Sophia, they were destined to become her prison.

In icon painting new fashions became apparent which involved an imaginative use of perspective, realistic landscapes, and even lifelike human faces. Portraits of non-religious subjects were now considered acceptable. Easel paintings were still less common than murals or frescos, however. Book publication, which hitherto had lagged owing to ecclesiastical censorship, increased modestly towards the end of the century. Until 1679 there was only one printing press, a state institution supervised by the Patriarch, and nearly all titles were designed for liturgical use. They included a Bible translation (1663). A second press, which lasted only four years, was directed by Simeon Polotsky (1629–

---

* Hughes, *Sophia*, p. 134.

80), a noted poet in the florid style then à la mode, and had a somewhat broader scope. Even so, few expressly secular works appeared, though among them were Alexis's law code of 1649 and a military manual. Yet some aristocrats built up libraries, mainly of foreign-produced books, while at a more popular level satirical tales and chivalric romances circulated in manuscript.

The most interesting literary developments were in the field of drama. The first performance of a stage play in Muscovy took place in 1672 in the court's suburban village of Preobrazhenskoye. Written and directed by a German Lutheran pastor, Jan-Gottfried Gregory, it was a tragicomedy on the biblical theme of Esther, performed mainly by foreign immigrant children with musical accompaniment by a native serf 'orchestra' – and lasted ten hours! Tsar Alexis, who watched it in solitary splendour from an armchair in the centre of the auditorium, was spellbound and at once ordered a 'palace of amusements' to be built within the Kremlin walls. Later dramatic presentations included Polotsky's *Judith and Holofernes* and (by another author) *Adam and Eve*. The latter contained many Baroque elements that featured in the allegorical plays given at the Habsburg court. Nevertheless Moscow was a world away from the dramas of Molière or the Restoration comedies of contemporary England.

The expanding foreign colony in Moscow which provided Alexis with his players breached the country's self-imposed isolation and was for this reason carefully watched by the Church and state authorities. Conversely, the free-and-easy manners of these mercenary soldiers, artisans, and merchants attracted to their ranks certain critically disposed members of the élite.

The first Russian free-thinker was Prince Ivan Khvorostinin, a former military commander and man of letters who declared roundly: 'There are no decent people in Moscow: they are all stupid, there is no one to talk to.' He stopped going to church and questioned Orthodox doctrine. Philaret had him arrested and sent to a monastery to mend his ways. He repented and died a free man in 1625. Another 'dissident' was Gregory Kotoshikhin (*c.*1630–67). A minor official in the foreign ministry, he got into a scrape and in 1664 defected to Sweden, where he penned a scathing but informative attack on the customs and institutions of his native land: corrupt government, criminality, loveless marriages, pride, ignorance, and oppression – these were some of the vices he deplored. Kotoshikhin was executed in Stockholm for murdering his landlord.

Far more influential than either of these men was the forward-looking statesman Athanasius Ordyn-Nashchokin, who strove to promote municipal reform and the advancement of trade, notably by working towards a rapprochement with Poland. His successor in the *Posol'sky prikaz*, Artamon Matveyev, and several other boyars of his time broke with convention by furnishing their homes in luxurious Western style, complete with mirrors, wallpaper, gardens, and other modern amenities.

The concept of the West as a source of comfort and cultivated manners owed much to the 'German suburb' (*Nemetskaya sloboda*),* to which, in 1652, Patriarch Nikon had ordered Western residents to be confined. The 'suburb' soon developed into a fine city quarter with four Protestant churches and an object of fascination to natives who managed to visit it. The future Peter I was one such, and his biographers' understandable fascination with his early life has led to exaggeration of the suburb's historical significance. On balance, in the age of 'Moscow Baroque', influences from Catholic Europe through the Ukraine were probably stronger than those from the Protestant north: only under Peter I would the situation change radically in that respect.

It is misleading to view Muscovy simply as a passive partner in relations with the West. As in all intercultural contacts between more and less 'developed' countries, the leaders in the recipient society borrowed what they reckoned was most necessary and affordable from the 'donor' society. In Muscovy's case this meant primarily military technology and only secondarily the artefacts of humane culture. These were quite reasonably seen at best as luxuries, at worst as a threat to the country's spiritual values – and, implicitly, to its socio-political order.

This cautious approach was most evident in the educational field. The first school, located at the Andreyevsky monastery outside the capital, came into being in 1648–9 as a private venture by the nobleman F. M. Rtishchev. He sought to emulate precedents in Kiev and the first teachers were Ukrainian monks. Opposition by conservative clerics

---

* Muscovites commonly referred to all Western Europeans as 'Germans', although many of them were Dutchmen, Swedes, Englishmen, or Scots.

prevented it from prospering. Later, in 1666, another school was set up by Simeon Polotsky, whose learned student Sylvester Medvedev planned to turn it into an academy which, like Mohyla's college in Kiev, would teach a broad range of subjects, including Greek, Latin, and Church Slavonic. Such a tolerant approach was not to the liking of Patriarch Joachim, who side-tracked the idea. Instead, he set up an institution in 1687 which ostensibly had much the same profile but was run by two *Greek* brothers named Leikhudes.

Medvedev was executed for alleged heresy in 1690 (one of the few such cases in Muscovy), but shortly afterwards Joachim followed him to the grave. The Moscow Academy spent as much effort controlling knowledge as disseminating it. Had the hierarchy taken a less bigoted stance and actively promoted theological education, the Church would have been better placed to resist assault at the state's hands under Peter I and later. It was also a misfortune for Russia that the seventeenth-century schism, which dealt a sharp shock to the ecclesiastical establishment, was a backward-looking, indeed chauvinistic, phenomenon. It was not intellectually productive in the way that the Protestant Reformation or radical Puritanism were in Western Europe and then in the New World.

CHAPTER 7

Expansion and Bureaucracy: The Age of Peter the Great

At the end of the seventeenth century it became clear to many in the upper reaches of Muscovite society that the country was in deep crisis. Radical changes were needed if it were to survive in a competitive world dominated by more advanced Western states. It was no longer enough to borrow selectively from the West: instead there had to be a fundamental reorganization of the governing structure, coupled with a reorientation of values, that could allow the people's suppressed energies to be harnessed to new tasks.

This tacit sentiment found expression in a remarkable ruler, Peter I ('the Great'), Alexis's son by his second marriage to Natalia Naryshkin. Born in 1672, he formally became tsar in 1682, jointly with his dim-witted half-brother Ivan, but did not take up the reins of government until 1696. But from then until his death in 1725 he dominated his country's history in a way that few other European monarchs have ever done theirs. Both physically and intellectually, Peter towered over his contemporaries. Nearly seven feet tall, he was endowed with inexhaustible energy and an indomitable will. His mind and body were in continual movement: travelling, learning, giving orders, supervising his subjects' manifold activities, punishing rebels or laggards. He had received only the rudiments of a formal education, but taught himself to command armies, build ships, and engage in diplomatic manoeuvres. He became a skilled carpenter and could claim competence in a dozen other trades – including dentistry, as some of his courtiers with bad teeth discovered to their cost! Dispensing with the Byzantine pomp and religious ceremonial that had surrounded earlier Russian sovereigns, Peter mixed freely and casually with people of the most varied backgrounds. In this way he was able to indulge his taste for alcohol and other crude forms of pleasure. From these encounters with commoners, in the 'German suburb' and elsewhere, came many of his associates in the work of reform, although others were boyars of distinguished lineage. Whatever their origin, Peter's 'fledglings' were expected to labour zealously in the common cause, sacrificing their health and even their lives if need be. For although Peter's tastes were above all practical, his activity was directed towards a lofty goal: the greatness of the new Russian empire that was being erected on the foundations of the old Muscovite state.

This vision was destined to remain half-realized. The most obvious reason for this lay in the defects of Peter's own violent, autocratic temperament: he was impatient, irascible and often needlessly cruel. But at a deeper level there were also 'structural' reasons. Wherever Peter was unable to take over existing institutions and beliefs, adapting them to his purposes,

he set out to destroy them and to replace them with new rational and bureaucratic ones. In so doing he created the modern administrative apparatus of the empire that had to lead society on to the path of full modernization. Yet at the same time he subjected the forces of independent initiative and thought to intolerable controls that stifled their productive potential and creative energies.*

This contradiction persisted throughout the imperial era and led eventually to revolution, only to resurface in the Soviet order that replaced tsarism.

Peter was less of a despot than either Stalin in the twentieth century or Ivan IV in the sixteenth. He was no megalomaniac. Though subject to fits of tyrannical fury, he retained an appealing human quality, a spontaneous vivacity and sense of fun, a capacity for affection and great physical courage. Characteristically, his death was expedited by jumping into freezing water in an effort to save some sailors from drowning, although its main cause seems to have been syphilis, brought on by his unconventional, lascivious lifestyle.

Peter's youth was disturbed. His father's remarriage split the Romanov family, and ambitious boyars exploited the breach. When only ten he witnessed the humiliation of the respected Artamon Matveyev at the hands of the rebellious *strel'tsy*: allegedly the experience gave him a lifelong nervous tic. During Sophia's regency the Naryshkins were sidelined and obliged to live away from the capital. They were not,

* Raeff, *Political Ideas and Institutions in Imperial Russia*, pp. 118–19.

however, repressed, and the boy Peter had the leisure to develop his contacts with foreigners in the 'German suburb'. He developed an interest in military pursuits and began to drill his companions into regiments and organize manoeuvres around a fortress built on the river Yauza near Moscow. All the paraphernalia of a miniature army were present – cannon and firearms supplied by the royal arsenal, barracks, stables, uniforms, money. Soon Peter had at his disposal two regular regiments, the Preobrazhensky and the Semenovsky. The officers were mostly foreigners, while the soldiers, drawn from the Muscovite nobility, were in effect, cadets at the first Russian military academy. These regiments became the nucleus of the Guards, the élite force in the regular Russian army which Peter built.

Discovery of an old English sailing-boat, which he later called 'the father of the Russian navy', awakened in him a passion for things nautical. From experiments on nearby lakes he progressed to sailing on the open water at Archangel, which he first saw in 1693. That year he accompanied some foreign merchantmen for many miles out to sea: 'it was one of the crucial experiences of his youth, indeed of his whole life'.* Russia's embryonic naval power was designed for use in southern waters. Russia was still nominally at war with the Turks. In 1695 an overland campaign against Azov failed, largely because the Turks could supply the fortress by sea. That winter the tsar built a fleet at Voronezh on the Don, which eventually comprised thirty sea-going vessels and about a thousand barges. It was instrumental in forcing Azov's surrender in July 1696. However, since the Kerch Strait remained in Turkish hands Peter's warships could not gain access to the Black Sea.

The need to boost the alliance against Turkey, coupled with Peter's personal desire for first-hand knowledge of other lands, led him to organize a 'Grand Embassy' to the West in 1697–8, in which he took part under a transparent incognito. For a reigning monarch to leave the country was an affront to Muscovite tradition. The journey had a serious purpose: to learn the secrets of Western might so that they might be emulated in Russia. By way of the Swedish Baltic provinces and Prussia the party reached the Netherlands, where for several weeks the tsar and his companions laboured as apprentice shipwrights in the

---

* R. Wittram, *Peter I: Czar und Kaiser*, Göttingen, 1964, i, p. 113.

wharves of the Dutch East India Company, first at Zaandam and then at Amsterdam. In their leisure hours they visited mills, workshops, schools, and various public institutions.

After four months in Holland, Peter went on to England. He sailed in the royal yacht presented to him by William III. This was the real climax of the journey. With his headquarters at John Evelyn's house at Deptford, conveniently near the King's Wharf, Peter was able to study the latest shipbuilding techniques. But he also visited Oxford, London, the Tower, the Mint, and, of course, Woolwich Arsenal. There were other visits to Chatham and Portsmouth for fleet reviews and mock naval battles. All of this Peter meticulously noted in his diary. From Bishop Burnett he learned of the advantages of a state-controlled Church. The lighter side of the English stay produced damages to Evelyn's house estimated by Sir Christopher Wren at £350. Wren's report noted a ruined lawn, destroyed furniture, pictures used for target practice, walls scratched and smeared.

After some four months in England Peter set out on his return journey by way of Vienna. He intended to go on to Venice, where some Russian nobles had been sent to study, but instead had to rush back to Moscow. News reached him of another rebellion by the *strel'tsy*. He had long suspected this force of disloyalty, although without good grounds. In 1689 they had not responded when called on to back an attempt to give the regent Sophia the crown. (Indeed, this affair had actually helped Peter, since it led to Sophia's deposition and the return to power of the Naryshkin faction.) On the present occasion about 2,200 musketeers marched on Moscow demanding satisfaction of service grievances, such as non-payment of a promised bonus. Some of them certainly hoped for a change of ruler, but there is no evidence that Sophia, confined in a Moscow convent, gave them any encouragement. The disturbance had already been put down, and 130 men hanged in public, before Peter returned. But for the tsar this was not enough. Intent on vengeance, he launched a fresh investigation to extract confessions of seditious offences that would justify the corps' destruction. Peter himself was among the torturers. Within three weeks 800 men were hanged by the Kremlin wall; a second wave of terror claimed several hundred more. Repression on this scale had not been seen in Moscow for generations. It was the first big test for the Preobrazhensky

Office. Formed to administer one of the Guards regiments, it became Russia's first regular secret police agency.

This merciless onslaught on a group of men identified with the old order was accompanied by another attack that had symbolic implications. Muscovite males wore their beards long. For some believers they were a sign that man was made in God's image. To Peter this was mere obscurantism; as well as adopting new modes of behaviour, his people had to *look* different. No sooner had he returned to Moscow than, to set an example, he shaved off the beards of his leading boyars. He also enforced the wearing of 'German' dress as distinct from the long-sleeved topcoats worn hitherto. Every Russian, except for the clergy and the peasants, had to comply with the new laws on pain of a fine. This effort to westernize the outward appearance of Peter's subjects had little success outside the court and military milieu. Most Russians preferred to pay the fine rather than lose their beards.

More significant were the measures taken to expand the army with a view to launching an offensive war against Sweden. Proprietors of every category were obliged to provide recruits, according to the number of their serfs. What the decree did *not* make clear was that these soldiers were never expected to return: they were 'immortals', destined to spend the rest of their days in a new permanent (standing) army, which silently superseded the old military formations. By 1700 seventy-one new infantry regiments had been formed. Each nominally had 1,000 men, organized, equipped, and uniformed in European style. They were under the command of foreign specialists, but most officers were drawn from the Russian privileged servitor class.

THE GREAT NORTHERN WAR

As the war with Turkey fizzled out in 1700, with only minor gains for Russia, Peter turned his attention to the north. In 1697 a mere youth, Charles XII, had come to the Swedish throne. It seemed an opportune moment to seize the Baltic provinces and so eliminate a major obstacle to trade with the West. Peter's ally Augustus II of Poland (and elector of Saxony) had already begun the assault; Denmark followed. On 19 August, once peace had been signed with the Porte, Peter declared war. He did not know that Charles XII would prove a formidable foe, or that hostilities would last twenty-one years, postponing and seriously distorting the reforms which Peter had set out to introduce.

Charles first knocked the Danes out of the war and then turned on his eastern enemy. The freshly recruited and as yet inexperienced Russian forces were encamped before the Swedish port of Narva. On 30 November, in a heavy snowstorm, the Swedes launched a surprise attack. One quarter of Peter's 40,000 men were killed or captured, the rest put to flight. All his precious artillery had to be abandoned. The tsar at first despaired but soon recovered his balance. Reconstruction of the army became his prime concern. Levy after levy was imposed on the peasants and townspeople, usually in the proportion of one man per twenty households. They produced about 138,000 men by 1709. Training, drill, and tactics were all revolutionized. Peter stepped up the production of flint-locks and bayonets, of siege guns and field artillery. New ironworks and powder factories in the Urals were the chief centres of arms manufacture. He made every effort to attract more and more military specialists from abroad; and in 1702 issued a decree inviting all foreigners to Russia, promising them religious freedom and their own law courts, as well as free passage and employment. To finance all this effort, Peter sequestered the Church's revenues and devised a plethora of new taxes; all in all, about 80 per cent of the state's income went to feed the needs of war.

For all his urging and impatience, Peter also needed time. Here Charles came to his aid. He failed to follow up his victory at Narva by a march on Moscow; instead he moved south and involved his forces in innumerable minor campaigns against the Poles. Peter himself kept Charles bogged down in Poland as long as possible by sending Augustus II reinforcements and money. But at the end of 1706 the Polish front finally collapsed. By the treaty of Altranstädt a Swedish-Polish peace was concluded. Augustus had to give up his throne and acknowledge Charles's nominee, Stanislas Leszczyński, as the new Polish king.

In the meantime Peter had strengthened his position in the north. In 1703 he took Ingria and founded, at the mouth of the Neva, the city that today once again proudly bears his name. From the start he intended to make St Petersburg his capital in order to symbolize the break with Moscow and make manifest the country's orientation to the West. In 1704 Dorpat and Narva were taken. The Russian forces under Sheremetev despoiled the Baltic provinces they occupied, for it was uncertain that Russia would be able to keep them.

In the interior, conscription and oppressive taxation caused a great deal of discontent. Rumours spread among Old Believers and others that Peter was the Antichrist. In 1705 *strel'tsy* and other troops garrisoning Astrakhan' rose in revolt, holding the city for nine months. Two years later the Don Cossacks rebelled once more, led by their hetman Kondratiy Bulavin. It was a replica of Razin's revolt, but did not win as much peasant support. It was ruthlessly suppressed by Prince Dolgoruky, who ordered villages and crops to be destroyed. Some 14,000 men, women, and children were put to death. Rebellions also broke out among the Bashkirs and other non-Russian nationalities in the Volga–Urals region.

To deal with these troubles troops had to be transferred from the western front, leaving the country open to invasion by Charles XII's forces. After driving the Russians out of Poland (1706), he crossed the border in January 1708 at the head of 50,000 men with the evident intention of marching on Moscow. The old capital hurriedly prepared to withstand a siege. But in September supply difficulties led Charles to make a fateful decision:

> He renounced the direct route eastwards to Moscow, with its endless prospect of burning villages, and instead turned his army south-east ... He plunged on in the direction of the Ukraine, there to join forces with the Dnieper Cossacks under the hetman Mazepa, and recoup his strength amid relative abundance for a fresh advance on Moscow in 1709.*

Peter sent Sheremetev with the main army to dog his footsteps on a parallel course, and a few days later himself struck at the Swedish baggage train with reinforcements under Lewenhaupt, which was proceeding southwards from the Baltic provinces, and severely mauled it. As he later claimed, 'This may be termed our first victory, for never before have we overcome a regular force ... it was the mother of Poltava.'

On 27 June 1709 this little fortress on the Vorskla witnessed one of the most crucial battles in Russian military history. Charles's forces

---

* Duffy, *Russia's Military Way to the West ... 1701–1800*, p. 24.

had received little aid from Mazepa, who managed to bring over only 2,000 men: his leadership was in question and many Cossacks had been intimidated by Russian punitive actions. The harsh winter and the siege had worn down the invading army. Charles was wounded and had to be carried around on a litter. He had only some 24,000 men available to fight twice as many Russians. The Swedes advanced at night, suffering heavy losses, only to find themselves facing two enemy lines, which marched towards them. In the ensuing clash Russian superiority in artillery proved decisive. The Swedes lost 10,000 men, twice the Russian toll; the rest fled towards Turkish territory but were forced to surrender. Only Charles and a few followers got across the Dnieper safely, there to plot revenge. Peter invited the captured Swedish generals to a banquet, where he is said to have toasted them as his teachers in the art of war. Many of their officers entered Russian service and contributed to the spread of Western ideas.

'Now indeed has the foundation stone of St Petersburg been laid,' Peter commented. Not only was Russia free from the threat of invasion, but she could exploit Swedish discomfiture at her king's enforced absence in order to revive the alliance. In Poland Augustus was restored to power; Peter could tighten his grip on the Baltic lands by taking Vyborg, Reval, and (in 1710) Riga; three years later the new Russian fleet defeated a Swedish squadron off Hangö. A small force was sent into northern Germany to help the Danes, and in 1715 Prussia and Hanover were brought into the allied camp. In the tyrannical duke of Mecklenburg Peter obtained a useful client, but his activities aroused misgivings elsewhere in Central Europe. Britain, too, was alarmed at Russian designs and the 'Quadruple Alliance' formed in 1715 creaked badly. Its squabbles frustrated a grandiose plan to invade the Swedish mainland, and after 1718 Russia again found herself all but isolated as Sweden's principal antagonist. Charles had meanwhile escaped from Turkish internment, but to his enemies' good fortune met his death in a minor engagement in Norway (December 1718). Direct peace talks in the Åland Islands dragged on for eighteen months and it was only after Russian troops had launched three destructive raids on the Swedish coast, and a British squadron appeared in the eastern Baltic, that the war was at last brought to an end.

By the peace of Nystad (August 1721) Russia returned to Sweden the Finnish provinces which she had occupied, but was granted title to part of Karelia, Ingria, Estland, and Livland (roughly, modern Estonia and northern Latvia). This put at her disposal a potentially valuable reservoir of educated Baltic Germans, many of whom entered the tsar's service. Russia had to pay monetary compensation and undertake not to interfere in Swedish internal affairs – a promise that was not always kept.

These terms signalled nothing less than Russia's emergence as one of the great powers of Europe. Her new status was exemplified by an active policy of forging dynastic matrimonial links abroad. Peter married a niece to the duke of Kurland (on the southern Baltic coast), and even aspired, vainly, to wed one of his daughters, Elizabeth, to the young Louis XV of France. He himself visited the French court in 1717 on a trip which also took him back to the Netherlands, this time not as a shipwright but as a prestigious ruler. It was only fitting that in October 1721 he should have taken the title of emperor, although some time elapsed before it was generally recognized abroad.

These successes were not matched by equivalent victories in the south. Indeed, at one point Peter very nearly found himself in Turkish captivity. In 1711 the sultan was prevailed on by the Tatars and the fugitive Charles XII to declare war on Russia. This gave Peter the extravagant idea – the stuff of the 'Eastern Question' for the next two centuries – that Russia could incite the Orthodox peoples of the Balkans to rise up against their Muslim 'oppressor' and create a situation that would allow Russia a leading role in the Balkans. There was indeed much combustible material in the region, and the rulers of Moldavia and Montenegro responded positively to Russia's summons. But the military equation was unfavourable to her designs. In July 1711 a Russian army under Peter's personal command was surrounded on the river Pruth. The tsar was saved by what seemed at the time a miracle. The Turkish commander was corrupt, and in return for a handsome bribe agreed to a lenient peace that obliged Peter merely to cede Azov and its hinterland, which he had gained some years earlier.* The deal

---

* Peter also promised to vacate Poland and allow Charles XII free passage home through that country. It is probable that Turkish moderation was due also to political-strategic considerations, especially the knowledge that Vienna, having defeated the Hungarian rebels, had a free hand for another campaign in the Balkans.

was later endorsed, not without difficulty, by the treaty of Adrianople (1713).

This settlement forced Peter to look further east for compensatory territorial gains. He had long dreamed of bringing Europe's trade with the Orient under Russian control. In 1715 he sent an officer, Volynsky, to reconnoitre the ground. He reported that Persia was in a state of collapse and an easy target. Appointed governor of Astrakhan', he was then entrusted with making military preparations. The newly minted Emperor Peter himself took charge of the campaign (1722–3), which brought the western and even southern shores of the Caspian under Russian control. But he had overreached himself and shortly after his death the newly acquired provinces had to be abandoned. The enterprise did at least give some hope to the hard-pressed Christians of Armenia and Georgia that Islamic rule might one day be ended with Russian aid.

Peter also sent an expedition across the desert to Central Asia (1717), but it was surprised and massacred by the khan of Khiva – an inauspicious start to Russia's relations with the peoples of that region. Diplomatic and commercial relations developed with China. Geographical discoveries in Siberia were promoted, as was the study of Eastern languages – including even Japanese, after a castaway on the Pacific shore turned out to hail from that as yet unknown country.

INSTITUTIONAL, SOCIAL, AND ECONOMIC REFORMS

For most of Peter's reign, Russia was at war. This very largely determined the nature, scope, and success of the tsar's activities as a reformer. Many of his reforms were desperate expedients born of immediate military necessity, but as he matured he came to see the need for greater consistency in his legislation. Throughout his career, he was inspired by the same vision of a people devoted to the state which had inspired the rulers of Muscovy since the fifteenth century. Peter was pragmatic in his approach and his reforms were addressed to two objectives: to educate the Russian élite in his own rationalist ethos and to harness all the resources of the country for total war. He shrank from no measure that seemed calculated to advance his purposes, however great the opposition he met with. 'The Tsar pulls uphill along with the strength of ten, but millions pull downhill,' wrote Pososhkov, an early critic of the Petrine regime. To drag these millions with him, Peter had to deploy a widespread system of spying and informing, in addition to the punishments traditional in Muscovy. He made his subjects, particularly the peasants, pay a heavy price for their country's rise to the status of a great power.

His chief innovations were the standing army and the fleet. Both armed services were organized on the Western pattern, with an eye to Prussian and English models respectively, but adapted to suit Russia's capabilities. The disparate forces of Muscovy were welded together to form an army that had conventional infantry regiments, cavalry squadrons, and artillery detachments (the engineers came a poor fourth), the whole supervised from 1720 by a War College. Its first head was Peter's favourite, the humbly born Field Marshal Alexander Menshikov. The artillery came under an experienced soldier, James Bruce, a russified member of an old Scots family. Foreigners played a prominent part in Peter's army, but sometimes proved unreliable, and so as soon as possible they were phased out in favour of Russians whom they had trained.

By the end of the reign the regular army was an estimated 204,000 strong, to which may be added 85,000 irregulars (and 15,000 sailors). Conscripts were supposed to receive pay, a pledge not always observed, and a food ration nominally worth half as much as their pay. This consisted of rye flour and groats, the basis of the gruel that was their principal fare. When on active service they were entitled to meat, wine, and beer, and so on paper at least were better fed than the average peasant. But soldiers served for life and had no leave entitlement. They were often employed as forced labourers on construction projects and discipline was harsh. The Military Statute (1716) prescribed ample use of corporal punishment, notably the dreaded penalty of running the gauntlet. 'Those who flee and are caught,' ordained Peter in 1708, 'are to be put to death without any mercy.' Nevertheless large numbers of men dared to desert. To bring them back a series of amnesties had to be proclaimed, with rewards for those who revealed their whereabouts. The bulk of Peter's soldiers, however, imbibed the new military ethos.

Officers were exempt from corporal punishment (except in the case of grave state crimes) and earned much higher pay, but otherwise endured conditions comparable to those of their men. Guards units, in principle composed wholly of noblemen, did best. Promotion to officer rank automatically conferred noble status. Figures for 1720 show that only 14 per cent were of non-privileged background (38 per cent if former low-grade servitors and foreigners are included). Peter's Table of Ranks (see below, page 93) of 1722 laid down strict rules governing promotion in all branches of state service. Although modelled on Western regulations, in practice it allowed *mestnichestvo* to survive in the form of clan rivalries over appointments, social privileges, and other bounties conferred by the autocrat. Eighteenth-century Russian nobles much preferred military service to civilian, as it conferred higher status. It can be argued that Petrine absolutism, with its militaristic character, actually delayed the political maturing of the nobility, of which there had been some modest signs in the late seventeenth century.

Much less attractive was service in the navy, for this was relatively arduous. In 1721 the fleet had 124 Russian-built sailing vessels, plus another 55 taken from the Swedes. There were also 416 man-powered galleys, which proved their worth in Baltic waters. Naval bases were constructed at Kronstadt (on an island outside St Petersburg), Reval, Vyborg, and elsewhere – by forced labour, needless to say, and at the price of many lives. Peter's Baltic fleet was expensive to maintain and his enthusiasm for it was not sustained by his immediate successors, who allowed it to rot away. One problem here was that Russia still lacked a merchant marine of her own, to serve as a reservoir of naval officers and nautical expertise, and so had to rely extensively on foreign (mainly British) know-how.

Financing the armed forces was always at the centre of Peter's attention. His early measures were desperate expedients: debasing the coinage, introducing direct taxes on beards, coffins, bathhouses, and the like. These devices yielded diminishing returns and prompted a radical reform of the fiscal system. In 1710 a new census was ordered, but in the chaotic conditions of the time it could not be carried out properly. There was widespread evasion: some householders took to the woods, others bribed officials to overlook their existence. After much confusion a system was gradually introduced (1718–24) that was simplicity itself (on paper!): the cost of the armed forces was calculated and this sum divided up between various provinces, districts, and local communities. Each of the tsar's non-privileged male subjects, irrespective of age, had to pay a poll tax. The base rate was seventy-four kopecks a year; peasants without landlords and townspeople respectively paid forty and fifty kopecks more. The proceeds accounted for about half the total state revenue and went almost wholly on the army, units of which were quartered in each district with the task of collecting their sustenance by the use of military force. There were Western (Swedish) precedents for such a 'cantonment' system, but as applied in Russia it proved a disaster. The rural areas effectively came under a chaotic military dictatorship. The regimental colonels and a baffling array of 'commissars' behaved like oriental satraps, flogging the wretched inhabitants and subjecting them to all manner of abuse in search of the elusive funds for their units' support.

The armed forces' total cost in 1725 is reckoned at 6.7 million roubles. This represented a much heavier burden on the taxpayer than in Muscovite times. Allowing for inflation and population growth (a rise from 4.5 to 6.3 million male peasants between 1678 and 1719), and taking indirect taxes into account, the demands of the fisc probably increased two and a half times over the period. What mattered was less the actual drain on peasant incomes (about 12 per cent of a day labourer's average earnings) than the cumbersome system whereby the poll tax was assessed and collected. These defects outweighed the positive effects of the tax in stimulating peasants to extend the cultivated area and so to increase their monetary income.

Peter's energetic efforts to create a modern bureaucratic administrative machine were frustrated by lack of funds and skilled personnel. In consequence the Muscovite vices of corruption, nepotism (clientism), and malfeasance persisted beneath the European veneer of the new institutional framework. Peter's initial measures did little more than destroy the old system. Authority was devolved to eight (later eleven) provincial governors. Their chief task was to secure recruits and funds; they lacked the resources to do anything constructive for those in their charge. After 1712 the pendulum swung back to the centralization characteristic of Muscovite government. In the seventeenth century there had been a jumble of nearly a hundred 'offices' (*prikazy*), including temporary ones; some were territorially based, others functional. These chanceries gave way to central executive bodies rearranged on functional lines as 'colleges'.* The most important were those for the armed forces (War College, Admiralty) and foreign affairs. Three others were instituted for financial matters, and three more for justice, commerce, and manufacturing. Above them stood the Governing Senate (1711), designed to act as the highest state institution. On paper it had broad executive and supervisory powers. But Peter, in a typical move, deputed a Guards officer to attend its meetings and forestall any improper conduct, a function that later passed to the procurator-general. Supported by a phalanx of procurators and 'fiscals', his job was to act as 'the sovereign's eye', i.e. to ensure legality throughout the administration. But how could this function be reconciled with the principle of autocracy? Elaborate rules were devised governing officials' conduct, but it was a task of generations to instil in them a modern bureaucratic ethos – for example, to distinguish between their own private interests and those of the state. Educational levels were low; poverty and family pressures encouraged bribe-taking; and decisions would often be inordinately delayed. In Imperial Russia, as earlier, corruption was not just an incidental factor but 'systemic': the oil that made the machine turn, so to speak.

Peter's government was certainly bureaucratic, but not in the Weberian sense (implying regularity, professional expertise, and observance of legal norms). No effective provision was made for a separation of powers (though the idea was mooted), and the executive, as an expression of the sovereign's will, was paramount. Old Russia had known consultative organs: the boyars' *duma* and the *Zemsky sobor*. But their powers derived from custom and they lacked clear institutional contours, let alone defined rights. In the later seventeenth century, as its membership expanded, the *duma* had lost weight, its place taken by informal consultations between the monarch and his closest advisers,

---

* The term reflected the then common European bureaucratic practice of collective decision making by boards. In Russia most decisions were actually taken by the college president and then endorsed by his subordinates. Relics of the old territorial system survived, e.g. in the Siberian Office, which lasted until 1763. Recent research has shown that the Muscovite *prikazy* did have regular budgets and followed elaborate procedural rules, but the clerks received no training and could only perform routine tasks. Peter's reform of the alphabet and introduction of Arabic numerals (along with the Western calendar) certainly helped to improve record keeping; documents ceased to be written on scrolls and the complicated old script was simplified.

called 'boyars of the tsar's chamber' (*komnatnye boyare*). After 1653 the Sobor was seen as an unnecessary and perhaps dangerous luxury. Although the merchants still called for one (1662), and in 1681 separate consultations were held with representatives of different social groups, the Assembly of the Land faded from people's memory. Not until 1767 would there be another national consultative body, and that failed to establish itself. In essence, such discussion of public issues was incompatible with the bureaucratic absolutism of the Petrine state.

At the local level, however, there was in practice greater flexibility, since Peter's militarization of the countryside was moderated after 1727 and there were few officials below provincial (*guberniya*) level. Here power continued to lie with owners of landed estates, in so far as they were not absent on service. Peter did much to change their cultural profile but left their power over their dependants intact. His sole intervention in the sphere of landlord–serf relations remained a dead letter. This was an edict of 1721 banning the sale of serfs as individuals, apart from their families, 'like cattle, a practice not found anywhere else in the world'. The situation of the mass of the population deteriorated during his reign. Since the poll-tax registers included household slaves and even vagrants, the scope of serfdom was now extended. The old distinction between serf and slave ceased to apply, and the bonded peasants' lot did indeed have much in common with slavery. They needed a passport, signed by the seignior (or where there was none, by a local official) to leave their area of residence.

Peasants could at least take satisfaction in the fact that their owners were themselves in bondage to the state. Peter forced the 'gentry' (now commonly referred to by the Polish term *szlachta*) to undergo instruction in some branch of practical knowledge, and even prescribed that those who failed the course should not be allowed to marry – another of his ineffective edicts. At age fifteen they had to choose which branch of state service to join. Sometimes the tsar examined and assigned them himself. Thereafter their progress – and incomes – were governed by the Table of Ranks. Men of non-privileged backgrounds (e.g. townspeople, clergy) could in principle enter state service and on reaching rank V (VIII in the armed forces) obtain 'gentry' status. Few of them got much higher than this, although there were fourteen ranks in all.*

---

* Actually thirteen, but old superstitions died hard!

The merchants and urban population (3 per cent of the total) stood to gain more immediate benefit from Peter's policies than either peasants or 'gentry'. As early as 1699 he had tried to reorganize municipal government by introducing elected burgomasters, but this did not depart from Muscovite tradition and turned out to be mainly a revenue-raising measure. In 1718 he took up the idea again, influenced by the (German) self-governing municipal institutions in the annexed Baltic lands. The town population was divided into three groups: prosperous members of the 'first guild', such as merchants and professional men; a second guild of artisans and petty traders; and commoners. The two guilds jointly elected a magistracy (council) responsible for all the town's affairs, on which, however, only members of the first guild could serve. Unfortunately this oligarchic system did little more than perpetuate the old order of things, especially as taxes were increased. Urban communities were riven by constant conflicts over distribution of the load, and the elected officials remained pre-eminently state servitors. Although empowered to perform beneficial 'police' functions (providing social services, fighting fires, and so on), they lacked the resources and will to carry them out.

Peter held to the mercantilist outlook then popular, with its emphasis on achieving a favourable balance of trade by government stimulation of domestic industry and protective tariff barriers. 'Our people will not undertake anything unless they are compelled to,' he wrote, 'therefore the Commerce College is to direct them as a mother does her children until they grow up.' Merchants were bullied into setting up companies and investing their capital in new state-run mining and metallurgical enterprises in the Urals. The first ironworks here was founded in 1698 by Nikita Demidov, an ex-serf whose family became one of Russia's first mercantile dynasties. By 1725 there were thirteen ironworks in the region, and four times as many in all Russia. Indeed, prior to the British industrial revolution, which introduced new technologies based on fossil fuels, Russia's wood-burning 'manufactories' led the world in iron output, much of which was exported. The first industrialists depended heavily on state aid in many ways, not least for assignments of forced labourers: vagrants and other marginal elements, such as orphans and prostitutes. In 1721 factory owners were allowed to buy populated estates, subject to a loose control by officialdom. This move was unpopular with nobles, who cherished their monopoly on land in private (secular) ownership, and, of course, with the 'factory peasants' themselves. They became one of the most oppressed groups in the population and frequently rose in revolt.

Conditions in the textile industry, centred around Moscow, were only slightly better. There was ample use of female and child labour. These relatively large enterprises at first produced sailcloth, uniforms, and other articles needed by the state, but soon catered to the civilian market as well. The same was true of those making paper (indispensable under a bureaucratic regime!), glass, and china. The chief natural obstacle to the development of a market was the great distances separating producers (especially in the Urals) from potential consumers. Peter made a start on this problem by building canals. One was designed to facilitate the transit of goods from the Neva to the upper Volga, another to link the Volga and the Don. The project remained incomplete until Stalin finished the job in 1952 – also by using forced labour!

EDUCATION AND CULTURE

It was in his treatment of the Church that Peter broke most radically with Muscovite tradition. The gradual secularization of Russian society had begun earlier. Alexis had worsted the patriarchate and, eager for more revenue, interfered in the administration of monastic estates. Peter took the process to its logical conclusion by ensuring that henceforth the Church should serve the largely secular objectives of the state.

Unlike his father, Peter regarded the religious sensibilities of his subjects with indifference or even hostility. Early in his reign, he organized his drinking partners into a 'Most Drunken Synod' at which the rites of the Church were openly mocked. Deprived of popular esteem by the schism provoked by Nikon's reforms, the Church lacked the moral authority to oppose him. In 1700, when the Patriarch died, Peter failed to appoint a successor and in 1721 he replaced the patriarchate by a Holy Synod, essentially a secular ministry of religion. The Church thereby lost any form of independent self-government at the national level. Peter restricted entry into monasteries and convents and insisted that those remaining in them help to care for the sick or engage in useful trades. Surplus parish clergy were conscripted into the army. In the longer term, the clergy were also profoundly affected by changes in the system of direct taxation that turned them into a closed caste. Out of all these changes emerged a clergy that very gradually became better educated and more efficiently administered. The costs were high, however. The churchmen felt slighted in status by the secular state while their efforts to emulate the gentry cut them off still further from the masses, who were already suspicious of them for accepting Nikon's reforms and for carrying out the new tasks imposed on them by Peter. Increasingly, peasants and Cossacks looked to the Old Belief and to new fundamentalist sects for religious enlightenment.

Church schools lacked adequate financial support and made little impact until later in the century. They were unpopular with pupils, not least because the teaching concentrated on Latin and was all but irrelevant to their later function as priests.

The seminary brought little return on the Church's crucial investment . . . most attention was on discipline, not moral upbringing [and so its graduates] often had only the haziest conception of Orthodoxy.*

Little better success, attended the tsar-reformer's efforts to promote secular education, at least in the short term. As always, his aims were utilitarian: to provide the hosts of experts that the new state required. Foreigners could be no more than a stopgap. Nor was it enough to send Russians abroad to study navigation, engineering, or other practical subjects. Several schools had the job of training future officers. In 1716 twelve 'cipher schools' were set up, so called because they taught mathematics. In both cases the pupils were conscripted.

When volunteers could not be found, recruits were raised for education just as they were for the armed forces or for pioneering work. Truancy was punished with the same severity as absence without leave from the army, but pupils defected from the schools just as peasants ran away from the landed estates and soldiers deserted from their regiments.†

By 1722 the number of cipher schools was said to be forty-two, with some 4,000 pupils, but five years later there were only 500 pupils in all the schools that were left. By 1744 the whole system had collapsed.

---

* Freeze, *The Russian Levites: Parish Clergy in the Eighteenth Century*, pp. 96, 98.
† Lewitter and Vlasto (tr., ed.), *Ivan Pososhkov, 'The Book of Poverty and Wealth'*, p. 83.

Apart from the lack of money and teachers, and the pupils' natural reluctance to prepare themselves for conscription into state service, the underlying reason was the growing stratification in Russian society. Nobles, for instance, did not relish their sons sharing a school bench with those of humble merchants or clerics.

Despite these disappointments, Peter's reign witnessed something of a 'cultural revolution' in Russia, even if its effects were at first limited to the privileged. Far more Russians travelled abroad, although only on official business. Foreign books were translated and published, most of them now on secular, technological subjects. The first Russian newspaper appeared, and public theatrical performances were given in Moscow's Red Square. The seclusion of noblewomen ended after 1718, when the tsar ordered the holding of *assemblées*, social gatherings at which men and women met, danced, and cultivated the rudiments of good manners. The idea caught on and within a few decades the court of St Petersburg had a reputation as one of the gayest in Europe. With its fine canals and gracious public buildings, the new capital was well on its way to becoming one of the continent's architectural marvels. In many respects it was a model of early town planning, even if life for its inhabitants was costly and unhealthy.

St Petersburg also had some pretensions to be a seat of learning, for Peter founded an Academy of Sciences, which came into being shortly after his death in 1725. For some years foreigners predominated among the staff and even the students at the university associated with it had to be imported from Germany; but in time the academy became a truly Russian institution and one of the world's leading establishments for scientific research. It had a museum of antiquities (*Kunstkamer*), in which the tsar kept curiosities that struck his fancy, such as botanical and mineral specimens. Archaeology was only one of several disciplines that could trace their beginnings back to this era. Some critics have dismissed all this activity as over-ambitious for a country that was such a newcomer to science, and certainly Peter was motivated in part by a desire to win international prestige. But he was also curious to learn, and in this as in so many other ways he set a pattern for a small but growing number of his subjects.

It is an exaggeration to conceive of Peter I as having artificially 'westernized' Russia, cutting her off from the supposedly 'organic' life of old Muscovy. This myth was spread by Slavophils and nationalists in the nineteenth century, and echoes of it can be heard even today. To a large extent he followed earlier precedents, and where he innovated he took care to explain to his subjects why the changes were necessary. But it is also true that his reforms were imposed from above, in a violent, arbitrary way which detracted from their success. The idea of the state power as the demiurge of progress was rooted in Western rationalism, notably in the thinking of German cameralists and Pietists who were influential at the time. When transported to Russia and implemented by a convinced autocrat and partisan of military measures, they produced results that did not justify their tremendous social costs. A recent Russian historian sees Peter's reforms as 'the apotheosis of statism'. Based on authoritarianism and coercion, they 'naturally gave birth to the apathy of the slave, the thievery of the official, the social dependence, and the indifference that became a sorry tradition of Russian history'.*

Certainly there was no rational reason for Peter's extreme nervousness at the threat of subversion, which led him to institute the harsh and cruel system of espionage managed by the Preobrazhensky Office. Characteristically, priests who heard their parishioners' confessions had to report to the secret police any suspicious remark. The mild-mannered Old Believers suffered greatly from this persecution, although Peter was initially not ill-disposed towards them and in 1714 permitted their communities to exist on payment of a tax at double the normal rate. They had to wear a distinctive red patch on their clothing to facilitate surveillance; for their womenfolk the regulations prescribed long cloaks and cocked hats.

Among Peter's notable victims was his son by his first wife, the tsarevich Alexis. In 1718 he was indicted for alleged sedition and died in prison from gruelling tortures in which his father is believed to have participated. There was indeed a barbaric streak in the tsar which contrasts with his feats as Russia's first 'enlightened' ruler. Peter initiated more than he achieved. If the pace of change slackened after his death, this was because the burdens imposed on the population were excessive. Like other early European advocates of Enlightenment, Peter put too much trust in mere legislation. It was not in his nature to balance goals against resources carefully, or to relate his ends to the

---

* Anisimov, *The Reforms of Peter the Great* . . . tr. J. T. Alexander, pp. 40, 296.

means available. Foreign advisers who thought in such terms, such as Heinrich Fick, a German official who at the tsar's command made a thorough study of the Swedish administrative system, found their elaborate proposals amended to suit the vagaries of court politics or the demands of the military.

Moreover, Peter's measures accentuated the divisions in Russian society. Bewigged and clean-shaven nobles or officials, dressed in Western style and living far away from their estates, had less and less in common with bearded peasants in *kaftans*, mired in their native villages. Imperial Russia became a land of two cultures which coexisted with little interconnection. The common people, steeped in poverty and illiteracy, clung with ingrained conservatism to their traditional beliefs and way of life. The privileged classes eventually came to speak a different language, think in different terms, and pursue different ideals. Up to a point this gap was inescapable, for the tsar could not have been expected to bring the fruits of modernity to all his subjects at once. Moreover, members of the upper classes were with few exceptions as yet neither free nor wealthy. But in so far as the socially privileged managed to improve their lot in the decades that followed, the social tensions would increase and, in the fullness of time, have dramatic consequences.

CHAPTER 8

The Birth of Civil Society

On the death of Peter the Great the throne passed to his widow, Catherine I. A simple Livonian serving girl, she had risen to become the emperor's consort and then his second wife. The death of their son and heir in 1719 dealt a blow to Peter's hopes of dynastic continuity. In 1724 he had Catherine crowned empress and may then have intended her to rule after him, but by a decree of 1722 he reserved to the sovereign the sole right to nominate his or her successor. This introduced an additional element of arbitrariness into Russian court politics. In the event Peter was unable to name his successor, and Catherine I owed her crown to a cabal, led by Menshikov, Peter's chief favourite, who conveniently had a Guards detachment at his disposal.

Over the next decades the throne was occupied by a series of weak or ineffectual rulers – three women, a boy, and an infant – while real power rested with an oligarchy drawn from senior aristocratic families, who appointed the leading officials. However, this vacuum at the centre, deplored by later monarchist and nationalist historians, was not necessarily a bad thing. It facilitated pluralistic thinking among the élite and allowed the central government institutions, notably the Senate, to find their footing and perform routine administrative business in a reasonably regular way. There was probably less wilfulness in law-making than there had been under the dynamic Peter I.

Continuity of policy was assured in most major policy areas. In the first place, the Russian empire continued to expand, buttressed by an army that won all the wars it fought. Secondly, the tacit compact between state and nobility ensured social stability – at high cost to the peasants, to be sure – and considerable economic growth. Thirdly, during the long reign of Catherine II ('the Great', 1762–96) the arts of civilization increasingly penetrated the upper classes, who gained a fair measure of autonomy *vis-à-vis* the central power. Although with few exceptions Russia's emerging intelligentsia was politically conformist, its very existence was a latent threat to the autocratic system.

EXPANSION OF EMPIRE

The Great Northern War had made Russia a major European power. Her interests extended from the Baltic to the Caspian. She had humiliated Sweden, made inroads on the Polish-Lithuanian Commonwealth, gained influence in German affairs, and waged the second of many campaigns against Turkey. These successes were now taken further as the new Russian empire enlarged its territory at the expense of its neighbours to the west and south.

Under a skilful foreign minister, Ostermann, Russia's international policy was based on an alliance with the Austrian Habsburgs (1726). The two powers had common interests in south-eastern Europe (or so at least it seemed) and were united in opposition to the French Bourbons, who sought to bolster Sweden, Poland, and Turkey as a cordon sanitaire against Russian expansion as well as a counterweight to the Habsburgs. In 1733–5 the two powers succeeded in imposing another Saxon ruler, Augustus III, on the Polish throne and defeating the French candidate, the native son Stanislas Leszczyński. This War of the Polish Succession (1733–6) saw the first clash of Russian and French arms, at the siege of Danzig, and in 1735 eight Russian regiments appeared on the Rhine in response to an Austrian request. They were too late to fight, but 'astonished everyone by their good order and discipline', or so a contemporary (C. H. Manstein) claimed.

The partnership with Austria was less successful against the Turks. Russian armies performed better than before against the Crimean Tatars, took the fortress of Ochakov near the mouth of the Dnieper, and later advanced into Moldavia. But in 1739 the Austrians, who were less doughty in the field, signed a separate peace and left their eastern ally no choice but to follow suit. The treaty of Belgrade partially made up for the disappointing outcome of Peter's Pruth campaign. It returned Azov on the Don (without its fortifications) and adjacent territory to Russia, along with another stretch of steppe to the south-west, but still denied her direct access to the Black Sea.

In the 1740s Russia became enmeshed in a network of incompatible commitments which prevented her from consistently aiding the hard-pressed Habsburg empress Maria Theresa in the War of the Austrian Succession. A pro-French (and pro-Prussian) party lobbied effectively at the St Petersburg court. Eventually another Russian expeditionary corps was sent to the Rhine (1748), but these were mercenaries paid for by Britain, Austria's ally, and Russia had no part in the peace settlement.

Her military and political role was much more substantial in the Seven Years War (1756–63), in which she took the side of Austria and France against Frederick II of Prussia. After clearing East Prussia, Russian armies repeatedly marched through Poland into eastern Germany, where they participated in several decisive engagements. At Zorndorf (1758) nearly 12,000 men fell in action. An effective long-distance supply system was built up, but often troops had to live off the land and their depredations, particularly in Poland, were a major by-product of the conflict. In 1760 a force of Cossacks briefly occupied Berlin. But just when Frederick's position was weakest he was saved by the fortuitous death of Empress Elizabeth (December 1761). Her successor, Peter III, idolized Frederick, and within months Russia's armies had withdrawn from the war without winning any compensation. Elizabeth had hoped to secure East Prussia, but such a gain would have alarmed Central European opinion. As it was, the Austro-Prussian struggle for hegemony in Germany lent itself to exploitation by Russia, who in 1779 became a formal guarantor of the territorial *status quo*. This symbolized her attainment of a pre-eminent status in European affairs, as did her sponsorship of the continent-wide Armed Neutrality league in the following year.

By this time Poland had suffered dismemberment by her neighbours. Each of them had its client among the aristocrats who called the tune in this elective monarchy. The death of the Polish king, Augustus III, in 1763 precipitated a contest for the throne in which Russia again managed to impose her will. Stanislas Poniatowski, the successful candidate, was a native Pole but an ex-favourite of Catherine II. She skilfully manipulated their relationship, and the grievances of the Orthodox believers, to force on the Polish Diet a treaty placing the country's archaic constitution under Russian 'protection' (1768). This provoked an insurrectionary movement which in turn led to intensification of the Russian military presence. Other states, not least Turkey, were alarmed, but the Germanic powers allowed themselves to be bought off. The first partition of Poland (1772) deprived that country of one third of its territory and population. Russia gained the districts of Polotsk, Vitebsk, and Mogilev, measuring some 93,000 square kilometres, and about 1.8 million people, most of them either Orthodox eastern Slavs (Belarusians) or else Jews.

Worse was to come. When the French Revolution broke out, the three partitioning powers affected to perceive a threat in its numerous Polish sympathizers, who in May 1791 adopted a democratic constitution. Desperate diplomatic manoeuvring by the Polish government, which in the interim had worked hard to consolidate its authority, was of no avail. In 1793 Russia joined with Prussia in organizing a second partition of the country. Catherine II's instruments were a 'confederation' of pro-Russian magnates and a force of 100,000 troops. This time Russia acquired 230,000 square kilometres and over 3 million people (three times more than Prussia). Most of them were ethnic Poles (and Roman Catholics), and so harder to assimilate. The rump Polish state was finally eliminated in 1795, after a desperate uprising led by Thaddeus Kosciuszko. By this cynical display of power politics Poland was wiped off the map until 1918, but its people's desire to recover their independence would complicate relations among the victors for the next century.

On the southern Baltic coast Russia rounded off her gains by incorporating the duchy of Kurland (roughly, southern modern Latvia), which had been within her sphere of influence for decades. From time to time she also intervened politically in Sweden, backing the oligarchic faction against royalist centralizers (as in Poland), but failed to undermine that country's sovereignty. A brief naval war in 1788–90 brought no territorial changes and did not affect Russia's Baltic trade. Exports from St Petersburg rose from 3.2 million roubles in 1760 to 38.2 million in 1799. This trade was

one of the important engines of economic growth. It had a major impact on the commercialization of agriculture, the growth of industry, the expansion of the money supply, and the accumulation of capital.*

Economic interests were still more to the fore in Russia's expansion

---

* Kahan, *The Plow, the Hammer and the Knout*, pp. 163–4.

Westward Expansion
— Muscovy, ca. 1650
– – – Russian Empire, ca. 1750
– – – – – Russian Empire, ca. 1800
·········· Polish partition borders
–·–·– Russian Empire, ca. 1815

```
0        200      400 Miles
0     200   400 Km
```

White
Sea

S W E D E N

FINLAND 1809

K A R E L I A

Abo

Helsinki   1743

BALTIC SEA

Gulf of Finland

Reval

ESTLAND
1721

Dorpat

LIVLAND
1721

Riga

COURLAND
1795

P R U S S I A

R. Neman

Vilnyus

KINGDOM OF
Warsaw
POLAND 1815

LITHUANIA   1772

WHITE RUSSIA
(BELARUS)
1795

R. Vistula

R. Dniester

R. Pruth

Kishinev

BESSARABIA
1812

T U R K E Y

R. Donau

Vyborg   1721

St. Petersburg

L. Ladoga

INGRIA

L. Peipus

R. Dvina

Minsk

Smolensk
1654/1667

Moscow

Chernigov

Kiev
Pereyaslavl
UKRAINE
1654/1667

Poltava

Khar'kov

R. Don

R. Bug

R. Dnieper

Odessa

Zaporozh'e (Sich)
1775

CRIMEAN

TATARS

KUBAN

BLACK SEA

1793

MAP 4. *Russian westward and south-westward expansion in the reign of Catherine the Great*

southwards. Initially the whole territory north of the Black Sea, from the Danube to the Caucasus, was still under Ottoman rule. The spread of Slavic (Russian and Ukrainian) settlers across the steppe was a long-term process. Peter's subjugation of the Dnieper and Don Cossacks helped to 'pacify' this wild region, although conflict with the Crimean Tatars was endemic. Military colonists were also brought in. A 'Ukrainian land militia' some 9,000 strong took shape in the 1720s. Its role was akin to that of provincial 'gentry' servitors in Muscovite times. After 1751 the government recruited Orthodox South Slav (mainly Serbian) immigrants for settlement on the Dnieper, and in 1762–3 two edicts invited all foreigners, except Jews, to install themselves in the empire's empty lands. Most of these newcomers were from southern Germany. By 1775 over 30,000 such settlers had established themselves west of the lower Volga.

In the meantime Russia's position in the south had been revolutionized by the striking success of Catherine II's first war with Turkey (1768–74). This originated in the Porte's concern at Russian interference in Polish affairs. It saw major engagements on land and sea. While one Russian army captured the Crimea, another advanced into the Balkans, defeating large Ottoman forces and appealing to the Christians to rise against their masters. A Russian flotilla under the command of Admiral Elphinstone, lately of the Royal Navy, sailed around Europe to assist them. It arrived too late, but totally destroyed the Turkish fleet at the battle of Chesme (July 1770). This was certainly a landmark in Russian naval history, but did not suffice to make the Turks give in. Peace talks led nowhere and the land war dragged on for four more years, during which Russia was wracked by the Pugachev revolt (see below, page 110). The treaty of Küçük Kaynarca gave Russia extensive footholds on the Black Sea coast that jeopardized the new independence of the Crimean khanate, which she pledged herself to respect. She also gained the right to navigate freely on the Black Sea and to maintain a church in Constantinople.*

All this opened up exciting new political and economic perspectives.

---

* The Ottomans also agreed to protect Christianity in their territories. These two concessions were later interpreted by Russian diplomats as giving St Petersburg a formal right to intervene on behalf of all Christians under Ottoman rule, which Turkey and other powers contested.

The Crimea was annexed in 1783. Its Muslim population was treated quite well, but many thousands preferred to emigrate. Catherine proposed to Joseph II of Austria joint action to 'liberate' (and partition) the whole Balkans. She dreamed of recovering Constantinople for Christianity, perhaps under her own grandson, portentously christened Constantine. But in the event nothing came of this so-called 'Greek project'. It took another costly war with Turkey (1787–91) before Russia could advance her frontier in the south-west from the river Bug to the Dniester. Here would soon be built the cosmopolitan port city of Odessa, a major outlet for grain from the fertile steppe lands that were now at last brought under the plough, stimulated by the new possibilities for export to markets abroad.

Already in 1793 wheat constituted over half the reported value of Russia's Black Sea trade. From the 1730s to the 1790s total average annual cereals exports nearly tripled. Russia's acquisition of 'New Russia', as these lands were called, had important demographic consequences, too. The state's centre of gravity shifted southwards, away from the infertile soil of the north and centre, on which Muscovy had been built, to the rich Black-Earth belt of the Ukraine. This made possible the population explosion of the nineteenth century.

Also significant for the future were the beginnings of Russian expansion in the Caucasus region. From the 1730s onward a line of forts was built from the Black Sea to the Caspian, manned in part by Cossacks of the Terek and Kuban' hosts. The first local Muslims to come under Russian rule were the Kabardinians (1774), who lived in the foothills west of the river Terek. South of the Caucasus range lay the Christian kingdom of eastern Georgia (Kartli-Kakheti). In 1783, at the request of its king, Erekle II, Catherine placed it under Russian protection. A military highway was built across the mountains, with a fortress at its northern end pretentiously named Vladikavkaz (literally, 'Rule the Caucasus'). But Russian interest in the region was episodic and its peoples had to face Turkish and Persian reprisals. In 1801 Tsar Alexander I unilaterally annexed Georgia. The balance of power in the Near East was being fundamentally altered in Russia's favour.

SOCIAL AND ECONOMIC DEVELOPMENTS

Eighteenth-century Russia is conventionally seen as 'the age of the nobility'. However, the emancipation of the *dvoryane*, or 'gentry', from the bonds of state service was a long-drawn-out process that affected only a relatively well-to-do minority. Their provincial cousins had no option but to soldier on, or at least to hope for jobs as civil officials. Few of them could make a decent living from their lands, despite improved management methods. Even aristocrats continued to look to the court as the source of power and favour. They tried to combine a westernized lifestyle with ownership of large estates populated by thousands of serfs in a state of rightlessness. In some sensitive minds this contradiction produced a psychological malaise that eventually engendered political dissent. But the overwhelming majority of nobles had come to regard their privileges, especially serf ownership, as their natural and even 'historic' right. To be sure, economically there was as yet no realistic alternative to bondage. It could only be reformed, and this implied state initiative. But timid efforts in this direction ran up against opposition by landowners.

It should be made clear that only about half the country's peasants were owned by secular lords. The others belonged either to ecclesiastical institutions* or to the state. There was a further legal distinction between the latter and so-called 'apanage peasants', who came directly under the crown. Finally, there were two categories of peasant, 'possessional' and 'ascripted', who were employed in industry. As even this brief review suggests, the traditional division of society into 'estates' (*sosloviya* = *états*) no longer fitted an increasingly complex reality. Some small groups, lumped together by officials as 'men of various ranks', managed to escape categorization altogether. By and large spontaneous economic processes were more powerful than autocracy's efforts to control social development.

The emancipation of the nobility from the state might equally well be seen as an emancipation of the state from the nobility. Now that the country enjoyed greater security, and its wars were fought from a

---

* After secularization of church lands in 1764 these were known as 'economy peasants' and were managed by state officials.

position of strength, why should the government retain the costly services of barely competent noblemen when a smaller civil and military establishment could do the job more efficiently? This idea was seldom expressed orally, and likewise the *dvoryane* rarely articulated their demands. The first occasion when they did so came unexpectedly in 1730. The sudden death of the young tsar Peter II led a group of oligarchs who comprised the Supreme Privy Council, an *ad hoc* senior executive body, to offer the throne to Anna Ivanovna, a niece of Peter the Great, on condition that she accepted certain limitations on her autocratic power. She was not to marry, levy taxes, dispose of crown estates, or punish nobles without the council's consent. Anna agreed to these conditions. However, although they stood to gain from such provisions, the mass of nobles rejected them since they were inspired by Western (Swedish) precedents and seemed to benefit the oligarchs. Not for the first or last time, jealousies among the leading families helped the autocracy to reassert itself. On arriving in Moscow, confronted by Guards officers rattling their sabres to show their discontent, Anna dramatically tore up the document she had signed and thereafter ruled repressively as absolute monarch.

Neither then nor later were Russia's 'gentry' interested in political reform, but rather in socio-economic advantages. These, up to a point, the government was willing to grant. In 1730 Peter's unpopular entail law (1714) was repealed. This had obliged landowners to bequeath their estates intact to one son instead of dividing them up among several heirs.* Two years later a military academy, the Cadet Corps, was set up whose graduates received commissions: ever fewer nobles suffered the indignity of having to rise through the ranks as in Peter's day. In 1736 the period of compulsory service was reduced from life to twenty-five years, although characteristically this edict did not come into effect until 1739, after the Turkish war. It was in any case a largely symbolic act, given the low life expectancy rates of the period. (For ordinary soldiers this reduction came in 1793.) When the Seven Years

---

* Though the idea was borrowed from Britain, the act's purpose was entirely traditional: to ensure that enough nobles would be available for state service. The edict had the incidental consequence of eliminating the old distinction between hereditary estates (*votchiny*) and those in conditional tenure (*pomest'ya*) in favour of the former. This remained in effect; it strengthened nobles' rights to land and was economically progressive.

War ended for Russia in 1762 and supernumerary officers were retired, Peter III issued a 'Charter of Liberties' freeing nobles from service entirely – if no war was in progress. They were allowed to travel abroad and even to enlist in foreign armies. Few could afford to do so. But gradually nobles came to spend more time on their estates, so bringing a new dynamic spirit to the countryside.

The charter did nothing, of course, to limit autocracy, and Catherine II had a free hand to define the nobles' role. After the Pugachev revolt (see below) she was more than ever convinced that the government needed their support, particularly in the expanded local administration (1775), where local nobles were given important positions. In practice the principles governing the Table of Ranks were frequently subverted, since officials won promotion merely for long service (or even for genealogical seniority) rather than for personal merit.

Finally, in 1785, a Noblemen's Charter codified many privileges they had previously secured *de facto*. It signalled the transformation of the state servitors of old into an authentic nobility. Like clergymen, *dvoryane* were exempt from corporal punishment – an important right in Russia, where beatings were administered so severely as to endanger life – and could not be dispossessed of title, estates, or personal status without trial. If a nobleman were convicted on a serious charge, his property passed to his heirs instead of being confiscated, as had been the practice hitherto. He could engage in commerce and industry, and exploit any mineral or timber resources on his land. New was the establishment in each province (*guberniya*) of a noble corporation, presided over by an elected marshal empowered to transmit its desires to St Petersburg. However, in practice these bodies generally acted as agencies of the local administration instead of serving to mobilize and express 'gentry' opinion.

Even so these reforms constituted a major step towards the birth of an autonomous civil society. Implicitly there was a compact between nobles and state: the former left politics to the latter in return for a free hand on their estates.

Noble property was highly concentrated. In 1777 only 16 per cent of owners had a hundred serfs or more, then considered the minimum for a successful career – but these owned 80 per cent of serfs! The great magnates had less than ever in common with the lower 'gentry', who had to struggle hard to survive economically. But all were keen to increase their monetary incomes, not least in order to buy imported luxuries. To this end proprietors who acquired land in the south would move their dependants there (although most inhabitants of this region were still free) and raise the dues paid by their serf householders. There was a gradual shift towards *barshchina*, which in 1797 was legally limited to three days a week. *Obrok* payments took an estimated 20 per cent of serf income in the late eighteenth century and taxes another 12 per cent. Even so peasant living standards were on the rise, except for peasants working for wages in industry. Those employed in artisanal crafts did best, and were encouraged by their masters to develop their skills and accumulate capital. Such wealth was, however, insecure.

The real hardship of the peasant serf lay not in his poverty but in his vulnerability. One bad season could bring famine with all its attendant horrors. And always there hovered above him and his family the threat . . . of being taken off the land, sold, sent into the army or to settlement in Siberia, brutally punished, whether innocent or guilty, abused, beaten or even killed.*

Particularly tragic was the plight of those domestic servants, of both sexes, who became talented artists or musicians but were entirely dependent on their master's (or mistress's) whim.

Rights of manorial jurisdiction were explicitly reaffirmed and in 1767 serfs were even prohibited from complaining about abuses to the authorities. In her early years Catherine alleviated the lot of church and factory peasants, as well as those in the Baltic, and granted a succession of amnesties to bring back Old Believer fugitives from abroad. But when she suggested (anonymously) to the 1767 Legislative Commission that serfs be granted property rights, as a step towards eventual emancipation, the idea was bluntly rejected by nearly all noble deputies. That year there were twenty-seven local peasant uprisings, which had to be suppressed by regular troops, and fugitives continued to trickle from central Russia to the middle and lower Volga region. The ground was being prepared for the fourth (and last) great popular insurrection, that of Emelian Pugachev (1773–4).

The Cossacks on the river Yaik, near the Siberian border, were the first to rise. The movement spread rapidly to the Bashkirs and workers

* De Madariaga, *Catherine the Great: A Short History*, p. 155.

in the Urals metal foundries. Government forces, busy in the Balkans, were unable to intervene, but managed to hold on to the strategic bases of Orenburg and Ufa. In July 1774 20,000 rebels suddenly appeared before Kazan' on the Volga and captured the lightly garrisoned city. Here as elsewhere officials and nobles were slaughtered, their property looted, and the citizens invited to govern themselves, Cossack-style. Pugachev's manifestos circulated among the peasants of the south-east, who responded by rising *en masse* and killing their oppressors. It mattered little whether they really believed that he was Russia's legitimate ruler, the resurrected Peter III. More important was the motley but relatively well-armed and organized force that the rebels managed to create. This was, however, no match for regular troops once peace with Turkey freed them for action. In August they defeated the insurgents. Betrayed and captured, Pugachev was taken to Moscow in a cage and sentenced to public execution by dismemberment. Secretly Catherine acted to allay the severity of the penalty. Understandably, perhaps, nobles were thereafter more distrustful of their serfs and commoners generally. The revolt set back the cause of agrarian reform. Relations between masters and men came to be governed by inertia, fear, and force.

The parish clergy, who in other circumstances might have played a mediating role, were unable to do so because they formed an isolated caste, little respected either by nobles whose lifestyle they aspired to emulate or by peasants who had to pay for their upkeep. Orthodox priests laboured in the fields like their parishioners. They were entitled to a plot of land when this was periodically redistributed by the village commune (*obshchina*, *mir*). On private estates this body existed at the owner's sufferance and in practice did his or his bailiff's bidding. The estate authorities used it to promote early marriages (sometimes even choosing the partners!), in order to ensure population growth and a plentiful supply of future taxpayers and dues-payers. The same rationale was behind the practice of periodical land redistribution. This was a mixed blessing: although it limited social differentiation among the peasantry, it was economically regressive. So long as ample land reserves were still available, the problem was manageable, but in the next century its harmful effects became apparent.

By 1800 the population had reached 35.5 million, as against some 18 million in 1724 and 23.2 million in 1762; part of the later increase was the result of territorial acquisitions. Severe local famines were frequent in the earlier eighteenth century. Peasants could hope to escape their impact by migrating southwards – although here there was a greater risk of epidemic disease. In 1771 plague struck Moscow, killing about one fifth of the city's inhabitants and 120,000 throughout the empire.

Cereal yields remained low: a 3:1 output to seed ratio in poor households in the centre, rising to 7:1 in 'strong' ones in the black-earth zone. Here livestock-raising became a commercial proposition and manure was more widely used as fertilizer. The distilling of liquor, a noble monopoly, leaped up. In 1796 the poet Gabriel Derzhavin produced 200,000 litres – a mere drop when compared with Prince Kurakin's 1,365,000 litres! Alcoholism was rampant in rural Russia – and highly profitable to the state, which from 1767 operated a tax-farming system. By the 1790s liquor receipts provided on average 38 per cent of total revenue. Drink 'had become an item of immense importance in social and ritual life, . . . a lever for extracting wealth which other institutions, such as serfdom and direct taxation, could not extract'.*

A monopoly on salt and customs dues, together with the poll tax, were the main other sources of state revenue. War expenses forced the government to introduce paper money (*assignats*) and to raise loans abroad. The rouble's value fell. Nevertheless more expenditure now went on non-military purposes and, most importantly, the economy was expanding. Russia had a favourable balance of trade (if one overlooks smuggling!), aided by a liberal tariff policy, and as we have seen exports rose considerably in value. The removal of domestic tariffs in 1753 gave a fillip to internal trade. All classes participated. This was a source of grievance to Russian merchants (as was continued foreign domination of international commerce). The first banks to appear (1754) benefited landowners in the main and played a modest role in stimulating the economy. As the market expanded, there was a shift from home-produced goods to those made by specialists, especially in the labour-intensive cottage (*kustar'*) industries, whose output was sold to itinerant pedlars or at fairs, many of which were now held in villages. Their total number rose from 627 in the 1750s to 4,044 in the 1790s.

* Christian, *'Living Water': Vodka and Russian Society*, pp. 46–7, 384.

Merchants were not a closed caste and, despite the institutional barriers, their numbers grew as (non-serf) peasants accumulated enough capital to join. Few new entrants reached the first guild, as the qualifications for membership in it were raised. These wealthier elements were often less enterprising than their humbler fellows. Their main aspiration was to join the nobility. Even so the merchantry 'was conscious of its economic power . . . and became more demanding not only in the area of profits and protection but also with regard to . . . security and the rudiments of civil rights' (A. Kahan). This new self-awareness was fostered by the leading role accorded to first-guild merchants by a major reform of municipal government undertaken in 1785.

Of entrepreneurs in iron and copper works between 1701 and 1800 72 per cent (113 out of 156) were merchants; for linen and silk the figures are comparable (78, 70 per cent), whereas woollen mills were predominantly in noble hands – indeed, three aristocrats controlled two thirds of the output catering for the armed forces (1791). In the iron industry the state's share declined from 28 per cent in 1725 to a mere 9 per cent by 1800. In the latter year output (101,000 metric tonnes) was 16.4 times greater than it had been in 1725. Copper output expanded at a similar rate to reach 2,559 tonnes by 1790; in that year silver production, which took off in the 1760s, amounted to 20 tonnes. The silver mines, situated in eastern Siberia, were worked largely by convict labour. In other branches of industry the general tendency was for hired workers to replace various categories of bondsmen, as their labour was clearly more efficient. (The difference was not, however, absolute since some serfs were paid wages.) Thus in the woollen manufactories hired workers accounted for 23 per cent of the labour force in 1797. Total employment figures by the end of the century in certain branches were as follows:

industry	size of workforce
Iron (1800)	159,000*
Wool cloth (1797)	25,900
Linen (1799)	29,300
Silk (1797)	8,900

* Includes 'attached' serfs (83,300). Figures to nearest hundred.

Other workers made weapons, paper, or glass, or mined copper and salt. To complete the picture one should note the key role played by skilled foreign specialists. From the 1760s Russia produced some experts, too, but the rapid pace of technological change abroad made it essential to recruit ever more foreigners. They formed sizeable 'colonies' in St Petersburg and Moscow, and (somewhat later) in such new towns as Odessa.

Catherine's government was non-interventionist: only in defence-related branches did state-owned enterprises set the tone. Private manufactories (i.e. water-powered works with a concentration of labour) had to compete with rural craft industries. In leather-working and milling the latter were more efficient. In textiles this was not the case; here the 'putting-out' system, with spinning and weaving contracted out to cottage industries, was often found to be most advantageous – as in the contemporary West.

THE ENLIGHTENMENT IN RUSSIA

By the 1730s St Petersburg had established itself decisively as the nation's 'first' capital. The architectural magnificence of Rastrelli's Winter Palace outshone that of Peter I's summer residence, Peterhof. Later Catherine II would outdo her predecessors. As part of a lavish construction programme, mostly in the classical style that now replaced the baroque previously in favour, she had the Scot Charles Cameron remodel her apartments at Tsarskoye Selo (the modern Pushkin) and built an elegant palace at Pavlovsk for her son Paul. These splendid edifices, set in extensive parkland, still draw tourists today. They were emulated on a smaller scale by Prince Potemkin and other wealthy aristocrats. The banks of the Neva were faced with granite, stone bridges built, and many streets paved. In a number of provincial towns, too, handsome squares, avenues, and public buildings arose as part of a grandiose state-directed effort to improve urban amenities. The poorer quarters were another story, to be sure, not least in St Petersburg with its grim climate.

The court patronized music and the arts. Dramatic and operatic performances were put on regularly from the 1730s, at first by foreign troupes and then by Russians, many of the dancers being pupils at the

Cadet Corps. The first native theatrical company dates from the 1750s. Significantly, it was founded by merchants from provincial Yaroslavl' who had a genuine interest in the stage; only later did the empress Elizabeth take it under her wing and grant it official patronage. Initially people attended performances just to keep up with current fashion, but before long they developed a critical taste. Plays by foreign, especially French, dramatists – Molière, Beaumarchais – vied with the works of self-taught playwrights such as Sumarokov and Kheraskov.

Known in his day as 'the Russian Homer', the latter was the key figure in a literary circle (*kruzhok*) centred on Moscow University. The long tradition of such informal groupings, destined to continue into the late twentieth century, can be traced back to the mid 1730s, when such a circle was formed by translators at the Academy of Sciences. Headed by Vasiliy Tredyakovsky, the members of this 'learned band' (as they were sometimes referred to)

took seriously their role as the appointed vehicle for making Western literature available to Russian readers, a mission for which they engaged in furious, if inconclusive, debates concerning grammar, style, and the literary vernacular.*

Russia's first genuine man of letters, Tredyakovsky came from an Astrakhan' clerical family and studied in Paris and The Hague before devoting himself to literature. As the basis for modern literary Russian he rejected Church Slavonic in favour of the spoken vernacular, expanding its vocabulary by an admixture of selected foreign terms. In verse he synthesized Slavonic and Romance forms to create a new, melodious medium of expression that a century later would reach perfection in the poetry of Pushkin.

Still greater was the impact of Mikhail Lomonosov (1711–65). As a fisherman's son from Archangel he had a hard struggle to gain an education, but was fortunate enough to be able to attend university at Marburg, where he came under the influence of the Pietist and humanist thinker Christian Wolff. (At that time German intellectual influences were far stronger in Russia than French.) In an age of limited scientific specialization Lomonosov was a polymath; Pushkin would eulogize him as 'the first Russian university', so broad was his learning. He did

---

* Marker, *Publishing, Printing, and the Origins of Intellectual Life in Russia, 1700–1800*, p. 50.

pioneering work in physics and chemistry which had applications in such varied fields as mineralogy, optics, electricity, and even astronomy: for example, he ascertained the existence of an atmosphere on Venus. Unhappily the means were lacking to put his findings to practical use. Not until 1871 did his essay *On the Multiplication and Preservation of the Russian People* (1760) appear in print. This contained many sensible propositions, but some of his other writings on topics in the humanities were disfigured by chauvinism and pettiness. This was in part a reaction to his niggardly treatment by the Academy, in which German scholars and officials called the tune. Lomonosov got his own back in 1755 by helping to found Moscow University, which now proudly bears his name. This was the first authentically Russian institution of higher (secular) learning. Within a decade about half the twenty or so professors were Russians and instruction was being given in the native tongue rather than Latin.

This had been the language of the first publications of the Academy of Sciences, and their readership was consequently small. However, it did put out a newspaper, in Russian and German, which lasted until 1917; its supplementary monthly *Notes* contained articles on a wide variety of popular scientific and other topics. Conceived by the worthy historian G. F. Müller, it was the first Russian publishing venture to cater to the public interest. Its sequel, rather unimaginatively called *Monthly Compositions* (1755–64), attained a record circulation of 1,250 copies, despite continual harassment of its editor by Lomonosov.

At this point Russian journalism took off, with the empress Catherine's active encouragement. She had a genuine if superficial interest in intellectual matters – Voltaire was among her many correspondents – and was herself something of a graphomaniac. Anonymously, she wrote and produced a short-lived periodical, *All Sorts of Things* (1769), modelled on Addison's *Spectator*. Her aim was to stimulate controversy, albeit within genteel limits. By 1774 sixteen magazines had appeared in the capital, half of them satirical in content, financed either by the court or by writers themselves. The best known was N. I. Novikov's *The Drone* (1769–70), which poked fun at Russian nobles' ignorant aping of foreign fashions or brutal treatment of their serfs. The long-held view that this outspokenness led an angry Catherine to close the journal down has no foundation in fact. Financial difficulties were responsible, and Novikov continued to enjoy imperial patronage. Censorship became necessary only after 1783, when an edict allowed anyone to set up a printing press, provided he registered it with the police. A veritable publishing explosion followed. In the last quarter of the century thirty-three presses in the two capitals and twenty-six outside them produced almost 8,000 titles, peaking in 1788 with 400 Russian-language books and journals.

The most active private publisher was Novikov. In 1779 he leased Moscow University's press and in 1785 founded his own Typographical Company. These enterprises, too, lost money, but Novikov was an idealist – and a convert to freemasonry to boot. 'He saw masonry as seeking moral perfection by means of self-knowledge and enlightenment in the light of Christian doctrine.'* These sentiments rendered him suspect to Catherine. Apart from philosophical differences – as a self-confessed 'Voltairean' she regarded masons as reactionary mystics – she was nervous at the masons' international links. With war and revolution looming in the West, they represented a security risk, especially as her estranged son and heir, Paul, was also a mason. In April 1792 Novikov was arrested and then sentenced without trial to fifteen years' imprisonment in a fortress.†

This unreasonably harsh action does not make Catherine a 'tyrant'. Though alarmed by events in revolutionary France, she launched no general wave of repression. The restrictive measures of her last years need to be judged in the context of her earlier reforms. These involved a humanization of the judicial system and a long overdue devolution of government. In 1775, partly in response to Pugachev's revolt, much administrative power was entrusted to forty-odd governors (in some provinces, governors-general, such as Potemkin, her chief favourite, who ruled New Russia). For the first time they were given adequate official staffs with well-defined functions, among these being to maintain welfare services such as hospitals and almshouses. A network of law courts was set up, largely on an estate (*soslovie*) basis, in which elected assessors advised the judge. So-called 'courts of conscience' tried cases where the parties were from different estates, as well as those involving children and others who deserved lenient treatment. Some provision

---

* W. Gareth Jones, *Nikolai Novikov: Enlightener of Russia*, Cambridge, 1984, p. 133.
† He was allowed to keep his physician and a servant. Released after Catherine's death, he lived quietly on his estates until 1818.

was made for habeas corpus. These measures did not ensure the rule of law – there were as yet no professional advocates, and courts relied on written procedure – but it was at least a start.

The same is true of Catherine's educational policy. Several private boarding schools and 'pensions' were set up, among them the celebrated Smol'ny Institute for girls. (In some respects Russia was ahead of the West in the treatment of women.) In 1786 came the outline of a nation-wide coeducational school system with a broad modern curriculum. By 1798 there were over 3,000 such schools with nearly 20,000 pupils, of whom one tenth were female. Perhaps as many were in church schools (which had revived in the interim); counting those in private or garrison schools, the total may have reached 62,000. The principal drawbacks to expansion, as before, were Russia's inadequate financial resources and social prejudice among the privileged. Many nobles and merchants still saw schooling as a luxury, and of course serfs were automatically debarred from attending. Characteristically, at Smol'ny noble and non-noble girls were taught separately.

As elsewhere in Europe at the time, literacy was all but confined to members of the élite groups. Even fewer people read books, journals, or newspapers. Methods of distribution were primitive: pedlars rather than bookshops, although there were a few of these in the capitals. Calendars, prayer books, primers or narrowly utilitarian works sold better than *belles-lettres*. The market for fine literature, whether translated or by native authors, was far smaller than in Western European countries at this time. Nevertheless by Catherine's death Russia did have a minuscule intelligentsia – that is to say, a group of individuals interested in ideas for their own sake and willing to suffer for them. This became clear in 1790 when Alexander Radishchev, a senior government official (assistant director of customs in St Petersburg), who had hitherto been cautious about expressing his dissenting views on social and political issues, published *A Journey from St Petersburg to Moscow*.

In form this was a series of letters by a young man travelling between the two cities, but the content was revolutionary. 'I looked around,' he began, 'and my soul was afflicted by the sufferings of mankind.' What did the traveller find on his grisly journey from the new to the old capital? He found serfs forced to toil six days a week on their master's land. He found officials and judges who would sell a verdict or a decision. He found corrupt businessmen. He witnessed a serf auction, where human beings were knocked down like cattle to the highest bidder. He saw a round-up of serfs, press-ganged into army service, as in eighteenth-century England, and – last but not least – a vainglorious monarch, wallowing in luxury and blind to his/her subjects' misery. Catherine read the book soon after it appeared and set down her criticisms.

It pained her inwardly to see ideals she formerly held (or still held privately . . .) perverted in the service of attacks on time-honoured institutions: absolutism and bureaucracy, nobility and serfdom, war in pursuit of national defence.*

Radishchev was sentenced to death, a penalty commuted to ten years' imprisonment in Siberia, but was released in 1796; he committed suicide in 1802. The rather naïve but sincere idealism of 'the first Russian revolutionary' inspired later generations of critically thinking intellectuals, some of whom would share his tragic fate under regimes far more oppressive than that of Catherine.

Born an obscure German princess, she took power by a *coup d'état* in which her husband, Peter III, met his death. As a character she was immeasurably superior to her immediate predecessors, especially the suspicious-minded Anna Ivanovna (1730–40) and the generous but idle Elizabeth (1741–61). Her statesmanlike qualities and patronage of the arts made her Russia's most enlightened ruler. Against this must be set her vanity, fondness for luxury, and many love affairs. These shocked contemporaries, and some earlier historians too, but today they seem of little consequence. 'Amid the welter of state duties and court routine, she sometimes felt achingly alone,' writes J. T. Alexander; 'a nymphomaniac she was not, but a normal person in an abnormal position.' In any case her excesses in private did far less damage than the cruelty and arbitrariness of her militaristic male successors, and many Russians living under Paul had good grounds for nostalgia.

* Alexander, *Catherine the Great: Life and Legend*, p. 283.

CHAPTER 9

Liberators and Gendarmes

The brief reign of Paul I (1797–1801) ended abruptly with a *coup d'état* that cost the emperor his life. Only recently has it received its due from historians. For many years the unhappy tsar was either ignored or represented as insane – a version that naturally appealed to those who benefited from the conspiracy. In fact he pursued rational, consistent policies of bureaucratic centralization at home and defence of monarchical legitimism abroad which were followed for the next half-century. Certainly Paul had a choleric, fickle temper; many of his decisions were arbitrary and vindictive; he was excessively fond of military minutiae and ceremonial. But in this he was behaving 'true to type' for a Romanov tsar.* It was the foreign-born Catherine who was the exception. As his recent biographer puts it:

Whatever else Paul may have been, he was in tune with the fundamental imperatives shaping Russian history. Tsarist absolutism, as he interpreted it, was far closer to the country's established traditions than Catherine's sophisticated enlightenment, and it is therefore not surprising that it was his rejuvenated autocracy rather than her creative innovations which survived . . . He was the first [Russian ruler] to attempt to cope with a radically modernizing world through an essentially conservative ideology.†

Acceding to power with a well-developed programme of (counter-) reforms, he regulated the succession to the throne, recentralized the administration, and curbed the newly won privileges of the nobility – which won him the plaudits of the common people. They did not share

---

* Genetically, Paul may *not* have been a Romanov at all if, as seems possible, his father was not Catherine II's husband, who reigned in 1761–2 as Peter III, but her lover Sergey Saltykov. But Paul worshipped the memory of Peter III, for whose assassination he held his mother responsible, had his mortal remains reburied in honour, and emulated his example – with equally fatal results!

† McGrew, *Paul I of Russia, 1754–1801*, p. 356.

the discreditable view of Paul held by large sections of the élite. The emperor's arbitrary style of rule stood in sharp contrast to the easy-going ways permitted during his mother's reign, and the censorship of Western literary works, and even fashions, deemed to reflect the subversive ideas of the French revolution led to disaffection. It was particularly rife in the army, whose officers felt threatened by his Prussian-style emphasis on discipline and order. Young Guardsmen were prominent among the nearly 200 people involved in the conspiracy. The *coup* stood midway between the 'palace revolutions' of the eighteenth century, initiated by a tiny coterie of courtiers, and the much broader social movement that produced the abortive 'Decembrist' revolts of 1825. Unlike the latter's leaders, the plotters of 1801 held conservative views on social and constitutional matters. They wanted to set up a regency council under the heir to the throne, Alexander. He was privy to their plans – but deeply shocked when he unexpectedly found himself hoisted to power by an act of bloodshed.

Alexander I (1801–25) had acquired a cosmopolitan education under the benign guidance of his grandmother Catherine II, who appointed as his tutor the Swiss republican LaHarpe. A sensitive soul, in his youth the prince dreamed of abandoning his responsibilities for some quiet retreat on the Rhine. Well-mannered and charming, Alexander also had an authoritarian, militaristic streak in his character. This uneasy combination of traits perplexed contemporaries, who called him a 'sphinx' or an enigma – and the labels have stuck. He skilfully dissimulated his true intentions and might dismiss a trusted adviser without warning. Judged by results, his reign was a disappointment, for although the tsar initiated several reforms, they were not implemented consistently and in any case fell short of what Russian society expected or needed. 'The only reforms Alexander carried out at home were concerned with governmental efficiency . . . [He] made no move during his reign that could have alarmed serf-owners.'* After 1815, moreover, Alexander fell under the sway of mystical notions and adopted a more repressive stance which led to widespread dissatisfaction and eventually to violence.

It would, however, be wrong to blame this tragic outcome wholly on the tsar's personal failings, his capriciousness or inconsequentiality.

---

* McConnell, *Tsar Alexander I: Paternalistic Reformer*, pp. vi, 34.

Far more important were the institutional constraints: any large-scale attempt at reform from above risked destabilizing the system. And foreign affairs continually intruded, for during Alexander's reign Russia faced a formidable foe in Napoleon I's French empire. In the eighteenth century the image of Europe had been a positive one for educated Russians, but now it assumed a more ambiguous, indeed dangerous, colouring. One result was the growth of Russian national consciousness among the élite. It was fortified by the grim experiences of invasion, defeat, and ultimate victory in the 'Patriotic War' of 1812. This epic struggle decided the fate of all Europe, not just Russia, and the ensuing peace settlement registered her paramountcy on the continent more firmly than before. In domestic affairs it marked the 'coming of age' of Russian educated society and a widening breach between the public and the autocracy. Hitherto the state power had stood in the van of the country's development. After 1815 it acted as a brake on its progress.

THE DUEL WITH NAPOLEONIC EUROPE

Paul I began his reign by dissociating Russia from foreign involvements, but he could not long remain indifferent to the French revolutionary regime's challenge to the European balance of power. He saw this threat as ideological as well as military. The empire was sealed off from 'jacobin' influences and offered shelter to French royalist émigrés. Allied to Austria, Britain, and even Turkey, Russia joined in efforts to curb French expansionism in Italy and the Low Countries. Under the experienced but eccentric Suvorov, a Russo-Austrian force scored major victories in the Po valley. Then Russian troops executed an epic, though costly, march across the Swiss Alps to join other forces operating to the north (1799). Suvorov arrived too late to prevent them suffering defeat and had to take up winter quarters. Russia's leaders resented the poor cooperation afforded by their Austrian ally. Relations with Britain soured, too: a joint Anglo-Russian force that landed in the Scheldt had to be evacuated to the Channel Islands, where many Russian soldiers died of neglect. Another source of friction was Malta. When Napoleon captured the island Paul took its knightly rulers (the Order of St John) under his protection, but when the British recaptured it they kept it. Russia embargoed British goods, withdrew from the alliance, and even sought a *rapprochement* with Napoleon, now First Consul and so in Paul's eyes a monarch of sorts. The policy switch did make sense, especially in the light of Russian designs on Turkey, but it was unpopular within Russia and the British reacted by helping to finance the 1801 *coup* that led to Paul's assassination.

On his accession Alexander quickly mended fences with London and countermanded his father's order for the dispatch of 22,000 Cossacks towards India. (The move was unrealistic, but significant in marking the start of Anglo-Russian rivalry in Asia, sometimes called 'the great game'.) He, too, wanted peace. But Napoleon was more of a threat to his neighbours than ever. Russia was outraged by the kidnapping and summary execution of the duc d'Enghien (1804), the tsar's distant relative. The following April an Anglo-Russian convention laid the basis for the Third Coalition against France. Austria and Sweden joined the new alliance, but Prussia vacillated until it was too late. Napoleon defeated the Austrians at Ulm and then routed a mixed allied force at Austerlitz (December 1805). It was the worst blow for Russia since Narva over a century earlier, and she had to withdraw her armies from Central Europe. Then, at Jena, it was Prussia's turn to go down to defeat. In the winter of 1806–7 Russian armies fought valiantly to defend their last continental ally. However, the battle of Friedland left Alexander no alternative but to make peace – not least because Russia was simultaneously engaged against the Turks. 'Containment' having failed, a temporary accommodation was essential.

On 25 June 1807 the French and Russian emperors met on 'neutral' ground, a raft moored in the river Neman near Tilsit. Skilfully the tsar pretended delight at Napoleon's offer of an alliance and promised to join the Continental Blockade of British goods. He was determined to win a breathing space and may have been tempted by the vision of a Europe partitioned into two zones of influence. The French alliance indirectly brought Russia some gains: after a campaign in Finland this Swedish province was incorporated into the tsarist empire. But in the Danubian principalities (modern Romania) the French played a double game, and in the Mediterranean Russia had to forfeit her recent acquisitions (the Ionian islands). It was economically disadvantageous, too, for it deprived landowners of their British export market, which augmented their natural dissatisfaction; there developed something of a noble *fronde*. These malcontents, who had supporters at court, relished every sign of growing tension between the incompatible allies. In 1809, when Napoleon called on Alexander to help put down an Austrian revolt, he deliberately procrastinated. Still more serious was French support for the duchy of Warsaw, the Polish mini-state that Napoleon had resurrected – 'a pistol aimed at Russia's heart', in the view of Russian nationalists. Late in 1810 Alexander allowed British goods to be imported on neutral ships and imposed a tariff on French wares. This was an act of provocation and both sides prepared for war. Russia managed to conclude peace with the Turks just in time.

Napoleon's *Grande Armée*, nearly half a million strong, was the greatest assemblage of men and material in the history of warfare to date. Only half the soldiers were French; the rest included Poles, Germans, Spaniards. Russia's sole ally, Britain, could render her only indirect financial support. The Russian generals were at loggerheads, her armies outnumbered and soon obliged to retreat. Two months after crossing the Neman, Napoleon took Smolensk. But already the invading armies were sorely depleted, while the Russians were more or less intact. Alexander acceded to public demand by sacking his war minister, Barclay de Tolly, unjustly suspect to some 'patriots', in favour of a Suvorov protégé, General Kutuzov. He continued the withdrawal but in September made a stand at Borodino. In an unusually bloody three-day engagement, involving some 130,000 troops on each side, tens of thousands fell on the field. The result was indecisive. Kutuzov retreated and reluctantly allowed the enemy to enter Moscow. Soon the city was engulfed in flames. It is unlikely that it was set on fire deliberately, as was once widely thought. Its wooden buildings, all but deserted, were exposed to the elements and there was a strong wind.

Napoleon had assumed that Alexander, stricken by such catastrophic reverses, would sue for peace. But he rebuffed all overtures. After a fruitless month in the ruined capital, Napoleon had no option but to retreat. Supplies were short and he was desperately far from base. Kutuzov barred access to the southerly routes, and so the invaders had to retrace their steps through the devastated countryside, continually harassed by Cossacks, partisans, and even peasants infuriated by enemy exactions. At Smolensk the once mighty *Grande Armée* was down to 60,000 men; at Vilnius, after a horrendous crossing of the wintry Berezina, only half that number were still able to fight. Scarcely one tenth of the invaders escaped the débâcle.

On the Russian side victory was owed to Kutuzov's prudent strategy, the resources of the army's recruitment system, and the political cohesion of tsar and educated society. But the attractive picture of an entire nation in arms, powerfully reinforced by Tolstoy's masterpiece *War and Peace*, has been qualified by recent research.

Peasant antagonism actually played very little part in the downfall of Napoleon ... What peasants did more than anything else was protect their own villages and fields from [French raiders]. Such operations could have very little impact on the course of the war. Although there may have been some peasant volunteers, the majority of recruits [to the popular militia, or *opolchenie*] appear to have been sent ... by their landlords ... In certain areas under French control there appears to have been a significant amount of collaboration ... The serfs showed the most serious commitment to the struggle only when they were in uniform.*

Though fallacious, the image of patriotic unity against the foe was historically important, since it deluded both supporters and opponents of autocracy as to the people's mentality.

Alexander sent his armies across the border to complete Napoleon's downfall. Aided by the resurgent Prussians and (less enthusiastically) Austrians, the allies decisively defeated the French near Leipzig (October 1813). In March 1814 the tsar entered Paris in triumph. Napoleon abdicated. Russian troops marching up the Champs-Élysées symbolized the new international order that would be established by the Congress of Vienna (1815). Russia participated in a (brief) allied occupation of defeated France.

If Russia's paramountcy in continental affairs was less than total, this was a result of differences among the victors. Alexander's scheme to resuscitate most of Poland as a constitutional monarchy under his sceptre went too far for his partners. He had to agree to what was in effect a fourth partition of that country. The tsar's subjects in his Polish kingdom received rights denied to native Russians – a discrimination that antagonized patriotic opinion. In France, too, Alexander took a 'soft' line, since he wanted the restored Bourbons to act as a counterweight to Austria and Britain. The 'Holy Alliance' (September 1815) was intended by the messianic-minded tsar as an eternal covenant

* Fuller, *Strategy and Power in Russia, 1600–1914*, pp. 213–14.

between Christian rulers to keep the peace. It was Austria's Prince Metternich, better attuned to the demands of *Realpolitik*, who turned it into an instrument for upholding the interests of the conservative autocrats who ruled Central and Eastern Europe.

Until 1822 periodic international congresses gave an appearance of solidity to this first all-European security pact. But Britain and France were reluctant to allow indiscriminate intervention to suppress popular revolutionary movements. These differences came to the fore notably over the Eastern Question. Alexander was torn between support for the legitimate rights of the Turkish sultan and sympathy for his rebellious Greek Orthodox subjects. The latter tendency won out, and under his successor Greece secured a precarious independence (1830). Its partisans were fortunate in that tensions between Russia and the Western maritime powers in the region were not yet so acute as to prevent common action against the Ottomans. In October 1827 the Russians joined with the British and French in destroying the Turkish fleet at Navarino bay. But for Russia the price of this was yet another costly bilateral confrontation with the Turks in the Balkans and the Caucasus (1827–8). This war was a prelude to much graver problems, for Russia's international might was less assured than contemporaries thought.

THE DECEMBRISTS

Alexander I's initial reforms awakened among his more enlightened compatriots hopes of a new golden age. An estimated 12,000 people arrested without trial during Paul's reign were released and the nobles' rights under their 1785 Charter reaffirmed. There was no persecution either of Paul's favourites or of his murderers (for this would have exposed Alexander's own complicity). Censorship restrictions were eased, the Secret Chancellery abolished (once again!), and a commission appointed to draft a new law code. These liberal moves were the work of Count Pahlen, but as the *coup*'s chief organizer his days were numbered. Instead Alexander relied on a circle of 'young friends' who met in secret to discuss policy. They favoured above all strengthening the autocratic power, ostensibly in the interests of reform, rather than a *de facto* power-sharing arrangement with the Senate. The aristocrats who advocated this alternative, sometimes called anachronistically 'the senatorial party', wanted a formal right to challenge decrees they thought harmful or illegal. This was granted (September 1802) – only to be nullified a few months later by a proviso that it applied solely to *earlier* legislation. Instead the Senate now actually lost power to the new ministries. These were wholly bureaucratic bodies that replaced Peter I's old 'colleges', whose power had already been whittled down by Catherine II. The 'unofficial committee' of the tsar's friends gradually broke up.

After Tilsit a new start became possible. It was identified largely with Michael Speransky. The son of a priest, he became a brilliant administrator, but his position depended entirely on the tsar's confidence. Proud and aloof, he was mistrusted in aristocratic circles. He was partly responsible, as an interior ministry official, for an 1802 edict improving the status of Russia's Jews. Promoted state secretary five years later, he set about reforming the bureaucracy. Many officials of noble origin had obtained sinecures by twisting in their favour the lax provisions of the Table of Ranks. Speransky wanted promotion to eighth rank to be by examination and persuaded Alexander to rule accordingly. His indignant critics maligned him as a jacobin. In fact he stood for a law-based monarchy that would gradually evolve towards constitutional rule as the populace learned to appreciate its merits. His 'general plan' (1809) envisaged a pyramid of institutions, headed by a State Council, each with clearly demarcated executive, legislative, or judicial functions. The national parliament ('State Duma') was to be more than a mere consultative body. This idea was only hinted at, for it clearly limited the tsar's power. Another problem Speransky side-stepped was emancipation of the serfs. Apparently he favoured it, as well as extension of property rights (and ultimately the vote) for liberated peasants, yet it was impolitic to say so clearly.

Of all these projects only the State Council saw daylight (1810), but in isolation it proved ineffective. Speransky was identified by his critics with the unpopular pro-French phase of Alexander's foreign policy. In March 1812, as the war clouds thickened, the tsar dismissed him. He survived to serve his successor, but never exercised the same degree of influence. Had his moderate ideas been implemented, there might have been no 'Decembrist movement'.

This term refers to the mood of dissent that spread in Russian educated society after 1815 and led to two revolts in December 1825. Dissenters were particularly prominent among Guards and other officers, but the mood of disaffection also embraced civil servants, landowners, and even some merchants – sons and grandsons of those who had drunk from the spring of Enlightenment under Catherine. According to the conventional interpretation, sensitive souls who had experienced the patriotic euphoria of 1812 and then the civilized delights of Europe after 1813 were appalled, on their return to Russia, by their country's miserable condition: serfdom, general lack of rights, corruption, and, above all, autocracy. This is, however, to over-simplify. Many dissidents never left Russia; their knowledge of European ways was derived from books. Those who went abroad were not necessarily impressed by what they saw there.

Paris is a nice town [wrote one officer in a letter home], a bit like Moscow, [which] is smaller and more populous. There a family has an entire house, whereas in Paris one finds a family behind each window. In short there's nothing to be envious about except perhaps the ladies.

Best of all he liked the zoo, which boasted 'an enormous elephant'. Another man, later a prominent dissident, found the worthy burghers of Hamburg unduly concerned with prompt payment of bills and similar mundane matters.* Thus 'the West' augmented reflective Russian officers' malaise at the way things were going at home but did not necessarily offer an appealing model for change. Exposure to it did not so much give them a taste for constitutionalism as lead to a heightened patriotism, coupled with a feeling that military action might help set things right.

Their natural pride as victors in a terrible war was offended by the return to peacetime army routine, with its humiliating emphasis on drill, turnout, and pointless ceremonial – the *Arakcheyevshchina*, as it was commonly called after Count Arakcheyev, Alexander's unpopular war minister. Another humbly born favourite, he was cast in a different mould from Speransky. He was a crude disciplinarian who treated subordinates brutally and tactlessly. He backed a pet scheme of the tsar's to set up a network of military colonies, where agricultural pursuits were combined with part-time soldiering. The idea had

---

* Cited in Keep, *Soldiers of the Tsar*, pp. 254–6.

eighteenth-century precedents and was not in itself unsound. However, as applied from 1810 onwards, first in Mogilev and Novgorod provinces and then in the south, it involved intolerable hardship for the settlers involved, whose officers had ample opportunity to engage in corrupt and tyrannical practices.

In 1819 a peaceful protest erupted among soldier-farmers at Chugu-yev near Khar'kov. Two thousand men, women, and children were arrested and 275 of them sentenced to death. Arakcheyev commuted the penalty to mass beatings in public. Of fifty-two who 'ran the gauntlet' – up to 12,000 blows! – twenty-five died; the rest were sent into exile. Next year trouble spread to the Guards. Men in the prestigious Semenovsky regiment, stationed in the capital, complained (legitimately) at malpractices by their colonel, Shvarts. Panic-stricken, the authorities over-reacted. The regiment was promptly disbanded, the 'ringleaders' punished, and the remainder dispersed to the south. Here they formed a potential reservoir of support for disaffected officers active in the secret societies that had meanwhile come into existence.

These began in the capital cities as informal associations (*artels*) formed by officers with cultured tastes. In 1816 two brothers named Muravyov secured permission to found a journal to promote pro-fessional military education. It served as convenient cover for a conspira-torial body, modelled on earlier masonic societies, with some thirty members who harboured political aims.* Alexander Muravyov favoured a *coup d'état*, but most of his comrades thought this too extreme. Internal tensions and security concerns led to the group formally disbanding, but this was only a tactical ruse that allowed the more militant members to set up a successor. Ostensibly, the Union of Public Welfare (1818–21) had cultural and charitable objectives. Its statute, based on that of the German patriotic student organization, the *Tugend-bund*, provided for an elaborate hierarchical structure designed to maintain control by the leaders – a device that would be emulated by many later Russian revolutionary activists, including the Bolsheviks. The union's members, 200 at its peak, knew about their radically minded counterparts in Naples, Piedmont, Greece, and Spain. They faced even tougher obstacles, since in Russia the élite was thinner and

---

* Usually referred to as the 'Union of Salvation', its national–patriotic orientation is better expressed by its full title, 'Society of True and Loyal Sons of the Fatherland'.

the autocracy stronger. Government spies were ubiquitous. Nearly all nobles backed serfdom, and the peasant masses were inaccessible to propaganda. The idealistic conspirators could hope to win over only a few soldiers. Even this required extreme caution, indeed subterfuge, in revealing their intentions. Outside Russian Poland, at least, there was as yet no popular constituency for ideas of limited government, whether of the Anglo-American or French jacobin variety.

These were the options earnestly discussed in the two regional bodies that replaced the union after it, in turn, underwent dissolution in 1821. The Northern Society was based in St Petersburg. Its chief theorist, Nikita Muravyov, drafted a programme that provided for retention of the monarchy, devolution of government on American federal lines, with central and local assemblies elected on a socially limited franchise, and civil liberties. The serfs were to be freed, but without any allotment of noble-owned land. This was a more conservative document than the *Russian Law* (*Russkaya pravda*) devised by Colonel Peter Pestel', leader of the southerners. Son of a Siberian governor, Pestel' was educated in Germany, joined the Guards, and was wounded in action. He had a remarkable intellect and organizational talent, but an associate rightly observed that he was 'a Bonaparte, not a Washington'. He stood for a republican form of government, to be introduced after an indeterminate era of revolutionary dictatorship, clearly under his own command. After emancipation all peasants were to receive enough land to feed their families, grants being made from a state land fund. This is why Pestel' has been called 'a socialist before socialism', although he accepted the need for private enterprise and stood for equality before the law, a jury system, and abolition of the standing army. Citizens were, however, to be denied the right of association and Russians were to be favoured over other nationalities. Jews, Pestel' argued, should either assimilate or be forced to emigrate. He probably did not advocate regicide, as his investigators alleged, but he was scarcely a liberal democrat.

These differences could not be reconciled before the dissidents had to act. On 19 November 1825 Alexander I died unexpectedly at Taganrog. This led to a dynastic crisis. The childless tsar had two younger brothers, Constantine and Nicholas. Constantine, who had entered into a morganatic marriage, had earlier renounced his claim to the throne, but this was unknown to the public, and even to Nicholas.

Accordingly he, along with the empire's dignitaries and troops, swore allegiance to his elder brother. When the truth came out, an oath had to be taken to Nicholas instead, who was unpopular (and knew it). The confusion gave the conspirators a splendid opportunity. They botched it badly. On 12 December some Northern Society activists decided to bring out their men, hoping that their mere presence on Senate Square would overawe Nicholas and stop him taking power. But they had no fall-back plan. Three thousand soldiers assembled. Nicholas, warned in advance by two delators, put together a larger force and stood firm as the wretched 'rebels', bereft of effective leadership, got colder and hungrier. When darkness fell cannon opened fire and cleared the square. Several dozen men are thought to have been killed, their bodies thrust beneath the ice of the frozen Neva. A follow-up insurrection in the south fared no better.

Nicholas I personally directed the ensuing investigation. Of some 600 individuals deemed to have displayed disloyalty, 289 were sentenced. About three quarters of them were serving officers; most were aged under thirty. There was a fair sprinkling of senior men (colonels), and some were of distinguished lineage. Five accused, including Pestel' and the poet Ryleyev, were executed and over a hundred exiled to Siberia, many of them for life; the soldiers were sent to serve in the Caucasus. No mention of the revolts was made in the press. Nevertheless a myth had been born which would inspire opponents of tsarism for generations. It was reinforced by the courageous decision of several exiled Decembrists' wives to share their husbands' lot. Arch-conservatives like Count Rostopchin mocked the conspirators as fundamentally misguided: 'Usually cobblers make revolutions to become grandees, but in Russia grandees wanted to become cobblers.' In fact 'Decembrism' was an early manifestation of a common modern phenomenon, an attempted revolution on the people's behalf by a section of the educated élite. Action by a 'military intelligentsia' is frequently characteristic of its early phase; later the activists are normally civilians who seek a social base in peasants and workmen, not just soldiers.

One may well ask what progress Russia actually made during Alexander I's reign, which had begun so auspiciously. Although there were few improvements in the empire's political institutions, much was done in the educational field and culture blossomed. By 1825 there were 337 district schools, twice as many as under Catherine, 48 state secondary schools (gymnasia) and 3 'lyceums', the most famous of which, at Tsarskoye Selo, could proudly claim to have produced Pushkin; it trained many senior officials and played an active role in intellectual life generally. There were three new universities, two of them in outlying areas (Kazan', Khar'kov). At revived older institutions – Tartu (then Dorpat), Turku (then Åbo), and Vilnius – the atmosphere was respectively German, Swedish, and Polish. Private individuals made a notable contribution to the basically state-run system. A school was founded at Yaroslavl' by one Demidov, and in Moscow Rumyantsev founded a library that today is one of the world's largest.

Even more important, . . . a professionalized intellectual life began to develop outside the schools and universities. Members of the social élite, along with a few representatives of the 'masses', enthusiastically threw themselves into intellectual and academic activities . . . Organizations and groups [developed] a passionate interest in culture or scholarship . . . Having dispensed with state patronage, they also hoped to avoid state control.*

Here was the rub: in the mystical, reactionary atmosphere of Alexander I's last decade the authorities looked askance at such tendencies. At two universities an obscurantist official, Magnitsky, tried to purge staff, students, and libraries of men and ideas deemed too secular, and hence subversive. Fortunately he was dismissed before irreversible harm was done, but reconciling the spread of 'useful' knowledge with the maintenance of political conformity would remain an acute problem for later tsars.

NICHOLAS I: OFFICIALDOM AND THE INTELLIGENTSIA

Nicholas I (1825–55) embodied to the full the bureaucratic and militaristic style characteristic of so many Romanov rulers. In appearance and manner a thoroughgoing autocrat, brave and honourable, he travelled tirelessly through his domains, dutifully checking on implementation of the decrees that issued by the thousand from his pen. Traumatized by the circumstances of his accession, he exaggerated the threat of

* Raeff, *Understanding Imperial Russia*, p. 132.

subversion to Russia's political and social order. Although he realized that there was truth in the Decembrists' indictment of administrative abuses, his efforts to remedy them were ineffectual. Formalism, complacency, and routine characterized his rule. Several official committees were set up to devise reforms, including improvements for the peasantry, but their findings were mostly pigeon-holed because it seemed too dangerous to tamper with the *status quo*. Still, even if only minor adjustments were made to the system of government during Nicholas's reign, at least a group of enlightened officials emerged whose expertise would bear fruit later.

Distrusting the regular government machinery, the tsar subordinated it to his personal Chancellery. This was divided into several sections. The First Section monitored civil-service appointments, while the Second Section was responsible for systematizing and publishing the empire's existing laws – an indispensable preliminary to any reform. This task was performed by the indefatigable Speransky, now returned to imperial favour. More important was General Benkendorf's Third Section, which was concerned with internal security. Nicholas saw it as a means of collecting reliable information, giving society 'moral guidance', solving minor conflicts expeditiously, and, above all, nipping potential subversion in the bud. Writers, religious dissidents, and foreign visitors were placed under especially close surveillance. The French traveller the Marquis de Custine, irritated by his over-solicitous escorts, commented sarcastically that 'the Tsar is the only man in his Empire with whom one can converse without fear of informers . . . He is also the only one so far in whom I have recognized natural feelings or sincerity of speech. If I were to live in this country and I had a secret to hide, I should start by confiding it to him.'* He exaggerated; nevertheless Nicholas's police–judicial system did depend to an extraordinary degree on his subjects' readiness to denounce each other for nonconformist behaviour, a practice that added to the general climate of suspicion and fear. By modern standards, to be sure, the empire was *under*-policed. Regular constables were sparse and ill-trained; even the celebrated corps of *gendarmes* numbered only a few thousand.† This

---

* *Letters from Russia*, p. 91.
† It was, however, supplemented by an Internal Guard some 145,000 strong, which performed such paramilitary tasks as escorting recruits, hunting down fugitives, and guarding public buildings (including prisons).

force was organized on military lines; its officers, in their sky-blue uniforms, were especially selected for intelligence and high moral character. They reported directly to the tsar and were often quite frank in criticizing abuses, including serfdom. Nevertheless on balance their activities were pernicious.

Particularly obnoxious was the use of paid journalists to influence public opinion covertly. This clumsy effort at thought control antagonized intellectuals, few of whom were oppositionists in the normal sense of the term. Indeed, such an opposition could not exist in Nicholas's Russia, for there was no legitimate outlet for dissent. After the revolutions of 1848 in the West, the tsar became still more afraid of subversion and tightened censorship restrictions further. Russians were once again forbidden to travel abroad, the intake of university students limited, and philosophy banned from the academic curriculum.

One casualty of this 'freeze' was the education minister, Uvarov. A distinguished scholar, he had in the previous reign held liberal views which as minister (1833–49) he found it expedient to temper. Nevertheless he promoted secondary schooling and was less eager than his imperial master to restrict university attendance to the privileged. By the 1840s Russia could claim a *non*-noble intelligentsia* numbering some 15,000 to 20,000. These men had been educated to fill official positions but could not be prevented from putting their knowledge to non-approved use. Uvarov was shrewd enough to realize that it was not enough simply to exclude modern ideas by administrative fiat: one needed to offer the young an alternative creed. To the French revolutionary formula of 'liberty, equality, and fraternity' he counterposed a triad of his own: Orthodoxy, Autocracy, and 'Nationality' were the three indestructible pillars on which the Russian empire allegedly stood. By 'nationality' (*narodnost'*) he meant national unity, having the (spurious!) patriotism of 1812 in mind. It did *not* mean nationalism in the contemporary European sense, as manifest among Frenchmen, Germans, Italians, or – especially – Poles. It was a value with which all the tsar's subjects were expected to identify, irrespective of language, religion, or 'race'. Yet it was clearly open to other interpretations; and so, too, were the first two elements in Uvarov's triad.

---

* Many of them were priests' sons or other 'men of all ranks' (*raznochintsy*, see page 107).

Contrary to his intentions, his 'doctrine' was fated to play an important role in the evolution of independent thought during the so-called 'marvellous decade' (1837–47).

Leading Russian intellectuals carried on passionate debates in 'solid' monthly journals, so far as the censors permitted, but more particularly in Moscow's aristocratic salons, where the atmosphere was freer than in official St Petersburg. To understand this controversy, which centred on the historic destiny of an abstractly conceived Russia ('the Russian Idea'), one has to consider the general European intellectual context. To simplify greatly, the rationalism of the eighteenth-century Enlightenment was widely seen as philosophically superficial, one-sided, and even socially dangerous. Had it not led to the excesses of the French revolution and Napoleon? German Idealism, and the Romantic movement generally, gave voice to these concerns. They exalted spirit over matter, intuition and imagination over reason, respect for the past over utopian hopes for the future. The political connotations were conservative, at least in stable, well-established states, where national and state boundaries by and large coincided. But elsewhere in Europe the new mood opened up existential questions: what *was* the authentic tradition of the country concerned? What principles should guide its political life? How far should its borders extend, and how should it relate to other peoples? The philosophical founder of modern nationalism, Herder, had been among the first to highlight the potential role of the Slavs, who had yet to fulfil their historic destiny. Even more important was Hegel, with his heady notion that a process of dialectical change was at work in human history, as in the development of ideas generally. Although Hegel was himself a conservative supporter of the Prussian monarchy, his ideas were capable of infinite adaptation – not only by East European nationalists but also, through a quirk of intellectual history, by internationalist socialists who received a dose of 'left Hegelianism' through Marx.

Russian students at German universities brought home the master's half-understood message and used it to give the intelligentsia's aspirations a modish philosophical camouflage. All the disputants were earnest patriots who resented their government's reactionary leanings and hoped to make a contribution of their own to the country's progress – at least in the world of ideas, so long as circumstances prevented practical action. Though united in basic outlook, they differed on the course to follow.

Chaadayev fired the opening shot with the publication in 1836 of his first *Philosophical Letter*, actually written seven years earlier. It caused a furore, since Chaadayev denied that Russian civilization had any intrinsic value. Since the Middle Ages the country had stood apart from European developments, in stagnant isolation:

Confined in our schism, nothing of what was happening in Europe reached us. We stood apart from the world's great venture . . . while the whole world was building anew, we created nothing: we remained crouched in our hovels of log and thatch. In a word, we had no part in the new destinies of mankind. We were Christians, but the fruits of Christianity were not for us.

Chaadayev's remedy was a *rapprochement* with Catholicism (to which he himself converted), but this option commended itself to few.* Most of his readers responded by searching the Russian past for positive achievements. A group that came to be called 'Slavophiles' (the theological writer Khomyakov, the brothers Aksakov and Kireyevsky) elaborated theories that in effect gave a 'popular', even subversive, twist to Uvarov's formula. For they, too, respected Orthodoxy – not the existing ecclesiastical establishment, subordinate to the state, but the *early* Church, which had had a conciliar structure, responsive to believers' needs. And they accepted Autocracy – not in its current bureaucratized form, which they held was a consequence of alien Germanic influence, but as it had supposedly existed before Peter I, when the *Zemsky sobor* had enabled the tsar to consult his people. Finally, by *narodnost'* they understood not national unity artificially imposed from above but a spontaneous patriotism rooted in such authentic native institutions as the self-governing *mir*, which exemplified the spirit of concord that naturally prevailed among simple tillers of the soil – in striking contrast to the urbanized, strife-torn West.

It might be objected that this idyllic picture of the rural commune was itself remote from the truth (see p. 179), and that Muscovy had really been an oriental despotism. But these objections miss the point.

---

* He was officially declared insane and subjected to a form of house arrest. In his later *Letters* and a brilliant riposte, *Apology of a Madman*, he modified his initial bleak assessment of Russia's history and rightful place in the world.

The Slavophils were not scholars but 'historiosophers' who were constructing an 'ideal type' or exemplar for the future. Their ideology

was clearly only an interesting offshoot of European conservative romanticism ... There are striking affinities with the ideas of such German romantic thinkers as [Schelling, Schlegel, and Franz von Baader] ... At a fundamental level [these similarities] were a function of social developments in the two countries ... Both Russia and Germany were economically backward and faced the need to modernize at a time when capitalism had already become established in more advanced countries ... Slavophile criticism of Western Europe was therefore essentially ... a critique of capitalist civilization from a romantic conservative point of view ... It was less defence of the present than romantic nostalgia for a lost ideal.*

Precisely this, and not scientific precision, gave it an emotional appeal that would endure (for example, in Solzhenitsyn) until our own day.

The so-called 'Westernizers' were a more diffuse group. The appellation is misleading, for they did not stand for rapid 'modernization' on Western capitalist lines. Although sympathetic to constitutional government, they were Romantics at heart, even if their outlook was slightly more rationalistic. They were less committed to Orthodoxy (or religion in general) and more appreciative of Peter I. On the other hand, like the Slavophils, they were of noble background (the literary critic Belinsky was an exception) and vehemently opposed to serfdom on moral grounds, but had just as little idea of rural Russian realities. The ideas of the French socialist Fourier evoked enthusiasm in their ranks, not least with the idealistic and gifted political writer Herzen and the more volatile Bakunin, dubbed 'the father of European anarchism'. Both men emigrated, since they found the intellectual climate in Russia stifling, whereas the Slavophils stayed behind. Khomyakov, however, was a strong admirer of England – whereas Herzen was disenchanted with the 'bourgeois' French revolutionaries of 1848 and reacted to their failure by preaching his own brand of 'Russian socialism', based on an idealized village commune. Even Bakunin began to talk of the Russian *muzhik* as the progenitor of European revolution. As these examples show, the two groups had much in common and should not be differentiated too crudely.

* Walicki, *A History of Russian Thought*, pp. 156–7.

Another point to bear in mind is that until 1848 official censorship, though severe, was not totally effective. Writers learned to express their ideas indirectly, especially in 'solid' literary periodicals, by means of such subterfuges as the use of 'Aesopian' language, a kind of code that initiates readily understood. A political message could be transmitted in a discussion of some historical topic, or else through literary criticism – with consequent harm to the appreciation of *belles-lettres*. The literary critic Belinsky in particular sinned in this respect, for his aesthetic judgements owed a lot to his radical socio-political commitment and his acerbic, didactic style set a fashion that lasted. 'Art for art's sake' was not a principle that appealed to Russians before the end of the nineteenth century.

For all its harshness, the Nicolaevan era was an age of great writers, who, however, suffered greatly in their personal lives. The impoverished Belinsky died of consumption in 1848, shortly before the *gendarmes* came to arrest him. Pushkin, that most gracious of poets, had to endure the emperor's personal control and was killed in a duel (1837). So, too, was the twenty-six-year-old Lermontov four years later. A Byronic figure, Lermontov is best remembered for his poetic evocation of the war-torn Caucasus and for the character of Pechorin, in *A Hero of Our Time* (1840). Pechorin embodies the frustrations of that characteristic figure of the age, the 'repentant nobleman'. Unable to put his talents to good use, he wastes his life in pointless soldiering, only to end his days in unfathomable despair. This was the aboriginal Russian realistic novel.

Gogol', who came from a poor Ukrainian gentry family, portrayed the world of the rural squire in all its triviality and vulgarity. *Dead Souls* (1842) was, however, far more than mere social criticism. The hero, Chichikov, the epitome of smooth imperturbability, decides to enrich himself by trafficking in the dead – the physically, and not the officially dead. He will buy from the landowner those of his serfs who have died since the last census. The 'souls' of the title are serfs, this being the term by which they were known in Russia. This macabre story is the pretext for a broad panorama of provincial life. Whom does Chichikov meet on his travels? Grasping, corrupt officials, miserly widows, slothful, brutal landowners, stupid noblemen, gamblers, and a whole array of living monstrosities. At the end it is clear that the 'dead souls' of the title are by no means the serfs but the whole world above them.

In his later years Gogol' became mentally ill. *Extracts from Correspondence with Friends* (1847), in which he praised autocracy and serfdom, shocked all educated Russians. Denounced by Belinsky as an obscurantist, he destroyed the manuscript of a sequel to *Dead Souls* before his death in 1852.

Despite such tragedies Russian writers of the era made a signal contribution to world literature. Music, too, was well represented by the composer Glinka (1804–57), among whose best-known operatic works is *A Life for the Tsar* (1836). Moscow's Bol'shoy theatre dates from 1824. The architectural glories of St Petersburg were enhanced by such notable neo-classical edifices as the Stock Exchange (1816) and the Virgin of Kazan' Cathedral (1801–11). Nicholas I's tastes were more eclectic, and St Isaac's Cathedral, completed after many vicissitudes in 1858, was a controversial addition to the city's skyline, since it did not accord with classical taste.

SERFDOM AND THE ECONOMY

The institution of serfdom was so entrenched that efforts, whether by government officials or the few 'improving landlords', to ameliorate the peasants' lot did not get far. Alexander I merely tinkered with the problem, for instance by decreeing in 1801 that serfs should no longer be advertised for sale (which, of course, did not stop them being sold). Two years later he permitted seigniors to free their dependants by mutual agreement, with provision of an appropriate area of land, but by 1860 only 384 had done so; 116,000 serf families were affected – a drop in the proverbial bucket. Nevertheless the practice of granting state peasants to private owners ceased, and in consequence the share of the population in servitude declined from just over half (10.5 million males) in 1811 to some 37 per cent fifty years later. This shift was owed in part to the practice of freeing surviving army conscripts who returned to their communities, as well as to the personal emancipation in 1816–19 of serfs in the three Baltic provinces. The land here, however, remained in the hands of their German lords, and the reform was of little immediate benefit to the peasants concerned. This kind of deal clearly could not serve as a model for the rest of the empire, although the Baltic precedent did at least put emancipation on the agenda.

During Nicholas I's reign public discussion of the subject was taboo. Benkendorf warned the tsar that serfdom was a 'powder magazine under the state'. In the south-west action was taken to impose legal limits on dues payable by serfs to their masters. But this was a political move aimed at protecting Orthodox dependants of 'disloyal' Polish landowners. Such contracts would have been strongly resisted by nearly all Russian nobles who continued to own estates – a declining proportion, but still a powerful vested interest which the government could not afford to alienate. Indeed, Nicholas once told a noble audience that he regarded the *dvoryanstvo* as a substitute police force. Thus the measures he took on the serfs' behalf, such as allowing dependants of bankrupt lords to purchase their freedom, or prohibiting the dispersal of serf families by sale at auction, were mere palliatives. More important were the steps undertaken in regard to state peasants, which were designed to encourage emulation elsewhere. As minister of state domains from 1837 Kiselev pushed through a reform that equalized peasants' land allotments and created rudimentary welfare facilities: schools, medical services, and agricultural advisory centres. These improvements were, however, offset by heavy tax burdens and continued administrative malpractice.

'Gentry' landowners were worried at their mounting debts. By the early 1840s over half their estates were mortgaged, and their obligations totalled more than two thirds the cash value of their serfs. Dimly they realized that surplus agricultural labour needed to be absorbed by industries and that the future lay with a market economy, yet they feared any major change that might endanger their precarious livelihood. Only a few magnates, particularly in New Russia, did well out of agriculture (e.g. sugar-beet cultivation) and reinvested their profits. Most wealthy nobles lived for the day, spending their income on conspicuous consumption – a lifestyle that the vast majority of squires, of course, could not afford to emulate.

What serfdom meant for the peasants has become clear from a recent study of the Gagarin family estate of Petrovskoye in Tambov province,

situated on fertile land some 500 kilometres south-east of Moscow.*
Their main adversaries were still the forces of nature, not their seignior
or the far-distant state power. When famine struck, as it did on three
occasions in this period (1821–2, 1833–4, 1848–9) they starved,
despite relief by the estate authorities, and mortality rates rose sharply.
Otherwise their food supply was ample: 'excluding . . . years of agricultural crisis, the peasants of Petrovskoe were . . . better nourished than
their French or Belgian counterparts at the turn of the nineteenth
century and certainly had a better diet than most persons living in
developing countries today'. Each husband-and-wife work team (*tyaglo*)
cultivated some 5.8 to 6.4 hectares of ploughland (8.7 to 9.6 ha including
fallow). Seed/yield ratios on the demesne were up to 30 per cent greater
than officially reported: for rye, an average of 1:6.2, for buckwheat
1:4.8. If peasants had a similar ratio on their allotments, this could
provide 'enough rye flour for 6.2 persons and buckwheat or millet for
7.8 persons'. Only 4.4 to 12.5 per cent of households fell below
subsistence level – mainly widows or elderly persons with children
below working age – and had to be assisted by neighbours. On average
each household had per capita 0.5 horses, 0.3 cows, 1.3 sheep, and 0.4
pigs. It is therefore 'unlikely that the serfs regularly suffered protein
deficiency . . . Meat was found on most peasant tables for major religious
holidays, parish festivals, wedding days and funerals.' Poultry, fruit
and vegetables were provided by kitchen gardens, which might be
spacious (up to 0.57 ha). By contrast, the peasants' accommodation
was crowded and insanitary, with dirt floors and no room for a bed;
most huts even lacked a chimney. Since stock had to be brought inside
in winter, 'the air was fetid from animal and fowl excreta. The walls
and ceiling were covered with soot and ash . . . It was impossible to
keep cockroaches out of the food; they even became a symbol of
abundance . . . and a sign of good luck.'

In the 1850s 45 per cent of Petrovskoye's children died before age
five. Survivors could expect to reach forty; but 'such circumstances
were common throughout much of pre-industrial Europe'. The birth-
rate was exceptionally high but stable. A woman who lived through
her child-bearing years would normally have six to seven children.

* For the following see S. L. Hoch, *Serfdom and Social Control in Russia: Petrovskoe, a
Village in Tambov*, 2nd ed., Chicago–London, 1989.

Serfs married young: males at age 20.1, females at 19.5 (early 1850s). 'Permanent celibacy was virtually unknown.' The estate and/or peasant authorities intervened whenever necessary to preserve the large three-generation household and so the authority of the family patriarch (*bol'shak*). Unregulated household division was perceived as a threat to stability and 'a male serf rarely left the paternal household as long as his father was alive'. Patriarchs and bailiffs cooperated to maintain a system ostensibly designed for the common good: it made for self-sufficiency, and thus prompt payment of dues and taxes. Periodical reallotment of land according to household size ensured that there was little social differentiation. But this did *not* mean harmony, as the Slavophiles fondly supposed. On the contrary, Petrovskoye was the scene of continuous rivalry between households and generations, which frequently erupted in violence. Theft, from neighbours or the estate, was a major problem, and the peasants were lazy in performing field work. Offenders were flogged – in two years, 1826–8, no less than 79 per cent of males suffered this penalty! – and, in the most serious cases, sent off as army recruits. Worst of all, the ferocious methods of repression engendered a culture of violence. The social climate in a Russian village was akin to that of a slave plantation in the American South. Prince Gagarin's peasants rebelled or fled relatively rarely; but in the empire as a whole the threat of revolt was real enough. It was a factor, though perhaps not the main one, in serf emancipation (1861) – 'from above, before they free themselves from below', to paraphrase Alexander II.

Serfdom was only one economic obstacle to economic growth. Another was financial instability. The Napoleonic wars played havoc with the empire's budget. Only gradually did a capable finance minister, Kankrin (1834–44), succeed in building up a reserve of precious metals and stabilizing the exchange rate for paper roubles (*assignats*). He also insisted on economy in government expenditure. Alas, his achievements were largely undone by the Crimean War. Russia's textile industry received a fillip from the Continental Blockade, but then suffered from the war of 1812 and the low-tariff policy in force until 1822. However, the domestic market expanded, especially from the 1830s onward. According to official data the number of cotton mills rose from 199 in 1804 to 1,200 by 1860, with respectively 8,000 and 152,000 employees: an eighteen-fold increase. This was the fastest growing sector. In the metallurgical industries the labour force grew by a factor of 13.6, while in paper manufacture and leather-working it more than doubled. By 1860 the total work force may have exceeded half a million (higher figures are encountered). Of these men and women perhaps 60 per cent were hired.

But the expansion of output was modest when set against that in Britain, then in the throes of industrialization. The iron industry, once the champion growth sector, stagnated until the 1850s. Russian enterprises were highly labour-intensive and productivity levels low. These deficiencies could be offset up to a point by importing modern technology, particularly in textile manufacturing, from Britain (where the export of such equipment was permitted in 1842). By the 1850s home-produced machinery output was catching up, at least quantitatively. Ivanovo, a village east of Moscow, earned the appellation 'the Russian Manchester'. The two capital cities were also becoming major industrial centres. Moscow's population grew from 270,200 in 1811 to 462,500 in 1863, St Petersburg's from 335,600 to 539,500.

The Alexandrovsk works in the latter city produced Russia's first railway locomotives. The 'iron horse' first appeared in 1837. It linked St Petersburg with the tsar's residence, Tsarskoye Selo. Nicholas and his ministers, however, feared the expense of construction – and the danger to 'public morals'. Kankrin thought that they would 'encourage frequent purposeless travel, thus fostering the restless spirit of our age'. Nevertheless by 1851 a railway line united Moscow with St Petersburg; there were, however, no lines south of Moscow, which prevented rapid supply of troops during the Crimean War. By then Russia's railway network measured a modest 1,046 kilometres, one fifth that of France. This was a rough indicator of the empire's growing lag behind the Western powers.

THE ROAD TO THE CRIMEAN WAR

The military balance was also becoming unfavourable to Russia. Nicholas took a keen interest in his armed forces, but typically concentrated on external formalities instead of weapons development and other technological innovations. About one million men were kept under arms at any one time, which made the Russian army by far the largest in Europe. This show of strength bolstered a posture that looked more aggressive than it was; it was one best termed 'coercive deterrence'.

Nicholas maintained such an enormous army and navy precisely because of the imposing impression he hoped they would make on Russia's enemies at home and abroad. The mobilizations, manoeuvres, naval demonstrations, even parades were all scenes in a theatre of intimidation that Nicholas staged for the benefit of his foes (Fuller, op. cit., p. 231).

The 'gendarme of Europe' was no trigger-happy interventionist, but sought rather to maintain the European equilibrium while protecting Russia from 'seditious' external influences. He saw these as stemming principally from France, for whose 'bourgeois' king Louis-Philippe he harboured contempt, and more immediately from his Polish subjects.

The Constitution granted in 1815 did not satisfy patriotic Poles and was frequently infringed by the Russian authorities. Opposition grew among the educated classes, particularly students and military cadets. In November 1830, encouraged by the July revolution in Paris and fearing they might be sent to suppress it, insurgent cadets seized the palace of the Viceroy, Grand Duke Constantine, and part of Warsaw. Constantine lost his nerve and ordered Russian forces to withdraw. The Polish revolt was a far graver security threat than the Decembrist uprisings. Fortunately for Nicholas, the less radical elements were prepared to negotiate. Few peasants joined the movement and no effective aid arrived from abroad. In February 1831 Russian troops returned in force and defeated the hopelessly outnumbered insurgents. Even so, trouble spread to the provinces (including parts of west Russia which some Poles regarded as historically theirs) and Warsaw was not retaken until September. Several hundred noble activists were exiled to Siberia and their estates confiscated. The Constitution was superseded by an 'Organic Statute' (1832) under which a new and more energetic viceroy, Paskevich, wielded virtually dictatorial power.

Nicholas cemented his victory by signing conventions with Austria and Prussia (1833) which pledged the signatories to uphold the *status quo* in partitioned Poland and to support each other in case of further trouble. Dynastic links were strengthened. But this reincarnation of the Holy Alliance was stronger on paper than in fact. In 1848, when revolution broke out all over Western and Central Europe, the tsar's threatening gestures alarmed the Prussian king, who could not afford to act too intransigently. At the behest of the new Habsburg emperor, Franz Joseph, Russian troops intervened to help put down a national uprising in Hungary (1849). This was a success in purely military terms, but did not bring Nicholas the 'gratitude' he expected from Vienna. Relations between the two courts were strained over the 'Eastern Question', which was leaving the tsar dangerously isolated diplomatically.

By 1825 Russia had not only consolidated her hold on Georgia, putting down several native risings, but had also taken all the territory north of the Caucasus. The regional governor, Yermolov (1816–27), constructed additional fortified lines, manned largely by Cossacks, and applied genocidal tactics against the (largely Islamic) Daghestani and Chechen tribesmen. Whole villages were put to the sword and women whose lives were spared sold into slavery or distributed among his officers. To critics he retorted that 'Asiatics see condescension as weakness . . . a single execution saves hundreds of Russians from destruction'.* The result was a holy war (*jihad*) which soon spread to several other Muslim peoples of the region. Adherents of clandestine Sufi sects provided leadership. The Russian command at first concentrated on gradually subduing the Circassians and then turned to deal with the imam Shamil, who adopted sophisticated guerrilla tactics. He avoided pitched battles and repeatedly inflicted heavy losses on the invaders. In 1845 command passed to Vorontsov, the experienced and relatively enlightened governor-general of New Russia.

He abandoned grand campaigns in favour of a *cordon sanitaire*, a gradual strangulation of the resistance . . . Instead of confronting the rebels with force, Vorontsov used diplomacy, including economic enticements, to drive a wedge between the rebel leaders and . . . [the] population . . . The new strategy . . . took a lot of the glory out of the Russian effort. It also limited the gore.†

After several setbacks, all Chechnya had been subjugated by 1853, although Shamil himself did not surrender until six years later.

* M. Gammer, 'Russian Strategies in the Conquest of Chechnia and Daghestan, 1825–59', in M. Bennigsen Broxup (ed.), *The North Caucasus Barrier: The Russian Advance towards the Muslim World*, London, 1992, p. 46.
† A. L. H. Rhinelander, *Prince Michael Vorontsov, Viceroy to the Tsar*, Montreal etc., 1990, p. 149.

This belated success released Russian troops for action against Turkey. Nicholas's main aim in this theatre was to keep the Straits closed to foreign warships. He wanted to maintain a weak Ottoman empire lest a more formidable enemy appear at the Porte. When the Egyptian khedive rebelled against the sultan in 1833, Nicholas moved to protect the latter, securing in return the promise he wanted regarding the Straits. But the treaty of Hünkâr-Iskelesi alarmed other powers, especially Britain, who had her own designs on the Ottoman empire. London saw the Near East as the crucial sector in the 'great game', and in 1837–8 there was a minor confrontation between the two powers in Afghanistan. (British russophobes also tried to help the Caucasian resistance, but to little effect.) The five-power Straits convention (1841) seemed to give Russia the guarantee she wanted.

Three years later the tsar visited Britain, where he was lavishly fêted. However, the agreement to consult in any future crisis did not dispel British misgivings, and Nicholas failed to realize that it did not bind the British government. For the next few years the power equilibrium held, but after 1850 the rise of Napoleon III, and an obscure dispute over religious rights in Palestine ('the Holy Places'), led to tension with France. Self-assured as ever, the tsar misread the signals. He assumed that Anglo-French rifts would prevent these powers from cooperating in the Near East, and that in the event of conflict he could obtain his ends by bluff, with Austria's tacit support. Reinterpreting the provisions of the treaty of Küçük Kainarca (see page 105), Russia demanded further rights to protect the sultan's Christian subjects and secretly prepared to enforce this claim by landing troops at the Bosphorus (December 1852). This was coercive diplomacy.

The Turks, assured of Anglo-French support, resisted pressure from Menshikov, the tsar's personal envoy to the Porte, who demanded a convention granting the Orthodox extra privileges. Attempts at compromise got nowhere. In July Russian troops occupied the Danubian principalities. Three months later Turkey declared war. Within weeks Admiral Nakhimov had sunk an Ottoman flotilla off Sinope. Thereupon British warships passed through the Straits into the Black Sea and the conflict became generalized.

It was an avoidable war, for which much of the responsibility lies with Nicholas, although the maritime powers were also not without fault. On the Anatolian front Russian armies performed well. Austrian pressure forced the evacuation of the eastern Balkans (August 1854), whereupon the allies landed in the Crimea. The campaign was costly for both sides. Russia lost some half a million men, mainly from disease, and incurred a budgetary deficit of 800 million roubles. The stubborn defence of besieged Sevastopol (October 1854 to August 1855) could not turn the scales in Russia's favour, for the correlation of forces was against her. The empire was on the brink of exhaustion. Her armies lacked essential supplies. Austria openly sympathized with the allies; even Sweden was hostile (there was some minor scrapping in the Baltic). In February 1855 Nicholas died in bitter disillusionment. His system was thoroughly discredited. There was now no alternative to peace – or to reform.

CHAPTER 10

From Reform to Assassination

ALEXANDER II AND THE GREAT REFORMS

Alexander II (1855–81) was not by nature a reformer, but had the wit to realize that substantial changes were necessary if the Russian autocratic state were to survive. However reluctantly, he confronted vested interests and introduced a number of measures, the most far-reaching of which was the emancipation of the serfs, arguably the greatest piece of socio-economic legislation attempted anywhere in the world hitherto.

When Alexander succeeded his father in February 1855, at a difficult moment in the Crimean war, his overriding priority was to make peace with the invaders. Not until this was achieved, by the treaty of Paris (March 1856), could he turn to domestic affairs. He was ably assisted by his younger brother, Constantine, whose liberal views had a consistency the emperor's lacked, and by a coterie of enlightened officials, notably in the interior ministry, who had forged contact with one another during the preceding reign. One venue for the reformers was the salon maintained by the new tsar's aunt, the progressive-minded German-born Grand Duchess Helen. Another was the Imperial Russian Geographical Society, which encouraged the collection of vital statistical data about agrarian conditions in various provinces of the empire.

Defeat in the Crimea at the hands of the Western powers shocked Russian public opinion and created a mood favourable to change. For a time many people harboured exaggerated expectations of what could be achieved within a few years if educated society worked together purposively with the government. This euphoria did not last and after 1861 public sentiment began to sour. While some intellectuals felt that the reforms did not go far enough, the former serf-owners were bitter that they had been forced to yield so much of their power. Alexander's own vacillations harmed his image. By the last years of his reign he had become isolated from his subjects and unpopular with the educated classes. Even in court circles he attracted criticism on account of an extra-marital affair. When revolutionary terrorists threw the bombs that ended his life on 1 March 1881, the horror generally felt in society at such a deed – he was the first Russian ruler to die a violent death since 1801 – was tinged with a feeling that the 'tsar-liberator' was himself partly responsible for his tragic fate.

In retrospect his reign deserves a more positive evaluation. Although the reformist impulse faltered as the years passed, it was never totally abandoned. One of Alexander's last acts was to sanction administrative changes that, had he lived, might well have become a starting-point for constitutional rule – for that 'crowning of the edifice' by parliamentary institutions that contemporary Russian liberals, with their eyes on Western Europe, yearned for. As it was, the reforms undertaken in local government, the army, education, and the judicial system went a long way towards modernizing autocratic rule and advancing citizens' rights. This was an age when Russian society demonstrated its maturity by forming a host of professional, charitable, and civic bodies. Economically, too, the empire took a great leap forward. State finances were put on a sounder footing and the basis laid for the industrial expansion that characterized the last fifteen years of the century. Above all, some 25 million peasants, the mass of them serfs, acquired personal freedom and allotments of land on secure (though collective) tenure – necessary preliminaries to the development of a sense of their own worth, along with entrepreneurial skills and a modicum of wealth.

Serf emancipation

Alexander's first moves on the 'peasant question' were cautious to an extreme. Addressing the Moscow nobles in April 1856, he coupled his historic remarks (cited above) that it was 'better to abolish serfdom from above rather than wait until it begins to abolish itself from below' with a denial of rumours that the government was planning immediate emancipation. Such ambiguity was at least partly deliberate. Neither the tsar nor the *dvoryanstvo* was really afraid of a new Pugachev revolt. Nor is it true, as was at one time widely believed, that noble landowners found serfdom unprofitable and wanted to move on to a more 'capitalistic' agrarian system. On the contrary, most of them were wedded to the *status quo* and deeply distrusted officials in St Petersburg, whom they suspected of persuading the tsar to act contrary to their interests.

Much therefore depended on the stand taken by Alexander himself, who was prone to veer irresolutely between competing pressure groups. He would have preferred the nobles to take the initiative – this was the message implicit in his Moscow speech – but they were reluctant to do so. Instead they filibustered in one after another of the bureaucratic agencies set up to consider 'improvements in the peasant way of life', as the current euphemism put it. The Secret (later Main) Committee on Peasant Affairs, established in January 1857, initially had ten members, of whom four owned over 1,000 serfs; three were princes and two counts. None could claim any real expertise on the matter under discussion; 'rank, wealth and long experience in Russia's service disposed them to look to the past rather than the future'.* This was hardly an auspicious beginning. But when they reported, true to form, that general emancipation was at present impossible, Alexander did not simply accept their verdict but turned instead to the young officials in the interior ministry. Aided by Nicholas Milyutin, the best brain among the reformers, the minister, Lanskoy, astutely manipulated 'gentry' opinion in the three north-western provinces of Vilnius, Grodno, and Kovno to extract from them a petition that their serfs be emancipated – *without* land, as had been done earlier in the Baltic. This gave the government a convenient pretext to order the local governor-general, Nazimov, to set up a committee of local nobles to draw up concrete plans for emancipation on a broader basis, with peasants having use of some 'gentry' land (November 1857). Before anyone could object, this 'rescript' was circulated to other provinces as an indication of the tsar's will. In this way the reform-minded officials seized the initiative. 'Alexander insisted on the fiction that he was not only acting in the gentry's best interest but with its overall support.'† Though duplicitous, this was a most useful device, since it exploited the nobles' traditional awe of the autocrat to prevent them effectively resisting the unpopular reform.

For the first time since 1767 the government gave leading citizens a voice in law-making, but the consultations were, as one deputy put it, 'like a dialogue between the chickens and the cook'. Much pressure

---

* Lincoln, *Great Reforms*, p. 68.
† Pereira, *Alexander II*, p. 56.

was exerted from above to ensure that the forty-eight provincial committees of landowners that were now formed came up with reasonably acceptable recommendations. Tours to several provinces left the tsar under no illusion about the state of landlord opinion, and in April 1858 he lurched to the right. Influenced by a magnate from the southern province of Poltava, he approved a programme to guide the provincial committees' deliberations which left them ample leeway to define the conditions on which emancipation was to take place. The main questions were: how much land would the *pomeshchik* keep and how much would go to the peasants? Would the former be compensated for the loss of his peasants' labour as well as their land? How were the peasants to pay for the land they acquired? 'Gentry' views varied according to personal inclination, age, and education, but were shaped mainly by local economic circumstances. Broadly speaking, those living in the northern and central (non-Black Earth) provinces were willing to be generous over land allotments, since the soil was unproductive and they derived their income mainly from the dues (*obrok*) which their serfs earned by off-farm employment. In the Black Earth provinces, on the other hand, where land was valuable, the seigniors wanted to retain as much of it as possible for themselves and to ensure a ready supply of labour by imposing severe conditions on their former dependants.

By the autumn of 1858 Alexander had moved left again. This time he was influenced mainly by Rostovtsev, a trusted adjutant-general in his suite and to all appearances the personification of a parade-ground officer from Nicholas I's reign: indeed, in his youth he had helped suppress the Decembrist revolt. But he was above all else a loyal servant of the emperor. He came round to the liberal view that the serfs must be granted some land at once for their use, and eventually receive title to it, while the government helped them pay for this land by means of a long-term redemption scheme. Rostovtsev's endorsement of these ideas convinced Alexander too, who now in effect ruled that the provincial nobles' proposals were to be vetted to ensure conformity with these principles. Rostovtsev was made head of the crucial Editing Commission, which had a liberal majority.

At this point, however, the empire's strained finances, which had been unbalanced by high military expenditure during the Crimean War and speculative railway construction projects, forced the government to cut back its projected investment in the land redemption scheme. The liberated peasants were now expected to bear the entire cost themselves, and the value was reduced of the state bonds that their former owners were to receive as compensation. On top of this, Rostovtsev fell seriously ill. On his death (February 1860) he was succeeded by Count Panin, one of the greatest lords in the empire who owned 20,000 serfs. The whole enterprise seemed to be in mortal danger. In the event the Editing Commission survived the fierce attacks launched against it by the 'planters' lobby'. The final stage came in the State Council, where at the last moment arch-conservatives managed to insert a clause permitting peasants to settle with their owners for 'beggarly allotments', one quarter the size of the local norm, in return for exemption from redemption payments.

This was only one of several blots on the vast corpus of legislation published on 19 February 1861.* The authorities knew that the statutes fell short of what the public, and in particular the peasants, expected. In churches across the land a high-flown manifesto was read out which few commoners understood. Troops were posted in force for fear of an uprising. The interior ministry reported 647 riots in the first four months after promulgation of the edict. The worst of these incidents, at Bezdna near Kazan', led to the massacre of dozens of peasant protesters who believed that the 'real' emancipation decree was being kept from them by the lords. In the popular view all land rightfully belonged to those who worked it, and therefore why should they be required to pay for it? This was an understandable, but unrealistic, reaction: given the nobles' leading role in Russian society there had to be a compromise between them and the state. Even so, it was regrettable that the shape of the peasant reform should have been defined less by the application of enlightened principles than by intrigue in the highest councils of the land. The inadequacies of the settlement, to be examined further in Chapter 11, would cast a pall over agrarian relations in the empire for the next half-century.

---

* Crown and state peasants were freed under separate legislation issued later, on more generous terms than the serfs.

Local self-government

One consequence of serf emancipation was to undercut the dominant position hitherto held by squires in the rural administration. They had been seen, and had seen themselves, as *de facto* agents of the central government. Angry at the loss of their serfs, they could no longer be relied on. At first the authorities toyed with the idea of imposing a system of military control, but fortunately wiser counsels prevailed. In 1859 the tsar opted for the representative principle, which meant devolving power and giving non-official, elected persons a voice in running local affairs. This was designed to appease both conservative and liberal nobles. The former, ever suspicious of the bureaucracy, hoped that the new rural councils would uphold their interests; the latter, headed by Unkovsky of Tver' (in the north-west), were idealists who saw these bodies as a step towards a constitutional order which would do away with class privilege. The statute of January 1864 provided for such councils, called *zemstva* (singular: *zemstvo*) to be set up at provincial and district level. Election was by indirect suffrage, with nobles, urban property-owners, and peasant delegates meeting separately to choose their deputies, who served a three-year term; members of the provincial assemblies were chosen by those in the districts. Each assembly elected its executive board, which functioned in permanence between annual sessions of the full council.

By 1880 zemstvos had been set up in thirty-four provinces of the empire, concentrated in its Russian heartland. They were, however, prohibited from communicating with each other on matters of common interest, and local governors were empowered to keep close watch on their activities lest they exceed their brief. The most serious deficiency was that zemstvos received no funds from the centre but had to raise their own taxes to meet expenditure on local needs. Despite these limitations they managed to achieve a great deal. Gradually the emphasis of their work shifted to public health and education. Hospitals and schools were built, and a growing number of employees recruited to lead the fight against disease and ignorance. To many thoughtful people the zemstvos came to embody hopes of a transition to a democratic order. Peasant taxpayers were less enthusiastic about them, but learned to appreciate their practical benefit. The assemblies were one of the few places where ex-serfs could meet and bargain with their former masters – admittedly with due deference – and so bridge the divide between people belonging to different social estates.

In June 1870 similar principles were applied to the government of large towns which increased the role of the elected element. Such an approach had been tried out in St Petersburg during the previous reign, but in most other urban centres the administrative system was wholly pre-modern. The handful of functionaries in charge were notoriously ill-trained, incompetent, and corrupt. The Slavophil writer Ivan Aksakov wrote privately in 1850 that 'out of every hundred elected officials two-thirds are swindlers, and out of every hundred petty bureaucrats one cannot find even two who are honest'.* By the time Alexander acceded urban government had virtually collapsed. Yet thoroughgoing changes were delayed, largely because defenders of noble privilege objected to the principle that most power should go to those who paid high property or business taxes, as in the West. In the end the liberals got the better of the argument. Despite a narrowly based suffrage, many of the new municipal councils recruited able administrators who took measures to pave and light the streets, develop urban transport, promote hygiene and welfare, and generally foster a spirit of civic responsibility. It would go too far to claim that the city fathers had an adequate grasp of the problems generated by rapid industrialization: the urban poor lacked proper housing and amenities, but the new system was at least flexible enough to permit further improvements to be made in the early twentieth century.

Justice

Early in his reign Alexander proclaimed his desire 'to introduce into Russia legal proceedings that are swift, just, merciful and equal for all', since respect for the law was the basis of civilization. The judicial statutes of November 1864 registered considerable progress towards that lofty objective – perhaps more than the population, whose legal consciousness was deplorably weak, could readily assimilate. As in the West, judges' independence was protected by the grant of life tenure. Cases were to be heard in open court before a jury, and could be reported in the press. This meant giving accused the right to counsel, so that a bar of professional advocates took shape. Most of the old

* Letter to Nicholas Milyutin, 31 May 1850, cit. Lincoln, p. 135.

class barriers were swept away, although lawsuits between peasants continued to be settled according to ill-defined customary laws rather than the norms of jurisprudence. This left plenty of room for cruel and arbitrary decisions. Another drawback was that political offences came increasingly to be heard by military or administrative tribunals, not by the regular courts.

Even so, efforts to bend the law to suit the state's purposes were stoutly resisted by prominent advocates, who eagerly took up cases of people victimized for their opinions and even came to the defence of revolutionary terrorists. Russian lawyers took the lead in the struggle for civil rights. Conservatives fought hard to contain the liberties granted by the 1864 statute, which they claimed were eroding national traditions and the authority of the autocrat; but the genie had escaped from the bottle and could not readily be put back. By introducing the principle of separation of powers, the judicial reform broke away from bureaucratic absolutism, the system whereby the empire had been governed since Peter the Great, and moved towards a modern pluralistic order.

Culture and education

In 1858 a pamphlet by an unknown parish priest was published anonymously abroad and copies smuggled into Russia. Much like Radishchev's *Journey* half a century earlier, it created a furore. The author, Bellyustin, deplored the clergy's subjugation to a 'crushing routine' that obliged them to combine administration of the sacraments with tilling the soil. They were exposed to constant humiliation by their parishioners and by the 'black' clergy – the upper caste of monks and bishops, into whose ranks they had no hope of rising. In response, reforms were attempted in the Russian Orthodox Church, but they did not solve the main problem, the clergy's social segregation. An unpopular drive to consolidate parishes (1869) led to 'a virtual civil war among clergy' and 'left behind a great dark cloud of pessimism and disillusionment'.* The Church's resistance to modernization meant that it could not offer an alternative to the secular materialism that was sweeping through the educated classes. In fact a fair proportion of young revolutionaries had studied in ecclesiastical seminaries, where

---

* Freeze, *Parish Clergy in Nineteenth-Century Russia*, pp. 376–8.

educational standards remained deplorable. (There was, however, some improvement at the higher level of religious academies.) A few Orthodox churchmen developed Protestant sympathies, but most priests showed little tolerance for Christians of other confessions or Old Believers, let alone for Jews or Muslims.

The reformers had better success in promoting secular education. A statute of July 1864 encouraged private individuals, as well as the Church and zemstvos, to set up primary schools. Among the devoted amateur educationalists was Korf of Yekaterinoslav province, who took a common-sense, pragmatic view of what his charges required; another was the novelist Leo Tolstoy, whose pedagogical philosophy was in advance of its time. The main problem here was cash: peasants could not be expected to pay high school fees, and upper-class benevolence had its limits. Nor could the zemstvos raise enough funds to sustain systematic endeavours, so that their performance was patchy, the north-eastern (non-gentry!) provinces doing best. By the early 1880s some 14 per cent of boys aged eight to twelve were going to school. The zemstvos alone had established over 8,000 schools and were contributing 43 per cent of the total spent on primary education; peasant communities provided 23 per cent and the education ministry 16 per cent.

The latter's activities were regarded askance by local teachers and zemstvo activists, who resented the imposition of bureaucratic controls. Dmitriy Tolstoy, minister of education, was a convinced centralizer, ever alert to the threat of subversion. He established a corps of school inspectors (in itself an unobjectionable step) and teacher-training colleges. Most of the ministry's effort went on secondary or higher education, which was of more immediate relevance to state needs. The number of secondary-school (*gimnaziya*) pupils quintupled during Alexander II's reign. But the emphasis which Tolstoy placed on classical languages, deemed politically 'safe', provoked most teachers and pupils, who thought them irrelevant.

Universities were teaching 60 per cent more students in 1880 than they had in 1859, but this hardly kept up with population growth. One of the main problems facing their administrators was student radicalism, which in 1861 led to disturbances in St Petersburg and elsewhere; despite this the university reform (1863) allowed these institutions a remarkable degree of autonomy. Although student organizations were prohibited, grants were given to the most deserving and the principle maintained that access should be open to young men from all classes. A start was also made on higher education for women, although they had to wait until 1878 before they were admitted to regular courses. Before then alternative study arrangements were available privately, and some went abroad. The upshot was that within a few years Russia could claim a higher proportion of women with higher education than any other country in Europe. They did sterling work, especially in medicine.

This was an age of cultural efflorescence: Tolstoy, Dostoyevsky, and Turgenev in literature; Mussorgsky and Rimsky-Korsakov in music; and in the pictorial arts, slightly less conspicuously, Repin, the marine painter Aivaozovsky, and others who worked mainly in the 'realist' style. In the sciences, too, Russia made a notable contribution: Mendeleyev (1834-1907), who taught at St Petersburg University from 1857, devised the periodic table of the known elements (and predicted the discovery of three others). Later he did important work in crystallography, organic chemistry (petroleum), and meteorology. A successful industrialist, he advocated developing Russia's rich mineral resources to achieve rapid economic growth – a view still novel in his day. It was as a professor at Moscow University that the botanist Timiryazev (1843-1920) began his work on photosynthesis. Of even greater practical significance, given the role of agriculture in the country's economy, were the discoveries of the soil scientist Dokuchayev (1846-1903), who was the first to advance the idea of soil zones. Russian geographers and explorers did first-class work. An adventurous army officer, Przewalski (1839-88), spent nine years from 1871 exploring inner Asia, whence he returned with thousands of zoological and botanical specimens, including the wild horse since named after him. He was a disciple of Semenov-Tyan-shansky (1827-1914), who after playing an honorable part in serf emancipation laid the foundations of the pioneering local statistical studies organized under zemstvo auspices.

On the negative side, Russian scientists were hampered by lack of funds (and public esteem) as well as by the country's technological lag. It was sadly characteristic that experiments made in the 1870s in using electricity for street lighting (by Yablochkov and Lodygin) should have been followed up abroad rather than in Russia, so that their names are less familiar than they deserve to be. Later on, as the political climate deteriorated, a number of scholars and scientists chose to work abroad. Among them was the mathematician Sofia Kovalevskaya (1850–91), who ended her days as a professor in Stockholm. Law and economics were two fields of study that suffered relative neglect for political reasons; historiography, by contrast, did surprisingly well.

Not that censorship was unduly restrictive: the bleak years 1848–55 were followed by an epoch of *glasnost'* (roughly, freedom of expression). In the first decade of Alexander's reign ten times as many new periodicals saw the light as in the previous ten years. In provincial towns the arrival of each successive issue of one of the 'thick journals', such as *The Contemporary* or *Notes of the Fatherland*, was keenly awaited by educated people. In April 1865 so-called 'temporary regulations' were issued – they lasted thirty-eight years! – which abolished preliminary censorship and instead held writers, editors, and publishers responsible for generating material considered dangerous. This was a double-edged sword, since simultaneously the supervision of literature passed from the (relatively liberal) education ministry to that of interior, whose chief had the option of imposing administrative penalties (including suspension of a journal for up to six months) if he did not want the case to go before the courts. On the other hand, some journalists were prone to abuse their new freedom. They now had to assume moral and legal responsibility for what they wrote, as in countries with a more liberal tradition. The learning process was not easy, since all too many Russian intellectuals were instinctively hostile to whatever officialdom did, and loath to evaluate policies fairly, with an eye to the country's modest resources.

The armed forces

Alexander II was not proof against the militaristic attitudes of his predecessors, and the empire's military predicament in the post-Crimean era played a large part in impelling him to take the path of reform. Nicholas I's vast conscript army had to be thinned down into a trained cadre force of full-time soldiers who could be supplemented by reservists in case of war. This meant reducing the men's service term and giving them a rudimentary education, so that they could understand orders. This in turn required recasting officers' training on more professional lines and updating the antiquated system of military justice. On the more technical side, it necessitated replacing muskets by rifles, increasing artillery firepower, and devolving authority to regional headquarters so that a more flexible response could be offered to local security threats. All these controversial matters were tackled, in the face of stiff opposition from 'old-guard' officers, by the tsar's brilliant war minister, Dmitriy Milyutin (younger brother of Nicholas, the architect of serf emancipation). But not until 1874, three years after the Franco-Prussian War, could he achieve his principal objective, a law introducing general conscription. In principle this treated nobles and commoners alike. In practice an element of social discrimination remained, since service exemptions were liberally granted on educational grounds, which of course favoured the élite, as well as to men whose family status was that of 'breadwinners'.

Milyutin's measures enabled the Russian army to build up sizeable reserves. It was unfortunate that, before they took full effect, the country became involved in another Balkan war with Turkey (1877-8). Although ultimately successful in military terms, it led to heavy manpower losses. Many long-standing deficiencies in organization and supply had yet to be remedied. The navy played little role in these hostilities, but the picture here was more encouraging, since as naval minister Grand Duke Constantine managed to effect several improvements which raised sailors' qualifications and morale.

RETRENCHMENT IN EUROPE, ADVANCES IN ASIA

Russia had to make do without her Black Sea fleet for over twenty years after the treaty of Paris. This was the heaviest blow inflicted on her by the peace settlement and patriotic opinion bitterly resented it. Actually Russia was treated with considerable magnanimity, partly because the allies were split. Britain stood out for tougher sanctions, but France saw Russia as a potential ally against Austria. The European map was about to be redrawn as, in the wake of the Crimean War, national movements came to the fore in Italy, the Balkans, and, above all, Germany. Russia, the dominant power on the continent since 1814, was now temporarily in eclipse, preoccupied with internal reconstruction. Reluctantly she had to reconcile herself to demilitarization of the Black Sea, loss of territory in southern Bessarabia that had given her control over the Danube, and the assumption by the Powers of joint responsibility for Christians under Ottoman rule.

Her objectives in Europe were now necessarily limited, but she could not afford to remain isolated. Alexander and his foreign minister, Prince Gorchakov, first worked towards a rapprochement with Napoleon III. In 1859 the Russians agreed to remain benevolently neutral, and even to mobilize troops on the Galician border, while Napoleon and his Piedmontese ally tried to drive Austria out of northern Italy. But St Petersburg was unwilling to go further, fearing Napoleon's unpredictability and imperial ambitions. The unification of Italy under French auspices, and by revolutionary means, disturbed Russian conservatives, and when Napoleon went on to give diplomatic backing to the rebellious Poles in 1863 the flirtation abruptly ended.

All along Alexander II had instinctively preferred a more traditional course, an alliance with the Prussian monarchy. Family ties between Romanovs and Hohenzollerns still counted for much. During the Polish uprising Berlin promised to return any insurgents who sought sanctuary on Prussian soil. The convention on this minor matter heralded twenty-seven years of collaboration. Bismarck in particular was always anxious to keep open 'the wire to St Petersburg', where he had formerly served as ambassador. He saw that Russian goodwill was essential to the successful pursuit of German unity under Prussian hegemony. In the brief wars against Denmark (1864) and Austria (1866) Russia stood aside, although far-sighted observers realized that the weakening of Habsburg power in Central Europe deprived Russia of her ability to exploit divisions between Berlin and Vienna. Moreover, the emergence on the empire's western border of a united Germany, endowed with vast industrial and military potential, posed a long-term threat.

The dangers were demonstrated all too starkly when in 1870 Prussia went on to defeat and humiliate France, and then proclaim Wilhelm I all-German emperor. Yet Russia made no real move to help the French, partly because she was alarmed at the revolutionary tendencies in Paris when Napoleonic rule collapsed. She had in truth lost much of her freedom of manoeuvre and found herself in the tow of the new Germany. There were benefits in this situation. In October 1870 the prudent Gorchakov felt that Russia was strong enough to denounce unilaterally the naval clauses of the treaty of Paris, which had for long been her principal goal. The other powers were busy with the war in the west, and Bismarck skilfully used his good offices to obtain their assent to the Russian move (convention of London, March 1871).

This was a useful sop to assuage patriotic public disquiet, which had been gathering force throughout the decade and, even in autocratic Russia, could no longer be ignored by the makers of foreign policy. After the Crimean War Slavophilism gradually disintegrated into a strident Russian nationalism, often cloaked as Pan-Slavism: the idea, by no means new – it had been mooted by the Croat Križanić already in the seventeenth century – that all the Slav peoples should be freed from Germanic or Turkish rule and united under the sceptre of the Russian tsar. (There was also a left-wing version, articulated *inter alia* by Bakunin, which assigned the leadership role to a future *democratic* Russia.) Pan-Slavism owed much to the Pan-German precedent and was prevailingly a conservative movement, which at its peak acquired chauvinistic and racist features. Initially, to be sure, it took a fairly benign form. Slavic benevolent committees were set up in Moscow and elsewhere to promote cultural contact with other Slavic peoples, particularly in the Balkans. Funds were collected to enable students from the region to attend Russian universities (where to their hosts' indignation they sometimes fell under the sway of radical ideas!). The greatest obstacle to realization of the Pan-Slav ideal, however, was Poland, a Slavic nation *par excellence* but united in hostility to Russia as the leading and most repressive partitioning power. Resentful at the failure of the 1863 revolt, the Polish public would have nothing to do with the Slav Congress held in Moscow four years later. Its practical results were accordingly slight, but the meeting made a big impression on Russian opinion.

In 1869 Danilevsky published a nationalistic tract, *Russia and Europe*, in which he predicted a titanic clash between the Germanic-Romanic and Slavic 'races' that would end with Constantinople becoming the capital of a great Slav federation. Less marred by ill-digested social Darwinism, and more influential, was *Opinion on the Eastern Question*, which appeared in the same year. Its author, General Fadeyev, argued that Russia should seek to destroy both the Austrian and Ottoman empires. The most strident spokesman for the Russian right was not really a Pan-Slav at all. Katkov, editor of the daily *Moscow News*, looked on the other Slavic nations as adjuncts to the pursuit of Russia's imperial interests. He advocated autocracy at home and a vigorous foreign policy directed against the Germanic powers, even if the price of this was cooperation with the French Third Republic.

Official St Petersburg was embarrassed by these emotionally laden criticisms. Gorchakov was essentially a *Realpolitiker* who recognized the practical limitations that kept Russia from taking a more adventuristic stance. He held to the principle of a European balance of power, sustained where possible by dynastic links, and for that reason welcomed renewal of the old alliance between the three eastern emperors (1873). He saw the British as Russia's main rivals and was even more afraid of revolutionary nationalism. Gorchakov was also a suave courtier who had one ear cocked to his imperial master's will, and in foreign, as in domestic, affairs Alexander vacillated. His foreign minister could rely on his colleagues at the war and finance ministries, who knew that the empire was not ready for further hostilities, but the tsar's other advisers pulled in the reverse direction. Indeed, Gorchakov was not even master in his own house, since all too often his ministry's Asiatic department (whose responsibilities included the Near East) pursued a line of its own. Until 1864 its chief was the fiery Ignatyev, who was then sent as ambassador to the Porte, where he had even more opportunity to make mischief and undercut the moderates at home.

A forward policy was most easily undertaken in regard to Russia's Asian possessions, which could be expanded under the pretext of bringing 'European civilization' to allegedly backward lands. The ethos of Russian imperialism had much in common with that of its British, French, and other Western counterparts. Perhaps there was less sense of racial superiority among Russian colonialists, who on the other hand were less intent on introducing modern notions of administration and law. The promotion of economic interests went hand in hand with considerations of national prestige. There was also an element of international competition, in the sense that advances were sometimes made in order to deny certain territory to an antagonist. Both Russia and Britain feared, or pretended to fear, that the other had aggressive designs on lands strategically situated between modern Kazakhstan and India. There was also an element of pure military adventurism, in that local generals eagerly exploited opportunities to win fame and glory by taking action that they confidently hoped would later be condoned by their superiors – who themselves were not above fraudulently claiming that these satraps had acted irregularly.

The first victims of Russian expansion, as we know, were the native peoples of Siberia. During the eighteenth century their lot worsened as their means of subsistence were destroyed by profit-hungry traders and settlers. The latter numbered some 900,000 in 1800 and 2.7 million fifty years later, most of them resident in the western regions. An administrative reform introduced by Speransky in 1822, ostensibly in order to encourage nomadic and semi-nomadic tribesmen to become agriculturalists, had the effect of greatly increasing tax burdens. Merchants bought up and then leased back land to natives at extortionate rates, while the sale of tobacco and vodka had even more devastating consequences. Epidemics of syphilis cost many lives. Only the Yakuts managed to adapt fairly well, at least at élite level, and to preserve their shamanist traditions under a Christian veneer – as well as their language, which was even adopted by some local Russians.

The pioneers' never-ending quest for more fur-bearing animals, sea otters, and whales led them across the north Pacific to the Aleutian islands and Alaska. Not only were the rich stocks of wildlife sadly depleted, but so too were many indigenous peoples: the Aleuts, for example, declined from $c.20,000$ before the conquest to 2,500 by the 1790s.[*] In Alaska government lay at first with the Russo-American company, founded in 1797, which built a chain of strong points and commercial outposts down the coast as far south as San Francisco (Fort Ross), where the Russians came up against the Spanish colonial empire. A principal object of this particular venture, abandoned in 1841, was to grow food for the fur-trappers and whalers farther north.

By the mid nineteenth century it had become clear that Russia's North American enterprise was uneconomic and strategically indefensible. Its survival depended on the continued goodwill of the United States. Relations were generally amicable, since both countries shared an antipathy to the British. In 1853 the energetic governor-general of eastern Siberia, N. N. Muravyov, recommended surrendering the far-off province in order to cement ties with Washington, and in 1867 this course was taken. Its sale, for a mere $7.2 million, seemed a good bargain at the time, but the discovery of Alaskan gold caused some Russians to regret it later.

---

[*] Forsyth, *History of Peoples of Siberia*, pp. 115, 150–52, 165.

The loss was easier to bear now that the empire's hold on the western shore of the Pacific was more solidly based. In 1850 Muravyov sent a flotilla down the river Amur and established an outpost near its mouth. This improved communications with Kamchatka and led to an interest in Sakhalin island, which was taken in 1875 (in an exchange for the Kuriles, returned to Japan). Nominally at least these were Chinese possessions, but Beijing was not then strong enough to resist encroachments on its borderlands. (These acquisitions would cause friction a century later.) By the 'unequal treaties' of Aigun and Beijing (1858, 1860) China was forced to recognize Russian sovereignty over a vast area of territory south and east of the Amur. This was the first revision of the border between the two powers since the treaty of Nerchinsk in 1689. Particularly valuable economically and strategically was the Ussuri valley. Close to its new border with Korea Russia established the port and naval base of Vladivostok (1860), whose very name ('Rule the East') symbolized her expansionist designs in the region. Although the Russians did not take part in the humiliating Anglo-French occupation and looting of Beijing, they secured the same commercial privileges as the other imperial powers and established a permanent legation in the Chinese capital.

In Central Asia they had to act more cautiously owing to British sensitivities. The first moves, against the Kokand khanate, were undertaken in 1863 when Anglo-Russian tension was acute over Poland and a diversion in Asia seemed opportune. Tashkent, the capital, fell in June 1865 to the impetuous Colonel (later General) Chernyaev and soon became the administrative centre of a new governor-generalship, Turkestan. Bokhara, to the south-west, an ancient focus of Islamic civilization, was captured in 1868 and became a Russian protectorate, in this way conserving a vestige of its former sovereignty. The same status was accorded to Khiva, in the lower basin of the Amu-darya, after it capitulated in 1873. The natives were outnumbered and outgunned. Some local chieftains were won over by promises of aid against their rivals. Those who sought to wage a *jihad* against the invaders were dealt with by punitive expeditions. One of these was led by Von Kaufman, a stern colonial administrator; another by General Skobelev, who became the object of a popular cult. This left the lands east of the Caspian Sea and north of Persia (Iran), modern Turkmenistan. In 1869 the Russians, having consolidated their rule over the Caucasus, established a base at Krasnovodsk on the eastern shore of the Caspian. The first campaign against the warlike Turcomans, however, ended in disaster and not until 1881 did their capital, Geok Tepe, fall to Skobelev's superior forces. The casualty figures are suggestive: 700 dead on the Russian side, 8,000 among the natives. Farther to the south-east the city and region of Merv, on the Afghan border, came under Russian rule in 1884. This provoked a crisis with Britain, which had established a kind of protectorate over Afghanistan. Here Russia's advance in the region came to a halt, except for a frontier rectification in the Pamirs in 1895 which established a buffer zone between the two empires in eastern Afghanistan so that their territories did not touch.

In the conquered lands Russian rule brought some benefits, such as the elimination of slavery and the construction of railways (mainly for strategic purposes). For good or ill the colonial administration did not interfere too radically in the native way of life. Educational levels, for instance, remained abysmally low. The main innovation was cotton cultivation, which provided a livelihood for thousands of labourers. Russian settlers did not enter Turkestan in force until 1910, but the situation was different farther north. On the Kazakh steppe by that date Russian colonists comprised 40 per cent of the population and posed a threat to the survival of the largely nomadic (or semi-nomadic) Kazakhs and Kyrgyz.

Anglo-Russian tension was most acute over the Turkish Straits, and in the 1870s nearly led to another war between the two powers. In 1875 revolts broke out against Turkish rule in Bosnia and Herzegovina, which spread to Bulgaria in the following year. The Turks suppressed the rebels with great ferocity, causing an international outcry but bringing them little in the way of concrete aid. Serbia and Montenegro went to war against the Porte. Their action was not, as many Englishmen then believed, instigated by Russia, for St Petersburg was keen to localize the conflict in cooperation with the other powers, but Russian patriotic opinion was mightily aroused. The Slavonic benevolent committees recruited several thousand volunteers for service with the Serbs and sent Chernyaev to take charge. But 'the lion of Tashkent' was unable to prevent the south Slav states' defeat. In Russia the public mood turned from euphoria to bitterness, and the government found itself under heavy pressure to go to war.

The first imperative was to ensure Vienna's benevolent neutrality. The Reichstadt agreement of July 1876 and two later conventions rewarded the Danubian monarchy with the right to annex Bosnia and Herzegovina when it chose;* in return, Russia could occupy Bulgaria on condition that it did not create a large Slav state in the eastern Balkans. After further diplomatic efforts to defuse the crisis proved unavailing, Russia declared war on Turkey (April 1877). Her troops performed reasonably well both in the southern Caucasus and in the Balkans, where after the costly five-month siege of Plevna they reached the outskirts of Constantinople. But the bilateral treaty concluded at San Stefano with the Turks (March 1878), devised mainly by Ignatyev, provided for the very 'greater Bulgaria' that Russia's rivals so dreaded. The British fleet, which was already in Turkish waters, moved closer to Constantinople and there was a mood of hysterical Russophobia in London.

Hostilities were averted largely thanks to Bismarck, who summoned the powers to a congress in Berlin and mediated a settlement whereby the San Stefano treaty was drastically revised, the projected Bulgaria being halved in size. Russia reacquired southern Bessarabia and in Asia Minor secured Kars and Ardahan, Batum becoming a free port. Nevertheless Russia's skilful negotiator in Berlin, Count Peter Shuvalov, and the government generally were lambasted by the nationalists. This contributed to the tsar's isolation at home and greatly strained Russo-German relations. Exasperated by attacks in the Russian press, Bismarck made Germany's alliance with Austria-Hungary (reinforced in 1879) the mainstay of his policy, while disaffected Russians, alarmed at the empire's ever greater dependence on the Germanic powers, toyed more seriously with the idea of a French accord. European diplomatic alignments were already assuming the contours they would have in 1914.

INTERNAL OPPOSITION

The tsarist regime had to confront not only the right but, more menacingly, revolutionary socialists and the leaders of several emerging

* This concession led to trouble in 1908: see below, page 258.

national minorities. The Populist* movement that ultimately brought about Alexander II's assassination has naturally received most attention. This distorts the picture, for in long-term perspective minority nationalism was an even greater threat to the empire's survival.

So far as the Poles were concerned, Alexander first tried conciliation, amnestying exiles in Siberia and allowing a medical school to be set up in Warsaw as the nucleus of a future Polish university. Its students soon became politicized, as did the landowners' newly established Agricultural Society. Once again, as in 1830–31, a split occurred between moderates and radicals that harmed the Polish national cause. The latter staged demonstrations that led to clashes with Russian troops. Despite this a semi-autonomous regime was set up in the kingdom under a viceroy, Marquis Wielopolski. It permitted the use of Polish in government offices and schools, but the patriots were not appeased. Wielopolski closed the Agricultural Society, which led to further violence. For the radicals the final straw came in January 1863 when youths with nationalist sympathies were made subject to the draft. Many of them fled to the woods and a guerrilla war got under way.

The insurgents were active not only throughout the Polish kingdom but also in the west Russian provinces (modern Lithuania and Belarus). This greatly alarmed the government, although the agitation here could be put down more rapidly than in Poland proper, where this took eighteen months. The outcome was never in doubt, for the rebels were vastly outnumbered and received only moral support from friends abroad. In 1864 peasants in the region were freed on more generous terms than in the Russian heartland. This somewhat Machiavellian move stopped them backing the insurgents, without however reconciling them to the *status quo* in the long term; ultimately possession of the land strengthened their national consciousness. Some 3,500 estates were confiscated and taken over by Russians; half the monasteries were closed and among the 20,000 exiles were many priests. General M. M. Muravyov, appointed virtual dictator of Vilnius province, had 240

---

* The term Populism is properly applied to those activists who, in 1875–8, tried to help peasants express their own aspirations for change instead of instilling socialist ideas 'from above', but it is commonly given to the entire agrarian socialist movement in Russia from its origins in the 1840s to its destruction by the Bolsheviks after 1917.

rebels executed in public, earning for himself the epithet 'hangman'. The region was placed in a 'state of exception', a handy device applied to many areas of the empire that became insecure, which meant that the new liberal judicial system introduced in 1864 did not apply there. Repression was followed by russification measures in the administration and school system; even on the railways and in banks leading positions now usually went to Russians. However, in the 'Vistula region', as the Polish provinces were now officially known, industry and commerce prospered from the 1870s onwards. Polish industrialists benefited from access to the vast Russian hinterland. Economic development fostered a climate of opinion termed 'realism' (in contrast to the earlier Romantic mood): this was a time for accumulating new energies that would later assume a socialist colouring and explode in 1905.

The historical grounds for Polish intransigence did not exist in the grand duchy of Finland, where the national movement was still in its cultural phase; this was also true of the more northerly Baltic provinces. In response to restlessness among the Finns, in 1863 Alexander convened the Diet for the first time since 1809. Thereafter it met regularly and passed a number of measures that assuaged public opinion: Finnish became the sole official language, schools were freed from church control, and a separate currency introduced. Under the 1874 military reform Finnish soldiers could not be made to serve outside the duchy. All this would change in the late 1890s, but for the present the Finnish experience showed that in certain conditions peaceful political development was possible for the empire's national minorities.

This was not the case in either Belarus or in Ukraine ('Little Russia', in official terminology), where the local languages lost the right to exist. The Ukrainian national movement began as a regional phenomenon, and so was regarded benignly by Russian intellectuals, including Pushkin and Gogol' (the latter, of course, himself of Ukrainian origin). Taras Shevchenko (1814–61), a symbolic figure to his compatriots to this day, was a former serf, freed by his master and encouraged to develop his artistic gifts. His verse created the modern Ukrainian literary language, much as Pushkin's poetry had done for Russian. In 1847 Shevchenko was exiled for ten years as a soldier to the Kazakh steppe, where his sufferings fatally undermined his health. The harsh penalty was owed to the appearance, at Kiev University in the mid 1840s, of a clandestine organization, 'the Brotherhood of Cyril and

Methodius'. Its main activists were two historians, Kostomarov and Kulish. The former was probably the author of an anonymous work with the quaint title *Book of Genesis of the Ukrainian People*,* which in quasi-biblical language recounted Ukraine's struggle against Polish and Muscovite conquerors and prophesied a golden age of Pan-Slav brotherhood (in which, however, Ukraine was apparently to be 'more equal than the others'!).

The members of the Brotherhood, a mere dozen or so, were arrested in 1847, at the same time as the so-called 'Petrashevtsy' in St Petersburg, a larger group whose ideas had a vaguely socialistic hue.† These police measures served to limit the impact within the empire of the 1848 revolutions in Central Europe, which *inter alia* did much to foster Ukrainian national consciousness in Austrian-ruled eastern Galicia. This region became a kind of 'Piedmont' whence progressive ideas percolated across the border into Russian Ukraine. Here the freer conditions of Alexander's reign permitted the formation of so-called *hromady* (= communities), in which intellectuals and students came together to promote educational and other cultural activities. Meanwhile in St Petersburg Kostomarov and others founded a journal, *Osnova* (*The Foundation*), which although published in Russian set itself similar goals.

The pro-peasant orientation of these cultural endeavours alarmed the authorities, who feared that Ukrainian malcontents might make common cause with the rebellious Poles (and also that Ukrainians were increasing faster than Russians). Interior minister Valuyev issued a secret circular (1863) banning literature (except *belles-lettres*) in Ukrainian, which he derogatorily called a mere 'dialect of Russian spoiled by Polish influences'. A more intelligent administration might have exploited Ukrainian-Polish tensions; as it was they were overlooked. Up to a point russification succeeded in putting a brake on the Ukrainian

---

* This title was modelled on that of a volume by the Polish patriot Adam Mickiewicz, a tribute to the 'copycat' element in the rise of nationalism throughout Europe.
† The main organizer, Butashevich-Petrashevsky, an admirer of the French 'Utopian' socialist Fourier, held informal discussions with friends on political and social questions. Some associates, notably Speshnev, planned to form a clandestine revolutionary society, but this did not materialize before the police struck. A secret court tried 122 individuals; Dostoyevsky was one of fifteen condemned to death, but their execution was stayed at the last moment and replaced by a sentence of exile with forced labour.

movement, although in the early 1870s it revived and obtained a precarious institutional base in the Russian Geographical Society's (innocuously titled) 'South-western branch'. The moderates followed the lead of the Polish-born scholar Antonovych, the radicals that of the democratic agrarian socialist Drahomaniw, who advocated reconstruction of the empire on federal lines. He was obliged to emigrate in order to escape a resurgence of the russification drive. Alexander's circular, issued from Bad Ems (1876), went further than its predecessor, and in particular endeavoured to stop literature in Ukrainian being smuggled in from Galicia, where at this time Lwów (Lviv) was becoming a flourishing centre of national culture.

As has recently been recognized, both Ukrainians and Jews played an important part in Russian Populism (*narodnichestvo*). The empire's Jewish population, the victim of some of Nicholas I's most repressive measures, experienced a movement of secular enlightenment (*haskalah*) which challenged the authority of the traditional rabbinate within their communities (*kahalim*). These communities were located within the so-called Pale of Settlement, an area comprising Poland and a zone extending from Lithuania to southern Ukraine. Jews had traditionally lived in a largely self-imposed isolation from their Slavic neighbours, from whom they were conspicuously distinguished by their dress and lifestyle. Heavy-handed government efforts to assimilate them into Russian culture largely failed until Alexander II opened the way to a *rapprochement* by relaxing certain legal disabilities. Those Jews, for example, who were first-guild merchants and holders of academic degrees were permitted to reside outside the Pale, and occupational restrictions on rural Jews were eased – temporarily, as it turned out. The improved climate encouraged some Jewish parents to send their children to Russian schools and a thin élite formed of assimilated Jews (bankers, industrialists, and professional people). It was generally *their* progeny who were attracted to revolutionary ideas.

Antisemites were, of course, wrong to see the Russian Populist movement as an 'alien Jewish creation'. Reacting to such charges, historians of Russian Jewry have tended to play down the Jews' role as one of mere 'technical assistance', for example helping fugitives to cross the border. Actually the percentage of Jewish activists rose from about 8 per cent in the 1870s to 25–30 per cent by the late 1880s. There were also a few 'generals of revolution' (Natanson, Aptekman), who were distinguished by a humanistic cosmopolitanism (although some other Jewish activists were caught up in the drift to terrorism). This moderate stance has been called 'a transfiguration of their Jewishness': having forsaken traditional religious beliefs, they found solace in a universal socialist credo.*

To some extent a quasi-religious idealism was characteristic of the Russian intelligentsia as well. Often they 'saw the light' while at school or university and sundered their ties to family and religion in order to devote themselves, in a spirit of exaltation, to the revolutionary cause. Intellectually, Populism was derived from Herzen's Romantic blend of enlightened Westernism and faith in the (unproven) redemptive capabilities of the peasant commune, once this inherently egalitarian institution had been freed from bureaucratic control. The task of educated youth – women as well as men – was to help the peasants realize their potential and build a more equitable social order, superior to that of Western 'capitalism'. Some enthusiasts hoped that, by taking its own road to progress, Russia might achieve socialism ahead of the conflict-torn West, but this 'messianic' element in Populist teaching was seldom clearly articulated.

After 1856 the first student circles concerned themselves with self-improvement and reading forbidden books (Darwin, Mill). There was a vogue for the latest in Western intellectual and scientific fashions. The protests of 1861, motivated largely by indignation at the terms of the Emancipation, involved the distribution of leaflets, some of them couched in inflammatory language. The youthful radicals were at first heartened by moral support from the *émigré* Herzen, whose periodical *The Bell* was very influential in the late 1850s, but he objected to the needlessly provocative tone of the 'men of the sixties'. They accordingly took their lead rather from Chernyshevsky and his associates on *The Contemporary*. Some critics called them 'nihilists', but this term is misleading: they were, on the contrary, zealously committed to their ideological principles.

The government, nervous at violence in the empire's capital, overestimated the radicals' importance and responded with unduly harsh repression. Chernyshevsky was arrested on trumped-up charges (July 1862) and *The Contemporary* suppressed. While in gaol he wrote a

* Haberer, *Jews and Revolution*, pp. 253–65.

novel, *What's to be Done?*, which provided disaffected youth with an agreeable model of an alternative lifestyle: emancipated from family bonds and the constraints of conventional morality, the 'new people' should form free cooperatives, treat their womenfolk as comrades, and steel themselves physically and emotionally for the struggle against all traditional authorities. When Chernyshevsky received a fourteen-year sentence to penal servitude in Siberia he was widely regarded as a martyr.

In default of any other charismatic leader the movement lost ground. Some followed the apostle of anarchism, Bakunin, but he was abroad; others were drawn to the 'rational egoism' of Pisarev, who met an accidental death in 1868. The Polish revolt caused the mood in Russian society to veer sharply to the right. This shift accelerated in 1866 when Karakozov, a radical student who belonged to a melodramatically named clandestine group, 'Hell', made the first attempt on the tsar's life. This individual act of terror proved counter-productive and led to the appointment of the conservative Tolstoy as education minister.

The left was rescued from the doldrums by Peter Lavrov, a former army officer whose *Historical Letters* (1868–9) pleaded for a more ethical brand of socialism. 'Critically thinking individuals', i.e. intellectuals, who had been educated at the people's expense, he argued, were under a moral obligation to repay their debt. Members of clandestine discussion circles in the two capital cities interpreted this as a summons to 'go to the people', bringing them the fruits of their knowledge both on the practical plane as teachers, midwives, and so on (a kind of development aid *avant la lettre*), and also on a more expressly political plane by making propaganda for social change. A minority of Bakuninists held that the peasants were already so alienated that a mere call to rebel would suffice to launch a new *Pugachevshchina*.

Both views rested on a misconception of rural realities. The results of the pilgrimage were disappointing, at least in the short term. Few activists managed to establish fruitful contact with the populace. Some 700 of them were arrested, occasionally after a tip-off to the authorities by their prospective disciples. It was clearly impossible to bridge the social gulf by such naïve methods. The key lay in forming durable clandestine bodies and concentrating efforts on artisans and urban workmen, who had shown themselves more receptive to novel ideas than peasants. Already in 1862 an attempt had been made to establish a nation-wide clandestine organization called 'Land and Liberty' – the two main planks in the revolutionary programme – but it had been quickly broken up by the police. In 1876 it was reformed under new leadership. The founders, Natanson and Mikhaylov, conceived it as a closely knit, disciplined body of propagandists, settled permanently in the villages, who would build support by articulating their contacts' immediate demands and grievances. They were to be directed by a militant nucleus, skilled in the arts of survival 'underground'. A sinister feature was a so-called 'Disorganization section', which included an explosives expert and a spy in the police. It carried out such 'technical' tasks as freeing arrested comrades – or assassinating informers.

A succession of violent clashes with police indicated that the movement was degenerating into terrorism. The zealots' anger was stimulated by brutal treatment of arrested activists, who were then put on trial. Increasingly conflicting views on the importance of violent deeds and peaceful propaganda jeopardized the organization's unity. It was a question of degree: few 'villagers' (propagandists) objected to using weapons in self-defence, but they recognized the danger in an obsession with conspiracy. The movement's noble ends were being compromised by the means employed to reach them, especially since, as a consequence of the discovery of dynamite, the revolver was giving way to the bomb.

In January 1878, directly after sentences were announced in the great 'trial of the 193', Vera Zasulich shot and wounded the governor of St Petersburg to avenge a prisoner whom he had ordered to be flogged. This was the signal for further *coups* which claimed the lives of the Kiev police chief, the head of the Third department, and the governor-general of Khar'kov. In April 1879 it was again the tsar's turn. The assailant, Solovyov, missed his target and was hanged, as were several others. In June some twenty-five Land and Liberty activists met in congress at Voronezh. (The venue had to be changed at the last moment because some comrades' singing attracted the attention of the local police!) The terrorists among them had pre-empted its decisions at an earlier conclave held nearby, where 'they sought to seize the mother organization for themselves [and] devised a scheme to pack the meeting with proponents of terrorism . . . The plan reeked of deception and conspiracy, but as things turned out it worked.'* The propagandists

---

* Hardy, *Land and Freedom*, pp. 104–5, 108.

present acquiesced in a compromise that gave the terrorists their way, Plekhanov alone dissenting. The victors took the name 'People's Will' (*Narodnaya volya*).

Plekhanov's group, 'Black Repartition' (i.e. all land to the peasants), which clung to the old tactics, was of little account, except in so far as its views subsequently evolved in the direction of Marxism. The eyes of the world were now fixed on the dramatic unequal struggle between the autocracy and a few hundred conspirators – in effect, the eight-man Executive Committee, for the 'People's Will' was a semi-fictitious body. Its leaders publicly revealed that their aim was to kill the emperor. Some leaders, notably Zhelyabov, son of a former serf who had attended university, thought that this might spark a popular upheaval, or else compel a new ruler to make constitutional concessions – although according to socialist theory these could benefit only the 'bourgeoisie', not the masses. In November 1879 Zhelyabov tried to blow up a train on which Alexander II was travelling, but the plot failed. A more sensational *coup* was staged in February 1880. A workman, Khalturin, who had secured a job in the Winter Palace, set off a powerful explosion under a hall where the tsar was expected to dine; eleven people were killed and fifty-six injured, but the ruler, who had been delayed, was not among them.

Security precautions were now stepped up, but remained amateurish. A 'supreme executive commission' under Count Loris-Melikov was granted emergency powers to coordinate government policy. While dealing ruthlessly with the men of violence, the 'dictator' eased the censorship and made gestures towards the gentry liberals. Since their emergence in 1862 the latter had devoted themselves mainly to practical work in the zemstvo. In 1879 they re-emerged, under Petrunkevich's leadership, and submitted 'loyal addresses' hinting at the need for a constitution. They also established contact with the revolutionaries, who, however, regarded them with contempt while valuing any practical aid they gave. Liberals made poor conspirators; their Zemstvo Union was infiltrated by police informers and achieved little.

In January 1881 Loris-Melikov submitted to the tsar a complex and cautious scheme whereby persons elected by zemstvos and munici-palities might participate in discussing new laws. Alexander II approved it, but before it could be published he was dead. On 1 March, as he returned from manoeuvres, a bomb was thrown at his sleigh which killed one of his escorts and a passer-by. The monarch stepped out to inspect the victims and their assailant. Thereupon a second bomb blasted his body. He died shortly afterwards.

With him died all hope of constitutional change for the next generation. His son, Alexander III, was a convinced partisan of firm autocratic government, and his views were reinforced by the manner of his father's death. As for the 'People's Will', Zhelyabov and four comrades were hanged and the remaining activists soon rounded up. The organization forfeited its public credit. Nevertheless the appeal of revolutionary violence lived on, to resurface with greater force in the early twentieth century.

CHAPTER 11

Economic Development and Social Change in the Late Imperial Era

THE RURAL ECONOMY

The edicts of 1861–6 freed peasant householders from servitude and assured them a modicum of inalienable land on their allotments (*nadely*), but did not bring economic prosperity or make them equal citizens. Right up to the 1917 revolution (and even beyond) most Russian villagers kept to the traditional three-field crop rotation system. They tilled the soil with primitive implements such as the ox- or horse-drawn wooden plough (*sokha*) and had little incentive to improve farming techniques. Egalitarian sentiment was fostered by retention of the village commune (*obshchina*), valued by the authorities as a device to facilitate collection of taxes and hinder excessive mobility. In Great Russian areas the commune periodically redistributed householders' strips of arable according to changing family needs. These strips were often situated far from the village and intermingled in a chequerboard pattern with those of other users. This led to petty conflicts over boundaries, water resources, and so on. There was too little pasture land for livestock or timber for fuel and building, since forests were largely a state or 'gentry' preserve.

Peasant housing remained squalid; rural roads were impassable for weeks on end; and low hygienic standards made for high mortality. In 1891–2 famine afflicted a vast region in south and south-east European Russia. With the ensuing cholera epidemic, it cost several hundred thousand lives. Foreign competition depressed the price of grain, but those who bought land had to pay dearly for it because demand was so heavy. To rent land was also costly, and those who concluded leases frequently fell into dependence on the lessor, who might well be their former seignior. To these burdens were added payments under the land redemption scheme and heavy indirect taxes on articles of mass consumption such as tobacco. In consequence arrears steadily mounted.

In sum the *muzhik* was poverty stricken and miserable. Unschooled if not illiterate, isolated from 'civilized' society in the towns, he blamed his fate on the greed of the upper classes and so posed a risk to political stability. In 1905–6, and again in 1917–18, these resentments flared up in agrarian unrest – which ultimately brought about the long-sought-after 'black repartition': that is, the expulsion of all 'non-toilers' from the countryside and an egalitarian distribution of all economic resources.

This dreary picture of Russian rural life after Emancipation prevailed until the 1960s, but today is increasingly questioned. It has its roots in the polemics of the time, when liberals and socialists opposed to tsarism were prone to partisanship. Often they based their arguments on misleading statistics (such as average income data). Their views left a deep imprint on later historiography. Today, however, scholars armed with insights drawn from anthropology, comparative rural sociology and development studies are challenging many propositions once regarded as axiomatic. The traditional interpretation has to be modified in many respects. More weight needs to be given to regional variations: whereas the south-central Black-Earth region was indeed overcrowded and depressed, the situation was much better in peripheral areas such as the Baltic, the south-east and (eventually) western Siberia. Crops other than cereals, on which attention was previously concentrated, and livestock-raising require greater attention, for they not only contributed significantly to overall output but also improved the country dweller's diet. This historical revision is not designed to rehabilitate the tsarist government's policies – although they may now indeed appear in a better light – but to show that Russian peasant farmers actively shaped their own destiny. Far from being just passive objects of solicitude on the part of officials or intellectuals, they adapted flexibly to the challenges of the market economy and took decisions that were rational in *their* terms, however perplexing or reprehensible they may have seemed to outsiders.

Notwithstanding these fresh insights, the Emancipation certainly did place a heavy burden on the former serfs. They remained legally tied to their village community, though not as firmly as they had formerly been to their seigniors. Nearly all householders were obliged to accept a land allotment and to redeem it by making (through the *obshchina*) annual payments to the government, which reimbursed gentry proprietors in the form of interest-bearing bonds. The amount was fixed according to the annual rent (*obrok*) paid during the period of 'temporary obligation' that preceded conclusion of an agreement.* These rents were set at a rate higher than the market value of the land. The scheme reflected the informal deal struck between reforming officials and gentry vested interests and took no account of peasants' ability to pay. Unrealistically, they were expected to redeem their land over a forty-nine year period before becoming owners of it. Naturally arrears built up and in 1882 redemption dues had to be reduced; in 1906 the whole scheme was abandoned.

Moreover, the amount of land allotted to householders was on average 4 per cent less than that which they had worked before Emancipation. In some southern provinces (Ukraine, lower Volga) peasants lost as much as a quarter, although in Belarus and Lithuania, where the soil was poor, they gained respectively 18 and 24 per cent more land. The so-called 'cut-offs' (*otrezki*) in favour of gentry proprietors offended peasants' natural sense of justice. As the rural population grew, so did complaints of a 'land shortage', and much was made of this grievance by the government's critics. Actually land endowments were generous by Western European standards: the average allotment of an ex-serf household measured 3.6 hectares; of a state peasant one 6.5–7.3 hectares. What really mattered was the quality of the land and the use to which it was put. It is true that peasants were often left with inferior land scattered in several strips. Yet recent research shows that they were able to improve cultivation methods and to diversify their crops, especially where villages were located near major communications arteries and urban markets.

The reformers saw the *obshchina* as a useful means of upholding order in the countryside. The elected village elder, along with the patriarchal family head, had the right to deny or issue the passports that had to be shown to the police by peasants who left their native

---

* The *obrok* was capitalized at 6 per cent, i.e. the total sum payable was calculated in such a way as to give bond holders 5 per cent annual interest, the other 1 per cent going on costs and amortization. The actual market value of the bonds fluctuated. If the contract was imposed by the proprietor instead of being freely negotiated, he forfeited 20–25 per cent of the sum that was otherwise paid to him directly by his peasants. The half million or so who took the 'beggars' allotments' had no obligations under the redemption scheme. In 1881 over one million householders who had not yet concluded a contract with their former proprietors were compulsorily brought into the scheme.

village to work elsewhere, whether for a season or a longer term. The chief object was to prevent the formation of a rootless proletariat, as in Western European cities, that might be driven to revolt by unemployment and unfamiliar harsh living conditions. This concern was not unreasonable and for a time at least the measure was effective in controlling migration from the countryside. It does not seem to have seriously inhibited industrial growth, as some manufacturers complained, for there was plenty of unskilled labour available: it was *skilled* labour that was short! In any case, the number of passports granted annually grew exponentially, from 1.2 million in 1861–70 to 6.2 million in 1891–1900 (and 8.8 million in 1906–10). This increase was particularly significant in the northern and central provinces, where off-farm earnings were essential to a peasant household's survival. In practice many youngsters left without proper papers and employers turned a blind eye to the fact.

The commune's role in regard to land use has likewise been misunderstood. Its decisions as to when to perform the major operations in the agricultural cycle (sowing, harvesting) were economically rational, given the climatic problems confronting farmers in Russia; broadly speaking, they were acceptable to those concerned – including the women who did so much of the farm work. Even the practice of periodic land repartition, so objectionable to contemporary liberals (and Marxists) on economic grounds, can be defended. Contrary to received opinion, it was rare for the communal authorities to take land from a prosperous, innovative household and allocate it to a poorer one. Due regard was paid to any improvements that had been made, so that what occurred at a repartition was a levelling *up* rather than a levelling down. (In any case, the wealthier peasants usually managed communal affairs and saw to it that their interests were looked after.) Neo-Populist writers (N. P. Oganovsky, A. V. Chayanov), who studied the family farm most closely, deserve credit for illuminating the mechanism of social relationships within the village, which were based on a cyclical demographic movement, and not on income or status differentials reflected in the area of land worked or the number of horses owned, as was generally supposed at the time. Possession of a large area of land might even signify that it was being farmed extensively, and so *less* efficiently, than a smaller area!

The key to the riddle lies in the nature of the patriarchal peasant family. Young couples were under intense social pressure to produce as many male heirs as they could. Daughters were held to be of relatively little account, whereas sons were welcome because they could provide for their parents if they survived to old age. Those families that were genetically advantaged and avoided accidents (illness, conscription, destruction of the farm by fire, and so on) prospered relatively to others. They were entitled to additional land and could build up their livestock herds, so accumulating capital that could be invested productively. But such prosperity was generally short-lived, for once sons grew to maturity they established independent households of their own; the 'extended' family fragmented, losing its predominant position in village life to more dynamic competitors. Poor households comprised those demographically disadvantaged, such as childless couples, widows, the sick, or drop-outs (e.g. alcoholics). Clearly, this basic model needs refinement and one should not overdo its applicability; yet it is closer to reality than others that were more popular at the time.

Successful households managed to improve both output and yields. Although statistical information on these points is rather shaky, it is estimated that in European Russia total agricultural output rose by 1.5 to 1.9 per cent per annum between 1860 and 1913. Part of this increase was, however, due to extension of the sown area. Between the 1860s and 1900s cereal crop yields on peasant allotment land improved by 40 per cent, and on privately owned land by 63 per cent. (About half of this was held by peasants!) When other crops (legumes, potatoes) and livestock are taken into account, the record is still more favourable. Between the late 1860s and 1914 the number of horses rose by 38 per cent (15.5 to 21.4 million) and of cattle by 46 per cent (21.0 to 30.7 million); moreover, the yield of milch cows was rising markedly. (Sheep and pigs were less plentiful than before.) Russian cattle herds were growing more rapidly than German ones and by 1913 the tsarist empire was exporting over a million head annually; commercial production had risen by 80 per cent in twenty years.

Food output kept pace with population growth and nearly everyone had enough to eat, although then, as later, working people's diet was nutritionally unbalanced, with an excess of carbohydrates. The peasant economy no longer stood at subsistence level. Farmers retained a greater share of their cereal crops for their own consumption or as livestock feed – a tendency taken further during the years of war and revolution. The once popular view that the village became impoverished between 1861 and 1905 can no longer be sustained.

Not government policy but market buoyancy was primarily responsible for this. In the 1900s farmers' surplus produce commanded a much better price than it had done in the depressed 1880s. Machinery was coming into use – although mainly on gentry estates – and as the livestock herd expanded more manure was available as fertilizer. More peasants adopted improved systems of crop rotation, and there was greater specialization between regions. This could create problems, too, as the First World War would show: the 'consumer provinces' of the north and centre were too dependent on produce that had to be transported from distant areas.

Gradually peasant farmers displaced their former seigniors as masters of rural Russia. By 1877 gentry proprietors owned only 59 per cent of the land that had been theirs at Emancipation; by 1914 this figure had fallen to 46 per cent. Sales were particularly common after the unrest of 1905–6, when some 12 million hectares passed into peasant hands. Nobles were most successful at farming in New Russia, the south-west (where they constituted a powerful lobby), and the Baltic provinces. As a rule they secured higher yields than peasants did, since they farmed less intensively. Pre-revolutionary rural Russia was not 'an empire of nobles': in 1912–13 peasants in seven northern provinces planted crops on 93 per cent of the sown area, and in eleven southern ones on 82 per cent.

However, one has to distinguish between land bought by peasants, whether individually or by their commune, and land that was rented: respectively about 26 and 40 million hectares in 1905. The former process was assisted, in a rather dilatory manner, by the state-sponsored Peasant Land Bank. This began operations in 1883, but was at first not allowed to hold land on its own account and two decades passed before it made loans on an extensive scale. From 1895 capital was provided by credit cooperatives as well. Even so, the lack of rural credit facilities was one of the main shortcomings of the post-1861 agrarian order. The government was much keener on helping gentry proprietors, who typically were granted a bank of their own in 1885. This deficiency explains why so many peasants had to resort to private moneylenders who charged usurious rates of interest.

In these circumstances leasing land was an obvious alternative, although the cost of this was sometimes inordinate. The most desperate tenants might have to conclude loans to tide them over for a few months until the next harvest. Those unwilling to accept such onerous terms had the option of leaving to work as seasonal labourers on the large estates in New Russia. This might mean a lengthy journey on foot, a degrading wait in a busy 'hiring market' such as the notorious Kakhovka (Tavrida province), and several weeks of back-breaking toil for sixteen hours a day, nights spent on straw beside the cattle – for wages that hardly justified the effort. Yet in 1900 some 2½ million men made the trek to New Russia alone.

Only slightly less uncongenial was the prospect of going off for good to farm new land in Asiatic Russia, where it was more plentiful. At first officialdom obstructed this movement of colonization, but with the construction of the Trans-Siberian railway after 1892 policy was reviewed. The luckier migrants travelled with permits that entitled them to a sizeable plot of land. The less fortunate went on their own, risking hunger or death from disease at some insanitary transit point. On arrival they might have to work as hired hands rather than as independent proprietors. In 1908, when this vast population movement reached its peak, three quarters of a million pioneers crossed the Urals. Many gave up the struggle and returned home (according to official figures, 18 per cent over the years 1896–1915). Even so, this exodus could do no more than temporarily absorb the natural increase of the rural population in the most densely settled regions.

This left the option of migrating to the towns. By the end of the century there were some sixty 'migrant cities', in which only a quarter of those registered as belonging to the peasant 'estate' were locally born.

They ranged in size from Moscow, which grew from 350,000 to over one million between 1856 and 1897, to new industrial settlements like Ivanovo-Voznesensk, which had expanded from a village of one thousand to a city of 54,000, and provincial commercial centres like Saratov, which grew from 61,000 to 137,000.*

The new arrivals had to live in insanitary suburbs and, if they were

* Brower, *Russian City Between Tradition and Modernity*, pp. 77–9.

lucky enough to find work, to accept lowly paid jobs. Only those who had acquired some skill could hope for assured employment. Agents sent out to the countryside by industrial firms chose recruits from particular areas, or even villages, that had supplied labour in the past.

Migrants often belonged to informal associations called *zemlya-chestva*, whose more experienced members helped to 'break in' newcomers to factory routine; often they provided shared accommodation. As a rule the distance which migrants travelled was brief, but those who went to work in far-off St Petersburg had to endure a long journey and grimmer living conditions. Some factory owners, notably in the Moscow region, who took a patriarchal view of their responsibilities erected barrack-like buildings to house their labourers. Depressing as these undoubtedly were, they were an advance on what many migrants had known in the overcrowded *izba* back home, and also superior to lodging-houses, in which workers might rent no more than a 'cot' or 'corner' shared with several others. In St Petersburg in 1900 there were 1.7 persons per room and 7.4 per apartment, and in 1914 60,000 of its inhabitants lived in cellars under abysmal conditions, or in one of the capital's thirty-four doss-houses. A British traveller recorded his impressions there in 1896:

We open the door and a warm unsavoury odour rushes out. It is a chamber perhaps 22 feet in length by 16 in breadth. A narrow passage extends to the opposite wall, between a couple of platforms . . . On and underneath these lie crowds of sleeping men: their low breathing is very audible, while some snorers combine to produce a greater effect . . . The licence of the lodging-house proprietor permits him to accommodate twenty-five people in this room: there are exactly forty-nine . . . For all this they pay five kopecks a night, and some relish the accommodation so much that they have engaged the right to sleep there for two years in advance.*

The point to stress here is that most urban migrants retained a link to their peasant communities, despite the changes that were taking place in their lifestyle and outlook as a result of exposure to urban life. Only gradually, perhaps after several generations, were these ties

* Bater, *St Petersburg*, pp. 327–9, citing J. Simpson, *Sidelights on Siberia*, London, 1898, pp. 145–7.

severed. Officially workers remained peasants in legal status. The *obshchina* kept them on its rolls and ensured that they paid their share of tax on their allotment and did not depart too crassly from the moral norms of the village. Those who transgressed the code might be arrested and returned under guard and punished for their misdemeanours. Even the threat of this sufficed to ensure a measure of conformity.

Aware that their families depended on their earnings, migrants would regularly send money home: in St Petersburg a study (1909) showed that 67 per cent of single workers did so. They would normally return home at least once a year, to obtain a renewal of their passport or to help with the harvest. The latter practice was more usual among artisans and workers in small-scale enterprises than among those in large factories, and still less common among the few who managed to become self-employed. These men looked down on those who went back as rustics; on the other hand, when illness struck or they became too old to go on working, men in every category tended to go back to their relatives and take up farming again. After all, the village did offer a rudimentary form of social security (the state made no provision for workers' insurance until 1912), and economic conditions in the countryside were becoming more attractive.

INDUSTRY

According to the first modern census, taken in 1897, some 80 per cent of the empire's population were employed in agriculture or related pursuits. But the industrial sector of the economy had expanded rapidly. The pace of growth accelerated after the mid 1880s. Under Witte, finance minister from 1892 to 1903, industrialization received energetic backing from the state. This did not, however, avert a crisis in the south Russian region (modern eastern Ukraine) after 1900, or a much more serious setback during the revolution of 1905–6. Thereafter recovery was swift, and the years prior to the First World War were something of a second golden age for Russian industrialists and foreign investors. The view that it represented a 'take-off to self-sustaining growth' (W. Rostow) is now in discredit. Present-day economic historians prefer to stress the basic continuities in Russia's industrial development and are sceptical of the once widely held notion that the key to this progress was state intervention, rather than the ability of business leaders to respond creatively to the opportunities of the expanding international market economy, in which the tsarist empire now played a far from insignificant part.

It would, however, go against the evidence to portray Russian merchants of the era as Western-style capitalists. Indeed, some would argue that 'capitalism' never became a reality (as distinct from a mental concept) and that pre-1917 Russia singularly lacked the 'business ethos' vital to a free-enterprise economy. Just as large modern factories coexisted with archaic crafts, so there were substantial differences between various parts of the empire.

Merchants in Moscow and the surrounding 'Central Industrial region' (as it was rather grandly called) were well known for their conservative outlook and old-fashioned lifestyle. Many came from Old Believer families and had risen up from the lower depths by displaying unusual thrift. Anxious not to jeopardize their status, they kept a low profile politically and took little interest in the wider world. They refrained from energetic lobbying through business associations (which existed from 1867 onwards), did not relish competition – they were hostile to Poles, Jews, and Western Europeans – and clung for decades to outdated business practices. (One man refused to keep any written accounts whatever!)

In defence of this group it should be added that they engaged in charitable activities and patronized the arts (see page 250); moreover, attitudes changed after 1905, when they formed a significant lobby in defence of their economic and political interests. Patriarchal attitudes did not imply softness towards employees. Moscow industrialists stubbornly obstructed the government's rather languid efforts after 1882 to introduce rudimentary legislation to protect the health of the women and children who toiled in their textile mills. Official factory inspectors did yeoman work in the face of such obstruction. In 1885 a major strike broke out in the Morozov family's works at Orekhovo-Zuyevo, an industrial agglomeration in Moscow province. It challenged the complacent assumption in educated society that Russian industrial workers, unlike those in the West, were incapable of organizing to defend their interests. The strikers won concessions over the imposition of fines for sub-standard work and the exorbitant prices charged in company stores; henceforward wages had to be paid regularly, in cash not kind. Even so, some factory owners clung to the view that external agitators had caused the trouble.

Moscow and the centre were not typical of the empire as a whole. Other regions on the periphery showed greater dynamism in exploiting natural resources and were more open to foreign influences – and capital. This was true both of Russian Poland (Łodż) and of the north-west, where the city of Riga became a flourishing port and industrial centre, as did, on a smaller scale, the naval base of Tallinn (then Reval) in modern Estonia. St Petersburg itself had 1¼ million inhabitants by 1897; when the First World War broke out the figure had almost doubled to 2.2 million (cf. Moscow with 1.8 million). The imperial capital remained an important centre of metal-working, textile manufacture, and food-processing. It also developed new branches of industry such as chemicals, rubber and electrical equipment, which owed much to foreign investment. The level of technology here matched that of contemporary Western and Central Europe. Labour productivity was generally higher than in the central region, with its heavy emphasis on textiles. Large enterprises employing hundreds and even thousands of workers prevailed: already by 1901 the Putilov works, which made industrial machinery and railway locomotives, employed over 12,000 men. Also important were shipbuilding, leather-working and brewing – while many tens of thousands of white-collar workers had jobs in banking, insurance, and government administration.

The most notable landmark on the labour scene in St Petersburg was a strike of 30,000 cotton spinners and weavers in 1896–7. They showed an unusual degree of resolution, won public sympathy, and were indirectly rewarded by a law which for the first time fixed the maximum length of the working day for male adults – at eleven and a half hours! To the modern eye this might seem a modest victory, but it has to be set against the frequency of public holidays in Russia: only 270 days in the year were actually worked. Employers in the north-west were scarcely less antagonistic to the interests of their dependants than their competitors in Moscow, but the risk of disturbances by organized labour alarmed officials, especially in the interior ministry, which took a stricter attitude towards such abuses than did Witte's subordinates in the finance ministry. Until 1906 the law forbade any association of workers that strove for higher wages or better conditions. Even when locally based trade unions were permitted in the wake of the 1905 revolution they faced continual harassment.

The great success story for Russian industry in this era occurred in the south, which by 1913 produced 64 per cent of the empire's iron and steel and 70 per cent of its coal: 1.5 milliard tons as against a mere 15.6 million in 1870. In 1869 John Hughes, a Welsh entrepreneur, set up a metallurgical plant at a village that became a major city bearing his name, Yuzovka (later Stalino, now Donetsk). High-quality iron ore was obtained from nearby Krivoy Rog (after 1884 by the newly built 'Catherine Railway') and output zoomed. New coal mines opened along the Donets river. Many entrepreneurs in this region were foreigners, or else Jews, Poles, or other non-Russians of the empire who had been trained as engineers. Capable organizers, they set up an Association of Southern Coal and Steel Producers, a pressure group which battled successfully for high protective tariffs (opposed by industrialists in Russian Poland) and cheaper freight rates on railways to the north, where their potential market largely lay. It was in the southern region, too, that industrialists first combined to manipulate the market for their products by setting informal output quotas and fixing prices higher than was warranted. In 1902 a syndicate, 'Prodameta', was formed which united thirty enterprises producing 88 per cent of the region's iron. Other such ventures followed, but in central Russia the textile industry resisted the trend. Cartels were unpopular with the general public, especially since they owed a lot to the influence exercised by foreign (mainly French) bankers and managers. High prices also resulted from the very considerable degree of vertical integration in Russian heavy industry, i.e. the concentration of power in the hands of corporations that controlled the market for raw materials and semi-finished goods, a process taken further during the First World War. The government contributed to this development, since it was eager to reduce dependence on foreign energy supplies, but made sure that it had the last word over industries with a defence application.

Most workers in the South Russian industrial region were immigrants from the north rather than Ukrainians from close by. Labour turnover was very high. 'The very idea of entering the mine or factory, dark and enclosed, was foreign and repugnant to the peasant. He had to be coaxed, wheedled or even tricked into entering the mine, and then into signing on for a winter season.'* Working conditions were initially as bad as anywhere else but later improved, especially in foreign-owned plants. The small Donets valley mines were the scene of frequent accidents and flooding. After 1884, and especially 1904, the employers' association did at least provide modest compensation to the injured or to the families of those killed, although many such claims were rejected. These enterprises were also ahead in technological innovation, introducing large-capacity blast furnaces and steel-rolling mills. More pig iron was produced per ton of ore in south Russia than in Germany, despite continued reliance on steam power rather than electricity.

Change here contrasted starkly with relative technological stagnation in the Urals region. In the north Caucasus (Grozny) and beyond, at Baku in modern Azerbaijan, oil extraction became a major enterprise towards the end of the century, the firm of Nobel playing a notable role, but thereafter Russia's share of total world output declined as new oilfields were opened up in the Near East and elsewhere. The Baku oil workers, who numbered 30,000 by 1900, were very mixed ethnically and their working environment appalling: the atmosphere was badly polluted by emissions of noxious gases and the ground awash with spilled oil.

It has been calculated that on average gross factory output grew by 5 to 5.5 per cent per annum over the thirty years from 1883 to 1913 (4.5 to 5 per cent if craft industry is included). A rough estimate for the annual increase of productivity per worker is 1.8 per cent; between 1900 and 1913 it grew by some 45 per cent. These figures look less impressive when one takes account of the immensity of Russia's empire. Growth per capita has been put at 0.75 per cent in 1860–85 and 1.25 per cent in 1885–1913. This was about half that of Sweden and only two fifths that of Japan. By 1914 the Russian industrial economy could take pride in its achievements over the past half-century, but it was still in a delicate state when disaster struck.

* Friedgut, *Iuzovka and Revolution*, i, p. 209.

COMMUNICATIONS AND FINANCE

The basic reason for this lay of course in the empire's natural handicaps of size and remoteness from the principal areas of global economic development. These handicaps could be overcome only by improving communications and encouraging foreign investment. The former was expensive, the latter threatened to erode Russia's economic sovereignty – or so at least nationalist critics alleged. To some extent industrial progress could be furthered by state action in such areas as tariff policy or subsidies for those sectors deemed to be of strategic importance (in the economic sense or literally so); less directly, the government helped by maintaining the value of the rouble and improving the infrastructure (education, public health, and so on). Only some of these activities can be considered here.

To contemporaries the railway was a veritable symbol of modernity. Psychologically, socially, and above all economically rail transport could revolutionize a backward district's way of life: it was, as Witte once said, 'a leaven which stimulates cultural ferment among the population'. Farmers could sell their crops at a more stable price and meet the needs of consumers living far afield. Untapped minerals could be exploited and the labour market more readily satisfied. The new means of transport performed a 'pump-priming' function, creating demand for rails, rolling stock, and locomotives; these nascent industries called forth others to supply them.

Moscow became the nodal point of lines reaching south to the steppe and Black Sea ports, east to the Volga and Urals, and west to Warsaw and the Baltic. Other lines linked St Petersburg to Archangel on the White Sea and, in 1916, even Murmansk. The last-named link, designed to speed the flow of Allied war supplies, was one of several that had military implications. This motive was uppermost in construction of the line from Krasnovodsk, on the eastern shore of the Caspian, to Samarkand and the Afghan border (1880–96) and another from Orenburg, in the southern Urals, to Tashkent somewhat later. Last but not least, it to some extent inspired the builders of the great Trans-Siberian railway, launched in 1892 and completed twelve years later (but for a stretch around the southern tip of Lake Baikal), just in time to convey troops to the Manchurian front in the Russo-Japanese war. Shortly before the First World War broke out the government, at French prompting, was actively developing a network of strategic lines in the western border region.

Total track length, a bare 1,000 miles in 1860, exceeded 33,000 miles by 1900 and 45,000 by 1917. In this expansion economic considerations were paramount, and the prospect of quick profits was a magnet for Russian and foreign entrepreneurs (John Hughes included). In the late 1890s railways accounted for one quarter of total net investment, or about 30 per cent if transport equipment is included; in 1899 they absorbed 64 per cent of the empire's iron and steel output. This was the second major construction boom. The first, twenty years or so earlier, had been disfigured by a great deal of speculation. Promoters did well out of government-guaranteed interest rates and were sometimes able to buy state-owned lines on highly favourable terms; when the state switched its policy, the least profitable lines were the first to be bought back by the government, so that again vested interests profited. By 1914 over two thirds of track were publicly owned and the government also had a sizeable stake in the private sector. Some 244 million passengers took the train (the equivalent of only one and a half journeys per inhabitant!); far more important were freight movements, first grain and then coal, timber, and oil. Goods carried over long distances benefited from a differential tariff introduced in the 1890s. A fair proportion continued to be carried by waterways. Roads, by contrast, suffered from neglect; for the automobile was making only a hesitant entry into the Russian lands, although the first Beijing to Paris road race in 1907 (won by an Italian, S. Borghese) showed the possibilities of this form of transport, and during the First World War Russia built not only vehicles for military purposes but even a few thousand aircraft.

Initially, when domestic industry was still very weak, the government adhered to a free-trade policy, reflected in the liberal tariffs of 1857 and 1868. Protectionists argued that higher rates of duty were required in order to safeguard producers from the competition of more advanced countries and that consumers would benefit ultimately from cheaper goods made at home, even if for the present they had to pay more. The government, hard pressed for revenue and anxious to increase customs receipts, responded to this pressure and ultimately accepted the reasoning behind it. From 1877 customs duty had to be paid in gold; thereafter there were several increases which culminated in a new general tariff (June 1891). Tension developed with Russia's chief trading partner, Germany, and thereafter St Petersburg adopted a differential system, based on country of origin, from which Germany was the principal gainer: in 1913 she provided 53 per cent of Russian imports and absorbed 32 per cent of her exports. Had economic self-interest dictated foreign policy, there would have been no reason for war between the two empires; as it was, nationalist passions held sway. Considerable amounts of German capital were invested in the electrical industry and banking, but its volume was surpassed by that of French (or Franco-Belgian) origin, while smaller shares were of British or American provenance.

Traditionalists (and radicals, too) feared this influx and complained at the mounting foreign debt, which by 1914 had reached some 8 milliard roubles; already at the turn of the century servicing it accounted for about one fifth of budgetary expenditure. Official attitudes varied. The ministries of interior and agriculture sided with the 'patriots', whereas Witte's finance ministry took the view that the risks were well worth while. It was partly in order to project an image abroad of Russia's financial stability that the gold standard was adopted in 1897.* Characteristically, it was opposed by both right- and left-wing opinion – both anti-capitalist – and had to be forced through on the tsar's personal authority. The measure proved a success, in that foreign capital flowed in plentifully, much of it from small French investors. If in 1860 foreign investment in the Russian economy had not exceeded 10 million roubles, and twenty years later 100 million, by 1900 the figure was between 700 and 900 million, and by 1914 some 1,750 million roubles. Over half of it was in mining and metallurgy, the rest in textiles, municipal utilities and banking. Taking into account the contribution which foreign-owned (or -managed) firms made to technological progress, and the relatively modest rate of profit which investors from abroad received on their securities, given the high risks they took,

---

* This involved an exchange of paper 'credit' roubles for gold ones at two thirds the former's face value. This was possible because previous administrations had accumulated a reserve of precious metal, so stabilizing and building up the value of paper money, and had rescheduled Russia's foreign debt on advantageous terms.

it seems that the pessimists were wrong in seeing foreign capital as a threat.

The Russian government did not automatically follow the dictates of its creditors, nor did it become over-reliant on any one source of credit ... French attempts to influence the tsarist government either came to nothing ... or simply coincided with [Russia's] wishes ... Foreign investors were at least as dependent on Russia as Russia was on foreign credit.*

To be sure, the influx of foreign money was not in itself a panacea for achieving rapid, balanced development. But all in all the so-called 'Witte system' made good sense, for the alternatives to it were either stagnation or else an advance at breakneck speed sustained solely by domestic savings and imposed by force, as would be accepted by Stalin after 1928.

An essential ingredient in achieving economic growth was a modern banking system. At first the State Bank had the credit field virtually to itself, but by 1900 there were over forty commercial banks with 150 million roubles 'on call' in their customers' accounts; by 1914 their value had risen to 800 million roubles. The six largest banks had a capital worth half that amount – an indicator of the degree to which financial power was concentrated in a handful of institutions. In 1890 post-office and other savings banks held 139 million roubles, invested by some 800,000 account holders; by 1913 the figures were 1.7 milliard roubles and 8.9 million depositors. This was testimony to rising prosperity, which was not confined to the propertied classes: later generations would recall with nostalgia an epoch when even a simple *muzhik* might think nothing of having a gold coin in his pocket.

Contemporaries accused the government of squeezing the peasants with heavy taxes. In the 1880s the burden was indeed shifted from direct to indirect taxation, which cost less to administer and could be levied on a wide array of consumer goods. Recent research has, however, questioned the extent of this burden. Was the growth of arrears perhaps a consequence of villagers' *unwillingness*, rather than inability, to pay, given their increased expenditure, on vodka in particular? It now appears that most goods subject to tax were bought by townspeople,

* Gatrell, *The Tsarist Economy*, p. 227.

and that, taking into account property taxes and the like, urban residents provided 68 per cent of total tax receipts (1901). But this question is still controversial, and there is no doubt that the government monopoly on alcoholic spirits, introduced in the 1890s and maintained despite much criticism because of its contribution to the treasury (28 per cent of revenue in 1913!), contributed to the scourge of drunkenness that afflicted people in town and country alike.

SOCIAL DIVISIONS AND FAMILY MATTERS

The empire's population rose at a hitherto unparalleled rate, from an average of 74 million in 1860/64 to 164 million in 1909/13. In the latter quinquennium the annual increase was of the order of 1.6 per cent, higher than anywhere else in Europe.* This was owing to the stability of the birth-rate (on average 50 per 1,000) and, from the mid 1880s, a fall in the average death-rate, from 37 per 1,000 in Alexander II's reign to 27 per 1,000 on the eve of the First World War. This drop probably owed more to improved nutrition than to better medical care. Russian peasant women were no more fertile than those in, say, Ireland, but they had what demographers call a 'non-European marriage pattern', i.e. they nearly all married, at a tender age, and had on average as many as nine children, half of whom died young (one quarter in the first year of life). The main reason for early marriage, as noted above, was cultural, in the form of strong community pressure to uphold the traditional lifestyle. Young people accepted it, at least until they came into closer contact with the urban world. Migrants to the towns, who rose up the social ladder and could afford to bring their families (or to marry townswomen), generally had fewer children. This was also the pattern in the more 'Europeanized' regions of the empire such as the Baltic provinces.

Officially, Russian society was still divided into estates (*sosloviya*). These no longer corresponded to social realities, but it is now thought

---

* These figures exclude Finland, Khiva, and Bukhara. Allowance should be made for those who emigrated: an estimated 1.25 million from 1860 to 1889 and 3.35 million between 1890 and 1915. About two fifths of the latter were Jews and one third Poles fleeing from discrimination and poverty.

(G. Freeze) that they were less of a barrier to mobility than earlier historians supposed. The 'caste system' was actually quite flexible.

At the top of the ladder were Russia's aristocratic magnates, who retained their importance throughout the period, and the gentry (*dvory-ane*). The former were better able than the latter to withstand the challenge of Emancipation, because of their greater wealth and superior educational levels. In 1900 seventy-nine aristocratic families each owned over 50,000 dessyatines of land (approximately 46,000 hectares); a good many of them had been among the largest serf-owners forty years earlier, although there was also some 'new blood'. They concentrated on livestock-raising and forestry, rather than arable farming, and possessed large tracts of rich timber land in the Urals. More important, however, as sources of aristocratic wealth were urban property and securities. At the turn of the century one of Russia's richest magnates, Count Platon Zubov, owned estates worth 2.7 million roubles, property in St Petersburg valued at 1.3 million, and 2 million roubles in stocks and bonds. He had a house on Nevsky Prospekt worth nearly half a million roubles which he leased profitably; 'his net return on capital of 12.5 per cent far exceed[ed] the rate a rural landowner could expect from his land'.* Income on this scale was beyond the dreams of even the highest salary-earners – a leading banker was paid 120,000 roubles a year – and all but a handful of industrialists.

The provincial gentry found it hard to become rural entrepreneurs; many who gave up farming altogether turned to the professions, admin-istration, or (reverting to type!) service in the armed forces. Those who lived off the income from land leased to peasant cultivators were hard hit by the agricultural depression of the 1880s and rising labour costs; regarded as parasites by many of their tenants, they were under pressure to sell out or face the prospect of violent unrest. This classic dilemma forms the backdrop to Anton Chekhov's *The Cherry Orchard* (1903), staged on the eve of the great agrarian revolts of 1905–6. But the peasant insurgents also dealt severely with those privileged proprietors, mainly in the Black Earth provinces, who adopted a modest lifestyle

---

* Lieven, *Aristocracy in Europe*, pp. 51, 115. The Bobrinsky family's possessions were valued at 17.5 million roubles (1897), of which 9.3 million was in land, 3.1 million in their famous sugar enterprises, and most of the rest in securities.

and tried to cultivate their holdings more intensively, increasing their demesnes at the cost of rented land (or renting it to merchants instead). During the agrarian revolts

the peasants . . . took special pains to destroy all indications of the proprietor's recent entrepreneurship – his prize-winning vineyards, his pure-bred dairy cattle, and his new mechanized agricultural equipment . . . Agricultural processing plants, from gigantic sugar refineries to . . . small flour mills and butter and cheese factories, appeared a special target of the peasants' destructive wrath . . .*

After 1907 the gentry took their revenge, so to speak, by developing new forms of organization which made them a force to be reckoned with in the empire's political life. Their representatives came to dominate the national legislature, as they did the provincial zemstvos, and lobbied against the government's modest efforts at reform – ultimately, so to speak, cutting off the branch on which they sat.

The better-off commercial groups have been discussed above. Their social inferiors, officially categorized as 'lower middle-class' (*mesh-chane*), consisted of office staff and shopworkers (including the self-employed) and artisans. The first two categories have yet to be thoroughly studied, but it is clear that their numbers increased significantly as commerce expanded, requiring the services of thousands of clerks, typists, messengers, and so on. In 1905 they took the lead in forming trade unions to struggle for higher wages, the eight-hour day, and improved working conditions. In provincial towns shops catered primarily for the better-off, since working people preferred to patronize street markets and bazaars.

A great variety of goods were produced by craft (*kustar*) industry, both in towns and villages. Artisanal work and petty trade were, as we know, an important income source for peasants in the non-Black Earth zone, particularly in the winter months. Crafts were fostered by liberal and Populist activists on the zemstvos as an allegedly more 'authentic' alternative to factory production, with its alien capitalistic overtones. Although many traditional handicrafts did indeed succumb to competition from technologically more up-to-date and cost-effective producers, as these critics noted with alarm, it is an exaggeration to see

* Manning, *Crisis of the Old Order*, p. 163.

the two types of industry as engaged in cut-throat rivalry. In the early twentieth century several branches of *kustar'* industry revived because they could work up factory-made semi-finished goods. Such craftsmen played a useful role in promoting retail trade.

Most urban *meshchane* were desperately poor. In Moscow nine out of ten could not afford to take part in electing the elders of their guild. In Nizhniy Novgorod artisans paid only 20 kopecks in municipal tax (1890), whereas the wealthiest merchants paid 1,700 roubles. Not surprisingly, the latter looked down contemptuously on the former. The situation of artisans and traders was particularly acute in the overcrowded towns and hamlets of those western provinces where the overwhelming majority of Jews were required to live. In this so-called 'Pale of settlement', craft occupations such as tailoring and cobbling were practically the sole means of subsistence for thousands of people, and competition was intense.

Russian society, as the foregoing remarks suggest, was badly fragmented, both vertically (among people of various nationalities) and horizontally. Its eventual collapse in revolution has naturally led historians to focus on the division between the *tsenzovye*, as the privileged groups were referred to (i.e. officials, nobles, merchants, and higher clergy) and the 'masses'. It is important not to assume that these tensions, which exploded in violence in 1905–6 and 1917–18, were a permanent or unchanging factor; nevertheless there was certainly an undercurrent of class antagonism even in relatively peaceful times. Among working people (peasants *and workers*: the distinction between these two groups, on which Marxists in particular insisted, was more apparent than real) violence was a fact of life, which normally found a relatively harmless outlet, for instance in ritualized fist fights, 'hooliganism', or gang warfare. Such lawlessness became a major problem in the years before 1914.

Then, as earlier, it might become politicized and take the form of anti-Jewish pogroms and assaults on members of the educated classes (even socialists who were dedicated to improving the people's condition). Radical activists did their best to direct mass violence into more acceptable channels by raising people's 'consciousness'. This meant engaging in educational and cultural endeavours, often on the margin of the law, as well as making revolutionary propaganda. A distinction was drawn between the latter and 'agitation', that is, mobilizing working people to take strike action or to demonstrate against their employers and the government (see page 217).

These activities required a sensitive understanding of popular psychology that was not easy to acquire, so great was the gulf between intellectuals and the 'masses'. Another obstacle was the abstract, ideological character of much socialist doctrine. Revolutionaries were prone, for instance, to underestimate the force of residual monarchist sentiment in popular quarters, especially among villagers: until 1905 at least, and perhaps beyond, the tsar was widely respected, if not as sacrosanct at least as a moral 'authority figure' who had the power to mediate between the 'just' and the 'unjust'. This sentiment, like the desire for a redistribution of property on egalitarian lines, was probably more marked among Great Russians than minority groups (Poles, for example, had no time for the Russian autocracy), and was kept alive by the retention, until Stolypin's reforms of 1906–10, of the repartitional commune.

The lack of any marked social divide between artisans, workers, and peasants should not blind us to the existence of subtle nuances in their lifestyle and outlook. Also important are distinctions of age and gender. Younger males tended to have more 'advanced' views than their elders or womenfolk. Among factory workers there were similar variations between those in metalworking, who inclined towards radicalism, and printers or railway employees, who were more interested in defending their professional interests by legal means. Here, too, regional differences might prove as important as occupational ones; another factor was the size of the enterprise concerned and its ownership (private or state, Russian or foreign). Peasants were more likely to become politically active in regions where population density was highest (south-central Russia, northern Ukraine, middle Volga) and less so in the forested zones of the north or Siberia – although violence could prove infectious and spread rapidly. Those peasants exposed to urban life (or the army) were often a medium through which 'modern' secular (and subversive) ideas percolated back into the village. In 1905 those who worked as hired hands on latifundia in the south took up strike action, a method of struggle associated with urban workers. This distinguished them from peasant rioters who ransacked landlords' estates and confiscated their property in a manner somewhat reminiscent of that employed by Pugachev's bands in the eighteenth century.

The 1897 census showed that literacy had made much greater headway in the urban (or industrial) milieu, as one would expect. Of male metalworkers 66.8 per cent could read and write; for miners the corresponding figure was 33.5 per cent. Among textile workers, who were predominantly female, the rate was 53.9 per cent for men but only 12.2 per cent for women. Country-dwellers, by contrast, lagged badly: taking the empire as a whole, only one citizen in five was literate (29.3 per cent of men, 13.1 per cent of women). Thereafter progress was rapid, and by 1914 the proportion of those who could read and write had risen to 44 per cent. Between 1900 and 1916 the number of pupils in elementary schools doubled, from 4 to 8 million, and by the latter date they encompassed over half the children aged eight to eleven. Moreover, in Moscow province in 1911 30 per cent of elementary school pupils were girls.

An education act passed by the Duma in 1911 (but rejected by the upper house) aimed to make primary schooling universal (and compulsory) within fourteen years. To judge by the increased appropriations belatedly made by the central and local authorities, this goal might have been feasible had not war and revolution supervened. True, peasants were at first ambivalent about the value of education, partly because they did not want their children to be taken from farm work, and partly because rural teachers were seen as 'outsiders' who cost the village money. But by the 1900s this attitude was changing. Younger men in particular sought to acquire the rudiments of knowledge and turned for aid to local intellectuals, most of whom professed radical or democratic sentiments. (Women teachers, who comprised 83 per cent of those at elementary level by 1914, were treated with greater reserve.)

In peasant eyes the rural intelligentsia acquired a new utility and the status of teachers and others in the local community improved as a result . . . In Pokrov district . . . the teacher A. M. Sobolev . . . argued that rural police were unnecessary and . . . [called] for election of officials trusted by the population. As a result, the peasants decided not to fill the police post.*

Free education for every child was one of the demands frequently put forward by peasants during the unrest of 1905–6, along with

* Seregny, in Wade and Seregny (eds.), *Politics in Provincial Russia*, pp. 347, 370.

redistribution of the land and reduced taxation. Rural intellectuals had an inflated idea of their role as 'enlighteners' and political leaders, and nervous government officials, too, were prone to overestimate their importance. Recent research shows that peasants responded creatively to the outsiders' teaching, taking from it what suited them and displaying skill in manoeuvring among the different groups of strangers (intellectuals, officials) with whom they came into contact.

Likewise, they adapted the traditional peasant family to changing conditions. As late as 1887–96 a study in Voronezh province showed that 42 per cent of households comprised two generations and 46 per cent three or more. But gradually the authority of its patriarchal head was being hollowed out and the household's joint property divided up. Often it was young married women members who took the initiative in this, perhaps because they wanted to escape subordination to their mothers-in-law, who under the old dispensation wielded extensive power over other females in the household. It must be stressed that the traditional family, although oppressive, allotted women a well-defined economic and social role. They were responsible for certain tasks, such as looking after poultry, spinning cloth, and keeping everyone fed, and accordingly were seen by their menfolk as a valuable asset. They had an independent source of income, which included whatever was earned during the autumn and winter months. Their children's upbringing, marital arrangements, and so on were also seen as 'women's matters'. In practice women could and did take action to mitigate their lot, even if they stayed on in the village. These positive characteristics of the traditional family offset its better-known negative features, such as the violent beatings frequently meted out to wives by their husbands. In serious cases these wrongs could be brought to the notice of the communal authorities and the courts, which could punish the malefactor or bring back errant husbands who deserted their wives. Nevertheless one can appreciate that young country girls were ambivalent at the prospect of marriage. On the one hand they feared subjection to their spouse and a set of potentially hostile in-laws; on the other hand marriage alone conferred respect and status within the community.

All in all it is not surprising that so many women sought to escape these burdens by joining in the trek to the textile mills (or to domestic service). For in the towns, despite all the hardship associated with factory work, they enjoyed a greater measure of independence. If they married another urban resident they were likely to have fewer children and their family responsibilities would be more manageable. Alternatively, where the husband went to work off the farm and left his wife behind, she played a greater role in the community than had hitherto been customary, and this to some extent compensated for the heavier workload she now had to bear. In Kostroma province, an area of heavy outmigration, women often assumed their husbands' places at the village assembly and were even chosen as elders.

Already by 1885 22 per cent of all workers in industrial enterprises subject to the factory inspectorate, i.e. with over fifty employees, were women; by 1909 the figure had risen to 31 per cent. In St Petersburg in 1913 women comprised 42 per cent of those employed in the chemical branch, 47 per cent of those producing foodstuffs and tobacco, and 68 per cent of textile workers. There was a tendency, even before the First World War, for industrial jobs to be increasingly taken by women. Their labour was less well remunerated than that of male workers – a state of affairs that men generally considered acceptable, even if they held radical views; the notion of 'equal pay for equal work' seemed to them novel and threatening. Indeed, trade-union activists, fearing female competition for jobs, often insisted that gender differentials be maintained and tried to exclude married women from the workplace altogether. Characteristically, in 1907 workers at Ivanovo-Voznesensk put forward a demand that their women comrades should get a half-day off each week to do the family washing! This was evidence, if such were needed, of Russian society's continuing lag behind the West. There was indeed a feminist movement in the tsarist empire, but it was a mild, middle-class affair.

Contrary to a view once widely held, by the eve of the First World War Russian society had come a long way from the days of serfdom, although it had yet to become 'modern' in the sense that this term is used in sociological discourse today. For the vast majority of the population, both in town and country, life had improved in many respects, but people's security remained precarious. Recent improvements could be swiftly nullified by some natural catastrophe, such as a row of bad harvests or a downward turn in the business cycle. Still more disastrous, of course, would be a man-made one, such as a major war, and in 1914 it was precisely that fate which struck the tsarist empire. Within three years it would be toppled by a revolution that promised much but, alas, brought a succession of new social cataclysms. The old society, with all its faults and hopes, disappeared for good.

CHAPTER 12

Towards the First Russian Revolution

'COUNTER-REFORM'

The shock of his father's assassination confirmed Alexander III (1881–94), who succeeded him, in the conviction that the liberal reforms of the preceding reign had been wrong-headed. The new tsar set out to strengthen authority at all levels of government, to eliminate subversive thinking among his subjects, and to bolster the interests of Orthodox ethnic Russians *vis-à-vis* minority peoples.

This entailed the dismissal of survivors from the previous administration, such as Count Loris-Melikov, who had toyed with the idea of constitutional concessions, and the progressive war minister, Dmitriy Milyutin. One year later they were followed into limbo by Alexander's own initial choice as interior minister, the former Pan-Slav activist N. P. Ignatyev, who had rather naïvely dreamed of bringing the autocracy closer to the people through a consultative assembly on the lines of the *Zemsky sobor*. Conservative functionaries and backstairs advisers who shared the tsar's political credo replaced them, but Alexander neither could nor would carry out a whole purge of the bureaucracy. He was not cast in a dictatorial mould but tried to work through the existing legal and institutional framework. In effect he was its prisoner, for over the previous quarter-century the nature of Russian officialdom had evolved. There were now far more people in authority who had received a decent education, and in particular some legal training. They were not necessarily liberals in the conventional sense, but men who based their conduct on Western models. They could use their influence to frustrate efforts to revert to the crude, arbitrary style of government of Nicholas I's era. In consequence the drive behind the so-called 'counter-reforms' of the 1880s was blunted.

The new tsar's bark was worse than his bite. Alexander certainly looked every inch an autocrat: tall and well built, he could reputedly bend a horseshoe with his bare hands. But his impressive exterior concealed a lack of self-confidence and a second-rate intellect. He found it hard to follow an intricate argument in debate and would delay taking difficult decisions by withdrawing to the solace of his family. Happily married to a Danish princess, he could not like his father be reproached for unconventional behaviour in private. Much the same was true of his son, Nicholas II (1894–1917), who adored his father and tried to model his conduct on his, but lacked his purposefulness. In different ways each of Russia's last emperors, while upholding the principle of untrammelled autocracy, lacked the personal qualities needed to make the monarchical system work, still less to adapt it to modern realities.

Contemporary critics of the tsarist regime made much of the sinister power allegedly wielded behind the scenes by Konstantin Pobedonostsev. Tutor and (intermittently) close adviser to both the last tsars, and simultaneously lay head (chief procurator) of the Holy Synod, this sour-minded moralist had few practical policy recommendations to offer. He restricted himself to intrigue against officials whom he suspected of partiality for individualism, constitutional government, freedom of the press, and so on – ideas which he eloquently castigated. Much more important than Pobedonostsev was Alexander III's intimate friend Prince V. P. Meshchersky, whose rabidly chauvinistic newspaper *The Citizen* the tsar secretly subsidized.

In 1885 Meshchersky began to send the tsar his weekly diary in addition to regular letters, and from this date his influence on Alexander grew to major proportions ... Letters and diary alike mix advice on state policy and personnel with the basest kind of flattery, juicy tidbits of gossip from the St Petersburg rumour mills, and protestations of the writer's abject prostration before the figure of his lord and master.*

Official rhetoric stressed the need for order and obedience to the law, yet the imperial administration was cumbersome, corrupt, and archaic. Much arbitrary power was exercised by gendarmes and other police officials. They ignored legal norms and took their cue from their superiors in the interior ministry, who in turn kept one ear cocked to each change of mood in the 'higher spheres'. Policy at the highest levels of government was devised in a manner that made for confusion.

* Whelan, *Alexander III and the State Council*, p. 75.

There was no central coordinating body, such as a Cabinet, since this would have infringed the autocratic prerogative. Neither was there a prime minister, for the same reason, although Witte's role as *de facto* economic overlord in the 1890s (prior to his sudden dismissal in 1903) gave him a commanding position which his colleagues bitterly resented. In those years inter-ministerial intrigue reached its peak in the barely concealed conflict between finance and interior, for the two agencies pursued different strategies on key issues. Under the pre-1905 system of administration each minister reported individually to the tsar, who in principle had the last word. He could issue 'nominal decrees' (*imennye ukazy*) which immediately had the force of law, but such interventions from on high were relatively rare. Routine legislation was drafted in the various ministries (or other executive bodies) and then submitted directly to the tsar. The more important decisions were taken after discussion in the State Council, which in the 1880s had some fifty to sixty members, most of them elderly dignitaries.* When there was disagreement, the council submitted majority and minority resolutions. On nineteen occasions out of fifty-seven Alexander III backed the stand of the minority group, i.e. the traditionalists; several times he amended *both* opinions submitted to him. Neither of his two predecessors had interfered so frequently, yet this increased activism did not mean that the autocrat was stronger than before – rather the reverse! On the other hand, it seems that state councillors who dissented from the imperial will did so largely for careerist or bureaucratic reasons, rather than on grounds of principle. They certainly did not seek to turn the council into an instrument of opposition. This was because even 'reformist' officials were not constitutionalists, still less democrats, but stood for a *law-based absolutism* that would take the lead in improving popular well-being. To outsiders this concept might seem to be a contradiction in terms, but it had broad appeal within Russia's educated élite (and indeed is still popular today). Even true liberals outside the bureaucracy took a paternalistic approach. They assumed that they knew what was

---

* The Committee of Ministers, which sought to reconcile differences over current legislation and other administrative problems, carried little weight. The Ruling Senate remained the empire's supreme judicial body; its First department had the function of publishing and interpreting laws, which was important.

best for the common people, whom they saw as potentially dangerous, and therefore in need of control, or 'tutelage', from above.

These assumptions shaped the course of the 'great debate' of Alexander III's reign, which focused on the question of local government. As in the discussions on emancipating the serfs a generation earlier, educated society was ranged between partisans of 'reactionary' and 'progressive' standpoints. But recent studies have shown that it is misleading to divide public opinion into two camps and to view the contest as one between good and evil. First, all the protagonists stood for some degree of supervision by the centre. Secondly, the institutions of rural self-government really *were* working badly. Peasants in positions of authority at village or rural district (*volost'*) level often lacked sufficient education and experience to fulfil their duties responsibly. Where judicial decisions were based on unwritten local custom, they could not but be arbitrary, even if they were acceptable to the parties concerned. Nor were the socially more inclusive zemstvos, despite the benevolent intentions of many deputies, gentry as well as peasants, always immune to corruption and mismanagement: overheads were high and the services rendered far beneath popular expectations. This was chiefly because their financial resources were so exiguous. Peasants were too poor to support them adequately.

In the long run the solution lay in bridging the social divide, improving education, and developing a sense of civic solidarity – in short, in democratizing Russian society. But this commended itself only to a radical fringe of educated opinion. The right-wingers now in the ascendant clamoured instead for the zemstvos to be integrated into the bureaucracy and for the electoral system to be reformed so that gentry representatives should play a leading role. They also wanted organs of peasant self-government to be supervised by a new body of officials, the 'land captains' (*zemskie nachal'niki*), drawn exclusively from local landowners but paid by the state. They would combine administrative and judicial powers and so could punish, by fines and gaol terms, recalcitrant peasant elders who abetted villagers in defaulting on tax payments. Conservatives saw such deviant behaviour as evidence of malicious intent, not of an inability to pay.

The 1880s witnessed a hard-fought struggle within the bureaucracy, and ultimately in the State Council, over the shape of this 'counter-reform', in which departmental interests played a part as well as ideology. The upshot was a law of July 1889 establishing the land captains. However, service in this function proved unpopular among landowners; the calibre of those appointed was low – many remained idle or became dependent on the village scribes they were supposed to control; and their activities were not properly supervised.

Uniform, efficient administration of the village was no closer to reality in the late 1890s than in the previous three decades . . . [The land captains] were perceived by peasants and non-peasants alike as one more step in the bureaucratization of the countryside . . . These efforts did little to arrest the massive growth of redemption and tax arrears . . . Land captains had little success in raising the peasants' social consciousness by organizing village welfare and charitable organizations. On the contrary, [those] who sought to regiment village life ran the risk of engendering anti-government feelings.*

In many ways the situation anticipated that which followed Stalin's collectivization of agriculture in the 1930s, when the degree of bureaucratic coercion was infinitely greater (see page 383).

Equally fruitless was the manipulation of the electoral system in the zemstvos (1890) and municipalities (1892) to favour the upper classes. The rural squires, as we know, were a declining force and in no position to spearhead a reactionary offensive in the countryside. Indirectly, the former measure fostered a mood of opposition which then assumed organizational shape. Zemstvo leaders and other public activists were foremost in trying to feed the starving rural masses during the famine of 1891, which was widely blamed on the insensitive, pro-business policies of the government. The 'third element' of zemstvo employees – doctors, teachers, statisticians – endeavoured to set up nation-wide professional associations that had a covert political agenda, as did the many committees to promote adult literacy.

When Nicholas II succeeded to the throne in 1894 some moderate zemstvo deputies submitted loyal addresses in which they hinted at the need for constitutional change. The nervous young tsar interpreted these mild suggestions as a threat to his power and tactlessly dismissed such aspirations as 'senseless dreams': 'let all know', he went on, 'that I . . . shall safeguard the principles of autocracy as firmly and unswervingly as did my late, unforgettable father.' This provocation

* Pearson, *Russian Officialdom in Crisis*, pp. 207–8.

brought a response from zemstvo deputies. Following the example of the professionals, they petitioned for the right to meet on a national scale in order to discuss matters of common concern. Such a gathering was indeed held legally in provincial Nizhniy Novgorod (1896). It marked the rebirth of Russian liberalism as a political movement.

The conservative drive to reshape local government had its corollary in measures to undermine the independence of the courts. The relatively fair-minded rural justices of the peace disappeared and judges were made subject to disciplinary boards. Only two of them were actually dismissed for alleged misdemeanours in Alexander III's reign, but all had to withstand considerable political pressure. Trial by jury was depicted as 'un-Russian' and emergency powers frequently invoked to ensure that cases were dealt with in camera or by special tribunals.

Likewise universities came under attack for spreading subversive ideas. Under a new charter (1884) teaching staff were to be appointed by the education ministry instead of being elected by their colleagues as before. Official inspectors maintained order among the student body, which lacked corporate rights. These measures were unpopular at all levels of the academic community. In 1899 disturbances at St Petersburg University were put down by Cossacks wielding whips and regulations issued whereby rebellious students could be sent to army disciplinary battalions. Next year they were enforced, whereupon public demonstrations took place in the two capital cities – the first of any consequence in the empire's history.

The intelligentsia objected with equal force to the government's tightening of censorship under new 'provisional' rules adopted in 1882 (they remained in force for over twenty years). Press organs were suspended or closed down, their editors debarred from taking other jobs in journalism. In Nicholas II's early years pressure was slightly relaxed, which led to an effervescence that could not easily be controlled by traditional methods.

Officials took the view (erroneously, as one might think) that subversive notions stemmed from the easier access to educational facilities now enjoyed by members of the lower classes. A general ban on their admission to school was suggested, but the tsar thought it too dangerous. Instead the education minister, Delyanov, issued an instruction (1887) which became notorious. School authorities were told to scrutinize the social and financial background of applicants and to reject those on behalf of

. . . children of coachmen, servants, cooks, washerwomen, small shopkeepers, and persons of a similar type, whose children, perhaps with the exception of those gifted with unusual abilities, should certainly not be brought out of the social environment to which they belong.

This was really a counsel of desperation, for such measures could only decay, not halt, expansion and 'democratization' of the school system: by 1914 39 per cent of university students and about half the pupils in secondary schools hailed from the poorer classes. This was perhaps the clearest example of the contradiction that underlay the whole strategy of 'counter-reform'. For the government remained committed to industrialization and economic growth, which inevitably led to tremendous social and cultural changes. These required adaptation of the political and administrative system, not stubborn adherence to 'authentically Russian values' which, on critical examination, meant little more than unthinking compliance with commands from above.

ETHNIC DISCRIMINATION

It was not long before Alexander III's reactionary course provoked a violent response that was at its strongest among the non-Russian minorities. For these peoples were now subjected to much more systematic ethnic discrimination. Why did the tsarist administration embark on a policy that so clearly threatened the cohesion of the realm? More was involved than mere national or religious prejudice within the ruling class, although this was certainly a factor. However reprehensible, indeed suicidal, this course may seem today, it did have a crazy rationale: it was designed to *avert* the danger of the empire breaking up into petty states as minority élites joined in the great surge of nationalism sweeping across Europe. Whereas the Austro-Hungarian Empire chose the path of conciliation and compromise (although fitfully and under pressure), tsarism opted for resistance to nationalism, even if this meant taking repressive measures. This was partly because Russia lacked a strong legal tradition, partly because her minorities, being less developed politically, seemed more manageable. Moreover, strung out along the border, the minorities represented a potential security threat in the event of major war. The government's critics argued that this threat could best be countered by treating these peoples with consideration and respect. But that would have meant behaving likewise towards Russians, too, whom the authorities deemed to be immature and therefore in need of protection against competition from their more developed neighbours. There was also a (well-substantiated) fear in high places that demographic growth was proceeding faster among non-Russians than Russians. These considerations were heightened by emotional phobias that, as we have seen, had their roots in Romantic political thought. Leaders who feel vulnerable, as did those of Imperial Russia, are unlikely to show statesmanlike tolerance and generosity.

The shift of attitude in official thinking implied that the source of the regime's legitimacy became ethnic instead of dynastic, exclusive rather than inclusive. Previously, all the tsar's subjects, whatever their origin, were expected to exhibit loyalty to the autocrat and were equally rightless. Now Orthodox Russians (including Ukrainians or religious converts, equated with them) occupied a privileged position, while the others were allotted inferior places on a graduated scale, with Jews and other 'aliens' (*inorodtsy*) at the bottom of the heap. However, this assumption was not articulated clearly. Tsarist nationality policy was not based on theory (ideology), but instead developed *ad hoc*, in response to various pressures within and upon the government. There was no central agency to coordinate policy and hence it was often contradictory. Officialdom refused to acknowledge publicly that a 'minorities question' existed. Even oppositionists critical of tsarism downplayed the issue. Well into the twentieth century many Russians, revolutionaries included, underestimated the complexity of inter-ethnic relations within the empire. They tended to assume that tensions would be attenuated by comradeship in the common struggle for progress, and that with the advent of democracy (and socialism) any remaining problems could be sorted out amicably. This was, of course, to downplay the tempestuous force of national sentiment, especially once it spread down from élites to the masses. Oddly, such illusions persisted even after the 1905 revolution had demonstrated the fragility of the imperial structure.

The widely used term 'Russification' should not be taken too literally. Assimilation was at best a long-term goal for Russian policy makers, and then only for other Slavic peoples (or certain small oriental groups). In this relatively civilized era there was as yet no question of compulsory population transfers or genocide. 'Russification' really meant taking administrative measures to homogenize local government, justice, and education; to foster use of Russian as the empire's official language; and, less significantly, to propagate Orthodoxy – along with an appreciation of Russian cultural achievements. Since any attempt to generalize about the various minorities' experiences is likely to mislead, a few highlights must suffice here.

After Poland, the Baltic provinces presented imperial policy makers with their greatest problem. Ever since Russian conquest of the region in the early eighteenth century the German nobles and burghers had enjoyed a privileged status. They had their own autonomous representative bodies and played a leading role in local government. This was now perceived in St Petersburg as anachronistic. On his accession Alexander III broke with tradition by omitting to confirm the Baltic Germans' privileges and subsequently the three provinces (Estland, Livland, Kurland) forfeited many of their ancient rights. These were, however, not abolished *in toto*; likewise the Lutheran Church survived an Orthodox assault, mainly over the vexed question of converts. The principal victim was the school system, where Russian was introduced as the language of instruction. So it was also in the University of Dorpat, which was given its purported 'old Russian' name of Yur'ev (now Tartu, Estonia). Educational standards, which were higher in this region than anywhere else in the empire, suffered in consequence, but for the 'Russifiers' the political benefits outweighed the costs. The offensive lost the government the goodwill of the hitherto loyal Baltic Germans. The drive for linguistic uniformity was taken to ridiculous lengths. It might have made sense to teach the lingua franca to the upwardly mobile, who needed it for their careers, but to make people speak Russian when buying a stamp or railway ticket was just silly.

These measures failed to win support for Russia among native Latvians and Estonians, as Slavophils like Yuriy Samarin had initially hoped. Among both peoples a process of national awakening got under way from mid century. The 'Young Latvian' movement, patterned on Mazzini's 'Young Italy', set up a cultural association (1868) which organized festivals of choral singing, collected folklore, and so on. To some extent this activity won support from the German community in Latvia, for both peoples shared the same faith and had similar grievances. On the other hand, the German élite was nervous at the Latvians' demographic and commercial dynamism. The patriotic leader K. Valdemars, an experienced seafarer, encouraged construction of a merchant fleet which by 1914 had over 300 vessels. In Estonia the national revival, which was more moderate politically, developed along similar lines. No fewer than 400 choral groups attended the sixth song festival in 1896. For linguistic and cultural reasons the main external influences here came from Finland.

In the grand duchy the *status quo* came under challenge from St Petersburg in the 1890s. The 'Russifiers' took the view that Finland's special status – it even had a small army of its own, for local defence only – was prejudicial to imperial interests. In 1890 it lost its separate postal service. Preparations were made to deprive it of two other symbols of sovereignty, its coinage and customs service, but energetic lobbying by the Finns, helped by certain Russian business interests, prevented the legislation from being promulgated. All the greater was the shock when in 1899 Nicholas II, who five years earlier had solemnly confirmed Finnish autonomy, declared in a manifesto that, 'We have considered it necessary to reserve to Ourselves final determination of legislative matters concerning the Empire as a whole.' Just which laws were covered was not specified, so that local Russian officials had leeway to act as they pleased. Students from Helsinki University skied around the countryside collecting signatures on a petition to the 'All-Highest' and a nation-wide passive resistance campaign ensued. It was effective in mobilizing support, also in Western Europe, but – as with the Poles in 1863 – foreign powers could not legally intervene on the Finns' behalf.

Simultaneously trouble was brewing in the empire's Transcaucasian provinces. In schools and other public institutions the Georgian language was replaced by Russian. The rector of the Tiflis (Tbilisi) theological seminary, who rashly referred to the native tongue as fit only for dogs, was assassinated (1886). Repressive measures against the culture of the proud and ancient Georgians stimulated a national revival which soon became politicized and veered left towards Marxism. Georgia would later become a bastion of (Menshevik) Social Democracy.

Simultaneously the Armenians were affronted by measures taken against their national Church, whose schools and charitable organizations were closed down. Their vigorous merchant class was portrayed in Russian propaganda as parasitic and disloyal. In fact the Armenian community had traditionally taken a pro-Russian line, partly from concern for fellow-nationals in the Ottoman Empire. However, they were disappointed when, in 1896, St Petersburg conspicuously failed to protect the latter from a Turco-Kurdish pogrom, and some turned to terrorism. In these circumstances the tsarist authorities acted with remarkable insouciance when, in 1903, they confiscated the possessions of the Armenian Orthodox Church.

Wisely, they did not interfere much with the religion or culture of Transcaucasian Muslims ('Tatars', as the Azerbaijani were then known), nor with those either north of the Caucasus or in Central Asia. Among the *inorodtsy* in the Volga valley a revival of Islam came about as an indirect response to the missionary activities undertaken from the 1860s onward by N. I. Il'minsky, an orientalist from Kazan', and his associates in the St Guriy Brotherhood. This agency energetically promoted, along with Orthodox Christianity, schooling and publications in local languages (for some of which alphabets had to be invented), and trained native teachers and priests. Il'minsky's influence eventually extended throughout Russia's eastern domains, but his very success created its antidote: a thin native intelligentsia able to develop in a different direction. A number of baptized Tatars reconverted to Islam. In 1883 Ismail bey Gasprali (in Russian: Gasprinsky), a Crimean Tatar who had studied in Paris and Istanbul as well as Moscow, established in the Crimea an influential newspaper, *Tarjuman* (*The Interpreter*). Widely read in various parts of the empire, it became a vehicle for the Islamic reform movement known as *jadidism*. It urged Muslims to borrow from, and even rely on, the scientific knowledge of the modern West, instead of rejecting it as heretical, in order to overcome Islam's internal weakness. Gasprali taught that, by dropping classical Arabic in favour of a Turkic vernacular language, Russia's Muslims could overcome their ethnic divisions and (it was implied) form a single united nation. The political aspect was deliberately played down, and outwardly at least Gasprali remained a loyal subject of the tsar, but by 1900 it was clear that these ideas had a great future in both empires, the Ottoman as well as the Russian. Native schools with a reformed curriculum proliferated and alarmed tsarist officials began to perceive a 'pan-Islamic' or 'pan-Turkic' threat. This was something of a chimera, since the emergent Muslim nations were widely scattered and had no common bond other than religion. For the present, the danger was confined to a few small circles of Volga Tatars and Bashkir intellectuals, whose radicalism was suspect to conservative mullahs and beys – and it was they who still controlled men's minds, especially in backward Central Asia.

The principal victims of tsarist ethnic and religious discrimination were the Jews, who by the end of the nineteenth century had grown to number some 6 million. All but a tiny handful were, as we know, crammed into the overcrowded 'Pale of settlement', where antisemitic prejudice was rife among the local Slavic population. A Jewish girl, G. Gel'fman, was one of Alexander II's assassins, and this touched off a spate of rumours which found a ready echo, not least among rootless and hungry agricultural labourers who had flocked to the south-western region in search of work. In April 1881 a quarrel in a Jewish-owned tavern at Yekaterinoslav led to a riot. Jewish homes and shops were looted and some people killed. The disorders spread to nearby villages. Later that year, and at Easter 1882, there were further violent outbreaks in Warsaw and Podolia province. In all 20,000 Jews were rendered homeless and casualties ran into the hundreds.

Though local pogroms had occurred before, notably at Odessa in 1871, this was the first example of massive rioting. Because the police did not act promptly to quell the trouble-makers, and some press organs were openly antisemitic, official connivance was suspected. This view has since been shown to be false, although the government was culpable in tolerating a climate of opinion that led ruffians to think that violence against Jews was permissible.

The pogroms were more the result of Russia's modernization and industrialization process than of age-old religious and national antagonisms . . . [Yet] officials felt quite comfortable enforcing very discriminatory legislation against the Jews, and . . . the Christian population . . . often drew the conclusion that the [Jews] were not fully under the protection of the law.*

* I. M. Aronson, in Klier and Lambroza, *Pogroms*, p. 51.

The authorities feared mass violence in any form and belatedly suppressed it. Most perpetrators received light sentences, supposedly from fear of further mob action.

The indirect effects of the pogroms were devastating. They were a prime cause of the Jewish emigration wave, for hopes of peaceful coexistence had been brutally shattered. To make matters worse, the authorities blamed the outbreaks on the victims. A host of discriminatory laws followed. In 1882 Jews were forbidden to settle in the Pale's rural areas or to trade on Christian holidays. Five years later an ethnic quota was introduced in secondary schools and universities, as well as at the bar. Jewish doctors were banned from taking jobs in the public service, while in the army Jews could not attain officer rank. Nor could they vote in local elections. This repressive campaign culminated in 1891–2, when in bitter wintry weather over 10,000 Jewish artisans were deported from Moscow, ostensibly because they lacked proper residence permits. Others were forced to leave their homes near the western frontier, where they were alleged to represent a security risk, and resettled in the interior. All this was accompanied by propaganda that increasingly bore racist overtones.

Far from Jews being 'Russified', they were ostracized and segregated so far as possible from the Slavic population. Contradictorily, antisemites in high places portrayed their enemies both as dangerous social revolutionaries and as the hidden power behind international capital. The notorious *Protocols of the Elders of Zion* were fabricated by tsarist secret police agents in 1895. Although an obvious forgery, the document was destined to have a long life. Such allegations appealed to the credulous in all classes who were unsettled by the rapid changes taking place in economic and social life. 'In Russia anti-Semitism was linked to pre-capitalist, pre-modern forms of organization. It was a "reactionary utopia" nurtured by a noble élite concerned for its privileged position in the state.'* Despite this persecution it was now that Russo-Jewish culture brought forth some of its finest fruits: in literature (Sholom Aleichem), music (the Rubinstein brothers), and the arts (Leonid Pasternak, Mark Antokol'sky). Some wrote in Russian, others in Yiddish or (increasingly) in Hebrew.

Ethnic discrimination went hand in hand with clumsy efforts to

---

* Löwe, *Antisemitismus*, p. 23 (cf. idem, *The Tsars and the Jews*, p. 111).

promote Orthodoxy as the official state religion. To symbolize its claims to pre-eminence, cathedrals were built in traditional Muscovite style in Warsaw and Riga. However, the layman Pobedonostsev's strict rule over the Church (1880–1905) did nothing to raise the tenor of its spiritual life, for the chief procurator's outlook was purely formal and bureaucratic. He actually feared any genuine Christian impulses among the faithful. In the interests of order, bishops' disciplinary authority over priests was reinforced and repressive measures taken against the Old Believers (c.20 million in 1900) and members of various dissident sects – which did not prevent Protestant Baptists from making considerable headway among peasants in the west and south. Leo Tolstoy's unconventional Christian pacifism did the writer credit but had a more limited appeal. Orthodox who converted (or reconverted) to other denominations were harassed. Until 1905 there was as little place in the tsarist empire for religious liberty as there was for political freedom.

These reactionary tendencies were strongly criticized by enlightened Russians, in the press and elsewhere. Liberals worried at the empire's poor image in Western Europe, for whose opinions and institutions they had great respect. The more radically minded considered themselves internationalists, part of the world-wide movement for democracy, socialism, and friendship among peoples. But it was hard for them to translate these high ideals into practice, particularly in conditions where political activity of any kind was all but ruled out.

THE RADICAL INTELLIGENTSIA

The eventual triumph of the Bolsheviks in 1917 has distorted historiographical treatment of radical politics during the 1880s and 1890s. First, it has highlighted ideological divisions between Populists and Marxists, who actually cooperated quite well at grass-roots level while their leaders disputed the fine points of revolutionary doctrine. Secondly, excessive stress has been laid on theorizing by intellectuals who, especially if they were forced into emigration, had only tenuous contact with their followers among the masses. Thirdly, the role of Russian organizations has been overemphasized at the expense of those formed by left-wingers among the minority peoples.

Certainly the catastrophe inflicted and suffered by the People's Will group in 1881 discredited revolutionary terrorism. Nevertheless this tactic did not forfeit its attraction entirely, despite the tough methods employed by the security police (popularly known as 'the Okhrana'), which included the use of *agents provocateurs* to infiltrate the radical milieu. In March 1887 a small group led by the student Alexander Ulyanov set out to kill Alexander III. The *coup* was averted and the conspirators hanged, but the episode has a secure niche in history owing to the role later played by Ulyanov's younger brother Vladimir, better known under his pseudonym Lenin.

It was not too difficult for members of clandestine Populist circles to integrate into their ideology such elements of Marxism as the concept of an inexorable class struggle culminating in a socialist revolution in which a major role would be played by industrial workers, the 'proletariat'. Most of them saw the peasants, too, as a (or *the*) revolution-ary force. However, the belief in the progressive potential of the rural commune was now somewhat attenuated, since evidence suggested that the peasants' social cohesion was being undermined by 'capitalist' influences.

This was the point on which G. V. Plekhanov, 'father of Russian Marxism', insisted strongly. The former leader of the minority anti-terrorist faction among the Populists now lived in far-off Geneva, where in 1883 he broke off negotiations for a common journalistic enterprise with some fellow-*émigré* narodniks and set up a new group, 'Liberation of Labour'. (So tiny was it that once, when its five members went boating on Lake Geneva, Plekhanov quipped with rare humour: 'Watch out, if this boat sinks, it'll be the end of Russian Marxism.') In a succession of programmatic writings he and his comrades, notably P. B. Axelrod and the now repentant ex-terrorist Vera Zasulich, devoted themselves to fierce polemics designed to show that the Populists' theories were utopian and unscientific. An erudite but intolerant man, Plekhanov accentuated the doctrinaire note in Russian revolutionary controversies. Precisely because of their vulner-ability in the underground or exile, Marxist intellectuals showed little understanding of politics as 'the art of the possible', but rather sought to demonstrate the abiding truth of their views by invoking scriptural authority. It was embarrassing, therefore, that Marx had shown more enthusiasm for the Populist terrorists than for his would-be Russian disciples.* This was because he thought that, given Russia's backwardness, a revolution there could do no more than touch off one in the more developed countries of Central and Western Europe, whereas Plekhanov's key concept was that 'the Russian revolution will either succeed as a workers' revolution or it will not succeed at all', as he put it in 1889 to an international socialist gathering.

He was contemptuous of the peasantry as inherently conservative: 'The proletarian and the *muzhik* are real political antipodes.' Revolutionaries should allow the historical process to work itself out and not try to anticipate events by seizing power on behalf of the people: this would result either in defeat or in a new despotism. Instead they should help workers acquire 'class consciousness' (i.e. socialist convictions) and bring about a 'bourgeois-democratic' regime which would create the conditions for capitalism to develop. This first stage was an essential preliminary to the ultimate socialist one, a fully fledged 'dictatorship of the proletariat' on an international scale. Yet Plekhanov was willing to envisage telescoping these two phases, arguing that the pace of advance depended on the amount of influence that workers brought to bear on the 'bourgeoisie' during the initial phase.

This was a weak point in the Marxists' intellectual armoury which would assume great importance in 1905 and 1917. Meanwhile Liberation of Labour concentrated on smuggling, with the aid of Polish and Jewish sympathizers, its theoretical literature into Russia. It was read assiduously by the organizers of clandestine discussion and self-educational circles, although its tone was too abstract for ordinary workers. Intermittently there was tension between these leaders and the rank and file, who were naturally keener on self-improvement than making revolution. Nevertheless during the 1890s Marxist ideas struck root in cities such as St Petersburg, Moscow, and Odessa and the rudiments of a 'worker intelligentsia' took shape. Gradually propagandists turned into agitators who sought to provide leadership in labour disputes, notably during the strike in St Petersburg textile mills in 1896–7. It was here that Yu. O. Martov, the future Menshevik leader,

* To Zasulich he wrote in 1881 that 'the commune is the *point d'appui* of social regeneration in Russia'. Engels later took a more ambivalent position and at the end of his life endorsed Plekhanov's position.

and Lenin won their revolutionary spurs, although police arrested both men before the strike began and exiled them to Siberia.

In the late 1890s Social Democratic ideas won many adherents in the educated classes, even becoming something of a vogue. A relaxation of censorship permitted Marxist periodicals to appear legally. The so-called 'Legal Marxists' (P. B. Struve, S. N. Bulgakov) questioned orthodox Marxist assumptions in philosophy and sociology, emphasizing the autonomy of the individual and advocating evolution rather than revolution. Plekhanov and his comrades treated these ideas as dangerously heretical. They were also alarmed by what they misleadingly termed 'Economism', roughly the view that initially priority should be given to industrial as distinct from political methods of struggle – although these tactics had proved successful in practice. There was also a Syndicalist tendency among some radical workers who resented the orthodox intellectuals' bossiness.

How were the scattered groups to be welded into a single party? The strongest local organizations were those of the General Jewish Workers' League ('Bund'), formed in 1897. Jewish activists were behind an effort to unite their Russian comrades which went badly awry: all but one of the delegates to the first congress of the Russian Social Democratic Labour party (RSDRP), held in Minsk in March 1898, were arrested. This left the field clear for Lenin and Martov, once back from Siberia. In December 1900, together with Plekhanov's Liberation of Labour group, they issued the first number of the newspaper *Iskra* (*The Spark*). Like Herzen's *Kolokol* forty or so years earlier, this was published in Western Europe – the six editors lived in various cities and kept in touch by correspondence – and conveyed to Russia through underground channels.

Lenin in particular saw the paper not just as an information medium but as a means of moulding the infant party to his own design. His chief instrument was a network of 'agents' – full-time professional revolutionaries who toured local committees to distribute the paper and keep them in line, purging dissidents where necessary. There was to be no room for laxity or federalism within the RSDRP. As a militantly revolutionary party it needed to be run along highly centralized lines. In this scheme, as he frankly admitted, there was an element of the 'jacobinism' that had characterized the 'People's Will' group. A succession of campaigns against real or imagined foes, including rivals on the left, kept the membership fully motivated. Lenin wrote that the rank and file 'should observe all the "laws and customs" of that "regular army" in which they have enlisted', and in another striking image likened himself to an orchestral conductor who knew just when to bring into play each group of musicians. 'Democratic centralism', as he called it misleadingly, provided no genuine safety valve for legitimate differences of opinion and ensured that the history of the RSDRP, and of its communist successor, would be one of continual schism.

A word about the character of the future Bolshevik leader is called for here. Born in 1870, he practised briefly as a lawyer before becoming a full-time revolutionary in 1892. His intellect was powerful but narrowly focused. What distinguished him from his colleagues was his unusually zealous dedication to the cause: 'He dreams about nothing but revolution day and night,' as Axelrod put it later. Lenin's total commitment to Marxism (from about 1891: previously his views were more heterodox) went hand in hand with a keen sense of tactical realism that enabled him to show flexibility where required, while persuading himself (and most of his followers) that every shift of position was ideologically correct. This versatility led to charges of cynical unscrupulousness by his foes. Indeed, Lenin did take a highly instrumental view of morality: what was good was whatever was expedient in the class struggle (as he defined it).

His nervous system was seriously overloaded and had probably never been very strong . . . The sound of the violin put his nerves on edge and he could not stand extraneous noise or bustle . . . When he got excited he would work himself up into such a state of bellicosity that he would be ready to take extreme, even cruel measures.*

Lenin exercised an almost hypnotic power over others and ultimately managed to transmit his fanatical credo and intransigent attitude to a vast number of people.

Few could have imagined Vladimir Ulyanov's brilliant future when he had only several dozen supporters. Resistance to his design for the new party was offered by local activists, not all of them 'Economists', as well as by followers of the Bund. The latter wanted their organization

* Volkogonov, *Lenin*, pp. 410–11.

alone to speak for the Jewish proletariat, with its special concerns, and to transform the RSDRP into a federation of equal national units. Influenced to some extent by the Zionist movement, the Bundists manifested an idea of Jewish identity which, in the opinion of their Russian (and Polish) comrades, smacked of nationalism. They stood for a Social Democratic party organized in a way that ignored its members' ethnic or religious backgrounds.

Matters came to a head at the RSDRP's second congress in 1903. The Bund's demands for autonomy were rejected and so its delegates walked out. This altered the balance of power among the pro-*Iskra* Russian faction, which beneath the surface was split over programmatic, tactical, and organizational issues – and not least over Lenin's personality.* Martov had viewed with growing distaste his comrade's duplicitous methods, but held his peace until the congress met. Here his formula on membership went through, but the Bund's withdrawal gave the Leninists a majority (Russian: *bol'shinstvo*, hence the term 'Bolshevik'). Thereupon they restaffed the party's central institutions so as to reflect the new line-up of forces. The upshot was total disarray: *Iskra* came under Menshevik (*men'shinstvo* = minority) control, whereas the Central Committee was Bolshevik. Although rank-and-file members of the two factions (or of neither) often cooperated locally, the schism was never really healed. The resulting polemics and intrigues greatly weakened the RSDRP on the eve of a revolutionary upsurge that it might otherwise have led.

The initiative in Russian opposition politics passed to the agrarian socialists and the liberals. During the 1890s Populism was temporarily eclipsed by the Marxists. Among intellectuals its banner was upheld by the sociologist N. K. Mikhaylovsky, editor of the prestigious *Russkoye bogatstvo* (*Russia's Wealth*). He warned of the perils inherent in Marxist determinism and crossed swords over this issue with Plekhanov. Meanwhile the so-called Legal Populists conducted empirical studies of rural life which served as the basis for the theories of a new Socialist Revolutionary party (PSR, commonly called 'SRs' to distinguish them from the 'SDs' or Social Democrats). This was a more mature body

---

* Formally, the reason for the schism was the definition of party membership. Martov stood for a broad, inclusive formula, whereas Lenin wanted to restrict membership to hardened professional revolutionaries, the others forming a fringe of sympathizers.

than the earlier 'People's Will'. It was formed in 1901 on the basis of several pre-existing regional Populist groups, notably in Saratov and Minsk. The SRs' ideology owed much to V. M. Chernov, grandson of a serf who grew up in Samara and studied in Moscow. (It may not be irrelevant that both Plekhanov and Lenin were of noble stock.) Chernov was influenced by Marxism, but he interpreted it in a non-doctrinaire fashion. The forthcoming democratic revolution, he averred, could come about only through cooperation between peasants, workers, and intellectuals; the struggle was not between antagonistic 'bourgeois' and 'proletarian' classes, as the SDs held, but between the people as a whole and the autocracy. More concretely, the SRs stood for socialization of all the land; noble and state domains were to be expropriated, without compensation, and transferred to local peasant communities, which would divide them up among individual house-holders in the customary way of the commune. Thereupon each house-hold was to be free to farm its land as it wished, aided by democratic central and local authorities as well as such civic bodies as agricultural cooperatives.

As regards the immediate interests of industrial workers, both Russian socialist parties took much the same line, advocating the right to strike, an eight-hour day, and so on, but the SRs objected to the idea of eventual proletarian dictatorship. Each party won support among industrial workers, but the PSR alone made headway among the peasants. This was to be expected, for their agrarian programme reflected egalitarian sentiments long current in the countryside. The PSR's Agrarian Socialist League successfully agitated for peasants to resist landlord 'exploitation' by refusing to pay rents or taxes. In the spring of 1902 serious riots broke out in two southern provinces (Poltava, Khar'kov) – the first major trouble of this kind since 1861. Though suppressed by Cossack whips and drumhead tribunals, they greatly alarmed officials, who were debating agricultural policy in a 'special conference' called by Witte. (This conference was attended by representatives of educated society, which was a considerable concession by the autocracy.)

Less justifiable, but undeniably successful in the short term, was the SRs' resort to terror. This was a legacy of the 1870s, but theorists now developed an elaborate rationalization for it – a veritable cult of the individual 'fighter' prepared to sacrifice his life for the good of the

People. A so-called 'Combat Group', initially led by G. A. Gershuni, organized the assassination of two successive interior ministers, D. S. Sipyagin (1902) and V. K. Plehve (1904). Other prominent victims included the education minister, N. P. Bogolepov (1901), and the governor of Ufa province. These *coups* invited emulation by anarchists and Social Democrats.

The RSDRP's attitude to terror was ambivalent. Although cool to the idea of liquidating senior functionaries, on the grounds that this deflected socialists from their task of building mass support, they tolerated the killing of alleged Okhrana informers, unpopular foremen, and the like, so that in practice there was not much to choose between the two parties. The authorities dealt firmly with terrorists whom they caught, but were unable to provide senior officials with complete protection. Understandably, many of them lost their nerve. Political terrorism helped to weaken a regime already uncertain of its course. One peculiarity of this struggle was the relatively high number of defectors from both camps. There were officials who leaked secrets to the opposition and revolutionaries – among them the celebrated double agent Ye. Azef – who were police informers in disguise.

It should be noted that the Okhrana did not, like its Soviet successors, have the power to try and convict offenders, who as a rule were dealt with by extraordinary judicial procedure. One of the agency's most remarkable (and, from the revolutionaries' viewpoint, insidious) operations was to set up ostensibly independent labour organizations that were actually under police control. These devious ventures were initiated by S. V. Zubatov, who like many Okhrana officers had been a revolutionary in his time. He did much to systematize the surveillance of political suspects and in 1900–1 went on to set up, with the consent of Grand Duke Sergey, governor-general of Moscow, a trade union. By settling workers' grievances against their employers this body earned their confidence to such a point that some 40,000 to 50,000 men turned out to demonstrate their loyalty to the tsar at a ceremony in the Kremlin. In the western provinces gendarmes managed to win over followers of the Bund, which led to armed clashes between rival labour organizations. Employers complained to the finance ministry. This was one reason why the experiment was brought to an end. Most historians write it off as a failure, but it did show how fragile 'class consciousness' still was among Russian workers.

Opposition to tsarism was not confined to extremists. In the late 1890s liberal zemstvo deputies began to demand the rule of law, civil rights, and parliamentary government. The more cautious, led by D. N. Shipov, stood in the Slavophil tradition and wanted a merely consultative assembly, but the radicals under I. I. Petrunkevich went farther. In 1902, together with professional men like Struve and the historian P. N. Milyukov, they founded a clandestine newspaper, *Osvobozhdenie* (*Liberation*), which like *Iskra* was published abroad and smuggled in. At this time Russian liberals stood some way to the left of those in the West. They supported universal (male) suffrage and far-reaching social and agrarian reforms; tactically, they advocated cooperation with the SDs. But the latter spurned their advances, fearing 'bourgeois' infiltration of the labour movement.

These antagonisms helped the government. Not only were the Russian left-wing parties at loggerheads, but the national-minority revolutionary groups, too, were divided. By 1904 these comprised Jewish, Polish, Ukrainian, Georgian, and Latvian SDs, the Polish Socialist party (PPS, which put national independence first), Finnish Activists and Armenian 'Dashnyaks', to name only the most important. One might have expected them to form a bloc or 'united front'. Such an endeavour was indeed made, at a conference held in Paris in October 1904, but it came to nought, even though it was secretly backed by the foreign power with which Russia was now at war – Japan.

THE FATEFUL ALLIANCE

During Alexander III's reign, uniquely, Russia was not involved in major hostilities. This was due less to any pacific intent on the tsar's part, as his admirers claimed, than to Russia's awkward diplomatic situation on a continent dominated by Bismarck. Apart from this, financial and military weakness obliged St Petersburg to observe restraint. In the Balkans a clumsy attempt to interfere in Bulgaria's internal affairs, which at one point led to the brief kidnapping of its ruler by pro-Russian officers, backfired badly. That country, which owed its independence to Russian arms, followed the Serbian and Romanian example by drifting into the orbit of the Germanic powers, leaving tiny Montenegro as Russia's only firm friend.* Hopes of winning control of the Turkish straits had to be postponed indefinitely.

Katkov and other nationalist spokesmen inveighed against the 'soft' pro-German orientation of official foreign policy, but Alexander realized that he had no choice. In taking this option he was supported by his plodding but worthy foreign minister, N. K. Giers. In 1881 the Three Emperors' alliance was secretly restored, with Russia now definitely its weakest partner. Six years later Katkov revealed details of the agreement, which earned him a private rebuke (foreign policy was wholly the tsar's domain). The nationalists were outraged by Germany's role in Bulgaria, perceived the Reich as a growing security threat, and called for a rapprochement with France. But this suggestion ran up against ideological reservations. Monarchists distrusted the Third Republic as inherently unstable and had no wish to see Russia dragged into war to help it regain the 'lost provinces' of Alsace and Lorraine. Even so, French military and financial lobbyists forged links with their counterparts in Russia. The two powers' chiefs of staff, Boisdeffre and Obruchev, met secretly at a château in the Dordogne owned by the latter's French wife, with arms exports a prime topic of conversation, and from 1888 onwards French bankers raised loans to assist Russia in postponing the day of reckoning on her international debts.

In the previous year Bismarck had all but closed German financial markets to Russia as a way of bringing her to heel. The Iron Chancellor was finding it ever harder to reconcile Germany's two allies, the Habsburgs and the Romanovs. He succeeded in fobbing off St Petersburg with a so-called 'Reinsurance treaty' that was of little practical worth. It saved Russia from isolation, but increased the pressures towards her 'fateful alliance' (G. F. Kennan) with France. In 1890 the irresponsible new Kaiser, William II, who listened willingly to militaristic advisers' warnings of a 'Russian threat', sacked Bismarck, allowed the Reinsurance treaty to lapse, and for good measure personally insulted the tsar. Only with difficulty could the latter be persuaded to pay the Kaiser a courtesy visit, and this went badly. Perhaps Alexander

---

* According to an apocryphal story, journalists asked its ruler how strong his army was. 'Together with our great Russian ally, one million.' But how large was it if Russian forces were subtracted? 'Montenegro never abandons its friends.' See Rogger, *Russia*, p. 181.

was secretly quite glad at the breach, for it freed his hands *vis-à-vis* the French. Next summer, welcoming a French naval squadron to Kronstadt, he bared his head as a military band played the *Marseillaise*, the anthem of revolutionaries everywhere.* A vague agreement of August 1891, providing for mutual consultation should either country's security be in danger, was converted early in 1894 into a binding military–political alliance. The entente was curiously precise as to the number of troops each party should field in the event of war with the future Central Powers, yet vague as to what would constitute a *casus belli*; nor were the signatories' war aims specified. If an adversary mobilized, the partners agreed to do so too, but no provision was made for *partial* mobilization. Thus, although its object was to deter Germany from aggression by threatening her with hostilities on two fronts, the pact actually signified an open-ended commitment to wage total war on the other's behalf, perhaps for no very good reason.

This interpretation owes much to hindsight. At the time each signatory thought it had kept its options open, and in the 1890s Russo-German (and even Russo-Austrian) relations remained on an even keel. But in 1905–6 it had become clear that Russia was France's junior partner, at least so far as European affairs were concerned.

Stymied in the Balkans, Russian expansionists looked to the Far East, where construction of the Trans-Siberian railway opened up exciting new possibilities *vis-à-vis* a greatly weakened China. Here Russia faced the rivalry of Japan, which in 1895 took the Liaotung peninsula, leaving Korea nominally independent. The former prize she was forced by diplomatic pressure to yield to the Russians, who planned to build there, on the shores of the Yellow Sea, an ice-free naval base to supplement that at Vladivostok, together with a commercial port.† Access was to be ensured by a railway spur line from Harbin, the nodal point on a southern branch of the Trans-Siberian which crossed the Chinese province of Manchuria, greatly shortening the distance to Vladivostok; the lines were to be guarded by troops. These

---

* When it reached the second verse, he exclaimed sharply, 'That's enough!'
† Respectively Lüshun (Port Arthur) and Ta-lien (Dalny). Formally, the Liaotung peninsula was leased, so that Chinese sovereignty was respected on paper, but this was cold comfort for Beijing.

concessions were exacted from China by two unequal treaties (1896, 1898).

Russia's leaders disagreed over the pace and nature of this classic imperialist venture. Witte, who launched it, stood for a relatively soft approach which emphasized economic aspirations; he saw China, and other Asian lands, as a vast potential market for Russian goods that could not compete in Europe. Military men like General A. N. Kuropatkin, and a group of courtiers with private interests in the area (notably a timber concession on the Yalu in northern Korea), took a tougher line. In 1900 the 'Boxer' uprising in Beijing gave Russian troops a pretext to enter Manchuria in force. Japan reacted by signing an alliance with Britain (so breaching the latter's 'glorious isolation'); the United States, too, was hostile to Russian expansion. Reluctantly St Petersburg agreed to withdraw its troops in phases, but then dragged out the process and, to make matters worse, infiltrated them into Korea.

Tension with Japan could have been defused if Russia had accepted a Japanese proposal for mutual delimitation of spheres of influence. But she fatally underestimated her adversary, a power written off by some chauvinists as racially inferior. The interior minister, Plehve, was widely thought to have wanted a 'short, victorious war' to stem the tide of revolution. In fact he was as aware as Witte of the dangers to internal stability, but the Russian policy-making process was confused. No minister dared disobey the tsar, who displayed blind overconfidence. On 8 February 1904 Japanese ships launched a surprise attack on Port Arthur and the war had begun.

It was easier for Japan to transport troops to the Far Eastern theatre than it was for Russia; the Trans-Siberian rail link was still rudimentary. No overall commander was appointed and there were sharp personal clashes at the top.

Talented leaders . . . were a scarce commodity in the Far East . . . Russian naval leaders . . . presented a picture of incompetence and sloth. The army seemed to possess more talented men in second-level positions, but too often the best officers were wasted by their superiors. Kuropatkin left the war ministry to assume command of the field army, but he was far from an ideal troop commander. Although he was a man of unquestionable courage, charm and intellect, he lacked resolution and decisiveness.*

* Menning, *Bayonets before Bullets*, p. 154.

Time and again Russian troops were forced to retreat after engagements that cost tens of thousands of lives. The soldiers fought well but morale began to sag once Port Arthur fell to its besiegers in December 1904 with the loss of 23,000 men. In May 1905 the Russian Baltic fleet, which had been dispatched half-way round the world to do battle, was annihilated in the Tsushima strait before it could reach the theatre of operations. This was an unparalleled catastrophe in Russia's naval annals – it seemed to mark the end of Peter I's dream of maritime greatness and stimulated domestic opposition to the war. This had been gathering steam for months. Isolated and discredited, the tsarist government found itself confronting revolution.

CHAPTER 13

Last Years of Empire

THE 1905 REVOLUTION

On Sunday, 9 January 1905, several columns of working men, totalling over 100,000, approached the Winter Palace in St Petersburg. Their aim was to present to the 'All-Highest' a petition listing their grievances. Some of the men were accompanied by their wives, others held icons aloft. They were met by a hail of bullets. Over a hundred fell dead, many more were injured. 'Bloody Sunday', as it came to be called, sent waves of revulsion throughout the empire. It fatally undermined the autocracy's prestige, at least among townsfolk: for what could be said in defence of a government so isolated from the people that it could not distinguish friend from foe? Ministers had been alerted to the march in advance but failed to countermand the troops' orders to disperse the crowds by force.

In 1904 the police allowed Father George Gapon, an idealistic and ambitious dissident priest, to set up a benevolent association for workpeople in the capital, much on the lines of Zubatov's trade unions. Gapon acquired a charismatic authority over his followers, who within a few months numbered tens of thousands. They met in clubs and tea-houses maintained by the organization, and it was here that they worked out the text of their 'most humble and loyal address':

Sire [it began], we, the workers and inhabitants of St Petersburg, ... come to Thee to seek justice and protection. We are destitute, oppressed, overburdened with heavy toil, treated with contempt ... Our endurance is at an end. We have reached that frightful moment when death is better than prolongation of our unbearable sufferings.

The document's tone was humble, but some of its demands were radical: an eight-hour working day, higher wages, elected grievance committees in factories, equality before the law, and 'freedom of speech, press, association and worship'. Without saying so precisely, it called for a constitutional order. Parts of the text ('brazen exploitation by capitalists') showed that socialist intellectuals had a hand in the drafting. But they were not in control of the movement – and nor was Gapon. He was as shocked as anyone by the shooting; 'tear up all portraits of the blood-sucking tsar', he cried, 'and tell him: "be damned, with all thine august reptilian progeny!" '

Nicholas, who had not been in the palace, further inflamed the situation by inviting a delegation of workers for tea and cakes. Conveniently attributing the trouble to traitors, he 'forgave' the workers for what had occurred, as though he and his officials were not rather to blame. Yet some genuine concessions were made. Workers were allowed to elect representatives to a government commission on industrial unrest. This unwittingly facilitated the emergence of genuine labour organizations. The wave of sympathy strikes that followed 'Bloody Sunday' was largely spontaneous, but as the year wore on radicals acquired considerable influence over the strike movement and sought to direct it to revolutionary ends. Even so the popular mood remained fickle and it is difficult to find any evidence of 'class consciousness'.

One reason for this fickleness was the growing unemployment caused by the strains of war and internal disturbances. Most workers depended wholly on their earnings and, if they had families, could not afford to remain on strike for long. Until the autumn at least they were more concerned with bread-and-butter issues than with larger political questions, such as abolishing autocracy. Radicalization came about in part because employers, though not as yet well organized, generally resisted wage demands or made only minor concessions. Textile workers, for instance, got their working week reduced by three hours (to sixty!) but had to make up for this by overtime. Humiliating treatment by foremen (some of them foreigners) was no longer taken lying down. Some who offended in this respect were exposed to public ridicule by being carted out of the factory in a wheelbarrow and dumped in a nearby pond, a variant of the old peasant custom of 'shaming' deviants. But such archaic methods were yielding to more 'modern' forms of struggle such as the creation of trade unions. They numbered several dozen by the end of 1905. Most were of necessity local bodies, since any effort to combine more broadly encountered official obstruction. Another development was the emergence of local councils (*soviets*) of workmen's deputies. The first of these appeared at Ivanovo in May. They sought to coordinate strike action within a given area and gradually became more politicized. Strikes cost the economy an estimated 23.5 million lost working days during 1905.

They were particularly violent in Russian Poland, where national and social grievances fused into an explosive mix. Industry in the region had been hard hit by the Russo-Japanese war; wages fell and unemployment rose. Five days after 'Bloody Sunday' Russian troops killed sixty-four civilian demonstrators in Warsaw, and on May Day another thirty-one. Terrorist bands raided armourers' shops and attacked public buildings. Polish opinion rejoiced at news of Russian defeats in the Far East. Students joined in street demonstrations, setting an example to their Russian counterparts. The government made minor concessions on cultural issues, while beefing up the military presence, but the army was fully engaged elsewhere. Altogether troops were involved in 2,700 police actions between January and October. Thoughtful senior officers were justifiably alarmed at the drain on resources.

The Baltic provinces were another scene of revolutionary disorders. The national movement was weaker in Estland (as Estonia was then known) than in Livland (northern Latvia) or Kurland, but the entire region was prey to agrarian unrest. Peasants refused to pay rent or taxes, or to work the estates of the 'Baltic barons', and then proceeded to set fire to their manor houses. In Transcaucasia the situation was even more serious. Railwaymen spearheaded a strike movement that spread to industrial workers in the major centres. In some parts of Georgia the authorities were rendered powerless and local revolutionary committees took over. They confiscated private and state land and distributed it to the peasants, some of whom formally revoked their loyalty oaths and swore allegiance to their new leaders. A general of Tatar extraction was sent with 10,000 men to restore order, but had to withdraw lest his men fraternize with the rebels. Months later he returned to wreak frightful vengeance.

Meanwhile in Baku Azerbaijani mobs had staged a pogrom of Armenian residents, who retaliated in kind against their neighbours and Russian officials whom they suspected (wrongly, as is now known) of conniving in the attack. Jews, too, were once again the target of mass violence. The worst antisemitic pogrom took place in Odessa in October. Altogether hundreds were killed and 7,000 to 8,000 injured in 690 separate outbreaks. Many of these attacks were condoned by local officials.

Most regions of rural Russia were afflicted by peasant disturbances, which fluctuated in intensity according to the rhythm of the agricultural cycle. The movement peaked in May–July 1905 (300 or more incidents reported monthly) and again in November, when the number reached 796; a third wave followed in the early summer of 1906. The peasants directed their anger chiefly at landowners and officials rather than the tsar's government *per se*. Sometimes they claimed that the autocrat had himself authorized their land seizures or other breaches of property rights. This was both an expression of 'naïve monarchism' and a deliberate ploy. The initiative was often taken by the wealthier households and communal leaders. Agitation by SRs and other outsiders was of lesser importance, but they were active in forming an all-Russian Peasant Union. At its inaugural meeting, held secretly near Moscow in July, delegates from twenty-two provinces called for the abolition of private property in land and the convocation of a democratic Constituent Assembly. Though not representative of all peasant opinion, the gathering pointed to a growing politicization of the agrarian movement. The union held another conference in November, but then was suppressed, along with other left-wing bodies, as the government recovered its poise.

The ebbing of the revolutionary tide during the winter of 1905–6 owed much to the timely conclusion of peace with Japan at Portsmouth (USA) on 29 August. This enabled troops to be brought back from the Far East. Their return was delayed by technical problems, which aroused much discontent among the soldiers. In Manchuria and Siberia mutineers seized control of several towns and imposed their will on the local authorities, including hapless officials of the Trans-Siberian railway. There was also trouble among garrison troops in various parts of the empire. These outbreaks were largely non-violent and focused on service grievances. They were quelled by a mixture of concessions and reprisals against alleged ringleaders. Sometimes men who had mutinied participated zealously in these punitive actions. Life in barracks was tough and offered little scope for revolutionary propagandists.

They could score better results in the navy, where educational standards were higher. In the Black Sea fleet there was a fair sprinkling of active revolutionaries. On 14 June the crew of the battleship *Prince Potemkin* refused to eat some rotten meat which the ship's doctor fraudulently pronounced fit for consumption. When a delegation complained, their spokesman, Vakulenchuk, was shot by an officer. Crying 'Long live freedom!', his companions fell on the commander, threw him overboard, and killed him as he struggled in the water. Several other officers, among them the doctor, were put to death or taken captive. Hoisting the red flag, the battleship made for Odessa, where the populace was in an ugly mood.

The strikers and demonstrators ... were astonished by the appearance of the *Potemkin* in the harbour and deeply moved by the deposit ... of Vakulenchuk's body on a bier, surrounded by an honour guard, near a set of marble steps leading up from the harbour ... At about 5 p.m. people turned violent ... Many in the crowd had consumed large quantities of vodka and thieves and vagabonds played an important role ... Once the tumult began, people looted warehouses at will, carrying off bolts of silk, champagne, tea, clothing ... Soon the entire harbour front was ablaze ... Shortly after midnight the troops began shooting indiscriminately into the crowd, which was hemmed in from all sides. Unable to escape, many people jumped into the sea, where they drowned ... According to credible accounts 2,000 people were killed and 3,000 seriously wounded.[*]

As the popular mood shifted to the left, Russia's opposition leaders moved in the same direction, hopeful that mass pressure could force the government to yield but also fearful of incipient anarchy. It is remarkable that the liberals were able to preserve their ascendancy for so long. For it was they who had first challenged the regime in November 1904, when a national congress of zemstvo representatives, meeting in private with official sanction, passed resolutions calling for the full range of civil liberties and a national legislature.[†] These demands were

---

[*] Ascher, *Revolution of 1905*, i. 171–2. The drama is the subject of one of Sergey Eisenstein's most famous films (1925).

[†] The majority wanted a parliament with power to control the executive, but a minority under Shipov would agree only to a *consultative* assembly. This divergence, which replicated that between westernizers and Slavophils in the 1840s, was papered over for a time but led to the formation of two distinct liberal parties, the Constitutional Democrats ('Kadets') and the more moderate Union of 17 October ('Octobrists') a year later.

widely endorsed at a series of banquets which mobilized educated opinion in the provinces on behalf of peace and radical reform.

Even after 'Bloody Sunday' there was still room for compromise between the liberals and government ministers, who were as usual divided. The key player here was Nicholas II. Determined to preserve his autocratic prerogatives, and misjudging the public's mood, he vacillated. On 18 February he consented to 'the participation of worthy men enjoying the people's confidence in the preliminary elaboration and discussion of legislative proposals', but simultaneously issued a manifesto denouncing 'ill-intentioned leaders who . . . seek to create a new government based on principles alien to Our Fatherland'. The public remained unimpressed, the more so since there were now in effect two interior ministers, A. I. Bulygin and D. F. Trepov, each identified with one of the two contradictory policies.

Zemstvo and municipal deputies held further congresses; academics, doctors, and other professionals formed associations which merged into a left-leaning League of Unions led by the historian Milyukov. Liberal lawyers drafted a constitution. Published in July 1905, it provided for the rule of law, civil liberties, and a parliament elected by universal, equal, direct, and secret male suffrage (the so-called 'four-tail' formula) – then still a radical idea even in the West. Had this draft been adopted, Russia would have become a monarchy on the way to a democratic *Rechtsstaat*. But instead, after earnest deliberations, details of which leaked to the opposition, the tsar approved the so-called 'Bulygin Constitution' (6 August). This provided for a legislature, the State Duma, elected on a socially restrictive and *indirect* suffrage; workers, for instance, would have no vote at all. Liberals disapproved, but most of them were willing to participate in elections to such a body while continuing to press for further concessions.

These elections were destined not to be held. In September labour unrest intensified. A strike by printers in the two capitals was followed by one of railwaymen. Both groups had built up relatively strong, militant organizations which were autonomous but under radical (especially Menshevik) influence. Meanwhile students had voted to throw open the universities to the public after lectures ended. This move was tacitly tolerated by Trepov, the tsar's chief confidant, who hoped it would let the masses blow off steam. But the reverse happened: the halls of academe resounded to revolutionary rhetoric and the socialists acquired an ideal propaganda forum. By mid October the strike movement on the railways had developed an unstoppable dynamic and the empire's communications system ground to a halt. Work ceased in most factories and the League of Unions brought out the professionals. It was Europe's first general strike.

For five days the strike movement made it virtually impossible for the tsar and his advisers to leave Peterhof, outside the capital. At last, realizing the gravity of the situation, Nicholas turned to Witte, who had regained stature by his role in the peace negotiations. He told the ruler that he had two options: either to yield or to install a dictator. When asked to take on the latter job, Grand Duke Nicholas, the tsar's uncle, is said to have gone with a revolver to urge his nephew to accept Witte's other proposal. Whether for this or other reasons, the tsar assented, and 17 October saw publication of his historic 'October Manifesto'.* This looked like surrender in distress.

Nicholas . . . had finally consented to a 'constitution' against his better judgement and with immense pain. Though his attitudes had not necessarily changed, his own isolation, public clamour, and the panic of his entourage had ruled out any other path. Everyone had abandoned him . . . [Nicholas] comes across as a passive object enveloped by formless chaos, carried along by an unfathomable fate.†

Once order had been restored, he would try to take back what he had granted so unwillingly, and to rid himself of Witte as well.

The premier's position was unenviable. Despised and hated by the right, he was distrusted even more deeply by the opposition. The liberals insisted that the government be purged of reactionaries, as an earnest of its proclaimed good intentions. But this Witte could not grant. Instead he made a point of giving the key job of interior minister to a particularly unsavoury character, P. N. Durnovo. This frustrated all efforts to bring about a *rapprochement* with 'society'. Real authority

---

* This instructed the government to implement 'Our inflexible will' to (i) grant 'the unshakeable foundations of civil liberty'; (ii) extend the franchise to those classes currently excluded; and (iii) 'establish as an immutable rule that no law can take effect without the State Duma's approval'. Simultaneously Witte was appointed *de facto* prime minister (chairman of the *Council* of Ministers, a new post) as head of a united government, which implied acceptance of the principle of cabinet responsibility.

† Verner, *Crisis of Russian Autocracy*, pp. 241–2.

lay with Trepov and other backstairs advisers of the monarch, who set about suppressing revolutionary unrest with a veritable 'White terror'.

What contemporaries called the 'days of liberty' were stained with blood. The signals were mixed. On the one hand the air was thick with threats and violence: pogroms and 'patriotic' demonstrations by the right, political strikes by the left. Censorship, on the other hand, all but vanished and press organs mushroomed, some of them preaching 'permanent revolution'. Radical *émigré* leaders returned from abroad; political prisoners were released. The Kadets, now established as a political party, and the socialists held mass meetings while policemen watched in embarrassment, biding their time.

The socialists' chief bastion was the St Petersburg soviet of workers' deputies. Some 500 strong, it owed its origin to Mensheviks and non-party radical intellectuals, who dominated its thirty-one-man executive committee. A leading role was played by Lev Trotsky, at that time formally a Menshevik. The local Bolsheviks at first took a reserved attitude, afraid that the body might escape party controls; only later did Lenin publicly advance the notion that soviets might serve as nuclei of a provisional revolutionary government. In practice Social Democrats of both factions, impelled forward by the rush of events, threw Marxist theory to the winds and cooperated as best they could.* In November the soviet leadership called a political strike. This antagonized employers and the middle classes generally, who now veered to the right. The government recovered its nerve and arrested the soviet's nominal head. Its other leaders responded by calling on people to withdraw all their savings, which they hoped would bring down the regime. However, the move fell flat and on 3 December the entire soviet was taken into police custody. The next step was to launch armed uprisings, although little sustained effort had been made to obtain weapons or to train urban guerrillas. In Moscow 1,000 or so

---

* Plekhanov apart, their leaders now held that the two phases of revolution (see page 217) were being telescoped and that events in Russia could ignite a Europe-wide socialist upheaval. Mensheviks tried to set up local centers of revolutionary power, while Bolsheviks strove to seize power at the centre, if possible by armed insurrection, and to form what Lenin called a 'revolutionary democratic dictatorship of the proletariat and peasantry' – as distinct from a proletarian dictatorship pure and simple, as advocated by Trotsky; in practice this meant a Bolshevik-led socialist coalition. These doctrinal subtleties would assume importance in Communist ideological polemics in later years.

partisans ('militiamen') manned barricades in the streets, but within days loyal troops with artillery had shelled them into submission. There was much damage to property and about 1,000 people, mostly non-combatants, were killed.

This was the first popular uprising in the Russian heartland since the seventeenth century. The 'forces of order' employed archaic methods of reprisal. 'Punitive expeditions' set out from either end of the Trans-Siberian railway. Suspects were arraigned before drumhead tribunals or shot out of hand. Similar methods were applied in the Baltic and Caucasus. Villages were burned down and atrocities perpetrated. Altogether at least 20,000 men and women, perhaps more, were sentenced to gaol and exile. Though effective in the short term, such violent repression doomed the chance, already slight, of reconciliation between government and public. This augured badly for Russia's first experiment in constitutional rule.

CONSTITUTIONAL POLITICS AND THE STOLYPIN REFORM

Having regained the initiative, the cabinet nominally headed by Witte and the tsar's courtiers could dictate the rules of the parliamentary game. On 20 February 1906 an imperial decree announced that the State Council, reformed so as to comprise as many elected as appointed members, was to constitute an 'upper house' of the legislature; the agreement of both chambers was required before bills could be submitted for imperial assent. By issuing a decree on his 'supreme Autocratic authority' Nicholas made it clear that he did not consider himself bound by the terms of the October Manifesto. (He would accept only that his autocratic power was no longer 'unlimited'.) Budgetary rules deprived the legislature of jurisdiction over one third of national expenditure, including the court and armed forces. Deputies could question ministers, but they had thirty days in which to reply. They remained responsible to the emperor. Since they continued to report to him individually, the Council of Ministers was not a true cabinet; the premier's authority depended on his imperial master's whim. While the Duma was not in session, emergency legislation could be passed under Article 87 of the revised Fundamental Laws (which could be amended only on the Crown's initiative); although the assembly had to approve any such measures when it met, this provision opened the way to abuse. The suffrage now admitted certain groups of industrial workers but was not general. The complicated system of indirect, multiple-stage voting in separate electoral assemblies (curiae) for various social groups was designed to give a privileged status to the upper classes and ethnic Russians. Paradoxically, however, it allowed a fair number of peasant representatives, as those who framed the Constitution expected them to back the government.

The elections were largely boycotted by the socialists, so that the First Duma (27 April–9 July 1906) was dominated by Kadets and other liberals committed to enlarging the assembly's powers. Its relations with the government were hostile from the start. Witte had meanwhile resigned, largely to escape constant badgering by high-placed reactionaries – but not before he had secured a vast loan from foreign bankers which enabled the regime to stay solvent for a year irrespective of the Duma's wishes. His successor, a bureaucratic nonentity, bluntly rejected the deputies' unanimous demands, put forward in an address to the throne, among them a proposed land reform that allowed the confiscation (with compensation) of landlords' estates. Behind the scenes efforts were made to bridge the gap between Duma and government, but the idea of a Kadet ministry was anathema to conservatives – as it was to most people on the left as well, where the mood was unsympathetic to what Lenin dismissed as 'constitutional illusions'. With agrarian unrest again on the rise, some radicals thought that a premature dissolution of the assembly would spark more insurrections. But this was to misjudge popular morale. When the Duma was dissolved 200 deputies travelled to the safety of Vyborg in Finland, whence they called for a nation-wide passive resistance campaign. Their appeal fell completely flat. Dissatisfaction was general, but this was no longer the time for mass protest.

Instead some extremists turned to individual acts of terror. Several hundred officials (including ordinary policemen, bank clerks, and so on) were among the victims. In August a bomb injured two daughters of the new premier, P. A. Stolypin, along with sixty-eight others (most of them petitioners) at his St Petersburg dacha; twenty-seven people lost their lives. Stolypin showed a calm courage that won him public sympathy. Unlike his predecessor he was a man of vision who wanted to make the new constitutional system work. A former provincial

governor with practical experience, he possessed statesmanlike qualities all too rare among tsarist officials. Yet even his warmest admirers
could not claim that he was unequivocally devoted to the rule of law.
He sanctioned (unwillingly, to be sure) summary trial by field court
martial of persons 'obviously suspect' of security offences. These
makeshift tribunals took no account of procedural norms, and within
eight months had put 1,144 individuals to death and sentenced 779
others to prison or exile. It is true that public order was under threat,
but

pacification achieved by such means was bound to widen the chasm between
state and society . . . Reliance on due process by the government . . . would
have gained the sympathy of large sectors of society. Equally important, it
would probably have engendered greater respect for the law . . . Lawless
conduct by the government made matters worse . . . and impeded emergence
of a genuine sense of citizenship.*

This helps to explain why the Second Duma (20 February–3 June
1907) was no more capable of constructive work than its predecessor,
whose fate it shared. Right- and left-wing extremists were more
strongly represented than before and the Kadets' moderating influence
reduced. Deputies constantly exchanged insults and had to be expelled
from the chamber. In a debate on the recruit levy a Social Democrat
member, Zurabov, incautiously declared that 'the army of autocratic
Russia always was and will be defeated'. Rightists interpreted this as
a slur on the army's honour. The police hunted for evidence to link
the SD parliamentary 'fraction' with treachery. This turned out to be
only circumstantial, but it sufficed for the government's purposes.
When the liberals rejected a peremptory demand to lift their SD
colleagues' immunity, dissolution followed. This time it was accompanied by a major revision of the electoral law which amounted to
a virtual *coup d'état*. The representation of the lower classes and
non-Russians was drastically cut back in an all too obvious attempt to
obtain an assembly that would cooperate docilely on the government's
terms. The 'first Russian revolution' was definitely over.

Behind all the political sparring loomed the problem of agrarian
reform. Already before 1905 prescient ministers, Witte among them,

* Ascher, *The Revolution of 1905* ii, p. 249.

had realized that radical measures were needed to give peasants a greater personal stake in their land. The subsequent unrest showed only too clearly that communal ownership, far from upholding order in the countryside as officials had complacently assumed since the 1860s, actually perpetuated egalitarian sentiment and provided revolutionaries with ample combustible material. Most peasants, especially in the empire's Russian heartland, took the view that land, like air, was 'God's' or 'no one's', and that it was therefore wicked for it to be appropriated privately, at least by those who did not work it with their own or their family's labour. Ideally, the great estates should be expropriated and their assets distributed among 'toilers' according to their needs, as determined by the communal authorities in the time-honoured way. As we have seen, this concept, renamed 'socialization', was picked up by the SRs and accounted for that party's successful agitation in the countryside. Liberals, too, were not immune to its appeal, although most of them thought that owners should receive compensation (at a 'fair' price, i.e. below market value). They realized that rural poverty had deeper causes and could not be alleviated by property redistribution alone; technical improvements, better credit facilities, and rural education were needed as well. But few democrats questioned the merits of communal institutions or practices so long as these were what peasants themselves seemed to want.

But precisely the repartitional commune was the principal target of Stolypin's ambitious programme of agrarian reform. He made no secret of its political objective: to create a class of property-owning yeomen farmers that, as in the West, would be a bulwark of stability, replacing the landowning squires in those areas where they were in decline and reinforcing their power wherever they were not. He sought to encourage the development of a civic spirit among the rural population. All but a shiftless few, so the reasoning went, stood to gain from the accrued wealth that would come from the application of modern farming methods by self-reliant individual proprietors. Ultimately Stolypin aimed to transform peasant psychology and so to strengthen the entire realm: 'We must raise up our impoverished, weak, exhausted land, since the land is the pledge of our future strength, the land *is* Russia.'

Convinced that his policy alone was correct, the premier introduced it while the Duma was in recess by resorting to Article 87, in clear breach of its purpose. A decree of 9 November 1906 gave every peasant

239

family head the right to claim as his own property his due share of allotment land, whether the communal assembly approved or not. If he secured an affirmative two-thirds vote (from 1910, a majority), he could also consolidate his scattered strips into a single plot. Official surveyors and other experts were sent to help reallocate the land in each village – the first time government administrators had reached down to that level. The separation process was supposed to be voluntary, but in practice was often effected under duress, particularly after 1910 when the land in all communes that had not experienced a general redistribution since Emancipation (about one third of the total) was transferred to individual ownership. Simultaneously other measures were taken to encourage migration eastwards, expand rural credit, and remove peasants' legal disabilities.

All this was done from above, in the paternalistic tradition of the Russian state and in the face of opposition from the intelligentsia. Not surprisingly, it encountered a patchy response among its potential beneficiaries. In evaluating the Stolypin reform, one must appreciate that its chief architect thought it needed twenty years of peace to succeed, whereas a bare three years lay between the reform's final legislative act (1911) and the outbreak of the First World War. (And already in 1911 Stolypin himself succumbed to an assassin's bullet.) It was most successful in those regions, especially in the west and south-east, where peasant communes were of the non-repartitional type or there was plenty of land available for the newly separated farmers. In the overpopulated centre it proceeded more slowly and had made relatively little impact before a new revolutionary upsurge gave the rural commune its long-awaited chance (see page 277). Altogether by 1915 about 2½ million householders,* about one fifth of all those eligible, had been granted title to their property. This measured 17.8 million hectares, equivalent to 14 per cent of allotment land or 9 per cent of all peasant land. Of such householders only 1.3 million had set up independent farms, and a mere quarter of these had actually established *khutora*, i.e. homesteads in their own enclosures, on the Western pattern.

The reformers greatly underestimated the extent and cost of the

---

* This excludes the 1.7 million householders converted to individual tenure automatically under the law of 14 June 1910.

work that needed to be done (e.g. digging wells, building roads) in order to make such farms economically viable. Many farmers ran into debt or still depended for services on their communally minded neighbours. Meanwhile those forced out of the village swelled the ranks of the urban working class. Stolypin deserves credit for imagination and determination, but it could be argued that he came on the scene half a century too late: his measures ought to have formed part of the Emancipation package. But this is admittedly unhistorical reasoning, for in the 1860s the government had been poorer, more dependent on the gentry, and less development-minded. In any case individual farming would once again figure on rural Russia's agenda in the 1990s, after the socialist (or pseudo-socialist?) solution, which Stolypin castigated, had been tried and found wanting.

Although the Third Duma was custom-made to fit the government's requirements and lasted its full term (1907–12), relations between legislature and executive were often strained. Initially leadership in the assembly lay with the Octobrists, who as their name suggests sought to cooperate with Stolypin's ministry on the basis of strict adherence to the constitutional provisions of the October Manifesto. They stood in the Slavophil tradition of Shipov, and were drawn predominantly from the landowning and business world. They backed the premier's agrarian programme, his efforts to extend local self-government, and even his chauvinistic measures against the Finns, who had won a measure of autonomy during the revolutionary upheaval.* But they could not stomach the administration's frequent breaches of legality – the harassment, for example, of religious dissidents and innocuous trade unionists.

In particular the Octobrists stood for an effective reform of the antiquated military and naval establishment so that the armed forces might be better equipped, technically and morally, to face the looming conflict with the Central Powers than they had been in the Far East. But this was to infringe on the tsar's prerogative, or so at least Nicholas

---

* The Finnish Diet had an SD majority and the kingdom's legal status was helpful to Russian revolutionaries on the run. In Poland the elections benefited R. Dmowski's National Democrats, who allied with the Kadets, rather than the strongly anti-Russian PPS. The Duma also had a few representatives of Muslim and other national-minority groups.

thought. In 1909 he provoked a crisis by angrily returning to the Duma a bill *increasing* naval appropriations because the assembly, merely by debating the matter, had exceeded its powers.

This friction undermined Stolypin's parliamentary support. In 1910 the premier turned away from the Octobrists to the right-wing Russian Nationalist party, which had been created the previous year. This was based on the Russian gentry lobby in the south-western provinces. As a special-interest group it was a less effective prop for Stolypin and ultimately helped to bring about his fall.

This occurred over a government bill to introduce zemstvos in the western provinces (March 1911), which the Nationalists endorsed as a weapon against the Polish gentry, whom they suspected of disloyalty, and other ethnic groups in the region. But the scheme backfired. The bill was defeated in the State Council by rightists who stood for aristocratic solidarity. Stolypin secured the tsar's consent to a highly unparliamentary move. Suspending the council for three days, he pushed the measure through under Article 87.

He had grown weary of the reactionaries' attacks . . . An exasperated man unaccustomed to . . . being thwarted, Stolypin appeared to be committing suicide . . . [He] clearly underestimated the intensity of the reaction to his decision. He had won a victory of sorts, but criticism in the capital was nearly universal . . . The most dramatic result of Stolypin's move was the near-complete evaporation of support for him in the Duma.*

The tsar, too, was displeased, and a few months later, when Stolypin was assassinated (by a double agent working for the revolutionaries and the police), his imperial master showed signs of relief. Of limited intellect himself, Nicholas could be really content only when served by men of mediocre talent.

One such was the next premier, Kokovtsov. His expertise lay in finance, and he was even less able than Stolypin to withstand intrigue by reactionaries at court. His tenure of power was marked mainly by scandals. One of these involved a charge of ritual murder against a Jewish clerk in Kiev, M. Beilis, which the justice minister insisted on pressing even though an investigation had established that the victim, a Christian boy, had been killed by thieves. It was a Russian counterpart

* Edelman, *Gentry Politics*, pp. 121–3.

to the Dreyfus case. Beilis's trial (1913) ended in an acquittal, to the undisguised relief of the public and the discredit of the government. Another scandal, which would have serious repercussions later, was linked to Gregory Rasputin. A licentious 'holy man' (*starets*) from Siberia, he acquired influence at court through his uncanny ability to ease the pains endured by the heir to the throne, the tsarevich Alexis, who was a haemophiliac. Rasputin also won backing from certain unscrupulous prelates of the Church, which brought that institution, too, into disrepute. Altogether it seemed by early 1914 as if the tsarist government's authority was crumbling. The constitutional order* established so reluctantly in 1905 stood on shaky foundations. Respect for the rule of law was certainly growing among officials and the public, but it remained far weaker than anywhere in the West (even in Wilhelminian Germany). Its most vocal critics were to be found on the right.

In 1905 conservative monarchists had set up political organizations to fight 'anarchy'. The most important of these groups was the physician A. I. Dubrovin's Union of the Russian People, whose message won support among lower-class tradespeople (shopkeepers, artisans) as well as from some workers and peasants. By 1907 the URP had an estimated 200,000 to 300,000 members.

Like other rightist organizations, the URP was not essentially an intellectual movement. Nor did its strength depend on the rationality of its programme or on a systematic philosophy. Often it simply used popular slogans – 'for tsar, faith and fatherland' was a favourite ... The Union believed that because of personal shortcomings Nicholas had disastrously compromised his calling ... [It] also emphasized the unity of the people themselves. This notion took on a distinctly chauvinistic meaning when applied to Russia's multi-national empire ... Relentlessly deploring ethnic particularism, the Union never conceded that the minority nationalities, like the Russians, might have valid aspirations of their own.†

URP and other right-wing extremists helped to instigate pogroms

---

* The appellation 'quasi-constitutional' given it at the time by Max Weber has stuck, but from a juridical viewpoint is incorrect, for the tsar's power *was* constitutionally limited, even though he refused to recognize the fact.
† Rawson, *Russian Rightists*, pp. 65–8.

and arranged the assassination of prominent Jewish politicians. Their outlook had racist features and may be termed proto-fascist, but they were held back from advocating dictatorship by their monarchist and religious convictions. The tsar sympathized with the URP and in 1906, when asked by the entire Council of Ministers to sanction a reduction of Jewish disabilities, replied that an 'inner voice' prevented him from doing so. In the Third Duma the far right had forty-nine seats (11 per cent of the total), but it was their hidden connections at court, in the Church, and in officialdom that made them dangerous.

Meanwhile, on the left wing of the political spectrum, the revolutionaries were in retreat. Their organizations were broken up and their leaders forced back into emigration. Party membership evaporated. The SRs were seriously discredited by the disclosure in 1909 that one of their principal terrorist organizers, Yevno Azef, had been a police spy (since 1893!). A minority advocated giving up illegal activities, but Chernov clung to the old tactics. Both they and their SD rivals were afflicted by factional schism. An effort to reunite the RSDRP in 1906 produced only superficial and temporary agreement. Even the Bolsheviks were split several ways. Lenin's supporters faced opposition from a 'leftist' (syndicalist) group under A. A. Bogdanov and A. V. Lunacharsky which developed its own religio-philosophical credo sometimes known as 'God-building'.

The notion of religion as collectivist self-sacrifice was widespread after 1905 and represented a powerful current of thought among the Bolsheviks. For Lenin, such thinking led ultimately to idealism, fideism and other 'swamps' of heretical deviation. But for Lunacharsky they became fused with a new vision of collectivism that combined syndicalist politics with a socialist religion of the future.*

This would lead *inter alia* to the Lenin cult in Josef Stalin's Russia.

The future dictator was already winning a name for himself by organizing bandit raids, euphemistically termed 'expropriations', to obtain money for the party's depleted funds. This drift to criminality, which Lenin approved of, alarmed some respectable socialists, such as Martov, who in 1911 published a pamphlet exposing the seamy side

* Williams, *The Other Bolsheviks*, p. 99.

of the Bolsheviks' clandestine activities. It caused a sensation, but the Menshevik leader was unable to turn his moral victory to political account. Ever anxious to achieve party unity, he and his comrades compromised. Subjected to a propaganda barrage as alleged 'liquidators' of the party's revolutionary tradition, the Mensheviks were eased out of the trade unions, pension funds, and other working-class bodies, most of which they had founded, by their Bolshevik rivals.

In 1912 a massacre of striking workers in the Lena goldfields led to a renewed upsurge of activism which the Bolsheviks were best placed to bring under their control. Lenin moved to Austrian Galicia, where he could influence events across the border. He focused his attention on 'legal' (i.e. officially tolerated) labour organizations and his daily newspaper *Pravda*, which the censors permitted to appear in St Petersburg. Earlier that year the RSDRP had been virtually taken over in a *coup* by the Bolsheviks, who threw out their critics, changed the rules, and chose new central bodies prepared to obey them. Though few realized it at the time, the scene was being set for their victory in October 1917.

CULTURAL EFFLORESCENCE

The thirty years after 1850 were the great age of the Russian, indeed European, novel. Ivan Turgenev constructed delicate portraits of cultivated men (and especially women) in the grip of emotional distress. The most 'Western' of Russian writers, his works were even more popular abroad than at home, where radical critics lamented his ambivalence on current political controversies. Leo Tolstoy gave realism a deeper meaning by his rich, multi-faceted depiction of Russian society during the Napoleonic era (*War and Peace*, 1869) and later in *Anna Karenina* (1877). The characters he created are as lifelike today as when he wrote. In the former novel Platon Karatayev, a simple peasant, incarnates the wisdom of the common folk. Though far more than an ideologue, Tolstoy shared the widespread belief among educated Russians that the *muzhik*, spared the debilitating effects of civilization, could act as a regenerating force.

Fedor Dostoyevsky, too, had a strong sense of Russia's world mission. In his *Writer's Diary* he predicted the West's imminent collapse in social conflict, whose 'destructive waves will break on Russia's shores'. Rather more prescient was his prophecy that revolutionary materialism would lead to totalitarian tyranny. In *The Brothers Karamazov* (1880) the figure of the Grand Inquisitor, a power-loving ecclesiastic who would crucify Christ again on His return lest He subvert the established order, is counterposed to that of the saintly *starets* Zosima. Dostoyevsky's characters, exceptional men in extreme situations who wrestle with existential problems, transcend reality and seemed overdrawn to literal-minded critics of his day. But he had no equal in plumbing the depths of the human soul; 'he understood better than most the psychology of poverty, humiliation, resentment, jealousy, cynicism and cruelty' (V. Terras). Even villains were drawn with such empathy that some readers were confused as to where the author stood. Dostoyevsky, for all his philosophical profundity, was a literary artist with an unsurpassed ability to represent ordinary people leading mundane lives and facing run-of-the-mill situations.

He died in 1881, Turgenev two years later. Meanwhile Tolstoy had undergone a religious conversion that led him virtually to abandon *belles-lettres*,* along with his 'sinful' earlier privileged life, and devote himself to spreading an ethical Christianity based on his appealing (but to some theologians, naïve) reading of the New Testament. He preached the doctrine of non-resistance to evil, which he saw as embodied in the Church and state authorities; social injustice was to be overcome not by violence but by following Christ's teaching to the letter. This message was proclaimed in a stream of pamphlets and in the free schooling which Tolstoy provided for peasants on his Yasnaya Polyana estate, south of Moscow, which became a place of pilgrimage for thousands of admirers. In this way the great novelist became the conscience of Russia. The establishment perceived him as a threat to order and in 1901 he was excommunicated by the Holy Synod. The action aroused a storm of protest and gave him a martyr's crown.

Meanwhile the literary banner had passed to worthy but less significant writers such as Nicholas Leskov (1831–95), who portrayed sympathetically the hard life of rural clergy, the talented but implacable satirist M. Ye. Saltykov-Shchedrin (1826–89), or the explicitly Populist

---

* Except for *Resurrection* (1899) and several tales, notably 'The Kreuzer Sonata'.

novelist Gleb Uspensky (1843–1900), who depicted with grim realism the peasantry's fate as the power of money took hold. Here literature reflected most clearly the social concerns that so preoccupied contemporary Russian intellectuals.

Painters of the 'Wanderers'* school played their part in upholding realist values. G. V. Perov (1833–82), for instance, depicted an Easter procession of villagers lurching along a muddy road after the customary halt at an inn. The most talented of his group, whose work at its best bears comparison with that of the French Impressionists, was Ilya Repin (1844–1930). His *Volga Boatmen* (1870) seemed to contemporaries to symbolize the oppressed people in their entirety. He executed some remarkable historical canvases, notably of Ivan the Terrible, aghast at having killed his son and heir, or the Zaporozhian Cossacks responding merrily to a harsh decree from the Turkish sultan (1891). Less flamboyant in his choice of colours was Vasiliy Surikov, who likewise depicted outstanding moments in Russia's past, such as Peter I's execution of the *streltsy*. Though never a 'Wanderer', Vasiliy Vereshchagin (1842–1904) was an expressly political painter whose work focused on the horrors of war – of which he himself became a victim when his battleship was sunk in action by the Japanese.

Meanwhile the world of Russian music was at first dominated by the 'Mighty Five'.† 'Aspiring to create works of profound content that expressed truthfully the thoughts of their contemporaries, they stressed the national and popular character of art and drew on folklore and folksong in developing their style' (C. de Grunwald). They won the support of the influential critic V. V. Stasov and of music-loving patrons at the imperial court. A Romanov grand duke was largely responsible for founding the St Petersburg Conservatoire (1863), whose first director was the world-famous pianist and composer Anton Rubinstein; his brother Nicholas soon afterwards assumed a similar function in Moscow. Mussorgsky was to Russian music what Wagner was to German. The themes of his two greatest operas, *Boris Godunov* and *Khovanshchina*, were drawn from seventeenth-century history. Their merit was insufficiently appreciated at the time, and it was only in

---

* Or better, Itinerants: the name given to those who in 1863 broke with the official Academy of Fine Arts and travelled around the country exhibiting their works.
† M. Balakyrev, C. Cui, M. Mussorgsky, N. Rimsky-Korsakov, A. Borodin.

subsequent versions by his friend Rimsky-Korsakov (1844–1908) that they acquired international renown. The younger composer wrote no fewer than fifteen operas of his own, most of them based on folk legends – *The Snow Maiden* (1882) and *The Golden Cockerel* (1908) are the best known – as well as many symphonic works. Peter Chaykovsky (Tchaikovski, 1840–93: he was a victim of the cholera epidemic that year) stood some way apart from his contemporaries and his music may be seen as more Western – or, one should rather say, more universal.

A culture that could produce so many gifted artists could scarcely be described as in the doldrums, yet that is what many contemporaries thought as the nineteenth century drew to a close. It was refreshed by two major developments. The first was the dramatic talent of Anton Chekhov, the second the lively response of Russian intellectuals to French Symbolism. This latter trend manifested itself initially in poetry but then encompassed all the arts.

The Russian stage had always striven for a sincere naturalism that contrasted with the artificial, melodramatic quality of much Western theatre. In 1882 the imperial authorities abandoned their monopoly over theatrical representations in the two cities. Whatever the motive (it may have been an attempt to divert people from politics), it encouraged private entrepreneurial activity which exercised a beneficial effect, as did the impact of foreign touring companies.

Trained as a doctor, Chekhov (1860–1904) was a humanitarian as well as a gifted writer of short stories and plays.

When a cholera epidemic threatened, he organized a campaign of preventive medicine. He induced wealthy citizens to build clinics . . . and the epidemic was averted in his area . . . He spent a year inspecting the penal colony on Sakhalin Island [and] on his return published a lengthy report which called for prison reforms. A more humane administration on Sakhalin resulted from his trip . . . Everywhere he went he planted trees. His goal was to make all of Russia a beautiful garden.*

The Seagull (*Chayka*, 1895) avoids direct treatment of social and moral problems, but their presence is implicit in the conditions in which the

---

* C.W. Meister, *Chekhov Criticism: 1880 through 1986*, Jefferson N C – London, 1988, p. 5.

action occurs, in the play's *mood*. The characters interact in a subtle way, sometimes seeming to talk past each other; there are moments of silence and little action in the accepted sense. Superficially, we witness the unhappy romances of Nina, a young actress, whose family seem bored with life on their country estate. But critics have discerned in the play elements of Greek tragedy, called it 'an inverted *Hamlet*', and acclaimed its truthful, compassionate understanding of the frailties of human nature. Once audiences learned to appreciate the novelty of Chekhov's dramatic technique, the play was a commercial success, notably at the Moscow Art Theatre.

This institution, founded in 1898 by Konstantin Stanislavsky and Vladimir Nemirovich-Danchenko,* also put on Chekhov's later master-pieces (*Uncle Vanya, Three Sisters, The Cherry Orchard*). These depicted the same milieu, a world of alienated individuals, overwhelmed by their frustrations, which they often vented in near-hysterical fashion. Chekhov himself believed in a better future for Russia but was neither a rebel nor an apostle of a return to religious values; indeed, he was rare among his contemporaries in that he refrained from preaching. Instead he reflected with sympathetic humour on the predicament and foibles of his fellow-men. The atmosphere of his dramatic works is redolent of a sense of foreboding that one also finds, expressed more philosophically, in Tolstoy and Dostoyevsky. Into the mouth of a character in *Three Sisters* he puts the words:

The time has come, an avalanche is moving down on us, a mighty, wholesome storm is brewing, which is approaching, is already near, and soon will sweep away from our society its idleness, indifference, prejudice against work, and foul *ennui*. I shall work, and in some twenty-five or thirty years everyone will work too.

This sentiment, not peculiar to Russia, expressed the apocalyptic mood of intellectuals all over *fin-de-siècle* Europe. Thinkers like Nietzsche and Sorel were suggesting that the old values were moribund, that forces of unreason and violence were struggling to the surface. In the tsarist empire the regime's repressive policies may have made critical minds especially susceptible to gloomy prognoses about the future course of events.

---

* It became world famous as the source of the 'Stanislavsky school' of natural acting.

Nietzsche was one of those, along with Baudelaire and the French 'decadents', who stood at the cradle of the Russian Symbolist movement, which soon developed along autonomous lines. The aspiring young poets D. S. Merezhkovsky (1865–1941) and his wife Zinaida Hippius reacted against the *civisme* and materialism hitherto so prominent in Russian *belles-lettres*, emphasizing instead the subjective traits of the individual, his or her emotions and ideals. They felt that critics and the general public lacked aesthetic judgement and set out to improve the quality of poetic diction which (as Goethe had said) should above all be symbolic rather than naturalistic. Hippius (1869–1945), who was the better artist, dealt with death and religious themes in her verse: 'I'm dying in insane sadness / Alas, I'm dying. / I'm striving for something I know not, / I know not what.' The world offered only 'false promises', yet the miracle of divine salvation gave life meaning ('Song', 1893). Her husband at first struck a less overtly Christian note, finding much to admire in Nietzsche and pagan antiquity.

Though scorned by intellectuals of realist persuasion, the Symbolists made headway in the 1890s, recruiting to their camp a galaxy of poets who would attain distinction later: Fedor Sologub, Konstantin Balmont, Valeriy Bryusov, and then Alexander Blok, Vyacheslav Ivanov, and Andrey Beliy. By the turn of the century their influence had extended to the visual arts and to religious philosophy. In 1898 Sergey Dyagilev (Diaghilev, 1872–1929), who would become famous as the organizer of the Ballets Russes, founded the journal *The World of Art* (*Mir iskusstva*), which was subsidized initially by private patrons, such as the Moscow merchant Savva Mamontov, and later from the tsar's personal funds. One of the editors was Alexandre Benois, another avid collector as well as an art critic. The group organized a succession of influential exhibitions. The journal's main idea was expressed in the phrase, 'Art is free, life is fettered.'

They sought freedom from the influence of the accepted realistic painters, avoided social and political commentary in their art work, and often focused most of their attention on the 'how' of art rather than the 'what'. Their tastes were eclectic and revealed equal support for Russian national art as well as foreign, especially French, styles.*

---

* Peterson, *History of Russian Symbolism*, p. 39.

Another forum of debate was a series of 'religious-philosophical meetings' held in St Petersburg from late 1901 onward. Characteristically, the initiative was taken by interested laymen rather than by the Church hierarchs, who looked on the venture with misgiving and got the meetings banned in 1903. The lack of an adequate institutional base would doom the whole enterprise of religious reform, with catastrophic results for Russia. It was indicative that the nineteenth century's leading Orthodox philosopher, Vladimir Solovyov (1853–1900), had likewise not been an ecclesiastic.* When, in 1905, Church reform came on the agenda, the reformist clergy split between moderates, who wanted to revive the patriarchate as a counterweight to the secular power, and liberals who sought a broader devolution of authority and other changes designed to open up the Church to the modern world and equip it morally to face the challenge of atheistic materialism. The schism benefited the minority reactionary faction, with which the tsar sympathized, and so all reform efforts were thwarted so long as the old regime existed.

While secular ideas made headway among the mass of believers, writers and artists evinced interest in matters of the spirit. Merezhkovsky represented Peter I as Antichrist in a novel of that title (1904). Publication of a volume of essays entitled *Signposts* (*Vyekhi*, 1909) unleashed a storm. Its contributors (Struve, Frank, Berdyaev, Bulgakov) called on intellectuals to forsake their shallow positivism and embrace religious values, 'the basic prerequisite for any consistent philosophy of life'. One of the most telling charges was that Russia's intelligentsia lacked respect for the law and a spirit of compromise; other critics pointed to their low level of cultural and philosophical awareness. Since the writers were liberal Kadets (and mostly ex-Social Democrats!), they laid themselves open to the accusation of having soiled their own nest. This was a superficial view, although it must be admitted that the *Vyekhi* group were better at raising questions than providing answers.

---

* His name is associated chiefly with the concepts of 'God-manhood' and 'divine wisdom', which he set forth mainly before the rise of the Symbolists, who, however, appreciated his significance. The first Russian philosopher to develop a comprehensive system, he opposed national chauvinism and advocated closer relations with the Roman Catholics, as a step towards fulfilment of his essentially humanistic vision of universal harmony.

Meanwhile Symbolist notions were propagated in a variety of small-circulation journals, such as *Vesy* (*The Scales*, 1904–9), *The Golden Fleece* (1906–9), and *Apollo* (1909–17) as well as in earnest discussions at Ivanov's St Petersburg apartment, nicknamed 'The Tower'. The most significant work was Beliy's novel *Petersburg* (1913–14), which spoke – like Joyce of Dublin – of the Russian capital's 'ominous unreality'. But as the movement expanded it began to disintegrate. In 1910 a controversy between Ivanov and Bryusov over its true nature brought about its eclipse.

Its intellectual heritage was carried on by the Acmeists, among whom were two gifted poets, Anna Akhmatova (1889–1966) and Osip Mandelshtam (1891–1938); they would achieve martyr status in the Soviet era. Three other young poets who likewise suffered a chequered fate after 1917 – Velimir Khlebnikov (1885–1922), Vladimir Mayakovsky (1893–1930), and Boris Pasternak (1890–1960) – were adherents of another post-Symbolist group, the Futurists. Following current fashion, the latter announced their existence in a bombastic manifesto, headed *A Slap in the Face of Public Taste*, in which they held up to execration not only the classics ('Pushkin, Tolstoy, etc.', as they called them derogatorily) but also several modernist colleagues. A few years later anyone who scorned convention so irresponsibly would risk life and limb.

This was the age of the avant-garde: painters who broke away from the conventions of representational art, drawing their inspiration from

the folk imagery of the *lubok* (peasant woodcut), primitive icons, children's drawings and even graffiti . . . Goncharova exhibited coarse peasant scenes in deep colours with abrupt shapes that ignored perspective. In his series of *Hair-dressers* (1907–9) and *Soldiers* Larionov showed works that were frankly barbaric. The colours were crude and hastily applied, figures and objects were over-simplified, distorted and quite out of scale; inscriptions were scribbled and even made to come out of people's mouths as in certain medieval paintings. Such work was later dubbed Neo-primitivism.*

Rayonism was another term used of Larionov's later work, while the schools of Expressionism, Cubo-Futurism, and Suprematism were

---

* S. Faucherau, *Moscow, 1900–1930*, Fribourg – New York, 1988, p. 61. The reference is to Natalya Goncharova (1881–1964) and her husband Mikhail Larionov (1881–1962).

associated respectively with Marc Chagall, Kazimir Malevich, and Vladimir Tatlin. Stage and costume design were revolutionized by Benois and Leon Bakst, most notably for productions of the Ballets Russes, which took Paris by storm in 1909. By then Moscow had become an artistic centre rivalling Paris, its rise assisted by the opening to the public of the great collections of contemporary French and Russian art assembled by such connoisseurs as Sergey Shchukin or the Morozov brothers.

The Silver Age of Russian art and letters, so termed by analogy with the Golden Age of Pushkin, was rich in diversity. But precisely this quality aroused antagonism among people of more conventional views, not just in the upper classes but also among ordinary people who, having acquired a basic education, were developing cultural interests. In so far as they were aware of modernist trends, they found them incomprehensible and even abhorrent. Instinctively they were more attracted by the notion (as yet implicit) that all cultural artefacts should be disciplined in the service of a single Great Idea (see page 386). At this time commercial publishers were flooding the market with cheap books and pamphlets, some just for entertainment but others of an 'improving' religious-moralistic or patriotic flavour. In 1913 alone the best-known firm, Sytin, put out 3.8 million copies of items devoted to the Romanov dynasty's three hundredth anniversary.

Many ordinary people were able to receive and exchange information through the printed word for the first time . . . Reading about fanciful characters and situations was a crude but simple way of acquiring useful ideas and symbols. The treatment of themes such as national identity, science and superstition, success and mobility, and crime and rebellion answered popular demand . . . Popular communication through the printed word facilitated the cumulative build-up of rebellious ideas and the spread of disaffection.*

There were obvious dangers here. Yet one should not lose sight of the positive effects of the concerts, plays, and lectures that were put on in workmen's clubs ('people's houses'), which had been established on private initiative in many cities. These functions were well attended. In summer ordinary folk went on organized excursions to the country. Sporting events acquired a rapidly growing audience, as did the cinema.

* Brooks, *When Russia Learned to Read*, pp. 353–4.

In 1908 Russia produced 6 films; by 1913 the number had soared to 116. Some of them were adaptations of literary masterpieces, others documentaries or farces. Even for working people life was not uniformly grey.

THE COMING OF THE WAR

Defeat in the Far East obliged Russia to seek compensation in the Balkans and at the Turkish Straits. But expansion in this quarter was more likely than ever to antagonize Austria-Hungary, nervous about the cohesion of her own domains and able to call for support on her powerful German ally. Policy makers in St Petersburg thought that they could contain this threat, not least because they had the (albeit reluctant) backing of France and, from 1907, Britain as well. None of the Entente powers sought a general war, but each was willing to run high risks in order to uphold its supposed vital national interests.

Russia's basic aim was to maintain the delicate balance of power between the two rival blocs, but she no longer had the military or economic strength to arbitrate in European affairs. Stolypin recognized the objective constraints on her freedom of action, but some other political and military leaders were less circumspect and a vocal section of the public was stridently nationalistic. Foreign policy was still poorly coordinated, despite the powers assigned to the new Council of Ministers, and Nicholas was no more able to impose his will in this sphere than he was in domestic affairs. He was prone to accept the overconfident assessments of Russia's strength offered by the armed services chiefs. Like their counterparts elsewhere, they assumed that a future war would be of brief duration and limited to a single theatre. More especially, the problem of mobilizing the army's vast manpower reserves, given the empire's inadequate communications, compelled military planners to adhere to a rigid timetable. This hindered the diplomats from responding flexibly when the balloon went up in 1914. Four years earlier some experts had proposed that, in the event of hostilities with the Central Powers, the exposed Polish salient should be abandoned as a costly liability. Unwisely, the idea was ruled out as politically inopportune. Instead a programme was launched to build strategic railways and fortresses in Russian Poland. This was costly – and counterproductive, since the lines could be used by a victorious enemy. Similarly, the impressive naval construction programme could bring little advantage to Russia unless she controlled both the Baltic and Black Seas, which was a doubtful prospect.

At least the strategists did not need to worry much about the security of Russia's Asian domains. *Rapprochement* with Japan was facilitated by mutual concern at intervention by other powers in the affairs of northern China. A convention of 1907 divided Manchuria into two spheres of influence. Later Russia raised no objection when Japan annexed Korea, while she herself fostered Mongolian 'autonomy' and increased her influence in Xingjiang (Sinkiang), China's westernmost province. This classically imperialist accommodation helped to settle differences with Japan's ally, Britain. An Anglo-Russian convention (1907), encouraged by the French, defined the two powers' relations in three disputed areas. In Tibet they acknowledged Chinese sovereignty and undertook not to intervene; Afghanistan was recognized as falling within the British sphere; and Persia (Iran) was carved into three zones. This did not put an end to the signatories' rivalry here, for the British, who got the southern oilfields, wanted more, and the Russians in the north tried to control the government in Tehran. They introduced a small military force, which touched off a nationalist revolt in 1909.

Anglo-Russian tension also continued over the Ottoman Empire. Britain would offer only a vague promise to support Russian ambitions at the Straits, while Russia suspected that the British (and Germans) were backing the Turks in promoting disaffection ('pan-Turkism') among her Muslim subjects. The 'Young Turk' revolution of July 1908 upset the Great Powers' calculations. It was welcomed by the Russian public, but official St Petersburg was worried at the prospect of instability in the Balkans, where the independent Christian states could be expected to challenge a weakened Turkish power. Now that so much of Russia's exports passed through the Black Sea ports, it seemed more vital than ever to ensure that the Straits remained in friendly hands.

Accordingly the foreign minister, A. P. Izvol'sky, proposed to his Austro-Hungarian counterpart, Count von Aehrenthal, a deal whereby

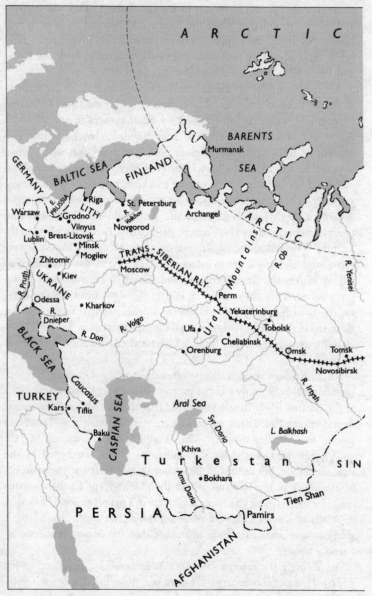

MAP 5. *The Russian Empire in 1914*

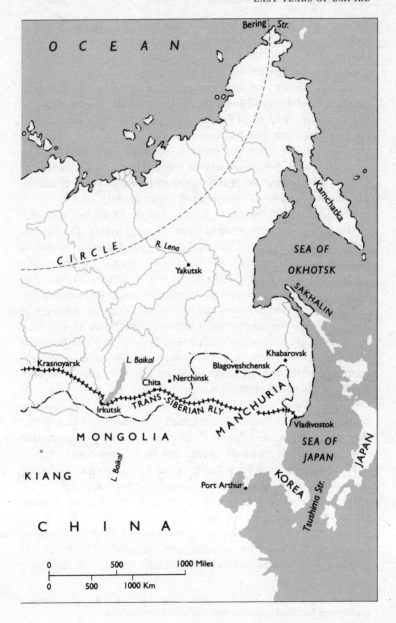

Bering Str.

O C E A N

Kamchatka

SEA OF

OKHOTSK

C I R C L E

R. Lena

Yakutsk

SAKHALIN

Khabarovsk

Krasnoyarsk

L. Baikal

Blagoveshchensk

Chita   Nerchinsk

TRANS-SIBERIAN RLY

MANCHURIA

Irkutsk

Vladivostok

MONGOLIA

L. Baikal

SEA OF

JAPAN

JAPAN

KIANG

Port Arthur

KOREA

Tsushima Str.

C H I N A

0   500   1000 Miles

0   500   1000 Km

Russia would be allowed to 'secure her interests'* at the Straits in exchange for Russian agreement to Austria's annexation of Bosnia-Herzegovina, which she had occupied since 1878. Before he could acquire the other powers' assent – and the British made no secret of their misgivings – Aehrenthal acted unilaterally by annexing the territory in question. Izvol'sky was discredited, and his humiliation was made worse when Germany insisted on Russia stating plainly whether she accepted the Austrian move. She had no choice but to agree. The crisis cost Izvol'sky his job; more important, it outraged the nationalists, or 'neo-Slavs' as they were sometimes called. Hostile to the Germanic powers, they backed the claims to the disputed province of Serbia, who wanted to unite all Serb speakers under her rule.

The disgruntled elements in 'society' and the Duma had associates in the politico-military establishment. N. G. Hartvig, the Russian envoy to Belgrade, played an unscrupulous role analogous to that of Ignatyev forty years earlier. These extremists led the way in creating a league of Balkan states (Serbia, Montenegro, Bulgaria, and Greece) which they hoped would serve as a barrier to Austro-German designs.

The Central Powers meanwhile had consolidated their influence in Turkey, where the scheme for a railway 'from Berlin to Baghdad' aroused the apprehension of rival powers. In 1911 the Turks faced war with Italy. Russia's envoy in Constantinople, Charykov, seized the opportunity (the foreign minister, S. D. Sazonov, was ill) to offer Turkey a guarantee of the *status quo* in return for concessions over the Straits. Politely, his interlocutors replied that the idea could be considered only if Russia's allies joined in – knowing full well that they would oppose it. 'Charykov's kite', as it is known to diplomatic historians, did not get off the ground and he was repudiated.

His colleague in Sofia belatedly warned St Petersburg that the architects of the Balkan league (of which he was one) might use it aggressively against Turkey rather than defensively against Austria. He was right. Lured by the hope of winning (Turkish) Macedonia, the league's members attacked southwards (1912). They were successful, but soon fell apart over division of the spoils. The Bulgarians attacked their Serbian and Greek allies, who rallied, won Romanian

---

* This meant revising the 1871 Straits Convention so as to allow Russian warships to pass through but possibly also as a first step towards territorial control.

support, and took Macedonia. The Bulgarians, embittered, looked to the Central Powers. The Serbs, for their part, found their hopes of winning access to the Adriatic blocked by Austria. In the eyes of Serbian extremists Russia was a lukewarm patron, so they tried to force the issue by provoking Austria, compelling St Petersburg to come to their aid.

Meanwhile Russo-German relations had been amicable, at least on the surface. Visits were exchanged at top level; economic ties were strong and largely trouble-free; there were no major bilateral disputes. The Russian foreign ministry took pains to assure Berlin that improved relations with Britain had no hostile intent, which to be sure did not allay German nationalists' fears of 'encirclement'. The greatest danger came from the partners' embroilment in obligations to their allies and clients. When Nicholas met his cousin Wilhelm II for the last time (June 1912) the mood was so friendly that the French were concerned. Paris insisted that in future no political questions should be discussed without prior French consent.

This stance was grist to the mill of Russian nationalists. In 1914 the climate worsened. There were hostile exchanges in the Russian and German press. The appointment of a German general to command Turkish forces on the Bosphorus set alarm bells ringing in St Petersburg. The affair had comic-opera aspects,* but seriously strained relations. The Russian navy responded by requesting a large sum (110 million roubles) to expand the Black Sea fleet. The head of the Military Academy warned graduating officers that war was 'probable this year' – a view that was widely shared, not only in Russia.

This jingoistic atmosphere makes intelligible Russia's reaction to the assassination by the Serb terrorist Prinkip of the heir to the Austro-Hungarian throne at Sarajevo on 28 June (N.S.). Russia used her influence in Belgrade to urge appeasement – even after the stern Austrian ultimatum of 23 July, which was designed to serve as a pretext for war against Serbia. 'You are setting all Europe alight,' Sazonov warned the Austrians. They rejected his overtures. The military machines had taken over. The Russian government decided to mobilize

---

* It was settled by granting General Liman von Sanders field marshal's rank, which made him too senior to hold the post in question. The British already had an admiral commanding the Turkish fleet!

thirteen corps against Austria, only to learn that a *partial* mobilization was technically impossible. Reluctantly, Nicholas agreed to *general* mobilization instead.* This touched off similar action by Germany, who demanded that the Russian measure be rescinded. Alas, this was no longer possible, either technically or politically. On 1 August the two empires found themselves at war. Three days earlier Austrian artillery had shelled Belgrade. France and Britain declared war on the Central Powers and the conflagration became general. At the time few realized that it would lead to the collapse not just of the Russian (and later the German and Austrian) empires but imperil the very survival of European civilization.

---

* Some earlier historians, especially in Germany, interpreted this as evidence of Russia's 'war guilt', but this is to overrate the importance of the immediate as against the long-range causes of the conflict.

CHAPTER 14

War and Revolution

ARMAGEDDON I

Russia entered the First World War gravely unprepared. In equipment and training her armed forces were no match for those of the Central Powers (Germany and Austria-Hungary, joined later by Turkey and Bulgaria). Russia's vast manpower reserves could not be mobilized at once lest agricultural production be disrupted. Initially family 'bread-winners' were exempted from conscription. Teenagers were recruited in their stead and virtually thrown straight into battle. Tens of thousands of soldiers met untimely death for lack of adequate weaponry. In 1914 there was only one machine-gun for 1,000 men. Even rifles were in short supply, so that on some sectors of the front advancing infantry were expected to equip themselves by picking up those of slain enemy troops. Domestic industry could supply only one in three of the rifles needed; the rest had to be imported, and this took time. Even more acute was the shell shortage. When war began Russian artillerymen had a stock of 1,000 shells per gun, only one third as many as their German counterparts. This would have sufficed for a mere ten days of fighting at the rate of fire reached in 1916. Infantry (and even cavalry!) attacks were launched without adequate artillery support.

Military planners, convinced that the war would be brief, had seriously underestimated the army's material requirements. There was a good deal of incompetence in the higher ranks. Neither the first commander-in-chief, Grand Duke Nicholas, nor his chief of staff, Yanushkevich, were up to their task. Some generals still believed, as Suvorov had, that bayonets were better than bullets. But these old maxims no longer fitted a war fought with modern technology. The troops' morale was brittle. The heavy casualty toll led to apathy and a search for scapegoats. Here the quality of NCOs and junior officers was particularly important. Most pre-war regulars fell in the first engagements, their places taken by men fresh from civilian life who lacked experience and tended to be critical of authority. By 1916 soldiers were mutilating themselves or deserting. Jobs in the swollen rear echelons were greatly prized, not least by educated men anxious to escape front-line service.

A dangerous gulf yawned between Russia's fighting men* and the civilian population, who were spared the sight of bloodshed on an unparalleled scale and tried to live normal lives. Some of them were actually better off than before: peasants, for example, who could consume produce previously exported, to say nothing of war profiteers. A few industrialists milked the state purchasing agencies and accumulated fortunes. The extent of such malfeasance was exaggerated by rumour-mongers. Since the press was subject to military censorship, it was not believed and people preferred to rely on informal means of communication. The general public was poorly informed; even well-educated citizens distrusted the authorities and lent credence to extravagant myths about treason in high places.

In fact Russia's wartime predicament stemmed less from human fallibility than objective circumstances. Of these the most important were her relative industrial backwardness and geographical isolation. The Western Allies, preoccupied with their own problems and ignorant of Russian realities, could do little to help. With both the Baltic and Black Seas under enemy control, the only possible supply routes were via the Arctic ports or Vladivostok and the (single-track!) Trans-Siberian railway. The Entente powers, riven by mutual suspicions, did a poor job of coordinating their military efforts. In the first weeks of war, responding to French pleas, the Russians launched an ill-prepared attack on East Prussia and were routed at Tannenberg. The Second Army commander, Samsonov, committed suicide. This catastrophe, as Alexander Solzhenitsyn writes, 'prefigured a thunderous cataclysm of incomparable force'.† It offset the otherwise significant gains scored

---

* They numbered 6.5 million by the end of 1914. By October 1917 over 15 million had been called up, of whom at least 2.3 million were killed or missing, 4.9 million wounded.

† In *August 14*, the first section of his epic *The Red Wheel*, Solzhenitsyn gives a graphic semi-fictionalized account of this campaign, fought over territory where he saw service in 1945. Of its last moments he writes: 'The mass [of soldiers] poured through the forest haphazardly, feeling their way. Those who had not eaten for two days were delirious;

in the south against the Austrians. In 1915 Russian forces were obliged to abandon both the territory won in Galicia (where the occupation authorities behaved towards the local Ukrainians with astonishing tactlessness) and Russian Poland. This strategic retreat was carried out well, but with heavy loss of life. Thereafter the front line became more or less stabilized along a line running from Libau on the Baltic coast to the Romanian border. Patriotic opinion blamed the loss of territory (which was not ethnically Russian!) on the country's leadership.

In May 1916 General A. A. Brusilov launched another offensive to help the French, hard pressed at Verdun, on Russia's south-western front. By November he claimed to have put one and a half million enemy soldiers out of action for the loss of one third as many of his own men. At the time this was rated a signal victory, but the historians' verdict is ambivalent. Certainly the advance weakened Austrian resolve and encouraged Romania to join the Allies; but this was a mixed blessing, since the Romanian forces were quickly overrun, and thereafter the eastern front stretched as far as the Black Sea coast, and further strained Russia's resources. Russia was also heavily engaged against the Turks in Anatolia, where Erzerum was taken in February 1916. Viewed in historical context, this was a remarkable triumph, but now it scarcely mattered, for the war's accumulating burdens were bringing the empire to the verge of collapse.

The initial patriotic euphoria waned fast. The tsarist government, instead of seeking to cooperate with 'society', rebuffed it. The Duma was summoned only rarely for brief sessions. As in 1905, liberals set up unions of zemstvos and municipalities to provide an alternative forum for discussion. Along with other voluntary agencies they tried to care for the wounded and the many thousands of refugees, mainly Jews and Poles, who poured from the war zone into the interior. Reluctantly, the authorities relaxed residence restrictions, but their efforts to relieve distress were amateurish. The scale of the disaster was simply too great for the creaky, tradition-bound administration.

---

with no water in their flasks, they stuffed their dry mouths with dirt; they no longer trusted their generals or saw any reason why they should be herded along. Some tore off their insignia so that they could not be identified; others just stepped aside or fell asleep on the ground . . . By the evening of the 16th the Second Army had ceased to exist and become a jumbled, ungovernable mob . . . (Russian edition, i, pp. 440–41).

Children in particular suffered badly. In coming to the people's aid, however, the liberal opposition also pursued a political objective: the establishment of a ministry enjoying public confidence.

This demand might well be thought quite reasonable. It was less radical than that advanced in 1905 – a government responsible to parliament – but it still went too far for Nicholas, and especially for his consort Alexandra, who continually urged the tsar to assert his autocratic prerogative. Her influence was all the greater once Nicholas, acting from a misguided sense of obligation and ignoring his ministers' advice, assumed the post of commander-in-chief (August 1915) and spent most of his time at general headquarters in Mogilev. This left the empire's government at the mercy of Alexandra, who was by now suffering from persecution mania. She convinced herself that God, through Rasputin, was commanding her to intervene in state affairs and 'save Russia' (and the monarchy, which to her were one and the same). In hysterical letters to Nicholas she denounced the ministers as 'rotten' and recommended that senior posts be given to nominees of Rasputin. 'Listen to Our Friend's counsels,' she implored, 'a country where a man of God helps the Sovereign will never be lost.' All too often the tsar meekly concurred with these suggestions, and the country came to be governed, on paper at least, by a succession of nonentities – this at a time of grave national emergency.

The opposition parties in the Duma, united since mid 1915 in a 'Progressive Bloc', derided the 'court camarilla', but their criticisms were vitiated by partisan bias and they did little to curb the evils of which they complained. For above all else they were 'patriots', devoted to winning the war and so unwilling to take determined action that might benefit the enemy (and the revolutionaries). Only towards the end of 1916 did some opposition leaders, notably the Octobrist leader Guchkov, sound out General Alexeyev, the army's chief of staff,* about a possible *coup d'état*, but their talks led nowhere. By then the initiative was passing out of the moderates' hands.

Popular opposition to the war was generated spontaneously by

---

* Actually *de facto* commander-in-chief, since Nicholas's role was purely nominal. The tsar did not interfere in operations and, apart from morale-raising efforts which had only perfunctory success, spent his time in leisure pursuits.

economic hardship and news from the front conveyed in soldiers' letters home. The conversion of industry to military production reduced the supply of consumer goods, and prices rose faster than wages. Workers in munitions factories did better than those in, say, textiles, but hours were long and conditions grim. Undernourishment and fatigue led to local outbreaks of cholera and typhus. Women were hired *en masse* for factory work. The proportion of industrial employees in large plants rose, particularly in Petrograd (as St Petersburg was now called) and in eastern Ukraine. So, too, did the incidence of strikes. A mere 170,000 working days were lost between August and December 1914; the figure was ten times greater in 1915 and in the following year reached 4.7 million.

As early as December 1915 police spies reported that women queuing for food were threatening to 'settle up' with shopkeepers unless they at once satisfied all regular customers with meat, and at an open-air market in Petrograd angry shoppers ventilated their frustration by damaging several traders' booths. In 1916 shortages of bread, fats, sugar, and other staples in the northern 'consuming provinces' worsened. This was partly due to declining agricultural output: harvests were down by 20 per cent on 1915 in the south, by 40 per cent in the north. Peasant farmers lacked able-bodied manpower and had less incentive than in peacetime to market any surplus they had. More important was the diversion of produce to feed the troops, and the strain which this imposed on the rail transport system. There was also a good deal of sheer administrative muddle.

Most working-class organizations and newspapers were suppressed in 1914–15. This gave special importance to the so-called Labour Group on the Central War Industries Committee (CWIC). The CWIC had been set up in May 1915 by Guchkov, P. P. Ryabushinsky, and other 'progressive' entrepreneurs. It aspired to bring together representatives of industry, labour, and the public (zemstvos and so on) in a joint effort to boost the war effort. Its myriad local committees busily set about allocating orders and raw materials to private firms. In practice the creation of this 'counter-bureaucracy' made administrative confusion worse, but the political consequences were important. The committees helped to mobilize public opinion against the regime, not least among industrial workers, who were allowed to send representatives to these committees. Many of the men elected were Mensheviks, who now had a chance to spread their ideas, and hoped to create a nation-wide labour organization.

Russia's socialists were split three ways over the war. Only a handful of 'defensists' followed Plekhanov's lead in backing the Allied cause. On the far left Lenin took an overtly 'defeatist' line, denouncing the war as 'imperialist'* and calling for the masses in all belligerent countries to rise up and end it from below. This stance was too extreme even for some radicals in the international socialist movement (referred to as Zimmerwaldists, after the Swiss village where they met in September 1915). The middle-of-the-roaders stood for 'revolutionary defensism', i.e. for low-intensity defensive operations only until diplomacy brought about a democratic peace according to the *status quo ante*, 'without annexations or contributions'.

By the winter of 1916–17 these ideas had gained wide currency. A soldier on the northern front wrote anonymously to a comrade: 'Don't go out on the attack ... Let's finish off our commanders, generals, ministers and Nicholas, then there'll be peace.' In another regiment, where three companies refused to fight, their commander reported that he had restored order by executing thirteen men in public. Soldiers in rear garrisons, anxious not to be sent to the front, were in mutinous mood. They interpreted after their own fashion Milyukov's suggestion in the Duma (1 November 1916) that the tsar's court was guilty of treason, and later the news that high-placed aristocrats had killed Rasputin (16 December). Violence on the right removed inhibitions about violence on the left. On 9 January 1917, the anniversary of 'Bloody Sunday', 145,000 workers came out on strike in Petrograd and were joined by some soldiers. On the 26th the interior minister had most members of the Labour Group arrested – in the circumstances a blatantly provocative act.

What happened next took everyone by surprise. A strike in the huge Putilov arms works prompted a lockout (22 February). Thousands of

---

* According to Leninist theory imperialism was 'the highest stage of capitalism', whose inherent contradictions had led to the war; its purpose was to redistribute the world's markets in the interests of the international bourgeoisie and to intimidate the working class. The task of the proletariat and its allies (peasants, soldiers) was therefore to 'turn the imperialist war into a civil war', so bringing about European-wide socialist revolution. Lenin expected the 'chain of international capital' to break at its 'weakest link', which by 1917 he had decided lay in Russia rather than in Germany.

embittered men were forced into the streets in wintry weather. On the morrow, International Women's Day, female workers queuing for scarce supplies* joined in the protest. By the 25th the strike had become general. Angry throngs surged from the industrial suburbs into the city centre.

Cavalry units and Cossacks . . . helped the police to scatter crowds of workers and beat demonstrators. Shots were fired at the people for the first time . . . At the City Duma building on Nevsky Prospekt, soldiers of the Ninth Reserve Cavalry regiment opened fire on the crowd, killing 9 and wounding 9 others. In many areas, however, the soldiers and Cossacks were passive . . . Male and female workers seized rifles pointed at them and pleaded with the soldiers to support the people . . . [That evening the city fell quiet.] But lights still burned brightly at the Alexander Theatre where the première of Lermontov's *Masquerade* was being performed, memorable for its . . . magnificent costumes, rich staging and the fabulously expensive tickets, while not far from the theatre crowds of people were demanding bread.†

The performance ended with the white figure of Death on the stage, as if symbolizing the end of Autocracy.

That evening Nicholas, away at headquarters, ordered the Petrograd military governor 'to end disorders in the capital tomorrow'. The action caused heavy casualties. Two Guards regiments which participated, on returning to barracks, mutinied and were speedily emulated by the rest of the garrison. Some soldiers went home, others merged with the crowds. A workers' revolt had become a revolution.

Nicholas still made a show of firmness. He prorogued the Duma, whose leaders he wrongly held responsible for the disturbances, and charged General Ivanov with their forcible suppression. But Ivanov's troops melted away, their movements sabotaged by angry railwaymen. The tsar's train, too, was prevented from returning to Petrograd, and it was at Pskov, in north-western Russia, that on 2 March he was persuaded by his generals to abdicate. He did so in favour of his brother, Grand Duke Michael, rather than his ailing son. Strictly speaking, this was illegal. Michael, who could read the writing on the wall, abdicated

---

* Food rationing had just been introduced in the city, but the system worked badly and there was a wave of panic buying.

† Burdzhalov, *Russia's Second Revolution*, pp. 131–3.

in turn the next day. He would have taken the throne only if asked to do so by a Constituent Assembly. For the first time in three centuries Russia was without a tsar – indeed, without a legitimate government at all.*

At once the empire's administration began to disintegrate. Power passed ostensibly to the former Duma politicians, but in fact to the self-appointed leaders of the Petrograd soviet of workers' and soldiers' deputies. This body had been formed one day before the new Provisional government of Duma politicians, which it looked on with suspicion. The Mensheviks and SRs who directed the soviet saw it as their role to support the government only in so far as it advanced the interests of the 'working masses' as they interpreted them. This attitude, based on ideological principle, helped to make Russia ungovernable and had to be dropped after a few weeks.

1917: WAR OR PEACE?

The foreign minister in the new Provisional government was Milyukov, the Kadet leader who for years had taken a strongly 'patriotic' line on international issues. He hoped that, by fulfilling her commitments to the Western Allies, Russia could win territorial compensation for her wartime sacrifices. These gains were to be made in eastern Galicia, at Austria's expense, but more particularly at the Turkish Straits. Here Russia could now hope for British goodwill, provided that her armies remained active in the field. But precisely their ability to fight was now in question. Allied material aid was arriving in amounts far below Russia's needs or expectations, partly because shipping was short and Russian ports congested, but also because Britain could not afford to meet Russia's orders for goods that she could no longer pay for. This apparently insensitive attitude aroused ill feeling in Petrograd, while

* Nicholas did confirm the appointment as prime minister of Prince G. E. L'vov, a liberal zemstvo leader, but this act conferred no real authority on the Provisional government he headed. This defined itself as democratic and sought to wield authority only until a permanent executive was chosen by a Constituent Assembly. Elections to this body were not, however, held until November, after the government's deposition by the Bolsheviks.

the British and French increasingly looked on revolutionary Russia as a liability.

The revolution further undermined military morale. Soldiers suspected that they were being denied truthful information as to what had occurred. Few officers could explain to their men why they should go on fighting now that there was no tsar to obey; some actually fled in panic, leaving soldiers to wonder whether they should not themselves choose their replacements. In any case they wanted better treatment at their officers' hands and so responded eagerly to the Petrograd soviet's invitation to 'join your brother workers' by sending delegates, one per company. On 1 March that body adopted its famous 'Order No. 1', which shook the army to its foundations. Although addressed solely to the Petrograd garrison, it was soon acted on by soldiers all over the country. It instructed them to establish committees in each unit or naval vessel, to obey orders only if they did not conflict with those of the soviet, and to keep all arms under their own control.

In no case should they be turned over to officers, even at their demand . . . Soldiers must observe the strictest military discipline, but . . . in private life cannot be deprived of those rights that all citizens enjoy . . . Standing to attention and compulsory saluting when not on duty are abolished . . . Rudeness towards soldiers . . . and especially addressing them as 'thou' are prohibited.*

A hierarchy of committees soon came into existence which officers had to accept with such good grace as they could muster. At first troops in front-line units could be persuaded to soldier on so as to protect 'the conquests of the revolution', but when offensive action was planned the men would discuss whether it was necessary or feasible. Mass meetings were sometimes addressed by outside agitators. Much persuasion was required to get soldiers to perform even the most elementary tasks. Officers who tried to reimpose conventional norms of discipline did so at their peril. Abolition of the death penalty (12 March) and of officers' powers of summary jurisdiction abolished the old system of military law without creating an effective replacement. Over Easter the Germans proclaimed a three-day ceasefire and fraternization took place

* Wildman, *End of Russian Imperial Army*, i, pp. 187–8.

on several sectors of the front. Thousands of Russian soldiers simply deserted.

Despite mutiny, disillusion and defeat Russia's enormous army was called on to launch another assault. The Allies needed desperately to hold back the German offensive on the Western Front, and Anglo-French pressure overcame the reluctance of the Russian high command and of Alexander Kerensky, who in May was to be appointed war minister in the new coalition cabinet.

A former lawyer, Kerensky was a fervent democrat and on paper at least an SR. He had been the only socialist in Prince L'vov's first cabinet, where he saw himself as the voice of 'revolutionary democracy'. He looked for support to the soviets and opposed what the left saw as Milyukov's 'imperialist' leanings. Within the cabinet Kerensky won over most of his colleagues to a 'revolutionary defensist' viewpoint that could scarcely be distinguished from 'Zimmerwaldism'. The foreign minister stuck to his pro-Allied position, using methods that smacked of duplicity, and on 20–21 April the conflict between the two men spilled over into the streets. Milyukov had to resign. He was followed by the war minister, Guchkov, who was aghast at the army's dissolution. The socialists had no alternative but to abandon their 'hands-off' stance towards the Provisional government. After talks in private they were offered five out of fifteen ministerial seats, Kerensky exchanging his justice portfolio for that of war. The shift of gravity to the left alarmed 'bourgeois' opinion at home and abroad.

Kerensky's sole qualification for his new job was his undoubted rhetorical talent. He toured the front lecturing the troops on the need for revolutionary discipline, which, he reasoned, could best be restored by a successful offensive. Yet his oratory, like that of Nicholas earlier, had only ephemeral effect. The operation on the south-western front, an ill-kept secret, was launched on 18 June as much for internal political reasons as for strategic ones. After initial successes the enemy counter-attacked (6 July) and soon the Russian retreat became a rout.

In spite of enormous numerical superiority, units of the XIth Army began to retreat of their own accord . . . Reliable reinforcements were not available. Casualties had cost [three] Russian . . . armies 58,329 men, including 6,905 killed and 36,240 wounded. They represented the picked troops and the reliable units. Without them there was little left to preserve order . . .

In one night alone the 'Death Battalion' . . . arrested approximately 12,000 deserters . . . Outrages . . . were committed on the populace. But owing to the lack of a death penalty . . . it was impossible in most cases to punish the culprits.*

Not just officers but members of the Petrograd soviet (including one of those who had drafted 'Order No. 1') were assaulted. Kerensky, who had earlier issued a high-sounding Declaration of Soldiers' Rights, now ordered disobedient men to be shot without trial. Many disillusioned soldiers viewed the Provisional government as no better than its predecessor and turned towards the 'maximalists' on the extreme left who stood for an immediate peace and for a second revolution hard on the heels of the first.

This movement was led by the Petrograd Bolsheviks, who demonstrated their growing strength by staging a protest march when the offensive was launched. (The demonstration had actually been called in support of the offensive by the moderate socialists, but was turned against its organizers.) The marchers carried inflammatory slogans: 'All Power to the Soviets!', 'Down with the Ten Capitalist Ministers!' The island of Kronstadt had virtually become an independent republic, ruled by its garrison of radicalized soldiers and sailors. On 3–4 July, under pressure from below, the Petrograd Bolsheviks staged a half-hearted insurrection. Some 400 lives were lost in street clashes before the action was called off.

The 'July Days', as they came to be called, cost the maximalist leaders some prestige, but their cause was only temporarily damaged. The Mensheviks and SRs, who dominated both the government (from which the Kadets now withdrew) and the central soviet executive, did not press their tactical advantage forcefully. They ordered some rebellious units to be broken up, but did not prevent the Bolsheviks from holding a party congress in Petrograd later in July. Kerensky, the leading figure in the coalition government, had been emotionally crippled by the failure of the offensive.

Where once he had spoken freely on all aspects of policy, he now seemed incapable of thinking hard about matters outside his own immediate sphere

---

* Heenan, *Russian Democracy's Fatal Blunder*, p. 121.

of competence . . . 'I summon all to sacrifices, to work and order [he declared on 15 July]. Any attempts, wherever they may come from, to create anarchy and disorder will be mercilessly repressed.' This was the new chastened Kerensky, his mood sombre, . . . his vocabulary increasingly traditional . . . The adoption of a synthetic authoritarian personality did not come easily to Kerensky and it did not always convince.*

Early in July he had gone on to succeed L'vov as premier, but the country's affairs were actually managed by an inner group of three (Kerensky and two left-wing dissident Kadets). A new cabinet was formed on 23 July. It had a socialist majority (eight against seven 'bourgeois' representatives) but it commanded little authority. It was even more dependent on the Petrograd (and national) soviet executive than its predecessor. Russian democrats, although still committed to prosecution of the war, were badly weakened and discredited at the very moment when they faced a double threat from extremists on the right and left.

Kerensky's choice as new commander-in-chief was the fiery and authoritarian General L. G. Kornilov, who accepted the job only on the proviso that the death penalty be extended to the rear. Such punishment was in fact rarely carried out, but its reintroduction was a powerful symbolic gesture and highly unpopular. The two men eyed one another with suspicion. Kornilov was the darling of the Kadets and conservatives generally, who hoped that he would act firmly to save Russia from anarchy. He cut a colourful figure, appearing for talks in Petrograd escorted by a bodyguard of Muslim troops armed with machine-guns. Officers' organizations and certain right-wing politicians plotted a *coup* against the government and soviet. Kornilov had fore-knowledge of their plans, but seems (contrary to what was long believed) not to have conspired himself. Following the fall of Riga to the Germans (21 August), he took over direct control of Petrograd military district and moved reliable forces there, among them the feared Caucasian 'Savage division'. These troops were designed to put down domestic enemies as well, but Kornilov evidently did not intend to act without the government's accord.

On 27 August he unexpectedly received a telegram from Kerensky

* Abraham, *Kerensky*, pp. 229–31.

dismissing him from office. The volatile premier, told that the general was acting treasonably, jumped to the conclusion that this was so without first verifying the information. He appealed to the soviet for help. Instantly an emergency committee of left-wing parties mobilized labour organizations and armed forces committees to 'defend the revolution'. Arms were distributed and communications disrupted. Scores of agitators persuaded the men in General Krymov's cavalry corps, which Kornilov had sent to Petrograd, to surrender; their commander committed suicide.

Kerensky himself took over as commander-in-chief. Kornilov and his leading associates were arrested. Many officers suspected of counter-revolutionary sympathies were beaten or killed by their men. The soldiers' spontaneous, unfocused 'trench Bolshevism' fused with the politicized, party-orientated variety which had hitherto been confined to committed activists. It expressed itself in violence and pogroms, as at Gomel' on 18–20 September, where several thousand soldiers went on a rampage. Characteristic of the troops' ugly mood was a letter written to a newspaper by a group of men on the Romanian front:

Did our new government really take power only to . . . continue the war for another three years? . . . Why did our brothers overthrow Nicholas II and put in Kerensky if not to get the war over with as soon as possible? . . . Give us real freedom now and not in the future . . . We're saying openly and directly that after 1 October we'll no longer hold our positions but will pick up our things and go home. Rather let [Kaiser] Wilhelm rule over us, at least we won't suffer any more.*

Alas, the five-man directory under Kerensky's chairmanship, which nominally governed the country, could not meet the popular demand for peace. Its all too evident weakness earned only contemptuous scorn from the Allies. Britain and France, confident that American aid would soon arrive, ignored desperate Russian pleas for talks about negotiating a settlement. Nor was a *separate* peace with the Central Powers a realistic possibility for Russians. Paradoxically, any leaders who dared take this path would have faced general ignominy as 'traitors': even

---

* Wildman, *The End of the Imperial Army*, ii, p. 238.

the Bolsheviks refrained from endorsing this option openly.* The harsh truth was that no political faction in Russia, maximalists included, could offer any easy way out of the country's predicament. It was just as difficult to end the war as to go on fighting it.

WORKERS, PEASANTS, NATIONALITIES

The Marxist-Leninist view of Russia's October 1917 overturn as a 'proletarian revolution' has distorted historical writing on the subject. The most important social group involved were not workers but soldiers. By destroying the old army from below they deprived the Russian state of the material force on which its existence in the last resort depended. Nevertheless the discontents of organized labour were a major factor; so, too, were those of peasants and members of various national-minority groups. Virtually the whole population was caught up in the revolutionary fever. Women, too, demanded equality; schoolboys contested their teachers; even clergymen rebelled against the Holy Synod.

Some Petrograd workers, on returning to their factories early in March, laid down tools after eight hours on the job. Their example was infectious and prompted concessions by local industrialists, backed by the Provisional government. The introduction of an eight-hour working day in the capital had symbolic significance. In Moscow and elsewhere similar concessions were secured by direct action on the part of the local soviet. Inflationary wage settlements undermined the economic well-being of smaller enterprises, which had to lay off employees and then close down production; another reason for doing so was the drying up of supplies of raw materials. Such actions were regarded by spokesmen for organized labour as evidence of malignant 'bourgeois' self-interest. The climate of industrial relations deteriorated. Between mid April and early July there was a rash of strikes,

---

* They called only for a *general* peace, in the hope, genuine or assumed, that all belligerent governments would be forced to negotiate under mass revolutionary pressure. For the same reason they did not publicly advocate that a future 'soviet government' should wage war by revolutionary means to bring about universal peace, which became the unacknowledged leitmotif of Soviet foreign policy under Stalin and later. This restraint was partly tactical cunning and partly self-deception.

most of them successful. Metalworkers and textile workers were the most active groups, notably in Moscow, but there was also unrest among shop assistants and other non-industrial employees. Nearly three quarters (71.5 per cent) of strikes were called over wages; but there was no lack of other demands that reflected a new concern for the dignity of the working man.

The provision [of] baths figured in a strike in Minsk; soap and boiling water were demanded by strikers in Nikolayev. Strikers at Krasnoyarsk leather factories, where the manufacturing process required the use of water and humid conditions, demanded special clothing . . . Workers . . . expected to be addressed with the formal 'you' and demanded that supervisors cease other forms of verbal abuse . . . In the Crimea, for example, striking waiters in late April demanded a dressing room [and] a table where they could sit and eat their meals.*

Some conflicts at the workplace could be settled by negotiation, and an array of conciliation boards was set up for this purpose. But the more radical workers scorned their efforts and went on to raise basic questions about the way industrial life was carried on. Factory committees took the initiative in pressing for 'workers' control', a term that at first meant giving the men's representatives the right to verify the firm's accounts but speedily came to signify the outright seizure of the plant. This desperate course was usually taken in response to threats by management to lock out 'trouble-makers'.

Labour militancy led employers to coordinate resistance by forming inter-branch associations, less from a concern to maximize profits (as much of the historical literature suggests) than in the hope of keeping industry's wheels turning and maintaining the country's defences. A Committee of United Industry was set up in Moscow in June, and another agency appeared in Petrograd (significantly, old entrepreneurial rivalries persisted). Both bodies took a strong anti-socialist line, at least in rhetoric. The Moscow industrialist Ryabushinsky famously declared that 'the bony hand of hunger' would soon grip Russian workers by the throat. In the hysterical atmosphere of the time his words were interpreted as a counter-revolutionary threat rather than as a needlessly provocative pointer to economic realities.

* Koenker and Rosenberg, *Strikes and Revolution in Russia*, pp. 168–73.

Employers received only tepid support from the coalition government, where the 'defensist' Menshevik I. G. Tsereteli took over as trade and industry minister from the liberal A. I. Konovalov. State intervention, begun under the tsarist regime with the formation of 'special councils' for defence, transport, fuels, and so on, was now expanded; prices of raw materials were controlled and joint boards set up with labour representation. All this would later be taken much farther by the Bolsheviks. At the time many socialists (and even liberals) looked on governmental regulation as a panacea for Russia's industrial ills. Controls did indeed have a certain rationale during the war emergency, but on a long-term view the bureaucratization of economic life was a mixed blessing, to say the least.

Meanwhile inflation surged ahead. The purchasing power of the rouble, 27 kopecks (1914 = 100) in February, declined to 6 kopecks by November. The amount of money in circulation doubled during the lifetime of the Provisional government, which, faced with sharply declining tax revenues and sources of credit, resorted increasingly to the printing press. Laws were passed taxing personal incomes and company profits, but with the economy in free fall they were no more than a declaration of good intentions. Almost equally alarming was the state of the rail transport system. By November one quarter of locomotives were out of service and fuel was running short. The government purged the old cadres and allowed the railwaymen's union* broad powers to supervise the movement of goods (27 May), but then took fright at its own boldness. For their part army leaders advocated 'militarizing' the railways, which helped to push the union leaders to the left.

In general, trade unions were a moderating force in 1917. They proliferated, and by the year's end numbered over 2,000 with more than 2 million members. They set up city-wide executives and in July a nation-wide Central Committee. The trade unions claimed authority over the factory committees, but these were generally under maximalist control and went their own way. Apart from harassing managers and technicians, these committees set up armed militia bands, ostensibly to defend industrial premises from hooligan and criminal elements.

---

* The All-Russian Union of Railwaymen, better known under the acronym of its central executive committee, Vikzhel.

These bands provided a ready outlet for those workers, particularly adolescents, attracted to violent means of settling disputes and soon came under Bolshevik influence.

The same was true, *mutatis mutandis*, of the urban soviets, of which there were nearly 1,000 by the end of 1917. They, too, developed a central executive body, with its own bureaucratic apparatus, which from midsummer functioned in effect as a parallel government. The leadership lay initially with the Mensheviks and SRs, but they failed to provide a clear sense of direction and after the Kornilov affair their authority was contested by Bolsheviks and others on the far left. These factional struggles were of more interest to committed intellectuals than to rank-and-file workers, who assumed that under 'soviet power' all left-wing parties would be represented in government according to the degree of popular support they commanded. This view was naïve since the Bolsheviks had ulterior intentions.

While Russia's cities were the scene of sharp political confrontation, the peasants carried out a veritable agrarian revolution more or less under their own auspices. This process began in a minor key when villagers took over privately owned land to graze their cattle on; they appropriated timber stocks needed for firewood, or compelled enemy prisoners of war to work on peasant plots. On larger farms, which depended on hired labour, land often had to be left unsown or crops unreaped. This gave peasants a welcome pretext to sequester them. Since the authorities wanted all land to be tilled, they did not object too strongly. Chernov, the veteran SR leader who took over as agriculture minister in May, sought to grant local land committees (popularly constituted bodies that leaned to the left) the right to decide how *all* land should be utilized, and especially to fix rents. This gave local peasant activists a green light. Some provinces, notably in the over-crowded south-central zone, were reduced to a state of near anarchy. Landowners, many of them women with husbands at the front, besieged the authorities with complaints at breaches of their property rights. Commissars were sent out, and sometimes troops as well, but they could do little to repress the agrarian movement.

This peaked in the autumn when landowners and their employees were assaulted, manor-houses burned down, and livestock or other moveable goods divided up among the villagers. As one victim in Ryazan' province put it:

The village assembly met to decide the fate of our property . . . At first they decided just to take all our belongings and leave the building. But this decision did not satisfy some of those present and another resolution was passed: to burn everything but the house, which was to be kept as a school . . . For two days they carried off whatever they could, . . . divided up the loot into heaps, and cast lots which group should get which . . . A sailor appeared, a local lad who had been on active service. He insisted they should burn down the house too . . . [After a nocturnal feast] the whole village assembled and once again the axes struck . . . They chopped out the windows, doors and floors, smashed the mirrors and divided up the pieces . . . At 3 p.m. they set light to the house from all sides.*

Such acts were more than wanton vandalism. They had a symbolic significance, and even a certain shrewd rationale, in that landlords whose houses had been destroyed could scarcely return to claim them back. The peasants wanted the non-toilers' property, not their lives, as in the days of Pugachev. Where they were killed, the blame usually lay with soldiers returning from the front. The communal or rural district (*volost'*) authorities tried to compile inventories of land and goods confiscated (though much property went astray). Landowners who did not flee to the towns, and eventually to White-held territory, were sometimes left a small plot of land, tools, and stock. Ordinary peasants showed a sense of fair play that was alien to the ideologized revolutionary activists who soon arrived to direct rural affairs, and the civil war put a stop to such laxity. Some manor houses were turned into schools (or, more often, offices), but most were left to decay.

The empire's various national minorities greeted the February revolution with enthusiasm. They shared the social aspirations of Russian workers and peasants, but also hoped for a devolution of power that would grant them cultural and political autonomy within a democratic federal structure. Some nationalist leaders already dreamed of independence, at least as a long-term goal. As the year wore on it became a closer prospect. Dissatisfaction grew apace because of the economic dislocation and the Provisional government's reluctance to make timely concessions. This stubbornness was owed partly to residual imperialist prejudice (especially among rightists and liberals), partly to the legalistic

* Cited in Keep, *Russian Revolution*, pp. 211–12.

notion that future relations between Russia's peoples could be decided only by a duly elected Constituent Assembly, and partly to the socialists' basic conviction that class loyalties were far more substantial than ethnic ones. By the autumn many minority leaders were leaning towards the Bolsheviks, who stood ostensibly for national self-determination up to and including the right to separate. Few appreciated the subtle qualifications attached to this offer – namely, that the choice must be exercised by 'proletarian' elements, in accordance with the general interests of international revolution as the Bolsheviks defined them. Lenin realized better than most the explosive potential of nationalism and sought to make it serve his party's purposes.

Between February and October 1917 a host of national movements came to the fore in the non-Russian regions, with a kaleidoscope of parties and groups whose views extended across the political spectrum. Some of them acquired rudimentary armed forces. Minority nationalism was primarily an urban phenomenon: intellectuals summoned the congresses, published the newspapers, and strove with varying success to acquire a mass base. In ethnically mixed areas rivalries developed that presaged inter-community violence in the near future.

In the entire Baltic region the presence of Russian soldiers and sailors was a complicating factor. The soviets set up in Finland were predominantly Russian, while the Finnish parties, led by the Social Democrats, sought to win independence by parliamentary means. They issued a proclamation of sovereignty, but Petrograd declared this illegal. Rising unemployment and food shortages led to a general strike (November). Yet the Finnish socialists did not try to seize power; instead a 'bourgeois' government secured recognition of independence from a reluctant Lenin and proceeded, with German aid, to quell a revolt by marauding soldiers and Red Guards whom the Bolsheviks were at that time too weak to help. In 1918 some 50,000 'Reds' died in the ensuing three-month civil war.

In Latvia the Bolsheviks were effectively in charge behind the front from July onward, whereas in Estonia the 'bourgeois' parties put up a stronger showing. In Ukraine the parties formed a Central Council (Rada), which in July clashed with the Provisional government over the grant of autonomy; Petrograd's subsequent efforts to limit the Rada's powers created bitterness in Kiev, where in November Ukraine was proclaimed a 'people's republic'. The Rada government had a democratic and socialist orientation, but this did not spare it armed conflict with the Bolsheviks.

Although the Ukrainian leaders tried to accommodate minority interests, both Russians and Jews in Ukraine looked on them with misgivings. Jews in the empire (now reduced to 3.3 million, including half a million refugees) benefited from the Provisional government's abolition of tsarist discriminatory laws but otherwise suffered great hardship. Officially viewed as equal citizens at last, they participated actively in Russian political life at all levels and in all parties. Specifically Jewish parties appeared, among which the Zionists predominated, their aspirations fortified by the Balfour declaration in November 1917. Some Jewish leaders wanted a national autonomous region somewhere in Russia, but these hopes were not compatible with the Bolshevik interpretation of 'proletarian internationalism'.

Meanwhile in Transcaucasia Russian control was under threat. In Tbilisi a moderate-controlled (Russian) soviet maintained a precarious stability, while in Baku its counterpart, consisting mainly of Russians and Armenians, faced opposition from the strong Azerbaijani 'Muslim Democratic' party (*Musavat*). Representatives of all the empire's Islamic communities met in Moscow in May. They voted in favour of equality for women, over noisy protests by the mullahs present. The Volga and Crimean Tatars, fairly well integrated into Russian life, were to the left of their co-religionists in Central Asia, where the socialist cause was upheld mainly by Russian immigrants and soldiers. They were contemptuous of the 'backward' natives, which would lead to conflict later.

LENIN TAKES POWER

At the beginning of 1917 few people gave much thought to the Bolsheviks. Lenin and his chief associates were in exile or emigration; the Central Committee had been broken up by the tsarist police. It was second-echelon activists, like A. G. Shlyapnikov in Petrograd, who were responsible for organizing their party's contribution to the February revolution. It can scarcely be distinguished from that of other left-wing groups. The uprising's essentially spontaneous nature was reflected in the initially non-partisan composition of the Petrograd soviet. In provincial soviets, too, members of all left-wing factions at first cooperated fairly harmoniously. In the resuscitated *Pravda* Kamenev and Stalin, who returned from Siberia and elbowed Shlyapnikov aside, followed the masses' mood by taking a conciliatory line towards the Mensheviks and even the Provisional government.

All this changed after 3 April, when Lenin arrived at Petrograd's Finland Station, his journey conveniently arranged by the German general staff.* While in Zurich he had greeted news of the revolution cautiously, wiring a comrade: 'Our tactics – absolute distrust, no support for the Provisional government. Distrust Kerensky above all. No alliance with other parties.' On arrival he adhered to this uncompromising line. Welcomed by the Menshevik chairman of the Petrograd soviet with the assertion that the workers' chief task was to defend the revolution, he ignored him and addressed the crowd: 'The dawn of the world-wide socialist revolution has risen . . . our Russian revolution marks its beginning.' Next day, in his 'April Theses', he set forth the new slogan, 'All power to the soviets!' The war could be stopped only by overthrowing capitalism; soldiers at the front should fraternize; land and banks should be nationalized, the police and army abolished. Some listeners thought he had taken leave of his senses. Had the 'bourgeois-democratic' phase of revolution been completed before it had begun? Lenin dismissed such criticisms as pedantic sophistry. What mattered most in a revolution, he knew, was *power*. This he was determined to win for himself and his party. The first task was to build support among workers and soldiers, so securing a majority in the soviets. Although he did not say so publicly, he saw these organizations as instruments of mass mobilization; later they would become the infrastructure of a single-party dictatorship.

Within weeks Lenin had won over his party to his views. Sceptics

---

* During the war the Germans secretly financed a variety of separatist and revolutionary groups, operating at times through an eccentric socialist entrepreneur, Alexander Help-hand ('Parvus'), based in Copenhagen. He helped in the intricate negotiations whereby a party of twenty or so Bolsheviks (and later a number of Mensheviks, including Martov) were enabled to leave neutral Switzerland and proceed, in a subsequently famous 'sealed train', to Russia via Germany and Sweden. This aid compromised Lenin politically in the eyes of patriots, but certainly did not make him a 'German agent', for his aim was to overthrow *all* 'imperialist' governments. Even so much German money did pass into Bolshevik hands and played some part, hard to specify, in ensuring their success.

like Kamenev concealed their doubts, overawed by the leader's intellect and the support he gained from the rank and file. In the summer Trotsky's group, called 'Inter-districtites', joined the Bolsheviks. Left-wing SRs broke away and under the fiery Maria Spiridonova formed their own faction, which took a broadly similar line. It appealed primarily to mutinous soldiers. On 1 June a conference of factory committees voted massively for a Bolshevik resolution on 'workers' control' after Lenin had addressed the throng. The Syndicalists present reckoned he had been converted to their views, for the Bolshevik commitment to centralized economic planning was nowhere in evidence. In Petrograd Anarchists and Bolsheviks cooperated in defending their revolutionary acquisitions (such as the sumptuous villas where each had established its headquarters). Thousands of enthusiasts took part in Bolshevik-inspired demonstrations. The 'July Days' episode threatened to bring the party to power before it had won control over the soviets, which was one reason why Lenin beat an embarrassed retreat. Trotsky, who was the better orator, was arrested. Lenin, accompanied by his lieutenant G. E. Zinoviev, shaved off his beard to disguise himself and took refuge in Finland, whence he gave Kamenev instructions what to do if he were killed. But as we have seen, the maximalists' discomfiture was only temporary and they were saved by the Kornilov affair.

Early in September Trotsky became chairman of the Petrograd soviet, which now had a Bolshevik majority, while Lenin placed an early insurrection on the party's agenda. Other members of the Central Committee were more circumspect, and he bombarded them with messages demanding immediate action: 'History will not forgive us if we do not seize power now.' They had one of his intemperate missives burned. Kamenev and other 'soft' Bolsheviks wanted a socialist *coalition* government resting on the soviets, and perhaps the projected Constituent Assembly as well. They saw no need for violence now that events were moving so rapidly in favour of the left. But precisely this factor made Lenin insist on insurrection: with acute psychological flair, he realized that this would separate hard-core activists from vacillating hangers-on. The party's military experts warned that its popular support was far from solid, but their advice was disregarded.

The Bolsheviks' intentions were common knowledge, but the Provisional government and the central soviet leadership seemed struck by paralysis. They called deliberative bodies designed to confer a

shadow of democratic legitimacy pending convocation of the Constituent Assembly, but these were just talking-shops. The Bolsheviks
demanded a second national congress of soviets (although the first had
been held as recently as June) to put the seal on their capture of so
many of these organizations. Fearing such an outcome, the Central
Executive Committee temporized. This antagonized the radicals
further. On 12 October they decided to set up a military revolutionary
committee in Petrograd. Characteristically, this idea originated with the
Mensheviks, but under Trotsky's inspiring leadership the committee
became the general staff of the insurrection. The uprising was timed
for 24 October, the day before the soviet congress was due to meet.*

That evening Lenin emerged from hiding and appeared, still beardless, at the conspirators' headquarters in the Smol'ny Institute, once a
finishing school for young ladies. He was nervous that the operation
which Trotsky was masterminding might still go awry. It was indeed
risky, for the Red guards and the revolutionary troops were an unreliable
rabble. But their adversaries' morale was even lower. Most of the
Petrograd garrison stayed prudently neutral. The city fell to the Bolsheviks by default, while life continued almost normally.

Trotsky's men put up posters declaring that 'the Provisional government has been overthrown'. Actually it was still in session, but without
Kerensky, who had left for the front in search of a few reliable troops.
They were not forthcoming. Defended by a posse of women soldiers
and military cadets, the ministers in the Winter Palace let themselves
be arrested by a man wearing pince-nez and a broad-brimmed hat
named Antonov-Ovseyenko. In Petrograd at least the *coup* was virtually
bloodless. But much blood was to be shed thereafter. Few imagined
that the unspectacular events of October 1917 heralded the start of a
new 'Soviet' era.

---

* This is the generally accepted version of events, which owes much to Trotsky's
self-serving account. There is good evidence that the date of the insurrection was not
fixed in advance and that the insurgents were forced to act by events.

CHAPTER 15

Red Victory

FIRST STEPS

To take power was easy for the Bolsheviks; to retain it was a far greater accomplishment, for the odds against them were high. They succeeded because their enemies, at home and abroad, were divided and because Lenin had a keen flair for tactical manoeuvre. He threw doctrine to the winds where necessary to stay in the saddle, and treated dissenters with scant respect. Bolshevism was an intransigent creed. It was contemptuous of public opinion, for it ruled not by sanction of the ballot-box but through its self-proclaimed adherence to the tenets of Marxist-Leninist ideology. But this was a flexible teaching which successive party leaders could interpret much as they deemed expedient. It allowed for temporary retreats and for compromise with 'class enemies' but never lost sight of the ultimate goal, the construction of a world-wide socialist (eventually, communist) order.

The ruling party* sought to extend its power by a mixture of persuasion and coercion. The former entailed mass propaganda, purveyed on such an extensive scale that historians have termed Soviet Russia the world's first 'propaganda state'. The latter included, along with military force of a traditional kind, the use of terror, not just against real or alleged 'counter-revolutionaries' but also against 'vacillating elements' among the masses. Being a worker or peasant was no protection against arbitrary action by the masters of the self-styled 'proletarian dictatorship'. Like the French jacobins before them, the Leninists sought to concentrate all power in their own hands in order to accomplish their revolutionary purposes. They scorned as 'bourgeois' conven-

---

* Known from March 1918 as the RCP(b) (= Russian Communist party (bolshevik)); later it became the All-Union Communist party and in 1952 the Communist party of the Soviet Union.

tional legal or moral restraints on the exercise of governmental functions. Citizens' political and civil liberties had to take second place to the basic socio-economic rights accorded to working people, such as free education or full employment. These were duly enshrined in the first Constitution of the Soviet state, or Russian Soviet Federative Socialist Republic as it was officially known. This state was seen, not as a means of conciliating discordant interests, but as the instrument through which the working class, as the new ruling class, implemented its will. It operated under the tutelage of the party, which was deemed to express the immanent interests of the workers, and by extension of the popular masses in general; it was 'the vanguard of the proletariat'.

Initially the Bolsheviks were little concerned with state-building measures, since they saw their regime as a provisional one, soon to be subsumed in an all-European socialist order. Within a few months this view was shown to be illusory. They adjusted well to the new realities, consolidating their domestic base by bringing the soviet organs under central control, creating a bureaucratic apparatus and, above all, by forging the Red Army, a force strong enough to worst all its adversaries in a three-year civil war. Together with epidemic disease and hunger, this conflict cost some 10 million lives, far more than Russia had lost in the conventional war that had preceded it.

Immediately after the October *coup* in Petrograd the Bolshevik government, called Council of People's Commissars (*Sovnarkom*), was endorsed – along with Lenin's decrees on peace and land – by delegates to the second congress of soviets, who then dispersed to help set up 'soviet power' in their localities. The congress also elected a new Central Executive Committee, but this supposedly sovereign assembly could not exercise any effective control over the people's commissars. Efforts to do so were nipped in the bud by Jacob Sverdlov, the Party's chief organizer at the time, who was appointed its chairman. He replaced L. B. Kamenev, who had helped to provoke a crisis by protesting at a Sovnarkom decree instituting press censorship. Calling for responsible government, four people's commissars and some other leading officials resigned (4 November). But Lenin asserted his will and torpedoed talks designed to replace Sovnarkom by a socialist coalition government. A few weeks later the Left SRs agreed to join Sovnarkom, which made it appear more representative of maximalist opinion, especially among soldiers and peasants. In the provinces, meanwhile, cities that initially had been run by committees elected by various democratic organizations gradually passed into the hands of Bolsheviks and their allies. They were assisted by leather-jacketed emissaries, mainly soldiers, sent from Petrograd or the front.

The most immediate threat which the Bolsheviks now faced came from the Constituent Assembly, the national representative body whose convocation had been the dream of Russia's democrats for generations. Earlier in 1917 the Bolsheviks had charged the Kadets, not unfairly, with seeking to delay the elections because they would yield a socialist majority. After October they could therefore scarcely delay them further or just declare them invalid, although they could expect support from no more than one quarter to one third of the deputies.* Lenin chose the tactic of letting the deputies meet but requiring them to endorse a declaration approving the government's actions to date. Several deputies were arrested and the Kadets outlawed as 'enemies of the people' (28 November). Troops and Red guards were mobilized. On 4 January 1918, the day before the assembly met, several hundred persons who demonstrated peacefully on its behalf were fired on and at least ten killed. The writer Maxim Gor'ky, once a Bolshevik sympathizer but now an eloquent critic, compared the shooting to 'Bloody Sunday'. The parallel was not inapposite, but the two incidents had a totally different impact: this was not a government to be trifled with. In the chamber the deputies stood their ground courageously. As sailors aimed rifles at them from the gallery, they rushed through bills on land reform and a general negotiated peace to show where they stood.

These gestures served a symbolic purpose, for democrats in several parts of the country would later invoke the Constituent Assembly's mantle to justify resistance to dictatorship. One may doubt whether an assembly so divided could have formed a viable government.

---

* The elections, held in November 1917, were fairly free and turn-out high. Of 41 million votes cast the Bolsheviks polled less than one quarter; they won about half the soldiers' ballots and did well in the two capital cities (45 and 48 per cent respectively), as well as in industrial centres. The Kadets performed poorly (2 million votes), the right and Mensheviks even worse. Seven and a half million votes were cast for national-minority parties. The victors were the SRs, with over 15 million votes. In terms of seats, the score was SRs 370, Left SRs 40, Bolsheviks 175, Kadets 17, Mensheviks 16.

But many parliaments do not have working majorities, and this is not normally taken to mean that the country is unfit for democracy ... The Russian population was not necessarily incapable of understanding democratic principles but it was concerned with local, not national issues; it did not understand the conflict between the soviets and the Constituent Assembly and political rights were at best an abstraction ... Lenin understood [better] the aspirations of the Russian people: peace, bread, land ... [but] the vast majority of Russians saw no reason why these should not be combined with democracy, coalition socialist government, and the Constituent Assembly.*

The dissolution of the assembly was endorsed by the third congress of soviets, held immediately afterwards. These bodies, Bolsheviks claimed, were inherently more democratic than any 'bourgeois' parliament. But this was a paper-thin excuse. When soviets disobeyed orders they were unceremoniously dissolved in their turn. In the spring of 1918 the Mensheviks and SRs made an electoral comeback, winning control of several town soviets, and helped to organize an assembly of workers' representatives in Petrograd. Strikes called in protest at deteriorating conditions were forcibly suppressed. In Tambov Red troops shelled the local soviet into submission. Several local uprisings broke out in central Russia and full-scale civil war seemed imminent.

Much anger was caused by the Bolshevik government's apparent surrender to German imperialism. The external menace to their power was even greater than the internal one. Lenin's initial peace decree was ignored in Allied capitals, leaving Sovnarkom no alternative but to enter direct talks with the Central Powers for a cease-fire and a separate peace. In these negotiations, held at the border town of Brest-Litovsk, Soviet Russia was at a considerable disadvantage. Not only did her frankly expressed revolutionary goals, and the plebeian image cultivated by her first representatives, make her suspect to the old-style diplomats across the bargaining table, but she no longer had a military force capable of defending the new state's interests. During the winter months the Russian army's dissolution proceeded apace. Many peasant soldiers simply went home, eager to claim their share of the land. The elaborate structure of army committees collapsed. General headquarters

* Williams, 'The All-Russian Constituent Assembly', pp. 127–9.

at Mogilev passed under the control of a mere ensign, N. V. Krylenko, who was a Bolshevik activist of long standing (and a member of Sovnarkom). He failed to stop mutinous soldiers lynching the old army's last commander-in-chief, General N. N. Dukhonin. On the Romanian front the Bolsheviks had a tough struggle to assert themselves. The situation was complicated by the presence of Ukrainian troops with their own loyalties and by Romanian claims to Bessarabia,* which its forces took over in January, ostensibly on behalf of their local kinsmen. On the northern front the army's strength had all but evaporated by February 1918, so that little resistance could be offered when German troops once again advanced.

The Soviet delegation's strategy at Brest-Litovsk was to gain time, and to wear down their adversaries by a propaganda offensive unequalled in diplomatic annals to date, until their bluff was called – or, as was hoped, revolution broke out in Germany. At issue was the fate of the belt of territory lying between Russia and the Central Powers, who had occupied most of it. All parties stood nominally for self-determination, but each interpreted this principle after its own fashion. For the German high command, which had the strongest voice in policy making in the east, the Reich's security interests demanded that any national rights accorded to the local peoples be fictitious. Ardent expansionists dreamed of turning the Baltic states and Finland (and also Ukraine!) into German satellites. Austria-Hungary, stricken by famine, cast an envious eye on Ukraine's supposedly immense grain reserves. Beyond lay further temptations: the coal and oil of the former Russian empire's southern provinces. The Soviet leaders had no illusions about their adversaries' 'imperialist greed', but overestimated the revolutionary potential of German and Austrian workers. On this point Lenin showed greater realism than Trotsky, his closest collaborator and the first people's commissar for foreign affairs, who took over in January as chief negotiator at Brest-Litovsk.

Assuming the role of prosecuting attorney, he subjected the representatives of the Quadruple Alliance to a withering barrage of revolutionary invective

---

* Most of the province became known as Moldavia (now Moldova). It has an ethnically mixed population. The largest element consists of people speaking a dialect of Romanian which after the area's reannexation by the USSR in 1940 was claimed to be an independent language.

... The peace conference became a courtroom in which [German foreign minister R. von] Kühlmann and Trotsky laboured to impeach each other and the different social systems they represented ... [Trotsky wrote to Lenin:] 'My plan is this: we announce termination of the war and demobilization without signing any peace ... We place the fate of Poland, Lithuania and Kurland on the responsibility of the German working people.' Internal conditions in Germany, he said, would make it impossible for her to attack Soviet Russia.*

Lenin concurred in this tactic, although he expected the Germans to attack anyway: 'This beast,' he remarked, 'springs suddenly.' He knew that with the army in its current state any attempt to wage a revolutionary war, as proposed by hotheads in his party, would end in defeat and the fall of his regime. Better to accept the German demands outright. But this course had the backing of only a minority of Central Committee members. Accordingly on 10 February Trotsky made his dramatic gesture of 'neither war nor peace'.† The Germans promptly denounced the armistice and ordered their armies to advance. Panic gripped the Russian troops, who had been ordered to demobilize. Dvinsk was captured by a few dozen enemy soldiers without a shot being fired in its defence. Clearly Russia had no alternative to capitulation, and Lenin's motion to this effect won a slender majority.

On 22 February he proclaimed 'the socialist fatherland in danger'. Martial law was declared in Petrograd and frantic measures taken to enlist 'all conscious revolutionary fighters' in the new Red Army. People of 'bourgeois' background had to dig trenches. There was even talk of accepting aid from the Entente powers, but nothing much came of the idea. On 3 March the treaty of Brest-Litovsk was signed. The terms were harsher than those originally offered. Russia lost the Baltic lands to Germany and made other territorial concessions to Turkey. She had to withdraw troops from areas of Ukraine they had occupied during previous hostilities against the Rada government and to recognize that country's independence, as also that of Finland and Georgia. More injurious to specifically *Russian* interests were the treaty's

* Debo, *Revolution and Survival*, pp. 67–9.
† This would later be held against him by Stalin and his followers, who obscured the fact that at the time the policy had Lenin's assent, however reluctant.

economic stipulations, although they could be evaded to some extent.* The real threat came from subsequent German territorial encroachment, especially from the military occupation of Ukraine. But there was actually little to choose between Bolshevik and Austro-German designs on that unfortunate country's resources and independence. As for Soviet Russia, by midsummer she was to all intents and purposes a German client state, liable to be snuffed out at any moment. For the time being the Germans preferred to let the Bolsheviks survive.

We have no interest in supporting the monarchists' ideas [wired von Kühlmann in May], which would reunite Russia. On the contrary, we must try as far as possible to prevent Russian consolidation ... and therefore support the parties furthest to the left.

Ultimately, and paradoxically, the Bolsheviks were saved from destruction at German hands by the Allied victory in the West, which forced Germany to abandon her Eastern European conquests.

CIVIL WAR

This victory, however, freed Allied forces and shipping for intervention in Russia's civil war on behalf of the anti-Bolshevik 'Whites'. Understandably, opinion among the 'Reds' was bitterly hostile to foreign meddling in Russian affairs, and this attitude influenced much subsequent historiography. In fact the threat which the Entente posed to the young Soviet state was far less substantial than that previously presented by the Central Powers, about which little was said since German-Bolshevik relations were a sensitive topic. In the West the muddle that afflicted Allied policy in Russia, and their forces' with-

---

* Germany was granted most-favoured-nation status and her investors were to be compensated for sequestrated property. Since governments were accorded the right to determine the conditions in which foreign-owned companies operated, Sovnarkom could legitimately, by nationalizing several hundred firms that had German capital (28 June), prevent them from being taken over. A supplementary agreement of 27 August alleviated the treaty's burdens, and after Imperial Germany's collapse it was unilaterally denounced by the Bolsheviks. By then 120 million gold roubles had been paid to Germany. Pro-Entente historians have condemned the treaty's provisions as unduly onerous, but they were arguably less so than those imposed on Germany at Versailles.

drawal in 1919 before the triumphant Reds, gave the intervention a bad image. With hindsight, however, one could argue that Allied aid helped to keep the Bolsheviks too busy fighting domestic foes to give decisive support to Communist revolutionaries in Central Europe at a time when that whole region was in post-war turmoil. By contrast, when a similar vacuum appeared in 1944–5, the Red Army quickly filled it.

In any case, what mattered was less the presence in Russia of Allied troops, which seldom became involved in actual combat, than the material and moral support offered to various White governments. This took the form of financial aid, weaponry – and political advice, which was less welcome. Allied representatives often acted at cross-purposes and their involvement was sometimes counter-productive. It also gave apparent substance to Red propaganda that their adversaries were just 'hirelings of foreign capital' devoid of genuine popular support.

Foreign intervention was not responsible for the civil war's outcome. The Whites were worsted for a variety of reasons: military, economic, and political. In the first place their forces were deployed around the periphery of the former empire, in regions remote from one another and without rich natural resources, whereas the (pro-Bolshevik) Reds never lost control of the Russian heartland, the centre of its communications network. It was easier for them to shift troops quickly by rail from one sector to another. They also inherited from the old army a sizeable stock of arms, munitions, and equipment. The higher population density in the central regions allowed the Reds to raise larger armies, which by 1920 had a paper strength of 5 million men. The White forces were far smaller, and their initial advantage in experience was more apparent than real. Command structures were top-heavy and generals used to conventional warfare found it hard to adapt to a highly mobile style of campaigning, in which relatively light forces advanced and retreated rapidly across vast stretches of territory, usually following the railways.

This was an archaic war in which modern military hardware (aircraft, tanks) was of little account. Both sides used cavalry to good effect, although the 'First Cavalry Army' of S. M. Budenny (an intimate of Stalin) and its opponent, led by K. K. Mamontov, were alike notoriously ill-disciplined. Soldiers on each side, often short of food, lived off the country and so turned the population against them. Rapine and robbery were commonplace. On balance the Reds were better at containing such anarchistic excesses and in inspiring their men with a belief in the righteousness of their cause. They also had more success in reconciling divergent civilian and military interests. Lenin headed a virtually omnipotent Council of Labour and Defence. As people's commissar of war, Trotsky displayed considerable organizational talent. He pushed through, with Lenin's support, the unpopular policy of recruiting former officers and NCOs, some of whom (e.g. M. V. Frunze, K. E. Voroshilov) made astonishing careers, reaching top positions in the Red Army.

A system of supervision by 'political commissars' ensured that commanders of 'bourgeois' origin remained loyal. If they did not, members of their families held hostage were likely to be shot. Communist activists by the thousand were sent to the front, where they acted as ginger groups, ensuring that central directives were followed, preaching the party's message to the rank and file, and alleviating their day-to-day hardships. There was no equivalent among the White forces, whose propaganda and intelligence activities were amateurish. 'Russia one and indivisible' could scarcely compete with the Reds' revolutionary promises of equality and abundance under socialism. They satisfied popular aspirations for material betterment and the utopian longings that gave psychological solace to many. Moreover, the former slogan antagonized the non-Russian minorities.

On the economic side, the Bolsheviks were able to channel the heartland's industrial resources into the production of war goods more effectively than previous regimes could, thanks to state monopoly of ownership, labour controls, and a centralized supply organization that put the troops' needs first, leaving civilians to fend for themselves. Workers in Soviet territory had their grievances, but by and large they preferred Red rule to White, especially in those areas (e.g. the Donets valley) that experienced both. *Mutatis mutandis*, the same held good for the peasants, although for Cossacks the priorities were reversed. Until the last phase of the struggle no White leader was willing to endorse the agrarian revolution, whereby the villagers had seized the land for themselves. In the Crimea General (Baron) P. N. Wrangel made a half-hearted move in this direction in mid 1920, but it came too late.

Most remarkably of all, the White leaders failed to establish an efficient, law-abiding administration over the territories they held. As military professionals they were suspicious of civilian politicians, especially those of democratic and socialist persuasion. Used to giving orders, they found modern participatory politics distasteful and sought to keep control in military hands, at least so long as fighting lasted. Under Allied pressure the main White leaders agreed that power should pass ultimately to a new Constituent Assembly, though privately they hoped for a monarchist restoration. In any case this long-term commitment did not imply respect for human rights in the present emergency, and the major White administrations were scarred by gross miscarriages of justice and official corruption. The worst offenders were in eastern Siberia and Mongolia, where the White movement degenerated into sheer banditry.

Robber bands could be found across the lines, too. Ukraine was terrorized by a succession of local warlords, notably Ataman N. Grigoryev and *batko* (father) Nestor Makhno. The latter assembled a sizeable force of cut-throats, the Revolutionary Insurgent Army, which waged guerrilla war against Ukrainian nationalists, Whites, and (eventually) Reds. These bands were among the worst perpetrators of antisemitic atrocities, which in general were opposed more effectively by the Bolsheviks than by the Whites. Peasant partisan bands, known as 'Greens', also operated in many areas. The chiefs' main purpose was to protect the local population against predatory outsiders. Most ordinary folk sought to avoid taking sides in the struggle for as long as they could. When forced to choose, their preference usually lay with the Reds, who were identified with land reform and presented a more plebeian image.

The conflict passed through three phases: low-intensity warfare in 1918, major confrontations in 1919, and partial internationalization in 1920 (when Soviet Russia fought independent Poland). This latter war ended in a compromise peace, as did the fighting in the Baltic, but by and large the Reds emerged as clear winners. It remained for them to reconstitute the tsarist empire in new guise by establishing or consolidating Red power in the borderlands, subduing the governments established there by various national minorities.

During the first phase of the war a small Red force under Antonov-Ovseyenko marched on Kiev and overthrew the democratic Rada government, only to be cheated of the fruits of victory by the Central Powers. The Rada returned, but before it found its feet was deposed in favour of a German puppet, Hetman Skoropadsky (April 1918). A russified Ukrainian with links to the old regime, he tried to cooperate with the nationalist politicians and to enact a land reform, but his regime's constructive measures were negated by its obligation to supply the Central Powers with the agricultural produce they coveted. Peasant rebellions broke out and the nationalists conspired against him. As the Central Powers' hold on the country weakened, Skoropadsky's regime disintegrated. In December 1918 power passed to a civilian Directory under two Social Democrats, V. Vynnychenko and S. Petlyura, but it was soon faced with a second Bolshevik invasion.

Meanwhile to the east General Alexeyev's tiny anti-Bolshevik Russian 'Volunteer Army' established itself in the Don–Kuban' area. It depended for military muscle on well-trained Don Cossacks under P. N. Krasnov, elected ataman in May 1918, but their separatist and pro-German tendencies made them suspect to the Volunteers. These rivalries hampered concerted operations against the Reds. An offensive northwards reached Tsaritsyn (later Stalingrad) on the Volga. The city's successful defence owed less to the presence there of Stalin and Voroshilov, as later myth would have it, than to the Reds' numerical superiority.

They faced stiffer opposition on the eastern front. In the summer democratic socialists formed a government at Samara on the Volga. Its efforts to conscript soldiers aroused popular resistance and in October it fell to the Reds. This 'democratic counter-revolution' was made possible by a freak of history: an anti-Bolshevik uprising by the 40,000-strong Czechoslovak corps. This force consisted mainly of Austro-Hungarian prisoners of war, and was *en route* to join the Western Allies via Russian Arctic and Far Eastern ports. Friction with local pro-Bolshevik forces at Chelyabinsk in the Urals in May led to the overthrow of Soviet power in the entire Volga–Urals region and Siberia, where it was thinly stretched. The fall of Kazan' posed a direct threat to Moscow itself. Trotsky rallied the Red defenders on the Volga, transferring troops there from the west. Revolutionary Latvian riflemen under Colonel I. I. Vatsetis were prominent in the Red counter-offensive, which by year's end had reached the Urals.

In all this the Western Allies played little part, but they landed a few troops in the north, at Murmansk and Archangel, and at Vladivostok in the Far East, ostensibly to protect their military supply dumps.*

In the second phase of the war the French intervened at Odessa in the south, partly to sustain the Ukrainians, while the British backed the conservative Great Russian elements farther east. The 'Volunteer Army' had now been superseded by the Armed Forces of Southern Russia under General A. I. Denikin, a larger body which controlled the northern Caucasus. In May 1919, having repelled several Red offensives and penetrated into the Don basin, which brought the Cossacks under his command, Denikin launched a major operation to the north. He faced Red forces which, though numerically superior, suffered from shaky morale. This time Tsaritsyn fell to its attackers, as did Khar'kov and then Kursk and Orel.

Only 120 miles north of Orel was Tula, the armoury of the Red forces, and 120 miles north of Tula was Moscow . . . As Skoblin, the Kornilov [division] commander, rode his grey stallion into Orel's main square, a piece of Soviet 'monumental propaganda' covered in red cloth was knocked over in a cloud of lime dust. Could Red Square be far away?†

But Denikin had over-extended his forces, while the Reds now had a new leadership under S. S. Kamenev and some 150,000 men. It was now that Budennyi's cavalry came into its own. The Whites' administrative failings were their undoing. By the end of the year the Reds had reached the Don and Denikin's forces were back in the Crimea, where he had to turn over command to his chief critic, Wrangel.

One of the Whites' major lapses was poor coordination. On the eastern front Admiral A. V. Kolchak, who in November 1918 had taken over in a *coup* from a democratic predecessor,‡ launched an offensive into European Russia in March 1919, before Denikin was

---

* This was largely a pretext (although the problem was a real one). The Allied forces in Murmansk initially cooperated with the local Reds, and effected a minor joint operation against the White (pro-German) Finns, but relations soon became hostile. Morale among Allied soldiers was low and they saw no reason to fight on behalf of poorly motivated local anti-Bolsheviks.

† Mawdsley, *Russian Civil War*, p. 196.

‡ This was the short-lived five-man Directorate of liberals and moderate socialists, chosen in September by the Ufa State Conference as a provisional all-Russian government. The *coup* had the backing of the head of the British military mission, General Sir Alfred Knox.

ready to strike. Taken by surprise, the Reds fell back and soon Kolchak's troops threatened the vital Volga bridges. But before reaching the river the Whites had to retreat. Battles in the Urals cost them their sole industrial base and they fell back in disorder on to the Siberian plain, following the Trans-Siberian railway line eastward as superior Red forces pursued them and peasants rose up in their rear. Few of Kolchak's men got past Lake Baikal. The 'Supreme Ruler' himself was handed over by Allied (Czechoslovak) troops to a local socialist group and so to the Reds, who executed him at Irkutsk (February 1920). Denikin and Wrangel were luckier: they emigrated and later wrote their memoirs.

In March 1920 small Red forces moved into the White enclave in northern European Russia, whence British troops had pulled out several months earlier. This front had only nuisance value. A more serious threat was the Whites' North-western Army, based in Estonia. In September 1919, led by General N. N. Yudenich of Erzerum fame, it reached Petrograd's outer suburbs before Trotsky rushed up troops to bolster the city's defences. Outnumbered, Yudenich withdrew in disorder to Estonia, where his tatterdemalion army was interned.

The third phase of the war was fought on two fronts only. The Reds, now greatly strengthened, were fortunate that Wrangel in the Crimea and Jósef Piłsudski in Poland failed to coordinate their operations. The 'black baron' approached Ukrainian politicians, but without success; and most of them were hostile to the Poles, with whom they had fought a bitter war in Galicia. This proved to be a crucial factor. Wrangel managed to instil better discipline into his men, but the need for supplies forced him to undertake a premature offensive into southern Ukraine (June). Within a fortnight he had doubled the territory under his control and smashed a Red counter-offensive. But he was short of fuel and received only lukewarm support from the Allies, who were tiring of the game. The balance of power was unfavourable and he faced an experienced Red commander.

Fresh from a string of triumphs that stretched from Siberia to Turkestan, the iron-willed Frunze was not a man to accept anything short of victory. 'Wrangel must be smashed . . .', he announced in his first general order . . . The Reds had a thousand more machine-guns than did the Whites, and although the numbers of tanks, armoured cars, armoured trains and planes on each side remained about equal, the Reds' were of higher quality and in much better repair . . . The proportion of Frunze's soldiers who belonged to the Bolshevik party or were candidates for membership rose to one in eight.*

The end came in November. In an orderly evacuation 126 ships carried no fewer than 146,000 refugees to Istanbul and eventually to safety in the West. Those left behind faced fearsome reprisals.

Meanwhile the Poles, who had won their independence when the Central Powers collapsed, had become involved in intermittent fighting along the Soviet border. Piłsudski, the chief of state, sought to extend Polish control over Belarusian and Ukrainian territory, as if to re-create the situation before the eighteenth-century partitions. In May 1920 Polish troops entered Kiev. But Ukraine did not rise in support and swiftly the tide of battle turned. The Reds, carried forward by a wave of revolutionary patriotism, soon reached the river Bug, roughly the ethnic border (the Curzon line). The Bolsheviks then succumbed to the temptation of invading ethnically Polish territory in the hope of stimulating the long-hoped-for German workers' uprising – 'probing Western Europe with Russian bayonets', as Lenin put it. He expected to take Warsaw within days (17 August). But the Poles rallied, their resolve stiffened by French support. Trotsky quarrelled with Stalin, who not for the first time took an insubordinate line. In order to aid the southern front he moved troops on his own authority and so exposed the Russian armies' left flank to enemy counter-attack.

The man most responsible for making what might have been an orderly retreat from Poland into a rout was Stalin. What his real motives may have been . . . will always be a matter for speculation. It is possible that he refused [M. N. Tukhachevsky] assistance out of pure resentment. He and Voroshilov . . . held numerous grudges against the commissar for War [Trotsky, who] had humiliated them in the battle for Tsaritsyn two years before.†

The clash was papered over, but would assume political importance later. The Soviet-Polish war ended with the treaty of Riga (March 1921), which gave Poland some of the coveted eastern Slavic lands. As

---

* Lincoln, *Red Victory*, p. 442.
† Fiddick, *Russia's Retreat from Poland*, p. 244.

Lenin explained later, 'The thought of another agonizing winter of war was unbearable. We had to make peace.'

RECONSTITUTING THE EMPIRE

The Soviets had to make concessions in the Baltic, too. Finland's independence owed much to German and then to Allied support. The country's relations with Russia were uneasy. Some Finnish leaders, notably the Russian-educated regent, General (later Field Marshal) Mannerheim, wanted to help the Whites and hoped to secure the ethnically related region of Karelia to the east. But when Mannerheim was voted out of office he retired, for he was not cast in dictatorial mould.* Finnish nationalism was generally moderate and the population had a well-developed civic sense. The presence of a British naval squadron in the eastern Baltic also played a role in persuading the Bolsheviks to put aside plans to revolutionize the country and instead to make peace (October 1920). The frontier ran along the pre-war border and gave Finland access to Arctic waters at Petsamo; eastern Karelia became an autonomous region within the RSFSR.

The Finnish example was followed by the Estonians and Latvians. Both countries had suffered a damaging Red invasion in November 1918 which turned popular sentiment against the radical left. They also suffered from the presence on their territory of German and White Russian forces. It was this that led them to negotiate peace with the Bolsheviks, who were willing to recognize their independence provided they did not help the 'counter-revolutionaries'. The new democracies won recognition from the international community but their security remained precarious.

This was also true of Lithuania. After a brief phase of Bolshevik rule, which saw Lithuania linked to Belarus in a single republic, its chief city, Vilnius, was taken by the Poles. However, an independent government at Kaunas managed to win popular support and to regu-

---

* In the 1930s this aristocratic statesman would return to help stabilize a democracy whose principles differed from his own when it faced a Soviet threat that led to the 'Winter War': see page 400.

larize relations with Lithuania's rapacious neighbours. In the entire Baltic region the political and socio-economic situation was inherently unfavourable to revolutionary designs and the local Communist parties remained weak.

Ukrainian national consciousness, which in 1917 had been confined to a thin intellectual stratum, developed rapidly under the impact of occupation by the Central Powers, White and Red Russians and Poles – not to mention the depredations of bandit gangs. Kiev was 'liberated' fifteen times in three years! The Western Allies were sceptical of Ukrainian nationalists' desire for independence and accorded them less help than to their counterparts in the Baltic. The Reds, who re-entered the country in the winter of 1918–19, made themselves unpopular with the peasants by requisitioning grain stocks and setting up state farms. They also alienated intellectuals by taking a contemptuous attitude towards Ukrainian culture. Much of the country rose up in an insurrection that had regionalist, anarchist, and chauvinistic features. To these angry mobs anti-Bolshevism automatically meant antisemitism. In Uman' district in May 1919 Grigoryev's men, maddened by alcohol, butchered 400 Jews. Fifty pogroms occurred at that time in three provinces and by 1921 the total had reached 2,000. Overall ethnic violence cost some 30,000 Jews their lives; a further 120,000 died through injury or sickness.

One consequence was that Jews naturally looked more sympathetically on Bolshevism. In 1918 the RCP had formed Jewish sections (*Yevsektsii*), whose task was 'to carry out the proletarian dictatorship on the Jewish street', which meant struggling against the Zionists. The latter's organizations were dissolved and their funds seized. Hebrew was declared a 'counter-revolutionary' language. However, the policy of repression was not carried out consistently. Religious beliefs survived, together with a growing awareness of Jewish national identity.

Communist policy on the Ukrainian question was likewise incoherent. The local Party was split into several factions on the issue, outright centralizers opposing advocates of limited national autonomy – and, logically, a compromise with left-wing agrarian socialists (known as Borotbisty, akin to the Left SRs in Russia). Lenin took an intermediate stand. He viewed the problem in tactical terms: the proposed alliance should be only temporary, with the 'proletarian' party absorbing the 'vacillating petty-bourgeois elements'. This line was adopted, but it did not put an end to dissidence. Ukrainian Communists remained critical of Moscow's centralizing policies, as did the population generally. The leadership had to tread carefully, and advocated 'soft' policies on economic and cultural issues.

The same problem beset policy makers in other minority regions where the war gave a fillip to local nationalism. Now that Russia had lost so much territory in the west (the Baltic states, Poland, Bessarabia), her Asiatic territories assumed greater significance than before. The capital's move from Petrograd to Moscow symbolized this geopolitical shift. The Bolsheviks hoped, by successfully resolving the national question in the east, to win credit elsewhere in Asia (China, India, Near East), where local revolutionaries were challenging the colonial order. In this way the 'imperialist' powers, apparently triumphant for the moment in Europe, could be undermined by a mass movement of the 'toilers of the Orient', inspired and aided by Soviet Russia.

This enticing prospect does much to explain the Reds' conduct in Transcaucasia and towards the Muslim peoples generally, all of whom experienced an upsurge of nationalist and revolutionary sentiment. In the former region an attempt was first made to set up a federal government, but by the spring of 1918 this had broken up in ethnic rivalry. Armenians and Azerbaijanis slaughtered each other once again, whereupon Turkish troops came in. When Turkey was defeated the British replaced them, but in minuscule strength, and their efforts to resolve local disputes proved unavailing. External intervention, partly motivated by interest in the oilfields, did not help the three independent republics, which were all highly unstable. Their governments confronted economic breakdown, empty treasuries, and lack of administrative personnel. Food shortages were chronic: in Armenia alone 200,000 died of starvation within a year, notwithstanding American relief. Its Dashnyak government was unable to carry out a land reform and wasted its energies feuding with its neighbours. Much the same could be said of the Musavat regime in Azerbaijan. The Menshevik government of the Georgian Democratic Republic, by contrast, was more solidly based. It established a pluralistic political system and a strong militia – although here, too, there was fighting with local minority groups, such as the Abkhazians. All three republics feared the Whites, but this did not make them fonder of the Reds, whom they saw not unreasonably as neo-imperialists.

Soviet rule was imposed on the region by external force. In the spring of 1920 the RCP set up a 'Caucasian Bureau' under Sergo Ordzhonikidze, one of Stalin's cronies.* Within two months a bloodless *coup* had deposed the Azerbaijani government. Armenia's turn came in December, after it had been further weakened by more fighting with the Turks. Armenian nationalists looked to Moscow for support in this struggle, but instead found their lands once again partitioned. For Soviet Russia the friendship of Kemalist Turkey, so important in her international revolutionary strategy, took first priority.

An element of duplicity also marked the reconquest of Georgia, carried out in contravention of a friendship treaty. Lenin dropped his objections to an invasion when G. V. Chicherin, the foreign commissar, assured him that neither Turkey nor Britain would intervene. In February 1921 Moscow staged a local insurrection which gave Red Army troops a pretext to cross the border. Fighting lasted for a month but the issue was not in doubt. A Georgian Bolshevik regime took over. Moscow accorded it extensive rights, but these were soon whittled away and a new Transcaucasian federation set up, this time under Moscow's control.

The Russian empire's disintegration in 1917–18 left its Muslim peoples scattered and their respective fates owed much to the vagaries of civil war. Many *jadid* (enlightener) intellectuals hoped to win autonomy, if not independence, under Bolshevik auspices, so setting an example for their co-religionists elsewhere. For them national liberation took precedence over class struggle, which they viewed as a European concept irrelevant to their own circumstances, and even dangerous in so far as it was manipulated to establish Russian control over the revolutionary movement in their lands. A Volga Tatar leader, Sultan-Galiev, emerged as the most articulate spokesman for these heady ideas, which anticipated those of the Chinese Maoists in the 1960s. To the Bolsheviks, and particularly to Stalin, this was a 'bourgeois-nationalist deviation' that threatened to undermine inter-

---

* As nationalities commissar Stalin at first had little to do, but from 1919 he used this office skilfully to build up a personal power base within the Party – government apparatus, relying heavily, but not exclusively, on fellow-Georgians.

national proletarian solidarity and the interests of its vanguard, the RCP.

In May 1918 Muslim revolutionary leaders proclaimed a Tatar-Bashkir republic at Kazan'. But the Bashkirs resented the secondary role allotted them in this state, which soon collapsed. In November 1919, when the war clouds had settled, another effort was made. It led to the setting up of two small autonomous republics, in each of which the native element was outweighed by the Russian. This was also the case in the Kazakh autonomous republic farther south, where there were many Russian settlers, and in Kyrgyzstan.

Central Asia proper went through turbulent times. Turkestani Muslims set up an autonomous regime at Kokand which the local Russian Bolsheviks regarded as 'bourgeois'. They besieged the city and massacred its inhabitants (February 1918), which did not help the Communist cause. The emirate of Bokhara became a centre of Islamic resistance, while Turkmenia briefly hosted a British military mission. In 1919 Moscow restored contact with its unruly vassals in Tashkent, who had been temporarily cut off by the Whites, and brought them to heel. Frunze purged both Russian and Muslim nationalist elements in the local leadership and then marched on Khiva, which fell in February 1920, and Bokhara, subdued in September. The two emirates had enjoyed the status of protectorates in imperial times. They now became 'people's republics' in which private property and Islamic law were allowed to co-exist with Soviet-type institutions. They remained unstable, the scene of a long-drawn-out war against the *basmachi*, anti-Communist guerrillas inspired by a fundamentalist brand of Islam, who received intermittent support from Turkey (Enver Pasha) and Afghanistan.

In the rest of Soviet Turkestan – to look ahead – the Islamic threat to Communism was contained by a neat administrative device, the division of the territory into autonomous republics differentiated on supposedly ethnic lines (1924). This ostensibly progressive measure was contested by nationalists who argued that it was artificial, since the languages spoken in these republics were interrelated and ethnic animosities were a thing of the past. But their opposition could not be articulated freely. During the 1920s Moscow tried hard to woo the native élite with liberal cultural policies and measures of modernization. Many ex-*jadids* were indeed won over and took an active part in public life. But the day of reckoning had only been postponed: Stalin still distrusted them.

And it was Stalin, rather than Lenin, who laid his personal imprint on the new constitutional and administrative set-up. Bolshevik policy towards the nationalities owed more to circumstance than ideology. In 1918 the principle of federalism, hitherto condemned on doctrinal grounds, was tacitly accepted and written into the RSFSR Constitution – although this was seen as a temporary tactical expedient pending creation of an all-European revolutionary order. 'Federalism,' wrote Stalin, 'is only a transitional stage to future socialist unity.' As this ultimate goal receded and the Bolsheviks willy-nilly settled down to governing those territories they had 'liberated', a federal solution to inter-ethnic relations grew more attractive. Even so it was not a question of adopting 'bourgeois' notions of federalism, based on *Rechtsstaat* principles, but of what might be called pseudo-federalism. For the central party leadership reserved the right to determine what powers should be allocated to the constituent units and how they should be exercised. Priority was given to 'socialist construction'. Accordingly all authorities were obliged to harmonize policy on matters of consequence, to present a common front to the 'class enemy', and to accept direction of the RCP – which most emphatically was *not* to be federated but was run hierarchically on so-called 'democratic centralist' principles. The rights of union republics, which were ostensibly sovereign, and of autonomous republics and regions, which were not, were determined from above and largely bogus. Characteristically, no provision was made for independent legal (constitutional) settlement of inter-republican disputes.

As the several non-Russian territories came under Bolshevik control, their governments concluded treaties with the RSFSR whereby they agreed to align their policies. This was a preliminary step to unification. A commission headed by Stalin was set up (August 1922), which reported in favour of 'autonomization', an ostensibly generous scheme which camouflaged a highly centralized structure. Ukrainian and Georgian Communists objected. Lenin, already ailing, vacillated. He told Kamenev that 'Stalin is in too much of a hurry' but rebuked the Georgians for their disobedience. Stalin said privately that Lenin was guilty of 'national liberalism', i.e. excessive softness. In December a congress of soviets endorsed the idea of a Union of Soviet Socialist

Republics. At that very moment Lenin belatedly realized the harmful implications.* Convinced that the Party had become infected with 'great-power chauvinism', he suggested that the Union's bonds be loosened. However, before he could act he was disabled by a stroke (his fourth): Stalin was saved.

But did Lenin really have a viable alternative? On one reading of the evidence, Stalin had a better grasp of political realities. Lenin's more liberal concept anticipated the kind of relationship that existed among East European Communist states after 1956 (see page 504). Could this have worked in the USSR of the 1920s, which by its own volition was isolated and embattled? Arguably the Soviet leaders faced a stark choice between Stalinist totalitarianism and a genuine federalism that would have implied democratizing the 'proletarian dictatorship'.

THE DRIFT TO DICTATORSHIP

Such a dictatorship was more aspiration than reality so long as the civil war lasted. Until about 1921 policy was determined largely by the revolutionized masses, or at least by their most active elements, and the country's new rulers had to adapt to these pressures from below. It was less a matter of the party or government imposing socialist ideas than of the 'centre' responding flexibly to the egalitarian sentiments of its actual or potential supporters. The elemental mass drive for revenge on former oppressors probably mattered more than the utopian dreams that animated some idealists, mainly intellectuals. In any case, people's first priority was to survive the economic chaos, and they were none too scrupulous about the methods they employed.

This chaos was due to the breakdown of the market under the stress of war and revolution. The Soviet state's fluctuating frontiers hampered attempts at economic regulation. Whether one lived or died depended mainly on local conditions. Russia was fragmented into countless regions, districts, and villages. Rural areas usually did better than urban

---

* The immediate reason was the tactless behaviour of Stalin stalwarts towards Georgian Communist leaders, one of whom was struck in the face by Ordzhonikidze. They had previously resigned *en masse* in an effort to win Lenin's support for their demands.

ones, and there was a great exodus from the cities. The population of Petrograd, for example, fell from 2½ million in February 1917 to less than ¾ million in August 1920. By the winter of 1919/20 the former capital wore a ghostly aspect.

The silence was accompanied by whiteness and darkness: deathly whiteness, sounds muted by the huge snowdrifts which were no longer cleared from the streets, darkness out of which terrifying white-sheeted figures on tall stilts appeared, leaping grotesquely after a lone fleeing pedestrian whom they would seize and strip naked of all clothes and possessions. All street lighting went for good in the spring of 1920. Zamyatin wrote of houses gliding past each other like ships in the mist; Shklovsky of the walls of heated rooms showing up from the street as 'occasional dark patches' in an otherwise silver city . . . [To cite Akhmatova:]

> In the west an earthly sun still shines,
> And the roofs of cities gleam in its rays,
> But here the white plague marks the houses with crosses
> And summons the ravens – and the ravens come.*

Inflation sky-rocketed. By 1920 50,000 roubles were needed to buy what one rouble had fetched in 1914. The 10,000 officials engaged in printing banknotes could not keep up with demand. Goods were bartered instead. This trade, although deemed 'speculative', was tolerated for want of a viable alternative. It was carried on in open markets, one of which was situated almost within sight of the Kremlin. To working-class families wages were less important than rations and, for the breadwinner, a meal in a factory canteen. The rationing system was socially discriminatory, those performing physical labour getting more. It was also notoriously corrupt. Far more tickets were issued than there were people entitled to them. There were reports of commissars eating lavish dinners, but on the whole privilege was then at a discount and everyone went short: to many this was just what the revolution was about. Townspeople went to the country to exchange domestic articles for food. So-called 'bagmen' did a roaring trade, bribing their way past the detachments of armed men who controlled the trains. All this black-market activity undercut the food supply

* McAuley, *Bread and Justice*, pp. 263–4.

monopoly, which tried to organize 'products exchange' (factory goods for foodstuffs) to prevent town and village from drifting apart.

This scheme did not work well. One reason was that factories were prone to do what they liked with their products. Here the interests of management and labour coincided. In any case there were fewer plants making consumer goods. The lack of raw materials led many to close their doors; social tensions on the shopfloor often forced managers and technical staff to flee in despair. Initially Lenin sought an accommodation with leading industrialists. He argued that 'state capitalism' was an essential preliminary stage to socialism: he was impressed by the achievements of the German war economy and took it as a model. But this moderate course was sabotaged by workers who took over plants in the hope of keeping them going and so maintaining their earnings. The Soviet leadership responded by laying new emphasis on the merits of labour discipline, 'Taylorism',* and one-man management. 'Workers' control' largely disappeared; employees who objected to this faced dismissal or worse.

The intensification of civil war made centralized control of industry still more urgent. Production was diverted to military ends. Major industries (metals, chemicals, fuels, textiles) were nationalized; and in 1920 state ownership was extended, on paper at least, to all factories making non-essentials. These measures created an ever-expanding bureaucracy – by September 1918 the Central Economic Council's central staff alone was 6,000 strong – without doing much for industrial efficiency. (It did, however, keep many former middle-class people alive.) In practice the planners' attention was focused on keeping key defence plants supplied. Output of textiles, which had a lower priority, was down to about one third of the pre-war average by 1920; total industrial output was then only 14 per cent of the earlier figure. Oil kept up better than coal; locomotives ran on wood fuel, and peat bogs were exploited to make up the deficiency. All this demanded

---

* Named after the American engineer F. W. Taylor, an apostle of the scientific organization of factory work, based on time-and-motion studies and payment by piece-rates. This had hitherto been denounced by socialists as 'capitalist exploitation', but the Bolsheviks argued that, with the means of production now in the workers' hands, their obligation was to help build socialism by working hard and raising productivity. The surplus product taken by the proletarian state was used wholly for the people's benefit, so that there could no longer be any question of exploitation.

technical and organizational ingenuity, but there was no gainsaying the fact that the Russian economy was rapidly slipping back into the pre-industrial era. Its relative backwardness was actually an advantage in disguise, for it made it easier to withstand the crisis and recover later.

The 'black repartition' of 1917–18 created a large, relatively homogeneous class of peasant smallholders, whose chief aim was to enjoy the fruits of their victory and to feed their families as best they could. This was not easy, given the lack of equipment (even simple tools were lacking); livestock could not be properly cared for and many farmers lacked experience. The young villagers who returned from the front or the cities were in revolutionary mood and unwilling to heed their elders' advice. They set up their own homesteads, which often led to generational conflicts. There was also intercommunal rivalry. To the Bolsheviks, with their dogmatic outlook on agrarian matters, it seemed as if the village were rent by *class* conflict: poor or landless peasants (*bednyaki*, *batraki*) versus wealthy exploiters (*kulaki*). In June 1918 a decree established committees of poor peasants (*kombedy*), whose task was to help armed urban 'supply detachments' requisition the surplus allegedly held by greedy 'kulaks'. Committee members were to be rewarded with a share of whatever was taken. In effect, if not in intention, this was a declaration of war on the peasantry as a whole. Chaos ensued.

As the sorcerer's apprentice discovered, useful tools can get out of hand. The committees ran into conflict with local soviets and began to challenge their authority . . . They all too quickly absorbed the lessons of their Communist instructors and decided that while the poor were inheriting the earth they might as well take over its governance.*

Desperate activists took grain wherever they found it, relying on the bayonet. In one village (Chernigov province) a supply detachment appeared before the assembly, lined up the 'poor' on one side and the 'rich' on the other, pointing their rifles at the latter; within a few minutes they had surrendered. Revolts broke out which officials were quick to brand as 'counter-revolutionary'. They were suppressed as in

* Atkinson, *End of Russian Land Commune*, pp. 193–4.

the days of serfdom: the ringleaders were shot and 'contributions' levied on the recalcitrant communities. Much of the grain collected by these crude methods went to waste.

Belatedly Lenin rediscovered the 'middle peasant' and urged that he be courted. The *kombedy* were dissolved and the rural soviets reactivated – but under the control of local party stalwarts. In the meantime the RCP had built up its rural cadres, although they were thinly stretched. A 'new' policy – it actually had been tried in 1916! – was introduced: quota assessment (*razverstka*), which amounted to a tax in kind. This was supplemented by various labour duties, such as cutting timber or maintaining roads, not to mention helping Red Army units as they passed through. Taken together, these burdens might account for half a household's income; they were many times greater than what peasants had paid in tax and rent before the war. It is generally thought that these exactions deprived peasants of any incentive to sow more than they needed to consume. This view has recently been challenged,* but everyone agrees that the arbitrary methods of exaction were unjust and demoralizing. Not surprisingly, state grain procurements in 1918–20 were far below pre-revolutionary levels, even allowing for territorial losses.

Peasants continued to protest in the only ways they knew, joining 'Green' partisan bands and taking violent revenge on their tormentors.

There were numerous cases when local Communists were locked in the building of the soviet and burned alive . . . In a letter to Lenin, Lunacharsky described one of these horrifying episodes in Kostroma province: '. . . The peasants killed, froze to death, and burned alive twenty-four of our comrades, having subjected them to horrible tortures. But at the same time I am not completely sure that the blame falls on the peasants exclusively . . . it started with machine-gun fire upon them.'†

By 1920 whole regions of the country were in uproar. The struggle was particularly intense in Tambov, where Alexander Antonov, a former SR activist, led some 20,000 'Green' fighters in a terrorist

---

* By Lih, *Bread and Authority*, pp. 254ff., who argues that 'the difficulties were caused not so much by what was taken out of the countryside as by the failure to put anything back in' – for which he holds the war and the Allied blockade more responsible than the Bolsheviks.
† Brovkin, *Behind the Front Lines*, p. 157.

campaign against the Red authorities. They replied in kind, burning villages, taking hostages, and executing captives or deporting them *en masse* to forced-labour camps.

In February 1921 trouble erupted in Petrograd, where Zinoviev wielded dictatorial power. Large-scale strikes broke out in protest at cuts in the food ration. Nearly one hundred factories shut down for lack of fuel. The price of bread tripled within a few days. Sailors at the nearby Kronstadt naval base, 'the pride and glory of the revolution', knew of these grievances and were seething with discontent. On 1 March a mass meeting endorsed a resolution demanding that soviets throughout the land be re-elected by secret ballot. Other demands included:

freedom of speech and press for workers and peasants, anarchists and left socialist parties; freedom of assembly for trade unions and peasant associations; . . . the liberation of all political prisoners [belonging to] socialist parties, as well as all workers and peasants; . . . a commission to review the cases of those held in jails and concentration camps; . . . equalization of the rations of all toilers.*

This was 'counter-revolution from the left', so to speak. Bolshevik propagandists who represented it as 'bourgeois' were far from the truth; nor were the sailors fresh recruits to the Baltic fleet, as was alleged, but rather revolutionary veterans who wanted a return to the ideals of October 1917 – 'soviets without commissars', not Western-style democracy. The authorities blockaded the island and, on 17–18 March, sent some 45–50,000 troops, their morale stiffened by party cadres, across the ice of the frozen Finnish Gulf to subdue the rebels. Documents published in 1994 show that 2,103 men were executed; 10,000 suffered lesser penalties.

For Lenin the revolt showed that the Bolsheviks had to retreat on the economic front while stiffening political controls. He recognized that the earlier policies had been in error, yet sought to justify them as imposed on the party by the harsh necessities of war. The misleading appellation 'war communism' stuck, but it is clear that Bolshevik

---

* Getzler, *Kronstadt 1917–1921*, p. 214.

extremism derived in large measure from ideological preconceptions: just how far is a matter for debate.*

There is less disagreement about the significance of ideology in building the Bolshevik party-state, although certainly this process, too, was in part a response to civil-war pressures. The dictatorial measures of the first months anticipated what would follow, as Mensheviks and other critics correctly foresaw. Their ability to express their opinions was greatly hampered by press controls, arbitrary police measures, and the exclusion of democratic socialists from the soviets (July 1918). Despite this harassment they maintained a presence in some of these bodies at local level and profited from the groundswell of opposition in the winter of 1920–21.

Mensheviks were also prominent in several trade unions, notably the printers', while the SR party retained its appeal for peasants, soldiers, and sailors. Some elements of the latter party actively supported popular revolts against Bolshevik rule, while the Mensheviks adopted the role of 'loyal opposition'. Their advocacy of workers' rights embarrassed the authorities, who bided their time until the civil war had ended, and then silenced these irritating critics for good. In 1922, in an unusual gesture, ten of their leaders were allowed to emigrate, as were 160 intellectuals. A number of prominent SRs, however, were arraigned in the first 'show trial' of Soviet history. Largely thanks to pressure by socialists abroad, they escaped the death penalty, but Stalin caught up with them later. Nor did the Left SRs or Anarchists fare much better. By these drastic measures Lenin's Communist Party secured for itself a monopoly of political power.

This did not happen all at once. For the first year or so after October the Bolsheviks ruled primarily through the government machinery (Sovnarkom and people's commissariats), soviet executive committees

---

* A leading student of this problem concludes that: 'Marxist ideology provided . . . [the] belief that political means could take the place of economic criteria; . . . disregard for the peasants' interest, in so far as they aspired to own land; justification of coercion . . . ; preference for central control as a substitute for the market; and finally, the urgency of modernization. Yet the effective shape which the first Communist economic organization assumed was highly dependent on specific Russian legacies, on emergency and on social pressure.' See Malle, *Economic Organization of War Communism*, p. 503.

(excoms), the Red Army, and the security police;* only from 1919 onward did the RCP assume the role of central directing force. The Cheka began shooting 'enemies of the people' as early as February 1918. Among prominent victims were the former tsar Nicholas II and his family, put to death in grisly circumstances at Yekaterinburg on 16 July 1918. The operation was master-minded from Moscow, and the false impression given that local Cheka organs were responsible. These did indeed have wide powers to arrest suspects, take hostages, and so on. There was no question of their actions being subject to judicial control, although the justice commissariat made efforts in this direction. An attempt on Lenin's life (30 August 1918) led to a wave of officially sanctioned 'Red terror' which cost hundreds of lives (1,400 hostages were shot in Petrograd and Kronstadt alone). Forced-labour camps, also (in part) under Cheka control, held about 50,000 prisoners by 1920. The total number of persons executed in four years has been put at around 140,000, plus an equivalent number who perished when insurrections were suppressed. The Don Cossacks were exterminated in an operation that verged on genocide; and Whites left behind in the Crimea were likewise slaughtered *en masse*. The Cheka had a frontier defence force and its own internal security troops, whose combined strength exceeded a quarter of a million as the civil war ended.

A well-justified fear of the Cheka's arbitrary power played a big role in subduing the population. Coercion on a less vicious scale was applied by and within the regular government machinery. Soviet assemblies met less regularly, and then simply to endorse decisions by their executives (in fact, by the local bosses). Soviet agencies were also subject to control from within, by their Bolshevik members who formed a 'fraction' or core group. The RCP's statute (1919) allotted it merely a surveillance role in state organs, but in practice its agencies took over the business of government at all levels, from Sovnarkom down to the humble rural district. Not all members of these bodies were necessarily Communists, but in practice the 'non-party men' had to follow the party line, whether it was a matter of passing resolutions, appointing

---

* The All-Russian Extraordinary Commission for Combating Counter-Revolution and Sabotage (*Vecheka*, *Cheka*), headed by the Pole Felix Dzerzhinsky, was set up by Lenin already on 7 December 1917 and came directly under Sovnarkom.

(previously nominated) functionaries, or implementing policy decisions taken on high.

Simultaneously within the RCP itself power came to be concentrated in its 'leading organs': the Politburo, which took decisions on day-to-day policy, the Orgburo, and the Secretariat. The latter two agencies were responsible *inter alia* for appointing party personnel, of whom registers were kept in one of the Secretariat's many departments, Records and Assignment (Uchraspred). This marked the origin of the subsequently famous *nomenklatura* (see page 334). Party members were kept under supervision for moral or political backsliding. Disobedient organizations might be summarily disbanded and their members transferred elsewhere; periodically the ranks were purged to maintain quality – or to eliminate dissenters. Turnover was high: between March 1920 and March 1921 membership rose from 612,000 to 730,000, but thereafter fell sharply – or so it would appear.* The centralization process, coupled with war-time pressures, put a stop to the free-and-easy debating style of early 1918, when a 'Left Communist' faction of ideological fundamentalists had enjoyed considerable leeway. In 1920 two opposition groups emerged. The so-called Democratic Centralists, who grew out of the Ukrainian Communist Party, wanted more intra-party democracy and a greater role for workers in managing the economy. Similar demands, in reverse priority, were put forward by the 'Workers' Opposition' of Shlyapnikov and Alexandra Kollontay, a well-known feminist. Neither group was a real threat to Lenin, but he found their appeals to the Party's conscience embarrassing. An open discussion on the role of trade unions under socialism (1920) led to squabbling and advertised the Party's disunity.

The Kronstadt revolt was the last straw. The RCP's Tenth Party congress (March 1921) marked a watershed in its history. All factional groupings were prohibited and agitation on behalf of trade-union autonomy declared an 'Anarcho-Syndicalist deviation' incompatible with party membership. The ban did not stop factionalism, but by striving for 'monolithic unity' the country's rulers took a big step towards totalitarianism. The sinister party-state regime which Lenin had created would be perfected by his successor.

---

* Since the statistics for 1920 are incomplete, there may actually have been a 30 per cent *drop* over the year. See Service, *Bolshevik Party in Revolution*, p. 148.

CHAPTER 16

Recovery and Consolidation

SOCIETY AND THE ECONOMY IN THE 1920S

The Bolsheviks' adoption of a 'new economic policy' (NEP) in March 1921 did not bring an immediate improvement in the condition of Russian society. During seven years of war and revolution the country had been living off its capital and was all but ruined. Drought and neglect led to a catastrophic famine in the Volga region and Ukraine in 1921–2 which cost several million lives; estimates of total human losses over the period 1914–22 range from 9 to 14 million. Thereafter the population rose again, following a fall in the death-rate, particularly among infants, and by the mid 1920s it had regained the pre-war level. This did not apply to all regions or age-groups, and there were nearly 5 million more females than males. The 1926 census also showed that the population had become much more mobile. People who had fled the towns *en masse* during the civil war now returned. They were joined by countless villagers in search of employment; their arrival placed an intolerable strain on tightly stretched local resources.

Particularly heart-rending was the lot of homeless children, the so-called *besprizorniki*. Initially numbering between 4 and 7 million, they thronged railway stations and city streets, living rough and earning their keep by begging, crime, or prostitution. Some were orphans; others had been lost or abandoned by parents who,

drained by the famine to the point where they could no longer support their young, brought them to the nearest orphanage . . . [and], if told by officials that no resources or space remained in a facility, frequently deposited offspring in the hallways or stairwells of the building or on the street outside . . . Even a good harvest failed to halt the flow of rural youths to cities, for most villages contained landless or at least impoverished families . . . Youths slept under boats upturned on river banks, . . . under bridges, in discarded trunks and barrels . . .*

Family ties, shattered by death and deprivation, were further weakened by the new regime's avant-garde policies. The civil codes of 1918 and 1926 facilitated divorce, which could be obtained on demand: one had merely to send one's partner a postcard stating that the relationship was at an end. The divorce rate in the early 1920s was twenty-six times greater than in the United Kingdom (England and Wales) and in Moscow there was one divorce for every two marriages concluded. Predictably husbands rather than wives made use of these liberal arrangements. Working-class mothers with young children suffered much hardship, since it was rarely practicable for abandoned wives to extract alimony payments.

In general women did not gain a great deal from the revolutionary turmoil. Certainly they were now citizens with the same rights as men, and so could, for example, vote in soviet elections, but this was of slight account. The ideal of complete sexual freedom entertained by vanguard feminists like Kollontay remained a mirage. It was frowned on by Lenin and appealed only to a tiny minority. In this time of uncertainty most women valued the security provided by a home and family more than trying to win personal independence through the pursuit of a career. The RCP's line on the 'woman question' was ambivalent. It encouraged women to join the Party, but by 1927 they accounted for only 12 per cent of members (as against 8 per cent in 1922). They were under-represented in leadership positions and the Party's women's department (*Zhenotdel*) did not have an influential voice. Most Russian males, whether Communists or not, continued to take a position that today would be described as 'male chauvinist'. In the countryside patriarchal norms were still held to; marriages were arranged by elder kinsfolk and young women without families were regarded with suspicion.

Those who had taken jobs in industry during the war were the first to be discharged once retrenchment became the norm. Thereafter the female share of the workforce grew slowly, approaching 30 per cent by 1929. Most women workers continued to be employed in textiles

---

* Ball, *And Now My Soul is Hardened*, pp. 12–14, 29–30.

and other traditionally 'female' (and low-paid) industries. On the other hand, literacy levels among women had risen and there was no longer any legal bar to their receiving an education. The proportion of female students in higher educational establishments did not surpass the 1913 level until the 1930s, by which time party policy had been recast in a more traditional mould.

The leaders visualized the NEP as a temporary compromise with capitalism whose duration would depend on circumstances. Since the economy's 'commanding heights' (finance, heavy industry, foreign trade) remained under state control, the reforms began in the agricultural sector. Subsequently they were extended in piecemeal fashion to internal commerce and to small-scale factory production of consumer goods. The requisitioning of crops characteristic of the civil-war period gave way to a tax in kind (later in cash, as the financial system stabilized) which was much less burdensome. As coercive measures of revenue raising had not been entirely abandoned the effect of this change was largely psychological. Peasants were allowed to 'dispose of' (not yet 'sell'!) any surpluses that remained. In the first famine-stricken year or so these scarcely existed. Fortunately the 1922 harvest was relatively bountiful. Much of it, not surprisingly, went to fill hungry peasant stomachs. The price of grain soared, leading to complaints by urban workers that they, supposedly the 'ruling class', were being sacrificed to their greedy, 'petty-bourgeois' country cousins. The next year the price 'scissors' moved the other way, and it was the peasants' turn to complain that industrial goods were beyond their reach.

Such swings were to be expected, for the state did not yet have the wherewithal to regulate the market. But they accentuated the strained relationship between town and country dwellers that had developed during the civil war. Propagandists, invoking Lenin, called for a close bond (*smychka*) between proletariat and peasantry, but all too often urban zealots regarded the village as a bastion of 'reaction' inhabited by selfish rustics, and looked forward to a new offensive against the 'class-alien' smallholders. For their part peasants recalled the violence recently done to them by men from the city and were wary of promises made in jargon they barely understood. As they saw it, they were at last masters of their property and so had every right to seek the best price available for its proceeds, even if this meant holding back deliveries or dealing with private traders rather than state purchasing agencies.

In official eyes such behaviour was 'speculative', if not actually 'counter-revolutionary', and showed that the village was in the grip of the dreaded kulak. Much energy was spent on trying to define class relations within the peasantry, but the results were disappointing. This was because the complex social structure of the traditional rural community did not lend itself to rigid categorization in Marxist terms. It made little sense to distinguish between so-called poor, middling, and rich households when practically all peasant families lived on the margin of subsistence, with holdings of about 4 dessyatines (10.8 acres) and a horse or a second cow was virtually a luxury. Kinship ties often counted for more than property or income levels, and a smallholder might well employ hired labour in one season yet hire himself out for work in another. Relationships tended to be interdependent as much as conflictual; where there was tension it was often between older peasants who held to the village's ancient rituals and younger ones who, having gained experience of life in the city, had taken to modern ways.

In Tver, for example, where outmigration and *otkhod* [off-farm work] had long been a basic fact of peasant life, ... the fashion of the 1920s for young male peasants was civil-war dress (Red Army uniforms or homemade imitations, worn with wide leather belts and *budennovki* [conical caps]). Young peasant women in the region were similarly attracted to styles of modern urban dress which their elders deplored.*

When used by peasants, the term *kulak* indicated a morally unscrupulous individual who scorned accepted norms of good-neighbourly behaviour, not a member of an exploitative socio-economic class. But it was on the latter grounds that such farmers, generally the more enterprising and efficient, were discriminated against in various ways, such as jobs and schooling, whereas the 'poor' (or dissolute!) were correspondingly favoured. Poor youngsters also had priority in admission to the Communist Youth League (*Komsomol*). In this manner the country's new rulers built up groups of supporters in the countryside. They were, however, a far from reliable force. Some were former kulaks or even priests who had concealed their true identity. Apart from this, their educational level was low. Ensconced in the rural soviets, and

---

* Fitzpatrick, 'Class Identity', in idem *et al.* (ed.), *Russia in the Era of NEP*, p. 24.

backed by urban emissaries (agitators, journalists), they tried to dominate the traditional rural organizations, the village commune and church parish. Where the 'outsiders' were atheist zealots, there was bound to be sharp conflict.

In 1925 the harvest was unusually good and by the next year grain output had almost regained its pre-war average – but there were now more mouths to feed and there was no longer any prospect of Russia recovering its old role as a major cereals exporter. In bad crop years grain actually had to be imported. Sugar beet, cotton, and vegetables did better, and by the mid 1920s the nation's stock of cattle and pigs (but not of horses) was likewise greater than it had been in 1916 (when the last livestock census had been taken). Fruit was rarer than before because so many orchards had been cut down during the revolution. Most of the successes came about through an extension of the crop area rather than by improving agricultural techniques. Motor vehicles (only 16,000 in the whole country in 1928!) and tractors were still objects of curiosity in the countryside. But there was progress: by 1928 metal ploughs were in use over nine tenths of the land and over half the grain was harvested and threshed mechanically. As in the developing world generally, agricultural mechanization was inescapable, but much depended on the way it was introduced.

The Bolshevik leaders faced the problem of feeding the cities, building a reserve for the armed forces and providing a cushion against crop failures. The 'procurements gap' would serve as a pretext for forced collectivization (see page 370). But officials, above all Stalin, understated actual grain marketings and distorted the picture by drawing a misleading comparison with 1913 (a particularly good year). In 1926 the proportion of grain marketed was actually around 21 per cent* of total output, as against about 25 per cent in 1909–13. Most historians have blamed this shortfall on the very nature of small-scale peasant farming, but this view is no longer convincing. Much could have been done to encourage producers to raise yields and sell more by spreading knowledge and offering more favourable (even subsidized) prices. But the political cost of this would have been high, especially for a revolutionary regime short of capital and committed to rapid industrialization at the peasants' expense.

* A. Nove; R. W. Davies puts it at 16–17 per cent.

In 1926–7 industrial growth became the main goal of Soviet domestic policy. By then the total value of industrial production exceeded that in 1913.* The output of coal and oil was comparable, while that of electricity had more than doubled (to a modest 3.5 md kWh). The engineering and chemical industries were also back to where they had been before the war, whereas iron and steel lagged considerably. Contrary to what is generally thought, consumer goods did not do better than producer goods, except in 1924/5, when the internal market expanded rapidly. Cotton fabrics, for instance, were only 89 per cent as plentiful as in 1913, although the industry had recovered swiftly from near-zero in 1921.

During the NEP steps were taken to dismantle the top-heavy system of industrial management by setting up semi-autonomous 'trusts' (= corporations) and introducing an element of competitiveness. Managers were told to rationalize their business methods and to adopt regular profit-and-loss accounting (*khozraschet*). The partial return to a market economy meant that many workers became redundant. The number of registered unemployed shot up from 160,000 in January 1922 to 1,240,000 two years later. Labour exchanges and trade unions could not do much to help them. There was a good deal of grumbling and even local strikes, especially in 1923 when the 'scissors crisis' was at its height and sales of industrial goods slumped. Metalworkers and printers were most active.

Wage and norm disputes were exacerbated by labour–management tensions. At the Dinamo metal factory, archival sources reveal a series of disputes over 'mistaken' wage calculations, 'abnormal' wage payments and 'exploitative' wage levels throughout 1922–3. Disputes were often precipitated by management's failure to fulfil collective-agreement provisions.†

In time-honoured fashion aggrieved workers laid the blame less on the country's rulers than on their immediate bosses in management or on trade-union functionaries. The latter were embarrassed by their

---

* In 1926/7 prices. The post-revolutionary 'economic year' ran from September to August.
† Hatch, 'Labour Conflict in Moscow', in Fitzpatrick *et al.*, *Russia in the Era of NEP*, pp. 62–3.

anomalous role as 'transmission belts'* of party policy instead of as spokesmen for the interests of labour. They had to confine their activities to bargaining over wages and conditions of employment, the scope of which was limited. Even so, a certain amount of wage-driven inflation occurred, once money (in stabilized roubles) had replaced rations as the means of remuneration. By 1925 the trade unions, which enjoyed a semi-autonomous status, had made good earlier losses and had 6.9 million members, 2.7 million of whom were industrial workers.

There was much controversy over schemes involving the 'scientific organization of labour', energetically propagated by A. K. Gastev's Central Labour Institute and its provincial branches. The main idea was to inculcate in young workers fresh to industry a modern work ethic which would raise productivity levels. In Russia these were notoriously low, not least because antiquated machinery kept on breaking down and spare parts were in short supply; accidents were also common.

For such lapses workers were prone to make scapegoats of the engineers and other 'bourgeois specialists' (referred to derogatorily as *spetsy*) who had stayed on at their jobs, mainly because they had nowhere else to go. Their relatively high salaries and other privileges, e.g. in housing, aroused jealousies which could easily be exploited by party activists. It was in this heated atmosphere that the show trial was staged of a group of engineers accused of sabotage at Shakhty, a coal-mining town in the Donets valley (1928). The trial was a sign that the period of enforced cooperation with non-Communist experts that was a feature of the NEP was coming to an end.

There was another group of people whose very existence typified the era: the 'nepmen'. These were private traders and artisans (*kustari*) who produced and dealt in a wide variety of consumer goods. Unlike the earlier 'bag-men', their activities had been reluctantly legalized in 1921, when nothing more was involved than peddling articles of food and clothing in the street. Such traders were often 'former people' who, having lost their property and civil rights, had no other means of survival. The more fortunate dealers then set up shops, and a tiny

---

* This term of Stalin's, which had a great vogue, was applied equally to the soviets, which functioned as the formal organs of local government under Party guidance, as well as to the other mass organizations which proliferated at this time.

minority went on to engage in wholesale trade. By 1926 commercial licences had been granted to some half a million people, for most of whom this activity was seasonal; the real number was much higher, and by the end of the decade there were an estimated 4½ million artisans alone. Nepmen accounted for at least 40 per cent of total trade and townspeople depended heavily on their services.

Muscovites bought approximately 70 per cent of their bread from private traders in 1924, and . . . nepmen were generally most dominant in the trade of dairy products, eggs, meat, fruit and vegetables, often accounting for 80 per cent or more of total retail sales towards the end of NEP. In the marketing of manufactured goods, the nepmen's share of retail sales was usually largest for haberdashery, textiles, common hardware and . . . leather goods.*

From 1926 the party and state authorities strove with increasing zeal to restrict this ideologically suspect activity, but failed to provide a satisfactory replacement: cooperative stores were notoriously ill-stocked. The result was a 'goods famine' that would endure for decades. It was most evident in rural areas, where there had always been fewer retail outlets. But even in Moscow, which in this respect was privileged over provincial towns for prestige reasons, queuing for scarce supplies became normal practice.

This was more than just a matter of poor organization. Increasingly during the 1920s the Party's economic philosophy shifted towards favouring heavy industry over factories producing consumer goods, as part of a system of centrally controlled state planning that left little place for market relationships. After 1927 even agricultural cooperatives came to be seen as ideologically dubious, although until then they had made considerable progress. They provided peasant farmers with credit to buy seed or tools and helped them sell their produce – activities which Lenin in his last writings had hailed as compatible with socialism, indeed as embodying its essential virtues.

As the economy revived in the 1920s Bolshevik leaders and officials engaged in heated controversy about investment priorities and the tempo of Soviet Russia's advance towards a new socialist order. The debate was conducted chiefly in ideological terms and the positions taken were as a rule inadequately buttressed by objective statistical

* Ball, *Russia's Last Capitalists*, p. 164.

information. On the contrary, such data were habitually abused for political ends. Yet one should recognize that contemporary economic theory in the West had little to say about the problems of developing a backward country, so that the Bolsheviks were pioneers in the field; it is hardly surprising that they should have made serious mistakes.

There was general agreement on the objective of industrialization. It was essential not only for Russia to survive as a major European power amid a capitalist environment, but also to provide her with a large and well-qualified working class, such she conspicuously lacked – for an accident of history had condemned the 'proletarian revolution' to triumph not in the advanced countries of the West, as Marxist doctrine had presupposed, but in a retrograde agrarian land that seemed to lack the very prerequisites of socialism. The formula that solved the ideological conundrum was 'socialism in a single country first'.* Since in 1918 Soviet Russia had repudiated her foreign debts, totalling about 15 milliard roubles, she could not expect much credit from 'capitalist' countries. Lenin had opened the country to foreign concessions, but by 1926/7 these accounted for less than 1 per cent of total industrial output. (They were important only in mining, especially of precious metals.) Industrialization therefore had to be financed by domestically generated savings, in the first instance by the hard-pressed rural population. But what would harsh exactions do to the *smychka*?

The debate consequently revolved largely around the questions how far it was safe to squeeze the (rich) peasants and how fast heavy industry should expand. To simplify the arguments greatly, the Party's right wing, led by Bukharin (who spoke for the largely silent Stalin), and even more forcefully officials of the finance commissariat, advocated a moderate, non-violent approach to the peasantry. They should be appeased by a supply of cheap consumer goods and so gradually persuaded to accept socialized agriculture, in the form of voluntary cooperative farming. (It should be noted that the few state farms or 'communes' set up during the civil war had since virtually disappeared;

---

* Usually associated with Stalin, it actually expressed a consensus among the leadership. The phrase should not be truncated; the word 'first' showed that fostering international revolution had not been abandoned, as some observers thought, but only postponed until it could be assisted by a greatly strengthened Soviet state, rather than coming about primarily as an authentic artefact of the popular will, as in the original Leninist view.

in 1927 they held only 1.7 per cent of the total sown area.) This moderation also characterized the economists* who drew up the country's first nation-wide plans, or 'control figures'. These were examples of what was called 'genetic' planning, i.e. they extrapolated from current output data to devise feasible targets. Another approach, dubbed 'teleological', took as its starting-point what was deemed desirable, so 'in effect making the market adapt to state aims rather than the reverse' (L. H. Siegelbaum).

The most articulate spokesmen for this latter viewpoint in the Party's top echelon was Trotsky, assisted by the economist E. A. Preobrazhensky. These leftists complained that current policies were feather-bedding the consumer, and especially the kulak, who should be heavily taxed in order to build up the capital necessary for rapid planned industrial growth, not least in the armaments field (for they discerned a new 'imperialist' threat in the offing). They spoke of 'primitive socialist accumulation' by analogy with the process, studied by Marx, whereby British capitalists had initially financed industrial expansion at high cost to the country folk. Historical references were much in vogue. Bukharin for his part once echoed Guizot by calling on Russian peasants to 'enrich themselves', for which he was rebuked by the more cautious Stalin. The leaders were divided by differences of emphasis rather than of fundamental *Weltanschauung*. In a more pluralistic political setting their viewpoints might well have been reconciled. Alas, tolerance was not a feature of Bolshevik political culture, and each leader sought to represent his position alone as ideologically correct.

Even so, in December 1925 the basic strategy of self-reliant industrialization was endorsed at a party congress, the Fourteenth. Planning officials thereupon drew up two alternative draft plans, designed to cover a five-year span, which were then reconciled. Capital investment in the first year was set at 916 million roubles, making possible a 24 per cent rise in capital-goods industry; consumer-goods output was to expand by only half as much. In the event the actual figure for investment in 1926/7 was higher (1,068 million roubles). This was due largely to pressure by left-wingers, encouraged by industrial successes and

* Many of the officials in the Supreme Economic Council (Vesenkha) and State Planning Commission (Gosplan) were former Mensheviks.

another record harvest. In October 1926 a party conference sealed their victory by resolving 'to catch up and surpass . . . the leading capitalist countries in a relatively brief historical period'.

A dangerous precedent had been set, in that balanced plans prepared by experts had been superseded by more optimistic variants adopted largely from political expediency. This style of decision making would set the tone in the Stalinist 'command economy' to which these early experiments in planning gave rise once NEP had been silently abandoned. Was rapid industrialization compatible with the previous policies? Most historians have assumed that it was not. However, recent research suggests that a slower, more orderly tempo of advance after 1927/8 would have made the Soviet economy stronger than it was by 1941. It is another question whether such a course would have been *politically* possible for a dictatorial regime such as existed in Russia by that date, which had a vested interest in irrationally forcing the pace regardless of cost.

THE BOLSHEVIZATION OF CULTURE

Seen in the light of what was to come, the NEP era has earned a reputation for liberalism, perhaps excessively so. Certainly it took time before the new regime was able to consolidate its hold on the world of learning and the arts. Most intellectuals opposed the October revolution, and many of them were among the 2 million or so Russians who emigrated. Of those who stayed behind many were driven, by material need or conviction, to stomach any moral qualms and to pursue their careers in Soviet organizations. During the civil-war years they had to endure great hardship. A fair number owed their physical survival to relief efforts undertaken by Maxim Gor'ky and his friends, who interceded on their behalf with the authorities. Vladimir Korolenko was another writer who pleaded for a humane approach. To his old friend Anatoly Lunacharsky, the education commissar, he wrote:

I sincerely wish that your heart may again register those emotions that once brought us together in the belief that the development of socialism must be based on the best sides of human nature, i.e. on civic courage and humanity even towards enemies. Let crudeness and blind injustice belong to a past that has gone for ever . . . Social justice is indeed very important and you are right to say that without it there can be no real freedom. But without freedom there can be no justice.*

Lunacharsky's replies betray embarrassment – he was one of the more liberal Bolshevik leaders – but the dictatorship operated according to a brutal logic that he was powerless to alter.

During the civil war terrorist measures were taken against religious believers. In 1917 the Russian Orthodox Church held an All-Russian Council (*Sobor*), the first such gathering since the seventeenth century. It elected Tikhon (Belavin) as Patriarch. He soon found himself at grips with the Bolshevik regime. In January 1918 the government decreed the separation of Church from state and deprived the Orthodox of their property rights; the Church also lost its juridical status and priests were made dependent on their parishes. Tikhon, who had not been consulted, protested and formally anathematized the Bolsheviks, but then changed his line and declared that the Church should keep out of politics. Some clergy sympathized with the Whites, but most accepted his instructions. This did not save them from persecution, which cost the lives of some 10,000 to 14,000 clergy and activist laymen, including several bishops.

Under this pressure the Church hierarchy split. Monarchist *émigrés* set up an administration of their own in the future Yugoslavia (1921) and repudiated Tikhon's authority. Within Russia a dissident movement emerged which had its roots in the anti-establishment tendencies evident among parish (white) clergy before the revolution. These Renovationists were split into several factions, the largest being the 'Living Church' led by Father A. Vvedensky, a sincere believer but a careerist; his associate, Archpriest V. Krasnitsky, had once been chaplain to a 'Black Hundred' organization (and had written a screed on 'socialism as the work of Satan'). These dubious characteristics made it easy for agents of the security police (from 1922 known as the GPU or OGPU) to penetrate the movement, which they could manipulate in order to subvert the patriarchal Church. According to recently published documents, a Politburo commission resolved in October 1922

---

* W. [V. G.] Korolenko, *Ohne Freiheit keine Gerechtigkeit: Die Briefe an den Volkskommissar Lunatscharski*, Berlin, 1993, pp. 29–30, 71.

to place a greater stake on the 'Living Church' group, coalescing with the leftists in it, to step up the struggle against the Tikhonites . . . , to strike at the Tikhonite bishops and replace them, [and] to recommend that the GPU do a good job in compromising priests . . . [*Ist. arkhiv*, 2/1993, p. 79]

In 1923 Tikhon was arrested. The Renovationists declared him deposed and took over key jobs in the hierarchy. However, so great was the public outcry that their police controllers decided to backtrack and instead to seek a bogus accommodation with the patriarchal Church.

Previously they had launched an operation designed to discredit the Tikhonites as opposed to measures of famine relief which they had actually been among the first to organize. Along with secular intellectuals who engaged in such charitable work, they were arrested and their funds diverted to other uses, for instance to the Comintern. The authorities then ordered the confiscation, ostensibly for relief purposes, of valuables held in museums and places of worship. Tikhon refused to allow the requisitioning of sacramental objects, but they, too, were taken. Believers protested and there was a violent affray at Shuya (Vladimir province). Thereupon Lenin wrote a top-secret memorandum urging

the shooting of a very large number of the most influential and dangerous Black Hundreds [i.e. church people] . . . the more we manage to shoot on this occasion the better. Now is the moment to teach those types a lesson so that they will not even think of resistance for several decades to come. [*Izv. TsK* 4/1990, pp. 191–3]

Some 8,000 priests, monks, and nuns are thought to have perished in 1922–3 alone. Tikhon was placed under house arrest, but released after he signed a declaration of political loyalty. 'Henceforth I am not an enemy of Soviet power. I finally and decisively disassociate myself from the foreign and domestic White Guard counter-revolution.' The document's terminology betrayed its police origin, but it served to confuse religious believers further.

Before Tikhon died in April 1925, he designated as locum tenens a bishop who was soon exiled to Siberia; he in turn was succeeded by Sergey (Stragorodsky), who faced both obstruction from the authorities – half the bishops were now in gaol – and opposition within the Church from left and right. In July 1927 he, too, was prevailed on to issue a loyalty declaration. He evidently expected it would preserve a skeletal organization for the Church, and possibly that the state would respect its undertakings. If so, he miscalculated. Soon persecution intensified to a point where religious rites could be performed only underground, at great physical risk to those involved. By 1928 the number of Orthodox churches (50,000 in 1917) had been reduced to an estimated 10,000; by 1940 they numbered 4,225, three quarters of them in the newly annexed western territories. A similar fate befell Catholic, Baptist, and Old Believer communities, as well as the non-Christian faiths.

Few intellectuals were bothered by the Churches' fate: overwhelmingly secular in outlook, they did not appreciate that they would be among the next victims. Some left-wingers approved of the 'scientific atheism' propagated by E. E. Yaroslavsky's League of (Militant) Godless, which claimed half a million members by the end of the decade. However, the crude methods its zealots often employed (e.g. exposure of saints' relics, interference with religious services) were unpopular, and later they turned to more subtle methods. One device was to encourage secular festivals in lieu of Christian rites such as baptism* or marriage. Churches were taken over and put to profane purposes. At workers' clubs ceremonies were held to mark notable events in the revolutionary calendar. It often proved difficult to create the appropriate atmosphere.

The decor was uniformly artless, routinized, and often inappropriate: red table cover, a bust or portrait of the leader, slogans on the wall, and a dais; and on particularly 'festive' occasions, the bric-à-brac of a bygone age – crêpe, paper lanterns, a fir-tree. Music was provided by a brass ensemble which offered 'flourishes' to punctuate the proceedings and endless renderings of the *Internationale*. Meetings were usually poorly timed, too long, and stilted . . .†

Rather more successful were the outdoor festivals staged in the early

---

* Enthusiastic parents gave their offspring secular and 'revolutionary' names such as 'Electricity' or (after Lenin) 'Vladlen' to symbolize the breach with the past. New names were also bestowed on many towns, streets, and factories. These changes helped to bewilder ordinary people.

† Stites, 'Bolshevik Ritual Building', in Fitzpatrick *et al.*, *Russia in the Era of NEP*, p. 299.

years of the revolution. Tens of thousands of people took part in didactic dramas, directed by professionals, to celebrate 'the mystery of organized labour'. In the most famous instance (Petrograd, 1920) they re-enacted the storming of the Winter Palace (in a suitably mythologized rendering). Apart from their agitational purpose, such carnavalesque shows had something in common with ancient Greek dramatic festivals (K. Clark). The participants seem to have enjoyed them. In the later 1920s they dropped out of fashion and were replaced by massive parades with a military flavour, or else by sporting events.

A leading role in the new ritual was played by the cult of the deceased Lenin. This was not just a political ploy by Stalin (as Trotsky thought) but an outgrowth of the ideas of Bolshevik 'God-builders' like A. A. Bogdanov and Lunacharsky. The latter supervised construction of a mausoleum in Red Square in which the ex-leader's mummified remains were laid to rest (in a sarcophagus designed by L. B. Krasin), to be respectfully viewed by the faithful. This was something of a substitute religion which appealed to simple folk, but basically an instrumental device to mobilize the masses around a symbol of the new collectivist society. Worship of an infallible leader was really 'the Party's cult of itself' (M. Malia).

Avant-garde artists now had a chance to demonstrate their talents before a vast audience. While the academic theatres struggled to survive under the patronage of Lunacharsky's education commissariat, which inherited this role from the monarchy, the innovative director Vsevolod Meyerhold and the Suprematist painter Kazimir Malevich put on a satirical play by Mayakovsky, *Opera-Bouffe* (1918), which drew on the traditions of Russian folk theatre. Although coolly received, its dramatic style set the tone for much later Soviet 'agitprop' (agitation and propaganda) productions, with their use of documentary material and start-ling sound or visual effects. The proletarian audiences which packed free performances at 'RSFSR Theatre No. 1' (founded in November 1920) relished the crude caricaturing of 'class enemies' but found the Cubo-Futurist sets and costumes less to their taste. Initially many pieces were adaptations of works by pre-revolutionary or foreign writers, but by the mid 1920s Soviet dramatists like F. Gladkov (*Cement*, 1925) or M. A. Bulgakov (*Days of the Turbins*, 1926) were contributing to the repertoire and the Soviet stage was winning international renown. Particularly striking was the success of the State Jewish Theatre (Goset), which performed plays in Yiddish in an Expressionist style stressing mime and rhythmic movement. The repertoire widened after 1929, when the actor S. M. Mikhoels took over as artistic director since the company's founder decided to stay abroad.

Emigration was still possible until the close of the NEP era – and took a heavy toll of Russia's cultural élite: the painters Kandinsky and Chagall, the composers Rachmaninoff and Stravinsky, the singer Chaliapine, the writers Kuprin and Balmont, to name only a few. There was also some movement in the reverse direction which brought in fresh ideas. Soviet Russia was not yet internationally isolated. Indeed, the lively cultural scene in Moscow and Petrograd held a fascination for many Western intellectuals. Some thought that the 'silver age' had miraculously revived. This was a benign view; with hindsight it would be truer to see the era as a pale reflection of its predecessor, soon to be eclipsed by Stalin's 'cultural revolution'.

One of the few writers who welcomed the Bolshevik revolution was the Futurist Mayakovsky. Art was henceforth to serve the masses, not the privileged few. But the Futurists placed art ahead of politics and had grandiose ideas about their own role in the new proletarian culture. They saw the revolution less as a struggle between classes than as an upsurge of youthful anti-conformism.

> A White-Guardist?
> Put him against the wall!
> It's time for bullets to crackle in the museums
> . . . Why are you waiting to shoot Pushkin
> And all the other White classics?

Lunacharsky was scandalized. Lenin, whose taste in art was conventional, later reproved his education commissar for showing the poet too much leniency. Still more critical was the reception accorded to avant-garde artists by the ultra-left 'Proletarian Culture' group, for whom such extravagances were merely proof of bourgeois decadence. To make amends, Futurists designed revolutionary posters – an art form that later became the object of a veritable cult in certain quarters – and helped to decorate the 'agit-trains' that toured the front keeping up Red soldiers' morale during the civil war. Other vanguard artists devoted themselves to revolutionizing the design of furniture, textiles, ceramics, and so on, as well as sets for stage and screen. In this way they sought to escape charges that their work was of no practical use to the masses.

For Constructivists revolution meant the advent of the machine age, which would render all art superfluous.

We do not measure our work by the ell of beauty . . . We *construct* our works with a sounding-line in our hands, our eyes as straight as a ruler, in a spirit as taut as a pair of compasses.*

Their ideas were particularly fruitful in architecture. In 1920 Vladimir Tatlin responded to the Bolsheviks' call for monumental architecture to celebrate the revolution with a visionary design for a colossal tower – taller than the Tour Eiffel in Paris – to be erected in Petrograd to honour the Third International. It was to contain several halls, revolving in harmony with celestial bodies, in which the world's new rulers would meet to solve its problems. Such a structure would have been impossible to build, yet the design was influential as an image of global harmony, 'a utopian reference point' (J. Milner). Rather more practical were early Soviet architects' efforts at town planning. These owed a good deal to pre-revolutionary precedents (rarely acknowledged!) as well as to the 'garden cities' concept devised in the West. Moscow, as the new capital, was earmarked for special treatment. Some of these notions (e.g. beltways and radial avenues) would eventually become reality – but as much for the glory of Stalin's state as for the convenience of the city's inhabitants.

The 'seventh art' was hailed by Lenin as the most important of all, since he appreciated its propaganda potential for the unlettered. Short agitational films (*agitki*) were the main attraction on the propaganda trains just mentioned. The themes treated were simple. *The Frightened Bourgeois* (1919) was a humorous sketch in which

as a result of the revolution a capitalist loses his appetite and becomes an insomniac. Then he is ordered to appear in a work battalion. Honest labour cures him immediately. Others were melodramas. In *For the Red Flag* (1919) a father joins the Red Army to take the place of his [inadequately] class-conscious son. The son, recognizing the error of his ways, goes to

---

* N. Gabo and N. Pevsner, 'Realist Manifesto' (1920), cit. in I. Antonowa and J. Merkert (eds.), *Berlin-Moskau*, Munich–New York, 1995, p. 158.

search for his father ... and saves the wounded old man ... and the flag from the enemy.*

Such films also taught elementary rules of hygiene and showed viewers, perhaps for the first time, what other parts of their country looked like. Newsreels, too, performed a useful service. Early Soviet cinema was the training-ground of a pleiad of subsequently world-famous directors. In 1922 Dzhiga Vertov embarked on a series of films, *Film-Truth*, in which he developed the technique of photo-montage and clashing opposites. It was taken up by Eisenstein, in whose first notable film, *Strike* (1924), the scene of strikers being repressed is followed by one of a capitalist squeezing a lemon. In *Battleship Potemkin* the ship itself is the 'collective hero'. *October*, made to command for the revolution's tenth anniversary, was less successful. Although Eisenstein's work is justly praised as innovative by film buffs, Russian audiences of the time preferred lighter material, including the foreign imports still freely available.

Silent films usually had a piano accompaniment which gave employment to struggling musicians. At the other end of the scale state symphony orchestras maintained their predecessors' high reputation. The ultra-left Russian Association of Proletarian Musicians was responsible for such harmless inanities as A. Avraamov's symphony for factory sirens and locomotive whistles (1923). More serious were experiments in atonal music by A. I. Lurye (who emigrated in 1922) and above all Dmitriy Shostakovich's First Symphony (1925).† Under Stalin, Shostakovich would 'give his people a voice through his music at a time when they had to keep silent' (L. Gackel).

The first step in asserting the Party's political control over the arts came with the suppression in 1920–21 of the 'Proletarian Culture' (*Proletkuľt*) movement. The ideas of these extremists, rarely proletarians themselves, posed a less potent threat to freedom of expression than those of the RCP, since they had no powerful organization behind them. Inspired by Bogdanov, an errant Marxist, *Proletkuľt* set up educational and recreational facilities for workers who were as a rule keener to acquire useful knowledge than to support cultural iconoclasm.

---

* Kenez, *Cinema and Soviet Society*, p. 35.
† Another musical innovator, Sergey Prokofyev, lived abroad until 1936.

The party leadership suspected the organization of ideological error – many of the activists were non-Bolshevik socialists – and strove to establish its own monopoly over adult education through Lunacharsky's commissariat. Lunacharsky himself was lukewarm about this and so the movement continued to exercise some influence in Soviet intellectual life until it was finally killed off in 1932.

Until 1925 the Party's leaders did not interfere directly in cultural matters and allowed artists and writers to form groups and to interact much as they pleased, so long as they did not voice overtly counter-revolutionary sentiments. In 1924 Lunacharsky urged writers to develop a 'muscular' proletarian literature that reflected the best (i.e. realist) traditions of the old intelligentsia, but added that 'freedom exists [only] for the revolution'. Neither he nor Trotsky (in his *Literature and Revolution*, 1923) could understand the motives that led the poet Alexander Blok, for instance – author of the ambiguous and controversial 'The Twelve' (1918)* – to appeal on his deathbed for preservation of that 'secret freedom' which Pushkin had striven for under Nicholas I. A mood of uneasy foreboding was also evident in Eugene Zamiatin's novel *We* (1921), one of the first anti-utopian works. It drew a chilling picture of a technologically advanced world in which human beings had been reduced to ciphers: the principal character is identified solely by his number, D-503. The work could not be published in the USSR until the late 1980s but enjoyed success in the West; it was the forerunner of Aldous Huxley's *Brave New World* and George Orwell's *1984*.

Many writers naturally took as their theme the great cataclysm they were living through. *The Naked Year* (1922), by Boris Pilnyak (real name Vogau), portrayed the cruelty and heroism of the civil war. Four years later his 'Tale of the Unextinguished Moon' described the fate of a stricken Red Army hero ordered by the Party to undergo surgery and dying on the operating table. Many took this as referring to the death in this fashion of Frunze, the army's commander-in-chief at the

---

* The poem depicts twelve ruffianly Red Guards tramping through the snow, intent on murder and robbery – with Jesus Christ, no less, at their head. It probably represented a mystical bow of reverence towards the elemental force of the Russian people, seen as creating a new world order based on non-bourgeois and non-Western (but Christian?!) principles.

time; this helps to account for Pilnyak's subsequent fall from grace and ultimate death in the Great Terror (1938).

Yuriy Olesha (1899–1960) was another early Soviet writer who, though not put to death, was silenced after 1937. Ten years earlier his novel *Envy* aroused criticism for its depiction of an artist's fate in a totalitarian state. Two poets committed suicide during these years: Sergey Yesenin (1925) and Mayakovsky (1930). In both cases personal motives seem to have been combined with political ones. Yesenin saw himself as a voice of 'peasant Russia', whose fate he mourned with unrivalled poignancy:

> The little thatched hut I was born in lies bare to the sky,
> And in the crooked alleys of Moscow I am fated to die.

One of Mayakovsky's last dramatic works, *The Bedbug*, portrays a worker turned official who indulges in a 'bourgeois' lifestyle. After his death he is miraculously resurrected in the future communist society, which puts him on show as a curio from the past. The implication, clearly, is that the revolution has spawned a soulless, bureaucratic monstrosity. Attacks on the play by officialdom only reinforced the writer's conviction that this was so.

Much fiction in the 1920s was experimental in form, and its exponents were accordingly dubbed 'formalists' by party-minded critics for whom content was what really mattered. Writers belonged to various contending factions, which engaged in furious polemics and fell broadly into two categories: 'fellow-travellers' (*poputchiki*), who sought to preserve their artistic integrity while supporting the revolution's nobler aims, and younger (self-styled) 'proletarian' writers who, though weaker in quality, had the backing of the literary–political establishment. Such support was openly advocated in the party's first resolution on literary policy (1925), which, however, allowed for free competition between rival trends and urged that 'fellow-travellers' be treated tactfully. A Union of Soviet Writers came into being as early as 1922, but a decade elapsed before it assumed the task of controlling writers' political orthodoxy. By 1928 a new cohort of cultural officials (and writers!) had come to the fore. They were less tolerant of 'deviations' from what they considered the correct 'proletarian class line'.

This was an ominous development, not least for the USSR's non-Russian peoples. During the NEP years the authorities took a relatively liberal attitude towards minority cultures. Philologists devised written scripts for those people, mainly in the north and east of the country, who still lacked them. Non-Russian languages were studied and taught in schools. Ukrainians, who made up 45 per cent of the non-Russian population (1926), profited greatly. Here as elsewhere a policy of 'indigenization' (*korenizatsiya*) ensured that cadre positions went by choice to natives.* This was designed to reinforce central loyalties, and up to a point did so, but paradoxically it also encouraged Ukrainian national consciousness. So, too, did the policy of cultural 'ukrainization'. The Party's objective was defined somewhat vaguely as to create 'cultures national in form but socialist in content'. Initially at least 'form' was allowed to have some real meaning. Thus street signs were in Ukrainian; 97 per cent of primary schoolchildren were taught in Ukrainian-language schools (1929), and of book titles published in that republic 80 per cent were in the vernacular (1930). Ukrainian was increasingly used on the stage or in broadcasting.

But local Russians and many officials in Moscow thought this policy was being carried too far. When the Ukrainian writer M. Khvylovyj advanced the slogan 'away from Moscow' (whose policies he deemed insufficiently proletarian!), he was denounced as a 'bourgeois nationalist' in disguise. Several million Ukrainians lived in neighbouring Poland, and Moscow feared that an overtly Western orientation by Ukrainian intellectuals could complicate Soviet foreign policy. There was also an underlying national-chauvinist sentiment. In 1927 Ukraine's education commissar, O. Shumskyj, was dismissed for allegedly pursuing 'a struggle against "Moscow", Russian culture and its greatest achievement, Leninism'. His successor, M. Skrypnik, was, however, able to continue the same policies more guardedly until Stalin's collectivization drive, which had a strong anti-Ukrainian component, led him to commit suicide (1933).

The activists in this campaign belonged to the new generation of 'promotees' (*vydvizhentsy*) – that is, upwardly mobile former workers or (more rarely) peasants who acquired a smattering of education and

---

* The Ukrainian share of local party members leaped from 23 per cent in 1922 to 52 per cent in 1927 (and to 61 per cent in 1933). This was, however, still below the Ukrainians' share of the republic's population (80 per cent) and 'ukrainization' was less evident at leadership level, both in party and government.

rose to positions of influence during NEP. Some of these 'cadres' made a positive contribution to the country's development as engineers, doctors, and so on; but the majority, lacking specialized skills, became party or state functionaries. They were the backbone of the *nomenklatura*,* or what is today sometimes pejoratively called the 'administrative–command system' of the Stalin era. They developed character traits that in some ways resembled those of tsarist bureaucrats: an arrogant, supercilious attitude towards ordinary citizens and a tendency to build up patronage systems (clientèles) or to abuse their office for personal gain.

Yet such historical parallels should not be overworked. The new revolutionary cadres were more plebeian in their origin and cultural tastes than the old. They were also less inhibited by respect for customs or individual rights. Some were descended from former lower-middle-class people (*meshchane*), but claimed, rightly or wrongly, to be authentic proletarians (faking a working-class identity was a common practice), while others were genuinely of worker or peasant stock. Contemporaries exaggerated the significance of class background. What defined Stalinist functionaries was not social origin but cultural (or, as some might say, *anti*-cultural) experience. For many the chief formative influence in their lives had been the civil war. Others acquired the habits of command later, through service in one of the four great institutional pillars of the Soviet state (Party, Komsomol, Red Army, Cheka/GPU). Practically all of them, though, had been through some form of schooling, which shaped their attitudes in an even more fundamental way.

In 1919 the Bolsheviks had dreamed of giving every child in the land, male and female, a general and polytechnical education to age seventeen, with priority for pupils of lower-class background. This goal was utopian and in 1923, when work began in earnest on building the new school system, it concentrated on children aged 8–11, as in the late tsarist period. By 1927 only half of this age-group had attended school, and only one third of the schools had the complete four-year range. This expansion was of advantage to girls in particular (in contrast to tsarist practice). Children of 'bourgeois' origin suffered adverse

---

* In the narrower sense, a list of official posts to which people are appointed by a party organization at the appropriate level, and of potential appointees; more generally, in Stalin's Russia and later, holders of official positions who enjoyed privileged status.

discrimination. Class selection criteria were stricter still for admission to the 'workers' faculties' (*rabfaki*) that were designed as an alternative to traditional institutions of higher or technical learning. By 1927 the *rabfaki* had 49,000 students, among them some of the country's most famous future leaders. Another 273,000 students were enrolled in trade schools, located in factories and the like.

At grass-roots level a campaign to overcome mass illiteracy achieved commendable results: the 1926 census showed that 51 per cent of those aged nine years or more could read and write;* for young adults aged 20–24 the figure was 81 per cent of males and 53 per cent of females. (The next decade saw further progress and by 1939 81 per cent of those aged nine or over were literate.) The most striking feature of this educational advance was its marked ideological-political content. From the earliest age children were gradually moulded in such a way as to absorb Soviet values: atheism, hatred of the 'oppressors', and so on. Indoctrination in the classroom was supplemented by social pressure from youth organizations (Pioneers for those aged 9–14, Komsomol for adolescents and young adults), as well as from the state-controlled media. The system would be perfected under Stalin, but its roots were planted during NEP, with the active aid of a segment of the intelligentsia, who thereby, willingly or unwillingly, forged their own shackles.

THE RISE OF STALIN

Lenin, fatally disabled by his third stroke, died in January 1924. The succession struggle began over a year earlier. It was more than a mere conflict between a few individuals in the Party's top echelon. It marked the rise of a new generation – of 'Stalinists', as they would soon proudly call themselves – who knew little or nothing of the Party's pre-revolutionary traditions or of Marxism, and who for that reason willingly supported a leader who seemed to embody their aspirations for a further rapid advance towards socialism. Trotsky, the most

* As against 23 per cent in 1897, but the comparison overlooks the significant improvement made before 1914; subsequently there was a sharp drop in literacy levels, as in cultural standards generally.

prominent Bolshevik to be worsted by Stalin, saw this 'new class' as a bureaucratic degeneration of authentic Leninism, and blamed his own defeat on underhand intrigues by his rival. There was something to this interpretation, which for long influenced Western historiography, but it was too partisan.

Stalin's personal characteristics certainly mattered in deciding the outcome, as did Trotsky's own inadequacies. Joseph Vissarionovich Dzhugashvili – he adopted the name 'Stalin' (= man of steel) around 1910 – had a phenomenal memory and capacity for hard work; he was also ambitious and inordinately vain. Never one to forgive a slight, he would mask his real feelings and bide his time until the moment was ripe for revenge. Lev Davidovich Bronstein (as Trotsky was born) was the paramount revolutionary intellectual, with a gift for the striking phrase, his arrogant demeanour concealing a basic shyness. Stalin was Georgian (perhaps Ossetian?), Trotsky Jewish. For all their differences of temperament and background, both men were 'hard' Bolsheviks who had earned their spurs in the revolutionary struggle. They had clashed on several occasions. When it came to bureaucratic in-fighting, Stalin was in his element whereas Trotsky assumed a posture of high-minded aloofness.

The contest between them (and other claimants) can be understood only in the contest of the Party's still uncertain hold on power and its aspiration, rooted in ideology, to exercise an absolute, 'monolithic' authority. This situation led to an apotheosis of hierarchical subordination and strict discipline. It created a climate of fear and jealousy in which disputes could not readily be settled by reasoned argument. By 1927 the Party, with 1.3 million members and a powerful organization, was a very different body from what it had been six years earlier. An important role in public affairs was also played by other agencies, which, although ultimately dependent on the Party, enjoyed a measure of autonomy.

The Red Army had only half a million effectives during NEP and was not engaged in any operations of consequence, but it did much to shape its conscript soldiers' opinions. It perpetuated the militaristic outlook of the civil-war years, the simple-minded view that social problems could best be solved by coercion.

Militarized socialism resulted from the merging of certain features of the

Red Army's military ethos with important aspects of Bolshevik socialism. It flowed from the rising fortunes of the army in the Soviet state's priorities, from the evolution of soldiers' status in the new social order, and from increasingly alarmist perceptions of international threats . . . Bolshevik socialism and Red Army military culture were fused in a set of political attitudes and behaviour that persisted throughout the 1920s.*

A slow purge rid the army of potentially unreliable elements, whose places were taken by freshly minted 'Red commanders'. They lobbied for a strict disciplinary code, introduced in 1925. This re-established a differentiated scale of penalties for officers and men, which marked yet another defeat for the old ideal of a 'communal' structure within the military. As the professionals recovered ground, the practice of dual command, whereby officers' orders had to be countersigned by civilian commissars, was gradually phased out. However, the army's Central Political Administration (PUR), which had overseen these watchdogs, remained powerful. It supervised party-political work among the troops – as its chief put it, 'educating the Red Army man in the spirit of internationalism, large-scale industry, and antagonism to religion'. Hundreds of agitators enrolled in military academies and then became officers. The proportion of servicemen who were in the Party tripled during the decade;† by 1927 two thirds of divisional commanders and 95 per cent of corps commanders held a party card. Officers sometimes chafed at civilian control, but this friction was much less significant than the development of a homogeneous military-political élite.

There was also a high level of party 'saturation' in the security police, militia (ordinary police), and courts: for example, 92 per cent of judges in the RSFSR were in the RCP by 1931. Together with the enhanced role allotted to the procuracy, this ensured that the legal system did the rulers' bidding. The principle of an autonomous judiciary, so valued by earlier Russian liberals, was repudiated by the Bolsheviks as a worthless 'bourgeois' prejudice. Oddly, a bar of advocates, organized into so-called 'colleges of defenders', was permitted to exist from 1922,

---

* Hagen, 'NEP, Perestroika . . .', pp. 52–3.
† 93,000 by 1929, or about 15–16 per cent; another 177,000 were enrolled in the Komsomol.

but these lawyers were under heavy pressure to acquiesce in the Party's demands.

Meanwhile the Cheka had been reborn in 1922 as the State Political Administration (GPU; in 1923, OGPU). Its role was less in evidence than before the NEP era or after it, but was nevertheless important. Between 1921 and 1928 it sentenced 21,282 people to death (*Ot. arkh.* 2/1992, p. 28). Those deemed 'socially dangerous', even if they had broken no laws, were still liable to arrest, summary trial and, if not shot, confinement in a prison or camp. Lenin made no secret of his view that terror remained essential to ensure the regime's survival. He drafted a loosely worded paragraph in the 1922 criminal code prescribing death or imprisonment for counter-revolutionary propaganda or agitation. The security police, like the courts, operated under the party chiefs' supervision and had wide discretion to interpret their wishes as might be expedient. On Dzerzhinsky's death in 1926 his successor, Menzhinsky – 'an ice-cold aesthete' (R. Gul) – maintained a close relationship with Stalin through the latter's personal secretariat. A post-Soviet study of hitherto top-secret documents shows that in December 1924 the OGPU had a staff of 20,877 (excluding secret informants). Of these 115 were employed in vetting citizens' private correspondence, which was carefully analysed for its political content (*Vop. ist.*, 5/1995, pp. 31–3).

A much larger OGPU enterprise was maintenance of prisons and forced-labour camps for political prisoners and so-called 'incorrigible' common criminals. Together these numbered in excess of 30,000 in 1927/8, more than 10 per cent of all those confined (240,000 to 270,000).* One much-feared group of camps was located in former monastic buildings on the Solovetsky islands in the White Sea. Here prisoners who transgressed camp rules were sent to a punishment facility (*izolator*) in which conditions were extremely harsh, and alleged 'counter-revolutionaries' were often put to death summarily for acts of 'disobedience'.† In 1925 most surviving political prisoners were transferred to the mainland and had to work as lumberjacks. Their

---

* In this era most prisons and camps, however, came under a sub-agency of the internal affairs commissariat, and penal policy was 'reformatory' in intent, if not always in practice.

† Jakobson, *Origins of the Gulag*, pp. 116–17.

number would grow vastly after 1928, once Stalin was firmly in the saddle.

In his so-called 'Testament' – two memoranda to colleagues – Lenin wrote that, 'Stalin is too rude and this defect, although quite tolerable in our midst and in relations among us Communists, becomes intolerable in the post of Secretary-General.' He suggested that some way be found of removing him from the position. Was this dissatisfaction more than a passing whim? Arguably by 1922–3 Stalin had already accumulated so much power that he had become indispensable. His mastery of the Party's Secretariat gave him control over official appointments, and he also headed the Workers' and Peasants' Inspectorate, set up to check the proliferating bureaucracy – in addition to the nationalities commissariat and much else. Though embarrassed by the late leader's displeasure, he skilfully averted the blow, even offering to resign. Zinoviev and Kamenev, his fellow-triumvirs who had taken over the day-to-day running of affairs, appreciated Stalin's devotion to humdrum organizational tasks while they concerned themselves with matters of apparently greater political import.

The three men were driven together by Trotsky's clumsy attacks. Convinced of his superior intellect, Trotsky committed one political error after another. Having spurned Lenin's suggestion (December 1922) to form a 'bloc' against Stalin, in 1924 he openly criticized Kamenev and Zinoviev for disloyal conduct on the eve of the October revolution. Thereby he laid himself open to counter-attack over his own dubious record as a bitter critic of Lenin before 1917. By appropriating the 'socialism in one country first' formula, Stalin showed an unexpected flair for ideological disputation. His message was precisely attuned to what the party cadres wanted to hear. Only nuances separated his theoretical position from that of Trotsky, but Stalin's control of the propaganda apparatus enabled him to magnify their differences and present the opposition as 'anti-Leninist'.

An element of manipulation was certainly involved: Stalin could and did stack party gatherings with his appointees, as Trotsky complained. But this was normal Bolshevik practice, and *all* the leaders now had their own patronage systems. Moreover, Trotsky undermined his case by admitting, in May 1924, that 'in the last resort the Party is always right ... The English have a famous saying, "My country right or wrong." With much greater historical justification we may say, "My

Party right or wrong".' This was more than a rhetorical flourish: all the Bolshevik leaders, aware how fragile their rule still was, saw party unity as the supreme virtue and factionalism as a mortal sin. This sentiment, an integral feature of Bolshevik political culture, fatally weakened each successive effort to challenge the supposedly 'Leninist' majority. One could not really complain at the lack of intra-party democracy if one believed that freedom of expression should be limited to those of whose views one approved.

After Trotsky's defeat Stalin allied himself with Bukharin and the right wing against his former partners, Zinoviev and Kamenev. In December 1925 Zinoviev's men were eased out of their bastion in Leningrad* by a new team under a Stalin loyalist, Sergey Kirov. Zinoviev and Trotsky had long been personal antagonists, and this rivalry added to the problems of the 'United Opposition' that emerged in 1926. It could not develop a realistic alternative to the current 'party line'. Policy issues were of course important in the succession struggle, and individual contestants could be plausibly identified with a position somewhere on a scale from left to right. However, some leaders were more consistent than others, and Stalin especially took care not to reveal his own stance too precisely. In a dictatorial body political debate can be conducted only indirectly, by allusion, and in secret; public and private opinions may well not coincide, and so the conventional terms 'left' and 'right' may be deceptive. There are accordingly good grounds to view personal and power-political considerations as uppermost in disputes among Soviet leaders and policy differences as secondary.

In July 1926 Zinoviev was expelled from the Politburo on suspicion of fostering opposition activity within the army. Three months later the dissidents admitted that they had violated party statutes and promised to disband, yet persisted in criticizing the ruling group. It was now Trotsky's turn to vacate the Politburo, where his position had long been tenuous. Lesser figures recanted their errors and were suitably rewarded. In 1927 the opposition leaders broadened the dispute by challenging the majority over foreign-policy issues as well as domestic ones. This allowed Stalin to present their action as treasonable. Trotsky and Zinoviev were expelled from the Party's 'parliament', the Central

---

* Petrograd was renamed Leningrad in 1924; it reverted to its original name, St Petersburg, in 1991.

Committee, and when they tried to hold a demonstration of their supporters in the street were thrown out of the Party as well.

This occurred in November 1927, precisely ten years after the Bolsheviks had seized power. Trotsky was exiled to Kazakhstan and one year later sent abroad. Zinoviev and Kamenev renounced their views and got back their party cards. Each recantation by an anti-Stalinist leader lost him a portion of his clientèle, since they were thereby discredited, and by 1927 their number had been reduced to a meagre handful – whereas when the conflict began Trotsky had enjoyed a good measure of support among Bolshevik intellectuals and army officers. Characteristically, in his heyday as war commissar (to January 1925), he had never dared to seek military backing against the Party, whose dictatorial rule he endorsed as enthusiastically as anyone.

Thus Stalin reached pre-eminence chiefly by taking advantage of his adversaries' failings and of the general situation. Much less importance attaches to his deviousness or other personal qualities, but these would assume enormous weight during the quarter-century when he ruled the USSR as outright dictator.

CHAPTER 17

The Revolution and the World

EUROPEAN AFFAIRS: THE FIRST DECADE

From 1918 to 1921 Soviet Russia was all but isolated internationally. With the fall of the Kaiser her formal relations with Imperial Germany came to an end, and the Allied Powers, bent on overthrowing the Bolsheviks, would deal with them only through unofficial emissaries. Chicherin, who soon succeeded Trotsky as people's commissar for foreign affairs, skilfully exploited these episodic contacts, and in 1920, as the civil war drew to a close, Russia managed to normalize relations with her newly independent neighbours in the Baltic. In March 1921 a peace treaty signed at Riga terminated hostilities with Poland, and the inauguration at this time of the New Economic Policy implied that henceforth Soviet Russia would make her influence felt abroad primarily by diplomatic means rather than by promoting revolution through the Comintern.

The Third (Communist) International, to give the Comintern its proper name, was founded in Moscow in March 1919, at a moment when it seemed as though the revolutionary upsurge in central Europe was about to rescue the hard-pressed Bolsheviks. In Hungary Béla Kun proclaimed a soviet republic, to which Lenin promised practical and moral support. However, within a few weeks it had succumbed to its domestic and foreign foes. Even more disappointing for Moscow were developments in Germany, the country which Lenin, like Marx before him, had considered the best-prepared for socialism. Not only did it stand at a higher level economically and socially than backward Russia, but its working class was relatively well organized and had a strong radical tradition. Ever since 1914 the Bolsheviks had inveighed against its Social Democratic leaders' willingness to compromise with the 'bourgeois' class enemy in defence of Germany's national interests. As seen from Moscow, the course of events after November 1918, when the Reich collapsed, gave further proof of the reformists' 'treachery'. The workers' and soldiers' councils that came into being, much as in Russia a year earlier, had not tried to take power. Instead they had made way for a Social Democratic government which looked west, hoping for tolerable peace terms from the Allies, rather than east to Bolshevik Russia. Internally the government based its power on parliament and relied for material force on the army, where right-wing elements were in the ascendant. In January 1919 the latter brutally suppressed the left-wing Spartacus League in Berlin. Its leaders, Rosa Luxemburg and Karl Liebknecht, were killed. These murders deprived German revolutionary socialism of its head and its heart. A few months later an amateurish attempt to seize power in Bavaria predictably ended in another defeat. Despite these setbacks the situation remained highly volatile all over the continent, so that the Bolsheviks were justified in hoping that they might bring the widespread mass discontent under their own direction.

Comintern was under Russian control from the start. The delegates to its first congress were hastily put together from revolutionary activists who happened to be in Russia at the time, so that the organization's claim to represent the international working class was paper-thin. For this reason the German leader H. Eberlein thought its establishment premature, but he was overruled by his more enthusiastic comrades. They willingly deferred to the Bolsheviks' superior experience, as the only socialists to have successfully brought off a 'proletarian revolution'. Yet dissidence was only to be expected in such a milieu. To impose proper discipline, and to guard against the infiltration of Social Democratic ideas, Lenin drew up a formidable list of twenty-one conditions which member parties (or prospective adherents) had to satisfy. These were incorporated into the statute adopted at the Comintern's second congress in July–August 1920, held in a mood of exaltation as the Red Armies approached Warsaw. Delegates undertook to conduct regular purges of reformist elements, maintain tight control over the party press, carry on agitation among soldiers and peasants, and set up parallel secret organizations for subversive activities. The Bolshevik principle of 'democratic centralism' was binding on each 'section' of this would-be universal party. Its hierarchical organization was headed by an Executive Committee (ECCI) chaired by none other than Zinoviev, party boss in Petrograd and a member of the Politburo.

It seemed as if nothing had been left to chance, but the very thoroughness of these provisions engendered suspicion, quarrels, and schisms. In Germany the Communist KPD succeeded in winning over several hundred thousand supporters of a middle-of-the-road group, but in 1921 the ECCI expelled two of its independent-minded leaders and persuaded their more docile successors to stage a general strike in the Ruhr as a prelude to an insurrection. The operation was poorly planned and lacked broad popular support. The KPD was discredited and forsaken by many disillusioned members, while the leaders found themselves blamed by Moscow for the failure.

The ECCI was not yet ready to conclude that revolutionary activism had no future – in October 1923 it sponsored another insurrectionary effort in central Germany, with similarly disappointing returns – but gradually Moscow's strategic analysis did change. It was argued that the capitalist system had entered upon a period of temporary stabilization. Sooner or later there was bound to be another era of revolutionary outbreaks, which would enable local Communists to take power with indirect Soviet aid, but in the short term the emphasis had to be placed on diplomacy. In institutional terms the Comintern's prestige and power declined while the status of the foreign affairs commissariat correspondingly improved. Chicherin took his cue from Lenin so long as the latter lived, but he himself had little standing in the Party. Stalin and other rising leaders regarded him with distrust, not least on account of his noble background and familiarity with European ways.

All were agreed, however, on the essentials of Soviet foreign policy. It functioned 'dialectically' on a dual plane, combining conventional diplomacy with revolutionary activities designed to undermine the capitalist order from within. This meant adopting a tactical line referred to as the 'united front from below', whereby the Communists launched successive campaigns on topical issues of general concern, designed to reach out to the 'toilers' who misguidedly backed the Social Democrats or other reformists. This was designed to isolate the reformist leaders and eventually force them to enter into joint action with their Communist rivals, who would ultimately enjoy mass support.

This tactic had to be applied with great subtlety if it was not to rebound against its initiators. In the industrialized countries it did not work well. Organized labour generally remained aloof from Communist advances, preferring to follow 'safe' leaders whom they knew (and had elected) to men who could be branded all too plausibly as 'agents of Moscow'. Nervous governments played up the Communist threat and took administrative action against those deemed subversive. In the United States in particular there was a wave of hysterical persecution of real or alleged extremists on the left. Only in Germany did the KPD represent a serious political force, and even there it could claim the support of no more than a fraction of organized workers. Elsewhere in Europe the local Communist parties were little more than sects. On the other hand, size of membership was not necessarily the most reliable gauge of their strength. Some trade unionists voted Communist party members on to their executives. This was the case with British coal miners, for example, who, threatened with lower wages for longer hours, precipitated a nine-day general strike in 1926. Moscow pinned high hopes on an Anglo-Soviet trade-union committee, set up the previous year, which symbolized – and did what it could to facilitate – the increasing radicalization of British unions. Responsibility for the strike's collapse provoked recriminations between Trotsky and Stalin. The former argued that his rival held to the tactic of conditional collaboration with Labour ('entryism', in party jargon) long after it had ceased to be productive, and advocated a more radical line that in the circumstances was even less realistic. Similar arguments were deployed in regard to the much more serious failure of Communist revolutionizing efforts in China, to be considered shortly.

For Moscow it was axiomatic that the chief objective of Soviet diplomacy should be to prevent the 'imperialist' powers from forming a new bloc directed against the USSR. Post-war Europe offered ample scope for Soviet wedge-driving, since the crippling Versailles settlement and its sequels ensured permanent friction between the victorious Entente countries and those that had taken Germany's side. Already in 1918 Bolshevik Russia had been closer to Germany than to any other possible partner, and as the civil war ended this orientation naturally regained attractiveness. It was only a question of time before the two pariah states of Europe came together. Lenin argued that

the Versailles peace has created a situation in which Germany cannot even dream of a breathing-space or of not being plundered . . . Naturally her only means of salvation lies in an alliance with Soviet Russia, a country to which her eyes are therefore turning . . . The German bourgeois government has an implacable hatred of the Bolsheviks, but such is its international position that, against its own desires, [it] is driven towards peace with Soviet Russia.*

Neither he nor Trotsky had any compunction about dealing with some conservative German generals who in 1920 approached the Soviet government, through a Turkish intermediary, with a view to secret military cooperation. Their objective was to evade the restrictive clauses of the Versailles treaty, while the Soviets hoped to acquire advanced weapons technology, in the form of tanks, aircraft, and even poison gas. According to an agreement concluded in October 1922, aircraft and engines were to be produced by the Junkers firm at a factory outside Moscow, while Krupp, Siemens, and other German enterprises set up business at Kazan', Zlatoust, and Samara. However, the output of arms and munitions was below Soviet expectations, and the OGPU (secret police) took a poor view of the scheme. Quite apart from the security risk, it made more sense strategically for the USSR to develop its own arms production, using know-how obtained from the Germans. Accordingly in March 1926 the Politburo decided to cancel Junkers's lease and to start building Soviet aircraft plants. Later in the year some details of the secret arrangements leaked out to the international press and the matter was discussed in the Reichstag. This further cooled the Soviet leaders' enthusiasm for such cooperation, although it continued in other forms, notably training senior officers and sending them to manoeuvres held in the partner country.

The flourishing military collaboration, along with formally correct diplomatic relations and the trade crucial to both countries, kept the Berlin–Moscow connection alive during the years 1928–1932 even as political relations between the two countries were declining rapidly.†

The two general staffs also exchanged intelligence information, especially about Poland. This country had from the start been the focus of their mutual concern, for neither power was fully reconciled to its existence. Poland formed the hub of the French-sponsored 'Little Entente' in Eastern Europe, designed (much as in the eighteenth century) to serve as a barrier against both German and Russian expansion. In the USSR memories rankled of the 1920 war, and the more

* Lenin, *Collected Works*, xxxi, pp. 475–6.
† Jacobson, *When the Soviet Union Entered World Politics*, p. 252.

nationalistic leaders also had an eye on the Ukrainian and Belarusian lands allotted to Poland by the Riga treaty of 1921. Warsaw's policy towards its national minorities was not beyond reproach; even so, few eastern Slavs in Poland were so alienated as to prefer incorporation into the 'Soviet family of nations'. Nor, for the moment, was Stalin anxious to acquire more discontented Ukrainians, but the problem of Russia's western borders remained unsettled and would loom large later.

The Soviet-German trade treaty of May 1921, following on one with Britain, raised hopes in Moscow of large-scale investment and generous credits. A number of Soviet-German mixed companies were formed and concessions granted to industrialists, but in terms of Russia's needs the amount of aid received was paltry. By 1928 Russia accounted for only 3.3 per cent of German exports, as against 8.7 per cent before the war. Disappointment was only to be expected, given more immediate priorities in the West and uncertainty as to whether the Soviets could be trusted to meet their financial obligations. In 1918 the Bolsheviks had repudiated their predecessors' foreign debts, estimated at about 15 milliard gold roubles (including nationalized private assets). The measure deeply shocked the international business community. Soviet spokesmen occasionally suggested deals in return for trade and diplomatic recognition, but these offers were received coolly. As in the case of German reparations to the Allies, Russia's creditors could only hope to obtain partial repayment of debt by providing further credits. Such generosity could scarcely be expected of the stolid financiers and politicians who ran Europe's affairs at this juncture. Moreover, the Soviet government adopted a strongly anti-capitalist posture and was reluctant to be tied down as to how any credits should be spent. Lenin made no secret of his belief that if one gave the bourgeoisie enough rope they would hang themselves. This celebrated phrase showed that he overestimated both the attractiveness of the Russian market to even the greediest foreign businessmen, and also the likelihood that cut-throat competition to enter it would intensify the supposedly inexorable 'contradictions of capitalism' to a point where the entire system would collapse.

Logically, certain Western creditors planned to set up an international consortium with a monopoly over commercial and financial dealings with Russia. By a skilful diplomatic move the Soviets managed to avert this threat. In 1922 a delegation led by Chicherin was invited to attend an international conference on the international debt problem at Genoa. The Russian delegates were 'quarantined' in quarters in nearby Rapallo. There, unknown to the other powers' representatives, Chicherin negotiated privately with the Germans. He exploited their fear that the Allies might give Russia the right to claim a share of German reparations, and thus he secured the agreement of Rathenau, German foreign minister, to a treaty which cancelled all mutual claims between the two countries and re-established full diplomatic relations. The terms of Rapallo were innocuous, the symbolism enormous. The Entente powers lost the capacity to control events in Eastern Europe, for the two outcasts had teamed up against the West. In effect, Soviet Russia had undertaken to support Germany's struggle against Versailles in return for German abstention from any common capitalist front against the USSR. In the meantime 'Genoa' was left to gather archive dust while other Western countries followed Germany's lead by granting the *de jure* recognition that Moscow so coveted. Britain did so in 1924, when the first Labour government took office (a step vigorously contested by Tory 'diehards'); she was soon followed by France, Italy, the Scandinavian countries, Austria, and Greece; of major powers, only the United States held out until 1933.

Recognition did not mean normality. France remained Europe's most militantly anti-Soviet power. Poincaré, who returned to office in 1926, insisted that the debt question be settled in France's favour before entering into any political agreement. Negotiations got nowhere. The Soviets argued that the accountants' figures should allow for the damage done by Allied intervention in the civil war. The British Foreign Office pursued a line that has been aptly called 'a policy of disregard'. As one Conservative minister put it in 1927, 'Until the burglar has given proof of his repentance, one doesn't hand over the spoons to him for safe-keeping.'[*] Whitehall was much exercised by the threat of Communist propaganda in India, Egypt, and elsewhere, to say nothing of Britain herself. Earlier in 1927 the London metropolitan police had raided Soviet commercial premises in search of compromising documents: little was found, but the incident led to a two-year

---

[*] Cited by M. J. Carley, 'Down a Blind Alley: Anglo-Franco-Soviet Relations, 1920–1939', *Canadian Journal of History* 29 (1994), p. 155.

suspension of diplomatic relations. Taken together with the assassination of a Soviet envoy in Poland and threatening events in the Far East, the breach caused alarm in Moscow. Stalin seems to have exploited the mood to stage a 'war scare' that served his own political purposes, and later to justify launching an all-out military build-up.

Meanwhile the Moscow–Berlin relationship fluctuated, for reasons that had most to do with Germany's fulcrum position in European politics. Balanced between the USSR and the West, each move she made towards the latter evoked Russian fears of a deal at her expense, and consequently some countermove designed to foster the 'Rapallo spirit'. Thus the treaty of Locarno, concluded among the leading European states in October 1925, which guaranteed Germany's frontiers in the west but not in the east, led logically to the German-Soviet treaty of Berlin (April 1926), whereby each signatory undertook to remain neutral if either were attacked by a third power. This was a game that Germany could play better than Russia, at least until the Great Depression struck.

SOVIET DILEMMAS IN ASIA

Moscow was better placed to win friends in Asia than in Europe. As we have seen (page 300), the Bolsheviks saw themselves as the vanguard of a vast movement of the peoples in what we now call the 'Third World' (most of whom were then under colonial rule), which they hoped would gravely weaken Western 'imperialism' and bring about its ultimate demise. For the time being, however, the USSR was too weak to give much material aid to revolutionaries in either the Near or the Far East, who had to make do with propaganda and occasional advice from itinerant Comintern experts.

These professional revolutionaries were drawn from several lands but operated under the Moscow centre's close control. By and large they took a cautious line. Given the infinitesimal size of the working class ('proletariat') in all Asian countries, they aspired to bring about a 'united front' embracing all social groups deemed 'progressive', including even the so-called 'national bourgeoisie' – that is, middle-class intellectuals and others whose outlook was generally reformist rather than revolutionary. In practice Comintern policy often came down to seeking cooperation with elements in the ruling élite who adopted an anti-Western stance from nationalist convictions, but whose social attributes might be defined in Marxist terms as 'feudal'. This opportunistic course entailed a high risk that the local Communists might end up as the losers, since it was easier for native political leaders to manipulate popular sentiment than it was for outsiders who tended to think in doctrinaire fashion and had little insight into non-European cultures. In particular Soviet officials misjudged the importance of religious motives in the Islamic world, just as they did in the USSR itself, as is clear from the vindictive treatment meted out to Sultan-Galiev, the Tatar national-communist leader.* Another factor was that Soviet state interests were best served by winning the goodwill of the governments in countries situated along its lengthy southern and eastern perimeter, however authoritarian their domestic policies.

These dilemmas first came to the fore in regard to Turkey, where the modernizing revolution of Kemal Atatürk challenged the Western powers' interests in the Near East. The Soviets, building on earlier *de facto* cooperation in Transcaucasian politics, concluded a treaty with the Kemalists in March 1921 which extended them generous political, military and even economic support. The Soviets chose to overlook the earlier arrest and murder of the entire local communist leadership. Soviet-Turkish friendship rested on a precarious foundation, a perception of temporarily shared state interests. It clearly could not serve as a first step towards an eventual communist-style revolution. In the short term the relationship was useful as a way of overcoming Soviet diplomatic isolation. In December 1925, despite further persecution of Turkish leftists, the two governments signed a non-aggression pact. Russia had a strong strategic interest in ensuring that the Turks prevented British warships from passing through the Straits into the Black Sea. Such an eventuality (albeit on a minor scale) was permitted under the terms of the Lausanne convention (July 1923), which Soviet Russia signed under protest and did not ratify.

Turkey also had some significance as a trading partner, as did Persia

---

* In 1923 Stalin had him expelled from the Party as a 'deviationist' and imprisoned without an opportunity to defend his views – the first occasion of such vicious repression of a comrade. Rearrested in 1928, Sultan-Galiev was sent to a prison camp in the north and died in captivity in March 1940.

(Iran). A treaty of February 1921 established diplomatic relations and confirmed Russian renunciation of earlier privileges in the country – but gave the Soviets a right to intervene if Persian sovereignty were infringed by a third power (meaning Britain, which in 1919 had reinforced her presence there, mainly because of Iranian oil resources). Despite this agreement some Soviet politicians, Stalin among them, backed a local adventurer in Gilan province, on the southern shore of the Caspian, who set up a ramshackle soviet republic and even marched on Tehran. His enterprise came to grief and the Soviet forces, in divisional strength, were obliged to leave Persia. The lesson of this affair was not lost on Reza Khan, who became dictator in 1923. At first Moscow looked on him benevolently, as a counterpart to Turkey's Kemal. But Reza took an even sterner line towards local communists (of whom there were far fewer), entered into deals with the British, and made himself shah (1925).

The Soviets encountered similar frustrations in Afghanistan, where in 1919 a reform-minded emir, Amanullah Khan, looked to Moscow for support in throwing off British protection. Lenin responded enthusiastically, declaring that it was the Afghans' destiny 'to unite all the enslaved Muslim peoples and lead them to freedom and independence'. Moscow offered aid, which notably included a squadron of Russian- and German-piloted warplanes, used to bomb rebel tribesmen. In London the War Office was alarmed at the supposed threat to India, but the British had no stomach for a fight in this still remote mountain kingdom, which for the next fifty years resumed its nineteenth-century role as a pivot in the 'great game' for mastery of the Asian heartland.

Farther east Soviet Russia re-established the pre-war tsarist protectorate over Mongolia. A gradual approach was taken: first of all a revolutionary party was formed on Soviet soil, then a provisional government of liberation, nominally under a theocratic monarch, in which Buryat Mongols and other russified elements were prominent. When the ruler conveniently died in 1924, a national assembly declared Mongolia a 'people's republic', which in every material respect was tied to the USSR. In the inter-war period this was the sole successful attempt to extend Soviet power abroad. The techniques employed anticipated those that were to be used by Stalin in Eastern Europe after the Second World War.

The most formidable barrier to Soviet expansion in the Far East

351

was Japan, which did not evacuate its troops from eastern Siberia until 1922 (and from northern Sakhalin three years later). Their departure owed as much to pressure by the United States as by Russia – an instance of 'intra-imperialist contradictions' advancing Soviet interests. In Japan itself communists were very much on the defensive, as indeed were all those who opposed Tokyo's increasingly militaristic policies.

The situation was far more hopeful for Moscow in China, which had fallen apart into warring rival fiefdoms. While Chicherin sought to normalize relations with the country's nominal rulers in Beijing, the Comintern, acting as the other arm of Soviet foreign policy, helped to foment revolution in the south, where a popular nationalist movement was on the upsurge. It was led by a broad coalition of political forces, the Guomindang (GMD), headed until his death in 1925 by Sun Yatsen, who inclined towards a rather vague Western-style democratic socialism. Its chief objective was to end the British presence in the treaty ports. Comintern leaders heartily sympathized, but also pursued more far-reaching goals: to encourage the Chinese Communist party (CCP) to penetrate the GMD, using 'united front' tactics, in order to eliminate or neutralize its right-wing and centrist elements, so turning it into a mighty force that would ultimately overthrow the Beijing government and reunite China under communist leadership.

The Reds' successes in the Russian civil war enhanced the appeal to some Chinese intellectuals of what they termed the 'Russian Way', and they were impressed when, belatedly, they heard of the 'Karakhan declaration' of July 1919, whereby Soviet Russia formally repudiated the substantial rights which the tsarist government had acquired in China. In many ways Marxism seemed irrelevant to Chinese conditions and upset traditional thought patterns, but in 1921 the founders of the CCP overcame any ideological reservations, at least on the surface, and proceeded to build a disciplined cadre party committed to the Comintern line as interpreted by successive secret emissaries: the Dutchman G. Maring (1921) and the Soviet diplomat A. Ioffe, who two years later held talks with Sun Yatsen. Chinese revolutionaries also went to Moscow for meetings and study. Among them was Jiang Jieshi (more familiar in the West under the name Chiang Kai-shek), who, although he developed doubts about the merits of Moscow's policies, for the time being kept such thoughts to himself. Another Comintern agent in China, known under the pseudonym Mikhail

Borodin, set up a military academy at Whampoa near Canton to train revolutionary activists and acquired considerable influence within the GMD.

Sun Yatsen's death led to the fragmentation of the GMD and eased the CCP's self-appointed task. In January 1925, apparently with Comintern backing, it set out on a new course which gave the 'united front' slogan a more radical slant, accentuating the role of the movement's 'proletarian vanguard', and called for the 'liquidation' of certain non-Communist labour leaders. This engendered a reaction among those who gave priority in the struggle to the advancement of Chinese national interests. In March 1926 Jiang purged a number of Communists from senior posts and even arrested some Soviet advisers. But Borodin managed to restore an appearance of harmony and four months later the GMD forces moved northwards in strength. The peasants who flocked to their colours engaged in revolutionary deeds which harmed propertied interests and threatened to upset the delicate political balance within the GMD. As one of its armies approached Shanghai in April 1927, local Communists rose in insurrection, only to be massacred by Jiang, who had no wish to be cast in the role of Kerensky in the proposed 'Chinese October'.

The débâcle led to bitter recriminations in Moscow. Clearly much of the blame rested with the Soviet and Comintern leadership, and not just with its agents on the ground, who had carried out orders. Stalin had

supported Jiang Jieshi throughout until . . . April 1927 [and] denied the existence of any significant cleavages in the revolutionary camp . . . He was in support of Borodin's efforts to establish a strong political alliance with the GMD Left and pushed for . . . land reform and the building up of new armed forces from among the workers and peasants . . . This leaves us to wonder how much he knew about the actual conditions and complexities of the Chinese situation . . . He bore the same responsibility [as local leaders] in overestimating the CCP's ability to manipulate the GMD and transform it into a Communist tool . . .*

In Stalin's defence it might be said that, once Moscow had decided on intervention in Chinese internal affairs (and all the Bolshevik chiefs

* Luk, *Origins of Chinese Bolshevism*, pp. 127, 123–4.

backed such a course), and given the difficulties of maintaining regular communication (by courier rather than radio!), there was little else he could have done. But the Moscow centre was already trying to assume an aura of infallibility, and so laid the blame on the CCP leader Chen Duxiu and other underlings. Moreover, it held to its former line long after it had ceased to be plausible. Then, as the GMD suppressed Communist elements elsewhere, the CCP was instructed to move left. It decided to launch a series of uprisings in the south with the aim of setting up a socialist state; but these 'autumn harvest insurrections' were crushed, as was an effort to create a 'proletarian commune' in Canton in December 1927.

Soviet revolutionizing policies in eastern Asia had suffered a major, albeit temporary, setback. Mao Zedong was one of several CCP leaders who realized that the Chinese revolution could succeed only by basing itself on the peasantry rather than the working class – and by keeping Moscow's interference at arm's length, without advertising the fact. This line was actually less novel than it might appear. In 1930, after Chen Duxiu's successor as CCP leader had been purged in turn, Mao took his place. Aided by officers trained at Whampoa, he set up a soviet republic in the southern province of Jiangxi (November 1931) and engaged the Nationalists in guerrilla war. But by this time the Japanese invasion of Manchuria had radically altered the situation in the Far East.

THE 'THIRD PERIOD', 1928–34

Engrossed in his fight with the 'left opposition', Stalin had no intention of letting his prestige suffer from a disaster abroad. When Trotsky and Zinoviev circulated a memorandum detailing his errors over China, he simply read them out of the Party and then turned on his right-wing ally N. I. Bukharin, who had succeeded Zinoviev as *de facto* Comintern chief. Bukharin advocated a flexible line in order to achieve working agreements with cooperative Social Democrats: 'The banner of unity,' he stated, 'is no mere manoeuvre.' Ironically, he was also the first to suggest that the Comintern should enter into a 'third period' in its history. In mid 1927 he presided over a leftward shift which undermined his credibility and prepared the way for his ouster. The new tactic was formally launched at the Comintern's sixth congress, held in the summer of 1928. The slogan was now 'class against class', signifying abandonment of the 'united front' and an all-out assault on the bourgeoisie in all its political manifestations, from fascism on the right through liberal constitutionalism to Social Democracy. Henceforth the moderate socialists, who were clearly the principal targets, found themselves insultingly referred to in communist jargon as 'social fascists'. This implied that there was in effect no real difference between their brand of reformism and the strong-arm methods favoured by Mussolini's followers – or by the up-and-coming German Nazis.

The term 'social fascist' had originated with Stalin (in 1924) and did not rest upon any profound political analysis. Not everyone in the Comintern accepted it willingly, but opposition was fruitless now that all the member parties had become 'stalinized'. The Soviet ruler made it abundantly clear that their task was just to obey orders from Moscow:

An internationalist is one who unreservedly, unhesitatingly and unconditionally is prepared to defend the USSR, because the USSR is the base of the world revolutionary movement ... Whoever thinks of defending the world revolutionary movement without and against the USSR goes against revolution and must slide to the camp of counter-revolution.

This harsh, categorical style characterized many of Stalin's utterances. He rarely spoke about Comintern after 1929, when a purge removed 16 per cent of the officials in its central apparatus and left the survivors trembling. They were now led by men of inferior quality supervised by Stalin's factotum, V. M. Molotov. There emerged 'a new type of proletarian leader, young, tough, unscrupulous and fiercely loyal', eager to hunt out heresy (if necessary, with the OGPU's help), and to impose 'a stultifying tactical and ideological conformity'.*

Since most Communist parties lacked mass support, the new tactical line was more aggressive in rhetoric than in reality. No violent uprisings were attempted during the 'third period'. The advent of the Great Depression in 1929 aroused hopes in Moscow that the long-awaited collapse of capitalism might be at hand, but optimism was tempered by fear that the international bourgeoisie might try to relieve social

* K. McDermott, 'Stalin and the Comintern', pp. 413–14.

pressures by waging war jointly against the USSR.* This anxiety accelerated the drive to modernize the Soviet armed forces that lay at the heart of the first Five-year plan (see page 377). The 1927 war scare had been a trifle forced, but all Communists took it for granted that sooner or later an armed attack was inevitable; their chief task was to delay its onset for as long as possible by using conventional and unconventional means.

The latter were of importance above all in the Weimar republic, where the depression unleashed a grave socio-political crisis. The KPD leaders, such as E. Thälmann, had their qualms about the 'social fascism' thesis but propagated it energetically. They assumed that the Nazis posed less of a threat than the Social Democrats, who backed the existing government. Some zealots even saw the former as potential allies. In the elections of September 1930 the Nazis won more seats in the Reichstag than the Communists, but this failed to shake Moscow's confidence. The next year the two extremist parties collaborated in a referendum which sought to bring down the Social Democratic provincial government in Prussia. By July 1932 the Nazis had won 230 parliamentary seats as against the KPD's 89, yet cooperation continued at street level (although rival gangs frequently clashed). The KPD rebuffed Social Democratic overtures for common action. Even after Hitler had assumed power as German chancellor, the ECCI declared: 'The establishment of an open fascist dictatorship, by destroying the masses' democratic illusions and freeing them from Social Democratic influence, is speeding up the process of Germany's evolution towards proletarian revolution.' By the time this statement was printed, Thälmann and other German Communists were under lock and key, many of them never to emerge.

The Nazi victory was not solely, or even primarily, the result of Communist blindness, but the rift on the left confused ordinary Germans and weakened resistance to Hitler. It was characteristic that for years thereafter Soviet political writers never produced a serious study

* 'There is a real possibility of a softening, if only temporarily, of all the sharpening contradictions among the imperialist powers', wrote the leading Comintern journal in February 1930. '[Their] implacable hatred of the world's only proletarian state acts as cement ... to fill in the cracks which threaten new internecine imperialist conflicts in the near future.' Cited by Haslam, *Soviet Foreign Policy 1930–33*, pp. 24–5.

of German (or European) fascism, for to have done so would have exposed the deficiencies of Marxist–Leninist 'scientific' analysis and of Stalin's strategy. Stalin reacted to Hitler's success by taking a more nationalistic line at home, while continuing to hold that disagreements among the Nazi leaders might lead the regime to fall. The Soviets also valued their commercial ties with Germany. Not until January 1934, when Hitler concluded a non-aggression pact with Poland which threatened Soviet security, did Moscow's line slowly begin to change.

Until then the Far East was seen as the principal danger area. Russia's Maritime province, which bordered on Japanese-occupied Manchuria ('Manchukuo'), lay exposed to attack. Collectivization had disrupted the local economy and the famished population was restless. Some residents recalled that the region had enjoyed a (largely spurious) autonomy in 1920–22. In 1929 a Special Far Eastern Army had been set up under Marshal V. K. Blyukher, but his efforts to make the region economically self-sufficient, and so more defensible, aroused suspicion in Moscow that he was fostering separatist tendencies. Partly for this reason, the Soviet response to Japan's invasion of Manchuria was relatively low-key.

Another factor was that no aid could be expected from the Chinese Communists, who were geographically remote and preoccupied with fighting the Nationalists. Relations with the latter had been severed in 1929, after a local warlord had seized Soviet Russia's last major asset in the region, the strategic Chinese Eastern railway, built under the tsar, which linked Chita to Vladivostok by way of Harbin. Blyukher won back control of it a few months later, but in 1931–2 the line was taken over by the Japanese. Moscow prudently decided on appeasement and entered into negotiations for its sale to the invaders, while simultaneously resuming relations with the Chinese Nationalists. The talks with Japan dragged out over three years, by which time Soviet defences in the Far East were in better shape.

In Europe, too, the Soviets managed to improve their position, both militarily and diplomatically, in the early 1930s. The ailing Chicherin was succeeded in 1928 (formally, two years later) by Maxim Litvinov, a cultivated Old Bolshevik. Although not a senior party man, he was allowed a certain autonomy in the decision-making process – or so at least it seemed to Westerners who identified him with a 'soft' foreign policy line. In February 1929 the 'Litvinov protocol' was added to the

Kellogg–Briand* pact of the previous year, whereby the signatories renounced war as an instrument of national policy. This brought its provisions into operation over much of Eastern Europe, since the Soviets' action was emulated by the Baltic states, Poland, and Romania. These were admittedly in large measure public-relations gestures: relations between the USSR and its neighbours remained cool. Nevertheless three years later non-aggression pacts were signed with the same states (including Finland but excluding Romania on account of the Bessarabian dispute) – and then also with France. The latter country's adhesion to the group was a straw in the wind which hinted at a possible rapprochement with the Western democracies in face of the common danger from an expansionist Germany. Another success for 'peaceful co-existence' was the recognition of the USSR by the Roosevelt administration in the United States.

But how far could such cooperation with the West go, given ideological differences and the history of discord since the revolution? Europe's statesmen treated the USSR as a marginal power. Western public opinion, too, was largely antagonistic, not least because of Stalin's dictatorial policies, although many people were impressed by the successes claimed for the Five-year plan. It was in these difficult circumstances that Litvinov endeavoured to win international support for a policy of collective security designed to deter Germany and other 'aggressor states'. For it was in Moscow's interest to preserve the *status quo* in Europe until Soviet defence capability had reached a point where the USSR could face with equanimity the challenge of the forthcoming 'second imperialist war' – and, ideally, intervene in it at some point in order to influence the outcome to its own advantage.

COLLECTIVE SECURITY

These reservations need to be borne in mind when considering Soviet approaches to the Western democracies between 1934 and 1939. With hindsight these seem more reasonable than they did at the time to British and French leaders, who were above all anxious to preserve the

* Named after the American and French foreign affairs ministers of the day.

peace even if this required appeasing the Central European dictators. In this game, played for the highest stakes, Soviet cooperation had its price, which rose as the years passed. One may well take the view that it would have been in everyone's interest to pay this price at the earliest opportunity if this would have prevented the outbreak of a new world war. But Soviet policy was no more disinterested than that of any other power, and responding to Moscow's overtures involved an element of risk. Perhaps the risk should have been taken, but the post-1945 era would show that the threat of communist expansion was real enough, even if Soviet power was less formidable in the 1930s than it would be after the Second World War. On the other hand, the Comintern's 'popular front' strategy did succeed in rallying people of all classes against fascism.

Emblematic of Moscow's new course was its entry into the League of Nations. Hitherto this international organization had been scorned as a 'bourgeois' device to maintain the exploitative Versailles settlement (and capitalist rule generally), but Nazi Germany's dramatic exit from the league in 1933 made membership in it appear more attractive. Geneva afforded Litvinov an invaluable public forum. He had already shown his rhetorical skills at the 1932 disarmament conference, held under the league's auspices, where Soviet proposals for total renunciation of military force, however impractical, struck the imagination of many. But the league proved unable to halt Italian aggression in Ethiopia and was clearly a weak reed to lean upon. Soviet security demanded the conclusion of mutual defence pacts with any power willing to help maintain peace – a policy that did not preclude keeping a wire open to Berlin.

After tortuous negotiations between Litvinov and the slippery Pierre Laval, whose preference was for a deal with Germany, and in the face of British opposition, the French and Soviet governments agreed in May 1935 that they would come to one another's aid if either were attacked. However, the agreement lacked the teeth of the old Franco-Russian alliance (for example, the League's Council was supposed to endorse its implementation) and military staff talks did not follow. A similar Soviet pact with Czechoslovakia laid down that each signatory would assist the other only if France did so first, a provision that likewise seriously weakened its utility.

Germany cried 'encirclement'. The Soviets made confidential

approaches to the Germans in order to explore the prospects of reducing tension, but they led nowhere. Berlin was willing to loan Moscow money, but shrank from political commitments. Instead Hitler sent troops into the Rhineland (March 1936) and mounted an anti-Bolshevik ideological crusade. Within months the USSR and the future Axis powers were engaged in a proxy war in Spain. Soviet involvement on behalf of the Spanish republican government against General Franco's rebels was on a limited scale, for Moscow was anxious neither to antagonize Germany nor to alarm France, where there was most public sympathy for the Comintern's appeals to form a broad anti-fascist coalition.

The shift in Comintern policy towards a 'popular front' strategy seems to have owed something to input by the non-Soviet parties, whose leaders were chafing at Stalin's lack of realism. At the carefully orchestrated Seventh congress, held after a long interval in July–August 1935, the Bulgarian G. Dimitrov was appointed Comintern president, a post long vacant. Stalin never acknowledged his earlier error but simply placed his imprimatur on new 'theses' which belatedly extended the hand of cooperation not only to Social Democrats but also to radical 'bourgeois' elements, indeed anyone willing to oppose right-wing extremism.

From sectarian rigidity the international movement was launched on to a path of complete extemporization. Old shibboleths and sacred principles were unceremoniously smashed as archaic icons . . . , swept away from the floor of the congress in an atmosphere of desperation induced by the overriding threat from Nazi Germany. World revolution was put off for better times.*

In 1936 the anti-fascist coalition government in Spain was followed by one in France. Moscow voiced approval of French rearmament and warned the French Communist party (PCF) not to press socio-economic demands too energetically, lest it drive the bourgeoisie farther to the right; for the same reason the PCF was told not to join Léon Blum's government but to lend it support. Soviet material aid to the embattled Spanish loyalists was kept within limits. The British and French governments clung to the fig leaf of non-intervention and the

---

* Haslam, *The Soviet Union and the Struggle for Collective Security*, pp. 58–9.

USSR could not afford to become too visible as the republic's chief foreign backer. In any case Stalin did not want socialism in Spain for the time being. A Soviet satellite at the other extremity of Europe would be indefensible.

Moreover, the republican forces included Trotskyists, Anarchists, and other left-wing dissidents whose views were anathema in Moscow. Accordingly, as they retreated into Catalonia before the victorious *franquistas*, many of these 'trouble-makers' were done to death by agents of Stalin's secret police, the NKVD,* which master-minded Soviet operations in Spain. Soon afterwards Stalin withdrew from an increasingly untenable situation by ending the aid programme to the Spanish left. The Great Terror now under way in the USSR (see page 393) was difficult to reconcile with the policy of collective security. Although the accused in the Kremlin's show trials were charged with treasonable links with Germany or Japan, Moscow assured Axis diplomats privately that these allegations were not aimed at them. On the other hand, it does not appear to be the case that the purges were aimed at pro-Western ('democratic') elements within the Soviet foreign-policy establishment who might have obstructed a projected deal between Stalin and Hitler. The NKVD's victims were 'liquidated' irrespective of any particular political views they may have held. The foreign affairs commissariat was badly stricken, losing an estimated 62 per cent of its senior personnel; Litvinov survived, albeit narrowly, whereas several prominent advocates of the 'Rapallo line' were shot.

One result of the Terror, above all the judicial murder of Marshal Tukhachevsky and the cream of the Red Army general staff, was to make an association with the USSR seem less desirable than ever in London or Paris. With the collapse of the *Front populaire* government the French resumed their search for agreement with the Axis. Neither they nor the British reacted when Hitler annexed Austria in March 1938. It was widely expected that Czechoslovakia would be his next target. Litvinov suggested making a joint commitment in advance to aid the Czechs if they were attacked, but the idea was greeted coolly. The British in particular had little sympathy for Prague's resistance to

---

* The OGPU had become the NKVD (People's Commissariat of Internal Affairs) in 1934.

German demands over the Sudetenland: as one senior diplomat put it frankly, 'Central and Eastern Europe must dance to Hitler's pipe.' The British favoured a four-power block with Germany and Italy to the exclusion of the USSR. It would, however, be going too far to say (as has often been alleged) that they actively sought to embroil the Axis powers in a war with Soviet Russia. 'Appeasement' meant buying Hitler off with lesser prizes, notably by sacrificing the Czechs, notwithstanding France's commitments under the 1935 pact. This was the road that led inexorably to 'Munich'.

Would the Soviets have come to the aid of the Czechs? *If* the French had abided by their undertaking, and risked war with Germany as a result, the answer is almost certainly yes – although the lack of a common border would have meant sending troops through Poland and/or Romania, a step which these states would have opposed.* In the absence of prior French action, the answer is almost certainly no, although claims to the contrary have been advanced. In 1938 Stalin was no readier for war than the Western powers (or for that matter even Hitler).

The cynicism of Munich shocked, but did not wholly surprise, the Soviets. The sell-out virtually destroyed any hope of an effective policy of collective security. The USSR was particularly indignant at its exclusion from the concert of European powers, and for several months lapsed into a defiant isolationism. Press commentators revived the Leninist notion that one gang of imperialists was no better than the other.

* Under pressure Romania did agree to such transit rights at the last moment, but on conditions so stringent as to make the provision of military aid to the Czechs scarcely possible. Air support alone would not have sufficed. Given transport and mobilization problems, one may doubt whether Soviet ground forces could have arrived in time to fight the Germans even if Romania or Poland had been well disposed. On the other hand, a strong diplomatic stand by the Western powers and the USSR, acting jointly, might have deterred Hitler from annexing the Sudetenland and even led to a military *coup* in Germany.

FROM MUNICH TO THE NAZI–SOVIET PACT

To understand Stalin's actions during the last critical year of peace in Europe we have to bear in mind his overriding fear of having to fight a war on two fronts.

The Soviets had few friends in the Pacific region. The United States, then in isolationist mood, sympathized with the Chinese as victims of Japanese aggression but lacked the political will to restrain Tokyo. Britain and France were anxious above all to safeguard their colonial possessions. As Japanese armies penetrated ever more deeply into China, Moscow urged the CCP, which after the celebrated 'Long March' was based in the north-west, to make common cause with the Nationalist regime in Nanking. But a 'united front' was even more difficult to bring about in China than it was in the West. Mao Zedong in particular placed a high price on such cooperation. Old animosities ran deep, and influential segments of the GMD, notably Jiang Jieshi and his intimates, continued to rate the domestic enemy as more dangerous than the foreign one. The Comintern executive could maintain only intermittent contact with the CCP leaders, who listened politely but all too often went their own way.

In November 1936 Germany and Italy concluded with Japan the so-called 'anti-Comintern pact' directed against the USSR. This was one reason why Stalin recommended a compromise solution of the 'Xi'an incident'.* Shortly afterwards the simmering Sino-Japanese war broke out in earnest. The USSR remained neutral but covertly supplied the GMD at its request with military goods (including 900 aircraft and 1,140 heavy guns, for example, within four years). Given the enormous transport problems this was a considerable technical feat. It led to a restoration of the Russian presence in Xinjiang; some of the arms found their way to the CCP.

Meanwhile Japanese military leaders were keen to exploit Soviet

---

* In December Jiang Jieshi went to Xi'an to urge wavering GMD generals to liquidate the CCP, only to be made their prisoner. Reluctantly, the CCP agreed, at Moscow's behest, that he be released unharmed in return for vague promises to reshuffle his government and adopt a more cooperative stance.

internal weaknesses as demonstrated by the Great Terror. Its ravages claimed a number of prominent victims in the Maritime province, including Marshal Blyukher, who was arrested in August 1938 and later tortured to death. In July he had led Soviet troops in a successful action to reclaim some fortified hills near Lake Khasan, on the Soviet-Manchurian border, which the Japanese had taken, but did not conceal from Stalin's spies his suspicion that the clash had been engineered by NKVD frontier troops in an effort to compromise him. The Soviet victory owed more to good intelligence work by the USSR's 'master spy' in Tokyo, Richard Sorge, than to the Far Eastern Army's proficiency, which left much to be desired. These shortcomings emboldened the Japanese to challenge Soviet control over Mongolia.

In May 1939, after staging over thirty minor incidents, they launched three forays against Soviet troops stationed on the Mongolian-Chinese border. Almost simultaneously Moscow learned through Sorge that Tokyo was negotiating a military pact with Berlin whereby the Japanese would intervene against the USSR if it fought Germany. Sorge thought (correctly) that such action was unlikely before 1941. Stalin did not always fully trust Sorge's information, but seems to have treated this seriously. Soviet forces in Mongolia were quickly built up and on 24 August General (later Marshal) G. K. Zhukov launched a major counter-offensive at Khalkin-Gol (Nomonhan).

By the time hostilities ceased on 16 September, the Japanese had since May suffered 18,500 dead and wounded – one of the highest casualty rates they had received in any engagement since the turn of the century. The Russians lost 9,824 men – significant in absolute numbers but, given massive Soviet superiority, few in relative terms. This was the first major action involving mechanized forces and unquestionably boosted Soviet confidence that the Red Army had recovered from the devastation wrought by the Terror. That bubble did not burst until the Winter War with Finland.*

For the moment the Japanese defeat deterred Tokyo from further adventures and gave the USSR a breathing-space in which to forestall the nightmare scenario of a simultaneous German-Japanese onslaught.

This was the background to Stalin's astonishing step of making common cause with Hitler. The Nazi-Soviet pact of 23 August 1939

---

* Haslam, *The Soviet Union and the Threat from the East*, p. 132.

set the scene for the outbreak of hostilities in Europe. When did Stalin decide on this drastic move? Most historians believe that he kept his options open for as long as he could and finally committed himself only at the last moment.* Moscow's first diplomatic response to Munich was to seek improved relations with Poland, but little came of this. Another confidential approach to Berlin yielded only an agreement to moderate mutual recriminations in the press. Soviet policy marked time until March 1939, when Hitler made the next move by annexing what was left of Czechoslovakia. A nominally independent 'Carpatho-Ruthenian' state made its appearance on the Soviet border, but this did not represent a serious threat and Stalin made light of it.

He could not, however, remain indifferent to the Western powers' reactions to the Prague *coup*. The British guarantees to Poland and Romania, given without prior consultation with Moscow, were more than unwelcome. Not only did they indicate that London preferred to deal with Warsaw or Bucharest rather than Moscow, but they rebuffed Soviet aspirations for a comprehensive Eastern European security pact. Addressing the Eighteenth Party congress on 10 March, Stalin criticized Western appeasement policies and warned that the USSR would not be 'drawn into conflicts by warmongers who are accustomed to have others pull their chestnuts out of the fire for them'. The remark is generally taken as a signal to Berlin that Moscow was ready to do business.† This move was followed by the dismissal of Litvinov (3 May), who was replaced by none other than Molotov: clearly Stalin wanted to tighten up the decision-making process – and, as most historians think, demonstrate Soviet dissatisfaction with the democracies.

* This interpretation has been forcefully restated by G. Roberts in *The Soviet Union and the Origins of the Second World War* (1995), who uses hitherto secret Soviet documents. It must be borne in mind, however, that even senior Soviet diplomats were not privy to Stalin's secrets. The Soviet leader consulted only with Molotov and a few cronies before taking vital decisions. The evidence does not support the view that he had been working towards a deal with Hitler since 1934. He had a grudging respect for his fellow-dictator and doubtless considered playing this trump card, but kept it in reserve, so to speak, because of the high risks involved. In effect, he wavered between a pro-German and pro-Western course.

† Roberts argues against this view on the grounds that Stalin still identified the fascist powers as the aggressors and made no follow-up move in Berlin to ascertain whether the message had been received.

Litvinov was summoned to the Kremlin where he received a thorough critique of the collective security policy. Understandably, he made no defence and accepted his dismissal in silence. The lack of reaction apparently infuriated Molotov and, as Litvinov was leaving the room, Molotov stood up and screamed, 'You think we are all fools!'*

Molotov told the German ambassador that 'a corresponding political basis' was needed if the current economic negotiations between the two powers were to succeed. The bait was not taken at once in Berlin, but Hitler had already decided to attack Poland and needed the Soviets' goodwill. On 26 July a subordinate German official told a Soviet interlocutor that the moment had come for the two powers to delimit their spheres of interest in Eastern Europe. The point was made still more forcefully a few days later by Ribbentrop. Molotov was guarded in his reply, evidently believing that he could set a leisurely timetable for the *rapprochement*. But the Germans were pressing hard, and by 11 August the Kremlin seems to have decided in their favour.

Since Munich Moscow's price-tag on a deal with the Western powers had risen: nothing less than a full-scale alliance would now suffice. The relatively junior Anglo-French military mission sent (by sea!) to Moscow for staff talks on a tripartite pact was unable to agree to making the Poles allow Soviet troops into their country to face the German army on their soil. The negotiations stalled, but already before that point the Soviets had lost interest in them. Ribbentrop flew to Moscow and within a few hours the two parties had agreed to both a non-aggression pact and a secret protocol. The latter specified that in the event of a 'rearrangement' of Polish territory the demarcation line was to run along the rivers Vistula, San, and Bug; Finland, Estonia, and Latvia were to fall into the USSR's sphere of influence, and its 'interest' in Bessarabia was duly noted. At dinner afterwards Stalin proposed a toast to Hitler's health: 'I know how much the German nation loves its *Führer*.' Later, according to one eyewitness, he said: 'If Germany should be forced to her knees, I would come to her aid

---

* Phillips, *Between the Revolution and the West*, p. 166. Litvinov was, of course, Jewish. Roberts claims that he was sacked only because he was sceptical about the Soviet initiative for a triple alliance with Britain and France. If so, why was the NKVD preparing a case against him in which he was to be branded an Anglo-French spy?

with a hundred Red divisions on the Rhine.' Europe's two mightiest dictators were poised to carve up the continent, each according to his own fashion.

CHAPTER 18

Stalinism

THE ASSAULT ON THE PEASANTRY

At its Fifteenth Party congress in December 1927 the Communist regime celebrated ten years of soviet power. The delegates approved a draft plan of economic development intended to create the basis for a socialist transformation of Soviet society. The plan assumed that growth would be rapid but balanced, with relatively modest, feasible annual output targets. This was to reckon without Stalin. In 1928–9 he consolidated his grip on the leadership, crushed Bukharin and other right-wing critics as 'deviationists', and initiated a second revolution that would end in bloody tragedy. The chief victims, as always in Russia's tormented history, were the peasants.

At the congress Stalin spoke of the need 'to turn the small and scattered peasant farms into large united farms, based on cultivation of the land in common ... not by pressure but by example and persuasion'. Nothing here suggested that a storm was imminent. But during NEP the relationship between the Party and the rural population had never been free from misunderstanding and potential for conflict. In the winter of 1927–8 a decline in the amount of marketed produce, especially cereals, brought this potential to crisis point.

By January 1928 only 4.9 million tons of grain had been procured by the state against over 7 million in the same period of the previous year. The total was not only well below state expectations for building a grain reserve and exports but was disastrously short of the minimum required to feed the towns and the Red Army ... There had been a fall of over 50 per cent in Siberian grain procurement compared with about 30 per cent in the USSR [as a whole].*

* Hughes, *Stalin, Siberia and the Crisis of NEP*, p. 104.

There were many reasons for the shortfall. Agricultural productivity levels remained low; peasant incomes had risen; there was a dearth of manufactured goods; railways were clogged and much grain left to rot because of inadequate storage facilities. Above all, in September 1927 the authorities had lowered the prices paid for cereals while increasing those for livestock. Naturally many producers held back on grain deliveries in the hope of a price rise in the spring. But for Stalin, as for the young party cadres in general, only one explanation really counted: 'kulak greed'.

From above and below there was pressure for a return to the coercive methods of the 'War Communism' era. Those officials who held out for rational economic management and maintaining the *smychka* were denounced for 'Rightist' sympathies. It became harder than ever to discuss the particular merits of various policy options. Advice by experts was suspect to zealots who believed that, as Stalin put it in November 1929, 'there are no fortresses that Bolsheviks cannot conquer'. In January 1928 the Leader (as Stalin would soon be styled) set out on a two-week expedition to western Siberia, where he hectored local officials to the effect that *they* would be held individually responsible for late deliveries. Peasants who hoarded grain were to be prosecuted as speculators. This implied that normal market relationships were no longer deemed legal. Judicial officials in the region were reluctant to enforce this provision, but 1,589 such cases were taken to court over the next five months. The accused, chosen arbitrarily from previously prepared lists, were sentenced to heavy fines or brief gaol terms; one quarter of the confiscated grain was loaned to local *bednyaki* (poor peasants) to stimulate class conflict in the village. Similar methods were employed in other grain-producing areas, to which 30,000 officials in all were dispatched.

In the Politburo Bukharin and other doubters were led to believe that these 'extraordinary measures' were temporary, and indeed by April 1929 the official line sounded more relaxed. But this was a tactical move. Stalin was captivated by the so-called 'Ural–Siberian' method of procuring supplies and intended to rely on it in future. Even so, statements were still made that NEP had not been abandoned. The confusion was in part natural, since Stalin was still feeling his way, but also in part the result of deliberate deception. It was officially maintained that the anti-kulak campaign was a spontaneous mass movement, whereas in fact 'only the iron fist of the plenipotentiary dispatched from outside . . . secured the obedience of the commune to the state'.* The exactions reinforced the natural cohesiveness of rural society, but peasant resistance caused pressure to be stepped up. The result was that in 1928/9 the procurement campaign brought in less grain than in the previous year (10.8 as against 11.1 million tons).

To break the vicious circle the party leaders resorted to a desperate measure: forced collectivization *en masse*. The draft Five-year plan had envisaged a 15 per cent target; this was raised to encompass the *entire* peasantry. 'Class enemies' were to be deported to forced labour in 'settlements' located in inhospitable northern and eastern regions of the country. This policy, too, was neither thought out nor announced in advance. At first relatively gentle methods were used. By mid 1929 about a million households had been induced to join collective farms (*kolkhozy*), over twice as many as had been in them a year earlier. These were overwhelmingly peasants without land or stock – and even they joined less from conviction than in the hope of getting state aid. Those who had something to lose were unresponsive if not actually hostile. Realizing that they would be persecuted if they became too successful, and were in any case ultimately doomed to forfeit their property, they cut back on the area sown to crop and slaughtered their livestock for consumption. There were cases of arson and murder of village activists or peasants who informed on their fellows. The collectivization drive was accompanied by much violence and the forcible closure of churches. Church bells were seized and melted down. At Gorlovka in the Donbas 4,000 icons were consigned to a bonfire in the town square as thousands of miners danced in celebration.

Early in 1930 a wave of terror struck the countryside. The slogan was now: 'Liquidate the kulaks as a class.' Squads of politically reliable workers, stiffened by police and soldiers, descended on the villages to 'persuade' their inhabitants to set up collectives. Objectors were humiliated (for example, being made to strip and drink water from a bucket like a horse) and assaulted, their huts ransacked and useful items 'inventoried', that is, stolen. By 20 February half of all households had been 'collectivized' – on paper. The new farms did not exist in a material sense: they lacked funds, buildings, and above all the tractors

---

* Taniuchi, 'Decision-making on the Ural-Siberian Method', pp. 95–7.

that embodied progress through mechanization. Infuriated peasant women led hundreds of local revolts.

Faced with this mass reaction, the activists grew nervous. Stalin was prevailed upon to beat another tactical retreat. On 2 March 1930 he published an article in *Pravda*, 'Dizzy with Success', blaming the excesses on local zealots. Peasants in collectives were to be allowed to keep some property. The turnabout annoyed subordinates who were thus fraudulently cast as scapegoats, and was interpreted by peasants as licence to forsake the farms in droves; by late summer the proportion of collectivized households had fallen to 21 per cent. Yet those who left found it hard to reclaim their property and in the autumn pressure was resumed. By July 1931 the percentage of households collectivized had climbed back to 53 (with 68 per cent of the sown area); three years later the figures were 71 and 88 per cent. A new agrarian order had taken shape.

A Politburo directive of January 1930 divided kulaks into three categories. The first, numbering 60,000, were to be shot or sent to forced-labour camps; 150,000 in the second category were to be resettled elsewhere. No figure was set for the third group, who were to be allocated land near their former homes. In practice these figures were disregarded and many of those taken were not kulaks (a term still vaguely defined) but those whom local activists deemed objectionable. Recently published studies show that about 600,000 households in all were affected, of which 381,000 were deported in 1930–31 alone – that is, about 1.6 million individuals. Millions of others fled to towns or construction sites. A few stayed on as independent farmers until the mid-1930s. They were subjected to crippling taxes and eventually lost their property – and their lives as well.

The Urals region alone received 571,000 deportees in 1930–31. Those who survived the journey built makeshift huts with whatever materials were at hand. The authorities were unprepared for them. Rations were issued irregularly, and only to those fit for work (42 per cent in March 1931). Winter clothing was scarce, and many malnourished settlers froze to death.

Especially harsh is the lot of new-born babies [wrote the Sverdlovsk OGPU chief] who are kept hidden in rags and hardly ever washed owing to lack of soap, and have to live in very cold, damp huts . . . Crowding and poor supply have led to outbreaks of typhus, measles, scarlet fever and scurvy; the percentage of infants who die is high.

Even children of twelve had their allotted tasks: 2 to 2½ cubic metres of timber to be felled daily. Norms were a third to a half higher than those of 'free' workers. In the coal mines of Chelyabinsk settlers died for lack of drinking water. Beatings were commonplace; in one case sadistic guards forced people to dig their own graves and lie down in them, but this practice was officially deplored (I. Ye. Plotnikov, in *Ot. ist.* 3/1994, pp. 159–67; 1/1995, pp. 160–79).

By January 1935 less than a million (974,000) of these 'special settlers' were left. This figure remained fairly stable for the rest of the decade. The decrease was due mainly to high mortality rates but partly to flight.* Successful fugitives tried to start a new life in a town rather than go back to their own village, where they were unwelcome.

Peasants seem to have contemplated the actual return of the dekulakized with a very wary eye. This was not so much because of any long-standing hatred of kulaks as because the return of the dispossessed would start a new cycle of recrimination and revenge and raise all kinds of awkward questions about the disposition of confiscated kulak property.†

The wave of repression eased off slightly after completion of the first Five-year plan, but official policy was incoherent. Secret OGPU reports reveal extensive dissatisfaction. Hungry peasants pilfered wheat from the collective fields. A draconian edict of 7 August 1932 laid down that anyone appropriating 'socialist property' be shot or, if there were mitigating circumstances, deprived of liberty for ten years. Over the next seven months 103,000 people were sentenced under this 'seven-eight decree' (as it was popularly called), of whom over 6,000 were put to death. In Ukraine and the lower Volga region whole villages were blacklisted, and the inhabitants deported, for failing to meet their procurement targets.

---

* According to official statistics published in 1990, between 1932 and 1940 no fewer than 629,000 escaped, of whom 235,000 were recaptured; 112,000 others were released. These figures are as yet unverified, and the category 'transferred' may in some cases conceal execution. The same reservations apply to the new figures on labour-camp inmates, who are not included here: see page 395.

† Fitzpatrick, *Stalin's Peasants*, p. 239.

A man-made famine now stalked wide swathes of Ukraine and other areas of the south. Brigades of activists scoured the countryside for hidden grain to fulfil unreasonably high quotas. During the winter of 1932–3 peasants lay in their huts, their limbs swollen from hunger, as unburied corpses piled up in village streets and squares. Hordes of refugees made for nearby towns, but many were turned back by police. The afflicted areas were sealed off so that their inhabitants had no access to urban products. The very existence of a famine was officially denied, lest the fact discredit the regime. Hence no international relief materialized, as it had in 1921–2. On the contrary, agricultural produce continued to be exported.

Stalin could at any time have ordered the release of grain [stocks] but held off until the late spring in the clear knowledge that the famine was now doing its worst . . . [He] regarded the weapon of famine as acceptable and used it against the kulak-nationalist enemy . . . The verdict of history cannot be other than one of criminal responsibility.*

By May 1933 Stalin evidently decided to change tack. A secret order to party and government officials claimed that 'three years of struggle have crushed our class enemies in the village', so that it was now possible 'to cease, by and large, the practice of mass deportations and sharp forms of repression'. This was indirect acknowledgement that Soviet agriculture was in a critical state. Grain output in 1933 has been put at 65 million tons (±4 per cent), scarcely more than in 1928 (63 million); potato and sugar beet production declined, and only vegetables and industrial crops performed better than before the Five-year plan.

Even more dramatic was the collapse of the livestock sector: cattle were down from 60.1 to 33.5 million head, sheep and goats from 107 to 37.3 million, pigs from 22 to 9.9 million, horses from 32.1 to 17.3 million.† The slaughter of animals was partly a protest against collectivization, but mostly owed to lack of fodder. The loss of horses

---

* Conquest, *Harvest of Sorrow*, pp. 326–30. Some historians are less convinced that the famine was a deliberate act of genocide aimed at Ukrainians. The nomadic Kazakhs suffered relatively even more than Ukrainians; they are thought to have lost half their total population, about 2 million persons (some of whom, however, managed to escape abroad). The total number of famine deaths (excluding those in the Gulag) is estimated at 5–6 million.

† Davies *et al.*, *Economic Transformation of the Soviet Union*, pp. 113–14, 287–9.

could not be made good by tractors, which were still scarce. Total traction power in 1933 was only three quarters of what it had been four years earlier, and in some areas cows were used to pull implements. Not until the late 1930s did the total amount of energy available to farmers substantially exceed the 1928 level. These truths were concealed by suppressing inconvenient statistics and inflating others.

The collective farm that emerged from the turbulence was a small unit, in some respects akin to the old village community (*mir*), but subject to close bureaucratic controls which corrupted, if they did not extinguish, entrepreneurial spirit among its members. Prominent among these agencies were machine tractor stations (MTS), which had political departments staffed by NKVD officials. A far greater share of agricultural produce now went to the state, whose requirements had to be met before any residue was disposed of, for instance as payments to the *kolkhozniki*.* Farms with poor land or communications might have next to nothing left for their members, who were supposed to be rewarded according to the number of 'labour-days' (*trudodni*) that they had worked during the year. The system was weighted so that tractor drivers, stockmen, and other skilled workers did better than ordinary labourers. The number of agricultural specialists tripled between 1928 and 1941, reaching 153,000, of whom 65,000 had higher education; but of the latter only one fifth actually worked on farms, the rest preferring indoor jobs.

On paper collective farms were managed democratically, but in practice the chairman was appointed from above and this automatically endorsed at a mass meeting. The first farm bosses were proletarian zealots with virtually no experience of agriculture. Only gradually did these 'trouble-shooters' give way to local men with better qualifications; even so their educational level remained low. Invested with virtually dictatorial power, they were prone to abuse it. Thousands of letters of complaint were written on this score, and when investigations revealed wrongdoing the culprit faced punishment for 'kulak tendencies'. It was not a popular job.

During the later 1930s *kolkhozniki* learned to adapt to the system

* In 1928/9 the state, as we know, had collected 10.8 million tons of grain; by 1933/4 this had risen to 23.3 million, and by 1939/40 to 30.7 million tons, leaving the peasants (in each year) with about 42 million, although in 1937/8 they did significantly better.

and even to exploit it for their own benefit, much as they had under serfdom. A 'model charter' (1935) confirmed each household's right to maintain a small private plot, essentially a kitchen garden, on which to grow vegetables and keep poultry (even a cow, but never a horse). These plots supplied two thirds of the potatoes, and almost all dairy products, meat, and eggs eaten by rural folk. Budget studies showed that they were consuming less of many foods in 1937 than they had done in 1923/4. Bread, the principal dietary item, was baked on the farm from grain produced in its 'socialist sector'. But it was their plots that kept the peasants alive. They could not be certain of earning much from their work in the collective fields, and this was anyway more likely to be paid in kind than in cash. A share of the plots' produce had to be delivered to the state – another practice reminiscent of serfdom. Any surplus could be sold legally at '*kolkhoz* markets' in nearby towns, at prices determined by supply and demand, or else on the black market. Peasants could also take up off-farm employment, as in times past, although for this they needed permission from the farm management and the local soviet. They would leave their wives behind to tend the plot, a job that was in any case regarded as women's work.

The state was not reconciled to its *de facto* compromise with private farming and the market. In 1939 it reverted to a more coercive policy. A tax was levied on peasant orchards; quotas for meat and grain deliveries were raised; and above all private plots were cut down in size. This offensive was justified ideologically by arguing that the 235,000 *kolkhozy* (1940) were but a half-way house to fully socialized agriculture as practised on the 4,200 state farms (*sovkhozy*). These were conceived as veritable 'grain factories' and marketed more of their crop than collectives could. Their workers, 1.2 million strong in 1937, received regular wages and as 'proletarian' state employees enjoyed a superior status, even if their living conditions were little better than those of *kolkhozniki*.

THE BATTLE FOR INDUSTRY

The prime purpose of all the burdens imposed on the peasantry was to extract capital to finance the rapid expansion and modernization of Soviet industry. This motive could not be stated plainly, and some specialists have since questioned whether the agrarian sector of the economy really contributed as much to the great industrial drive as commonly thought. But it is generally agreed that the material and human resources had to be found at home, for foreign capital was no longer available, as it had been before the revolution. For ideological as well as strategic reasons, the leadership sought to make the Soviet economy as autarkic as possible, while relying heavily on advanced Western technology in the initial phase. The Great Depression abroad added to the authorities' problems. It upset Soviet expectations of increased foreign trade. It also fostered the belief, ultimately shown to be illusory but widely held at the time, that Soviet planning was inherently superior to the chaos of the capitalist world.

In 1929, when the first Five-year plan's 'optimal variant' was drafted, the leadership hoped to accomplish miracles: to build a number of capital-intensive grand projects, to achieve spectacular increases in industrial output, to change the structure of industry, and to improve living standards – all this within five years! In December 1932 the plan was even said to have been completed within a mere four years. This was partly propagandist boasting, partly self-deception. Statistics were freely manipulated and experts who dissented suppressed. 'The Plan' was a fiction, a psychological device to mobilize the population behind the vast endeavour. What emerged in 1928–32 was a 'command economy' in which resources were allocated centrally according to the leaders' priorities, with little thought for consumers; output targets were set arbitrarily and frequently altered, to the consternation of subordinate officials; and an atmosphere of feverish haste prevailed in which failure to meet prescribed plan indicators, unpunctual delivery of material, or industrial accidents would be ascribed not to the bureaucratic system of management, which was sacrosanct, but to sinister counter-revolutionary 'wreckers'.

This had been the charge against the Shakhty mining engineers in 1928, whose trial set a precedent for that of the so-called Industrial party in 1930, former Menshevik planning officials (1931), and specialists working for the British Metro-Vickers company (1933). The latter case was intended as a warning to Western industrialists, who nevertheless continued to sell their know-how for Soviet gold. Stalin preferred United States firms to European ones, as their technology was deemed superior and American industrial achievements were highly regarded.

Hugh L. Cooper, builder of the largest dam in the Tennessee valley, moved on to the Dneprostroy hydroelectric project and won a contract entitling him and his team to every amenity while the surrounding population starved. He was one of the few foreigners with access to Stalin. The Leader gave his name to the pig-iron complex constructed at Kuznetsk, near Penza, by the Freyn company of Chicago; the celebrated motor-vehicle works at Gor'ky (Nizhniy Novgorod) was built by Austin Motors under a licence from Ford. The giant tractor plants at Stalingrad and Chelyabinsk owed their existence to the International Harvester and Caterpillar companies respectively. The former, which at one time employed no less than 730 US engineers, was described by one of them in euphoric terms:

The assembly building, bristling with an endless forest of lathes, drills, gear-cutters, and a hundred machines that only a specialist could name, all of them bearing American trade-marks, stretched 446 yards long and 105 wide, enclosed by glass walls that let in light like a studio.

He added, however, that the conveyor belt, whose normal speed was two feet a minute, ran at only one quarter that pace. Importing technology was one thing: using it efficiently another. Even so, by the end of the decade freshly trained young Soviet engineers were successfully operating vast industrial complexes and copying their design elsewhere.

Particularly important was the growth of the arms industry. In 1929/ 30 the USSR produced 899 aircraft, less than a quarter of them for combat. By 1940 total output was over ten times as great (10,565) and fighters accounted for three quarters. The equivalent figures for tanks are 170 and 2,794 – fewer than in 1935 (4,803) because designers were switching to more powerful models. The output of artillery systems expanded from 952 units to about 15,000. The Soviet arms build-up was not steady but proceeded in spurts, as was true of industry generally. Between 1930 and 1932 its share of total industrial production more than doubled, to 5.7 per cent. This was already greater than in 1913 and much larger in absolute terms. By 1940 the proportion had increased to 22 per cent. The Soviet metallurgical industry learned to make the high-grade steel and alloys necessary for modern weapons, along with sophisticated machine tools for precision work. The defence sector had first claim on scarce materials and its workers enjoyed higher pay and better conditions – although the talented A. N. Tupolev, arrested in

1938 like countless other specialists, had to design some of the world's finest aircraft while confined in a special prison (*sharashka*), where his entire construction bureau toiled under NKVD supervision!

Their fate emphasizes the stark contrasts that marked the Soviet industrialization drive: on one hand giant projects and the latest in modern equipment, on the other slave labour and a 'free' work force that was poorer than before and had no right to organize. The trade unions' powers were further curbed. Their chief purpose was to boost output and productivity by championing officially sponsored campaigns of 'socialist emulation' between enterprises or branches of industry. They also managed leisure and cultural facilities for the working-class élite. Bargaining with management over working conditions (but not wages, which were set centrally) was largely a formality.

Soviet planners gave top priority to capital investment and the manufacture of producers' goods. According to official data, during the first Five-year plan the output of 'Group A' industry increased nearly threefold, from 8.4 to 23.1 milliard roubles, whereas that of 'Group B' (consumer goods) grew by less than double (13 to 20.2 milliard roubles). The figures for individual products make the point more clearly. Oil output rose from 11.6 million tons in 1928 to 21.4 million in 1932, pig iron from 3.3 to 6.2 million tons. But that of cotton fabrics stood at the same level in 1932 as in 1928 and of woollen fabrics actually declined. By 1940 the output of oil and pig iron were respectively 2.7 and 4.5 times greater than in 1928, whereas cotton and woollen fabrics had risen by 48 and 19 per cent.

Townspeople's diet deteriorated during the early 1930s and did not recover the quantity and quality of the NEP years for several decades. From 1929 to 1935 bread and other basic foodstuffs were rationed. Meat consumption was halved. Yet workmen, especially if they were privileged 'shock workers' (*udarniki*), were better fed than some other groups. In 1932 real wages stood at 52 per cent of their 1928 level, and in 1937 at 63 per cent.* The drop in personal income was offset to some extent by the provision of 'free' educational and health services. Also on the credit side was the ending of unemployment (1931) and the fact that many families had two breadwinners. Workers' wives were virtually obliged to take jobs in order to make ends meet. By 1939

* Figures for Moscow, but broadly indicative of the general situation.

women comprised 43 per cent of all industrial employees. Many of them performed heavy manual labour – tasks hitherto reserved to men: in coal mining nearly one quarter of the workforce was female. As before, there was much sexual harassment at the workplace. Women workers tended to be younger than males and to change jobs more frequently.

High labour mobility (50 per cent in 1929!) became an enduring feature of the labour scene. It had something to do with the massive influx of youngsters from the countryside. No less than 23 million rural-dwellers moved permanently to the cities between 1926 and 1939, a migration rate unprecedented in world history.

At the beginning of 1931 nearly one-third of all industrial workers had been employed for less than a year. By the end of the first Five-year plan the average worker had two to three years' work experience as compared with eight in 1929. The proportion of workers with five or more years' *stazh* [length of employment] had fallen to around a third.[*]

By the end of the decade, as the rate of increase slowed, the proportion of young people declined. They were, however, still numerous in the vast plants established in new towns such as Magnitogorsk in the Urals or Komsomol'sk-on-the-Amur in eastern Siberia. As the latter's name proudly indicated, these were pioneer ventures in which adolescent zealots were the standard-bearers.

Military strategy was one motive behind the effort to locate more factories in eastern regions. The drive slackened off in the mid 1930s, so that less was achieved in this respect than anticipated. By 1939 14.9 per cent of large-scale industry was situated in or beyond the Urals (including Central Asia), as against 11.2 per cent in 1928. Eastern Siberia and the Far East accounted for a mere 2.8 per cent of the total (1928: 1.7 per cent), yet this region produced nearly twelve times as much as it had before the drive began.[†]

[*] Davies *et al.*, *The Economic Transformation*, p. 97.
[†] Measured in 1926/7 prices. This measure inflates the growth rate and does not allow for deterioration of quality. On this basis contemporary Soviet statisticians claimed a 6.4-fold increase in industrial production in the period 1928–40, or 16.8 per cent per annum. Of several independent Western estimates using index numbers (1928: 100) the best, by W. Nutter (1962), gives 286 for civilian industry only and 312 for all industry including armaments. Post-Soviet Russian economic historians concur in this order of magnitude. Since the workforce also tripled, from 4 to 13 million (1928–40), there was

Managers were under heavy pressure to fulfil allotted plan goals. This was their legal responsibility, so that any backsliding was likely to land them in serious trouble. They would commonly engage in bureaucratic intrigue to get their factory's targets lowered, build up concealed stocks of raw materials or fuel, pad output statistics, and employ 'fixers' (*tolkachi*) to obtain scarce supplies by underhand methods.

'Taut planning' . . . was a framework in which political bosses exercised effective personal power in their trouble-shooting moments, sometimes at cross-purposes with one another despite the highly centralized hierarchy . . . Party bureaux and the government . . . issu[ed] numerous decrees and directives which, succeeding one another with conflicting messages, added up to a stream of policy proclamations rather than to an effective, enforceable legislation.*

Despite the plethora of controlling institutions there was no agency capable of settling conflicts impartially and imposing rational choices. The hectic atmosphere, with one campaign rapidly succeeded by another, encouraged waste. Entire industrial complexes might lie unfinished because funds were lacking to complete them, or men be left idle for weeks owing to a shortage of spare parts; they would then frantically have to work overtime to catch up. These problems were less in evidence during the second quinquennial plan (1933–7) but were never entirely overcome. They would become far more serious after the war and eventually bring about the collapse of the command economy. But at the time the leadership played down the costs of the industrialization drive, taking comfort from its successes in areas of key concern to the state.

What did workers themselves think? Few saw themselves as part of a new ruling class, as the propagandists would have it. But many were sustained by the hope that their current sacrifices would be made good by future abundance under socialism.† They tended to blame

---

no overall growth in per capita productivity, although the picture differed in specific industries.

* Andrle, *Social History of Twentieth-Century Russia*, pp. 165–6.

† The first Five-year plan was officially said to have laid the *foundations* of socialism, which now had to be 'completed', enabling the USSR to pass into the higher stage of (full) communism.

shortcomings on local foremen or bosses rather than on the system. There was a good deal of grumbling over food shortages, poor housing, and so on – even the odd riot – but this did not translate into political opposition.

Party leaders and functionaries defined working-class identity, and most workers outwardly conformed to this definition . . . When peasant migrants left the factory and returned to their neighbourhoods on the outskirts of Moscow, they reverted to the language, cultural expressions, and modes of behaviour expected by fellow villagers . . . Workers accepted the self-representation 'working class' as part of their public persona, but they did not internalize it as a guide for their behaviour or allow it to deter their pursuit of individual interests.*

A small minority – shock-workers and, from 1935, Stakhanovites – identified themselves with the regime. Alexey Stakhanov was a Donets coal miner who managed, by cheating, to exceed his output norm fourteen times over and achieved celebrity status. Workers elsewhere were urged to emulate his feat and were rewarded by privileges such as interest-free loans. In November 1935 labour heroes were invited to the Kremlin for a congress in their honour, where they were accorded VIP treatment. 'Proletarian justice' was meted out to fellow-workers or managers who obstructed the campaign. But soon routine set in. Stalin's old crony Ordzhonikidze, the heavy industry commissar, who committed suicide in February 1937, argued that spectacular individual achievements were all very well, but it would be better for all workers to improve their efficiency over the long run. Stakhanovites were unpopular with ordinary workers, under pressure to join the movement. As they did so, the material privileges granted to these high achievers were reduced, and their zeal evaporated.

Shop-floor tensions were rooted in the differentiated industrial wage structure introduced after 1931, when Stalin lambasted egalitarianism as a 'petty-bourgeois' vice. Payment by piece-rates, formerly condemned as exploitative, came back into favour. The top decile (10 per cent) of wage-earners got three times more than the lowest. The aim was to encourage the more enterprising to improve their skills and take

---

* Hoffmann, *Peasant Metropolis*, pp. 213–15.

on responsibility. Extensive training facilities were provided in factories, but few workers showed a proper 'socialist' concern for high productivity. Accordingly the carrot was followed by the whip. Like other urban residents, workers had to carry internal passports (1932) and, from 1938, 'labour books' in which any misconduct was noted. In practice managers often turned a blind eye to such remarks when hiring job applicants, so that these controls did not abolish the labour market. Changing employment was a practical alternative to going on strike, which was illegal. As war neared, disciplinary measures were tightened and absenteeism made a criminal offence.

CULTURE IN RETREAT

Those who ran the economy, along with engineers, scientists, teachers, and others in white-collar occupations, formed the Soviet intelligentsia – a term which had now changed its meaning. It no longer signified educated people who thought independently but a class of officials – brain-workers who in one way or another served the state, as the sole employer. Within this broad élite those appointed to their jobs by a party agency at the appropriate level comprised the *nomenklatura*. In the 1930s these men (and a few women) were in the main young, upwardly mobile party members of approved proletarian background.

During the first Five-year plan era the last old professional administrators were purged. Young Communist (Komsomol) zealots would march into government offices and denounce those serving there as incompetent or corrupt leftovers from the tsarist regime. In 1929–30 about a million and a half employees were put through the mill by Rabkrin inspectors, stiffened by *ad hoc* groups of workers; 164,000 of them were fired. The operation was presented as part of a general campaign against 'Rightism' by class-conscious proletarians, but was in fact a bureaucratic measure stimulated from above. The cadres that took over were poorly equipped to perform their new tasks, which explains why there were so many technical breakdowns and administrative snarl-ups at this time. A massive adult education drive was initiated. By early 1933 233,000 Communists were full-time students, 166,000 of them in higher schools, with engineering the favourite discipline.

Others attended military and party schools. About 100,000 college student were former workers.*

This new élite would dominate Soviet affairs for the next half-century. Leonid Brezhnev, for example, who led the country from 1964 to 1982, was still a candidate member of the Party when he entered the Timiryazev Agricultural Academy in 1930; he then took a job in a metallurgical plant in Ukraine and enrolled as a student in a local institute, graduating in 1935. A diploma of some sort and a party card were prerequisites for success in most spheres of life. One unintended consequence was that the Party became an élitist organization, notwithstanding its proletarian image and ideology.

Members of the 'new class' enjoyed material privileges, such as access to special stores, holidays at government-run sanatoria, even official limousines and country cottages (dachas). They no longer took their meals in the same canteens as ordinary folk but had their own, where the food was much better. All this was clearly a potential source of corruption. But neither could these benefits be translated into private property, nor did these functionaries enjoy security of tenure: what the state (or Party) gave it could just as readily take away. Accordingly Soviet bureaucrats valued most the *power* they wielded over their dependants. This owed much to privileged access to information in a society where decisions were often taken in secret. The system encouraged officials to behave arbitrarily, contravening the rules, on the tacit understanding that they might be held to account later if higher authority so wished. Their careers, and even physical survival, depended on the network of personal contacts they managed to build up. This explains the development of informal 'family circles' or clientèles. Such linkages were both vertical and horizontal. A successful provincial secretary (*obkomsec*) promoted to the Central Committee apparatus would bring with him men who had previously served in his bailiwick; likewise someone sent down as a factory manager would first cultivate fellow-bigwigs in the local Party, NKVD, and other 'machines'.

From the centre's viewpoint these alliances threatened its control, and campaigns would periodically be launched to destroy them. Stalin's purges and Great Terror can be partially (but only partially) explained

* Fitzpatrick, *The Cultural Front*, pp. 135–6, 159–60.

in this way.* In some respects Stalinist rule revived 'feudal' practices characteristic of the Muscovite service state, with its centralism and hierarchy of nobles dependent on the Crown. The two polities also shared a sense of their own superiority *vis-à-vis* the outside world and a self-defensive isolationism. However, the parallels should not be taken too far, for the Stalinist autocracy pursued a revolutionary mission. By reshaping society to its own design, it sought to alter human nature itself, ultimately on a world-wide scale. For all their preoccupation with humdrum everyday tasks, party activists did not lose sight of this utopian goal, which was inherent in Bolshevism. This accounts for their devotion to the cause, which in the 1930s at least involved more than mere careerist aspirations, as well as their readiness to tolerate, and help inflict, catastrophic human losses as the necessary price of progress. The official ideology, known as 'Marxism-Leninism' (*not* Stalinism!), taught that the USSR was constructing a model socialist society according to scientific precepts. Intellectuals were more likely to be impressed by these claims than common folk, since science enjoyed high prestige.

In 1929 the Academy of Sciences was in its turn purged of 'class enemies' and persuaded to accept as members leading Bolsheviks with scholarly credentials such as Bukharin and Lunacharsky – who thereby were politically downgraded, for at the time they were under attack as 'Rightists'. Over a hundred of the academy's staff were arrested in this operation, many of them in connection with a plot said to involve an eminent pre-revolutionary historian, S. F. Platonov. Some returned to favour later when cultural policy stabilized. In the mid 1930s the academy moved to Moscow, into the very premises earmarked for its highly politicized rival, the Communist Academy, whose institutes it took over. But this victory was bought at a high price. As the Party's protégés, scientists and scholars who contributed to the country's advance could expect high salaries and public acclaim. Some were allowed a modest share in policy making. But this collaboration demanded the sacrifice of the intellectual freedom essential to academic research.

A number of academics, above all in the natural sciences, accommodated themselves to these pressures, persuading themselves that they

---

* This is a principal argument of those Western 'revisionists', notably A. Getty, who have sought to depict the Terror as a rational bureaucratic device to control disobedient subordinates, playing down the Leader's criminal pathology. See below, page 394.

were carrying on an earlier tradition of serving the people. In the social sciences this was harder. Historians, for instance, had to take great liberties with the truth if they were to survive and have their work published. Both pre-revolutionary liberal-minded professional historians and their Marxist successors of the 1920s, who followed the teachings of Mikhail Pokrovsky, came to grief. Archives were closed to independent researchers and links with foreign scholars broken off. From 1934 onward the way was open for a new school which took its cue from the Kremlin. Its adepts managed, by manipulating the record, to reconcile (pseudo-)patriotic values with the demands of the class struggle and the 'personality cult'.

Philosophy, law, and biology were likewise perverted for political ends. Some disciplines disappeared: political science, sociology, and theoretical economics. Two of Russia's greatest authorities in the latter discipline perished in the camps: the mathematical economist N. D. Kondratyev, who opposed Stalinist methods in the name of truly scientific planning, and the 'neo-Populist' agrarian specialist Chayanov. Another prominent victim was the world-famous biologist N. I. Vavilov, who was denounced by partisans of the 'Michurin school' of applied genetics headed by the charlatan Trofim Lysenko. The latter falsified experimental data to substantiate extravagant claims that biological characteristics, being acquired, could be changed by manipulating the environment. This theory neatly complemented the Stalinist view that social engineering could produce a 'new Soviet man'. On the practical plane it held out the hope of near-miraculous increases in farm yields.

The new élite's artistic tastes were philistine. In 1928–9 the various 'proletarian' cultural bodies launched an all-out assault on 'bourgeois' values. Leopold Averbakh, head of the radical writers' organization RAPP, questioned the political loyalty of 'fellow-travelling' comrades: 'They accept the class struggle,' he intoned, 'but they speak of humanism, not class hatred . . . as if there could be anything more humanist than the class hatred of the proletariat.' Writers like Bulgakov or Andrey Platonov, who failed to measure up to these standards, were silenced; the former's plays were no longer performed* but the satirist

---

* After a telephone conversation with Stalin he was given a minor job in the MKhAT theatre, where in 1935 two of his plays did go into rehearsal, only to be banned. Thereafter he devoted himself to a remarkable novel, *The Master and Margarita*, which *inter alia* contained references to his fate at the censors' hands. He died in poverty in 1940.

Zamyatin, exceptionally, was allowed to emigrate (1931). Two years later the poet Osip Mandel'shtam incautiously wrote some epigrammatic verse highly critical of Stalin:

> We exist in a land grown unreal and strange.
> Ten steps away no one hears the talk we exchange.
> But when chances for half-conversations appear,
> They turn to the Kremlin mountaineer . . .
> Like horseshoes he forges decrees in a line,
> One for the groin, the head, brow and eye.

He was arrested but, after representations by colleagues, sent into exile, where he attempted suicide; four years later he was sentenced to hard labour in the Gulag, where he died of cold and hunger. His sufferings were later chronicled by his widow in two volumes that became classics (*Hope against Hope*, *Hope Abandoned*). Of 2,000 writers arrested during the Terror, three quarters lost their lives. Their letters, diaries, and manuscripts were confiscated; a few texts survived in police archives to be published after 1988.

The dissolution of RAPP and its artistic and musical counterparts in April 1932 encouraged literati to hope for a 'thaw'. They were compulsorily enrolled in the Union of Soviet Writers (USW). Its most prominent figure was Maxim Gor'ky, who in 1928 had returned from years of voluntary emigration, in a blaze of publicity, only to find himself playing a courtier's role that compromised his moral integrity. In 1933 he travelled with other celebrities along the Belomor canal joining the White Sea to the Baltic, which had been built by forced labour, and helped to produce a book praising this enterprise, which had supposedly turned criminals into honest, hard-working citizens. It was in fact but a visible island in what would shortly become the highly secret 'Gulag Archipelago'. Gor'ky, who died in 1936 (probably murdered at Stalin's instigation), also contributed to the formulation of the new doctrine that would henceforth guide writers and artists: 'socialist realism'.

Whatever its intentions, in practice 'socialist realism' limited writers' freedom to select themes and treat them as they thought fit. It did not mean depicting reality in its true colours, but rather propagating a mythologized world-view acceptable to the cultural controllers. These officials' taste ran chiefly to epics glorifying current achievements, written in a style readily accessible to the masses, in which heroes of sterling character were pitted against villainous reactionary forces. Where tsarist censors had simply hindered writers by chopping out subversive references, the functionaries of Glavlit sought to force literature into a preconceived mould.

In *The Quiet Don* (1928–40) Mikhail Sholokhov came closest to their ideal. This was a massive chronicle of revolutionary changes in that region (where he lived) from the civil war to collectivization. Yet the most 'positive' character, the cossack Melekhov, is more ambivalent about Bolshevism than he really ought to be. Likewise, the hero in the blind Nikolay Ostrovsky's semi-autobiographical *How the Steel Was Tempered* (1932–4) is a worker turned writer, whose struggle is waged as much against ill health as against class enemies. The author's stylistic gifts and sincerity raise his work far above the level of the 'production novels' that were turned out by the dozen. The construction of Magnito-gorsk, for example, was the theme of Valentin Katayev's novel *Time, Forward!*, while Yuriy Krymov's tale 'The Tanker *Derbent*' centred on a Stakhanovite mechanic in the Caspian oilfields; F. Panferov performed the same service for collective farmers (*Volga Peasants*, 1928–37). To be sure, pulp fiction as a literary genre was also popular in the West. The Soviet brand, whatever its aesthetic deficiencies, may have suited the needs of some newly literate readers.

The 'socialist realist' canon applied equally to the visual arts and even to music. Painters depicted healthy sportsmen and sportswomen (A. Samokhvalov, *Girl in a Football Jersey*, 1932; A. Deineka, *Goal-keeper*, 1934), for

the cult of strength, of the muscular athletic body symbolized . . . the social strength of the young state. Sculptures were created along green park alleys, whose expressive Spartan force was an essential element in the urban setting and a symbol of man's victory over nature or the younger generation's triumph over the 'rotten past' of pre-revolutionary Russia.*

Deineka was a former Constructivist who moved with the times. In *Ever High and Higher* (1934) Serafima Ryangina showed two smiling

---

* I. Leskova-Lamm, 'Kommunismus und Kitsch', in G. Gorzka (ed.), *Kultur im Stalinismus: Sowjetische Kultur und Kunst der 1930er Jahre*, Bremen, 1994, p. 184 (with illustrations).

young builders, one male and the other female, on scaffolding (without safety harnesses!) high above a landscape dotted with electricity pylons – romantic comradeship in a modern industrial setting. In 1937, at an international exhibition in Paris, the Soviet and Nazi pavilions, which faced each other, offered a comparative view of totalitarian art. The former was dominated by V. I. Mukhina's colossal bronze of a worker (male) and collective farmer (female) triumphantly holding aloft a hammer and sickle.*

Monumental architecture embodied the mood of the age. A competition was held to build a vast Palace of Soviets near the Kremlin, on land cleared by the destruction (1931) of the Cathedral of Christ the Redeemer, a national shrine marking the victory of 1812. This was a pointless act of vandalism. The palace was never built. The winning design, as amended by cultural bureaucrats, catered for an edifice 415 metres high (8 metres more than the Empire State Building!) with an 80-metre-tall statue of Lenin on top. It was too heavy to be practicable and eventually the site was turned into a public swimming-bath. In the 1990s the cathedral was rebuilt, using modern techniques, to symbolize the resurrection of Orthodoxy (and Russia).

Stalinist architecture did have a certain rationality, since it was designed to serve as a backdrop to organized mass demonstrations, such as those held on May Day or the anniversary of the October revolution, when the leaders took the salute atop Lenin's mausoleum. Equally ritualistic (and militaristic) were the parades of physical-culture activists. In this homogenized, collectivistic society there was no place for the individual.

In the world of music, too, the spotlight was on the chorus, preferably chanting airs drawn from folklore which all could join in singing. Shostakovich's Fourth Symphony (1935–6) was condemned for its disharmonies and not performed until 1942. His opera *Lady Macbeth of Mtsensk*, based on a work by Leskov, played to full houses in Leningrad and Moscow for two years until Stalin saw it (26 January

---

* It was later re-erected in front of the All-Union Agricultural Exhibition, 'a garden of socialism in which nature was recreated in a world deprived of its Creator, . . . an ideological greenhouse' (G. N. Yakovleva in ibid., p. 147). The central pavilion bore plaster mouldings of giant vegetables, wheatsheafs, etc., and each union republic's edifice had characteristic local motifs. For decades this was second only to Lenin's mausoleum as a tourist attraction in Moscow.

1936) and took umbrage at the explicit bedroom scene as well as the 'decadent' music. A philippic appeared in *Pravda*. The composer, distraught, took refuge in working for the cinema, while the dictator called on Soviet musicians to produce serious, life-affirming classics. It was a call that evoked a certain resonance, for many composers, like artists in other cultural spheres, concealed their inner doubts for fear of ostracism and punishment. In a sinister way Stalinism forced intellectuals to compromise themselves and in effect become their own censors. Many of them adopted one attitude in public but another in private.

The damage done was less evident at the popular level. Even during the Terror ordinary citizens joked, danced, and went to the circus or cinema. There was ample light entertainment, even jazz (Soviet-made, for choice) – although one band leader was actually arrested on the podium. Radio was becoming a mass medium (4.4 million receivers by 1940). Foreign films were seldom screened, but home-produced ones were popular, especially if they dealt with such modern topics as aviation. In 1938 Eisenstein was persuaded to make a historical epic, *Alexander Nevsky*, which had a strong anti-Teutonic slant; after the Nazi-Soviet pact it was withdrawn and replaced by a cinematic version of *Die Walküre*. History does not record whether Hitler got the point!

By this time all children in the RSFSR were spending at least four years in school and illiteracy had been greatly reduced: according to the 1939 census 89 per cent of those aged 9–49 could read and write. School buildings and other facilities were still inadequate – instruction was given in shifts by overworked and underpaid teachers – but the trend was in the right direction. Experimental methods were no longer tolerated in the classroom. Schools had a well-defined authority structure and again followed prescribed curricula with examinations and diplomas. Uniforms were worn and in 1940 fees were introduced for entrants to universities and technical schools. Likewise family policy became more conventional; divorce was made harder and abortion criminalized.

Contemporaries saw all this as a 'great retreat' from iconoclastic revolutionary principles. It was much more than this. Russian nationalistic (indeed, imperialistic) values were integrated into the official ideology, which was instrumentalized in the service of the ruling clique.

CULT, PURGE, TERROR

The brutal measures employed against the peasantry were justified ideologically by the argument that 'progress towards socialism is bound to aggravate the class struggle'. Bukharin, the Party's chief theorist, called this 'idiotic illiteracy'. Confiding his fears to Kamenev in July 1928, he compared Stalin to Jenghis Khan: an unprincipled intriguer, he cared only for power and wrought vengeance on all who opposed him; his policies could lead only to terror and bloodshed. His prophetic words made no impact on Kamenev, who rejected his advances, and in February 1929 Bukharin and his fellow 'Rightists' were censured for 'factionalism'. They were eased out of their jobs and excluded from the Politburo.

In 1930 the party machinery was overhauled. Henceforth the country was governed through the General Secretary's personal secretariat and a 'Secret Department' within the Central Committee's enlarged apparatus – and through the security police. Stalin's dictatorial pretensions were obvious, but until the mid 1930s his regime retained oligarchical features. There was still opposition among the party élite, although it could not be articulated: secret informers were everywhere. In 1930 two hitherto loyal Stalinist regional leaders, S. I. Syrtsov (Siberia) and V. V. Lominadze (Caucasus), criticized the confusion over economic policy and planned to get Stalin dismissed. They were 'unmasked' and downgraded.

The method of [their] removal marked a significant turning point in the institutional development of Stalin's dictatorial regime, for it graphically demonstrated that . . . he could dispense with leading members of his network who held key positions in the core executive at will, without any pretence of adherence to Party rules.*

Another prominent victim was M. N. Ryutin, who in 1932 circulated a seven-page 'appeal to all party members' which indicted Stalin for breaking with Leninism and muzzling criticism; collectivization by terror, he declared, had brought the country to the verge of disaster.

---

* Hughes, 'Patrimonialism and the Soviet System', p. 562. Lominadze died a natural death in 1935; Syrtsov was shot in 1937.

Ryutin and twenty alleged confederates were expelled. Among those implicated in the affair were Zinoviev and Kamenev, who had failed to report the document when it came into their possession. Stalin is said to have demanded Ryutin's execution as a terrorist, to which Kirov, the Leningrad leader, objected. Consequently he was given a ten-year prison term, only to be shot in 1937. This incident may have turned Stalin's suspicious mind against Kirov, too.

Since December 1929, when his fiftieth birthday was marked with fulsome praise in the press, the Leader had been the object of a growing cult. In public he affected a modest stance – he was a consummate actor – but privately he fostered the glorification. Absolute power brought out paranoid traits in his character. Intensely vain and ambitious, he condemned others for his own faults, which he could not admit even to himself. As his leading biographer writes:

The individual experiences his own failings as those of others . . . Stalin's is a classic case. From youth onward projection became second nature with him . . . In later years, the more there was in his conduct that he had to deny and censor out of [his] consciousness, the more he found to hate, blame and punish in others . . . Stalin's mental world was thus sharply split into trustworthy friends and villainous enemies – the former being those who affirmed his idealized self-concept, the latter those who negated it.*

Those who caused him some offence would be labelled 'double-dealers' or 'enemies of the people'. In November 1932 his young wife, Nadezhda Alliluyeva, committed suicide from despair at his brutality towards her and the people at large. This protest, too, he treated as betrayal. He would not visit her grave, yet brooded over the tragedy for years thereafter.

Convinced that the Party had been infiltrated by supporters of Trotsky and other secret oppositionists, Stalin in January 1933 ordered a purge of 'class-alien and hostile elements'; there were five other vaguely defined categories of undesirables. In all about 22 per cent of party members were expelled, generally after engaging in public self-criticism. Some were recent recruits from the countryside, others local officials. Yet the purge did not achieve its purpose. The operation created a sense of insecurity that actually strengthened clientelism (the

* Tucker, *Stalin in Power*, pp. 163–4.

formation of private networks) and contributed to the discontent with Stalin's leadership that emerged at the Seventeenth Party congress, held in January 1934.

Dubbed 'congress of victors', this stage-managed assembly witnessed an unexpected challenge behind the scenes to the General Secretary's authority. Delegates evidently backed a move to depose him in favour of the more popular Kirov. When ballots were cast, Stalin came so low down the list that he ordered the results falsified.* Most historians believe that this episode led the dictator to plot Kirov's murder. If so, he will have arranged this orally with G. Yagoda, the OGPU chief – who later confessed to his part in the killing (without, of course, betraying his master's presumed role!) – and a senior Leningrad security official, I. Zaporozhets. The evidence of Stalin's complicity is circumstantial. The assassin, a disgruntled Communist named L. Nikolayev, may conceivably have acted alone for personal reasons, in which case Stalin will have merely exploited the murder for his own purposes.

Whichever is the true version, he came to Leningrad on the following day (2 December) with a top-level delegation and launched a hunt for former Zinoviev supporters, who he claimed were behind the crime. A decree ordered judicial agencies 'not to hold up execution of death sentences' for terrorism; the verdicts were to be carried out 'as soon as sentence is passed'. This directive 'became the basis for massive abuses of socialist legality', as Khrushchev put it in his 1956 'secret speech' (see page 454). Nikolayev and others were put to death; Kirov's chief bodyguard, a potential witness, met his end in a staged motor accident – presumably to conceal official complicity in the murder.

Meanwhile Yagoda's fearsome deputy, the dwarf-like N. I. Yezhov, set to work with Stalin's close cooperation to fabricate materials for a show trial in which Zinoviev and Kamenev would be the star performers. In this pseudo-judicial farce, investigators intimidated and tortured prisoners to make them confess to counter-revolutionary crimes which even their torturers knew they had not committed. Court proceedings (before the Supreme Court's military collegium) were in public, but the verdicts had been decided beforehand by Stalin and his associates

---

* An investigation in 1989 could not, however, establish the number of adverse votes or confirm the destruction of ballot papers. Kirov is said to have told Stalin what was afoot and refused to take any part in it.

(notably Molotov, Kaganovich, and Zhdanov), who communicated their wishes to the judges. The USSR chief prosecutor, Vyshinsky, cruelly lambasted and mocked the accused. There was no question of them getting a fair hearing. At mass meetings in factories workers demanded the death penalty for the 'traitors'.

Very few people actually believed that since 1932 respected Bolshevik politicians had formed a 'Trotskyite-Zinovievite counter-revolutionary bloc' which had plotted to kill Stalin and seize power. This extravagant notion was put forward in a secret letter by Yezhov circulated to local party organs in the Central Committee's name (July 1935). It took more than a year before sixteen Old Bolshevik leaders, including Zinoviev and Kamenev, were brought to trial (August 1936). All of them were shot at once. Even so, Stalin was not yet satisfied. 'The OGPU was four years late in this affair,' he wired Politburo colleagues from Sochi on 25 September. 'Yagoda was clearly not up to the task.' Yagoda was accordingly replaced as head of the NKVD by Yezhov, and the Great Terror ('*Yezhovshchina*', in popular parlance) began in earnest.

The police apparatus was purged and investigators told to hunt out former 'Rightists' and frame them, too, as confederates of the other ex-oppositionists. In January 1937 came a second show trial involving seventeen former leaders who had been implicated in statements made under duress by their comrades. The charges were now broadened to include, still more improbably, association with German and Japanese agents, not just (non-existent) agents of the exiled Trotsky. After the trial the Central Committee met in plenary session. Its recently published minutes show that the delegates were in a state of near-hysteria. Hoping to save their skins, they vied with one another in exposing alleged 'anti-Soviet activities' in their organizations and vowed to eliminate all hidden enemies.

During the following months more and more people were arrested. Over a million and a half party members had at some time been expelled, and they were regarded as especially dangerous. Repression from above invited an orgy of denunciation from below. Vengeful employees eagerly informed on their bosses; neighbour turned against neighbour; some malicious or frightened people told on members of their own family. Women flax-workers, oddly, were particularly vigorous in exposing the crimes of (male) managers and engineers.

The Terror struck all segments of the Soviet élite (and some ordinary folk, too). It fell most heavily on non-Russians in the minority republics or individuals with foreign contacts. The rapid turnover of economic managers harmed industry's performance. Particularly grave was the impact on the Red Army leadership, which Stalin (and Voroshilov, his defence commissar) had long suspected of disloyalty. After torture – there are identifiable bloodstains on his interrogation record – and secret proceedings in the Supreme Court's Military Collegium, Marshal Tukhachevsky was shot in June 1937, along with other Red Army chiefs. Nearly 40,000 armed forced personnel were arrested, relatively few of whom survived the camps to be 'rehabilitated' when war came. Of 899 officers in the high command, 643 were taken, of whom 583 perished. Among major-generals and colonels the casualty rate was 59 per cent, among lieutenant-generals 93 per cent. In the party hierarchy, too, death came most frequently at senior level: of 139 Central Committee members elected in 1934, 98 were shot. In 1939 Stalin spoke of half a million members recently appointed to leading positions.

Victims were chosen in arbitrary fashion. Most of them had no association with any opposition tendency and a number were loyal Stalinists of unimpeachably proletarian credentials. Some were arrested and shot simply so that local NKVD functionaries could fulfil quotas assigned from above. In August 1937 their superiors decided that 259,450 individuals should be arrested and 72,950 of them shot; in March 1938 an even more lethal operation set figures of 57,200 and 48,000 respectively. In practice these quotas were often exceeded, either with or without the centre's permission. Retribution was meted out by 'trios' (*troyki*) of NKVD, procuracy, and party emissaries dispatched from Moscow. They paid no heed to judicial formalities, even the mock 'trials' by drumhead tribunals of which several dozen were staged in the first months of the Terror. Relatives of those 'repressed' were as a rule not told of their fate.

Some of those who passed through the hands of NKVD interrogators featured on lists which Yezhov submitted to Stalin and other leaders, who placed the figure '1' or '2' against the names: a '1' meant execution, a '2' deportation to the Gulag. Very few were spared. Khrushchev in 1956 spoke of 383 such lists, but the real figure was greater. In the Gorbachev era the State Security Committee (KGB) acknowledged 681,692 executions by its forerunner in 1937–8, but many more will have succumbed in detention or been 'liquidated' without any record. The true figure is probably nearer one million. Many more (perhaps 4 to 5 million) were sent to the Gulag, where people survived on average for only one to three years.

The term Gulag (more properly, GULag) refers to a department of the NKVD set up in 1930: the Main Administration of Camps. More generally, it indicates the penal system in general under Stalin. This ceased to be reformatory in spirit, as in the 1920s, and became fiercely punitive. The number of camp and colony* inmates rose from about 30,000 in 1928 to 2.6 million in 1933. These were mostly common-law offenders rather than political prisoners, although the two categories cannot be neatly differentiated. From 1929 inmates deemed capable of physical labour were obliged, like the 'special settlers' discussed above, to help fulfil the plan. Failure to meet high-output targets brought instant reprisal, such as a cut in rations or dispatch to the dreaded 'isolator'. Soon a network of camp complexes extended across the country. Conditions were particularly harsh in the goldfields run by Dal'stroy in the Far East (Magadan district). The OGPU developed an interest in expanding its economic operations, and this was a subsidiary reason for the massive influx of prisoners. According to recently published official statistics, by January 1935 the Gulag held 1,939,000 inmates (not counting gaol prisoners); five years later the figure was 2,658,000 (plus 190,000 in gaol). Unfortunately these data, if correct, give no idea of the inflow or outflow (through death, release, transfer, etc.); the statistics on these matters are confusing and require independent verification.

Even judged in economic terms the forced-labour system was incredibly wasteful. Morally, politically, and juridically it was an abomination. 'Politicals' suffered more than common criminals, who often served as auxiliary guards. Apart from the *sharashki* (see page 378), there were special camps for women, children, and those driven insane; the existence of execution camps is also well attested. After 1988 civic activists who began to exhume some sites (such as Kuropaty in Belarus) came across tens of thousands of human remains.

---

* Corrective-labour colonies (ITK) catered for short-term prisoners and in theory had a lighter regime than corrective-labour camps (ITL), where the regimes were of three degrees of increasing severity.

In Stalin's day the very existence of the Gulag was an official secret. It was never mentioned in the media, but ordinary people knew about it from rumour. Some thought it a good thing. Still more remarkably, a number of innocent victims of repression released in the 1950s, when the Gulag was partially dismantled, remained loyal to the Party.

By late 1938 it became apparent to Stalin that the Terror had achieved its ends: Soviet society had been coerced into conformity and a new generation of politically more reliable functionaries placed in commanding positions. That many of these individuals were soulless bureaucrats, incapable of initiative, was of little account, as was the loss of innocent lives. 'You can't make an omelette without breaking eggs,' the saying went. Yezhov was disgraced and in 1940 went the way of his victims. His successor, Lavrentiy Beriya, was a deceptively respectable-looking but vicious sadist. A Georgian, he owed his rise through the police and party hierarchy to shameless flattery of his all-powerful compatriot. After he took over,

arrests and executions continued, but on a smaller scale . . . Beriya brought a cold efficiency to his work, creating a feeling of purpose and stability among his subordinates. He did not bombard the population with news of plots and conspiracies, but attempted instead to establish a semblance of calm and 'business as usual' within the country. Police powers did not diminish, they simply were less dysfunctional.*

The torture of prisoners, which Stalin had explicitly sanctioned, continued, but the victims of repression were targeted less irrationally. Often they were entire national-minority groups. This practice had begun several years earlier, when for security reasons Poles living in the western borderlands were resettled *en masse* in Kazakhstan, and was then extended to Greeks, Karelians, Koreans, and others. After the territorial annexations of 1939–40 over a million people from these western areas joined the flood: Ukrainians, Belarusians, Jews, and Balts. Those deemed most dangerous, on political or social grounds, were killed or sent to camps, while the rest joined the 'special settlers'. All toiled and suffered under NKVD control in what one survivor ironically called 'Beriya's gardens'.

Rule by terror was the essence of Stalinism. No previous tyrant

* Knight, *Beria*, pp. 92–3.

since ancient times had dared discipline his subjects in such ruthless fashion. Whether Stalinism was totalitarian* remains a matter of opinion. Resistance was widespread. Inevitably it was in the main passive (except during the war), but it helped to inhibit the regime from achieving all its goals. Yet undeniably the Stalinist leadership did largely succeed in coopting and reshaping Soviet society. The 'progressive' image which it presented to the world had little to do with reality, but it appealed to a generation confronted by the threat of fascism.

---

* The term is vehemently contested by 'revisionist' historians in the West but accepted by many of their post-Soviet colleagues. *Inter alia* it implies, correctly, that there was no institutional check upon the ruler's power. Writers who used the term in the 1950s were prone to treat it as a static 'model', underestimating the system's ability to change and mellow, but critics eager to correct this error fell into a worse one. 'Totalitarianism . . . did not mean that such regimes in fact exercised total control over the population (since this is impossible), [but] that such control was their basic aspiration . . . It did not mean that such regimes were omnipotent in performance, but rather that they were omnicompetent in their institutional structure . . . It was not Soviet society that was totalitarian [but] the Soviet state.' [Malia, *Soviet Tragedy*, pp. 13–14]

ON THE EVE

The Soviet-German non-aggression pact on 23 August 1939 was followed, five weeks later, by a treaty of friendship that guaranteed the
two powers' new borders. This agreement transferred Lithuania to the
Soviet sphere of influence in exchange for a slice of ethnic Poland.
Fifty years later these treaties stimulated a massive protest in the Baltic
republics that was a factor in the USSR's collapse. At the time they
were denounced as a breach of international law. Stalin now became
Hitler's *de facto* ally.

The switch confused Communists abroad, who were obliged once
again to change their line: the enemy was no longer fascism but the
new 'imperialist war'. Hardliners in the British and French parties
came out against their countries' military preparations, so laying themselves open to punishment for sabotaging the war effort. Meanwhile,
under a credit agreement signed on 19 August, the USSR exported
to Nazi Germany large quantities of raw materials – oil, timber,
non-ferrous metals, and agricultural produce – to a total value of 672
milliard marks.* Soviet deliveries continued until the eve of the German
invasion on 22 June 1941, for at this time Stalin was more anxious than
ever to appease his partner.

Initially he reckoned that the USSR stood to gain whichever way
the war went in the West: a German victory would eliminate Britain,
which of all capitalist powers he disliked the most, and perhaps lead

---

* Plus 70 milliard marks for transport services; in exchange the USSR received
industrial goods worth only 462 milliard marks, for only one quarter of the machines
and other equipment that had been promised by Germany actually arrived; some imports
did, however, have a military use. Source: A. A. Shevyakov in *Vop. ist.* 4-5/1991,
pp. 164–70.

the Nazi regime to mellow; alternatively, a long-drawn-out struggle between Germany and the Western democracies would re-create the situation of 1918, but with the Soviets, having built up their military might, better able than then to exploit the warring peoples' misery for revolutionary purposes. As Zhdanov explained to a select party audience in November 1940,

a socialist government's policy is to use the contradictions between imperialists, in this case their military contradictions, to expand the position of socialism whenever the opportunity arises . . . Ours is an unusual neutrality: without fighting we get some territory [laughter]. To maintain this neutrality we have to be strong . . . The role of the bear [Russia] is to go round the forest and demand payment for each tree while the wood-cutter cuts the timber.*

He was less than truthful in representing Soviet territorial acquisitions in 1939–40 as conflict-free. Admittedly, few Red Army lives were lost when, on 17 September, Soviet soldiers marched into eastern Poland to claim a share of the spoils. Shattered by Hitler's blitzkrieg, many Poles hoped that the Soviet presence might shield them from the worst. An even warmer welcome was given by non-Polish elements of the population, some of whom wrought vengeance on their former 'oppressors' before order was re-established. But it soon became apparent that the occupiers were intent on outright sovietization. In October elections held under duress produced a 91 per cent vote in favour of the territories' incorporation in the Belarusian and Ukrainian Soviet republics. A start was made on adapting economic and cultural life to the Soviet pattern, for instance by expropriating private property and introducing atheistic teaching in schools. NKVD officials sought out actual or potential enemies. Some they killed on the spot, the rest were deported eastward, at times on foot, in four waves. First to go were males from the 'privileged classes' (February 1940), followed two months later by their dependants and by Jews. The latter comprised the bulk of the third group, which left in June; thousands of others, aware of the Nazi threat, moved east of their own accord.

Former Polish officers, policemen, and politicians met a particularly tragic fate. Most of them were interned in three camps at Katyn

* Nekrich, 'The Dynamism of the Past', in Wieczynski (ed.), *Operation Barbarossa*, pp. 231, 233 (retranslated).

(Smolensk district), Starobel'sk near Khar'kov, and Ostashkov (Kalinin district). On 5 March Beriya reported to the Politburo that they were conducting anti-Soviet agitation – 'they are only waiting to be freed so as to have a chance to struggle actively against Soviet power' – and proposed that their 'cases be examined by special procedure with application to them of the supreme penalty – shooting'. Stalin and five colleagues agreed. No fewer than 21,857 individuals were summarily put to death (*Vop. ist.* 1/1993, pp. 17–22). When some of their bodies were discovered at Katyn by the Germans in 1943, the Soviets angrily denied any responsibility and blamed the Nazis instead. They held to their version, despite mounting evidence of its falsity, until the truth was at last revealed in 1992. The number of victims was greater than previously suspected, and of course there had been no judicial proceedings whatever.

Annexation of eastern Poland was swiftly followed by strong-arm measures to improve Soviet security in the Baltic. Moscow demanded that neutral Finland cede a strip of land in Karelia and several islands covering the approaches to Leningrad. The Finns reckoned that this would compromise their sovereignty and refused. On 24 November a staged border incident gave the Soviets a pretext to invade. Viipuri and Helsinki were bombed. The Finns, far from being intimidated, resisted stoutly and soon showed themselves masters of winter warfare. Within Finland there was minimal support for the puppet government set up close to the border under the Finnish Communist leader Otto Kuusinen. The war dragged on for months, creating a risk that the Western powers might intervene on the Finns' behalf. The USSR was expelled from the League of Nations as an aggressor state. By March the Finns, having lost ground to fresh Red forces, had to sue for peace. They were granted reasonably moderate terms, but inevitably now looked for support to Germany. Kuusinen's 'government' was forgotten. Defence commissar Voroshilov admitted his share of the blame for the Red Army's poor showing – it suffered some 200,000 casualties – and on 8 May gave way to the more professional S. K. Timoshenko. The conventional ranks of general and admiral reappeared, discipline in the armed forces was tightened, and pressure stepped up on the three Baltic states of Estonia, Latvia, and Lithuania.

Already in October 1939 their governments had been coerced into allowing 70,000 Soviet troops on their soil, ostensibly for their joint defence. As Russian historians now concede, the popular response to this was lukewarm at best.

Most people adopted a reserved attitude ... Few believed that the Baltic states could stay completely independent and neutral ... The majority understood that the decisions were dictated by circumstances ... Given anti-German sentiment, especially in Latvia and Lithuania, the 'solution' offered by the Soviet government seemed to many a lesser evil. [A. G. Dongarov and G. N. Peskova, in *Vop. ist.* 1/1991, p. 39]

In Lithuania some people were appeased by the return of Vilnius, the former capital, from Poland (which had seized it in 1920). The foreseeable Soviet takeover ensued in June–July 1940. As in eastern Poland, sovietization followed, the three states being brought into the USSR as separate union republics. One year later 40,178 Balts were deported to the interior.* Among them were several politicians who had signed the earlier agreements. Shortly afterwards the USSR took two territories from Romania: Bessarabia, which had been allocated to her sphere by the Nazi-Soviet pact, and northern Bukovina, which had not.

The immediate reason for these annexations was Soviet discomfiture at the unexpected speed and scale of German victories in the West. When France fell in June 1940, Britain alone remained at war with Germany. Moscow was worried lest the two belligerents conclude a compromise peace at Soviet expense, but Winston Churchill's resolute stand brought relief. Even so, Britain's special envoy to Russia, Stafford Cripps, initially got a cool reception in Moscow because he was thought to be trying to foment Soviet-German enmity. There was evidently some disagreement among Stalin's advisers. Molotov, hitherto strongly identified with a pro-German stance, seems to have shifted his ground. In any case, when he visited Berlin in November 1940, he behaved provocatively. His talks with Ribbentrop ended

in an underground bunker, owing to an inconvenient appearance of the RAF over the German capital. While Ribbentrop was delivering the usual monologue about how Germany had already won the war, Molotov interrup-

* *Ist.* 1/1996, p. 138. V. N. Zemskov's figure of 25,586 (*Ot. arkh.* 1/1993, p. 4) is too low. *Émigré* historians had previously estimated the total at 41,000: Misiunas and Taagepera, p. 41.

ted and impishly inquired that, if that was really the case, he would be interested to learn whose bombs were currently raining down on Berlin.*

Two weeks later he told the Germans that the USSR would associate itself with Germany, Italy, and Japan if German troops were withdrawn from Finland and concessions made in Bulgaria, the Persian Gulf, and northern Sakhalin. He was evidently deluded into believing that Hitler would not attack the Soviet Union.† Actually the Führer's irritation at Molotov's demands was probably a factor in leading him to sign Directive No. 21 (18 December), which gave concrete shape to 'Operation Barbarossa'. Preliminary planning for an invasion of Russia had been set in motion on 31 July 1940, when Hitler took the momentous decision not to hold back the invasion until he had eliminated Britain, so risking a two-front war.

This was the one eventuality that Stalin did not reckon with, for he considered his partner to be basically a rational being ('a very able man, but greedy and prestige-conscious, unable to match military aims to capabilities', as he later told an American diplomat). There are several other plausible explanations for his apparent obtuseness in the face of the many warnings (at least eighty-four, according to one tally) he received to the effect that the Germans were preparing a massive attack. He reckoned that their military build-up was bluff, and that if a breach came it would take the form of a diplomatic démarche that would allow Moscow to negotiate and, if necessary, make concessions – here he was mindful of the Brest-Litovsk precedent of 1918. Another historical memory may have played a part: in 1914 Russia's hasty mobilization had provoked the enemy to respond, and he did not want to repeat the mistake. Apart from this, some (but not all) of his underlings were prone to report what they knew the Leader wanted to hear, while 'bourgeois' sources of information were written off as tainted by self-interest: when the German ambassador von der Schulenburg, at great

* Waddington, 'Ribbentrop and the Soviet Union, 1937–1941', in Erickson and Dilks (ed.), *Barbarossa*, p. 25.
† V. V. Lavrov (*Voenno-ist. zhurnal* 2/1996, pp. 16–23) argues that Molotov was trapped into making a statement on Soviet designs in the Middle East which Germany could then leak to Britain in order to keep the two powers apart; this may have had something to do with Rudolf Hess's secret mission to Britain (10 May 1941), which aroused deep misgiving in Moscow.

personal risk, warned Molotov 'in the spirit of Bismarck' that an attack was imminent, Stalin quipped that 'disinformation has reached ambassadorial level'. He had an inflated idea of his own capabilities as supreme decision maker. This encouraged complacency and flattery: shortly before the foe struck, Beriya told his boss that his wise policy had made invasion impossible.

The colossal misjudgement may thus be considered in part an *institutional* phenomenon. After the Great Terror few officials were willing to hazard independent, realistic opinions. Most underestimated the damage done by the purges to the Red Army's command structure, despite the lessons of the Finnish war. By 1940 the USSR had 4.2 million men under arms and defence outlays represented 32.5 per cent of the budget. The weapons build-up was proceeding apace, but much of the technology was outdated: fighter aircraft, for instance, had poor gunnery and were unstable in flight. Officers' intellectual level was low: of 579,000 officers (1941) 56 per cent had secondary, 7 per cent tertiary education, but 12 per cent had no military training at all (*Ist. arkh.* 2/1995, p. 23). Yet the leadership insisted on taking an offensive posture. Addressing military academy graduates on 5 May, Stalin declared:

From time to time we have taken a defensive line, pending re-equipment of our army ... But now that we have reconstructed the army and given it sufficient technology for modern warfare, now that we are strong, it is time to pass from defence to attack ... We have to reconstruct our education, propaganda, agitation and press in an offensive spirit. [*Ist. arkh.* 2/1995, p. 30]*

Up to a point he was a victim of his own propaganda and had lost touch with realities.

* Some historians, Russian and Western, have claimed that Stalin was preparing a preventive strike against German forces which 'Barbarossa' forestalled – as Nazi propagandists alleged at the time. That this was not so is clear from the Soviet troops' disposition. Zhukov did indeed draw up plans for a blow towards Lublin, but there is as yet no evidence that they were adopted. If Hitler had not invaded, Stalin *might* have ordered an offensive, say in 1942, by which time his forces would have been in better shape and the Germans' attention deflected elsewhere, but this is speculation.

ARMAGEDDON II

Incredibly, therefore, the Wehrmacht achieved a complete surprise, tactically and strategically. Of 5,400 Soviet aircraft deployed close to the front, 1,200 were destroyed in the first few days of fighting. The USSR's numerical superiority in manpower and weaponry was of little avail as troops were surrounded and taken captive *en masse*, or else fell back in disorder. They had been stationed too far forward and lacked adequate reserves close at hand. On the morning of 22 June soldiers who were fired on had to ask permission before firing back (although some disobeyed).

The Germans, 3 million strong, with 3,500 tanks and 2,700 warplanes, advanced in three army groups towards Leningrad, Moscow, and Kiev. Hitler's objective was to reach a line from Archangel to Astrakhan within six weeks by employing the blitzkrieg tactics that had worked so well in the West. At first the advance seemed unstoppable: 89 out of 164 Red divisions were lost and confusion reigned. However, pockets of resistance formed behind German lines. Near Smolensk a three-week counter-offensive prevented total encirclement and put the Germans' timetable out of gear. In fact the blitzkrieg had already failed, although this was not yet evident, and a war of attrition lay ahead in which Soviet resources outmatched those of their adversaries.

Initially Stalin failed to grasp the immensity of the challenge: he ordered Kiev to be held at all costs, which lost the army over half a million men. On 22 June he left it to Molotov to announce the outbreak of war and, according to some accounts, panicked – although the list of his visitors (since published) shows that he kept busy round the clock. Not until 3 July did he speak to his people, memorably addressing them as 'brothers and sisters' in language free from party jargon. He called for all-out resistance and a 'scorched earth' policy: there was to be no surrender.

The message was generally well received. People volunteered to join up without waiting for their call-up notices. To coordinate the war effort a five-man State Defence Council (GKO) and a general headquarters (*Stavka*) were set up; so, too, was an Evacuation Council, which worked day and night to save machinery in industrial plants at risk: 1,523 large factories were sent to the rear, along with many of their workers.

Thousands toiled to dig defence installations. The GKO, which took nearly 10,000 decisions during the war, dealt mainly with technical questions connected with the mobilization of manpower and resources, but did not overlook police duties. In July several generals were shot, among them D. G. Pavlov, the western front commander, and nine associates who were made scapegoats for Moscow's sins of omission – a vindictive act that scarcely improved army morale. (Later such repressive measures were seldom publicized.) Hundreds of ordinary folk met a similar fate for spreading 'defeatist' ideas. On the railways 412 'counter-revolutionary acts' were reported to the end of August; 2,524 individuals were sentenced, of whom 204 were shot (Yu. Khelemsky in *Ist.* 5/1994, pp. 107–12). In Moscow the total number of such offences between 20 October and 13 December was 2,610, and for other crimes 71,825; military tribunals executed 357 individuals.

By this time the enemy was nearing the capital where the population, seeing many of their leaders (though not Stalin) leave for safer areas, panicked. Harsh measures were taken to restore order, and there was no repetition of panic when, at the end of November, German advance units reached the suburbs.

At this moment of dire crisis the system stood the strain. Though shaken, its institutions continued to function and enough of its supporters remained loyal to its goals to ensure its survival . . . Local officials, rank-and-file party members, ordinary citizens were thrown back on their own resources. Left to their own devices by the government, they coped.*

Even greater fortitude was mustered by the citizens of Leningrad, which enemy forces had all but surrounded by September 1941: only a precarious route across Lake Ladoga linked the metropolis to the outside world. So began a siege destined to last 872 days, which has no parallel in the history of warfare. Not expecting such a disastrous turn of events, the authorities were slow to build up food reserves or to evacuate the city's inhabitants. Of 3.2 million only 600,000 or so managed to leave before the ring closed. The city was repeatedly

---

* Barber, 'The Moscow Crisis of October 1941', in Cooper *et al.* (eds.), *Soviet History 1917–53*, pp. 213–14; for daily life in Moscow, see also M. M. Gorinov in *Ot. ist.* 3/1996, pp. 3–28.

bombed and shelled, but its worst enemy was hunger. During the bitter winter of 1941–2

water mains burst . . . , trams stopped running, electricity and heat disappeared, and the city sank into cold and darkness. The elegant cultural capital . . . was homogenized into a listless, moribund mockery of a real city. Food was the obsession, survival the only goal . . . When bread rations were lowered for the fourth time on 13 November, the recipe was also changed and cellulose added . . . Somebody described it as 'black, sticky, like putty, sodden, with an admixture of wood pulp and sawdust'.*

Heroic effects were made to grow substitutes and to supply the city by a makeshift road across the frozen lake. But in January–February 1942 death from starvation and disease claimed 200,000 lives. The overall figure was probably close to a million, higher still if military casualties are included. For obvious reasons little was said about this tragedy at the time. It is an open question whether Stalin did everything possible to relieve the city, against which he seems to have harboured a grudge. But the decision to lay the siege, and so avoid responsibility for feeding its inhabitants, was Hitler's.

The Axis forces, inadequately prepared for wintry conditions, suffered too. They ran short of food and clothing, and their heavy equipment bogged down in the proverbial Russian mud. In January 1942 the Red Army, emboldened by its feat in holding Moscow, launched a counter-attack and pushed the invaders back in places by up to 300 kilometres. But the Soviet forces were too thin on the ground and poorly supplied. They did not attain their objectives. Stalin was trying to do too much too soon. Simultaneous counter-offensives were launched in the south which failed to recapture Khar'kov but made some gains in the Crimea.

This peninsula was the scene of further action in the spring of 1942. The Red Army had to evacuate, although the port of Sevastopol' held out for several weeks before surrendering with the loss of 90,000 men. Another effort to retake Khar'kov ended still more disastrously. The Germans were preparing 'Operation Blue', a major offensive designed to cross the Volga and reach the Caucasian oilfields. On the northern flank the Red Army staunchly held on to Voronezh for six weeks,

* Moskoff, *Bread of Affliction*, pp. 192–3.

delaying the advance, but farther south the invaders moved ahead rapidly, winning control of the vital Don basin by capturing Rostov on 27 July.

The next day Stalin issued his draconian order no. 227, in which he accused the troops at Rostov of having shown cowardice. He commanded that NKVD 'defence detachments' be set up behind the lines to shoot deserters. The watchword was, 'Not one step back!' But the enemy crossed the Don and seized Maikop, where the oilfields had been destroyed, and spread out across the north Caucasian plain; symbolically, mountain troops planted a swastika flag atop Mount Elbruz.

But the German hold on this distant region was weak. Everything now depended on Stalingrad, 'the city of Stalin' on the Volga, which in mid-September came under fierce attack. Hitler was determined to seize it, not least for psychological effect, while Stalin, conscious of his role there in 1918, was equally determined that it should not fall. From a military standpoint the great battle was unnecessary, for the Volga could have been cut elsewhere. Each street, each building was bitterly contested in hand-to-hand fighting. The remnants of the population cowered in the cellars. On 19 November Soviet forces under A. M. Vasilevsky and Zhukov struck Field Marshal von Paulus's Sixth Army in the rear. The Germans' Romanian and Italian allies gave way; soon over 250,000 troops found themselves trapped. Hitler ruled out surrender. A relief force under von Manstein was halted and on 31 January 1943 von Paulus and his staff were captured, along with 91,000 surviving soldiers. The victory gave an immense boost to Soviet morale and probably decided the outcome of the Second World War. Churchill later called it 'the hinge of fate'.

Henceforth it was the invaders who had to retreat, although this was by no means a continuous process: in March 1943 they temporarily recaptured Khar'kov, which had fallen into Soviet hands a month earlier. This operation prepared the way for the Germans' last throw, a summer offensive in the Kursk area ('Operation Citadel'). It evoked a massive counter-attack and turned into history's greatest tank battle (6,000 armoured vehicles were engaged on each side). By now Soviet KV and T-34 tanks were superior in firepower to all but the latest German Panzers, and the Red Army – thanks mainly to Allied aid – was fast becoming a motorized force. By the end of the year it had liberated most of Ukraine and central Russia. The ancient cities of Smolensk and Kiev were back in Soviet hands, as was the Crimea, while to the north the ground was laid for Leningrad's liberation on 15 January 1944. After an artillery barrage of 220,000 shells, troops entered the stricken city. The tsarist palaces of Peterhof and Tsarskoye Selo were among the buildings that lay in ruin.

The façade of the Catherine Palace was intact. But . . . the great hall was gone, so was the Amber Room . . . Under the Cameron Gallery a 500-pound bomb had been placed. Fortunately it had not gone off . . . Just beyond the Half-Moon stood a great linden tree . . . [with] four great hooks which swayed from a limb . . . 'That's where the Nazis hanged their victims' [said an officer]. Olga Berggol'ts [a heroine of the siege] wrote a brief poem:

> Again from the black dust, from the place
> Of death and ashes, will arise the garden as before.
> So it will be. I firmly believe in miracles.*

THE HOME FRONT

It is a truism to say that the Soviet victory was brought about by the stoicism which troops and civilians displayed in extreme conditions. Other contributory factors include military leadership, efficient mobilization of economic resources, the enhanced role of women, an upsurge of Russian patriotism, and Allied aid (not necessarily in that order). More important than any of these was revulsion against Nazi barbarism. In the USSR serious discussion of such matters was at first taboo – every success was automatically attributed to Stalin – and even later narrowly circumscribed; only in recent years has the picture begun to clear.

Vasilevsky, Zhukov, V. I. Chuikov, I. S. Konev, K. K. Rokossovsky – these are only a few of the generals whose names became household words, not only in the USSR. Nearly all of plebeian origin, they owed their promotion to professionalism as demonstrated on the battlefield. Victories, each marked by gun salutes, earned them Stalin's grudging respect, although he did not forget civil-war cronies such as Voroshilov.

* Salisbury, *The Siege of Leningrad*, pp. 567–8.

He treated all his commanders roughly, uttering crude threats and setting tasks impossible to fulfil, while controlling their execution through men who enjoyed his special confidence. His arbitrary interventions in strategy became less frequent once he had gained more experience in military matters, but even so no one could feel secure; moreover, his dictatorial manner was aped by others, Zhukov included. About fifty senior officers disappeared during the war as a result of NKVD action; several others committed suicide.* The chief controlling agency in the armed forces was the political directorate (PUR), led until June 1942 by L. Z. Mekhlis. A coarse fanatic, he had played a vicious role in the pre-war military purge and

could, without raising his voice, accuse an officer who had volunteered to cross enemy lines of scheming to return to his family; . . . or have a division commander cashiered after leading his troops out of encirclement because the tattered officer objected to being called a bandit.†

Yet even this sinister individual at times made common cause with commanders to help them get extra supplies. On occasion political officers (commissars) would utilize party channels for the same purpose.

Despite personal and institutional rivalries, inevitable under such stress, the machinery of command held together well. The GKO ensured that there was none of the tension between front and rear that there had been during the First World War, leading ultimately to revolution. Convalescent soldiers toured arms factories to egg on their workers, and the latter sent morale-boosting delegations to the front. Even senior generals adhered to a lifestyle that was modest by Western standards. They might draw better rations than their men, but they were not separated from them by a social gulf. The same applies with greater force to junior officers and NCOs, who learned leadership skills in combat and shared soldiers' everyday hardships to the full. Tales of men hurling themselves at the enemy with the cry, 'For the Motherland! For Stalin!' owed something to the propagandists'

---

* Not counting the Pavlov group. See Woff, in Shukman (ed.), *Stalin's Generals*, p. 362.
† Colton, *Commissars, Commanders and Civilian Authority*, p. 164. He behaved in this way after being demoted. In September 1943 the new PUR chief, Shcherbakov, received a report from the Bryansk front that Mekhlis was feared and hated by officers there because he arbitrarily replaced them with his own stooges. See *Ist.* 3/1995, appx., pp. 144–5.

imagination. There were deeds of heroism aplenty, but the troops knew what awaited them if they retreated without permission. According to another Stalin order (no. 270 of 16 August 1941) anyone who surrendered was officially regarded as a traitor.

On paper Red Army strength doubled to 10 million in the first week of war. Altogether 30.6 million individuals were mobilized, equivalent to 16 per cent of pre-war population. In 1945 the USSR had 11.6 million men and women under arms, four fifths of them in combat roles. Scarcely less dramatic was the mobilization of labour resources for work in war industries. The output of munitions was twenty to thirty times larger than it had been in the First World War, and twice as great as that of Nazi Germany. In 1944 aircraft production (40,246) was four times what it had been in 1940. For tanks and self-propelled guns the increase was ten-fold (2,794 to 28,963), for artillery pieces and mortars over double (53,800 to 129,500), against which must be set the very heavy losses incurred, especially in 1941: for example, 91 per cent of pre-war tank stock. In 1944 the USSR produced 439,100 machine-guns, 2,450,000 rifles and 219 million shells and mines.* These feats were made possible by 'effectively allowing the civilian economy to fall away'. The USSR also received significant amounts of military goods from the United States under the Lend-Lease agreement, including nearly 15,000 aircraft, over 7,000 tanks, and 132,000 machine-guns.†

Another factor that explains the rapid expansion of military production is that contingency plans for industrial conversion had been laid in advance. It was fairly easy to switch from building tractors to tanks, and in many other instances there was intelligent improvisation.

In Moscow a children's bicycle factory began making flame-throwers . . . A woodworking shop producing abacuses and screens turned over to making pistol cartridges. A furniture factory started turning out anti-tank mines, cartridge boxes and stretchers. A typewriter works began making automatic rifles . . .‡

---

* Harrison, *Soviet Planning in Peace and War*, pp. 118, 250; Gatrell and Harrison, 'Russian and Soviet Economies', pp. 436–7.
† ibid., p. 258.
‡ Barber and Harrison, *Soviet Home Front*, p. 135.

Things did not always go smoothly, of course: there were coordination problems and bottlenecks in labour supply. It took time before factories evacuated from the war zone to the Urals or Siberia could reassemble their machines and start up production again. Of 118 aviation plants covered by these emergency measures, only nine were working properly by the end of 1941. Precious equipment sometimes rusted away in the open air.

Women and juveniles comprised much of the labour force. The former's share rose from two fifths in 1940 to nearly three fifths in 1943. Retired people went back to work and peasants unfit for combat were assigned to industry. Villages were all but stripped of the able-bodied, which in turn adversely affected food supply. Since the recruits to industry were largely unskilled, on-the-job training became more important than ever. The women who entered employment generally remained at the bench rather than moving up into managerial positions. About 800,000 served in the armed forces; many saw action and won distinctions.

The forced labourers in the Gulag also made their contribution to the economy, which went unacknowledged at the time. About a million of them perished from overwork and lack of food: in 1942 mortality was around 21 per cent. Another million (975,000) were released to serve in army penal battalions which were given the most dangerous tasks, such as clearing minefields. A 'Polar division' which helped defend Murmansk from the Finns was composed wholly of prisoners (E. S. Senyavskaya in *Ot. ist.* 5/1995, p. 33). Prisoners built a railway line from Komsomol'sk-on-Amur to the Pacific coast at Sovetskaya Gavan', but got precious little of the US aid shipped through the new port (O. P. Yelantsev in *Ot. arkh.* 3/1995, pp. 90–9).

Practically everyone in the USSR went hungry during the war. Agriculture was already in a parlous state and the retreats of 1941–2 led to the loss of much valuable land. Desperate efforts were made to save the harvest from the invader, and what had to be left behind was often burned – with dire consequences for the population remaining in occupied territory. In the unoccupied regions, by 1943 agricultural products available per head had sunk to 56 per cent of the 1940 level (42 per cent for cereals). Meat became a rarity, potatoes and vegetables the main standby. They were grown on private plots, which were allowed to expand, and on farms maintained by enterprises. These had to set aside part of the product for the procurement authorities, who acted just as ruthlessly as before the war. In general, however, the intensity of state controls was somewhat relaxed. The authorities realized that, since they could not feed people properly, they had to let them make their own arrangements. In effect this was an unacknowledged 'mini-NEP'.

A rationing system was introduced for all essential foods, but most rural folk were excluded from it and many items were supplied irregularly or not at all. The bread ration was honoured best and provided four fifths of all the calorie intake. Manual labourers got more than office workers or dependants; there were supplements for small children, Stakhanovites, and workers in the Arctic (except prisoners!) or in dangerous occupations. In 1944 the latter were entitled to 1,200 grams a day, but office workers got only one third as much. It was therefore essential to have access to an allotment or to buy food in a collective-farm market. Those unable to do so, for instance abandoned children or the sick, were likely to perish, although the medical services did what they could.

Hunger had many aspects – some starved, most were poorly fed and nourished, and some suffered illness as a consequence of malnutrition . . . There was nothing selective about the tyranny of food shortages; for most people life was lived on the margin for most of the war.*

Food received under Lend-Lease accounted for one third of total tonnage in 1941–3; its psychological importance was immense. The bulk of these supplies came via the Pacific route, some through Iran or by convoy through Arctic waters, where ships were liable to enemy attack. A recent calculation puts American aid at 4,324,000 tons; Canada sent 437,000 and Britain 154,000 tons (short tons (907 kg.)). 'This would have sufficed to feed an army of ten million for 1,688 days, i.e. for the whole war' (M. N. Suprun in *Ot. ist.* 3/1996, p. 53). Most of the imported food did indeed go to fill out Red Army rations; the tinned meat was particularly welcome.

Earlier historians, especially in the USSR, were less generous in their evaluation of Lend-Lease. They were also prone to exaggerate the role of official propaganda in determining civilian morale. This

* Moskoff, *The Bread of Affliction*, p. 220.

fluctuated with the tide of battle, as was to be expected, as well as distance from the front. Rumour was probably as potent a source of information as the tightly controlled media. On the other hand it mattered greatly that party agencies de-emphasized themes associated with socialism in favour of patriotic ones. In 1942, when orders were introduced to mark military prowess, they were named for eminent tsarist commanders like Suvorov or Kutuzov. Historians praised Russian cultural achievements in earlier centuries, and countless journalists followed suit.

In a striking breach with past policy, the regime reached an (admittedly somewhat bogus) accommodation with the Orthodox Church. As soon as war broke out Metropolitan Sergey (Stragorodsky) backed the cause of national defence and called on the few remaining clergy to help collect funds for the war effort. In all 150 million roubles had been donated by October 1944.

Our Orthodox Church [ran a pastoral letter of June 1941] has always shared the nation's destinies ... Together with it she has borne both trials and successes. Neither shall she abandon her people today. She is invoking Heaven's blessings on the impending national struggle.*

Sergey's motives were to win more liberty for believers. Stalin did not respond at once, although atheistic propaganda ceased. It was probably the mass opening of churches under German auspices, plus concern for Allied opinion, that led in September 1943 to a surprise meeting in the Kremlin between Stalin, Molotov, and the last three metropolitans allowed to function on Soviet-held territory. The story goes that when asked why there were so few bishops (most had perished in the purges), Sergey replied: 'One reason is that, when we train someone for the priesthood, he may land up a marshal.' Stalin is said to have smiled at the allusion and reminisced about his studies at a seminary. In any case a synod was called which elected Sergey to the patriarchate of Moscow. He died a few months later and was succeeded by Alexis (Simansky, 1944–70). The compromise, which allowed restoration of seminaries and a patriarchal journal, was played up in propaganda and made a contribution to believers' morale. But the ecclesiastical hierarchy was

* Cited (slightly amended) from Pospielovsky, *The Russian Church under the Soviet Regime*, i, p. 195.

penetrated by NKVD agents and the few churches allowed to operate were situated mainly on 'liberated' territory.

In the same way patriotic Russian sentiment was manipulated by the regime to serve its ulterior ends. To a limited degree the war did bring the authorities closer to the people and reduce the gulf between what was propagated in the media and the realities of people's everyday lives. At first, when told of Nazi atrocities in the occupied areas, the public had sometimes reacted sceptically, but all too soon eyewitnesses confirmed that the grim picture was all too true.

NAZI OCCUPATION

According to Nazi racial theory the Slavs were 'sub-humans' (*Unter-menschen*), vastly inferior to those of pure 'Aryan' stock, and Jews had no right to exist at all. Hitler saw the war in the East as one of annihilation. The inhabitants were to be 'reduced': that is, starved, killed, or deported eastwards, so freeing 'living-space' (*Lebensraum*) for Germanic settlers, who would exploit ruthlessly as their slaves the few natives allowed to remain. Any human concern for the subjects of the 'master race' was dismissed as dangerous sentimentality. Nor was there any question of freeing the non-Russian peoples from 'Russian domination'. Himmler was explicit on this point. So, too, was Erich Koch, *Reichskommissar* of central and southern Ukraine. As he explained in August 1942,

There is no free Ukraine. The purpose of our work here is to see that Ukrainians work for Germany, not that we make Ukrainians happy. Ukraine has to deliver what Germany needs. This task must be carried out without any concern for losses . . . Germans in the *Reichskommissariat* must proceed from the standpoint that we are dealing with a people that is in every respect of lesser value . . . The Ukrainians' educational level must be kept low . . . Furthermore, everything must be done to destroy the birth-rate in this space.*

In practice genocidal policies were applied with greatest consistency against Jews and Romany. In regard to the other Soviet peoples it was

* Cited by A. Kappeler, *Kleine Geschichte der Ukraine*, Munich, 1994, p. 218.

often obstructed by conflicts among its executants or else took second place to military exigencies (or to the demand for slave labour in the Reich). SS extermination squads (*Einsatzgruppen*) set to work wherever the Germans conquered. Officers in the Wehrmacht – claims to the contrary notwithstanding – actively helped the squads, as did criminal elements in the local population, notably Ukrainians and Latvians.

These collaborators acted from a variety of motives: pseudo-patriotism, antisemitism, and also just to ingratiate themselves with the occupiers, perhaps in the hope of material gain. In Kiev, for instance, Jews were denounced by neighbours eager to lay hand on their possessions, be it only a piece of cloth. Those arrested were herded out of town to a nearby gully, Babiy Yar, where they were beaten, stripped, robbed, and mown down in batches by machine-gun fire. At this site alone as many as 200,000 people are believed to have been killed; in 1943, as they retreated, the Germans tried to dig up as many bodies as they could to destroy the evidence of their crime. Nevertheless a boy who lived through these horrors, Anatoliy Kuznetsov, lived to tell the tale in a documentary novel, *Babiy Yar*.*

Another major execution site was situated outside the Latvian capital, Riga. Of the 93,000 Jews resident in this republic in 1939, 12,000 were deported by the Soviets (of whom one third survived) and the rest killed in 1941–3 by the Nazis, either locally or at Auschwitz. The victims included 20,000 Jews brought to Riga from Central Europe. In Lithuania, where the pre-war Jewish population numbered about 200,000, three quarters were murdered in the last six months of 1941 alone. In 'Transnistria', as the region around Odessa was called, where Romanians were in charge, 40 per cent of the Jewish community survived, although the occupiers aided the *Einsatzgruppen*, as did some local German (*volksdeutsch*) and Ukrainian residents. Altogether the Nazi Holocaust took the lives of nearly 2 million Soviet Jews, roughly half of whom had previously lived in the newly annexed territories.†

---

* The Soviet edition (1966) was heavily censored, since for political reasons the authorities sought to conceal the specifically antisemitic orientation of German genocidal policy. The monument eventually erected at the site, in response to popular pressure, represented the victims simply as 'anti-fascist' Soviet citizens. The atrocity was, however, reported accurately in Soviet media at the time.

† Dobroszycki and Gurock, *The Holocaust in the Soviet Union*, pp. 98, 134ff., 183ff., 201.

Other groups of the population in the occupied zone also died *en masse*. Casualties were particularly heavy among Soviet prisoners of war. Captured Communists, if their political affiliation was discovered, were summarily shot according to the so-called *Kommissarbefehl* (6 June 1941). Initially their captors left prisoners under guard in the open without food or medical aid, so that they starved to death or succumbed to epidemics and wounds. Of 5.7 million soldiers captured, about 3.3 million paid with their lives (M. E. Yerin in *Yop. ist.* 11-12/1995, pp. 140–41). In 1943 the Germans came to realize that their labour might be of value. Some were deported to Germany, where they were often worked to death or else sent to concentration camps. Soviet civilians, too, were abducted for forced labour in the Reich. The total number of such workers has been put at 2.8 million. A lucky few found conditions tolerable and chose not to return to the USSR after the war (see page 429). The lot of the rest was aggravated by Soviet non-adherence to the Geneva convention on the treatment of prisoners of war. Stalin's harsh and vindictive order no. 270 of 1941 encouraged some prisoners to join formations set up by the Germans, although their main motive was just to survive in atrocious conditions. In the circumstances it is remarkable that only about a quarter of a million did so: 50,000 in General A. A. Vlasov's 'Russian Liberation Army', 45,000 in Moslem units, 48,000 from the Baltic states, and 35,000 Cossacks, according to one recent tally (plus 196,000 civilian collaborators: L. Reshin in *Znamya* 8/1994, p. 179; higher figures are encountered).

Vlasov was a Soviet commander taken prisoner in July 1942, whom German military propagandists placed in charge of a Russian national committee. He took an ambivalent line towards the Nazis, who distrusted him and would not allow his movement to operate in occupied Soviet territory. It carried on propaganda against the Communists among Soviet prisoners, but not until September 1944, by which time the Germans had been forced out of the USSR, did Himmler authorize the setting up of Russian military formations. They did not fight the advancing Reds. In 1945 Vlasov and other leading collaborators were handed over to the Soviets, who executed them the following year. Fortunately for the Allied cause, the Nazis failed to exploit the widespread anti-Communist sentiment among the USSR's multinational population. This helped to doom their entire *Ostpolitik*, which was not only criminal but suicidal.

Its immediate result was to stimulate resistance by partisan bands. This became a serious military factor from mid 1942. By the next autumn one tenth of all German divisions on Soviet soil were fighting guerrilla groups, which enjoyed considerable support from the local population. Stalin initially approached them cautiously, since many had a nationalist or non-political orientation, and it was not until May 1942 that a 'central staff for partisan warfare' was set up in Moscow to send aid, with the object of bringing them under control. In Belarus, where the swampy wooded terrain was suitable for such operations, partisans blew up bridges to impede German communications and struck at troop concentrations before vanishing back into the forest. By January 1944 the guerrillas are estimated to have numbered 150,000 on the central sector of the front alone and to have killed 100,000 of the enemy for the loss of half as many of their own men. The principal victims, however, were civilians: as many as a quarter of a million people may have been killed, mainly in the course of German reprisals. Over 600 Belarusian villages were burned to the ground together with their inhabitants.

A WAR OF LIBERATION

Sixteen months after freeing Leningrad the Russians were in Berlin. Their campaigns of 1944–5 delivered a succession of massive blows. These involved deep penetration of enemy lines and encircling operations – the same strategy earlier employed by the Wehrmacht. The Germans were now inferior in numbers and equipment. The Red Army had a three-to-one overall superiority in manpower. On the central front in 1944 it had nine to ten times as many tanks as the enemy and could lay down concentrated artillery barrages and crippling salvoes of Katyusha rockets.

The first major offensive, in southern Ukraine, rendered untenable a long enemy salient and by the end of March 1944 Zhukov had crossed the Dniester on a broad front, reaching the Romanian border. In August, when the Russians entered that country in force, King Michael deposed the fascist Antonescu government, surrendered, and turned against the Axis. Bulgaria proclaimed herself neutral but the USSR declared war. A coalition government with strong Communist participation took over and the army came under Soviet command. These changes threatened German forces in Greece, which were withdrawn, setting the scene for a long-drawn-out civil war between Communist guerrillas and a government backed by the Western powers. From Bulgaria Marshal F. I. Tolbukhin advanced into Yugoslavia, made contact with Tito's partisans, and on 19 October captured Belgrade. Meanwhile Marshal R. Ya. Malinovsky had entered Hungary, crossed the Tisza and turned towards Budapest. Here the Germans, having virtually taken over the country, prepared to counter-attack.

They offered still more stubborn resistance on the vital central front. On 23 June – shortly after the D-Day landings in Normandy – four Soviet army groups with a hundred divisions struck westwards, taking Minsk and Vilnius. To the south Konev surrounded and captured Lviv (25 July). In these battles the Germans lost more men than at Stalingrad. The Russians were now operating on pre-war Polish soil and by 31 July had reached the outskirts of Warsaw. The Polish Home Army, which was loyal to the exiled government in London and suspicious of the 'committee of national liberation' which the Soviets had just set up in Lublin, rose in revolt. The insurgents fought a desperate two-month struggle against overwhelming odds which ended in the systematic destruction of the Polish capital by the Germans, but Rokossovsky's forces did not move to help them until it was too late. Many people, in Poland and the West, suspected Stalin of bad faith. For the rest of the year Soviet forces remained on the Vistula.

On the Finnish front the Russians broke through the Mannerheim line in June, re-establishing the 1940 frontier, and later moved into northern Norway. An armistice in October knocked Finland out of the war.* South-wast of Leningrad the Red Army fought its way into Estonia (September), approached Riga from the east, and reached the Baltic coast near Memel. With difficulty the Germans managed to

---

* The peace treaty of 1947 gave the USSR a common border with Norway in the Arctic and some Finnish territory west of Lake Lagoda, as well as a fifty-year-lease (given up in 1956) on a naval base near Helsinki. On the whole the country was treated with greater leniency than East European states that were considered of greater strategic importance.

evacuate some of their encircled troops by sea. Without pausing to clear up this pocket, Soviet forces moved on into East Prussia until temporarily halted by fierce counter-attacks.

As 1944 drew to a close Marshal A. I. Antonov, the new chief of the general staff, and his officers planned a great offensive into Germany. Personal rivalries and differences over strategy complicated their task. Partly in response to appeals on behalf of the Anglo-American forces struggling in the Ardennes, Soviet troops at last crossed the Vistula. In southern Poland Konev took Craców and reached the upper Oder, as did Zhukov farther north, after a bitter battle for Poznań. Rokossovsky stormed into Danzig, cutting off more German troops to the east, and on 9 April Königsberg finally fell. Meanwhile Budapest had been taken (February) and Soviet troops marched into Austria, encircling and capturing Vienna (13 April). Nazi Germany was at its last gasp, but Hitler still refused to surrender, although overtures were made to both the Western Allies and the Soviets, which fostered their growing mutual suspicions.

On 17 April the final drive on Berlin began. Since the Allies were now advancing into central Germany, this operation made little military sense. But Stalin wanted the supreme prize for the Soviets, and was helped in achieving this aim when Eisenhower turned his forces south into Bohemia. A last-minute Soviet effort to 'liberate' Prague first was stalled. The assault on the German capital began with the usual destructive artillery barrage. It was in ruins when, after fierce fighting, the Red flag finally flew from the Reichstag. For a time Soviet soldiers were encouraged to take revenge on German civilians, and there was an orgy of rape and plunder.

After the German surrender to Allied representatives at Reims on 7 May 1945, the Soviets insisted on repeating the ceremony in Berlin the next day – a symptom of the discord that was already overshadowing world affairs. Having borne the brunt of the war against Hitler, the USSR expected to play the master role in shaping the post-war international order. Stalin also wanted large-scale material compensation for the losses that his country had suffered in the titanic conflict.

THE GRAND ALLIANCE AND THE ORIGINS OF THE COLD WAR

The disputes between the wartime Allies over strategy, and more especially over the disposition of territories freed from German occupation by the Red Army in 1944–5, would eventuate in forty years of cold war between East and West. There was nothing inevitable about this unfortunate development, although the fundamental disparity between the political and social systems of Stalin's USSR on one hand and the Western democracies on the other was bound to cause tension. Stalin had no preconceived plan or timetable for the expansion of Soviet power. It was rather a matter of his exploiting opportunities as they arose, taking advantage of the forbearance shown by his Western partners. They were above all anxious to keep the USSR in the war, and the ratio of forces within the alliance obliged them to heed Soviet wishes. For his part, Stalin feared that the Anglo-Saxon powers might make a deal with Hitler and so also had to display prudence.

Apart from restoring the 1941 boundaries, he did not seek to annex large areas to the USSR, not least because this would have tilted the ethnic balance further against the war-ravaged Russians. He was content with a slice of East Prussia (the district of Königsberg, renamed Kaliningrad) and the Carpatho-Ukraine, which before the war had belonged to Czechoslovakia. This gave the USSR a direct frontier with Hungary and for the first time in history placed all Ukrainian lands within the same state. For the same reason the Ukrainian SSR also took over the much-fought-over city of Lviv (Polish Lwów, German Lemberg). As for the rest of Eastern Europe, Stalin reckoned with indirect Soviet rule through broad coalition governments representing all 'democratic' (i.e. non-fascist) currents of opinion, but with Communist-directed popular fronts playing the leading part (and Soviet agents active behind the scenes). As a Marxist who thought dialectically, he expected these mixed regimes – 'people's democracies', as they came to be called – eventually to turn into Soviet clones committed to 'socialist construction'. But this was envisaged as a gradual process that need not harm maintenance of good relations with the West. Similarly, Europe's division into two blocs need not result in belligerent confrontation.

Stalin's optimism on this score, which at first sight seems ridiculous, was based on the assumption that all capitalist countries would be rent by grave economic crisis and social unrest, forcing their governments to yield before Soviet armed might. More specifically, a defeated Germany under Allied occupation would no longer play any active role in Europe; France, Italy, and Britain would be reduced to second-rank status; and the United States would return to isolationism. Accordingly no major obstacle would hinder the peaceful sovietization of the continent. As Stalin put it in a subsequently famous conversation with the Yugoslav leader Milovan Djilas in April 1945: 'This war is not as in the past. Whoever occupies a territory also imposes on it his own social system. Everyone imposes his own system as far as his army can reach. It cannot be otherwise.' This doctrine left much unsaid: precisely which territories were to be within the Red Army's reach, and when?

Stalin's strategic concept was inherently flawed. It owed a lot to wishful thinking and sought to combine incompatible aims. Not only did it misjudge the potential of Western capitalism, but it also assumed, contrary to good sense, that in Eastern Europe socio-political harmony could be brought about by relatively non-violent methods that would neither antagonize the local peoples nor alarm their friends abroad. Whatever the chances of such an outcome in, say, Bulgaria or Czechoslovakia, it was totally impracticable in Poland, given the troubled history of Russo-Polish relations since the eighteenth-century partitions. The Katyn massacre and the Warsaw uprising ruled out any genuine reconciliation with the *émigré* Polish government in London. The Grand Alliance would collapse mainly over the Polish question, although there were many other points of friction, some of which dated back to its initiation in the summer of 1941.

At that time the USSR had its back to the wall and was desperately anxious for succour from the West. The July 1941 Anglo-Soviet mutual assistance pact studiously avoided the term alliance and was largely of symbolic importance. Britain alone could not do much: Churchill sent Stalin valuable intelligence gained from cracking the enemy 'Enigma' codes and there was some limited naval cooperation in the Arctic; the two powers also took control of Iran to establish a circuitous communications route. The situation improved after December 1941, when the United States entered the war and began to supply the Lend-Lease aid already discussed (page 412).

In May 1942 the USSR and Britain entered into a formal alliance valid for twenty years. The problem of post-war Soviet frontiers, which came up in negotiations for this treaty, was for the moment diplomatically side-stepped, although privately the British were prepared to concede Soviet reacquisition of the Baltic states. The Americans, as foes of *Realpolitik*, were opposed on principle to deals on such matters until victory was won.

The divisions between the Anglo-Saxon powers were not concealed from Stalin, who pressed hard for an immediate second front in France in 1942. This call was taken up by the left in Britain and elsewhere,* although such an operation was not then militarily feasible. Stalin suspected that the delay was politically motivated. His Western partners were embarrassed that they could not do more in the Channel – a costly raid on Dieppe showed what the odds were – and in August Churchill had to go to Moscow and confess that no invasion could be mounted that year. Stalin reacted badly. He was only partially mollified by the Allied bombing of German cities and the prospect of landings in the Maghrib. In Egypt Montgomery's offensive at El Alamein (November 1942) was partly designed to relieve pressure on Stalingrad, but this too was cold comfort to Soviet strategists.

The outcome of the great battle on the Volga shifted the balance of forces within the alliance in the USSR's favour and the correspondence between the three leaders frequently struck a sour note. In April 1943 revelation of the Katyn murders led to a diplomatic breach between Moscow and the London Poles. Churchill tried to patch up relations in the interests of Allied unity, but the problem would not go away. Where were the new Poland's borders to lie and what was to be the shape of its future government? On the first of these issues at least the outlines of a settlement emerged in November 1943, at the first

* The Comintern line shifted once again after Hitler attacked the USSR and its member parties became vociferous advocates of intensifying the war effort; thus the British Communist party (CPGB) was allowed back into public life and a situation evolved that resembled the popular fronts of the 1930s, although the revolutionary implications were soft-pedalled. The dissolution of Comintern in May 1943 was a propaganda move which did not inhibit Soviet control of the member parties, many of whose leaders were anyway of necessity in Moscow, while the rank and file played a notable part in anti-fascist resistance movements all over Nazi-occupied Europe, above all in France, Italy, and the Balkans, receiving intermittent advice and aid from the Soviets but displaying autonomous tendencies.

conference of the 'Big Three' (as journalists irreverently termed them) at Tehran. It owed more to Churchill than to Stalin. The USSR was to incorporate the territories east of the 1920 'Curzon line', which more or less coincided with the 1941 border and also with the ethnic frontier between Poles and eastern Slavs. Poland was to be compensated in the west at Germany's expense, but the details were left vague. For their part the Lublin Poles reckoned with a border that ran along the rivers Oder and (western) Neisse, so incorporating Silesia, whose 6 million or so German inhabitants were to be expelled and replaced by settlers from the east. If this were done, the new Polish government, faced with the prospect of lasting German enmity, was bound to lean heavily towards Moscow, and no subsequent Western efforts to right the balance could succeed.

The Tehran conference was the most crucial of three inter-Allied summit meetings and demonstrated the perils of this form of diplomacy. Stalin was better prepared for the encounter than his partners and skilfully played on their differences. He backed American insistence that the Allied landings in France be concentrated on the Channel coast* and also consented to the USSR joining the United Nations and entering the war against Japan once hostilities in Europe were over – two points to which President Roosevelt attached great importance. On Germany the Soviets were still noncommittal: they were less inclined than the Western Allies to dismember the country but favoured total disarmament, sizeable reparations and a drastic purge, as was clear from Stalin's casual but chilling suggestion that after the war 50,000 German officers should be summarily shot. Moscow had previously sponsored formation of a 'national committee for a free Germany' and a corresponding military organization, both of which were designed to serve as the nucleus of an eventual pro-Soviet German regime. Austria was to become independent, at least nominally.

The Tehran conference was a Soviet success and encouraged Stalin to take a forceful line. In December 1943 he obtained from a subservient

---

* The operations in southern France, which Churchill favoured, were to have an auxiliary character. In October 1944 Stalin did recommend that Britain should land forces from Italy in the northern Adriatic and strike out for Vienna, but he was keen to keep Western forces out of the Balkans, lest they threaten Soviet pre-eminence in that region.

Eduard Beneš the promise that Czechoslovakia, when liberated, would have a strong Communist representation in government, and the two powers signed a treaty of friendship and alliance. Since the Poles were loath to follow suit, tougher measures were taken against them. In July 1944, as Soviet forces entered that country, Moscow set up in Lublin the nucleus of a Communist-led government (six months later it formally assumed that title) rivalling the one in London. Home Army soldiers were arrested and the Warsaw insurgents, as we know, left to their fate. These *faits accomplis* brought protests by the Western Allies, whose military successes after D-Day encouraged them to adopt a more robust attitude *vis-à-vis* Moscow. They sought at least to improve the Lublin Poles' image by adding to them selected non-Communist politicians from London, but this could in the circumstances confer only a fig leaf of democratic respectability.

Friction also developed over high-handed actions by the Soviets in occupied Romania and Bulgaria. The latter was rapidly becoming a satellite state. In October 1944 Churchill casually suggested to Stalin a peculiar deal whereby Soviet and Western influence in the Balkans should be shared according to a percentage formula: respectively 90:10 in Romania and 10:90 in Greece, 75:25 in Bulgaria and 50:50 in Yugoslavia and Hungary. Leaving morality aside, how was influence to be defined? Stalin and Molotov evinced interest, but nothing came of this impracticable idea; the big battalions were in any case on the Soviet side. Even so, until the spring of 1945 Stalin urged moderation on the Yugoslav partisans (and prevented a putative merger of that country with Bulgaria) and avoided direct involvement in the Greek civil war, while preserving freedom of action in the other lands under Red Army control. The outlines of the future bloc were clearer here than in Central Europe.

At Yalta in the Crimea (February 1945) Stalin acted the charming and genial host. The Allies' main task was to decide what to do about Germany. Agreement had previously been reached on establishing occupation zones, and when this was ratified the French were granted a zone of their own. (Stalin's contempt for France had been somewhat mitigated by an encounter with the formidable Charles de Gaulle, and the two states were now formally allies.) The amount due to the USSR in reparations was set at $10 milliard, but only 'as a basis for future discussion'. Western niggardliness encouraged Soviet dismantling teams to take whatever they could move, without any concern for the impact on the German economy, which was supposed to be treated as a single unit. (In the event much of this precious equipment went to waste.)

Stalin had better success in ensuring that decisions in the UN Security Council could be vetoed by any member, so frustrating American plans to make this body an instrument of world government (on Western principles, it was understood). In the UN General Assembly the USSR won *de facto* triple representation, for Ukraine and Belarus were each given seats alongside the USSR (*not* the RSFSR!), although everyone knew that their sovereignty was bogus. Last but not least, Stalin got his way over Poland, whose form of government he bluntly declared 'an internal matter'. A few weeks later sixteen non-Communist Polish leaders were lured into a trap, spirited off to Moscow and later tried as 'traitors'. Yalta was not really the 'sell-out' some American critics later alleged it to have been, for the key concessions had been made earlier. They could be justified up to a point by the need to ensure that the Red Army fought Japan as well as Germany. But the Western statesmen's attitude may well have fortified Stalin's conviction that, by winning leverage in Eastern Europe at the price of straining the wartime alliance to the point of breakdown, he could speedily attain his maximum objectives.

Soviet demands now escalated. The handshakes on the river Elbe and the euphoria of VE day were soon forgotten as the Allies vied with each other for supremacy in Germany. The Allied Control Commission was from the start the scene of bitter wrangling over dismantling, de-Nazification, and covert Soviet backing for political activities in their zone designed to further the Communist cause. However, Stalin's policies were not consistent, and he was still uncertain whether to aim for control of part of Germany or the whole: the demand for a Soviet presence in the Ruhr, for instance, suggested the latter. But this may have been just a bargaining counter, destined to be dropped in return for concessions of greater value (especially on Poland, where in July the Western Allies had to concede the legitimacy of a Communist-controlled regime). The same was probably true of Soviet claims in the Baltic (Danish Sound) and Black Sea (Turkish Straits), or for a voice in the disposal of Italy's former colonies.

The last summit, at Potsdam in July 1945, registered the East–West stalemate. In President Truman the Soviets faced an American leader who took a blunt, no-nonsense stand towards their pretensions; the sudden termination of Lend-Lease was a straw in the wind. Psychologically, if not yet militarily, the balance of forces now favoured the United States owing to the success of the Manhattan Project. Stalin probably knew of the US atomic bomb before he was told of it, which is why he showed no surprise at the news. But vast scientific and labour resources were at once assigned to matching American nuclear capability. For at a stroke the West's technological superiority had destroyed the original *raison d'être* of the territorial shield Stalin had spent such effort to build. The Soviet leader had overreached himself, yet he could not retreat gracefully at an hour when Russia had scored her greatest ever military victories. On being complimented that Soviet forces had reached Berlin, he retorted that Alexander I had got to Paris. Stalin's USSR had acquired an empire that no tsar could have dreamed of, but in the decades to come it would be as much a liability as an asset, beyond Russia's resources to sustain.

CHAPTER 20

Building an Empire, 1945–53

HIGH STALINISM

Stalin's imperial pretensions were particularly perverse in that he ruled over a country devastated by war. According to recent estimates total casualties numbered 26.6 million, of whom 9.1 million were members of the armed forces (N. A. Aralovets in *Ot. ist.* 3/1996, p. 194). Some writers offer higher figures. The loss of so many young males upset the demographic balance and reduced the birth-rate. Secret MVD reports show that in 1945 the natural increase of population was only 639,000 (1940: 2,480,000); in the following year it more than tripled, but in 1947 suffered a 15 per cent decline, thereafter climbing back to 89 per cent of pre-war (Yu. M. Degtarev in *Ot. arkh.* 2/1996, pp. 27–33). If so-called 'indirect losses' are included, i.e. children unborn because of war-time casualties and dislocation, the shortfall leaps to 44 million. For in 1946 the USSR had only 168.5 million inhabitants, not the 212.5 million it should have had given the level of 1939.* For many years the scale of this disaster was deliberately concealed and a false figure of '20 million dead' put into circulation.

Material losses were reported more fully. In September 1945 a government commission announced that 30 per cent of pre-war capital stock had been destroyed; in the occupied territories the proportion was as high as two thirds.

The German fascist invaders completely or partially destroyed and burned 1,710 towns and settlements and more than 70,000 villages and hamlets . . . more than 6 million buildings . . . 31,580 industrial enterprises . . . 65,000 kilometres of railway lines . . . 7 million horses, 17 million cattle and oxen

---

* Erickson, 'Soviet War Losses: Calculations and Controversies', in Erickson and Dilks (ed.), *Barbarossa*, p. 257; a 1.7 per cent annual growth coefficient is assumed.

... 40,000 hospitals and other medical establishments ... 43,000 public libraries.

These figures cannot be independently verified, but no one doubts that in 1944–5 large tracts of the country lay waste. The task of reconstruction was immense.

For this reason Soviet citizens looked forward to a long period of international peace, reduced military expenditure, and relief from the insuperable burdens they had been called on to bear during the war. In fact they faced new hardships and sacrifices. Paradoxically, the Allied victory led to the reimposition of Stalinist rule in all its ferocity. The defeat of fascism was officially hailed as proof of the superiority of Soviet 'socialism'. The propagandists' claim was not entirely false, since the Red Army could not have marched from Stalingrad to Berlin unless the state had been able to mobilize and direct vast resources towards a single end. Nevertheless credit for victory rightly belonged to the USSR's peoples, whether as soldiers or civilians, who owed their survival mainly to their own efforts, often achieved by behaviour that went against the wishes of authority.

Front-line officers in particular had developed a sense of their worth as human beings and citizens; they had no wish to be treated once again as mere cogs in a soulless bureaucratic machine. Many years later a veteran told an interviewer:

In school we had all believed the myths about the all-powerful Supreme Leader. The military catastrophe of 1941–2 forced us for the first time to question Stalin and threw us back on our own resources. So for many of us those first two years of war coincided with a spontaneous de-Stalinization. We felt that everything depended on us personally, and that gave us an extraordinary sense of freedom.[*]

For many the hope of a better life was linked to closer relations with the Western democracies. When elections were held to the Supreme Soviet in December 1945, people in Yaroslavl' and elsewhere defaced portraits of official candidates, shouting, 'They'll get us into war again,' and called for genuine constitutional rule 'as in the United States or Britain' (V. Kozlov in *NR* 4/1993, pp. 468–75). What the security

---

[*] Tumarkin, 'The Invasion and War as Myth and Memory', in Wieczynski (ed.), *Operation Barbarossa*, p. 277.

police termed 'hooligan acts' were rare, but the mood of disaffection was widespread. The regime responded with repressive measures and calls for vigilance *vis-à-vis* new external enemies, as fearsome as the fascists: the United States and its allies, whose 'aggressive' policies threatened to undermine Soviet security and socialist values. Without foreign foes Stalinism could not survive.

The first to experience its vindictiveness were Soviet prisoners of war repatriated from Central Europe, along with civilian deportees and those termed 'internally displaced persons'. By December 1946 these individuals numbered 5.4 million, of whom 1.8 million were armed forces personnel. Among the 3.6 million civilians, Ukrainians slightly outnumbered Russians; over half were women or children.* Much fewer were brought back subsequently; about half a million found refuge abroad. All repatriates had to pass through so-called 'filtration camps', where they were made to do forced labour and often maltreated, before their fate was decided. Some real or alleged collaborators were shot out of hand.† This embarrassed the Western powers, which had, for reasons of expedience, handed over 2 million of them to the Soviets, a practice later abandoned; these unfortunates were considered especially suspect. Of the remainder some were entrusted to the authority of the defence commissariat (now ministry), which sent them mainly to penal or construction battalions, while at least 600,000 formed a 'special contingent' under NKVD/MVD control. Among those who landed in the Gulag were all returned officers. Finally, about half the repatriates were allowed to return to civilian life, but not to reside in the three largest cities or near the border. They remained under surveillance as 'exposed to the influence of fascist propaganda' and suffered administrative harassment for years to come. Despite the grim conditions these prisoners had endured under the Nazis, and their generally good resistance record, Stalin saw them all as a security threat. They had seen too much of Western ways and so could expose the 'big lie' on which his system largely rested. In July 1945 the NKVD issued an order equating *all* repatriates, not just collaborators, with

---

* 'Yakovlev Commission' report, *NNI* 2/1996, p. 99; for earlier estimates, see Zemskov in *Sots. issled.* 5/1995, p. 10; M. I. Semiryaga in *Vop. ist.* 4/1995, p. 20.

† Military tribunals alone sentenced 157,593 repatriated persons to death between 1941 and 1945; others will have been liquidated by the NKVD.

enemies of the state. I. Ya. Tryapitsin, a veteran ex-prisoner who lived to be interviewed by the (post-Soviet) 'Yakovlev commission', recalled that

When we left the filtration camp we were all happy, even though we were under escort, and hoped our condition would soon improve once we got back to the motherland. But as we passed through our country our joy gave way to nervous expectation. On reaching the Murom area we were met by machine-guns and dogs. Instead of the shouts in German there was the order 'move smartly' in Russian. From the frying-pan we had fallen into the fire . . . We all wondered why we were still alive. ['Yakovlev commission' report, p. 103]

In the first post-war years the Gulag population expanded to a size hitherto unknown and then stabilized. In January 1949 there were 2.36 million inmates of camps and colonies (in roughly equal shares) plus 2.30 million in settlements. Four years later the total reached 2.46 million in camps and colonies plus 2.75 million in settlements. To these should be added (in each year) several thousand in gaol – and foreign prisoners of war, who came under a different branch of the MVD, known as GUPVI.* The latter numbered 2.66 million in June 1945, including 1.81 million Germans. After August 1945 they were joined by 520,000 Japanese prisoners seized in the lightning Manchurian campaign. In some respects, e.g. rations, Axis prisoners of European origin enjoyed better conditions than did Soviet repatriates – probably because they were expected to return home one day. All had to work. Mortality rates were initially very high (37 per cent in 1942–5) but improved subsequently. The MVD also maintained camps outside the USSR, notably in the Soviet zone of Germany, to which some German prisoners were later dispatched. To complete the picture, in 1945 some 700,000 Soviet citizens served sentences 'without deprivation of liberty' at their workplaces.

The special-settlement inmates (exiles) were now overwhelmingly from the non-Russian minorities. Their inflow, which had begun before 1941, was augmented that year by the Volga Germans (whose autonomous republic was liquidated) and their compatriots from other parts of the USSR. In March and May 1944 Stalin turned over to

* Main Administration of Prisoners of War and Internees.

Beriya's mercies a number of ethnic groups deemed disloyal: principally north Caucasians (Chechens, Ingush, Karachay, Balkars), Crimean Tatars, and Kalmyks; another group comprised three Turkic peoples from Georgia (December 1944). These operations were carried out in a matter of days by NKVD troops who were awarded medals for their 'excellent conduct' (A. I. Kokurin in *Ot. arkh.* 5/1993, p. 101). In October of that 'year of the great migration' the security police reported holding 2.22 million settlers, of whom 602,000 were from the north Caucasus and 225,000 (not all Tatars) from the Crimea; Kalmyks numbered 93,000 and Germans 589,000. Also listed were 45,000 'first-lings' of two groups which would become prominent in the Gulag after the war: Balts and Moldavians.

The blows that struck the Baltic peoples after 1947 were heavier than in 1941. The total number 'repressed' seems to have been around 270,000. In January 1953 there were 172,000 special settlers from that region (only 14,000 survivors of the pre-war contingent); over half as many others found themselves in camps or colonies (96,000 in January 1951). The 'Moldavians', who were taken in July 1949, numbered 36,000 (V. I. Tsaranov in *Ot. ist.* 2/1996, pp. 71–9). Far larger was the Ukrainian contingent, which is put at 175,000. They are described in police sources as followers of two nationalist guerrilla leaders, S. Bandera and A. Melnyk, but many non-collaborators were also swept into the net. There were 69,000 people from the Black Sea coast, 57,000 ex-'Vlasovites' and 9,000 Jehovah's Witnesses (exiled in 1951). The total influx into the settlements has been put at 600,000 (N. P. Popov in *Ot. arkh.* 2/1992, pp. 20–31; Zemskov in ibid., 1/1993, pp. 4–19). It is not yet clear what proportion of people in any of these categories were sent to camps and colonies. Normally conviction led to a term in camp followed by exile, but settlers who were found guilty of miscon-duct might be relegated to a camp. The system was inherently arbitrary. In February 1948 the Politburo issued a secret decree that political offenders and those with 'anti-Soviet ties' (i.e. contacts abroad) should not be freed on expiry of their sentence, but instead were to be dispatched *indefinitely* to some remote eastern region (*Ist.* 2/1994, pp. 92–3). At this time many people who had served out their term before the war were rearrested – on the old fraudulent charges! – and sent back to the Gulag.

The first post-war years were known among *zeks* (as prisoners were colloquially called) as the time of the 'Great Hunger'. Rations were inadequate to sustain the health of men and women who had to perform back-breaking physical labour in extreme conditions, under constant supervision by guards and 'trusties' (the ratio of informers to prisoners was officially set at 1:8). Survival was less problematic for those who secured jobs as camp doctors, accountants, or norm-setters. One such was the writer Lev Razgon, who many years later described vividly the way camps were run. There was, for instance, extensive collusion between administrators and criminals to falsify output statistics and steal prisoners' food. Colonel Vypol'zov, an 'art-lover' who took over the Ustvymlag camp complex in 1948, arranged for convicts to produce splendid items of ceramics with which he bribed his superiors. Other commandants, emulating noble grandees in the eighteenth century, put together convict orchestras, whose musicians were relegated to prisoner status once the fad passed. More usual was a taste for sadistic practices such as reading out to the inmates at roll-call lists of those shot for 'refusing to work'.*

The most famous post-war *zek*, Alexander Solzhenitsyn, was a serving officer arrested in 1945 for criticizing the dictator in correspondence opened by the censor. His account of the system, written in the 1960s on the basis of evidence painstakingly accumulated from hundreds of fellow prisoners, brought him world fame when it was published in the West as *The G U Lag Archipelago* (1973–5) and fostered a long-overdue reassessment of the entire Stalin era (see page 488). A good deal of information was available at the time about Soviet prison camps from former inmates who had defected, but many people in the West treated it sceptically. Within the USSR itself knowledge of the Gulag was also widespread, even though released prisoners were pledged to secrecy about their experiences, but it was dangerous to discuss such matters, even in private, given the ubiquity of delators. Fear of 'the organs' (i.e. the security police) helped to keep the population docile. Even so a resistance movement began to form in the camps after 1948. It was spearheaded by Ukrainians, Balts, and others inspired by national (or in some cases, religious) convictions. It was in part a reflection of the desperate armed struggle waged by scattered guerrilla bands in rural areas of the reannexed territories (Lithuania,

* Razgon, *La Vie sans lendemains*, pp. 121–6.

western Ukraine). Local outbreaks of protest by camp inmates were easily put down by MVD troops, but in 1953 the death of Stalin, followed by the arrest of Beriya, gave a fillip to prisoners' morale. Riots at Noril'sk and elsewhere, although suppressed with heavy loss of life, played a part in making the new party leadership adopt a reformist course.

For the 'free' population, too, Stalin's last years were a time of severe trial. Already before the war had ended there were signs of an impending reversal to pre-war political practices. Propagandists stressed the Party's role *vis-à-vis* the armed forces and action was taken to train the many soldiers who had joined the AUCP(b) during the war to think according to ideological precepts. Stalin, from June 1945 promoted to the rank of 'generalissimo', felt threatened by his generals' overbearing manner. Zhukov was recalled from Germany and, after a spell in the defence ministry, sent to cool his heels as chief of Odessa military district.

There were now two security agencies: the MGB, run by the vicious V. S. Abakumov, and Beriya's MVD. The split was evidently designed to reduce the latter's power, perhaps because Stalin suspected him of not being sufficiently antisemitic, but he remained in charge of the nuclear weapons programme as well as of the prison camps that supplied its needs, and was still very much a member of Stalin's inner circle.

The 'Boss' (as intimates called him, but not to his face) liked to play on the personal rivalries of his intimates, none of whom, even Beriya, could feel safe. Ageing fast, Stalin seldom appeared in public. Even an interview or statement was a rare event, treated as an oracular utterance and an outstanding contribution to Marxist-Leninist 'science'. The cult of his person was taken to ridiculous lengths. On his seventieth birthday in 1949 his portrait, suspended from a balloon and illuminated by searchlights, appeared in the night sky above the Kremlin. Scholars and poets hailed his genius with appropriate epithets – 'father of the toiling peoples', for instance – and his image, carved in wood or stone, was ubiquitous. Each day newspapers gave first place to stylized messages addressed to him by ordinary folk. All this glorification served to mask the absence of normal political discourse and to convey the impression of a Leader and people inseparably united in mortal struggle against foes at home and abroad.

At a victory reception in May 1945 Stalin toasted the Russians as 'the most outstanding of all the nations in the Soviet Union'. The war gave a fillip to Russian chauvinistic sentiment which the regime cleverly exploited to manufacture popular support. This did not mean, as some naïve Westerners thought, that Marxism-Leninism had been cast aside, but was just a manipulative device. Its chief targets were those minority peoples, or more specifically their intelligentsia, who were (or might be) attracted to Western ways of thought. They were condemned as 'rootless cosmopolitans', a term that had an antisemitic ring to it.

This campaign is customarily known as the *Zhdanovshchina*, although it did not move into full gear until after Zhdanov's* death (31 August 1948) and probably owed a lot to Malenkov (as well as Stalin himself, who liked to stay in the background and pull the strings). Already in 1946 Zhdanov had led an attack on Soviet intellectuals, whom he accused of 'kowtowing before bourgeois culture'. The humanist poet Anna Akhmatova was singled out for public humiliation, along with the humorous writer Mikhail Zoshchenko. The latter had written a story about a monkey that escaped from a zoo, spent a day observing life in a Soviet city, and found the experience so disheartening that it returned with relief to captivity.

Under Zhdanov's tutelage 'socialist realist' writing became still more didactic and schematic. Censors and other literary functionaries tried to shield it from the 'decadent' modernist tendencies current in the West. During the war there had been a certain *rapprochement* between literature and real life, manifest in the novels of Konstantin Simonov (*Days and Nights*) or Vasiliy Grossman (*Life and Fate*, completed in 1960 but not published in the USSR until 1988). Alexander Tvardovsky wrote a popular poem, 'Vasiliy Tyorkin', which depicted soldiers' sufferings and hopes for a better future. After 1946 few such works were permitted to appear. Writers often chose to consign their manuscripts to a drawer, awaiting better times. Superficially, this era in Russian literary history had a precedent in the last years of Nicholas I's reign, which later critics called 'an age of censorship terror' – although the phrase is more applicable to the twentieth-century situation.

In the visual arts, too, the war led to a thaw.

Although works such as *Hymn to October* (1942) by Alexander Gerasimov

---

* Zhdanov had charge of party affairs, while Malenkov and Beriya concerned themselves with government and security matters respectively. The arrangement was purely one of convenience and did not become institutionalized. Each sub-leader had his own clientèle.

... never stopped appearing, the new tendency ... to ease up on politically correct requirements [led artists to respond] with a resurgence of interest in such previously neglected and ideologically suspect genres as landscape painting, still-lifes, and scenes of everyday life.*

Even paintings on the war sometimes achieved spiritual depth and brought in religious motifs, as in the Kukryniksy group's *The Fascists Flee from Novgorod* (1944), where the ruined cathedral, 'an image of a disfigured human being', is 'illuminated by light from afar, a glimmer of freedom'. During the *Zhdanovshchina* artists were required 'to heed the Party's advice' both in the selection of subject matter and in the style of treatment. Gerasimov's work became more iconographic, as in *The Oath* (1949), where he depicted Politburo members lined up hierarchically. There were fewer portraits of the Leader than one might expect, because the theme was risky and artists fought shy of it. But Stalin remained the final arbiter in disputes.

In January 1948 it was the musicians' turn to come under fire. Composers were told to pay more heed to Russian folk themes, and an opera entitled *The Great Friendship* (by V. Muradeli) was singled out for ideological errors. Prokofyev and Shostakovich were both criticized for alleged 'formalistic' tendencies in their work. The film director Eisenstein had to confess to lack of vigilance. He was said to have taken too negative a view of Ivan the Terrible in the second part of his film dedicated to that ruler. Stalin in person lectured Nikolay Cherkasov, the actor who played the tsar's part, on the progressive role the *oprichnina* had supposedly played in undermining the boyars – in the circumstances an ominous but self-revealing remark. Eisenstein died a broken man, and the number of Soviet films produced, which by 1947 had regained the pre-war level, sank to a mere five in 1952. Those that were produced had an anti-Western slant.

M. Romm's *Secret Mission*, screened in 1950–1, accused the United States of having carried on separate negotiations with the Nazis ... Famous dramatists and theatre people literally vied with one another in trying to satisfy Stalin, who attached enormous importance to film releases and censored most of them himself ... The former allies who had organized Lend-Lease

---

* Glants, 'Images of the War in Painting', in Garrard (ed.), *World War II and the Soviet People*, pp. 106–7.

supplies were insistently represented as actively preparing to unleash a third world war. [V. S. Lel'chuk and E. I. Pivovar in *Ot. ist.*, 6/1993, p. 67]

Even the circus administration ordered programmes to be put on with anti-American themes!

The spirit of the age was expressed most vividly in the vast skyscrapers constructed in the capital – at a time when housing for the masses was still desperately short. These office buildings, hotels, and apartment blocks for the privileged few, with their pseudo-classical ornaments, were designed as prestigious monuments symbolizing the triumph of socialism. In 1947 Moscow's eight-hundredth anniversary was celebrated with great pomp and the city acquired a quasi-sacramental character. It was seen as a model for the whole country, which would thus take on a homogeneous appearance: the same urban layout, vast squares for public rituals, and rows of identical apartment blocks.

Historians played a fateful role in developing the Stalin cult and a heavily ideologized view of the past. They emphasized Russia's achievements throughout the ages. From Kievan times onward, so it was claimed, she had triumphantly resisted foreign aggression, and her empire had been built largely with the minorities' consent; in any case, tsarist rule had benefited them indirectly by enabling them to escape conquest by foreign imperialists and allowing their intellectuals to become acquainted with progressive Russian thought. Somehow the glorious deeds of select rulers, such as Peter I (but not the German Catherine II!), generals, explorers, scientists, and so on, were reconciled with Marxist concepts such as the inexorable succession of socio-economic formations. All scholarly writing had to have the proper dosage of citations from Stalin, Lenin, and Marx/Engels (in that order!), however relevant or irrelevant they might be. Faced with these pressures, many historians sought refuge in remoter periods, but even there they were not immune from criticism by ambitious colleagues. The atmosphere in the profession was one of suspicion and distrust.

Much the same was true of the other social sciences. In 1947 the Hungarian-born economist E. Varga got into trouble for holding that Western capitalism had been so transformed by the war that revolutionary upheavals were unlikely; this implied that the USSR should take a soft line in foreign policy. He was lucky to escape with a demotion.

N. A. Voznesensky, a leading planner who in 1947 joined the Politburo, wrote a popular textbook that, although ideologically orthodox, seems to have aroused Stalin's jealousy. In any case, the next year he was implicated in the so-called 'Leningrad case' and paid with his life – the only top-flight leader to suffer such a penalty in these years.

Among natural scientists there were some who benefited from nuclear weapons research and other secret programmes, even if they were obliged to live in 'closed cities', designated only by number, whose very existence could not be mentioned in public. But biologists suffered greatly from the activities of Lysenko, whose fallacious theories enjoyed support in high places. The scientific establishment resisted, but they were unable to stop him placing his protégés in leading positions.

Curiously, this campaign came to fruition only after the expiry of Zhdanov, who was lukewarm towards it. Whether or not he died of natural causes, his disappearance led to a new constellation of power within the Kremlin. It strengthened the position of Malenkov, who had suffered a temporary downgrading in 1946, and of Molotov, although he was unwilling or unable to rescue his (Jewish) wife from imprisonment at the Boss's command. Malenkov used the Lysenko affair to discredit Zhdanov and then, no doubt with Beriya's aid and Stalin's tacit assent, helped concoct a case against the Leningrad leader A. A. Kuznetsov, whom Stalin had earmarked as his heir apparent (Yu. N. Zhukov in *Vop. ist.* 1/1995, pp. 33–4). In September 1950, after a secret trial, Kuznetsov and Voskresensky were among six men sentenced to be shot; in all at least 200 officials were either 'liquidated' or imprisoned. The victims were all rehabilitated many years later.

Malenkov was a guiding spirit behind the case staged against members of the wartime Jewish Anti-Fascist Committee, that had international ramifications. Although the USSR was one of the first to recognize the new state of Israel in May 1948, official sympathies soon veered towards the Arab countries. Soviet Jews gave an effusive reception to Israel's first ambassador in Moscow, Golda Meir, on her arrival later that year, and the security authorities suspected a Zionist conspiracy. Stalin's latent antisemitism had been inflamed by developments in his own family (his daughter Svetlana married a Jew); Malenkov shared his prejudices. In January 1948, on Stalin's orders, Abakumov arranged for the committee's chairman, the much-loved actor–director Solomon Mikhoels, to be murdered in what was falsely described as a motor accident. Two Jewish scholars were then coerced into giving false testimony against other members of the committee. One item of 'evidence' was a scheme put up in 1944 by a veteran Bolshevik trade-union official, S. A. Lozovsky, to create a Jewish autonomous republic in the Crimea. This was now represented as a treasonable idea. The investigation dragged on until 1952, when the case came before the Supreme Court's Military Collegium. The presiding judge found the evidence insufficient to convict and protested, only to be told by Malenkov: 'The Politburo has approved the sentence three times: carry it out!' Thirteen defendants were condemned to death, six others to prison and exile. Thousands of Jews lost their jobs and the last remaining Jewish cultural institutions were closed down.

Antisemitic motifs also featured in the trials staged at this time in the East European satellites, along with the charge of ritual murder, which had already made its appearance during the Great Terror. Like many despots, Stalin was afraid of death and doctors. He suffered from advanced cerebral arteriosclerosis. When his personal physician incautiously suggested that he should scale down his activities he flew into a rage and cried: 'Put him in irons!' In January 1953 Dr Lydia Timashuk, a police informer, who presumably acted on MGB (and Stalin's) orders, alleged that Kremlin doctors had killed Zhdanov and another party leader. Those arrested were mainly Jewish. Rumours circulated that all Soviet Jews were to be rounded up and deported to the east.

After the long-overdue Nineteenth Party congress (October 1952) changes in the leading organs suggested that Stalin was planning a new purge that would have removed all or most current members of the Politburo. But on 1 March, after one of his customary nocturnal drinking bouts, the dictator suffered a burst blood vessel in the brain. The other leaders, when told, failed to seek medical aid promptly. The delay was probably not deliberate; they were afraid of being held to account, if he recovered, for whatever the doctors had or had not done. On the evening of 5 March he breathed his last. No individual in human history to date had acquired such vast power or caused the death of so many millions of his fellow human beings. Stalin's expiry marked the end of an era, but the political system he had built would survive him for over thirty years.

RECONSTRUCTING THE ECONOMY

The effort to break the United States' nuclear monopoly, and Stalin's expectation that a new world war was due in twenty (later: five) years' time, necessitated a new drive to develop the arms industry. In August 1949, long before Western observers had expected, the USSR successfully detonated an atomic weapon. The achievement owed a lot to luck: a Soviet spy, the physicist Karl Fuchs, defected with top-secret plans. But the subsequent development of a thermonuclear device (1953) owed more to the input of Soviet scientists and engineers.

The arms drive drained resources of skilled manpower, burdened the state budget, and distorted the balance of the industrial economy. The fourth Five-year plan (1946–50), like its pre-war forerunners, devoted a vast share of funds to capital investment. Once again consumers had to tighten their belts. By 1950 the output of producers' goods, expressed in index numbers (1940: 100), had more than doubled to 205, while goods in 'Group B' had increased by less than a quarter (123). Until 1951, when the pre-war level was exceeded, fewer pairs of boots and shoes were produced annually than there were inhabitants. The same was true of knitted garments, which rose from 183 million items in 1940 to only 198 million in 1950, but thereafter surged ahead (341 million in 1953). Radio receivers were relatively abundant (over a million sets produced in 1950), but refrigerators and TV sets would remain luxuries until the later 1950s. Even run-of-the-mill domestic objects were scarce and had to be bought on the 'free' market rather than in ill-stocked state shops.

People grumbled at low wages, which in 1945 were 60 per cent of pre-war, and the high cost of living. They also resented having to buy low-interest state bonds, the cost of which was deducted from their pay. On the other hand most consumers appreciated the practice of reducing the price of certain commodities each spring: 'Comrade Stalin always keeps his promises,' wrote one Moscow housewife to a friend, in a letter intercepted by the police in 1952 (A. Krayushkin and N. Teptsov in NR 2/1992, pp. 282–96). Few questioned the basic principles of the 'socialist' command economy. In the early years at least it was widely recognized that war-damaged industries had to be reconstructed before popular demands could be met. But the consensus between rulers and ruled, like the euphoria after Victory Day, was sorely tested once it became clear that the prospect for ordinary folk was one of apparently endless hardship. In the countryside especially many people were hard hit by a currency reform in December 1947 which wiped out nine tenths of the savings that they had managed to accumulate during the war.

The measure could be justified as a way of mopping up surplus purchasing power, and so keeping down inflation, at a time when it was not yet possible to increase the supply of goods. Maintaining a sound currency took priority over satisfying consumers. The planning officials took a long-term view and concentrated attention on boosting output in key sectors like fuel supply. By 1950 the Donets coalmines, which had been flooded during the war, were producing more than they had ten years earlier; three years later total coal output, at 320 million tons, was nearly double what it had been in 1940. Still more significant was the tripling of natural-gas output (to 6.9 milliard cubic metres), for in the decades to come this energy source would gradually take the place of fossil fuels. Already by 1947 the Dnepropetrovsk hydroelectric power station, a symbol of 'socialist construction' in the 1930s, had been brought back on stream. Pre-war steel output was exceeded in the following year, reaching 38.1 million tons (1940: 18.3 million). Altogether the reconstruction drive proceeded at an impressive pace, much faster than after the fighting in 1914–20. The defects of centralized planning and control, which would loom large in later years, were less evident at a time when what mattered most was quantitative growth in priority areas.

Agriculture continued to be the proverbial 'Achilles' heel of the Soviet economy'. Collective farming was restored and extended to the newly annexed (or reannexed) territories in the west. A decree of September 1946 confiscated 14 million hectares of land which peasants (and factories) had taken over during the war and farmed on their own account. Shortly thereafter collective farms' delivery quotas were raised and other burdens imposed on them: they had, for instance, to maintain their own reserves of seed. Procurement prices were kept low but taxes increased. These measures were followed by a drive to force *kolkhozy* to amalgamate. Ostensibly this was done to achieve economies of scale, but there was also an ideological and administrative aspect: larger farms, like *sovkhozy*, would be easier to control. The role of the M T S was enhanced and party members, usually war veterans distinguished for valour rather than agricultural know-how, took over leading functions. Between 1946 and 1948 21,285 collective-farm chairmen and 14,569 other rural activists were put on trial for reprehensible conduct (V. F. Zima in *Ot. ist.* 5/1995, p. 48).

One of their replacements' chief tasks was to restrict farmers' activities on their household plots, for in official eyes these were a relic of capitalism. By 1952 the number of cows, sheep, goats, and pigs in private ownership was considerably below pre-war levels. Only half the households on *kolkhozy* had a cow of their own, yet each had to deliver 210–50 litres of milk a year, as well as other produce, which they had to beg, borrow, or buy from their neighbours. In that year farmers' incomes were only 60 per cent of what they had been in 1928 – and even this was an improvement on 1949 (50 per cent). A mere fifth of their earnings came from work in the collective fields, for most farm managements had little surplus to distribute once they had met the state's claims.

According to no less an authority than N. S. Khrushchev, by this time the countryside looked as if the Tatar hordes had just passed through. Not surprisingly, the drift to the towns, especially of young people, accelerated, despite bureaucratic efforts to restrict it. In 1952 the actual grain harvest was 92.2 million tons – not the 130 million claimed by the party leadership on the basis of the fraudulent measure called 'biological yield'. This was less than in 1940, when there had been fewer mouths to feed. And 1952 was a 'good year'! The USSR had fewer head of cattle than the tsarist empire in 1916, and total traction power (animal and mechanical) was one fifth less than in 1928.

Stalin ignored these realities and clung to fantastic policies such as a grandiose plan for the 'transformation of nature' which owed a lot to Lysenko. It involved planting shelter belts of trees to prevent soil erosion and constructing a network of irrigation canals. The latter scheme was ecologically dubious and in the event most of the effort was wasted. Like the skyscrapers of Moscow, the costly project ignored realities: notably that farmers had no incentive to farm and that many people were going hungry.

In 1946–7 famine struck a belt of territory in the south. As with its predecessor in 1932–3, it was kept secret and the authorities refused to help the victims until it was too late. In Moldova alone over 300,000 were affected by dystrophy and 36,000 died. Doctors were told to report the cause of death as septic angina. In Ukraine the mortality rate was 1.7 times greater than in the previous year. When Khrushchev told Stalin that there had been cases of cannibalism, he was charged with softness: 'They are deceiving you by appealing to your emotions to make you distribute all the reserves.'

The government spent only half its reserves on feeding the hungry and knowingly set course for famine . . . It took deterrent measures to force people to work. A decree . . . of 2 June 1948 ordered over 23,000 people who refused to perform agricultural labour to be sent, without any investigation or trial, to special settlements for up to eight years . . . In this way, under the guise of reinforcing discipline, repressions were organized . . . which country folk called a second dekulakization. [Zima in *Ot. ist.* 1/1993, pp. 37, 47–50]

THE EXPANSION OF SOVIET POWER IN ASIA

The Soviet-Japanese neutrality pact of April 1941, and Tokyo's sub-sequent decision to move against the Western powers in the Pacific instead of aiding Hitler against the USSR, were crucial factors in the Soviet victory. Until 1942–3 Stalin remained nervous about Japanese intentions and was slow to withdraw troops from the east to fight in Europe. Thereafter he could afford to take a stronger line and, as we have seen, promised his allies to wage war on Japan once hostilities had ended in the west. The growth of American power in the Far East gave this task added urgency, and on 9 August 1945 1.6 million Soviet troops under Malinovsky crossed the Manchurian border. Their numerical preponderance ensured that the campaign was brief. It cost a mere 9,000 casualties and brought the USSR significant gains: Manchuria, the Kuriles, southern Sakhalin, and four off-shore islands.* Stalin would have liked control of Hokkaido as well, but this the Americans refused. In Manchuria, apart from the Japanese prisoners

---

* Iturup, Kunashir, Shikotan and Habomai were seized in late August (*after* the Japanese surrender!). They had not previously been Russian possessions and were later heavily fortified. They are still (1997) a major impediment to a normalization of relations between Russia and Japan.

of war (and White Russian *émigrés*, who were forcibly returned), there were large industrial resources that could be dismantled, not to mention ample consumer goods. Thereafter in the Soviet Far East

just about everyone trafficked in war trophies. Japanese watches, pens, stockings, paper fans, cosmetics, toothpaste, dolls, cigarettes and chocolates turned up in state stores as well as on the black market. Among bureaucrats, Nippon Electric telephones enjoyed the status of desk icons.*

Such actions contravened the treaty of friendship and alliance signed in August 1945 with Nationalist China, now resurgent. Under this agreement, a follow-up to Yalta, the USSR regained control of the Chinese Eastern (Changchun) railway, leased for twenty years, and the territories on the Liaotung peninsula (Lüshun and Talien, which the Russians called Dal'ny and Dairen) ceded in 1905. Stalin relished this avenging of a historical slight. In Mongolia the *status quo* was reaffirmed. In effect the USSR now had a sphere of influence in north-eastern China which to Chinese opinion (Communists included) looked like imperialism writ large.

Stalin did not trust Mao Zedong, whom he suspected (not without reason) of putting national interests first, and urged him to come to terms with Jiang Jieshi. For a few months the Chinese civil war subsided, but when it flared up again in May 1946 the Soviet leader acted to prevent Mao's defeat, not least because this would have left the USSR confronting an alliance between Nationalist China and the United States. The more victories Mao won over the Nationalists the closer Stalin veered to his side, and by October 1947 he made this support explicit. The Manchurian arms dumps yielded enough *matériel* for a Communist army of 600,000, and Soviet engineers were sent to repair the shattered railways. Even so Moscow did not believe that a victory for the Chinese Communist party (CPC) was on the cards and to the last maintained diplomatic relations with the Nationalist government. This upset Mao, who warned A. I. Mikoyan, the first senior Soviet envoy to visit his headquarters, against 'false friends [who] tell you one thing but do another'. It was soon clear that the Communists would win.

Stalin was faced with a valuable, but unpredictable, partner. China's

---

* Stephen, *Russian Far East*, p. 244.

size and vast population, together with the CPC's greater experience of revolutionary war, meant that it could not be treated as just another satellite. Stalin was willing to accord the CPC a leading role in eastern Asia, where prospects for revolution now seemed brighter than in Europe, but he was anxious to restrain Beijing from trying to seize Taiwan (whither the Nationalists retreated) since this risked embroiling the USSR in a confrontation with a nuclear-armed United States for which Moscow was not yet ready. He was also worried that Mao, despite his proclaimed policy of 'leaning to one side' (i.e. to the USSR), might seek a *rapprochement* with the West.

This ambivalence explains why, in October 1949, when the Chinese People's Republic (CPR) was established, Moscow at once recognized the new regime but 'forgot' to send congratulations, and why the two Communist powers took nearly two months to conclude their treaty of alliance (14 February 1950). Each of the two oriental emperors was sensitive on questions of protocol and eager to score points off the other; they used language that deliberately obscured their true aims. To Mao's chagrin, the eventual treaty was not so different from that with Jiang in 1945, and so 'unequal'. For although the Changchung railway system was restored to Chinese sovereignty the Soviets retained certain rights over it; similarly, the Soviet bases on the Liaotung peninsula were to be returned, but not until peace had been made with Japan;* on the other hand China regained full control of Xinjiang and Tibet. The Soviets were obligated to aid China if she were attacked by Japan (or a power allied to Japan), but only if a state of war had been declared – a wording that allowed Stalin to avoid *open* involvement in the Korean conflict of 1950–53.

Soviet troops had entered Korea in 1945 but were then withdrawn and by 1948 the peninsula had been in effect partitioned along the 38th parallel between the Communist PDRK (People's Democratic Republic of Korea) in the north and the US-orientated Republic of Korea in the south. In the spring of 1949 Kim Il Sung, the PDRK

---

* Or 1952 at the latest. The term of the lease was thus much shorter than that set in 1945. In the event the Korean War delayed Soviet withdrawal from Lüshun until 1955. Soviet-controlled resources in Manchuria were returned, but no compensation was offered for goods removed to the USSR. A low-interest loan was granted of $300 million, which the Chinese thought too modest a sum.

state and party leader, who owed his position to Soviet backing, visited Moscow. Stalin encouraged him to launch guerrilla attacks on the south and to foment uprisings there, but refrained from endorsing his plan for a major offensive. Kim was told to consult Mao first.

The Soviet leader said, 'If you should get kicked in the teeth, I shall not lift a finger. You have to ask Mao for all the help.' Stalin here manoeuvred himself into the enviable position of having everything to gain and nothing to lose . . . The onus for the attack, whether successful or not . . . , would rest solely on Mao and Kim.[*]

By April 1950 the Soviet leader had adopted a more activist stance and sent Soviet generals to plan a PDRK invasion of the south. The campaign, which started on 25 June, was expected to last a month at the most. But the aggressors underestimated the Western powers' ability to mount a successful counter-offensive, which, by October, had taken their troops to the river Yalu. Stalin now vacillated. At one point he was even reconciled to an American presence on the Soviet border. But Mao was determined to aid the North Koreans so long as he got Soviet air support – and this was duly provided. The final decision was probably expedited by American bombing of a Soviet airfield near Vladivostok. In any case, between November 1950 and the armistice of Panmunjom (July 1953) the 64th aviation fighter corps, based in Manchuria, flew over 63,000 missions and claimed to have shot down 1,309 United Nations aircraft for the loss of 335 planes and 120 crew (Yu. N. Semin and S. N. Ruban in *Vop. ist.* 11/1994, p. 4). The MIG-15 fighters were initially superior to those of their adversaries. Most dogfights took place over the Yellow Sea, away from the area of ground combat. This was the first and only time during the cold war that Soviet and American forces actually clashed.

One result of the Korean War was to increase East–West tension. Moscow was pleased that this kept China in line, but could no longer hope to install pro-Soviet regimes in Japan or elsewhere in the northern Pacific.

In the Middle East Stalin enacted a curious replay of his 1922 Gilan adventure. In 1945–6 Soviet troops in Iran backed an attempt to set

---

[*] Goncharov *et al., Uncertain Partners,* p. 145.

up a puppet state in southern Azerbaijan, but international opposition forced abandonment of the enterprise. The Soviets could not afford to antagonize independent Muslim states and it was not until the Israel-Arab conflict developed that they gained political leverage in the region. Likewise pressure on Turkey for concessions at the Straits and in eastern Anatolia brought no dividends but indirectly fostered that country's adherence to the Western alliance (1951).

EASTERN EUROPE: THE COLD WAR INTENSIFIES

Europe remained the focus of Stalin's attention. He aimed, as we know, to guarantee Soviet security by constructing a belt of dependent states and keeping Germany divided. From 1947 at the latest this objective took automatic precedence over maintaining good relations with the wartime Allies, and tension between them swiftly mounted. Soviet policy was not wholly consistent. The drive to exploit the material resources of the new 'people's democracies' so as to accelerate the USSR's economic recovery was bound to alienate the peoples concerned and whittle away any goodwill they had initially felt towards those who had liberated them from the Nazis. The pace of sovietization varied from country to country: it was faster in Poland, Romania, and Bulgaria than in Hungary and Czechoslovakia, where a shaky democratic interlude lasted for two years or so. But throughout the region Soviet policies were broadly similar, little distinction being made between pro-Allied countries and those that had leaned towards the Axis. Processes that in the USSR had taken decades were telescoped in a few years: in agrarian policy, for example, the confiscation of large estates and the distribution of land to peasant smallholders was swiftly followed by collectivization on the Soviet model. By 1949 economic and political integration had reached a point where six of the seven countries concerned (those mentioned above plus Albania – but *not*, significantly, Yugoslavia) could justly be termed Soviet satellites.

During the first three post-war years the USSR forged a network of defensive alliances that bound these countries to itself against a potential new threat from Germany (or her Western backers) and sought to isolate them from the West. Meanwhile their internal political life was transformed by gradual elimination, through what critics called 'salami tactics', of the non-Communist parties: first conservatives and liberals, then agrarian spokesmen for the peasant interest and Social Democrats. Each group was successively accused of sympathy for fascism or alien 'imperialist' forces and all power assumed by Popular Front-type coalitions in which the local Communist party pulled the strings. Political manipulation took the form of electoral fraud or the promotion of schisms in rival groups. It was supplemented by acts of terror, such as the arrest of prominent politicians, business leaders, churchmen, and others, as well as by massive propaganda campaigns that exploited popular distrust of the privileged classes and the general desire for social change.

These activities were master-minded by Soviet agents, operating either openly or secretly. In Poland, for example, the armed forces came under the command of a Soviet marshal, Rokossovsky, who was of Polish descent, supported by a pleiad of Red Army officers who made life difficult for those Polish soldiers who had returned after serving in the West. More sinister was the power exercised by itinerant MVD/MGB functionaries such as the notorious General F. Belkin. Within the local Communist parties leaders who had spent the war in the underground were edged out by 'Muscovites' like Bierut in Poland, Gottwald in Czechoslovakia, or Rákosi in Hungary. They adopted a Stalinist style of rule, even to the extent of promoting their own 'personality cults', while giant statues of the Great Leader were erected in the respective capitals (except Warsaw); Katowice, for instance, became Stalinogród.

Measures were taken to remodel each country's institutions on the Soviet pattern, with a collective presidency, rubber-stamp legislature, and even a local counterpart to *Pravda* as tone-setting official party organ. An official spokesman summed up current Soviet doctrine as follows:

it is not true that each country follows its own road to socialism ... The general laws of the transition from capitalism to socialism ... developed by Lenin and Stalin on the basis of the Bolshevik Party's experience and the Soviet state are obligatory for every country.*

* *Kommunist*, July 1948, cited by H. Carrère d'Encausse, *Le Grand Frère: l'Union Soviétique et l'Europe soviétisée*, Paris, 1983, p. 104.

In the educational system this meant privileged access for children of proletarian origin and political indoctrination. Instruction emphasized the superiority of Soviet (and Russian) culture and children were obliged to learn Russian. The Catholic and Protestant churches did their best to resist harassment, while in Romania, as in the USSR itself, Uniates were coerced into merging with the Orthodox.

Copying Soviet experience involved the staging of several show trials. The first victims (1947) were 'bourgeois' politicians like the Bulgarian N. Petkov or the Romanian J. Maniu, but the following year those in the dock included Communist leaders suspected of placing national interests ahead of loyalty to the USSR ('proletarian internationalism'). After 1951 even a Stalinist with 'Muscovite' credentials might be arrested, gaoled, tortured, and executed. Among those killed were Ana Pauker in Romania and R. Slánský in Czechoslovakia, both of whom were Jewish. Meanwhile the local parties were ruthlessly purged. In the Soviet zone of Germany there were no such trials but repressive measures were taken against Jewish party members.

In several East European countries mixed companies, set up with Soviet participation, served to channel resources to the USSR on terms beneficial to the latter. Trade links with the West were sundered and local economies reorientated eastwards. In January 1949 a Council of Mutual Economic Aid (disrespectfully termed by Westerners 'Comecon') set out to harmonize the national plans of its member states, but some years elapsed before its activities made much impact. Earlier, in June 1947, the US administration had launched the European Recovery Programme ('Marshall Plan'), in which the East European states were invited to participate. Several were keen to do so, and initially even Moscow was tempted by the idea. But when Molotov came to Paris for talks he discovered that implementation of the programme was to be supervised by a central agency, which in the Soviet view would compromise the participants' economic sovereignty. This was basically why Stalin changed course, so deepening the breach with the West.

The Soviet Union chose to abandon . . . the search for co-operation and agreement and to seek instead to protect its interests by independent manoeuvring, the gathering of strength, and the judicious deployment of its powers.*

Logically, it followed up this step by founding, in September 1947, a substitute for the old Comintern, the 'Communist Information Bureau' (Cominform). Membership was restricted to the ruling parties in Europe (except Albania) plus those of Italy and France. At the inaugural conference Zhdanov delivered a blistering attack on the latter for 'parliamentary pirouetting', i.e. lack of revolutionary zeal. Yet their 'soft' line had been endorsed by Stalin, who reiterated his approval when an anxious Maurice Thorez came to Moscow afterwards to seek guidance (Narinsky in *NNI* 1/1996, pp. 18–30). This suggests that on occasion the Kremlin spoke with more than one voice. Presumably Stalin wanted Zhdanov to be identified with a tougher stance on East–West relations, embodied in the doctrine of irreconcilable conflict between the 'two camps' of socialism and imperialism.

The onslaught on the French and Italian Communists was obediently delivered by two Yugoslav delegates, who soon discovered that

there was a price to be paid for the harsh attacks they were urged to deliver. For in a deceitful political scheme strikingly similar to the factional struggles in the 1920s, Stalin . . . instigated the Yugoslav left[-wingers] to censure the gradualist right, all the while contemplating the next round when he would use the right, by then properly humbled, to bring the self-righteous and stubborn Yugoslavs under control.†

Marshal Tito had been the most zealous of Stalinists, faithfully emulating his master in sovietizing his country's institutions and economic life – so much so that Cominform headquarters were located in Belgrade. But, like Mao later, he owed his power to leadership of an autochthonous revolutionary movement, not to being a Moscow stooge. Tito placed a high valuation on his international prestige, and that of his party and state. He harboured grievances against Stalin for not having backed

---

* Roberts, 'Moscow and the Marshall Plan', pp. 1382–3. The immediate cause of the rejection was a warning from a chastened Varga that the plan would lead to the formation of a bloc of 'bourgeois' states and equally minatory telegrams from the Soviet ambassador in Washington, N. Novikov. See Narinsky, 'Soviet Foreign Policy', pp. 108–9.
† Gati, 'Hegemony and Repression . . . in the Eastern Alliance', in Leffler and Painter, *Origins of the Cold War*, p. 190.

the Yugoslav partisans more energetically and, specifically, for luke-warmness towards Yugoslav claims on Trieste. But the breach of 1948 came over his efforts to build a league of East European parties that would look to Belgrade rather than Moscow.

Stalin was outraged: 'I shall raise my little finger and there will be no more Tito.' He fired off eight hysterical letters accusing the Yugoslavs of placing their national interests first, rejecting Soviet advice, and spying for the imperialists. Highly placed Soviet secret agents in Yugoslavia redoubled their activities and economic cooperation was suspended, threatening the country with ruin. But Tito stood firm. The dispute was taken to the Cominform, which promptly left Belgrade for Bucharest, denounced the 'Titoist' leadership (June 1948), and urged Yugoslav cadres to effect a *coup*. Neighbouring states staged border incidents and acts of terrorism, but to no avail. Instead Tito revised his party's doctrine, democratized its structure, and sought aid from the West. The Soviet-Yugoslav schism was the first successful heresy within the world Communist movement. It revealed the brittle-ness of Stalin's East European empire, which rested ultimately on the threat of force that 'big brother' could deploy.

Nevertheless in October 1949 the bloc was enlarged to admit another state, the German Democratic Republic (GDR). Its appearance was really a confession of failure: Stalin was unable to achieve his fundamental objective, a united Germany aligned with the USSR. It was not for want of trying. From the start the Soviet Military Administration in Germany, under Marshal Malinovsky, acted high-handedly, frustrating efforts to reach agreed solutions with the Western powers of such contentious issues as denazification or, especially, reparations. The latter were exacted by mixed companies (SAGs) which siphoned off an estimated \$30–35 million worth of goods, notably heavy machinery and vehicles, electrical equipment and optical instruments – far more than had been proposed at Yalta. Meanwhile political and socio-economic life in the Soviet zone came under control of the Communists, who in April 1946 effected a shotgun marriage with a Social Democratic faction to form the Socialist Unity party (SED). This was then purged of deviant elements and so groomed for acceptance into the fraternal band of Moscow loyalists.

The reparations drain placed on the Western powers the burden of feeding the people in their zones. They reacted by merging the British and American zones (1947) and then taking steps to set up a democratic West German federal government. Soviet rejection of the Marshall Plan, and especially the Prague *coup* of February 1948, greatly accelerated the process of West European unification, with Germany as a key partner. This development came as an unpleasant surprise to Stalin, invalidating his strategic assumptions. In protest at Western moves Sokolovsky walked out of the Allied Control Commission (March 1948) and on 24 June Soviet forces imposed a total ban on the movement of people and goods to and from the Western sectors of Berlin, which were cut off from West Germany by 150 kilometres of Soviet-held territory.

The Berlin blockade had a political purpose: to frustrate a currency reform in the Western zones that would make economic recovery possible. But neither was this objective attained nor were the Western powers forced out of Berlin. Over 322 days Allied planes conveyed 1.7 million tons of essential goods to isolated West Berlin. None of them was shot down, for Stalin feared an American nuclear response: sixty bombers armed with atomic weapons were based within striking range of Soviet territory. There was an element of bluff on both sides, and after informal talks the blockade was called off (May 1949). By then the West had improved its defence posture by forming NATO (April) and forging ahead with preparations to create the German Federal Republic (FRG), which was to have its own army (but no nuclear weapons), integrated into NATO. From the USSR's viewpoint this posed a real threat to its position in Eastern Europe. The balance of power had tipped against it and little comfort could be gained from creation of the GDR: its population was smaller and unreconciled to Communist rule, and the economy less developed than that of west Germany, whither there was ample opportunity to escape, despite the controls exercised by the 'people's police' and ultimately an army.

This weakness explains successive Soviet approaches to the West, most significantly in March 1952, for negotiations on restoring a united but neutral Germany with limited armed forces. This was unacceptable to the Western powers for three main reasons. First, it could not be imposed from outside on west Germany, which enjoyed incomparably greater popular legitimacy than did the east German regime. Secondly, such a Germany would be exposed to Communist infiltration and manipulation. Thirdly, the spectre loomed of a new Rapallo, but this time with Moscow clearly calling the tune. Better to keep Germany divided, even at the price of continued confrontation between the two blocs in the heart of Europe – a viewpoint that had tacit support in Moscow, too.

East–West tension levels remained high even after Stalin had passed from the scene. The goodwill felt towards the USSR in 1945 in Western Europe had largely disappeared and there was little popular support for revolutionary socialism, Moscow-style. In late 1947, at the Cominform's behest, the French and Italian Communists launched general strikes, but the movement fizzled out ineffectively. Thereafter they drifted towards reformist positions, whatever their leaders might say in public.

There was more mileage for Moscow to be gained by exploiting fears of nuclear war. Millions signed the Soviet-backed Stockholm Peace Appeal. Yet pacifism never became a mass force, since it was obvious that disarmament – and more especially arms control, as the essential preliminary step – could not be brought about unilaterally from below but required negotiation at governmental level to ensure a balanced, graduated reduction of military strength. Paradoxically, the awesome nuclear deterrent limited the freedom of action of all nuclear powers, the USSR included, although Moscow was reluctant to admit this in public and was willing to use its military might as a means of winning political advantages. In a nuclear age Stalinism was out of date, although this fact had yet to be reflected in a revision of strategic doctrine.

CHAPTER 21

From Neo-Leninism to Stagnation

THE POLITICAL SCENE UNDER KHRUSHCHEV

The deceased Stalin's closest comrades were agreed that a new course was necessary, involving material concessions to the populace. But they differed as to how it should be brought about and were loath to make any substantial change in the way the country was ruled. Not trusting each other, they made a show of commitment to 'the Leninist principle of collective leadership', listing Presidium* members in alphabetical order and even opening all doors of their limousine simultaneously when alighting from it. The Stalin cult soon fell out of fashion. The 'doctors' plot' was pronounced fraudulent and proceedings against the accused dropped. To symbolize the new spirit of openness tourists were allowed to visit the Kremlin.

In institutional terms the security police lost ground to the Party (now known as the CPSU). An *ad hoc* redistribution of senior posts, brokered while Stalin still lay on his deathbed, had to be amended a few days later (14 March 1953). Malenkov ended up heading the government (chairman of the Council of Ministers) while the post of Party First Secretary was assumed – formally not until September – by the remarkable N. S. Khrushchev (1894–1971). Nikita Sergeyevich gloried in his humble origins and was ambitious, temperamental, and irascible, but cultivated a folksy manner that contrasted with that of his more staid, secretive colleagues. Like them he had risen to power in the 1930s and bore a share of blame for the Terror. He had been primarily responsible for a decree of June 1948 exiling disobedient peasants. Yet he seems to have preserved a residue of moral sense that, along with political calculation, led him to dissociate himself from Stalin's worst excesses.

* From 1952 to 1966 the Politburo was known as the Presidium.

In his self-serving but invaluable memoirs he claims to have been the guiding spirit behind the *coup* of 26 June 1953, which deposed the fearsome Beriya, head of the (reunited) security services, who had sought to gain respectability by making pseudo-liberal moves after Stalin's death. Later that year Beriya and six other senior security officials were shot, after a trial behind closed doors in Stalin style, and several dozen more were purged. In 1954 a Committee of State Security (KGB) took over the police. It was under party control, which meant that the *nomenklatura* had less to fear from its operations than the population at large. A secret party commission was set up to investigate the repressions of the Stalin era. As Khrushchev appreciated better than most, its report would be political dynamite.

In February 1955 Malenkov had to admit publicly to errors over agricultural policy, which had once been in his charge but was now Khrushchev's main stamping-ground. The government came under N. A. Bulganin, who was also defence minister. Another Khrushchev ally was Molotov, the foreign minister, although the two men disagreed over the scope of the 'new look' in foreign policy. Molotov had to publicly acknowledge having made an ideological error, but retained his seat on the Presidium where, with other Stalinist holdovers like Kaganovich and Voroshilov, he intrigued against the First Secretary.

Personal and political rivalries ran deep, as became clear at the momentous Twentieth Party congress, held in February 1956. In a dramatic nocturnal address to the delegates (usually called his 'secret speech') Khrushchev denounced the once deified Stalin as a criminal who had inflicted grave harm on Party and people.

Stalin deviated from [the] clear and plain precepts of Lenin. Stalin put the Party and NKVD up to the use of mass terror when the exploiting classes had been liquidated in our country and there were no serious reasons for the use of extraordinary mass terror. This terror was actually directed . . . against honest workers of the Party and Soviet state, against whom were levelled lying, slanderous and absurd accusations . . . Confessions of guilt . . . were obtained with the help of cruel and inhuman tortures.*

Khrushchev cited graphic details of these abuses, promised that the victims would be (posthumously) rehabilitated, and went on to expose

---

* Cited from the translation in Dmytryshyn, *USSR: Concise History*, pp. 506–8.

Stalin's failings as war leader and interpreter of Leninist doctrine. He did not mention the repression of the kulaks, nor did he suggest that there might have been any merit in the views of Bukharin or Trotsky. They remained unmentionable, and the 'secret speech' was scarcely a truthful guide to Soviet history. Yet it was politically astute. It threw doubt indirectly on Malenkov and other old-guard party leaders, and conveniently blamed all abuses of 'socialist legality' on the 'cult of the individual', i.e. on Stalin, not on the system that had produced such horrors. The CPSU retained a mantle of infallibility and its monopoly of power. His listeners were relieved to hear that no massive new purge was in the offing.

Nevertheless, by speaking so plainly, Khrushchev undermined the Party's legitimacy. The revelations sparked popular disturbances, even revolution, in the East European satellites and threw international Communism into disarray. Later in 1956 he had to backtrack and praise Stalin as a 'great Marxist'. This was a damage-limitation exercise carried out under duress. His rivals sought to exploit his discomfiture. In June 1957, while Khrushchev was absent from Moscow, they secured a majority vote in the Presidium for his resignation and the institution of a rotating chairmanship – clearly intended as the first step in a general return to Stalinist policies. But Marshal Zhukov, who had come back as defence minister, aided by KGB chief Serov, alerted Khrushchev and got the Central Committee to meet, ferrying the provincial delegates to Moscow in military aircraft. Most of these men were Khrushchev appointees and sympathetic to reform. They condemned the reactionary leaders as 'deviationists', recalling their former crimes, and after several days of hectic debate forced them to climb down. To humiliate Molotov he was named ambassador to Mongolia; Malenkov and Kaganovich were sent to Kazakhstan and the Urals respectively to manage industrial plants. In March 1958 they were followed into the wilderness by Bulganin, who had vacillated during the crisis. Khrushchev himself took over as prime minister. Zhukov, too, fell from grace, probably because he was keener than the new leader to rehabilitate army officers victimized during the Terror. He was succeeded at defence by Marshal Malinovsky.

The military-industrial lobby was none too happy that Khrushchev had acquired so much power – on paper even more than Stalin! There was a controversy over the allocation of resources to defence and especially over the First Secretary's preference for a strategy based on missile-based nuclear weapons rather than massive conventional forces. Middle-ranking party functionaries, too, had their grievances. In stark contrast to his predecessor, Khrushchev enjoyed travelling around the country, making contact with ordinary folk and keeping local officials on their toes. Those in rural areas would have to render a detailed account of their activities in public and were reprimanded for any irregularities the leader discovered – and he fancied himself an agronomic expert! To be sure, malefactors were now just relegated and no longer faced fearsome penalties, but the more relaxed atmosphere made them readier to defend their interests.

From 1957 onward Khrushchev waged a campaign to reduce the central bureaucracy. In most economic ministries, including agriculture, staff was drastically thinned, so that officials faced the dismal prospect of leaving the comforts of Moscow for some provincial outpost, where they might even have to do physical work. In 1961 Khrushchev proposed filling senior jobs by rotation, so denying their holders security. The next year he devised an ill-thought-out scheme to divide all party agencies into two departments, one for industrial and the other for agricultural affairs. This threatened the Party's internal cohesion and put at a disadvantage those who performed non-economic functions (which indeed was its purpose); in the long run it would have made the Party superfluous.

Intellectuals, who pulled less weight than officials in Soviet society, were also disgruntled at Khrushchev's clumsy interventions in artistic and literary matters. He summoned several conferences at which leading writers were upbraided for heretical opinions expressed in their works. Cultural policy went through successive phases of 'thaw' and 'freeze'. In 1953–4, and again after the Twentieth Party congress, writers regained courage and took a sharp tone in condemning bureaucratic abuses – a popular theme. Each time the censors were told to tighten the noose. In 1962 the pendulum swung left once more when Khrushchev casually allowed A. Tvardovsky, editor of the main literary review *Novyi mir*, to publish a short novel by Alexander Solzhenitsyn. *One Day in the Life of Ivan Denisovich* described the typical day of a Gulag inmate. This deceptively simple narrative made what Solzhenitsyn's biographer calls 'a universal statement about the human condition' that put him on a level with Tolstoy or Dostoyevsky. It was the first major breach in the wall of secrecy surrounding the Gulag (which Khrushchev had not mentioned in his 1956 speech!). Apparently the leader misjudged the story's import and reckoned that its publication would help him overcome opponents in the Central Committee.

By now the Stalin question had become a political totem. At an extraordinary Party congress in 1959, and especially at the next regular one in October 1961, Khrushchev used this issue as a device to embarrass those who questioned his innovations. On the second occasion leading delegates were required to express their opinion individually. Only a minority condemned Stalin, but his mummified body was removed from the Lenin mausoleum, where it had lain alongside Lenin's since 1953, and reburied nearby. Khrushchev deprived his Stalinist rivals of party membership but was unable to have them indicted for their crimes. His associates in the Presidium were second-raters and some were making ready to betray him.

The leader also could not have things his own way over the Party's new programme, which was intended as a guide in moving from socialism to full communism within twenty years or so, by when material abundance would have been achieved. It set detailed projections for the output of the sinews of industrial might. This was to overlook built-in limitations of the command economy and to assume that current growth rates could be sustained indefinitely. Khrushchev's colleagues agreed with outside observers that the idea was utopian, but were unable to prevent its formal adoption at the Twenty-second Party congress. Within a few years the document would be forgotten in embarrassment.

More immediately Khrushchev's position was undermined by disappointing results in agriculture, his priority area: after a bumper grain crop in 1962, the next harvest was the lowest since 1954. A conspiracy took shape; the seventy-year-old leader got wind of the plot, but he was fatigued and offered no resistance. On 14 October the Central Committee met to hear Suslov denounce him for 'hare-brained scheming' and he was deprived of his posts.

That he was allowed to retire on a state pension was a measure of his achievement. He had made the USSR a more civilized place and freed millions from the Gulag. This did not mean the rule of law or democracy. The KGB remained powerful and pluralism was not on the agenda. Efforts to breathe new life into the soviets and trade unions got nowhere. Khrushchev's reforms were paradoxical, in that they were *not* intended to westernize or modernize political life but to return the country to a pristine Leninist state, to recover the dynamism of 'Great October'. This was not a feasible goal, since long ago the revolution had become bureaucratized; moreover, Khrushchev wanted to keep, and even expand, the imperial structure Stalin had created. Yet the drive for reform, misdirected though it was, had a certain tragic grandeur, and for many Soviet citizens these were years of hope.

BREZHNEV'S RUSSIA

As Khrushchev's successor the plotters of 1964 chose Leonid I. Brezhnev (1906–82), an experienced party functionary who for four years had served as Soviet president.* Of greater account was his close knowledge of the defence industry; earlier in his career he had been a political commissar and risen to major-general's rank. Sturdily built and beetle-browed, Brezhnev in middle age was a cordial, sociable man who treated comrades with courtesy. He lacked Khrushchev's emotional drive and fondness for experimentation, being rather the managerial type of leader. There was also a devious side to his character – like Stalin, he could act a part well – and when, in the mid 1970s, his health began to give way, his vanity came to the fore. He fostered a personal cult that had even less justification than that of his forerunners. He suppressed all mention of Khrushchev and tried to stop him writing his memoirs, but sanctioned a positive reappraisal of Stalin. In 1966 he assumed the latter's title of General Secretary of the CPSU. There was no return to mass terror, so that it is inaccurate to call Brezhnev's rule neo-Stalinist. He did not seek to change Soviet institutions, but rather to keep the system ticking over while reinforcing the USSR's military might.

Brezhnev was good at reconciling differences between spokesmen for various lobbies within the establishment. This made Kremlin politics less conflict ridden. Potential rivals like Podgorny or Shelepin were phased out of office gradually and suffered no harm. The new

---

* In the conspiracy against Khrushchev his role had been less important than that of N. V. Podgorny, A. N. Shelepin, or M. A. Suslov.

leader had an invaluable ally in Alexey Kosygin, a competent technocrat who took charge of routine government affairs, leaving Brezhnev free to assume the role of international statesman – or to go hunting, his preferred leisure activity.

The uneventful Twenty-third Party congress (1966) confirmed Brezhnev's personal authority. Subsequently he carried through a bloodless purge of the party apparatus, but after 1971 the watchword became 'stability of cadres'. This made for complacency, and even for corruption. There was a risk that functionaries who enjoyed job security and ample privileges would treat their office as a sinecure and a source of private gain, while paying lip-service to a socialist ideology in which they no longer really believed.

This degeneration stemmed from a long-term social process. The generation of *apparatchiki* who had won positions of power in the 1930s, in the wake of the revolutionaries purged by Stalin, was confronted with a new wave of officials whose experience dated mainly from the 1950s. (The intervening age cohort, which had grown to maturity in the war years, had been thinned by heavy casualties.) They were less likely to be of proletarian background than to be the sons (rarely, daughters) of serving officials and so better educated, with a technical orientation and experience in a particular branch of the economy: oil extraction, for example. Ambitious youngsters usually made careers through the regional party apparatus, after a brief apprenticeship as engineers or enterprise managers, and their professional skills were less important than their general *savoir-faire* and, above all, personal contacts as part of a cliency network. They were less likely to be boorish 'trouble-shooters' with a smattering of political knowledge (*politgramota*) who moved rapidly from one task to the next, as had often been the case under Stalin (and to a lesser extent under Khrushchev), but rather specialists who spent most of their working life in a single province or type of job. The result was that ambitious, competent men in early middle age faced a 'promotion block' in the form of less well-qualified oldsters with a dogmatic conservative outlook. It was symptomatic that the average age of Central Committee members rose from fifty-six in 1966 to sixty-three in 1982; for the Politburo the figures were fifty-five and sixty-eight. Of Central Committee members elected in 1966, 44 per cent were still there after the Twenty-sixth Party congress fifteen years later.

Characteristically, the Party's 'parliament' met regularly during Brezhnev's rule (its statutes now provided for a five-year interval between these gatherings instead of four as heretofore). Equally characteristically, the delegates were more concerned with stock-taking than with innovating. Policy decisions continued to be taken by the Politburo and Secretariat on the advice of the latter's two dozen or so departments – the real powerhouse in the Soviet polity. Their operations were enshrouded in secrecy. Most departments were concerned with verifying the work of various government ministries and other official bodies. Others, such as 'Agitprop', dealt with ideological matters. Of the Party's central staff 63 per cent are said to have had higher education, although their academic credentials were sometimes rather dubious. Much effort was expended on teaching 'scientific communism' (i.e. Marxism-Leninism) to the public at large. By the mid 1970s the Party had 1.3 million propagandists (out of a total membership of 14–15 million) and forests of timber were felled to print editions of the 'classics' (18 million copies of Lenin's writings alone in 1973!).

Party officials comprised the core of the *nomenklatura*, i.e. those who owed their jobs to selection by a party organ. They numbered three quarters of a million (1970), or roughly 3 million with dependants. The figure for 'specialists' was much larger – 25.2 million in 1977 – and for those who had completed at least seven years' schooling higher still: 95 million in 1970, 161 million in 1986; higher-education graduates numbered 8.3 and 20.1 million respectively. Thus in the late Soviet era the country was acquiring something of the middle class that it had hitherto conspicuously lacked. One in three employed citizens was doing non-manual work. Such a society could no longer be governed effectively by crude dictatorial methods.

Nomenklatura members enjoyed privileges and perquisites of power, strictly graded according to hierarchical status. Only the most senior functionaries qualified for a chauffeur-driven ZIL limousine, with curtains that could be drawn across the windows to protect them from eye contact with the plebs; lesser fry had to be content with a Chaika or Volga saloon. Railway stations or airports had reserved lounges so that dignitaries could avoid mixing with the masses, and on vacation by the Black Sea they stayed in spacious villas far from the bustle of overcrowded beaches. The famed 'Kremlin hospital' was actually a complex of medical establishments run in part by the KGB, which included a state-of-the-art rehabilitation centre on the Volga. Expenditure on health care for VIPs was on the rise at a time when the share of the state budget under this heading was falling (from 6.6 per cent in 1960 to 4.6 per cent in 1985).

Yet all such privileges could be forfeited if a functionary for some reason fell out of the charmed circle – although even in prison he might be treated better than others. Such perquisites were less extensive than those enjoyed by members of élites in capitalist countries. What made them scandalous was their existence in an impoverished society where other values were supposed to prevail. Moreover, the greatest rewards went to administrators who performed a political or security function rather than to economic leaders, who were therefore likelier to satisfy their wants by engaging in corrupt transactions within the 'second economy' (as the black market was known). Doctors, teachers, and other professionals got lower salaries than they deserved, while unproductive nonentities were cosseted and had invisible sources of revenue beyond the wildest dreams of ordinary people.

Political patronage was another aspect of the problem. Cliency networks were a substitute for legitimate opposition and a way of keeping the system functioning. Some leading officials were more active than others in maintaining such 'family circles', and they mattered more in the economic administration, for example, than they did in the armed forces. Protectionism was partly a consequence of the fact that the state was the sole employer. Already Lenin had entrusted high office to his wife and brother-in-law. Stalin made his son Vasiliy, a confirmed alcoholic, a lieutenant-general in the air force (but allowed another offspring, Keto Svanidze, to perish in a German prison camp). Khrushchev's journalist son-in-law, A. I. Ajubey, became editor of *Izvestiya* but lost office along with his patron and was thereafter ostracized.

Brezhnev showed less compunction in such matters than his fore-runners. His son Yuriy became a first deputy minister of foreign trade and a candidate member of the Central Committee. His eccentric daughter Galina married an unscrupulous MVD official, Yu. M. Churbanov, who was promoted rapidly from lieutenant to colonel-general.

This appointment, as well as the placement of Brezhnev cronies in other

461

militia posts, eventually proved the undoing of the Party [General] Secretary himself . . . Widening corruption did much to undermine the credibility of party rule in the 1970s; by the end of the Brezhnev period it was rampant at all levels of the militia apparatus and in all regions of the USSR.*

Churbanov's immediate patron, the interior minister N. A. Shchelokov, ran a special store for members of his clique, who retailed luxury imports on their own account. When his misdeeds came to light in 1984 he committed suicide. Four years later Churbanov received a twelve-year sentence. The Uzbek party boss, Rashidov, had a network comprising several thousand clients, one of whom was a *sovkhoz* chairman, Adylov. He ran his farm like an oriental sheikhdom, with its own harem, police force, and prison in which opponents were tortured and murdered. Yet Rashidov won ten Orders of Lenin. He kept in with Brezhnev by lavish gifts, among them several limousines for his private collection. When he showed them proudly to his mother, she is said to have commented: 'They're fine but what will you do if the Reds come back?'

There was no lack of agencies whose task was to investigate and suppress abuses of power, but they got in each other's way. They were part of the problem, not a solution to it. Under the intelligent, unscrupulous Yuriy V. Andropov (1914–84), who took over the KGB in 1967, the 'organs' regained much of the power they had forfeited under Khrushchev. In 1973 Andropov became a full member of the Politburo, an honour shared with the defence and foreign ministers (D. F. Ustinov, A. A. Gromyko). The trio acted as a kind of 'inner cabinet'. As Brezhnev's faculties faded, Andropov had an opportunity to take over but failed to do so. Evidently he preferred to influence policy making from behind, as it were. Consequently Brezhnev's illness (arteriosclerosis) was concealed and as a lesser evil he was permitted to continue in office although he could not carry out his duties. In 1976 he acquired marshal's rank and was referred to as Leader, the term once used of Stalin. His banal ghost-written memoirs were made obligatory reading and even won him the country's most prestigious literary prize. In 1977, on the revolution's sixtieth anniversary, he became head of state as well as party chief and gave his name to a new

* Shelley, *Policing Soviet Society*, pp. 46–7.

Constitution.* In reality the USSR was marking time or, as M. S. Gorbachev would put it later, 'stagnating'. When Brezhnev died in November 1982 Andropov at last took over, but by then he, too, was in ill health. He had scarcely embarked on a campaign to reimpose discipline, which included a purge of the MVD's ranks, than death claimed him. State funerals were becoming routine in Moscow. His successor was the unimaginative K. U. Chernenko, a former ideological functionary who suffered from severe emphysema and survived only until March 1985, when Gorbachev's selection as General Secretary inaugurated a new era in Soviet history.

DISSENT

A major concern of the KGB was to suppress critics of the Soviet system who became internationally known as 'dissidents'. Although only a few thousand people, most of whom were intellectuals, became actively involved in the Democratic movement, it expressed popular aspirations for greater liberty and posed a major threat to the regime, which for ideological reasons was vehemently opposed to any unauthorized expression of opinion.

The movement's origins can be traced to the cultural ferment of 1956, when writers took the lead in awakening Russia's conscience about Stalin's crimes and their ongoing legacy. It was then that the novelist and poet Boris Pasternak, who had submitted the manuscript of his epic *Dr Zhivago* (see page 487) to two Soviet journals but received no reply, handed a copy to an Italian publisher's agent. The work then appeared abroad, without official Soviet consent, and helped to win for its author a richly deserved Nobel Prize (1958). Critics in the USSR took exception to what they erroneously saw as his disrespectful view of the Bolshevik revolution. A hate campaign was launched in the

---

* This document, like the 1936 'Stalin Constitution', which it replaced, was meaningless in real terms since citizens' rights were granted 'in conformity with the interests of the people and in order to . . . develop the socialist system' (art. 50). Soviet society was defined as one of 'mature socialism' in which the Party was 'the leading and guiding force, the nucleus of its political system . . . and of social organizations' (art. 6). Citizens' duties (e.g. military service) were now spelled out more fully and minor changes made in the country's institutional arrangements.

media; Pasternak was expelled from the writers' union and compelled to renounce the prize. The affair accelerated his death in 1960, after which his simple grave outside Moscow attracted countless pilgrims who valued his artistic truthfulness.

In Russia literature has always been a sensitive medium for the expression of discordant views. During the Khrushchev era public poetry readings became occasions when the cultural élite – not just professional people but members of the *nomenklatura* – gathered to acclaim writers such as Yevgeniy Yevtushenko or Andrey Voznesensky and to manifest peaceably their respect for universal human values. But any effort to form a clandestine organization was soon nipped in the bud. Between 1958 and 1962 police uncovered four such groups in the Baltic republics and a dozen in Ukraine; several activists were shot. For obvious reasons the authorities were particularly alarmed by the cultural efflorescence among the minorities. Correspondingly, one of the dissidents' strengths was their appeal to people of different ethnic background. Many of them shared the experience of gaol or camp, and this helped to break down barriers. They developed a mutually acceptable programme based on the principle of defending elementary human rights which were enshrined in UN documents that the Soviet government had signed but blatantly failed to observe in practice. By invoking them the human rights activists embarrassed the regime and put it in the dock before international opinion.

The first to employ this technique were religious believers (chiefly Protestants) who resisted oppression of their churches in Khrushchev's last years, but it soon caught on elsewhere. In a practice known as self-publishing (*samizdat*) bold spirits typed up manuscripts in multiple copies and distributed them, usually by hand, among friends with the request to do likewise. The chain-letter method was effective but risky and liable to interruption at any moment. It became harder once the KGB registered all typewriters in the country and checked the typefaces used in such documents. Some of these documents reached thousands of individuals, but as the recipients could not reply there was only a limited exchange of ideas. The situation improved when such material reached the West and was rebroadcast by the BBC or other stations, even though such transmissions were regularly jammed. By 1971 about 700 items had reached friends abroad, who got some of them printed (*tamizdat* = 'published over there').

By the late 1960s the trickle of *samizdat* had become a flood. Literary almanacs gave way to essays on topical themes, memoirs, and materials on the cases mounted against fellow-activists. What began as cultural dissent became more political after 1965, when the police arrested two writers, Andrey Sinyavsky and Yuliy Daniel, who had poured scorn on socialist realism and satirized the Terror. After a farcical trial they were sentenced respectively to seven and five years behind bars. Their detention sparked the first of several rallies before Pushkin's statue in Moscow's Mayakavsky Square. The demonstrators (the first since 1927!) were treated leniently – Brezhnev was still feeling his way – but the trial's Stalinist echoes stirred the intelligentsia. A wave of petitions followed, signed by some of the most prestigious people in the land, like the physicist Kapitsa or the ballerina Plisetskaya. In May 1967 Solzhenitsyn wrote an open letter to delegates attending a USW congress protesting at censorship. The union's first task, he declared, should be to defend writers, not help persecute them. Solzhenitsyn had not been invited to the meeting and his letter was officially ignored, but in the corridors it was the focus of attention. For the next five years he fought a stubborn battle to preserve his precious manuscripts, but in February 1974 was deported abroad – although several Politburo members, including Shelepin and Gromyko, would have preferred to keep him in a Soviet gaol. Andropov compelled several other leading critics of the system to emigrate, although there was no legal provision for such a penalty.

The wave of protest peaked in 1968, partly under the influence of the 'Prague spring' (see page 505). On 25 August, when news reached Moscow that Warsaw Pact troops had invaded Czechoslovakia to suppress the movement for 'socialism with a human face', seven dissidents demonstrated in protest. Their courageous action saved Russia's honour at a moment when the Soviet regime faced world-wide condemnation. In April of that year the first issue appeared of a clandestine information bulletin, *The Chronicle of Current Events.* The neutral title was deliberately chosen to reflect the editors' non-partisan stance. The Democratic movement, as it came to be known, had no institutional structure and sought to avoid the ideological partisanship that had disfigured the opposition before 1917.

In addition to 'normal' surveillance methods (informers and electronic 'bugs' concealed in telephones or apartment walls) the KGB resorted to a range of more sinister procedures. Dissidents were put on trial in courtrooms packed with police agents in disguise. The system of forced-labour 'colonies' (as they were now called) survived the dismantling of the Gulag. They contained relatively few political or religious offenders (contemporaries estimated their number at around 10,000) amid a mass of criminal convicts. Most camps were now situated in less northerly latitudes than before: Kazakhstan, for example, or the Mordovian republic east of Moscow. In those with a 'strict regime' conditions remained grim, and there were occasional riots or protests. The most serious abuses occurred in a dozen or so 'special psychiatric hospitals', where political offenders were confined along with genuine mentally ill patients, some of them rapists or murderers, and injected with painful drugs that had no therapeutic value.

Dissidents succeeded in drawing international attention to their plight. The eminent nuclear physicist Andrey Sakharov argued cogently that a superpower which oppressed its law-abiding citizens could not be a reliable partner in détente. This idea made headway in the West and found expression in the 1975 Helsinki accords. A three-man Moscow Human Rights Committee, set up in 1970, secured affiliation with a non-governmental body recognized by the United Nations. This did not save it from repression but at least won the victims sympathetic media coverage abroad. In 1971–2 a police crackdown depleted the Democratic movement's ranks, although there were also some notable recruits, above all among scientists. Sakharov, whom the KGB at first feared to touch because of his international prestige, struggled on manfully and in 1975, to the regime's consternation, won the Nobel Peace Prize. A fellow physicist, Yuriy Orlov, set up a watch group to monitor the Soviet government's observance of its undertakings at Helsinki, which in six years produced 195 reports on human-rights issues as well as numerous appeals on behalf of people arrested. Sakharov's turn came in 1980, when he was seized by police and shipped off to Gor'ky, a closed city where he was kept under house arrest and, when he went on hunger strike, forcibly fed. Despite this persecution his views remained sagely moderate. If Solzhenitsyn was the movement's prophet, Sakharov was its saint.

The KGB's forceful methods seemed to have extinguished the Democrats, but it was a hollow victory. For during these decades civil society, which had been atomized under Stalin, revived – a tender growth to be sure, and more firmly rooted in some of the national republics than in Russia.

THE AWAKENING OF NATIONS

In the 1920s tsarist discriminatory policies had been repudiated and a major effort launched to promote the economic and cultural development of the national minorities, even at some cost to Russian interests. Stalin's revolution from above put a stop to such liberalism. He suspected members of the minority élites who had joined the Party of being 'bourgeois-national deviationists' in disguise and they suffered severely in the Terror. The task of 'socialist construction' gave priority to fulfilment of all-Union plans for economic development and the policy of ironing out national disadvantages was quietly side-tracked. In theory Soviet culture was 'national in form but socialist in content', but this formula was emptied of all real meaning. At its worst it allowed non-Russians to sing Stalin's praises in their own tongue or to reflect approved Soviet themes in their folklore. Similarly, the 1936 Constitution established a pseudo-federal state structure. Minorities were well represented in such decorative institutions as the Supreme Soviet but could not bargain to safeguard their interests because the key decisions were taken by the leadership of the supra-national Party, supposedly in the best interests of the population as a whole.

Paradoxically, though, precisely this fictional set-up ensured the USSR's ultimate dissolution. For, on the one hand, the Communists carved up the Union's territory on largely ethnic lines, granted non-Russians a significant presence in party and state bodies, and allowed the use of local languages. But, on the other hand, they made sure that all these rights were purely formal and dependent on current party policy, which was neither clearly enunciated nor challengeable in the courts or elsewhere. Thus in reality union republics, national regions, and the like had no more genuine autonomy than any Russian province; measures were taken to promote Russian, as the empire's *lingua franca*, at the expense of local languages; all-Union symbols had precedence over national ones; and minorities were prevented from giving expression to their own cultural values wherever their overlords deemed that this posed a threat to 'proletarian internationalism', i.e. to Moscow's authority.

This was the glaring discrepancy that led minority peoples to resent the gulf between promise and reality. Sooner or later they would seek to fill the empty forms with real content and employ them to advance their own interests. Without realizing it, the post-Stalin regimes allowed scope for minority élites to develop a national consciousness that either they had previously lacked or else had lain dormant during the Stalin era.

Its emergence was a gradual process, the pace of which differed from one ethnic group to another, as did the impulses behind it. National-minority activists, especially in emigration, saw it as a natural response to 'russification', but this is to over-simplify a complex phenomenon. What can be stated with assurance is that the Soviet leadership gravely underestimated the nationalist challenge, holding to the complacent delusion that, as Brezhnev put it in 1972, 'in the USSR the national question has been resolved completely and irrevocably'. Material progress was thought to have reconciled the minorities to Soviet rule.

Certainly economic issues had a relatively low ranking on their scale of grievances. The location of industries and the amount of capital invested in them were matters decided by the central planners on the basis of strategic and technical considerations. Local politicians might lobby informally for higher inputs but had no independent control over the flow or use of resources. From minority leaders' perspective, economic development was a mixed blessing: it brought higher incomes but also an influx of non-natives, mainly Russians, who might take the best jobs. Central Asians, for instance, wanted little part in it. The regions that grew fastest were those best equipped by nature and history for the race to modernity. The more advanced included not just European Russia but the Baltic republics as well as (parts of) Ukraine.*

* The latter republic did less well than the Baltic and may have contributed more to all-Union funds than it received. Unfortunately one cannot tell what price goods would have fetched if inter-republican trade had been conducted on market principles. Nor can one 'unscramble' the value to the peoples involved of central defence expenditure on their behalf or of belonging to a rouble zone with a stable currency. Another problem is that Soviet national income data relate to *regions*, not peoples. Measuring regional inequalities involves the use of 'variation coefficients' which may be weighted in countless different ways.

The gap between them and the less advanced regions seems to have widened after the mid 1970s (as in many other countries!) because of growing birth-rate differentials and other natural causes rather than government policy.

In regard to living standards, Central Asian residents did less well than Russians, but those in the Baltic republics better. People in the latter region had higher savings deposits, superior housing, and more supplies in the shops. In Estonia meat consumption was 87 kg. per head (1984) as against 66 kg. in the RSFSR; for cars the figures were respectively 10.4 and 3.9 per 100 households. Even so inter-regional differences were less striking than those between town and country. The key point is that greater material well-being did not necessarily imply greater readiness to accept the *status quo*.

Characteristically, a smaller proportion of Balts and Central Asians was willing to be co-opted into joining the CPSU, although everywhere the rate was upward. In 1982 67.8 per 1,000 Soviet citizens* belonged to the Party; among Russians and Belarusians the figure was higher (77.4, 70.6), for Ukrainians slightly lower (67.2), but it was only 56.1 among Estonians, 45.9 among Lithuanians, 34.8 among Kyrgyz and 26.8 among Tajiks. The champions were the adaptable Georgians, with 82.6 per 1,000 – but in the southern republics careerism often mattered more than ideological commitment, which was why their parties were periodically purged for alleged corruption, a charge that might mask *political* dissidence.

In the non-Slav republics real power lay with Russians (or at any rate Slavs), who also dominated the KGB and the armed forces. During Brezhnev's rule more natives were appointed to leading positions, especially in Ukraine and Belarus. These men often found themselves in an ambiguous situation, for they were obliged loyally to carry out the centre's policies yet were keen to build up their local support by dispensing patronage – and even by tolerating a measure of national sentiment. In practice they enjoyed a degree of elbow room within their 'baronies' so long as they did not contest central policy making.

One of the first to exploit these possibilities was P. Ye. Shelest, whom Khrushchev appointed first secretary of the Ukrainian party

---

* Of all ages: these data need adjustment to account for birth-rate differentials between republics.

organization in 1963. He protected officials in trouble for national leanings and surreptitiously fostered greater use of Ukrainian in teaching and administration. In 1970 he wrote a propaganda tract that went too far in praising Ukrainian historical achievements for Moscow's taste, and this served as a pretext for his dismissal two years later. His successor, V. V. Shcherbitsky, was also a Ukrainian but took a tougher line on cadres policy and much else. Another skilful tactician was A. Sniečkus, who ran the Lithuanian Party from 1940 to 1974 and made the country virtually his own fiefdom – which did not prevent patriots regarding him as a Moscow stooge. In May 1972 R. Kalanta, a Kaunas student, immolated himself to protest measures of russification, in this drastic step emulating earlier acts of self-sacrifice in Kiev (and Prague).

Particularly worrying to Balts was the influx of Russian settlers, drawn to the region by its rapid economic development. (Whether Moscow had a hidden political agenda in this migration is not yet clear.) Estonia and Latvia suffered most from this, along with Moldova and Kazakhstan. In Central Asia generally Slav immigration was offset by a high native birth-rate, and from the mid 1970s the boot was on the other foot: as in Quebec, the natives 'got even through the cradle'. In Kazakhstan there was a heavy Slav population inflow in the 1950s, associated with the 'virgin lands' drive (see page 476), but during the 1970s and 1980s the titular nationality recovered ground, rising from 32.6 per cent in 1970 to 39.7 per cent in 1989, while the Russian share declined by 4.6 per cent. In the Baltic, over the twenty years from 1959 to 1979, the native (i.e. titular republican) share of population fell from 62.0 to 53.7 per cent in Latvia and from 74.6 to 61.5 per cent in Estonia. This was partly the result of a very low indigenous birth-rate, but in the later 1970s there were signs here, too, of recovery. As a Catholic country, Lithuania held up better and there was less danger of natives being 'swamped' by Slavic settlers.

Nowhere was there any immediate risk of assimilation or 'ethnic genocide', as some alarmists suggested. This was for two reasons. First, there was little intermarriage between Slavs and non-Slavs, despite official encouragement of such matches. In the Central Asian republics and Azerbaijan, Islamic custom forbade native women to wed non-Muslims and this rule was strictly adhered to. On reaching the age of sixteen children of mixed parentage had to choose their national allegiance (entered in their passport), but opting for Russian brought few advantages and the decision was almost always taken for family or personal reasons rather than political ones.

Secondly, linguistic assimilation, i.e. the replacement of one's native language by Russian, was a long-drawn-out process likely to take generations. The preliminary step was for non-Russians to become bilingual. To judge by census data, even this occurred at a leisurely pace, except among Jews, Germans, and non-Russian Slavs. In 1970 *more* Baltic respondents reported that they spoke their own tongue 'first' than in 1959, and each group recorded a score of over 95 per cent; in Transcaucasia and Central Asia (but not Kazakhstan) the figures were even higher. Moreover, when linguists tested actual levels of competence in Russian they found them much lower than had been stated to the census-takers, and most of those who were genuinely bilingual were emigrants to the RSFSR.

Officialdom responded to this bad news by stepping up tuition in Russian to children and adults, as well as by limiting the publication of books and journals in local languages – although in general this was extensive. Such measures reinforced minority spokesmen's view that the covert purpose was russification. In 1978 thousands of Georgians demonstrated in favour of a constitutional formula that declared Georgian to be the state language, and Moscow caved in. Kazakhs in Alma-Ata protested against ethnic bias in the admission of university students. Muslim officials dragged their heels in implementing a decree making Russian obligatory for first-graders in schools and replaced Russian loanwords with terms of oriental origin. Patriotic intellectuals kept alive the memory of folk heroes like Hmelnyckyj in Ukraine or episodes in history such as the 1915 Armenian genocide. Discrimination over jobs and access to higher education led many Soviet Jews to conclude that their identity was at risk if they stayed in the USSR, but applications to emigrate ran into bureaucratic obstruction. The United States intervened on their behalf and during the 1970s some 200,000 left the country.

The fate of the Crimean Tatars was still more poignant. In 1956 a secret decree rehabilitated the 'punished nations', but the Tatars continued to be regarded officially as traitors. They were refused permission to return from Uzbekistan to their homeland, which in the meantime had been settled by Slavs. In Mustafa Jemilev they found a charismatic leader who organized petition campaigns and demonstrations. In 1967, after a decree belatedly annulling the treason charge, about 100,000 set off for home but nearly all were turned back, and in 1978 the few allowed to establish themselves in the Crimea were forcibly removed.

The Tatars achieved the highest degree of 'national mobilization' but the most successful in setting up clandestine organizations were the Muslim peoples of the north Caucasus and Central Asia. The Sufi brotherhoods, mystic sects of great antiquity, constituted a 'parallel Islam' with deeper roots in the populace than the official religious establishment. Their adherents were hard for the authorities to detect since their creed allowed them to dissimulate their opinions and even to join the Party or Komsomol. This explains why the press sometimes indignantly reported that apparently loyal Communists were performing religious rites. The brotherhoods' following was put at half a million (1979), but their very nature prevented them from assuming an integrating function.

In Western Ukraine and Lithuania national and religious opposition merged to form an equally potent brew. In 1971 a Lithuanian Catholic petition secured over 17,000 signatories. A *samizdat* journal, patterned on that of the mainstream dissidents, published sixty-seven issues between 1972 and 1985, and included a fair amount of secular material. Several groups came into being in the Baltic which declared national independence as their ultimate objective, unrealistic as this seemed at the time. As in the nineteenth-century national revival, song festivals were popular and there were rallies at which zealots displayed patriotic symbols. Throughout the western republics the example of upheavals in Eastern Europe proved infectious: Hungary in 1956, Czechoslovakia in 1968, Poland in 1980–81. The immediate impact of such manifestations of discontent was slight, but even some party functionaries shared their compatriots' sentiments, and as soon as the centre showed irresolution the emotions held at bay for so long would burst forth with unexpected vehemence.

National feeling was not confined to the minorities. Russian intellectuals, too, became alarmed at the slowdown in demographic growth, the high incidence of alcoholism, poor housing, and other social ills prevalent in the RSFSR. The ethnic Russian population grew by 13.1 per cent between 1959 and 1970 but by only 6.5 per cent over the next intercensal period; in 1979–89 it fell to 5.7 per cent. Meanwhile Tajiks, for instance, could show figures of 52.9, 35.7, and 45.5 per cent. Across the USSR life expectancy fell during the 1970s, and Russians died at an earlier age than Balts or Armenians. Alcohol killed one third more people in the RSFSR than in the Union as a whole (19.3 as against 14.4 per 100,000 population in 1985), whereas Muslims stayed sober. Heavy drinking was a drain on the economy and led to absenteeism, crime, and domestic violence. One in two urban marriages in the RSFSR ended in divorce (1978) and the real rate of family breakdown was higher still, since many couples chose just to separate, so avoiding expensive legal formalities. The number of illegitimate children was on the rise and Russia had one of the world's highest abortion rates. On top of all this were the adverse effects of environmental pollution.

These grievances could not be discussed straightforwardly in the media, and the Russian national movement mainly took a literary, religious, and aesthetic form (see Chapter 22). There was, however, a political lunatic fringe whose spokesmen adopted a racist and fascist ideology. A manifesto of 1970 contended that Communist international-ism threatened the Russians' 'biological degeneration'. 'For us the nation is primary and all else derivative.' The anonymous authors (M. F. Antonov et al.) recommended expulsion of the Jews from jobs in science and culture and restoration of a 'united indivisible Russia'. Russian intellectuals were quick to dissociate themselves from such extremism, but some people in the ruling apparatus (especially KGB officials) played along with it. Presumably they viewed it as a means of embarrassing the Democrats. But at a deeper level this cooperation marked the début of an unholy alliance between Communists and right-wing Russian nationalists that would flower after the USSR collapsed in 1991.

Could timely concessions to the minorities, and more freedom gener-ally, have averted disaster? Theoretically yes, but in practice no, for the Soviet imperial structure, based on the power monopoly of a single supra-national party, did not permit genuine bargaining between interest groups. Tito's federal Yugoslavia displayed far greater flexi-bility towards its constituent nations, but that country broke up even more violently than did the USSR.

CHAPTER 22

The Paradoxes of 'Mature Socialism'

Why did the USSR collapse? One prime reason was the inability of the socialist command economy to satisfy consumer needs and to sustain growth rates comparable with those in other developing countries. The Soviets could send human beings into space but could not ensure that their people were adequately housed, clothed, and fed. In part this was owing to the demands of national defence in a bipolar world of nuclear-tipped intercontinental ballistic missiles. But basically an unbalanced allocation of resources was inherent in the system, inherited from Stalin, of centralized bureaucratic management of the economy. Prices were set administratively, without regard for actual production costs or value to purchasers, and market relationships were severely restricted. It is true that when the war-time direction of labour was abandoned in 1956, its supply was indeed largely determined by supply and demand; people were also allowed to build their own homes on a cooperative basis and so-called 'commission stores' did a lively trade in second-hand domestic items. But these were no more than marginal concessions to the frailties of human nature, as was the tolerance extended in practice to black-market operations.

Otherwise all economic activity was conducted under the aegis of state agencies whose actions were supposed to conform to the requirements of the national Plan. Officials set targets for the output of various goods and sought to ensure that these were met by verifying mountains of indices in regard to quantity, quality, productivity, and so forth, while enterprise managers expended an equal amount of energy in trying to evade these controls and to cover up the myriad tricks they engaged in to give an impression of compliance. Statistics were freely manipulated to register successes that as often as not existed only on paper. The centre, in turn threatening and cajoling, tried to make economic actors behave in a rational, responsible manner, but the system made for inefficiency and waste. Ordinary people could not ignore the flood of instructions from above, and even made a show of obeying them enthusiastically, while keeping an eye open for a secure niche that would enable them to get by with minimal effort. This was not too difficult since socialism guaranteed everyone a job. Incomes might be low, goods scarce, and social services deficient, but life was tolerable for most people. At any rate few dreamed of exchanging it for the risks of capitalism, even if tales of abundance in the West excited general envy.

THE LAGGING VILLAGE

Nowhere were the vices of the command economy more evident than in the agricultural sector, since farming is by nature not an activity that lends itself to centralized direction. Khrushchev was the first (and last) Russian ruler to place the peasant at the centre of his government's attention. But he contemplated no substantive change in the collectivized system that Stalin had built. His approach was essentially bureaucratic, which is why his constant tinkering produced poor results. Certainly, agricultural output rose during his tenure of power: cereals from 98.8 in 1953–6 to 132.1 in 1961–4, meat from 6.3 to 9.1 (million tons, annual averages). But how much did this owe to government action? Some improvement on the abysmal situation in 1952 was bound to occur, and the size of the annual grain harvest remained subject to sharp fluctuations.

In September 1953 the prices paid by the state for deliveries of crops and livestock were raised significantly and compulsory quotas reduced, as were taxes, while farm debts were written off. By 1959 producers were getting seven times more for grain than in 1952. Quotas were now flexible, negotiated between farm managements and local officials, who, however, held the whip hand. It was far more profitable to produce grain than cattle or dairy products. Farms which concentrated on the latter were almost certain to run into debt. In a departure from earlier policy, peasants were encouraged to keep cattle on their allotments, but this fostered proprietorial tendencies that made the authorities nervous. They restricted the supply of feeding stuffs and put other obstacles in the way of the private sector. Even so, in 1958–65 this accounted for around 45 per cent of the meat and milk produced, and an even higher proportion of potatoes and eggs, although it comprised a mere 3 per cent of the sown area.

Another beneficial venture was to bring under cultivation vast expanses of steppe in northern Kazakhstan and western Siberia. These so-called 'virgin and idle lands' had previously been used by native Kazakhs and others for grazing cattle, so that the term was a misnomer. In fact the scheme continued a colonization process begun under the tsars. The guiding idea was that wheat grown here on giant *sovkhozy* would feed the burgeoning urban population while smaller farms with poorer land in European Russia would concentrate on fodder grains. This was in itself not unsound, but Khrushchev underestimated the costs, which were higher in the east, as well as climatic factors. The lack of rainfall and wind erosion made the harvest in these regions particularly uncertain. Much of the grain procured was infested with weeds, and after bumper crops in 1956 and 1960 output levelled off. Extending the sown area was a short-term expedient, a less problematic alternative to intensifying production in traditional farming areas, where yields were higher, which would have necessitated ideologically unacceptable concessions to peasant self-interest.

The First Secretary scorned scientific advice where it contradicted his own inclinations, for instance over leaving land fallow or under grass. In this he followed Lysenko. Like Stalin, he believed that Communists could defy nature and perform economic miracles. The grasslands were to be ploughed up and planted with maize (corn), a crop which was better than hay. If it did not grow as well as in Iowa (where Khrushchev was impressed by a model farm he visited), then it should be harvested when half-ripe. Not everyone was convinced, but he waged a mighty campaign to plant maize everywhere. Yields were disappointing and after his fall the drive was abandoned. It was much the same story with mineral fertilizer. After successive offensives, each launched with a propaganda fanfare, output rose from 7 million tons in 1953 to 31 million in 1965. Twenty years later it was 112 million tons, so that here at least the effort was sustained, but the fertilizer was rich in noxious chemicals. Farmers first let supplies accumulate in untended heaps in the open, where it spoiled, and then spread it around far too liberally.

They also did not take proper care of their mechanical equipment. This problem, too, owed a lot to politically inspired mismanagement.

Khrushchev at first expanded the powers of the machine-tractor stations (MTS), but in 1958 suddenly reversed course and abolished these agencies, which were prone to meddle in the affairs of the farms they supervised. They were replaced by *repair* stations, which were intended merely to help farms maintain the tractors and combine-harvesters that were sold off to them – all at once, at a high price that not only bankrupted poorer farms but also had to help pay the repairmen's considerable salaries. Like many of Khrushchev's measures, the reform had not been thought through but was imposed by *diktat*. One adminis-trative reorganization followed hard on the heels of the last. Farm managements were 'strengthened' by an infusion of party members, when what they needed were well-trained agronomists and fewer unproductive personnel. Devolution of authority to the provinces was a step in the right direction, but it benefited local officialdom rather than farm managers, let alone their employees. Officials frowned on the idea of letting them work in small (family) teams, known as 'links', on the principle of the traditional *artel'*, as this would have endangered their own control and made them redundant.

Under Brezhnev the Party's approach to agriculture was less haphaz-ard and more concerned with achieving long-term results. Investment was boosted massively and by 1970 was 58 per cent greater than it had been five years earlier. Subsequently it stabilized at around 26 per cent of total investment (higher if one includes industries servicing rural needs), more than double the proportion under Stalin. This amounted to paying a lavish subsidy which the state could ill afford. To keep urban consumers quiet, in the mid 1970s beef was sold in the shops at 2 roubles a kilo, although it cost farmers 3.50 roubles to produce. Despite these hand-outs most farms again fell into debt because their revenues were so unpredictable and they were not allowed to choose the type of activity that would maximize their profits. Livestock raising continued to be uneconomic whereas technical crops (e.g. cotton) sold well, with cereals in the middle range. The payment of bonuses to those farms which delivered more than their quotas accentuated the gulf between them and the laggards less well endowed by nature (remote location, poorer land). The farms handicapped in this way fell victim to a vicious cycle: they could not attract skilled personnel and their young people, seeing misery all around them, fled in vast numbers.

Matters were made worse by the policy of amalgamating collectives into larger units and recategorizing them as state farms which enjoyed privileged status. By 1985 the number of *kolkhozy* had fallen to 26,200, as against 36,300 twenty years earlier, while *sovkhozy* had doubled to 22,700. The latter now held more land than the former, most of it sown to grain, whereas the collectives still had more (unprofitable) cattle. By Western standards these beasts were thin, gave relatively little milk (2,200 kg. per annum in the early 1980s), and took a lot of looking after. Privately owned cows were in even worse shape, because farm managements allocated them poor-quality fodder: sometimes even hay ran short. When there was no fodder left, peasants would slaughter their animals *en masse*.

Much precious food went to waste because of inadequate storage and transport facilities. Rural roads were left in a primitive state and trucks had a brief life. Official statistics, which took little account of rural realities, registered higher output in most branches – meat was said to have risen from 11.6 million tons in 1966–70 to 16.2 million in 1981–5 (annual averages) – but not cereals, which in the last pre-Gorbachev quinquennium probably stood at the same level as in the early 1970s. Performance was so bad that no figures were released. In years of poor harvest much grain had to be imported from the Americas to make good the deficiency. For non-cereal items Soviet consumers still depended heavily on the peasants' household plots, which in 1979 produced over a quarter of the country's milk, 29 per cent of the meat, and 30 per cent of the eggs. Rural dwellers' food requirements were met almost wholly from this source, for there was little to buy in the village shop (assuming there was one) except the occasional tin of fish.

Some small Russian rural communities now faced the threat of being declared 'non-viable': the houses left to rot away and their residents compulsorily moved to an ugly urban-type settlement. Nationally minded intellectuals protested at the scheme as did the people directly concerned. It was eventually dropped for lack of money, but many villages did indeed disappear from the map as they were deserted by their inhabitants. This was a flight from poverty and general neglect – from boredom, as 40 per cent of respondents told pollsters in Smolensk province (1970). Some 16 million rural residents migrated between 1959 and 1970. Thereafter the average annual loss rate (which fluctuated markedly) was estimated at 630,000, and by 1985 the rural share of the total population had shrunk to 34.4 per cent, as against 46.7 per cent twenty years earlier. The efflux to the towns was a Slavic (and Baltic) phenomenon; there was no comparable movement in Central Asia, for example. As a result many rural communities in European Russia were made up of women and the elderly. Girls who did not leave the countryside when in their teens but married local lads were bound for life to their husband's household, as in the old days, as well as to his farm. They found themselves doing much of the agricultural labour – even women of pensionable age put in eighty-three days a year (1971) – but with little chance to rise much above the level of 'livestock brigadier': less than 2 per cent of collective-farm chairmen were women. With domestic duties on top of those they performed in the fields, their lot was even harder than that of urban women.

In some respects, to be sure, matters improved. From 1965–6 peasants were entitled to a pension. It was smaller than that of ex-workers, since they were expected to feed themselves from their plots. From 1976 collective farmers qualified for internal passports, although years passed before all got them. This emancipation from state controls was primarily of symbolic or psychological importance. It did not stop townspeople looking down on their country cousins as backward, an attitude fostered by continuing official emphasis on the supposed virtues of the proletariat; however, there was also a reverse tendency in that nationally minded intellectuals 'rediscovered' the peasant and spent their holidays in rural surroundings. Statistics showed that rural incomes were catching up on those in the towns: the gap was put at one third in 1970, 19 per cent in 1985. Nevertheless it remained significant in cultural terms. As many visitors noted, the peasants – largely female – in their kerchiefs who sold their wares at stalls in urban markets actually *looked* different from their customers. The arrival of television in country cottages did little to bridge the divide, and may have accentuated it by presenting an idealized picture of the outside world.

THE INDUSTRIAL ECONOMY

Unskilled immigrants to the towns faced several years' hardship; they lived in crowded and primitive dormitories before they could hope to acquire the skills, wage rates, and lifestyle of regular workers, who now enjoyed the rudiments of a welfare state. In 1956 a reform of the wage structure made life easier for the more highly skilled while slimming down differentials and introducing a minimum wage. Old-age pensioners and invalids also got a better deal, although they still belonged to the impoverished urban 'under-class', which included single-parent families and those with many dependants. The existence of this social group went unrecognized officially. The regime did not regard social security benefits as an individual entitlement (as was then the case in the West). Social policy in this regard was also not a matter of public discussion. The policy makers' priority was to maintain full employment, on the assumption that the resulting labour force would have the capacity to fulfil all targets set by the Plan. This was a wasteful approach to human resources that became ever less adequate as the supply of hands from over-populated rural regions dried up. The low level of labour productivity in the USSR was a major obstacle to sustained industrial growth, yet efforts to give workers incentives to perform more efficiently risked undermining the principles of state socialism; on the other hand, it was clearly impossible to resort to Stalinist methods, with direction of labour and a vast force of expendable convicts. The conundrum was insoluble.

Under Khrushchev workers' incomes grew by over 3 per cent per annum in real terms (1960–65), but in the 1970s the rate of increase tailed off. Even so it was in these 'good years' that working-class families, especially if they had two or more breadwinners, managed to acquire a variety of consumer goods taken for granted in the modern industrialized world: refrigerators and washing machines, TV sets and telephones, clocks and cameras – rarely cars, however, since public transport in large cities was remarkably cheap, thanks to lavish subsidies. The quality of these domestic articles was often sub-standard and repairing them might well necessitate calling on the services of someone operating *nalevo* ('on the left', i.e. illegally). There were also waiting lists for the most desirable items, such as tape recorders, which came into fashion in the 1980s, although there were ways of jumping the queue. Urban women had to line up for hours to obtain even basic food items, the supply of which remained uncertain. Those unable to find what they wanted put their money into savings banks, whose deposits rose to astronomic levels: from 19 milliard roubles in 1965 to 221 milliard twenty years later. About 100 milliard more may have been 'kept under the mattress' by people engaged in the second economy, i.e. the semi-licit or illicit markets.

Rising prosperity did not mean that wage earners were satisfied. They might not question the principles of the system (whose workings were imperfectly understood), but few believed official claims that the Party and state had the people's interests constantly at heart. Most realized that material conditions were superior in the West. Discontent was registered by 'go-slows' in the workplace, absenteeism – often the result of heavy drinking – and a tendency to change jobs with disconcerting frequency. Labour mobility ran at about 30 per cent per annum and was particularly prevalent in small plants and low-priority industries such as food processing. If workers who left also changed their occupations, the money spent on training them was largely wasted.

On occasion grievances led to industrial action. The first major such incident occurred in 1959 in the virgin lands. Three years later a strike over wage cuts and food-price rises at Novocherkassk in the Don valley, which the authorities mishandled, led to a confrontation with troops in which twenty-four were killed and thirty-nine wounded; subsequently 114 of the protesters were convicted in secret trials of banditry and other offences. But such violence was rare, since party or trade-union officials normally nipped disaffection in the bud.

In 1978 an unemployed worker tried to set up a 'free trade union' in Moscow. He and his comrades were arrested and sent to a special psychiatric hospital, but shortly afterwards a more representative body appeared, the Free Inter-professional Workers' Association. It had a following of about 300, half of whom were workers. The degree of support was scarcely overwhelming. A counterpart to Polish 'Solidarity' was impossible in the USSR, not just because of police controls but also because Soviet wage earners, however much they grumbled over norm setting, piece-rates, and the like, saw themselves as beneficiaries of a system in which, as the saying went, 'You pretend to pay us and we pretend to work.' They had neither enough incentive to back it energetically nor enough to subvert it.

The authorities recognized that many enterprises were overstaffed yet were loath to adopt the capitalist solution, unemployment. In 1967 a campaign was launched to persuade managers to shed surplus labour. Named after Shchekino, the site of a chemical combine near Tula, the experiment was initially a success: within three years over 1,000 jobs had been cut with a 114 per cent gain in labour productivity. The scheme was emulated elsewhere and by 1983 nearly a million jobs had been saved. But those dismissed had to be found other work. Ideological and institutional constraints prevented the emergence of a true labour market.

Likewise efforts to improve the system of planning and management ran into the sand. Under Khrushchev the watchword was devolution – but the 105 regional economic councils set up in 1957 were reduced to 47 six years later as the centralizing trend reasserted itself. After Khrushchev's fall the new bodies were abolished and power once again concentrated in Gosplan and the top-heavy industrial ministries – among them one for 'Medium Machine-Building', a codeword for atomic weapon production. Ustinov, the defence minister, occupied a key position in the economic bureaucracy, but it was Kosygin who in 1965 gave his name (unofficially) to the next effort at administrative reform. This reduced the number of indicators that enterprises had to meet and shifted their emphasis from quantitative targets to the amount of goods sold or profit made. Managers and workers got bonuses for achievement in this respect. Enterprises were encouraged to forge horizontal links as an antidote to the existing parallel bureaucratic 'empires', each with its vertical line of control. This reform produced giant state firms called (rather misleadingly) 'corporations'. Their managers were urged to apply up-to-date Western techniques, including the use of computers. They made some progress in this respect, but Soviet technology in data processing lagged badly – partly because Stalin had banned cybernetics as a bourgeois pseudo-science. In the 1950s (mathematical) economics recovered and the best brains applied their talents to the task of creating an optimal model national Plan. The exercise was interesting theoretically but took too little account of concrete realities. On the factory floor the scientific boffins' fancy notions were unwelcome. All too often foremen discarded their computer printouts and got on with the job in traditional fashion. But the basic reason for the Kosygin reform's failure was not cussedness or ignorance on the part of those lower down the ladder, but its inconsistency: unless one allowed prices to find their own level, how could one determine an enterprise's rate of profit – or even have meaningful statistics?

If one goes by the (error-prone) official data, the picture is one of a flourishing, expanding economy. Over the twenty-year span 1965–85 the output of the staple producers' goods continued to grow: iron ore from 153 to 248 million tons, steel from 91 to 155 million tons. The fuel balance shifted away from coal (up 26 per cent) and even oil (up 2½ times) to hydroelectric power (up 3 times)* and natural gas (up 5 times). A network of pipelines extended across the USSR and into Central Europe. Over six times more synthetic resins and plastics were produced in 1985 (5 million tons) than twenty years earlier. Nearly 6 million refrigerators and over 13 million TV sets left the factory gates, roughly three and a half times more than in 1965; moreover, 30 per cent of new TV sets were in colour.

One conspicuous absentee from the list is housing space, which rose by only 15.7 per cent, to 113 million square metres. In urban areas this worked out at around 9 square metres of 'living space'† per capita – the norm set in the 1920s. The advance in this sector had been swifter during the Khrushchev era, when row upon row of apartment blocks, built using prefabricated sections, had appeared in and around Soviet cities. The authorities also facilitated cooperative and private building projects, but in the 1960s the former, and in the 1970s also the latter (mainly financed by enterprises), came to be seen as ideologically suspect, which led to a dip in the overall growth rate; not until 1983 was the 1960 figure significantly exceeded. In the new apartment blocks quality was not the first consideration. Tenants frequently complained of shoddy workmanship, but most young couples, compelled to spend the first years of married life with their parents in cramped conditions, were glad to have a roof over their heads.

As in other industrial countries, family life increasingly came under strain, not least because of the housing shortage. By the late 1970s one in two urban marriages in the RSFSR ended in divorce. Unmarried couples, single parents, illegitimate children, abortion (either in official clinics or privately, in even less hygienic conditions): these were common features of the urban scene. As we have seen in Chapter 21, in the Slavic republics the birth-rate was falling. In 1981 the authorities,

* Including some electricity derived from coal and nuclear power; by 1985 the latter accounted for 10.8 per cent of total power supply.
† Excluding 'communal space', such as kitchens and corridors.

after years of complacency in this regard, adopted a natalist policy, increasing maternity leave for working mothers and the allowances paid on the birth of the first two children. These measures helped to check the decline for a time, but their impact was necessarily limited so long as the public health sector was so gravely neglected. In the 1970s* infant mortality rose and life expectancy fell – by two years on the average; for men the drop was greater than for women, partly because they drank more. Medicines were often hard to come by and many hospitals lacked even elementary facilities such as running hot water. Sometimes payment of a bribe was required to gain admission. Chronic diseases – diphtheria, scarlet fever, hepatitis, cancer – were on the increase, their spread hastened by industrial pollution.

Not until the USSR collapsed did the environmental cost of frenetic industrialization become apparent. Its apostles had seen nature as a foe to be conquered. Pressure to achieve rapid results led to neglect of the laws on environmental protection or workplace safety, which looked good on paper but were poorly enforced and so could be circumvented by ambitious local officials or enterprise managers. Nevertheless an informal 'Green' lobby emerged in the 1960s. It originated in an attempt to conserve Lake Baikal, the Earth's largest natural reservoir of fresh water. This unparalleled resource was threatened by a scheme, backed by the military, to build two pulp and paper mills on its shore. The campaign had only limited success but did at least establish the conservationists' credibility.

Dozens of towns across the land had to endure severe atmospheric pollution from motor traffic and industrial sources before filters were affixed to factory chimneys emitting effluents. Even so in the late 1980s sixty-eight Soviet cities were officially declared unhealthy to live in. Oil wells in the Caspian, nickel production at Noril'sk in the Arctic, mercury poisoning in Bashkiria (Bashkortostan): the list of danger spots was endless. Particularly tragic was the fate of the land-locked Aral Sea, the size of which shrank by 40 per cent over the thirty years 1960–90 as a result of the diversion of river water into canals to irrigate the surrounding salty desert – which won out in the end, despite belated

---

* Perhaps earlier: statistics here are unreliable since they exclude deaths within the first week after birth.

efforts to reduce the rate of evaporation. Cancer of the oesophagus here was fifteen times the all-Union average.

The armed forces were among the worst offenders. From 1960 onward the Soviet navy regularly sank unserviceable reactors from atomic-powered vessels, and even nuclear submarines, in Arctic waters. In the Kazakh steppe, which for years was used as a test site, deposits of radioactive waste rendered large areas unfit for agriculture. In 1957 a serious nuclear accident took place at a closed city in the Urals and over a 1,000-kilometre radius the population had to be secretly evacuated. In 1979 in another accident in the same region at least forty-two people died, this one being connected with the manufacture of biological weapons. The use of nuclear energy for civilian purposes became important in the 1970s. Dozens of plants were built using a design that had serious flaws. Their constructors and operators were under great pressure to bring them on stream as swiftly as possible. This led to neglect of time-consuming safety measures. One result was the world's first peace-time nuclear catastrophe, at Chernobyl (Ukraine) on 26 April 1986. But already before Gorbachev's accession to power in March 1985 it was plain that the country was in what he would call a 'pre-crisis state'. The paradox was that the gravity of the situation was not appreciated either by ordinary citizens or by those in positions of responsibility – or even by intellectuals critical of the regime.

THE INTELLIGENTSIA IN FERMONT

In 1959 Khrushchev launched a major offensive against organized religion, ostensibly on the grounds that the fragile compromise established by Stalin with the Orthodox Church during the war had been a deviation from Leninism. The regime stepped up atheist propaganda, fostered secular rituals, arrested clergy on fabricated charges, and closed churches or even razed them to the ground. Over the next seven years the number of Orthodox priests and registered parishes was reduced by nearly half. A law of 1962 in effect made it a crime to give young people religious instruction, even in private homes.

The wave of repression affected Jews and Muslims as well as members of other Christian confessions. In 1960 leaders of the Evangelical community,* which was strong in the Baltic, were forced to order clergy to restrict baptisms and missionary work. This evoked protests by churchmen and lay activists, who organized effective resistance and brought about a schism. The KGB-controlled agencies which supervised religious affairs were embarrassed and made concessions to . heal the schism while continuing to repress the 'extremists'. Baptist leaders were arrested, as were a number of laywomen who tried to bring up their children in the faith. These cases attracted sympathy outside church circles and helped to foster the human rights movement.

In Catholic regions opposition by religious believers, as we have seen, merged into the drive to safeguard national minorities' identity. The situation of the Orthodox was more complicated, since its traditions and hierarchical structure laid it open to state control. In 1961 an episcopal council, or Synod, made priests employees of their parish councils in a bid to keep them in line. KGB agents present at the meeting forced the measure, which was uncanonical, through. Prominent dignitaries, including the Patriarch, would tell foreign visitors that believers enjoyed religious liberty although they knew the contrary to be the case. This was taking collaboration too far and compromising the Church morally, as dissident priests and laymen pointed out. A. Levitin, a fervent Christian teacher who took a lowly job as church watchman, wrote tracts exposing the errant hierarchs. So, more famously, did Solzhenitsyn in his *Lenten Letter* to Patriarch Pimen (1972), in which he called on him to sacrifice himself like the martyrs of yore. Naturally the Patriarch ignored the appeal, but religious ideas became an important current in the Russian national movement.

The Orthodox revival, like dissent generally, began with writers who looked for inspiration to the religious philosophers of the turn of the century, a tradition that, although arbitrarily curtailed by the revolution, had survived among *émigrés* in the West. For only by rediscovering one's spiritual roots could one hope to make sense of the successive tragedies that the intelligentsia and people had lived through during the twentieth century. Their fate called to mind Dante's circles of Hell – and Christ's Passion.

Anna Akhmatova (1889–1966), last of the Acmeist poets, had been

---

* In 1944 the Protestant churches were forcibly amalgamated under the title 'Evangelical Christians and Baptists'.

banned from publishing her verse in the 1920s; she survived by becoming an expert on Pushkin, whose fate in some ways resembled her own. In *Requiem*, begun during the purges and completed in 1961, she acted as 'remembrancer' for the generation that had perished in the 'satanic years' of Stalinism. 'It is a polyphonic memorial to the victims of violence, written for the women who, like the poet herself, waited for months outside prison gates for news of their sons' (I. Schäfer). All of human history served Akhmatova as a source of recondite learned allusions, so enabling her to preserve a link to the universal culture from which Russian writers had been so cruelly excluded. After her public denunciation in 1946 she lived in semi-seclusion, but enjoyed the respectful adulation of perceptive lovers of literature at home and abroad.

One of her young protégés was Joseph Brodsky (1940–96), whose 'Christmas Poem' (1965) ended with a tribute to God's gift to man of the miracle of life. At that time he was serving a sentence of forced labour after a mock trial, but in response to international pressure was released before his term expired. The victory of life over death, the hope of divine redemption for mankind, is the principal motif in Pasternak's *Dr Zhivago* – Yuriy Zhivago's very name means life – and on a symbolic plane its 'hero' is a martyr to the aesthetic ideals that the revolution threatens to extinguish. The work closes with a cycle of sacred poems, ostensibly by Zhivago, in one of which Christ speaks from the garden of Gethsemane:

> And on the third day I shall rise again.
> Like rafts down a river, like a convoy of barges,
> The centuries will float to me out of the darkness
> And I shall judge them.

In Solzhenitsyn's tale 'Matryona's House' (1963) the central character is a simple peasant woman who dies helping a man who seeks to exploit her natural goodness. Her neighbours had failed to see that 'she was that Righteous One without whom, as the proverb says, no village can stand . . . And no city. Nor our whole land.' The 'proverb' was actually a reference to the Book of Genesis, excised in self-censorship, and the story can be read as an indictment of godless materialism. The theme recurs in his major works (*Cancer Ward*, *First Circle*, *The Red Wheel*), which could not be published in the USSR until many years later but in 1970 won him the Nobel Prize. Like Tolstoy, Solzhenitsyn sees a continuous struggle between good and evil being fought out within each individual's soul. It is not a matter of states or systems, human artefacts which he holds in slight esteem. His moralistic outlook led to misinterpretation of his views in the West, where he had to live for twenty years after his expulsion in 1974.

His ideas are not particularly original and owe much to the Slavophils as mediated through *Vyekhi* (1909): modern industrial civilization, with its hectic pursuit of individualism, is doomed without a regeneration of spiritual values which Russia, purged of the Communist legacy, would be well placed to provide. Her Church and people, so his reasoning goes, have preserved something of the old collegial and community spirit (*sobornost'*), which can serve as a moral centre in reconstructing the country on Christian humanist principles. Just how this beneficent process is to be brought about Solzhenitsyn (again like his nineteenth-century forerunners) does not explain – precisely because he is not a 'political man'; yet he is neither an authoritarian nor an imperialist, as detractors have alleged. His brand of Russian cultural nationalism, together with his exemplary civic courage and vast literary output, were influential in shaping the 'village prose' movement, which eventually became a serious political force.

This took shape in the 1960s, although its origins go back at least to 1952, when V. V. Ovechkin wrote *Sketches of Rural Daily Life* in a style still compatible with the 'socialist realist' canon. The early short-story writers and novelists (F. Abramov, Ye. Dorosh, V. Belov) who exposed bureaucratic wrongdoing risked official displeasure by displaying excessive empathy with the victims. One after another, taboos were broken – by mentioning Old Believers in north Russia, for instance, or describing ecological damage. Darya, the heroine in the Siberian writer Valentin Rasputin's tale 'Farewell to Matyora' (1976), is rather like Solzhenitsyn's Matryona. She defends her home, a metaphor for rural values in general, from destruction by hard-faced men from the big city, including her own son, who are intent on building a hydroelectric plant.

The 'Russophile' writers did not directly challenge official orthodoxy: national (and religious) motifs were expressed in a subdued manner, but the allusive 'Aesopian language' was intelligible to readers. They were implicitly subversive, although there were also points of contact with the ruling ideology. Under Brezhnev the system of literary controls, while outwardly still rigid, became more flexible. The boundaries of 'socialist realism', which had always been ill-defined, were quietly extended to accommodate authors who wrote in various moods, exploring the depths of human psychology, man's relationship to nature, or conflict between parents and children.

Particularly alarming to the more conservative members of the USW establishment was the emergence of writers who appealed directly to young people: Yevtushenko, for instance. Although suspect to some dissidents, who thought him too ready to compromise with the cultural controllers, he could nevertheless be a thorn in the side of officialdom. At poetry readings he made a point of mentioning exotic lands that his youthful audience would have loved to visit. Also deservedly popular were balladeers like Bulat Okudzhava, Alexander Galich (Ginzburg), and Vladimir Vysotsky, who sang emotional, sometimes ironical, lyrics that punctured official pieties, using the spicy vernacular of the underworld. Already in the 1960s the USSR faced a pale reflection of the 'alienated youth syndrome' that was shaking certainties in the West, and the authorities had to respond to it flexibly. One technique was to permit publication of science fiction and spy novels that would have been scorned in an earlier age. But Vladimir Voinovich's naughtily satirical novel *The Life and Strange Adventures of the Soldier Private Chonkin* could only appear abroad.*

Party policy towards the visual arts underwent a similar silent evolution. Its beginning was unpromising: in December 1962 Khrushchev's visit to an exhibition of abstract paintings in Moscow's Manège gallery turned all signals from green to red. 'Bourgeois decadence' had no place in a socialist society. In 1974 his successors acted with equal firmness: when non-representational artists held a private showing of their works in a park in the capital, the KGB had the offending canvases bulldozed into the ground. Yet several members of the establishment were at this time beginning to collect modernistic works of art and even to commission their portraits from controversial painters such as Ilya Glazunov, whose *Mystery of the Twentieth Century* and

---

* The same was true of books about the Terror and Gulag by Yevgeniya Ginzburg (*Into the Whirlwind*), Georgiy Vladimov (*Faithful Ruslan*), or Varlam Shalamov (*Kolyma Tales*).

Return of the Prodigal Son drew upon a repertoire of Christian and patriotic motifs. Artists who looked to the West for inspiration rather than to the Russian past had a harder time, to be sure, but the two trends were not necessarily antagonistic. A veritable cult grew up around Andrey Rublev, the medieval icon and fresco painter, and in the former monastery where he lay buried a museum of religious art appeared which specialized in restoration work.

Rublev's achievement was celebrated in a brilliant film by the director Andrey Tarkovsky, who, however, had to put up with a lot of obstruction from the official body concerned with cinematic affairs, Goskino. In 1983 he was denied permission to prolong his stay in Italy, where his work was greatly respected, in order to complete *Nostalgia* – his last film, for he died of cancer shortly afterwards. The authorities even stripped him of his citizenship, a penalty imposed (contrary to the law) on many other cultural figures who emigrated in these years. Tarkovsky's work had a mystical streak, most evident in *The Stalker* (1980), which featured a terrifying journey through a landscape rendered desolate by a strange explosion.

Architects, by contrast, had greater scope. They were kept fully employed on housing projects for the masses as well as public buildings, bridges, and war memorials. Monumental triumphalism was now at a discount since the authorities had become more cost-conscious. Khrushchev explicitly condemned Stalinist excesses in this domain. The national revival led to greater appreciation of the value of ancient buildings, including churches, and in 1965 an association was created to help conserve them; by 1982 it claimed 15 million members. Although, like any other public body, ultimately under party control, it owed its existence to civic initiative and – like the Greens – was proof of the educated public's growing maturity. Aesthetic considerations concerned people no less than did the belated realization that the country's heritage had been severely damaged by a revolutionary approach to industrial development.

An important role in this intellectual shift was played by distinguished scholars like D. S. Likhachev, an expert on early Russian culture who did much behind the scenes to help colleagues in trouble for their ideas. Historians, too, made a modest contribution, for example in the analysis of birch-bark documents which archaeologists discovered in the remains of medieval Novgorod. But it was tempting to interpret such evidence in a chauvinistic sense, as indicating that Kievan Rus' had been more advanced culturally than had actually been the case – a tendency that had begun under Stalin (and received a different slant at the hands of some Ukrainian scholars). When one historian, A. A. Zimin, questioned the authenticity of *The Lay of Igor's Host* he stirred up a hornets' nest. The gifted dissident political writer Andrey Amalrik first clashed with authority when, as a student, he submitted a thesis on the Varangians that portrayed them too favourably.

In each institute political watchdogs controlled what was written or discussed. Scholars were now permitted to attend conferences abroad, but each application was vetted carefully and might be arbitrarily refused at the last moment. Similarly, foreigners working in Soviet archives had to put up with deliberate obstruction. Historians working on sensitive topical themes suffered most from all this. Alexander Nekrich, who showed Stalin's responsibility for the defeats of 1941, lost his job, was expelled from the Party, and later emigrated. But no one was safe. Most scholars stomached their doubts and conformed, at least outwardly, to official dictates. The result was that an entire generation grew up knowing little about their country's true history, since they had been fed on a diet of lies and myths. This would account for the explosive force of *glasnost'* after 1988 (see page 523).

Sociology, suppressed under Stalin, made a comeback in the 1960s as a recognized academic discipline, although public-opinion polling was closely controlled: one could not, for example, inquire into or report on political disaffection. Nevertheless local leaders needed reliable information about the public mood, and encouraged such surveys as a counterpart to the data collected by the KGB. Sociologists stood a better chance of having their work published if they used mathematical methods, and the same was true of economists. Political science, as commonly understood, scarcely existed, but in 1982 Tatyana Zaslavskaya, a reform-minded scholar working in Novosibirsk (where the atmosphere was freer than in Moscow), startled the academic community by delivering a swingeing attack on the existing socio-economic system. Her report, which was (deliberately?) leaked to the West, served as one source of inspiration for Gorbachev's *perestroyka*.

The fall of Khrushchev cost his protégé Lysenko his job, to the relief of Soviet biologists. Members of the powerful USSR Academy of Sciences were listened to more attentively than before on professional matters, but the institution was far from being a focal point of dissent. Only a few scientists (mainly physicists) had the courage to back Andrey Sakharov in his defiant stand for human rights, since lavish privileges kept most of them politically docile. Sakharov's nobility of character went hand in hand with a rare dedication to scientific integrity. His work on the hydrogen bomb, which in 1953 earned him entry to the academy at the youthful age of thirty-two, led him to appreciate the genetic dangers inherent in the testing of nuclear weapons. He was instrumental in persuading the Soviet leader to negotiate the ban on such tests being conducted above ground (1963), a landmark in the effort to bring nuclear arms under international control. The implications of this success were lost on most of his scientific colleagues (except for those associated with the Pugwash movement), who were caught up in the military-industrial complex and saw it as their patriotic duty to help boost Soviet power – at any price. Theirs was a closed world, far removed from the preoccupations of ordinary folk.

It would be wrong to portray Brezhnev's 'mature socialism' in monotonously dark colours. As we have seen, the mass of working people accepted it *faute de mieux*. It offered them not just job security but also the leisure to enjoy a variety of private pursuits. City residents could go on to the theatre, at affordable (subsidized) prices, or visit a plenitude of museums. The cinema was losing ground to television, but it remained a popular medium, with 4.1 million seats sold in 1985. Failing that, there was the circus – Moscow's was the best in the world – and clubs, run by trade unions or the Komsomol, which organized concerts, dances, film shows, and lectures. In winter one could take the children skiing or skating (or for that matter play chess, as popular as ever); at other seasons there were woods to walk in and mushrooms to pick. Statisticians calculated that employed urban males had 3½ hours' free time on a working day – but women only 2 hours; on holidays the figures were 8 and 5½ hours respectively. Of this the men spent half an hour with their children, another half-hour reading, and 1¾ hours in front of the TV set (or listening to the radio); study and civic activities absorbed a mere 3 minutes – the same as for women, who with their 'double burden' of work and house-keeping read less and spent 27 hours a week on domestic duties, as against under 12 hours for men.* Relatively little time was spent in active sports; as

---

* The last data are for the early 1970s, the others for March 1990.

elsewhere, watching them was more popular. Professional football, hockey, and other games were played to a high standard, and at international events Soviet athletes ran off with the lion's share of the prizes. They were subjected to rigorous training schedules – not least for the Moscow Olympic Games in 1980 – since prowess on the sports field was seen as symbolizing the country's strength.

Officialdom looked askance at the percolation from the West of a hedonistic 'youth culture', yet by the mid 1970s Moscow could boast its first discothèques and a few years later they had proliferated. As elsewhere in the world, rock-and-rollers wore flamboyant costumes and idolized crooners who sang lyrics with dubious texts and adopted an exuberant lifestyle. In an age of tape recorders and video cassettes it was no longer possible to seal off the country from 'alien' influences. Partly this was a generational problem: men and women who had been through the war and suffered much for the sake of lofty ideals could no longer understand their grandchildren who laughed off their concerns as antiquated or behaved in a manner that to their elders seemed *nekulturny* (vulgar). A few youngsters became hippies or punks. On the anniversary of Hitler's birthday in 1982 some fifty 'heavy-metal boys' congregated in Moscow to mark the occasion. Unimportant (and untypical) in itself, the incident was an affront to the intelligentsia, not only to *apparatchiki*. It was a way of expressing a deep psychological malaise, a search for alternative 'values' by a generation that had lost its forefathers' faith in revolutionary socialism or industrial progress – and to whom the cause of human rights and democracy mattered little either. This was, so to speak, the 'under-side' of the intelligentsia's struggle for truth and justice. Viewed historically, it was a delayed reaction to criminal violence by the Stalinist state, which had unwittingly created a counter-culture in its own image.

CHAPTER 23

The USSR as a World Power

BURDENS OF EMPIRE

The post-Stalin Soviet leaders initiated an unparalleled build-up of the country's armed strength. In the 1950s the bomber gave way to the ballistic missile as the principal means of delivering a nuclear or thermonuclear charge to a hostile target. Khrushchev saw the strategic rocket forces, which became a separate service in 1959, as a virtual substitute for ground troops. These, he thought, would play only a minor role in a future war fought with nuclear weapons. This view was challenged within the military as too single-minded, and later the USSR – like its principal adversary – prepared for various possible scenarios, including limited wars involving conventional arms alone. The official strategic doctrine placed a high premium on professional efficiency and a vigilant concern for national security. The rulers also manipulated the population's understandable fear of a new armed conflict so as to create a veritable 'defence psychosis' that made them ready to accept a high degree of social mobilization for warlike tasks.

In 1956 the party leaders revised Lenin's assumption that war was inevitable between the socialist and capitalist (imperialist) countries. It was now argued that the risk of Western aggression could be minimized by the might of the USSR and its allies in the Warsaw pact (formed in 1955), aided by their friends in the developing countries. The 'correlation of forces' between the two blocs was shifting rapidly in favour of the East. The task was to assist this supposedly inexorable process by all means short of provoking war, and simultaneously to build up the country's defences and consolidate its socialist system. This stance did not exclude the use of armed force as a political and psychological weapon to overawe potential foes. Growing Soviet strength, the argument ran, served the cause of peace and so threatened no one. The USSR did not even seek military superiority over the

United States but was content with a position of parity. In the strategists' idiom this was known as 'mutual assured destruction' (MAD for short!), and was a fact of international relations from about 1969. By that date the USSR had deployed some 1,140 intercontinental missiles (ICBMs) as against 1,054 for the USA. It still had a smaller total number of warheads than the Americans, for they had more submarine-launched missiles (SLBMs) and bombers, but by May 1972 the total figures were equal, too.

What really mattered was not the absolute number of weapons but the capability of each side to (a) strike a pre-emptive blow that would annihilate the adversary and (b) maintain a credibly invulnerable missile force that could respond in kind even if the country had been completely devastated. In such a situation it clearly made sense to try to limit the arms race so as to preserve the existing equilibrium, or 'balance of terror'. The two super-powers had a common interest in managing their adversarial relationship in such a way as to favour the continued modernization of their armed forces while excluding such unwelcome developments as the attainment by one side of a technological break-through the other could not match, a conflict breaking out inadvertently, or either being attacked by a third party (such as China, which entered the nuclear club in 1964).

To the Chinese such putative Soviet-American arrangements were suspect as 'co-hegemonism', and in the 1970s world politics became tripolar rather than bipolar. The USSR had to prepare for nuclear war against two potential adversaries. However, it took time before the Americans and Chinese mended fences, and fortunately for Moscow there was never any prospect of them acting jointly against the USSR. Likewise, the path to a Soviet-American *rapprochement* proved stonier than initially expected. The limited East–West détente of the early 1970s gave way after 1979 to a new phase of bitter cold-war confrontation which did not end until, under Gorbachev, the USSR renounced its exclusivist ideological world-view and sought to reach a genuine partnership with both its former adversaries – so inadvertently bringing about the collapse of the Soviet 'security state' and of the USSR *tout court*. This apparently self-destructive course was adopted because Moscow recognized that the latest twist in the arms-race spiral would be ruinously expensive for a country that still lagged far behind its rival technologically and economically. In this way the world was spared

495

MAP 6. *The Soviet Union*

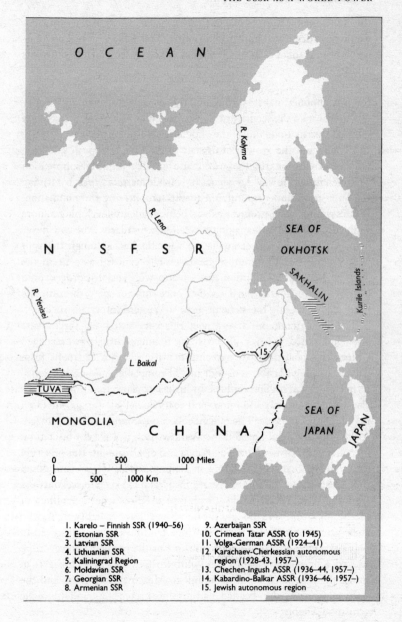

O C E A N

R. Kolyma

R. Lena

N S F S R

SEA OF

OKHOTSK

SAKHALIN

Kurile Islands

R. Yenisei

L Baikal

15

TUVA

MONGOLIA

C H I N A

SEA OF

JAPAN

JAPAN

| 0 | 500 | 1000 Miles |
| 0 | 500 | 1000 Km |

1. Karelo – Finnish SSR (1940–56)
2. Estonian SSR
3. Latvian SSR
4. Lithuanian SSR
5. Kaliningrad Region
6. Moldavian SSR
7. Georgian SSR
8. Armenian SSR
9. Azerbaijan SSR
10. Crimean Tatar ASSR (to 1945)
11. Volga-German ASSR (1924–41)
12. Karachaev-Cherkessian autonomous region (1928-43, 1957–)
13. Chechen-Ingush ASSR (1936–44, 1957–)
14. Kabardino-Balkar ASSR (1936–46, 1957–)
15. Jewish autonomous region

the unimaginable horrors of a nuclear exchange which, had it occurred, would have destroyed human civilization. This was a very real possibility in the mid 1980s as the nuclear clock ticked on remorselessly towards midnight.

For Soviet policy makers throughout this period the overriding priority was to maintain the security of the socialist bloc. There were two main internal threats to its unity: the widening schism between the USSR and China and the growth of dissent in the East European satellites. On several occasions this took a dramatic form that required suppression by armed force. However, violence only made matters worse, by driving the opposition underground and further embittering the population. It undermined such progress as was being made in developing a more sophisticated style in managing bloc affairs. Similarly, Moscow never managed to achieve a reconciliation with Beijing, although the split between the two Communist giants cruelly exposed as a myth the Marxist-Leninist assumption that a world-wide socialist order would put an end to international conflict once and for all – the ultimate rationale for waging the struggle against Western imperialism.

The honeymoon in Sino-Soviet relations lasted for three years after Stalin died. In 1954, after visiting Beijing, Khrushchev assuaged Chinese national pride by agreeing to withdraw Soviet troops from Talien, hand over control of four mixed companies, and grant a long-term loan of 520 million roubles. Industrial construction projects were also aided generously and for several years Soviet advisers proliferated in Chinese factories. The alliance became more institutionalized. Although China did not join the Warsaw pact, it was kept briefed on its policies, for instance on Yugoslavia and disarmament. But precisely these policies evoked misgiving in Beijing, where it was considered that Moscow was too soft on 'revisionism' and too keen to seek favours from the West. Mao was also displeased at Khrushchev's handling of 'de-Stalinization'. He thought the new Soviet leader a lightweight, who lacked the qualities of a Stalin – or of Mao himself, who deserved to play first fiddle in world Communism. For the moment, however, he backed Khrushchev against his Politburo foes and in October 1956 urged the rebellious Poles to submit to Moscow. Both men, and the party apparatuses they headed, had absolute pretensions, and this made schism inevitable.

The chief stumbling-block was security, but this fact was carefully concealed in the two parties' ideologically coloured polemics, which by 1962 had become public knowledge. For a time the disputants pretended to be attacking Yugoslav 'revisionism' and Albanian 'dogmatism' respectively. In 1961, at the Twenty-second CPSU congress, the Chinese delegation walked out in protest at condemnation of the latter country (which then took China's side in the dispute, the only one in Europe to do so). Mao's first bid for leadership of the international Communist movement dated from October 1957, when he raised objections to the Soviet formula allowing for a 'peaceful transition to socialism' (*Ist.* 4/1996, appx., pp. 109–14). Chinese bellicosity was mainly verbal, and Beijing's efforts to promote militant sectarian groups in the parties of third-world countries were seldom successful. Most of them tried to sit out the dispute, and if compelled to choose opted for Moscow as it had more aid to offer them.

In 1957 Khrushchev rashly tried to buy Mao off by agreeing to deliver a sample atomic bomb. But next summer the Taiwan Strait crisis (when Chinese forces shelled off-shore islands held by Taiwan) graphically illustrated the dangers of such action, which threatened to drag the USSR into a conflict with the Americans. Khrushchev reneged on his promise – but apparently not before Mao had already decided to pursue a policy of self-sufficiency in defence policy as in much else. Recalling unhappy pre-war experiences, he looked on Soviet military advisers in China as a potential fifth column and rejected Moscow's proposals for cooperation in defence. Frustrated, Khrushchev withdrew *all* Soviet advisers (1960), so plunging China's economy into disorder. But instead of making Mao relent, this caused all factions in the Chinese leadership to rally behind him in rejecting Soviet bullying. When Khrushchev fell from power, the Chinese were pleased but did not pick up the olive branch extended by his successor. Instead, Maoist China sank into the abyss of the so-called 'cultural revolution', an orgy of blood-letting that in many respects recalled Stalin's Great Terror.

Alarmed at these developments (and at the Chinese atomic bomb), Moscow built up its forces along the border and in Mongolia. The number of divisions stationed in the east rose from fifteen in 1968 to forty in 1973. At one point the Soviets hinted at a possible pre-emptive strike against China's main nuclear-test site at Lop Nor. To this sabre-rattling Beijing responded in kind. In March 1969 there was skirmishing along the Soviet frontier in the Far East. Other less-publicized 'provocations' took place elsewhere, and nomads in the border regions sought safety by moving to one side or the other. But the Sino-Soviet dispute was only secondarily about territorial claims. For prestige reasons Beijing wanted Moscow to disown the 'unequal treaties' imposed by the tsars in the nineteenth century, but it had no immediate plans to occupy the Soviet Far East, as many Russians feared. The stakes were in fact much higher: world survival in the nuclear age.

When Mao said that populous China could survive an atomic war between East and West, did he mean to be taken literally? Moscow could not be sure and denounced him as a warmonger. Its greatest fear was of a *rapprochement* between Beijing and Washington. In 1972 this seemed imminent when President Nixon visited the Chinese capital before attending a 'Summit' in Moscow. But the USA was tied down by the war in Vietnam and needed both Communist powers' aid to extricate itself. Less Machiavellian than either, it abstained from trying to deepen the schism by allying with one or the other; nor did it furnish China with advanced military technology, despite informal approaches to this effect. Moscow's China policy was to keep that country isolated – and, if possible, encircled either by capitalist states (Japan, Taiwan) or friendly Communist ones like North Korea and, eventually, the Democratic Republic of Vietnam (DRV).

From 1960, when it launched its revolutionary war against South Vietnam, the DRV had been a major recipient of Soviet aid, including jet aircraft and SAM missiles. This was of greater military consequence than the aid given by China. The country was a focal point of their rivalry, with Beijing preaching the virtues of 'people's revolutionary war' and Moscow providing most of the muscle for it. Yet the Soviets took care not to challenge US interests directly, and simultaneously backed efforts to reach a negotiated solution to the conflict (in Paris, from 1968), whereas the Chinese disapproved of these bipartite talks between the Americans and North Vietnamese. In 1972 Moscow overrode the DRV's interests when it received President Nixon despite his provocative order to lay mines off North Vietnamese ports, a move that even put Soviet supply vessels at risk. By sea and overland Soviet weapons continued to flood in.

The North's eventual victory (1975) was a tonic for Moscow, which promptly consolidated its hold over the new dependency. Hanoi welcomed Soviet aid in reconstructing its devastated country, but did not completely align itself with Moscow. It refused to allow the Soviet navy control over Camranh Bay, a splendid natural harbour which the Americans had developed into a major base. In 1979, however, the DRV relented on this point because it had become involved in a proxy war between the Soviets and Chinese. Beijing backed the murderous Pol Pot regime in neighbouring Cambodia (Kampuchea). Fortified by a friendship treaty with Moscow (November 1978), Hanoi invaded Cambodia and overthrew Pol Pot, only to be attacked in turn by China (February 1979). Fortunately for Moscow, this was a limited offensive designed 'to teach Vietnam a lesson' and the Chinese soon withdrew, while the Vietnamese extended their rule throughout Indo-China. They remodelled their economy in Soviet fashion and redirected trade towards fellow-members of Comecon. Vietnam was home to thousands of Russian advisers and the Soviet navy patrolled in strength the waters of the South China Sea.

Farther south, the states united in the SEATO pact barred Soviet expansion. None of the three major post-war insurgencies (Philippines and Malaya in the 1950s, followed by a half-hearted *coup* in Indonesia on 1 October 1965) owed much to Moscow. The USSR had previously backed Indonesia lavishly with weaponry, which ended up in the hands of the anti-Communist Suharto regime. In a wave of repression the new government slaughtered hundreds of thousands of real or alleged Communists, including their leader, D. N. Aidit. The setback was not too gravely felt in Moscow because it had placed its bets on President Sukarno, the neutralist leader, rather than Aidit, who sought guidance from Beijing. Even so, Jakarta in 1965 was a replay of Shanghai in 1927, and underlined the fragility of revolutionary enterprises in distant regions where Moscow did not call the tune.

For different reasons the Soviets made no headway in Japan, which remained solidly within the American sphere. Commercial relations remained on a modest scale, and plans to attract Japanese investment in Siberia failed to get off the ground, not least because Moscow refused to contemplate any concession over the occupied northern islands. In 1978 there was an anxious moment when Tokyo patched up relations with Beijing, but the danger passed.

By then Mao had at last joined his ancestors (1976). Once again Brezhnev extended an olive branch, but to no effect. Years passed before a shift in Chinese internal policies took some of the chill out of the Sino-Soviet relationship; even so, the basic differences persisted. Beijing made normalization conditional on a reduction of Soviet military strength along the northern border and in Vietnam, but, instead of yielding, the USSR tightened the ring around China by invading Afghanistan (December 1979) – although this was not the main reason for taking such a hazardous step, which helped to precipitate the Soviet regime's downfall.

India had been a key player in Soviet Asian strategy since 1955, when Bulganin and Khrushchev paid a much-publicized visit to that country. Four years later, when Indian and Chinese troops clashed on their Himalayan border, Moscow urged a peaceful settlement. It was the first occasion that it had failed to endorse publicly the claims of a Communist state against a non-Communist one, and this issue, too, played a part in the deterioration of Sino-Soviet relations. When hostilities erupted again in 1962, Moscow backed India still more forcefully. China thereupon looked to Pakistan. In 1965 Kosygin summoned the two south Asian rivals to Tashkent, where he imposed a ceasefire in their current clash over Kashmir. This marked a high point of Soviet influence in the sub-continent. Six years later, when they again nearly came to blows over the crisis in East Bengal (thereafter Bangladesh), Moscow aided India by staging a naval demonstration – but taking good care to avoid contact with American warships engaged on a similar mission. Indian gratitude was tempered by concern lest she endanger too obviously her non-aligned status, and so she refused to endorse Brezhnev's appeal for an all-Asian collective security pact, while receiving him warmly as a visitor (1973).

Soviet-Indian amity was severely tested by the invasion of Afghanistan. At the United Nations most non-aligned states condemned it, but India held aloof. She was afraid that if Pakistan became too overtly embroiled on behalf of the Muslim resistance, and therefore too reliant on US military aid, she might threaten India with nuclear weapons. Accordingly New Delhi turned to Moscow for further armed assistance, which was granted on more favourable terms than by the West. For the sub-continent the danger in the 1980s was of being drawn into a Soviet-American conflict rather than a Soviet-Chinese one. Often wrongly underestimated in Europe, this was an important if subsidiary arena of East–West confrontation, which fortunately for all the players in the game did not have fateful consequences.

Turning to Eastern Europe, in this theatre the danger of war was mitigated by the NATO powers' tacit willingness to regard the countries of that region as lying within the Soviet sphere and to refrain from exploiting any potential for intervention on their peoples' behalf. (Popularly, this restraint was often attributed by Western critics to the Yalta agreements, although there is no historical basis for this.) Moscow's problem was not any threat of 'imperialist aggression', as it tirelessly reiterated, still less of 'German revanchism', but the fact that the socio-political order it had so violently imposed on Eastern Europe under Stalin was at variance with the interests and preferences of the mass of the population. Only a narrow élite of *apparatchiki* was committed to Moscow, and even their loyalty was at times suspect. In brief, the region was both a declining strategic asset (because of the changing nature of the military threat) and a growing political and economic liability.

The post-Stalin leaders began by trimming the wings of the Hungarian dictator, M. Rákosi, and obliging him to share power with Imre Nagy, a leader of reformist inclinations. Thereby they unleashed expectations of change all over Eastern Europe that could not be satisfied. A few days later, in June 1953, a protest over higher work norms in East Berlin led to a popular upheaval in the GDR that had to be suppressed by Soviet tanks. Moscow's reconciliation with Titoist Yugoslavia in 1955, with its explicit recognition of the principle of 'different roads to socialism', encouraged 'national Communist' tendencies throughout the bloc. Up to a point the growing diversity had the Kremlin's blessing, since it was anxious to make Communist rule less unpopular by devolving responsibilities to local leaders, while ensuring that they maintained their single-party regimes intact and took their cue from 'the Centre'.

That there were limits to Soviet pragmatism became clear in 1956. Khrushchev's 'secret speech' shook the USSR's standing everywhere. In June Polish patriots sacked party and police headquarters in Poznań. Four months later crisis broke. The Polish Party's former chief, Władysław Gomułka, who had been imprisoned for 'Titoism' and had become a popular hero, returned to power. Soviet troop movements indicated a readiness by some in Moscow to 'restore order' by force, but in the event Khrushchev accepted the arrangement. Marshal Rokossovsky was withdrawn as Poland's defence minister and subsequently it was agreed that the Red Army's presence in the country should be made less conspicuous. The 'Polish October' left the peasantry de-collectivized and the Catholic Church with a fair degree of autonomy.

No such peaceful compromise was possible in Hungary, where tension between hard-liners and reformists in the Party was much more acute. Nagy, who had been ousted in March 1955, came to symbolize resistance to Muscovite hegemony. The Hungarian revolution began on 23 October 1956 with student demonstrations for his reinstatement. Quickly the movement spread to workers with economic grievances and then to the entire nation. Moscow's top-level emissaries, Mikoyan and Suslov, agreed with Nagy to withdraw Soviet troops and allow political pluralism. With the hated secret police in dissolution, it seemed that the insurgents had won. But on 31 October fresh Soviet forces invaded the country. Nagy was seized and, after a secret trial, executed (1958). Thousands of Hungarians were killed,* many more fled abroad. The decision to intervene was taken at the last moment but *before* Nagy's decision to leave the Warsaw pact (1 November). The real reason was Moscow's fear of losing control over the bloc and being seen as weak by the Western powers. The latter were distracted by the Suez crisis and the US presidential elections – factors that also entered into the Soviet leaders' calculation of the risk.

Hungary's grim fate taught Communist rulers elsewhere that they could not press their own parties' interests too strongly without being considered traitors to the principle of 'socialist internationalism'. The Italian leader Togliatti coined the term 'polycentrism', but this reflected an idea, not harsh current reality. In 1958 Yugoslavia again found itself under fire for ideological backsliding. Kept at arm's length by Moscow, Tito took on a new role as leader of the non-aligned countries. He also opened up his country to the West, which made Moscow nervous. From 1966 onward the Romanian leader N. Ceauşescu began to take an independent line, forging diplomatic links with West Germany,

---

* The Moscow archives give a figure of 2,260 killed, wounded and missing, but Hungarian sources put the figure at 21,000; 211,000 escaped to the West. See P. Gosztony in *NZZ*, 23 October 1996.

Israel, and China, and even hinting at territorial claims against the USSR over Bessarabia and northern Bukovina. But as he kept his population under iron control Moscow let him get away with such *lèse-majesté*.

Romania was odd man out when in 1968 the Warsaw pact states invaded Czechoslovakia to repress Alexander Dubček's reformist Communism ('socialism with a human face'). Unlike the Hungarians earlier, the Czech and Slovak leaders sought change *within* the system, not to overthrow it. They wanted 'socialist legality' and greater economic efficiency; to these demands non-party intellectuals added an end to censorship and democratization of the country's political life. All the reformers professed friendship for Moscow and loyalty to the Warsaw Pact, but this was not enough to make the 'Prague spring' acceptable to the Kremlin. It feared that pluralism in Czechoslovakia, even if brought about non-violently, would be emulated elsewhere in the bloc and lead to its dissolution – and even to Germany replacing the USSR as the hegemonic power in the region. (This alarmist view was propounded notably by the GDR's Erich Honecker as well as by Polish hardliners, who were listened to in Moscow, as also in Kiev, where the Ukrainian party boss Shelest feared the percolation of Western ideas through Slovakia.)

Armed intervention in Prague by twenty Warsaw pact divisions during the night of 20–21 August 1968 was a walkover militarily but a complete political disaster. Fewer lives were lost than in Hungary, but the impact was equally crippling. As intellectuals and reform-minded officials were forced to become dustmen or watchmen, Moscow promulgated the 'Brezhnev doctrine' in an effort to justify such drastic measures: all parties in the bloc had to put first their 'responsibility to all the socialist countries and the entire Communist movement' – in other words, the USSR knew best and there was no longer any room for 'separate roads to socialism'. One casualty of 'normalization' under G. Husák, who replaced Dubček in March 1969, was the long-standing amity of Czechs towards Russia. They were not reconciled by an infusion of Soviet aid that did little to remedy the country's underlying economic malaise.

More aid had to be pumped into Poland in the wake of serious labour unrest that broke out in Gdańsk in December 1970 and was repressed at the cost of forty-five lives. Although the workers' immediate demands were mainly economic, there was an undercurrent of political disaffection to which intellectuals (and the Church) were able to give expression. For the moment it was kept in check by the replacement of Gomułka by E. Gierek, who embarked on a policy of borrowing extensively from the West in order to pay for imports of consumer goods. By 1979 Poland's foreign debt was twenty times what it had been in 1971. Already in 1976 this burden prompted a squeeze on living standards that evoked further mass protests – and the formation of a Committee for Workers' Defence (KOR) which the Gierek regime had to half-tolerate. The political situation in Poland was more fluid than elsewhere in Eastern Europe, and moral authority lay with the Church, not the Party.

This helps to explain the extraordinary success of the 'Solidarity' movement in 1980–81. Initiated in Gdańsk's giant Lenin shipyard (a focus of the protests ten years earlier) by the Catholic electrician Lech Wałęsa and his comrades, it was soon joined by peasants and professional people. Moscow became increasingly anxious, and with good reason: this was a proletarian revolution in what was supposed to be a citadel of socialism! Poland was more populous than Czechoslovakia and strategically more vital, with a strong army, so that an invasion by her neighbours risked provoking civil war and even NATO intervention. After dithering for months, during which time 'Solidarity' became a truly nation-wide organization and even called on workers abroad to emulate its achievement, Moscow decided to act, but only indirectly, by mobilizing its few supporters within Poland. On 13 December 1981 General W. Jaruzelski, who had accumulated the offices of defence and prime minister (and was also party first secretary), imposed martial law. He acted at the USSR's behest,* and, in his own estimation at least, to prevent a still greater evil. There was little overt resistance but Polish society, far from being pacified, remained sullenly resentful and even more alienated from the regime than before. It was much the same situation in Czechoslovakia and in Hungary – where, however,

---

* Especially Andropov's: the Soviet ministry and some other Politburo members favoured direct intervention (V. I. Voronkov in *Vop. ist.* 10/1995, pp. 92–121). One element in Soviet planning was an unwillingness to undertake military action in Poland and Afghanistan simultaneously.

Moscow did permit a limited economic liberalization. It had no long-term solution for the region's problems.

One weakness was the lack of any institutional mechanism for settling differences among the leaders of European Communist parties. After Cominform was abolished in 1956, relations with each party were handled in deepest secrecy by departments of the CPSU Secretariat. This was little to the taste of those parties that had to compete openly for electoral support. The Italian and Spanish Communists were in the forefront of the so-called 'Euro-Communist' movement, which in the late 1970s embarrassed Moscow by calling for greater openness, democracy, and equality. The PCF, however, held aloof from this trend, as did smaller parties with sectarian followings. Realists in the CPSU *apparat* recognized that the Leninist dream of revolutionizing the Western industrialized world was a mirage.

Paradoxically, this deduction was reinforced by the growth of the 'new Left' in the late 1960s, for this intellectual movement took off in the direction of pacifism, anarchism, and even Maoism. Its leaders showed disdain for the 'mature socialism' that existed in the Soviet bloc, and even joined bourgeois spokesmen in characterizing it as imperialistic. But if the chances of achieving world-wide socialism were foreclosed, had not Soviet foreign policy lost its *raison d'être*?

THE USSR AND THE NON-ALIGNED COUNTRIES

For a time a credible substitute for the advanced countries of the West seemed to have been found in the great arc of 'third-world' territories that stretched from Latin America by way of Africa and the Middle East to South-East Asia. Long regarded by Soviet theorists as the soft underbelly of imperialism, these former colonial lands appeared to offer exciting prospects. Their national élites were keen to modernize their societies rapidly and bore an animus against their old masters which they expressed in the United Nations and in other international forums, sometimes using an idiom that owed much to Marxism-Leninism. Their leaders could be wooed by personal diplomacy; young cadres were invited to study in the USSR, and Moscow gave economic assistance to help develop the state sector at the expense of private business. Soviet ideologists viewed these countries as 'national democracies' that had embarked on a 'non-capitalist path' leading eventually to socialism. Hostile outsiders saw Soviet policy, especially the grant of military aid, as one of imperialistic infiltration that ultimately risked depriving the new nations of their highly prized sovereignty.

This interpretation, as it turned out, exaggerated the dangers, but equally Soviet policy makers overestimated the speed with which they could move events in the direction desired. Over the three post-Stalin decades they encountered more setbacks than successes. All too often promising investments of Soviet funds and political prestige turned into costly burdens. There was also a constant risk that their clients would use Soviet aid corruptly and unproductively, divert it against local adversaries, or even drag their patron into unwanted confrontations with the United States, so jeopardizing détente.

In the Khrushchev era economic aid was distributed liberally among a wide array of recipient states, but after 1965 there was a switch to concentration on a favoured few, together with a shift to military hardware – which incidentally helped to keep Soviet arms factories turning. Initially payment was in local goods or soft currency at low rates of interest, but as third-world debts to the USSR mounted it became more insistent on a material *quid pro quo*. Between 1954 and 1985 Moscow extended an estimated $97.9 milliard of economic aid, of which about half went to two acknowledged socialist countries, Cuba ($38.4 md) and Vietnam ($9.3 md). Other recipients included India ($4.4 md) and, rather surprisingly, Turkey ($3.4 md), whereas Ethiopia, Syria, Iran, and Angola each obtained about $1 md.* Some idea of the extent of military aid can be gained from data for arms transfers (1961– 85), which show Syria as the chief recipient ($21.5 md), followed by India ($15.2 md), Libya ($14.6 md), and Egypt ($14.1 md); Vietnam, Iraq, and Cuba did about half as well as the three last-mentioned states.†

The extent of Soviet assistance to developing countries was far smaller than that from Western sources, but Moscow excelled at

---

* Light (ed.), *Troubled Friendships*, p. 195. These are American (CIA) estimates. A high margin of error is possible, since aid offers were not always taken up and converting them to hard currency raises many problems.

† 1985 US dollars. See Brzoska and Ohlson, *Arms Transfers to the Third World*, pp. 338–51.

exploiting its political and psychological impact. The first major project, the Bhilai steel-making complex in India (begun in 1955), is a case in point. So, too, was Egypt's prestigious Aswan High Dam, opened in 1964, which the Soviets offered to help build after the USA had turned the scheme down. India's strategic significance has been discussed above; here we may consider briefly the Middle East, Black Africa, Cuba (as a potential gateway to Latin America), and, last but not least, Afghanistan.

Khrushchev's wager on the Arab states was a means of outflanking the 'northern tier' of neighbouring Middle Eastern countries (Turkey, Iraq, Iran) that were briefly joined in the Western-orientated Baghdad pact. This alliance broke up after the 1958 Iraqi revolution, which the USSR supported. It saw Abdul Kassim, the Iraqi nationalist leader, as a useful counterweight to Nasser in Egypt, whose plan for a union with Syria, forming the United Arab Republic, did not suit Soviet interests. Moscow preferred to deal with the Arab countries individually and misjudged the force of Arab nationalism, with its emphasis on hostility to Israel; it would have liked them to adopt a more explicitly anti-American stance and grant more leeway to local Communists, who both Kassim and Nasser suppressed ferociously, as the Turks had in an earlier age (see page 350).

The arms deal with Egypt in 1956 was the first such pact with a non-Communist country. In the Suez crisis later that year Khrushchev rattled his atomic armour in a (largely propagandist) bid to halt the Anglo-French offensive. This support, and the Aswan project, brought the USSR much Arab goodwill, but it still wielded less influence in the region than the West, and the conservative Islamic monarchies remained strongly anti-Soviet. The shah's Iran agreed not to allow Western missiles to be stationed on its territory, but Algeria's flirtation with the USSR during the war against the French ended in 1965 when Ben Bella, the nationalist leader, fell from power.

Under Brezhnev the Soviet position at first improved. The Black Sea fleet's Mediterranean squadron now patrolled Near Eastern waters, keeping a watch on its US counterpart. A large loan was given to Syria for construction of the Euphrates dam, but the Ba'athist regime's bellicose anti-Israeli stance, and that of its Egyptian ally, nearly embroiled the USSR in the Six-Day War of 1967. It lost much military hardware to the Israelis. Moscow tried to recoup the blow to its prestige by rebuilding the Arab states' armies. Meanwhile British withdrawal from Aden (1966) opened up new possibilities for Soviet-Egyptian involvement in the south of the Arabian peninsula. When Nasser began the 'war of attrition' along the Suez Canal (1969), the Soviets helped by supplying aircrew and an air defence system with SAM missiles, but sought to steer clear of any direct confrontation with the Israelis or their American backers. Officially, Moscow committed itself to supporting the ambiguously worded UN resolution 242, which like the Arabs it interpreted as referring to an Israeli evacuation of *all* occupied territories, and in practice it cooperated with Washington in imposing a cease-fire, despite the entreaties of its clients Syria and Iraq.

This carefully nuanced strategy came unstuck after Nasser's death. Extensive Soviet arms deliveries encouraged his successor, Anwar Sadat, to launch the Yom Kippur offensive against Israel in 1973. This time the Soviets, who must have had foreknowledge of the attack, resupplied the Arab forces massively while the war was still in progress, and there was a moment when they even offered to send ground troops; a world conflagration seemed likely. But subsequently Sadat, irritated by the extensive Soviet military presence in Egypt, demanded the recall of Soviet advisers. Moscow had no choice but to comply. Later Sadat denounced the Egyptian-Soviet friendship treaty and turned for backing to the United States, which by the late 1970s had bolstered its position in the region at the USSR's expense – this despite the 'oil-price shock' administered by OPEC, which the USSR (although not a member of that organization) predictably backed with enthusiasm. President Assad's Syria continued to look to Moscow, and received some benefit during her involvement in the Lebanese civil war. On the other hand, there was little mileage for Moscow either from Libya's radical Muslim leader Qaddafi or from the Iranian revolution of 1978–9: early hopes of gains for the secular, pro-Soviet Tudeh party were set at naught by the victory of Ayatollah Khomeini's Islamic fundamentalists. To make matters worse, the latter threatened the security of Soviet Central Asia.

Soviet interest in Black Africa dates back to 1960, when the collapse of the Belgian Congo led to a civil war in which the USSR backed the lost cause of Patrice Lumumba (who subsequently gave his name to a Moscow college for training third-world students). It remained marginal until 1974, when simultaneously the Portuguese and Ethiopian empires fell apart. Moscow sent some 15,000 Soviet-equipped Cuban troops as proxies to save the Angolan leader A. Neto's 'progressive' MPLA government from its domestic challengers, who were backed by the USA, South Africa, and even China. Thereafter it established a solid presence in the former Portuguese colony (as it did, to a lesser extent, in Mozambique). They were seen as front-line states in the struggle against apartheid; the South African ANC also received Soviet aid.

Ethiopian links with Russia were of longer standing. Within the ruling military council, known as the Dergue, the USSR backed the faction of Mengistu Haile Meriam, who took over in 1977 and developed into an unsavoury despot. Cuban troops and Soviet advisers poured in, and helped repel a Somalian incursion into the Ogaden desert. They went on, less justifiably, to repress Eritrean and other movements for national self-determination. The costs of this intervention were high: not just Mengistu's successive requests for more aid and association with a notoriously brutal regime, but the loss of Somalia, for until then (from 1969) that country, under Siad Barre, had taken a pro-Soviet line and given the USSR's Indian Ocean squadron excellent port facilities at Berbera. In 1977 Barre accordingly denounced the friendship treaty he had concluded with the Soviets three years earlier and sent their advisers packing. The beneficiary, predictably, was the United States. Moscow policy makers could take comfort from the fact that Ethiopia was a larger prize than little Somalia, but both countries were too impoverished, and too backward socially, for Communist experiments. In truth the Horn of Africa (including the two Yemeni states) was a worthless substitute for Egypt, the heart of the Arab world.

Cuba was a different matter altogether. Its location challenged US claims to hegemony in the Caribbean, and Fidel Castro's charismatic personality commanded sympathy in the non-aligned movement and beyond. After the 1962 missile crisis (see page 515) Moscow lavished aid, buying most of its exports in return for oil and so ensuring that this lonely socialist island in the New World did not founder. The heavy burden (estimated in 1973 at $1.5 million a day) was thought politically worth while, especially given Cuba's readiness to involve herself militarily in African adventures. However, efforts to export Castroism to Bolivia and other Latin American countries proved ineffectual, at least until the 1980s, when revolutionary movements emerged in El Salvador and Nicaragua. The Soviet military presence in Cuba was of necessity restricted, but in general army and navy officers had now become quite familiar with service conditions in distant tropical areas. The USSR had constructed an ocean-going 'blue-water' fleet, which, aided by long-distance transport planes, could bring Soviet armed strength to bear in conflicts virtually anywhere on the globe's surface – what strategists inelegantly called 'global reach'. Never before in landlocked Russia's history had there been such a massive expansion of armed power, but was it affordable?

On the whole this awesome might was used prudently, but in December 1979 the Soviet leadership* acted with uncharacteristic recklessness by intervening directly in Afghanistan's revolution. Its motives were mixed. It was dissatisfied with the extremist policies of Hafizullah Amin, who in September had overthrown and murdered his factional rival, Nur Muhammad Taraki, and was confident that Moscow's chosen protégé, Babrak Karmal, would win more popular support. Behind this move lay a desire to offset Iranian influence in Afghanistan and in the Muslim Central Asian republics. The military obstacles to winning control of the entire country were vastly under-estimated, as was the diplomatic fallout. Secret American military aid, funnelled to the guerrillas via Pakistan, helped fortify their resistance. The war dragged on until 1989, when Soviet losses were officially put at 14,500 killed and 50,000 wounded (the real figures were probably higher). Between 1984 and 1987 the financial cost of the war (excluding economic aid) rose from 1.6 to 4.1 milliard roubles a year (*Ist.* 3/1995, appx., pp. 153–6). This débâcle showed the perils of trying to intrude Soviet military power into a region where Marxist notions were irrelevant and Russians, however beneficent their intentions, were seen as hereditary foes of Islam. In the Middle East religion was a much stronger force than it had been half a century earlier in Central Asia.

---

* The decision was formulated by a committee consisting of Andropov, Gromyko, Ustinov, and B. N. Ponomarev, and then endorsed by two of these men, Brezhnev, and Suslov in the Politburo. See G. M. Kornienko in *NNI* 3/1993, pp. 107–18.

WESTERN APPROACHES

After Stalin's death the Kremlin removed some minor points of friction with the Western powers, agreed to a cease-fire in the Korean War, and adopted a 'new look' in foreign policy, based on the principle of 'peaceful coexistence between states with different social systems', which it was claimed (inexactly) had good Leninist authority. Diplomatic links were established with a number of countries hitherto outside Moscow's orbit. In 1955 the Soviet leaders went to Geneva for a 'summit' conference with their Western counterparts. This meeting, and subsequent visits to London (1956) and other capitals, improved the general climate of East–West relations but did not bring any progress on the German question, the chief stumbling-block. Moscow objected vehemently to the 1954 Paris accords, which brought the FRG into NATO, as well as to Western moves, however skilfully camouflaged,* to give Germany indirect access to nuclear weapons. The Soviets feared, perhaps with exaggerated memories of their 1941 defeat, that she could drag her NATO allies into a war to regain the lost eastern territories – a fear that was also manipulated by Moscow to keep Poles and Czechs in line. Two steps were taken in the hope of reducing tension in Central Europe. First, in 1955 Moscow reversed its stand on an Austrian state treaty and agreed to the withdrawal of all Allied forces from that country on condition that it became permanently neutral like Switzerland. This move was designed to encourage creation of a neutral buffer zone, stretching from Sweden to Yugoslavia, of states with a limited amount of conventional arms. The idea did not, however, get off the ground. Secondly, Chancellor Adenauer was invited to Moscow and the two countries established diplomatic relations. The FRG got back its last prisoners of war, but neither it nor any of its Western allies would consider extending recognition to the GDR (or 'Soviet zone', in official West German parlance).

Meanwhile, negotiations on disarmament were held in Geneva. The

---

* First the proposed European Defence Community (EDC), which was torpedoed by French opposition, and then the 'multilateral force' (MLF) plan, which would have given each NATO member state a finger on the nuclear button.

USSR held out for a phased general ban on nuclear weapons, to be controlled by an international inspectorate whose powers would be progressively expanded as confidence built up. For the West this did not offer sufficient guarantees against cheating. They wanted the control measures established and perfected *first*, and did not conceal their view that, so long as the two blocs existed, general disarmament was a pipe dream. The Soviets equated the proposed thorough control measures with espionage. Such a negative stance made sense in the light of their military inferiority, which they were desperately trying to overcome.

On 4 October 1957 the USSR launched the world's first artificial earth satellite, Sputnik I, whose innocent beeps surprised and fascinated the Western public. The USSR's evident lead in the technology of space exploration, and more especially its ability to launch ICBMs, vastly enhanced its international prestige. The subsequent race for the moon with the Americans was an extraordinary waste of resources for both rivals, but at the time it had a considerable propaganda impact. Of greater concern to us here is the effect which Soviet successes in space – Sputnik II, which put a dog called Laika into orbit, the Lunik rocket that photographed the dark side of the moon (1959), and the first human cosmonaut, Yuriy Gagarin (12 April 1961) – had on the Soviet government's attitude to international affairs. The leadership became much more self-confident, indeed over-confident, of the country's ability to compete with the United States. Frequently it warned the West of the 'annihilating blows' its rockets could deliver in the event of war.

In November 1958 Khrushchev tried to settle the Berlin question by force. He gave the Western Allies six months to negotiate a new settlement, proposing that the Western sectors should temporarily become a 'free city' (memories of Danzig!), failing which the USSR would unilaterally abrogate its rights in favour of the GDR. The Western powers rejected this ultimatum, which in the event was allowed to lapse. In 1961 a military confrontation on the sectoral boundary was narrowly averted, and the East Germans built a forbidding wall to keep their people from fleeing westwards. The Berlin Wall would stand until 1989, a grim symbol of the cold war, complemented by barbed wire, searchlights, and a 'death strip' along the inter-zonal frontier. In a sense these fortifications were monuments to the failure of Soviet foreign policy, since the second Berlin crisis, like the first, led to a moral and political victory for the Western alliance.

This setback was probably a motive leading Khrushchev to challenge the United States nearer home. Another was American threats against Communist Cuba, as manifest in the Bay of Pigs fiasco (April 1961). He dispatched to the island a force of intermediate-range missiles* with supporting troops and equipment. Their existence was detected; Washington's warnings were ignored; and on 22 October 1962 the world stood on the brink of thermonuclear war. After six anxious days the crisis was defused. Faced with a US 'quarantine' of the island, Khrushchev turned back the ships still *en route* and later withdrew the missiles. Soviet claims that their purpose had been purely defensive (deterrent) had little weight, since conventional arms would have sufficed for that purpose. They had been designed to alter the strategic balance between the superpowers on the cheap, as it were, and the Soviet leader's bluff had been called: in return he received only vague American promises to abstain from further threats against Cuba (and to dismantle some outdated missile systems in Turkey).

The Soviet humiliation harmed Khrushchev's position as leader, widened the Sino-Soviet schism, and upset Castro; but its most important consequence was to accelerate the Soviet drive to attain parity with the United States. Paradoxically, the crisis was also followed by the first major step towards international control of nuclear arms: the agreement of July 1963 banning tests above ground. (Previously the USSR had suspended and then resumed testing unilaterally, with serious adverse effects on the health of people living near the test areas.) One reason for Moscow's grudging move towards acceptance of arms *control*, as distinct from disarmament, was technological: one could now survey, from satellites in outer space, most military activity on the ground, while underground nuclear explosions were detectable, within a certain radius, by unmanned 'black boxes'. There was accordingly less need for intrusive probing – as by the high-altitude U-2 spy plane, shot down over the Urals while traversing Soviet territory on

---

* More precisely, twenty-four medium-range (*c*.1,000 miles) and twelve intermediate-range (*c*.2,000 miles) missiles and about forty bombers capable of carrying nuclear weapons. Not all of these armaments actually arrived.

1 May 1960, an incident which embarrassed the United States and led to the breakdown of the Paris 'summit' shortly afterwards.

By 1963 Moscow, anxious to prevent war breaking out by accident, agreed to the installation of a direct secret telephone link ('hot line') to Washington. Two years later it realized that it was to its advantage, despite Chinese objections, to join the Western powers in signing a treaty on nuclear non-proliferation (NPT). This pact (1 July 1968) more or less coincided with Soviet agreement to an American proposal for talks on the limitation of strategic arms (SALT). 'When it comes to maintaining peace,' said foreign minister Gromyko, 'the USSR and the USA can find a common language.' The negotiations got under way the following year, in Helsinki and then in Vienna, and eventuated in the SALT I agreement formally concluded during Nixon's visit to Moscow in May 1972.

This was one of several bilateral accords that formed the basis of a shaky détente between the superpowers. It was founded on the concept that up to a point their security interests were compatible. For the five years to come they could each modernize their strategic arms, for instance by increasing their range or improving their accuracy, but not exceed a given number of launchers and warheads. Even more important was an agreement on limiting complexes of defensive anti-ballistic missiles (ABMs), which were seen as 'de-stabilizing' the balance of military power. In June 1973 the two superpowers went on to sign a pact 'on preventing nuclear war' which obliged them to refrain from threatening or using force against each other or their allies, and to consult urgently if hostilities seemed likely. In effect this laid down a vague code of good behaviour which neither party could really comply with to the other's satisfaction. This helps to explain why détente proved short-lived, although there were concrete reasons for this as well.

Meanwhile the diplomatic scene in Europe had been transformed, largely thanks to the *Ostpolitik* of the FRG's socialist chancellor, Willy Brandt – although the changes can be traced back to 1965, when the leaders of the ruling Communist parties, meeting in Bucharest, issued an appeal for an all-European conference. At the time the idea aroused little interest in the West, but it would eventuate, in a different form, in the Helsinki accords of 1975. As seen from Moscow, Gaullist France's withdrawal from NATO's integrated command (1966), three years before the alliance's term expired, created dangers (a renovated, German-dominated NATO) but also opened up the prospect that European security could be reshaped in line with Soviet interests. Within Germany the Hallstein doctrine* and the dream of recovering the 1937 frontiers were increasingly seen as no longer realistic, whereas a more constructive attitude towards the Eastern countries, provided that it was coordinated with the Western Allies to avoid any suspicion of a 'new Rapallo', could secure better conditions for the people of the GDR, mitigate the worst consequences of Germany's division, and prepare the way towards the country's eventual peaceful reunification. The chief loser from such a *rapprochement* would clearly be the GDR's hardline leader Walter Ulbricht, who won over to his viewpoint his counterparts in Poland and Czechoslovakia (the so-called 'iron triangle') and lobbied energetically in Moscow.

The Soviet leaders vacillated. Kosygin was less reserved than Suslov or the military, while Brezhnev, eager to chalk up foreign-policy successes, stood in the centre. In 1968 bilateral talks with the FRG got under way, briefly interrupted by the crisis in Prague, and by July 1969 Gromyko could announce Soviet readiness for talks on two levels: with Bonn on the mutual renunciation of force, and with the Allies on the status of Berlin. The German socialists' subsequent victory at the polls, followed by adhesion to the NPT, cleared the way for the treaty of Moscow (12 August 1970). The FRG formally accepted existing frontiers in Europe, including the Oder–Neisse line, as 'inviolable' (Gromyko had wanted 'immutable'), while specifying its allegiance to NATO and, in an accompanying letter, its commitment to peaceful reunification.† The deal was supplemented by other German treaties with Warsaw and Prague, and in September 1971 by a quadripartite pact on West Berlin. This, too, was a compromise, which weakened the Western sectors' links with the rest of the FRG in exchange for assured transit rights.

The easing of obstacles to inter-German communication undercut

---

* Named for a senior German diplomat (and EEC president), this barred the FRG from maintaining diplomatic relations with any state that recognized the GDR.
† This was needed to convince the treaty's many domestic critics that it did not betray German national interests. Brandt argued that it conceded only what had long since been lost.

the feeble legitimacy of the GDR regime and foreshadowed its ultimate collapse. Elsewhere in Eastern Europe, including the USSR, non-Communist states could now supervise observance of human rights, as detailed in 'Basket 3' of the Helsinki accords, in exchange for their recognition of the post-war borders. In the short term the accords seemed to have given the East the better bargain, since expressions of international concern at violations were routinely ignored. But on a long-term view most benefits accrued to the West, since the USSR and its allies were put on the defensive and forfeited credibility.

This was one factor in the evaporation of détente after 1975. More serious blows were the expansion of Soviet influence in Africa and the continued deployment of Soviet ICBMs (SS-19s, SS-20s) in Eastern Europe and the USSR itself. The West saw the former as a breach of agreed behavioural norms and the latter as evidence of a deliberate drive for military superiority. The experts preparing SALT II (due to follow in 1977) found it hard to define parity precisely, and when they did so their interpretation was questioned, especially in the USA. The final straw was the invasion of Afghanistan. Reluctantly, President Carter withdrew the draft treaty from the Senate's agenda. Already before his Republican successor took over in 1980, Western rearmament was well under way. NATO planned to station intermediate-range cruise and Pershing missiles in several Western European countries, whence they could reach Soviet targets within minutes, giving the defenders no time to identify them and respond.

Moscow could at least exploit politically the widespread public opposition to this scheme, and welcomed the apparent fulfilment of a long-term Soviet objective, the 'de-coupling' of Western Europe from the United States. But the military implications were grave, especially in the light of President Reagan's threat to construct, in the western USA, an invulnerable system of mobile strategic missiles (MX) as well as a defensive anti-ballistic missile system in space (SDI). Whether or not these projects were feasible, technically or economically, they presented the Soviets with a challenge they could scarcely meet. By 1983 talks on arms control were breaking down and the scene seemed to be set for Armageddon III.

The arms problem overshadowed all other aspects of East–West relations, from diplomacy to economics. In 1980 the supply of American grain, which for years had been exported profitably to the USSR, was cut off in reprisal for the invasion of Afghanistan, and many Western states boycotted the Moscow Olympic Games. A propaganda element was involved here, for neither move was crippling. Similarly, the USSR could get round the embargo imposed by an international committee (Cocom) on trade in strategically valuable raw materials or equipment. On balance the 'second cold war' probably strengthened the Soviet regime, by giving the leaders a pretext to dig in their heels and consolidate their hold over the population: 1984 was not quite as sinister as George Orwell had predicted, but the situation was worse than at any time since Stalin.

Viewed in historical perspective, Soviet foreign policy had failed abysmally. The accretion of military strength, impressive as it was in many ways, had not improved Soviet security, and the USSR had precious few friends abroad – except in some developing countries that demanded an unduly large share of its meagre resources. The goodwill it had encountered in the 1950s was largely lost. The time was propitious for what Gorbachev could call 'new thinking' in international affairs.

CHAPTER 24

Gorbachev and After

PERESTROYKA

A reformist CPSU General Secretary is as rare as a liberal Pope. Yet in 1985 one such came to power, in the person of Mikhail Sergeyevich Gorbachev, and initiated changes that had consequences as unintended as they were overwhelming: the collapse of the Soviet order six years later. For the first three years of that tumultuous epoch the establishment maintained its grip on power. But in 1988 Russian 'society', as often before, took matters into its own hands. Civic activism from below unleashed a veritable revolution in which the non-Russian nationalities took a leading role. The USSR had to withdraw from its 'outer empire' in Eastern Europe, and this encouraged spokesmen for the minority republics to demand national sovereignty, and independence from Moscow, for themselves also. The Russians, who found a leader in Boris Yeltsin, followed their example. In vain did Gorbachev seek to transform the USSR into a genuine federation of equal sovereign states. Too much tension had built up beneath the surface over the previous decades, and the CPSU had lost its aura of invincibility. It was grievously split and faced challenges on all sides. Even so, the process of disintegration was on the whole remarkably non-violent. For this much of the credit is due to skilful management by Gorbachev and his advisers, who at successive critical junctures resisted the temptation to unshackle the vast repressive machinery they still commanded.

The leader's character, as so often in Russian and Soviet history, offers a clue to understanding what happened, although a fuller explanation requires one to consider ideological, institutional and socioeconomic factors as well, to say nothing of the international context. Born in 1931 in Stravopol' territory (in southern Russia), Mikhail Sergeyevich lost two members of his family to Stalin's terror but, like most of his generation, grew up as a convinced Stalinist. His excellent work record and native intelligence earned him a place at Moscow State University (1950), where he graduated in law. Later, back in Stavropol', he secured a second academic degree in agricultural economics and entered on a successful career in the local Komsomol and party apparatus. His swift rise to the centre of power owed something to contact with the high-ranking dignitaries who frequently visited the spas of the region, as well as to his achievements in boosting production. By 1978 he was in Moscow as a CC secretary with responsibility for agriculture; appointment to the Politburo followed a year later.

Outwardly Gorbachev adopted a conformist stance, but, as he told friends in private, his faith in ideological orthodoxy had been shaken by Khrushchev's 'secret speech'. He realized that the Soviet system had become mired in bureaucratic rigidity and corruption. Gorbachev was at heart a pragmatist who thought that by allowing greater public initiative the Party could recover its revolutionary ardour and take the lead in speeding up economic development and modernizing Soviet society. In this he resembled Khrushchev, but whereas the latter employed high-handed coercive methods, Gorbachev preferred the arts of persuasion. He spoke fluently and with a conviction that won him respect; he was the first Soviet leader who could use television to good effect. Both reformist party chiefs faced opposition from vested interests in the *nomenklatura*, but Gorbachev was less willing to bend under pressure and more ruthless in dismissing critics who obstructed his measures. He was also luckier in that party officials had come to recognize that change was inevitable, and were readier to compromise than their predecessors had been in the 1960s. By 1985 it was clear to thinking people generally that the gerontocracy was leading the country into an impasse.

This did not mean that the fifty-four-year-old Gorbachev's selection to succeed the ailing Chernenko as General Secretary was a foregone conclusion, or even that there were any evident policy differences within the Politburo. During Chernenko's brief spell in power Gorbachev chaired its sessions (and controlled the Secretariat), but jealous rivals, who feared his superior education and intelligence, keenly watched his performance. In December 1984 he delivered a relatively outspoken address to ideological functionaries in which he used three terms that would become hallmarks of his policy in later years: democratization, 'openness' (*glasnost'*), and 'reconstruction' (*perestroyka*).

Their implications were far from clear, but the speech was understood by insiders as setting out his credentials for the top job. When his colleagues nominated him as General Secretary three months later, they suppressed their reservations and Gorbachev reassured them that 'we have no need to change our policy [which] is correct and truly Leninist'.

At this point he saw himself as a continuer of the disciplinarian line taken by Andropov (with whom he had been closely associated), but his views were flexible, not to say chameleon-like. As he came to realize that the chief obstacle to 'accelerated development' lay in the *nomenklatura*, he assumed the guise of a 'new Lenin' – the reflective Lenin of 1922 who was ready to act unconventionally to destroy the bureaucratic monster engendered by the revolution. When neo-Leninism in turn failed to yield results, Gorbachev moved to an essentially Social Democratic position, favourable to political pluralism and the market, while taking care to disguise its radicalism in a cloud of ambiguous rhetoric. 'Reconstruction' turned out to be a rubbery term that meant different things as the pace of change speeded up. Gorbachev's statesman-like qualities were most evident in foreign affairs; at home he responded to events as much as he shaped them, particularly after 1989, when his personal popularity, which had previously reached an unprecedented peak, rapidly declined, while his international prestige remained high.

On taking over, Gorbachev moved smartly to cut out dead wood in the party and government apparatus. His main rival, G. V. Romanov, disappeared amid rumours of scandal: he was reputed to have borrowed precious tsarist silverware for a private party. Among those promoted were fellow 'Andropov men' like N. I. Ryzhkov, Ye. K. Ligachev, and the KGB chief, V. M. Chebrikov. All of them would soon fall out with their master once his growing radicalism threatened party supremacy. He got on better with the new foreign minister, E. A. Shevardnadze, a former associate who replaced the long-serving Gromyko, kicked upstairs to become head of state (until Gorbachev took the job himself in 1988). Equally important were the General Secretary's behind-the-scenes advisers, who had a considerable influence on policy making. A. N. Yakovlev, whom Brezhnev had 'exiled' to Canada an ambassador in 1973 for attacking the 'Russophile' chauvinists, became in effect the chief architect of *perestroyka*.

In March 1986, when the CPSU held its Twenty-seventh Party congress and elected a new CC, 40 per cent of its members were fresh to the job and their average age had declined; by mid 1987 over half the powerful provincial party secretaries (*obkomsecs*) had been dismissed. In many outlying areas this purge was associated with a drive against corruption. No fewer than 25,000 policemen (under the interior ministry) were sacked, of whom 1,500 faced criminal charges. Even the KGB felt the winds of change, but as in the 1950s, it was cleverer at weathering the storm and remained a major hindrance to progress towards turning the USSR into a 'law-governed socialist state' – a term that implied abandonment of the Party's monopoly of power and the *nomenklatura*'s privileges. At the 1986 congress this delicate issue was not tackled and most of the rhetoric ran on traditional lines, although the Party adopted a reformist programme and statute. The emphasis was less on political change than on economic development, as shown by the adoption of a grandiose national plan for the rest of the millennium, which was soon forgotten.

Within a few weeks this complacent attitude was subjected to severe shock. On 26 April 1986 an explosion destroyed reactor block 4 in the atomic power station at Chernobyl, north of Kiev. It was the world's first major peace-time nuclear disaster. Clouds of radioactive fallout spread north to the Baltic and even reached Western Europe. The population was evacuated from a thirty-kilometre zone around the site, but 10,000 square kilometres were contaminated to some degree and hundreds of thousands of people exposed to radiation; the loss to the economy was incalculable. The authorities were laggard in responding to the disaster and at first tried to conceal its extent. Gradually it became clear that reactors of this type, originally designed to produce plutonium for the military, had serious design faults and that the accident was the result of negligence. Politically, the fallout was no less important: it showed up the defects of Soviet-style bureaucratic management and fondness for secrecy. Years later Gorbachev called it a turning-point in the development of *glasnost'*.

With increasing boldness the media began to voice critical opinions. The popular journals *Ogonek* and *Moscow News* investigated a range of topics hitherto taboo. Their circulation soared, as did that of the literary magazine *Noviy mir*, now edited by the environmentalist and writer S. P. Zalygin. Already in 1985 Yevtushenko had signalled the advent of literary 'openness' with a self-critical poem, 'Fuku'. Several works long held up by the censor were allowed to appear. Among them was Anatoliy Rybakov's *Children of the Arbat*, which dealt truthfully with the Stalin years (and gave a memorable portrait of the dictator). A sequel appeared in 1988, by which time Soviet readers keen to discover what, when, and why things had gone wrong could acquaint themselves with Pasternak's *Dr Zhivago*, Vasiliy Grossman's Second World War novels, or memoirs by Yevgeniya Ginzburg and Nadezhda Mandelshtam. Belletristic works by *émigrés* (Zamyatin, Brodsky, even Solzhenitsyn) appeared, as did translations of modern Western classics such as George Orwell's *1984*. Still more influential were cinematic masterpieces like Tengiz Abuladze's *Repentance* and A. Prokshin's *Cold Summer of '53*, which touched on aspects of the Terror. Mikhail Shatrov's plays encouraged audiences to look afresh at Lenin and the revolution. Cinema and theatre workers were more radical than writers, whose union retained a strong conservative element. In 1987–8 hundreds of informal organizations, mainly pursuing cultural ends, sprouted all over the country as people took advantage of the new intellectual freedom. The atmosphere of exaltation resembled that of the late 1850s or of 1905–6. It was as if a magic spell had been broken.

Professional historians were slower to react, since they had been so thoroughly tamed. It was one thing to discuss 'deformations of socialism' under Stalin, another to find merit in Bukharin (rehabilitated in February 1988, fifty years after his judicial murder) or even Trotsky, still another to question the views of Lenin or Marx. Yet within a few months all these steps had been taken and the ground was littered with fallen idols. School authorities had to ordain that no history examinations should be held in 1988: the old ideological verities were discredited but revised textbooks had yet to be written. To fill the void, some Russian patriots resurrected the memory of Stolypin and Nicholas II, and a small but noisy organization, *Pamyat'* (Memory), revived the antisemitism of the Union of Russian People.

A far worthier civic body, Memorial, sought to commemorate the victims of Stalin's Terror, whose mortal remains were exhumed by the tens of thousand at Kuropaty (near Minsk), Vynnitsa in Ukraine, and many other mass-killing sites. In November 1988 a national 'conscience week' drew attention to the plight of surviving Gulag veterans. Memorial activists received some assistance from local authorities, but there was no systematic official effort to pursue in justice those responsible for grave breaches of human rights, even symbolically. Not until 1991 were steps taken to rehabilitate *en bloc* all those who had been 'repressed'. Likewise, the authorities clung for as long as possible to their self-serving interpretation of the Katyn massacre, despite Polish pressure.

There was a strong ethical component in the efforts made to come to terms with the past, to which the various religious communities tried to respond. Gorbachev had been baptized as an infant but was not a believer. In November 1986 he called for 'a decisive and uncompromising struggle' against religion, but that was his last such statement, for he soon realized that a compromise with churchpeople could aid his cause. Some consecrated buildings that had been taken over for secular use were restored to their rightful owners. In June 1988 the millennium of Russian Orthodoxy was celebrated in style (with Moscow, not Kiev, as the focus!). Previously Gorbachev had received the Patriarch,* in the first such meeting between Church and state leaders since 1943, and promised that freedom of conscience would be guaranteed by law. Such a law was indeed passed in October 1990; it allowed churches to set up their own schools and, once registered, to own property. The CRA was abolished, as were restrictions on the import of religious literature. By 1991 the Russian Orthodox had some 12,000 churches (1985: 6,806); the number of Catholic parishes had grown by half (to 1,525), while Islamic places of worship numbered 2,300 (1985: 392) – a much faster expansion. Protestants registered a modest increase (to 624) and Jewish synagogues a decline (91 to 70), largely because many Jews emigrated at this time. In November 1989 the Ukrainian Uniate church was legalized. This was not to the liking of those Russian hierarchs who had benefited from its suppression (in 1946) and who showed little eagerness to re-examine their own compromised past.

In February 1986 Gorbachev authorized the release of the leading Jewish 'refusenik', A. Shcharansky, a founder of the Moscow Helsinki group, who promptly left for Israel. The persecution of dissidents continued for a while, but later that year, in a still more spectacular intervention from on high, Andrey Sakharov was brought back to Moscow from enforced arrest in Gor'ky. He was the most prominent of the deputies whom the Academy of Sciences (after conservative

---

* Pimen died in 1990, to be succeeded by Alexii II.

foot-dragging) elected to the reformed legislature, where he became a leading liberal member. Opinion polls showed him to be one of the most popular figures in the land, and his death in December 1989 evoked a nation-wide display of grief.

By this time the political situation had been transformed by institutional changes, forced through by Gorbachev in the teeth of opposition by his colleagues, party *apparatchiki*, and the military. Serious divisions within the leadership emerged in the summer of 1987 when, with Gorbachev absent from Moscow, Ligachev and Chebrikov came out with hardline statements calling for discipline and criticizing the civic groups as disloyal. Gorbachev also faced criticism from the left, by Yeltsin, whom he had appointed party secretary in Moscow. Yeltsin was more zealous than most local bosses in dismissing corrupt functionaries and curried popular favour by talking to shoppers in queues, taking public transport, and convoking meetings at which he would answer citizens' questions frankly. When he touched on the *nomenklatura*'s privileges, he incurred Ligachev's wrath and decided that Gorbachev's reforms did not go far enough. In October 1987 he broke an unwritten convention by openly criticizing Ligachev at a meeting of the Party's CC. Clientelism and bureaucracy, he declared, were thriving as never before. At once he was denounced for 'political adventurism', sacked from his post, and shortly afterwards from the Politburo, too. Personal ambition played a part in his outburst, as he himself later conceded, and the row had important consequences: he never forgave Gorbachev for humiliating him.

In these circumstances it was remarkable that Gorbachev managed to hold on and even consolidate his position. He did so by summoning an extraordinary party conference,* a device that allowed him to mobilize grass-roots support for his policies against foes in high places without waiting for the next congress. To avert the blow they arranged for publication in a conservative paper of a letter, ostensibly written by a hitherto unknown Leningrad chemistry teacher, Nina Andreyeva, in which the reformers were characterized as rootless intellectuals eager to restore capitalism (13 March 1988). Some anxious weeks passed before Gorbachev, who was abroad at the time, counter-attacked. The

---

* As distinct from a *congress* (held at five-year intervals); the last such conference had been in 1941.

pre-conference electoral campaign was unusually lively, for it witnessed an open struggle between reformists and conservatives, the central authorities for once intervening on behalf of the former. Abuses called forth vocal protests. Multi-candidate elections had been abandoned in the 1920s. Most party functionaries found their reintroduction shocking, as they did the publicity given to the debates when the conference convened (June 1988). Some radicals called for the right-wingers to resign. After stormy discussions the assembly endorsed a scheme of Gorbachev's that emasculated the Secretariat and took a big step towards constitutional government.

Henceforth the Party, while keeping its political monopoly, was to yield governmental power to the soviets, according to Lenin's original scheme. This was not democracy: the local party boss was normally to be soviet chairman, but only after a free election. The main legislative body, the Supreme Soviet, was to become a real parliament, meeting in regular sessions instead of just for a few days to rubber-stamp decisions taken elsewhere, as previously. It could amend the Constitution and determine the main lines of policy. In March 1989 fiercely contested elections were held.* They were not conducted according to Marquess of Queensbury rules: some seats were reserved for official candidates, and party bodies had ample opportunity to vet and harass candidates. In many constituencies only one name appeared on the ballot paper. Yet turn-out was high (89.8 per cent) and in several places leading party officials went down to defeat. In Moscow Yeltsin, now on the rebound, was vindicated at the polls by a 89.4 per cent affirmative vote.

When the congress met in May, Gorbachev was duly elected chairman, but support for him was far from unanimous. The Supreme Soviet convened the next month and proved to be an equally rumbustious body. Nominees for ministerial jobs were quizzed and several of them rejected. This quasi-democratic system did not work well. There were no proper parties ('fractions') in the Western sense and little respect for procedural rules. The same was true of the reformed legislatures in the various republics (except in the Baltic). A major weakness of the USSR legislature was that Gorbachev, the chairman, had not stood for popular

* To a Congress of People's Deputies, a 2,250-man 'super-legislature' from which the 542-member Supreme Soviet was to be chosen.

election but owed his position solely to his party office. Moreover, the new arrangements had scarcely taken shape when he proposed another fundamental change. He was now willing to jettison the notorious article 6 of the Brezhnev Constitution, which legalized the Party as 'the force that directs and guides Soviet society', a step he had hitherto strongly resisted in public. In exchange he wanted parliament to elect him *President* of the USSR, an office modelled on the French (Fifth Republic) and American precedents. Only his eventual successor, not he himself, was to be popularly elected. A mere two thirds of the deputies voted for this (15 March 1990), and a simple majority quite reasonably wanted the new President to surrender his party post. This he would not do. As has been well said, he wanted to be Luther and the Pope. Supposedly above all parties, yet the leader of one, he was fatally weakened in the forthcoming contest with Yeltsin, who owed his position as *Russian* (RSFSR) leader to a democratic vote. Gorbachev's presidency of the USSR lasted less than two years in which he was on the defensive, desperately trying to hold the country together. When the USSR collapsed he and his office disappeared into limbo, along with the CPSU.

REVOLT OF NATIONS

Gorbachev shared with Khrushchev (and most other party leaders) an inability to comprehend the explosive potential of suppressed national feeling. He had made his career in a region where ethnic tensions were not particularly acute and adhered to the comfortable Leninist belief that any such animosities could be assuaged by timely socio-economic reform. He was a rationalist for whom efficiency mattered more than equality among nations and failed to see that, for example, cutbacks in non-essential investment in the national republics would upset local leaders who, for instance in Central Asia, depended heavily on allocations from the centre. In the past Brezhnev had tacitly tolerated an accommodation with local élite interest groups that *perestroyka* now threatened to subvert. Of fifty-five ministers at all-Union level appointed between 1985 and 1987, fifty were Russians, as were almost all Politburo members. In December 1986 the replacement of a native by a Russian as party first secretary in Kazakhstan touched off serious unrest. Kazakh students in Almaty (then Alma-Ata) destroyed Soviet symbols – including, rather unfairly, a bust of Brezhnev! – and twenty-six people were killed in the mêlée. This was an ominous warning which the 'centre' was slow to heed, although Gorbachev did at least now acknowledge that the nationality question had not been solved, as propagandists had long asserted, and called on social scientists to study such issues more intensively. Alas, the more they did so, bringing Stalin's legacy under critical scrutiny, the more vociferously did the minorities demand radical change. Criticism of Moscow's centralist cultural policies had a clear political subtext.

Among the civic organizations formed after 1987 were bodies in several non-Russian republics that coalesced into 'popular fronts', ostensibly in defence of *perestroyka* but actually to advance demands for the native language to be declared official, in preference to Russian, for a halt to Slav immigration, or for action on environmental issues. By 1988 street demonstrations in the Baltic states, Moldova, and elsewhere were attracting tens of thousands of participants. Old national flags were brought out of the cupboard and displayed in lieu of the hammer and sickle. The republican CPs could not remain immune to this pressure from below. Frequently they split. In most minority republics a majority of the local party cadres favoured concessions to their compatriots. Those who remained loyal to the 'centre' had difficulty in discovering what its policy was. By and large Moscow stressed the advantages of unity in a new, reformed federation – thereby acknowledging that the existing federation was bogus and straining its own credibility. The rights actually to be conceded were left to be fixed by negotiation, but the social climate was too bitter for peaceful settlement of disputes, while even Moscow hardliners shrank from imposing control by force and so abandoning *perestroyka*. Not until 1990 did a law specify how a national republic might in practice exercise its nominal right to secede from the USSR. The law's complicated provisions remained on paper, for history was being made elsewhere.

The first major popular demonstrations anywhere in the Union took place in Riga, the Latvian capital, in June 1987 to commemorate compatriots deported just forty years earlier. On the fiftieth anniversary of the Molotov–Ribbentrop pact over a million Balts linked hands in a human chain that stretched from Tallinn in Estonia to Vilnius in Lithuania. Other rallies marked the winning of independence after the

First World War. In Estonia and Latvia the movement at first focused on cultural issues, partly because of the strong Russian presence. This was less of a problem in Lithuania, where in 1988 a popular front (*Sajūdis*) took shape that represented no less than 1,000 local civic bodies. Notably, half its founding members were Communists anxious to show solidarity with the people, but within months they had yielded influence to radical nationalists led by the musicologist V. Landsbergis. *Sajūdis* and its counterparts in Estonia and Latvia won striking victories at the polls and dominated the local legislatures, where deputies passed laws changing the status of the native language, restoring symbols of national sovereignty, and rewriting their republics' constitutions in a democratic sense.

The Estonians were the first to take this provocative step (November 1988). They wrote into their republic's laws the provisions of the UN human rights charter, as a precaution in case the Soviets should invade. In the event Moscow just declared their action invalid and a 'war of laws' followed. However, the Baltic states' dependence on energy imports from Russia was a source of weakness. So, too, were the Russian immigrant communities in their midst, which with aid from Soviet troops began to organize resistance. There was trouble over Balts who deserted from the armed forces and the KGB carried out several terrorist acts.

In March 1990 Lithuania declared herself independent. Soviet tanks were brought up, but Gorbachev would not give the generals a green light for drastic repression. Instead he placed an embargo on energy supplies. Reluctantly the Lithuanians were persuaded not to implement their independence declaration while talks were held to reduce tension. But they did not give in and established ties with other dissident republics, including Russia, where Yeltsin, now in charge, gave the Baltic cause verbal support. Moscow conservatives, who hated Yeltsin and scorned Gorbachev for vacillating, planned to restore the centre's control by effecting military *coups*, much as in 1940. They knew that the Western powers would not intervene and were in any case busy in the Persian Gulf. In January 1991 Soviet troops stormed a media centre in Vilnius and announced that a national salvation committee was taking over. Fourteen Lithuanians were killed, 150 injured – in full view of television watchers around the world. A smaller-scale operation was mounted in Riga, but Gorbachev, concerned at the international impact, called off the one planned in Tallinn and then disowned the plotters, of whose plans he was, of course, aware. The extremists cried betrayal. The Balts boycotted an all-Union referendum on a new federal treaty and instead voted massively for independence. They even won some Russian residents to their side.

A similar situation developed in Moldova. Measures of linguistic russification had long been unpopular with the native population, who comprised two thirds of the whole (Ukrainians and Russians each accounted for about 13 per cent). Here, too, there were unpleasant memories of 1940, although so long as Ceauşescu held power in neighbouring Romania (which had possessed the area between the wars) few Moldovans wanted rule by Bucharest. Massive demonstrations brought concessions on cultural policy, but then events took a more violent turn than in the Baltic. Local Russians set up their own 'Trans-Dniestrian' republic to act as a counterweight to newly independent Moldova. General A. Lebed''s Soviet army (the Fourteenth) at first looked on approvingly, but in 1992 imposed a precarious truce that ensured for Moscow a dominant influence in the region.

There was much more violence in Transcaucasia, and here, too, Russian intervention – more political than military – yielded ambivalent results. The initiative in dissolving imperial bonds was taken by Armenian nationalists who wanted to annex Nagorny Karabakh, a mountainous area inhabited mainly by their compatriots, which Stalin had awarded to Azerbaijan. Baku treated it as a colony and discriminated against the inhabitants, but wanted to keep control. As in 1905, Muslim fanatics responded with pogroms of Christian Armenians resident in Azerbaijan. Hundreds of thousands of people fled in each direction as fighting broke out between rival militia bands. Occasionally Soviet troops also became involved, but Moscow's main concern was to mediate the dispute, not least to ensure that the border with Turkey and Iran remained under its control. It was unwilling to sanction the territorial changes Armenia wanted lest this serve as a precedent elsewhere, so that negotiations broke down. By 1991 both republics had seceded. Oil-rich Azerbaijan held the stronger cards, but the Armenians had more friends abroad. Their country suffered from a blockade by its neighbours and the effects of a disastrous earthquake.

In Georgia the nationalist upsurge led to the formation of patriotic societies which, like civic bodies elsewhere, espoused cultural aims with political undertones. Activists sought to restore the country's pre-1921 independence yet refused to countenance similar demands by smaller peoples (Abkhazians, Ossetians) resident in Georgia, suspecting that their claims were manipulated by Moscow. Again there was fighting in which Russian soldiers sometimes became embroiled. In April 1989 interior ministry troops wielding shovels and firing poison-gas shells attacked a crowd of peaceful Georgian demonstrators, most of them women, in the capital, Tbilisi, killing (according to unofficial sources) thirty-six. It was the worst such incident for many years and radicalized the national movement. The first free elections (October 1990) brought to power a loose coalition headed by a former dissident, Z. Gamsakhurdia. He staged a referendum in which 98.9 per cent of those voting favoured independence, but then took an authoritarian line that led to his overthrow in 1992. He was replaced by Shevardnadze, formerly Gorbachev's foreign minister (and prior to that the republic's party boss). Though more pro-Russian, he took care not to infringe too overtly the national sovereignty that the fiery Georgians were so proud of.

Continuity in the leadership during these turbulent years was still more marked in Central Asia, where modern secular nationalism was less developed and popular mobilization episodic. Violence was confined to a few localities and directed mainly against fellow-Muslim outsiders (such as Chechens) rather than Russians. However, the latter felt unwelcome and many of them chose to leave, so reversing the migration flow of earlier decades. In 1990 the Uzbek party chief I. A. Karimov, emulating Gorbachev, managed to get himself elected as president by the local legislature. His example was followed elsewhere, notably in Kazakhstan (N. Nazarbayev); Kyrgyzstan's leader, by contrast, was an eminent scientist, A. Akayev. All these men were eager to maintain close relations with Russia. This made good sense, given these republics' ethnic make-up, their continuing need for foreign (largely Russian) expertise, and the proximity of China. Only in Tajikistan was politicized Islam a factor. This republic, bordering on Afghanistan, could not remain aloof from events there, and by the end of 1991 the scene was set for a complex conflict between rival clans, regions, and ideologies. But as a whole Central Asia avoided the great upheaval some outside observers had predicted, and kept neighbouring Islamic states at arm's length.

The national awakening extended to many oriental groups, Islamic or not, that lacked union-republic status: Chechens, Ingush, and others in the Caucasus, Tatars of the Volga and Crimea, even Sakwa (Yakuts) and the small peoples inhabiting northern Russia and Siberia. They had no shortage of grievances, but seldom could these be assuaged even if their neighbours were well-disposed. After staging massive protests in Moscow the Crimean Tatars who had been deported by Stalin were allowed to return, where they were treated badly by the Ukrainians and Russians who had settled on their ancient lands. The Volga Tatars were better off economically (oil!) and eventually reached a mutually profitable deal with the Russians, as did the Bashkirs in what is now called Bashkortostan. The northern forest peoples suffered from the economic breakdown, which in particular meant that no funds were available to repair the decades of ecological damage that had undermined the basis of their way of life.

Of the three Slav peoples, the Belarusians had traditionally displayed the feeblest sense of ethnicity, so that the strength of the national revival here came as a surprise. It owed much to the effects of Chernobyl. A popular front, 'Renewal', founded in June 1989, did well at the elections but failed to win control of parliament. Even so the deputies proclaimed Belarus sovereign in July 1990. Their move did not necessarily imply secession, since most people, especially old party cadres, wanted to remain within a reconstituted USSR and did not care for market economics.

Ukrainians, by contrast, were divided regionally over their attitude towards Moscow. Those in the west were the most nationally conscious, whereas areas such as the Donbas and Crimea had large russophone populations whom local Ukrainians found it politic not to offend. By and large there was little tension, and the local Russians were prepared to give Ukrainian nationhood conditional support; Ukrainian patriots for their part were more anti-Soviet than anti-Russian. The popular front, here called *Rukh* ('the Movement'), was slower to emerge, partly because Kiev under Shcherbitsky was a bastion of Communist hardliners, and when it did its electoral success was patchy: it won a landslide victory in the west but only one third of the seats in Khar'kov. In mid 1990 *Rukh* gained force when the Ukrainian CP leadership switched its line and sought common ground with the patriots. L. Kravchuk, a former party official, became *Rukh*'s chairman. He pursued a centrist course, seeking to accommodate Moscow over the potentially dangerous Crimean question, which gave Russian nationalist extremists a lever to meddle in Ukraine's affairs.*

In Russia itself the political scene was chaotic, and none too promising from the viewpoint of those who hoped for a stable democratic order to emerge. The extremists in *Pamyat'* and other bodies (such as V. Zhirinovsky's LDRP)† were vocal but numerically weak and organizationally divided. At the other pole stood the (genuine) liberal democrats, who were also split into several factions which periodically came together to form electoral blocs. Party-building was an even more painful business in the 1980s than it had been in the 1900s, testimony to the regression of Russian political culture during seventy years of dictatorship. Perhaps the most significant group was the RCP (Russian Communist party), which in 1990 broke away from the CPSU to denounce Gorbachev's slide towards capitalism.

Yeltsin had no party behind him once he had melodramatically resigned from the CPSU. His authority rested on his position as elected chairman of the RSFSR legislature (later as elected President), and in a less formal sense on his reputation as a people's tribune who inveighed against the 'centre' 's malpractices and Gorbachev's in particular. The gap between the two men was not really as wide as it seemed at the time. Yeltsin stood for democracy, pluralism, and a market economy, while Gorbachev held fast to the 'socialist option'. Yeltsin wanted the future Union to be a loose confederation, whereas Gorbachev preferred a reformed federation in which the CPSU and central planners would continue to play a leading role. Yeltsin wanted the CPSU to forfeit its behind-the-scenes role in public life and decried the KGB as 'a monster'. With hindsight it is clear that both leaders were lukewarm about privatization and wanted Moscow to have the last word within the (former) empire.

The dyarchy at the centre (which faintly resembled that under Vasiliy Shuisky during the Time of Troubles) seriously impaired its

---

* The Russians were in a majority in the Crimea and did not care for the attribution, by Khrushchev in 1954, of their region to Ukraine, even if Kiev granted it autonomy. Gorbachev and Yeltsin were both disposed to let sleeping dogs lie.

† Although this party had the words 'liberal democratic' in its title, this was a demagogic feint. Some observers suspected that it originated with the KGB, which Zhirinovsky, however, energetically denied.

authority. Foreign opinion sympathized with Gorbachev. Within the USSR educated people veered towards Yeltsin, the first popularly elected leader in Russian history. Ordinary folk, however, resented both men's preoccupation with a partisan struggle that brought little apparent benefit. Democracy still had the allure of novelty, but there was an undercurrent of support for extremists, whether 'Red' or 'Brown', who stood for strong government and the maintenance at all cost of the social safety net. Ideologies were at a discount and Russians generally were even more confused than they had been in 1917.

ECONOMIC DECLINE

Gorbachev's experience as an agricultural scientist and manager did not equip him for the role of economic supremo and the experts he consulted gave contradictory advice. Few realized that the command economy needed not reform but replacement. In June 1985 Ligachev warned that any changes would occur 'within the framework of scientific socialism, without any deviations towards a market economy'. This was a shot across Gorbachev's bows, since he was interested in Hungary's 'new economic mechanism' and Deng Xiaoping's reforms in China.

His first steps were designed to boost discipline rather than effect structural change. In November 1985, in a move reminiscent of Khrushchev, he set up a 'state agro-industrial committee' with broad supervisory powers, which accomplished nothing and disappeared, unlamented, four years later. Scarcely more effective was another committee established to monitor product quality. Industrial decision making was once again decentralized, this time to enterprise level, but firms still had to meet mandatory state orders. Managers often used their new powers to increase the factory wage fund, so buying labour peace but adding to inflation, instead of investing in new technology. Yet this was the principal object of the drive for 'accelerated development': by 1990 one third of industry's capital stock (especially in engineering) was to be replaced so as to bring Soviet products (and productivity) up to Western standards. Gorbachev did not appreciate that the over-extended Soviet budget could not afford to finance this effort. One could not simultaneously modernize equipment, boost output, improve quality, and produce new types of goods – all this without running further into debt.

True, over the next few years the supply of foodstuffs and consumer durables expanded, but mainly by exploiting reserve capacity. By 1989 inflation was running at 7 to 10 per cent per annum and the budget deficit had quadrupled. Government expenditure was increased by the Chernobyl disaster and the 1988 Armenian earthquake, while revenue from oil exports was hit by a fall in the world price. Hitherto the state had benefited massively from the proceeds of the vodka monopoly. Ligachev was the chief proponent of a temperance campaign (begun timidly under Andropov) that by 1989 had halved the number of alcohol-related deaths and raised Russia's flagging birth-rate. The drop in consumption (from 13.4 to 5.6 litres per capita in the RSFSR, 1984–8) was certainly desirable morally and socially, but it alienated many people and, above all, cost the state some 28 milliard roubles in lost revenue – one reason why the temperance drive stalled after 1988.

Instead of being drastically curbed, government expenditure rose relative to the GNP (from 49.7 per cent in 1985 to an average of 52.4 per cent in 1987–9). Cuts in the defence sector had yet to make themselves felt; the new industrial equipment was expensive; and still more costly were consumer subsidies, which doubled between 1985 and 1990, from 58 to 111 milliard roubles. A. Åslund, who offers these data, calculates that the domestic state debt rose from 18.2 per cent of GNP to 42.8 per cent by late 1989.

The general public did not appreciate the gravity of this situation; but neither did those in charge, at least until 1989. Certainly Gorbachev's views were evolving. The ban on economic activity by individuals and their families, imposed in the early 1930s, was rescinded in 1987, but two years later a mere 300,000 people were employed in private enterprise. Five million others worked in cooperatives, which produced goods worth about 3 per cent of GNP; these were most prominent in the service sector (catering, repairs) and performed many jobs hitherto done illegally. Yet the black market expanded, for these businessmen (*biznesmeny*, a pejorative term) could not obtain enough materials from public sources. Those who got rich quickly aroused envy among the egalitarian-minded, especially blue-collar workers and pensioners. This neo-NEP was almost as unpopular as its forerunner. As for organized labour, it remained remarkably docile until 1989, when miners in several coalfields set up independent trade unions and bargained over wages. Those in the Kuznetsk basin were among the most radical: reckoning that their pits were more modern, they toyed with the idea of privatization under Yeltsin's aegis. But most industrial workers held to a more traditional outlook, and the same was true of farm employees.

The peasants' entrepreneurial spirit had been unnaturally distorted, if not destroyed, by collectivization half a century earlier, so that Gorbachev did not really have a 'Chinese option' (i.e. to follow Deng's lead). To stimulate incentive, he revived the scheme for collective contracts he had advanced unsuccessfully several years earlier, whereby several households (or 'links') would commit themselves to perform specified tasks more or less as they wished (see page 477). But farm managers failed to tie payments to results. More successful was a policy switch on private plots, now belatedly recognized as consonant with 'socialist agriculture'. Their holders were allowed to do on them what they wanted (for instance, raise cattle), and by 1990 the plots' share in the nation's food supply had risen by several percentage points.

Gorbachev then took a more innovative step by authorizing farms to lease unexploited land and buildings to anyone willing to take them on. 'The people,' he intoned, 'must once again become full-fledged masters of the land.' However, the land remained in state ownership; collective and state farms were not disbanded. Such a move would have been unpopular with most rural workers, especially women and the elderly, who had become reliant on them. The response to this reform was sluggish, partly because the pioneers were harassed by local officials, and in Russia at least real progress had to wait until Yeltsin took over: in 1991 the number of individual farms rose tenfold (to 40,000); even so, they were far from dominating the rural landscape.

Meanwhile both Gorbachev and Yeltsin had begun to grapple with the formidable problem of transition to a market economy. This meant freeing prices, which would inevitably leap to levels that people could not afford. On three successive occasions Gorbachev's liberal advisers (L. Abalkin, G. Yavlinsky, S. Shatalin) presented him with reform plans involving extensive privatization. Each time he drew back from the brink. Yeltsin was more venturesome, at least in words (the last such scheme was set in motion by both leaders jointly), but his RSFSR government could do little so long as the USSR remained in being. Some Western economists consider that a more resolute course should have been taken earlier; others hold that the command economy was unreformable. Foreigners had little input into the reform process prior to 1992, but the USSR was treated quite generously by its trading and financial partners (even, grudgingly, by the IMF). Germany in particular was lavish with support (75 md marks committed by late 1991), for reasons that had much to do with international security.

ENDING THE COLD WAR

From the start Gorbachev took an activist, self-confident approach to foreign affairs. In this he was ably assisted by Shevardnadze, who proved to be a flexible politician, in sharp contrast to the stodgy, bureaucratic Gromyko. Moscow's 'new thinking' implied a fundamental revision of Soviet concepts and behaviour. The old ideological class-based attitude to international politics was jettisoned in favour of an emphasis on common human values. The prime objective was to save civilization by ending the arms race, for in a world of interdependent states, it was now held, security was mutual and could be achieved only by dialogue, not threats; nuclear deterrence was out of date.

Already before Gorbachev took power the USSR had rejoined the arms control talks, which were pursued with fresh vigour. The new leadership held to the doctrine that a 'reasonable sufficiency' of arms had been attained. The deployment of medium-range missiles was temporarily halted. In July 1985 the USSR unilaterally suspended its underground nuclear tests in a moratorium that eventually lasted for eighteen months, and later that year, in Washington, Shevardnadze offered to halve nuclear weapon stocks in return for curbs on research into SDI. In December Gorbachev flew to Geneva for the first of several 'summits' with US President Reagan. The meeting led to a constructive personal *rapport* between the two leaders and a vague agreement to accelerate arms-control negotiations. At these talks the Soviets proposed the phased elimination of all nuclear weapons by the year 2000 – a goal rendered somewhat less unpalatable to the West by Moscow's apparent readiness to allow international on-site inspection of (certain!) defence installations. The Soviets also agreed to allow such inspection of military manoeuvres, to serve as a confidence-building measure. Western governments were under growing pressure from public opinion, which welcomed each Soviet initiative and made Gorbachev a popular figure abroad. His acceptance in May 1986 of the American 'zero option' plan for intermediate- (and short-)range 'Euromissiles' came as something of an embarrassment, especially to the British and French, with their independent deterrent strategy, since their nuclear forces would be affected as well.

Gorbachev sprang another surprise on Reagan at their second meeting, at Reykjavik in October 1986, by agreeing to eliminate *all* nuclear weapons so long as the 1972 ABM treaty was strictly observed (i.e. work on SDI had to be confined to the laboratory). Later he yielded on this point, too. The way was now clear for the signature, in Washington on 8 December 1987, of a treaty that eliminated all 'Euromissiles'. The cuts were asymmetrical: the Soviets had to destroy four times as many SS-20s as there were cruise missiles and Pershings. This signified adoption of a purely defensive strategy. Logically, the next year Moscow pledged unilateral cuts in its conventional forces (a reduction of half a million men), declared it would withdraw from Afghanistan, backed arrangements to end regional conflicts in the third world, and accepted the legitimacy of Western concern for the observance of human rights within the socialist bloc. Even more important was an unpublicized decision not to use force to stop the USSR's East European allies from choosing the political systems they wished – an abandonment of the 'Brezhnev doctrine' that was fated to produce unexpectedly swift and dramatic results.*

Soviet European policy had to take second place to the effort to reach a grand compromise with the United States, a goal that had overriding priority. Already in 1984 Gorbachev, on his first visit to

---

* Some critics claim that this revolution in military and foreign policy could be attributed to Soviet inability to match American technological superiority, and that this was responsible for the West's cold war 'victory'. This is to take too narrow a view. Gorbachev apparently acted on the assumption that SDI was an impracticable scheme that could if necessary be countered without undue effort. By and large the military and scientific lobby preferred hawkish policies and it took much persuading (not least by Marshal S. Akhromeyev) to win its support for disarmament and *perestroyka*. This is not to deny that a large element of *Realpolitik* was involved in the change of policy, which was designed to improve the USSR's security in the long run by reaching mutually profitable bargains with its erstwhile foes.

London, had impressed Margaret Thatcher ('I like Mr Gorbachev. We can do business together,' she memorably declared), and the British premier played a mediating role in overcoming Reagan's initial hesitations; in 1987 she visited Moscow to the plaudits of the crowds. Unlike his predecessors, Gorbachev succeeded in establishing cordial relations with many Western leaders irrespective of their political colour. His personal charm (and the gracious elegance of his wife Raisa) became a major asset to Soviet diplomacy.

The chief problem, of course, was Germany. Initially, as the NATO country most favourable to the deployment of 'Euromissiles', it was the main target of Soviet criticism. The East German leaders were openly critical of *perestroyka* and exerted pressure in Moscow, where proponents of 'new thinking' on the German question, Shevardnadze among them, were still very much in a minority. Chancellor Kohl did not help matters when he once rashly compared Gorbachev's rhetoric with that of Goebbels, so setting off a mini-crisis. But later the two statesmen established a remarkable rapport. Soviet insistence on West Berlin's special status held up conclusion of a technical cooperation agreement with Bonn, but a compromise formula was found and in July 1987 Gorbachev hinted to President von Weiszäcker that Germany's division would not last for ever: 'history will decide'. He was thinking in terms of decades and, like all decision makers in the West, assumed that for the foreseeable future the two German states would form part of an eventual new all-European security structure, to be based on the CSCE.*

The NATO allies were dubious about such ideas and scornful of Gorbachev's notion of building a 'common European home' in which all peoples on the continent should co-exist amicably. Yet by 1988 this idea was assuming realistic shape. The Soviet leader was willing to accept that Western international agencies such as the EEC and the Council of Europe could serve as the nucleus of future unity, and in July 1989, visiting Strasbourg, he even voiced tepid approval of NATO: sovereign states were free to cooperate for their security as they wished, so long as this promoted détente. He had previously made a wildly

---

* The Conference on Security and Cooperation in Europe (now OCSE), which had developed out of the arrangements for monitoring the 1975 Helsinki accords: see page 518.

popular tour through the German Federal Republic and signed a declaration pledging 'unqualified respect for the norms and principles of international law, especially the people's right to self-determination'. This was a hint that free elections would be allowed in the GDR and elsewhere in the east, so overcoming the continent's schism.

No one anticipated that this would occur within months, under revolutionary pressure from below, as governments toppled from Pankow to Sofia. Suddenly the USSR was stripped of its security belt established so painfully in the 1940s and a power vacuum created that the West was poised (but none too eager) to fill. Hanging over this void, the Warsaw Treaty Organization simply withered away. Soviet troops in Hungary, Czechoslovakia, and Poland were gradually withdrawn as these countries swiftly reasserted their independence. But what was to be the fate of the half-million men left stranded in the former GDR? That could be settled only by a bilateral deal with Bonn, backed by simultaneous quadripartite agreements with the other Second World War allies.

In 1990–91 Moscow cut its losses and executed a brilliant damage-limitation exercise. The so-called 'two plus four' talks led to a settlement whereby the newly reunited Germany, freed of the last Allied restrictions on her sovereignty, might remain in NATO and thus firmly linked to the West, but with an army reduced in strength,* and committed to acceptance of the Oder–Neisse frontier, along with other borders in the east. (This meant that the north of former East Prussia, Kaliningrad district, remained awkwardly isolated as a Soviet, later Russian, enclave.)

The Western Allies harboured reservations about these agreements, but Bonn worked hard to allay fears that a resurgent Germany would dominate Europe or play the 'Rapallo card'. The same problem overshadowed Germany's relations with her eastern neighbours. In regard to the USSR, and later Yeltsin's Russia, suspicions were allayed by economic aid (not least to build housing for relocated Soviet troops). But nothing Bonn or its allies did could appease the nationalists and Communist hardliners. The award to Gorbachev of the Nobel Peace

---

* No Allied troops or nuclear weapons were to be stationed in the former GDR, where the Bundeswehr incorporated some elements of the former army. The last Soviet troops left Germany according to schedule in August 1994.

Prize (October 1990) did him little good at home, where he was increasingly blamed for the loss of Eastern Europe as well as for the socio-economic breakdown.

These world-shaking events deflected attention from Soviet policy in Asia. Already in 1985 Sino-Soviet relations improved, and next year, speaking at Vladivostok, the Soviet leader offered China cooperation in railway construction and exploitation of the Amur. This signalled concessions on the disputed border, from which some Soviet troops were withdrawn. A similar gesture was made in Afghanistan and the DRV urged to evacuate its forces from Cambodia. This went some way towards fulfilling Beijing's conditions for normalization. However, when Gorbachev visited the Chinese capital in 1989 his successes were nullified by the massacre of demonstrators in Beijing's Tiananmen Square. Privately he was disgusted, but he kept a tactful silence and, less justifiably, imposed restraint on Soviet reporting of the affair.

Efforts to better relations with Japan did not get far, for reasons discussed earlier (see page 442), but there was modest compensation in Korea: Moscow established ties with the South, so all but isolating the PDRK. For former Soviet clients in the third world the new message was chilly: henceforth they had to stand on their own feet. Moscow disengaged itself from southern Africa and urged its Angolan protégés to seek peace with their foes. Cuba was badly hit. Its vast debt (80 per cent of all money owed by third-world countries) led the Soviets to cut oil deliveries and press for structural reforms. Like the East Germans, the Cubans censored Soviet publications critical of Castro. Gorbachev paid a visit in the spring of 1989, but professions of friendship could not conceal the rift. Meanwhile in the Middle East the last Soviet troops had quit Afghanistan (February 1989), leaving Najibullah's regime to face the *mujaheddin* as best it could. Steps were taken to resume diplomatic relations with Israel and the PLO urged to seek a compromise settlement. The supply of Soviet weaponry to Ethiopia tapered off and Moscow welcomed moves towards ending its civil war: the former pawn on the world chessboard had become an embarrassment.

COLLAPSE AND RENEWEL

The USSR did not, as is sometimes said, implode. It fragmented as centrifugal forces asserted themselves and challenged Moscow's authority, already gravely undermined by the Gorbachev/Yeltsin schism. The President tried to keep the crumbling empire together, mainly by peaceful means. He gave the *coups de main* in the Baltic only qualified support, acting in part under duress: in November 1990 a leading right-wing deputy, the 'Russian-Latvian' Colonel V. Alksnis, warned Gorbachev to restore order at once or face the consequences, and in Red Square a lone gunman fired shots at him. The appointments he made that winter, notably of V. Pavlov as premier, showed that he was leaning tactically to the right. Shevardnadze resigned, in a blaze of publicity, as a protest against impending dictatorship. But who was to be the dictator, Gorbachev or one of his nationalist-Communist critics? They had neither an obvious leader nor an alternative to *perestroyka*.

As in 1917, the rumour mills worked overtime. While conspirators in the security establishments wove their intrigues, hundreds of thousands took to the streets in support of democracy. Yeltsin took advantage of the situation. He could not prevent Gorbachev from holding a referendum on turning the USSR into a union of sovereign equal states (17 March 1991), but he could put a second question on the ballot paper: should Russia have its own President? Seventy per cent of voters favoured the idea, and after a noisy campaign Yeltsin was duly elected to that office on 12 June. He owed his victory in large part to a schism in the Russian CP. A reformist group under Colonel (later General) A. Rutskoy broke away. Two years later his ally, and vice-presidential running-mate, would become a bitter enemy.

Fortified by the referendum results, Gorbachev swung left again. Turn-out was high (80 per cent) and 76.4 per cent of those voting wanted to preserve the USSR. But the question was phrased so as to make it a 'motherhood issue': who would not want a renewed federation that promised sovereignty to its constituent republics and full guarantees of minority rights?* The details still had to be hammered out in

---

* The referendum was not held in the Baltic states, Moldova, Georgia, or Armenia.

talks held at Novo-Ogarevo, outside Moscow. The task was like trying to square a circle: a process that in Western Europe was taking decades had to be forced through in months, by leaders of states that lacked a democratic culture, and in an atmosphere of growing crisis. Each draft agreement promised more to the republics. The last, published on 14 August 1991, was a red rag to the plotters.

Early in the morning of the 19th tanks rolled into central Moscow. A state of emergency was imposed by an eight-man committee representing the chief organs of state power (interior ministry, KGB, army). Gorbachev, then in the Crimea, was said to be ill – a transparent subterfuge. The plan was presumably to win him over, eliminate Yeltsin, and then Gorbachev, too – much like General Kornilov in 1917. But the *putsch* was half-hearted and poorly organized. The soldiers did not know what to do, the conspirators faltered. Yeltsin addressed the crowds from atop an armoured vehicle – another echo of 1917. He declared the *coup* unconstitutional and called for resistance. This was courageous. He went on to show who was now master: when Gorbachev, freed from arrest, returned to Moscow, his rival publicly humiliated him, exploiting the fact that the conspirators had been his appointees.

The events of 19–22 August spelled the end of the Soviet system. The initiative passed from Moscow to the union republics. Those not already independent announced that they were taking this ultimate step. Gorbachev resigned as CPSU General Secretary. The Party's Central Committee disbanded and its property came under public control. On 29 August all its operations were formally suspended, but the ban was not enforced rigorously. The KGB, too, survived under other sets of initials, and may even have gained in importance now that the CPSU was in eclipse.

While Yeltsin built up an apparatus and brought various Union agencies under his control, Gorbachev pursued the talks on federation, the auspices for which were worse than ever. On 18 October eight of the twelve states still in the USSR agreed to set up an economic community. Ukraine was not among them, and even Yeltsin's Russia harboured reservations. There were too many difficult decisions, such as how to share out the USSR's national debt.

By this time the economy was virtually in free fall. Inflation was leaping by 2 to 3 per cent a week. Industrial production dropped off. Wages lagged ever farther behind prices. Those who had savings watched them melt away. As during the civil war, the printing presses worked overtime but there were not enough banknotes to meet demand. Meat that sold for 5 roubles in Poltava cost ten times as much in Moscow because Ukraine suspended exports. In St Petersburg, as Leningrad was now again known, the mayor announced food rationing, then changed his mind. Air transport was grounded for lack of fuel.

The only remedy was a swift transition to market relations, or so the pundits argued. But who would willingly bear responsibility for the resulting social dislocation? Even the most insistent reformers aimed to maintain the purchasing power of the poor.

The final blow came, rather unexpectedly, from Ukraine, where in a referendum on 1 December 90.3 per cent of voters endorsed independence. A few days later leaders of the three Slav republics, meeting near Brest-Litovsk, announced that the USSR was moribund. Its successor was to be a Commonwealth of Independent States (CIS), which eight non-Slav republics promptly agreed to join. On 25 December Gorbachev delivered a moving valedictory address. The Red flag over the Kremlin gave way to the Russian tricolour. But there was little rejoicing: the present was grim enough, the future still more uncertain.

The USSR's sudden collapse was a traumatic shock for Russians. Scarcely anyone had expected such a dénouement. Other twentieth-century empires had frittered away gradually. It was easier for the peoples of Eastern Europe, and even for minorities in the CIS, to adapt to new conditions than it was for citizens of the region's hegemonic nation. Before and after 1917 Russians had tended to assume that their leading role within their imperium was in the best interests of those over whom they ruled. This attitude carried on after 1991 in regard to their neighbours in what was now called 'the near abroad'.*

Matters were complicated by the presence of some 25 million Russians in the other CIS states, whose grievances and aspirations could be exploited by demagogues. Fortunately for international peace, the diaspora was itself too diversified to act as an effective political force, but there were many points of tension, notably the Crimea and the

---

* The Russian Federation used in its title the term *rossiiskiy*, rather than *russkiy*; the former had imperial connotations.

Baltic. In the former friction developed over the status of Sevastopol'
and the fate of the Black Sea fleet. In the latter Russians complained
about discriminatory citizenship laws. By 1996 Belarus, under an
authoritarian ruler, had drawn closer to Moscow. The two countries
(with Kazakhstan and Kyrgyzstan) formed a customs union as a first
step towards closer integration. Within the Russian Federation the
Chechens' yearnings for full sovereignty led to a bitter and ultimately
unsuccessful war which grievously harmed the Yeltsin regime's image
at home and abroad.

The East European nations sought protection within an expanded
NATO, an idea Moscow regarded with alarm. It countered with an
alternative 'European security architecture' that was unacceptable to
the West. The danger of a new cold war was, however, kept at bay. In
general Russia's relations with the United States and its allies developed
positively. There was practical cooperation in a host of fields, on a
scale that could not have been dreamed of a decade earlier. Nuclear
arms were gradually withdrawn to Russia from the three other republics
where they had been deployed. The former rivals for world supremacy
carried out an extensive programme to destroy their surplus destructive
capability. Russia might no longer be a superpower (a status Moscow
had anyway never openly claimed), but so long as she possessed a
nuclear deterrent she was still a force to be reckoned with – dangerously
so, since her political order was still unstable.

The 1993 Russian Constitution guaranteed human rights, civic
freedoms, and democratic institutions, but like that of 1906 its provisions were not always observed in practice. The federation was
admitted to the Council of Europe, yet the rule of law remained as
much aspiration as fact. There was political interference in the judiciary,
and offenders imprisoned in labour colonies (which still existed, though
unpublicized!) endured grim conditions. City streets were no longer
safe and gang warfare claimed many victims.

On the other hand, turnout was high in the 1996 presidential elections, which were in the main fairly conducted and resulted in a
victory for Yeltsin, who despite his tarnished image promised better
government than his Communist rival. The Communist party (now
KPRF) was the most highly structured, and with its Agrarian allies
appealed especially to those who pined for the security afforded by the
old system. But its ideology was in tatters and the 'Reds' had no realistic

chance of turning back the clock. Nor could the nationalistic right ('Browns') maintain their initial high standing in the polls. *Faute de mieux*, people were still willing to give liberalism and democracy a chance. In a country that had experienced little of either this was encouraging. Yet it was also true that civic culture was weak. All too few Russians were willing to accept public responsibilities. The weight of the paternalistic tradition was evident in the tendency of prominent figures to attract clients and to bestow favours in return for their support. (Not that patronage is unknown in mature democracies!)

The authoritarian past manifested itself in arbitrary rule-making by the executive and occasional heavy-handed treatment of the media. Journalists objected, and some paid for their professionalism with their lives. It was dangerous to inquire too closely into *mafiosi* with connections in high places. Press circulation fell from the high level of the later 1980s, and publishers generally had a thin time: the demand for their wares existed, but the means did not.

So it was, too, with the arts, which could no longer be subsidized extensively as in Soviet times. In 1994 the number of concert performances was half what it had been four years earlier and theatre-goers had shrunk from 54 to 33 million. In 1995 the entire CIS produced only thirty films, one tenth as many as in the USSR's last years, and average cinema attendance fell from thirteen visits a year to one. This, of course, tells us nothing about artistic quality (Sergey Bodrov's *Caucasian Prisoner* dealt boldly with the war in Chechnya), and if the box office gave priority to American products, this was for economic rather than aesthetic reasons.

The americanization of Russian culture was frowned on by intellectuals generally. Even some ex-dissidents (V. Maksimov, A. Zinoviev) took an anti-Western position. Those of a neo-Slavophil (or better, Russophil) persuasion argued that the nation's organic unity had been brutally sundered; materialistic egoism was triumphing over shared virtues. Theirs was 'a nostalgia for the sickness of Sovietism' (G. Nivat). Reformers countered that at least the new invaders came with peaceful intent; they had brought 'only about as much thievery as there always used to be in Russia, making allowances for differences of scale' (L. Anninsky).

There was no longer much demand for the products of giant factories, geared mainly to the needs of the military-industrial complex, and their workforce was largely idle. There was, however, relatively little unemployment (1995: 3.2 per cent), since the authorities feared to toss surplus labour on to the street: better to keep people on the payroll even if they received only a nominal wage. Strikes were organized, notably by desperate miners, but achieved little. By the mid 1990s it seemed as if the decline in industrial output was 'bottoming out' (1994: −21 per cent; 1995: −3 per cent), but official statistics were very misleading. They did not include the earnings 'on the side' that enabled many people to survive. In 1995 GNP was put at half what it had been ten years earlier. Inflation, astronomic in the first post-Soviet years, fell to a monthly rate of 1.2 per cent (June 1996), but the rouble's future seemed in doubt even though the government hoped to make it convertible. The budget deficit, which had been 10 per cent of GNP in 1994, fell to about 4 per cent the next year. The chief problem was a notoriously inefficient tax system. The well-to-do had their own rules.

The most obvious feature of this 'insider capitalism' was the mafia. Gangsters dealt in raw materials or products belonging to the state or dubious corporations, while others speculated on the financial market. The proceeds were salted away abroad or else spent on luxuries (for instance, villas under close guard). All this was a far cry from the modest enrichment permitted to the old *nomenklatura* (which provided many recruits to the new élite). These inequalities made people angry and aroused misgivings even among ardent Western advocates of the market. Yet the 'Paris Club' of Russia's creditors was induced to be forgiving over the country's $55-milliard external debt, and the IMF likewise was lavish with loans: $6.3 milliard in 1995, followed by a promise of $10 milliard over the next three years – this despite the slow progress being made in privatizing the economy.

It is too early to attempt a balance sheet of the Yeltsin years. What contemporaries called 'transition' (usually without specifying *to what*, but with the West implied as the model) involved greater hardship, and encountered stiffer opposition, than optimists had anticipated in 1991. But where it was a matter of altering ingrained habits of thought and conduct, the process was bound to take generations. Russia had suffered worse crises – the Time of Troubles, the revolutionary years 1917–22, the Second World War – and had survived. She would do so again.

ABM: anti-ballistic missile.

Academy of Sciences: highest academic body in Russia/USSR, with branches in various union republics and dozens of institutes, founded 1726.

Agitprop: Agitation and Propaganda Department (of CC of CPSU).

apparatchik: colloquial term for officials in party or government apparatus; functionary.

artel: informal group for cooperative agricultural or artisanal work.

assignat: paper rouble, whose value fluctuated *vis-à-vis* that of precious metals.

ASSR: autonomous Soviet socialist republic; a territorial-administrative division for certain (ethnic) regions, with fewer formal rights than a union republic.

barshchina: corvée; compulsory labour performed by serfs for their master (seignior).

bednyak: in Communist terminology, a poor peasant.

besprizornik: lit. 'one deprived of care'; a homeless waif.

Black hundred: term used by adversaries of right-wing band supportive of autocracy and using violence against 'disloyal elements' such as Jews, intellectuals.

black repartition: general redistribution of landed property, stock, and equipment.

Bolsheviks: *see* RSDRP.

boyar: in medieval era, senior or wealthier noble; in Muscovy, holder of first noble rank.

CC: Central Committee (of CPSU).

CCP: Chinese Communist party.

Centre, the: all-Union party and government organs; in Comintern affairs, the directing bodies in Moscow.

Cheka: All-Russian Extraordinary Commission for Combating Counter-Revolution, Sabotage and Speculation; the security police, December 1917–22, when it was renamed GPU (State Political Administration), in 1923 OGPU (Unified GPU).

chin, *chinovnik*: rank, rank- (or office-) holder in military or bureaucracy.

CIS: Commonwealth of Independent States.

clientelism: informal arrangement, in a bureaucracy, whereby a patron confers favours on subordinates in return for political support.

Cominform: Communist Information Bureau: body coordinating activities of certain European Communist parties, 1947–56.

Comintern: Third (Communist) International, 1919–43: an agency to promote proletarian solidarity and revolution, directed from Moscow.

Cossacks: to eighteenth century, free warrior bands in southern steppes, composed originally of fugitives from Muscovy or Poland-Lithuania; in imperial era, frontier defence forces organized in communities ('hosts'), often used as police auxiliaries.

CP: Communist party.

CPR: Chinese People's Republic, 1949–.

CPSU: Communist Party of the Soviet Union; successor to RCP(b), 1918–25 and AUCP(b), 1925–52.

CRA: Council for Religious Affairs; government agency under party control to supervise Christian Churches and other faiths.

CSCE: Conference on Security and Cooperation in Europe.

cult of the individual: euphemism current after 1953 for terror and other excesses committed by and under Stalin.

dacha: suburban land allotment, usually with cottage or hut, in rare cases a villa.

delation: informing authorities of other people's allegedly disloyal or suspicious thoughts or conduct.

DRV: Democratic Republic of Vietnam.

druzhina: in medieval era, a prince's military retinue.

duma: council; earlier historians inaccurately called the Muscovite ruler's informal advisory council the 'Boyarskaya Duma'.

Duma, State: lower house in bicameral national legislature, 1906–17, also in post-Soviet Russia.

dvor: homestead, household; a ruler's court.

ECCI: Executive Committee of the Communist International.

FRG: Federal Republic of Germany, 1949–.

GDR: German Democratic Republic, 1949–90.

General Secretary (of CPSU): the chief officer, from 1953 to 1966 known as First Secretary.

glasnost': 'openness' as distinct from secrecy, implying something less than freedom of information.

GMD: Guomindang (Kuomintang), a coalition of democratic forces in China.

GNP: gross national product.

Gosplan: State Planning Commission (Committee).

gost': in Muscovy, a merchant of the highest category.

Greens: in civil war, peasants who formed bands for local self-defence against Red or White marauders.

Group A/B: broadly, capital/consumer goods.

Guards: in imperial era, privileged regiments with many nobles serving in the ranks.

guberniya: in imperial era, province; the main administrative division, sub-divided into *uyezdy* (= counties) and *volosti* (rural districts).

Gulag: properly, GULag: Chief Administration of Corrective Labour Camps, a department of the NKVD; loosely, the Soviet penal administration under Stalin, which maintained ITK (corrective-labour colonies) and ITL (corrective-labour camps), and also supervised 'special settlers'.

hetman or *ataman*: elected chief of Cossack band.

ICBM: inter-continental ballistic missile.

inorodtsy: lit. 'those of other stock': subjects of the tsar belonging to none of the recognized Christian confessions.

jadid: among Muslims, enlightener, advocate of secular modernization.

jihad: holy war, as preached by Muslims.

Kadets: Constitutional Democrats; the chief liberal party, active 1905–17.

KGB: Committee for State Security, 1954–91; successor to Cheka, GPU/OGPU, NKVD, MVD, MGB.

kholop: slave.

khozraschet: profit-and-loss accounting.

kolkhoz: collective farm.

kolkhoznik: peasant or other worker resident on a *kolkhoz*.

kombed: committee of village poor.

Komsomol: Communist Youth League, the CPSU's chief organization for adolescents and young adults.

korenizatsiya: in 1920s, policy of staffing party and government posts in non-Russian areas with natives rather than Russians.

KPD: Kommunistische Partei Deutschlands.

kremlin: fortified area in medieval Russian town.

kruzhok: informal intellectual discussion circle.

kulak: derogatory term for relatively well-to-do peasant.

Marxism-Leninism: 'scientific communism': from mid 1920s, official term for the ideology of the CPSU, adherence to which was obligatory for all Soviet citizens.

maximalists: in 1917, term used by moderates of Bolsheviks, Anarchists, and other left-wing extremists.

Memorial: civic organization dedicated to commemorating victims of state repression in Soviet era.

Mensheviks: *see* RSDRP.

meshchane: members of the estate (*soslovie*) of townspeople, comprising most merchants, artisans, etc.

mestnichestvo: in Muscovy, practice of filling major appointments (military and civil) according to a noble candidate's genealogical and/or service record.

MGB: Ministry of State Security, 1946–53.

militia: in Soviet era, regular (as distinct from security) police.

MPLA: People's Movement for the Liberation of Angola.

MTS: machine-tractor station, 1928/30–58.

muzhik: patronizing term for peasant.

MVD: Ministry of Internal Affairs, 1801–1917, 1946–.

nadel: land allotment of peasant household.

nakaz: list of grievances (= *cahier de doléance*); instruction, esp. to Legislative Commission by Catherine II, 1766.

narodnichestvo: Populism; ideological and political movement favouring socialism based on peasants' communal institutions.

narodnost': concept of a nation bound by organic links.

NEP: New Economic Policy, 1921–8.

nepman: trader or small manufacturer permitted to conduct business by the NEP.

NKVD: People's Commissariat of Internal Affairs, 1917–46; from 1934, security police, successor to OGPU.

nomenklatura: list of official positions to which holders were appointed by a party organization at the appropriate level; more generally, party or state officials enjoying privileges.

NPT: non-proliferation treaty, pledging signatories not to acquire or develop a nuclear weapons capability.

obkomsec: secretary of a provincial party organization (*obkom*).

oblast': province; in Soviet era, chief administrative division of a (union, autonomous) republic.

obrok: annual payment by serfs to master for use of land farmed on their own account.

obshchina: village community, responsible for organizing routine agricultural tasks and in some areas periodically redistributing communal land among householders, with obligations to the state as well as to its members.

Octobrists: Union of 17 October: moderate liberal party, active 1905–17.

opolchenie: militia, esp. national levies organized in 1611–13, 1812, 1854–5.

OPEC: Organization of Petroleum Exporting Countries.

oprichnina: tsar's personal domain, 1564–72, in which selected servitors (*oprichniki*) used terroristic methods to press claims against nobles deemed disloyal, their kinsmen and servants.

otkhod: practice of leaving farm for labour in industry, transport, etc.

Pale: in imperial era, area of western Russia in which most Jews were obliged to reside.

Pamyat' (= Memory): right-wing antisemitic organization formed in 1980s out of movement to preserve historical monuments.

PCF: Parti communiste français.

PCI: Partito comunista italiano.

PDRK: People's Democratic Republic of Korea.

perestroyka: lit. 'restructuring': a reform of the economic and institutional order initiated from above.

plenum: full assembly, esp. of members of the CC.

pogrom: violent destruction by criminal bands of lives and property, esp. of Jews.

Politburo: Political Bureau of the CC of the CPSU, the Party's supreme decision-making body, from 1952 to 1966 known as Presidium.

pomest'ye (pl.: *-a*): estate or plot of land granted to a seignior (*pomeshchik*) on conditional tenure in return for state service; from early eighteenth century, any noble estate.

posad: commercial quarter of a town, inhabited by artisans, etc. (*posadskiye lyudi*).

Posol'sky prikaz: in Muscovy, foreign affairs chancellery.

PPS: Polish Socialist Party.

prikaz: in Muscovy, central government chancellery.

procuracy: state agency for supervising observance of legality by officials and for prosecution of criminal offences, 1722–1918, 1922–.

procurement: purchase of agricultural produce by state organs, through sales and obligatory deliveries at state-determined prices.

PSR: Party of Socialist Revolutionaries (SRs); agrarian socialist party, active 1901–1920s.

PUR: accepted acronym for Central (Main) Political Administration of the Armed Forces, responsible for political education and reliability of troops.

purge: of CPSU: periodical cleansing of the ranks, involving verification of performance and loyalty; members found wanting were relegated or expelled, but under Stalin often met a harsher fate.

RAPP: Russian Association of Proletarian Writers.

raznochintsy: lit. 'men of various ranks', who did not fit into the official social structure based on *chin*.

Razryad: in Muscovy, military service chancellery (for privileged servitors).

razverstka: or *prodrazverstka*: quota assessment, a system for allocating taxes, labour duties, and agricultural produce between individual regions, districts and villages in a rough-and-ready manner.

RCP(b): Russian Communist party (bolshevik); *see* CPSU.

Red Army: properly, Workers' and Peasants' Red Army (RKKA); from 1946, Soviet Army.

Red Guards: militia bands set up by workers, esp. in 1917, and later integrated into Red Army.

RSDRP: Russian Social Democratic Labour party (SDs), 1898–, which in 1903 split into Bolshevik and Menshevik factions; in 1918 the former took the name of Communists: *see* CPSU.

SAG: in Soviet zone of Germany after 1945, mixed company used to exact reparations; similar companies existed elsewhere in Eastern Europe and in China.

SALT: strategic arms-limitation talks.

SAM: surface-to-air missile.

samizdat: lit. 'self-publishing': writings produced and circulated without submission to censorship.

samoderzhets: independent or autocratic ruler.

SDI: strategic defence initiative.

SDs: *see* RSDRP.

SED: Socialist Unity party (Germany).

Senate: properly, Ruling Senate: organ for supervision of legality and coordination of administration, 1711–1917.

serf (Rus.: *krepostnoy* = bondsman): privately owned peasant (to 1861).

show trial: pseudo-judicial proceedings held for demonstrative effect and to deter potential opposition, in which the court showed prosecutorial bias and the sentence was predetermined by the political authorities.

sloboda: in Muscovy, settlement in or outside a town on privately owned land whose residents enjoyed tax-free status.

smerd: in Kievan era, (nominally) free peasant with own household.

smychka: close union between rural and urban workers.

sobor: council, esp. in Orthodox Church.

sokha: simple wooden plough.

soslovie: official social category, members of which lacked the defined rights characteristic of a Western European 'estate of the realm'.

soviet: council, originally of workers' deputies, later also of soldiers, peasants, etc.; in Soviet era, formal organ of state power, operating under party guidance.

Sovnarkom: Council of People's Commissars: the Soviet government (or those of individual union republics), 1917–46, when it became Council of Ministers.

'special settlers' (Rus.: *spetsposelentsy*): category of prisoners in Gulag under Stalin performing labour assignments under NKVD supervision, whose regime was generally less rigorous than that of camp or colony inmates.

SRs: *see* PSR.

Stakhanovite: adherent of party-directed movement to achieve feats of industrial output, setting a model for other workers to emulate, 1935–41.

starets: hermit, holy man.

State Council: chief consultative and administrative organ, 1801–1917.

Supreme Soviet: legislature at all-Union or union-republic level.

Table of Ranks: system for categorizing senior military and bureaucratic office-holders, theoretically with fourteen grades (*chiny*), 1722–1917.

troyka: group of three; in USSR, specifically, a three-member board with special powers to sentence accused without following regular judicial procedure.

trudoden' (pl.: *-dni*): work-day, a unit of account for calculating remuneration of *kolkhozniki* for work in a farm's 'socialist' sector.

tsar': from fifteenth century, autocratic ruler of Muscovy; from 1721, also known as *imperator* (= emperor).

tsenzovye: persons enjoying electoral privileges by virtue of a property qualification (*tsenz*).

udarnik: shock worker, rewarded for superior performance, 1927–35; succeeded by Stakhanovite.

ukaz: decree.

Ulozhenie: law code adopted in 1649.

Uniates: Catholics of Slavo-Byzantine rite, 1596–.

union republic: a constituent state of the (federated) USSR.

URP: Union of Russian People: chief organization of radical right, active 1905–17.

USSR: Union of Soviet Socialist Republics.

USW: Union of Soviet Writers.

uyezd: *see guberniya*.

veche: in medieval era, town assembly.

Vesenkha (properly, VSNKh): Supreme Council of National Economy, 1917–32.

volost': *see guberniya*.

votchina: patrimony; land held hereditarily as private property.

voyevoda (pl.: *-y*): military governor, seventeenth to eighteenth century.

Warsaw Pact (properly, WTO, Warsaw Treaty Organization): military alliance of Eastern European Communist states, 1955–90, counterpart to NATO.

Yezhovshchina: popular term for Great Terror, 1937–8, which downplays Stalin's responsibility.

zek: popular term for prisoner in Gulag.

zemlyachestvo: informal association of persons from same area, esp. migrants to towns.

zemsky nachal'nik: judicial and administrative post, held by local landowner, with supervisory rights over peasants' organs of self-government, 1889–1917.

Zemsky sobor: Assembly of the Land: name given by historians to consultative organ of clergy, nobles, townsmen, and (occasionally) state peasants, convoked irregularly, 1566–1653.

zemstvo: organ of local self-government in (some) rural areas, 1864–1917, the organizational basis of Russian liberalism.

Zhdanovshchina: popular term for drive against cultural and political nonconformity, 1947–.

Zimmerwaldist: during First World War, advocate of negotiated peace on basis of return to pre-war territorial *status quo*, without annexations or reparations.

This list, confined to books in English, concentrates on recent titles. Many of the works mentioned contain detailed bibliographies. London = L, New York = NY. The following abbreviations are used for post-1988 periodicals cited in the text:

Ist. arkh.	*Istoricheskiy arkhiv*
Izv. TsK	*Izvestiya Tsentral'nogo Komiteta KPSS*
Ist.	*Istochnik: Dokumenty russkoy istorii*
NNI	*Novaya i noveyshaya istoriya*
Ot. arkh.	*Otechestvennye arkhivy*
Ot. ist.	*Otechestvennaya istoriya*
Vop. ist.	*Voprosy istorii*

A. *Encyclopedias and General Reference*

Basic data

A. Brown, M. Kaser, G. S. Smith (eds.), *The Cambridge Encyclopedia of Russia and the Former Soviet Union*, Cambridge 1994; J. Paxton, *Encyclopedia of Russian History from the Christianization of Kiev to the Break-up of the USSR*, Santa Barbara CA 1993; J. L. Wieczynski (ed.), *The Modern Encyclopedia of Russian and Soviet History*, 59 vols., Gulf Breeze FL 1976–. In R. Auty and D. Obolensky (eds.), *Companion to Russian Studies*, 3 vols., Cambridge 1976–80, vol. I is on history.

Atlases include J. Channon and R. Hudson, *The Penguin Historical Atlas of Russia*, L 1995; P. R. Magocsi, *Ukraine: A Historical Atlas*, Toronto, 1986.

Of the many volumes of readings containing source materials, D. H. Kaiser and G. Marker (comps., eds.) covers a wide range of socio-economic and cultural issues: *Reinterpreting Russian History, 860s–1860*, Oxford 1994. cf. G. V. Vernadsky *et al.* (eds.), *A Source Book for Russian History from Early Times to 1917*, 3 vols., New Haven CT – L 1972.

B. *General Histories*

Three introductory accounts are: E. Acton, *Russia: the Tsarist and Soviet Legacy*, 2nd ed., L – NY 1995; J. M. Thompson, *Russia and the Soviet Union: An Historical Introduction*, 2nd ed., Boulder CO – Oxford 1990; P. Dukes, *A History of Russia: Medieval, Modern, Contemporary*, 2nd ed., Basingstoke – L 1990.

N. V. Riasanovsky, *A History of Russia*, 5th ed., NY – Oxford 1993; and D. MacKenzie and M. W. Curran, *A History of Russia and the Soviet Union*, Homewood IL 1977, are more substantial textbooks. Older, but still useful: M. T. Florinsky, *Russia: A History and an Interpretation*, 2 vols., NY 1953.

The multi-volume *Longman History of Russia* (gen. ed. H. Shukman, Harlow – NY) contains the following titles: S. Franklin and J. Shepard, *The Emergence of Rus, 750–1200*, L 1996; J. L. I. Fennell, *The Crisis of Medieval Russia, 1200–1304*, 1989; R. O. Crummey, *The Formation of Muscovy, 1304–1613*, 1987; P. Dukes, *The Making of Russian Absolutism, 1613–1801*, 2nd ed., 1990; D. Saunders, *Russia in the Era of Reaction and Reform, 1801–1881*, 1992; H. Rogger, *Russia in the Age of Modernization and Revolution, 1881–1917*, 1983; M. McCauley, *The Soviet Union since 1917*, 1981, 2nd ed., 1993.

National and regional histories

FINLAND: E. Jutikkala and K. Pirinen, *A History of Finland*, rev. ed., NY 1973.

BALTIC PEOPLES: D. Kirby, *The Baltic World, 1772–1993: Europe's Northern Peoples in an Age of Change*, L – NY 1995; T. U. Raun, *Estonia and the Estonians*, 2nd ed., Stanford CA 1991; A. Bilmanis, *A History of Latvia* (1951), repr., Westport CT 1970; A. E. Senn, *The Emergence of Modern Lithuania*, NY 1959.

POLAND: N. Davies, *God's Playground: A History of Poland*, 2 vols., Oxford 1981.

JEWS: S. Baron, *The Russian Jew under Tsars and Soviets*, NY 1964; see also section E below.

UKRAINE: O. Subtelny, *Ukraine: A History*, Toronto (1988) 1994.

GEORGIA, ARMENIA: R. G. Suny, *The Making of the Georgian Nation*, Bloomington IN – Stanford CA 1988; id., *Looking Towards Ararat: Armenia in Modern History*, Bloomington – Indianapolis IN 1993.

AZERBAIJAN: A. L. Altstadt, *The Azerbaijani Turks: Power and Identity under Russian Rule*, Stanford CA 1992.

CENTRAL ASIA: E. Allworth, *The Modern Uzbeks: from the Fourteenth Century to the Present: A Cultural History*, Stanford CA 1990; M. B. Olcott, *The Kazakhs*, Stanford CA (1987) 1993.

TATARS: A. A. Rorlich, *The Volga Tatars: A Profile in National Resilience*, Stanford CA 1986; A. W. Fisher, *The Crimean Tatars*, Stanford CA 1978.

(Most of the above Stanford CA publications are in the *Studies in Nationalities* series, ed. W. S. Vucinich.)

SIBERIA: Yu. Slezkine, *Arctic Mirrors: Russia and the Small Peoples of the North*, Ithaca NY – L 1994; J. Forsyth, *A History of the Peoples of Siberia: Russia's North Asian Colonies, 1581–1990*, Cambridge 1992.

FAR EAST: J. J. Stephan, *The Russian Far East: A History*, Stanford CA 1994.

COLONIAL EXPANSION IN GENERAL: M. Rywkin (ed.), *Russian Colonial Expansion to 1917*, L – NY 1988.

Social and economic

J. G. Blum, *Lord and Peasant in Russia from the Ninth to the Nineteenth Century*, Princeton NJ 1961, takes a predominantly social approach; R. E. F. Smith and D. Christian, *Bread and Salt: A Social and Economic History of Food and Drink in Russia*, Cambridge 1984.

Cultural

J. H. Billington, *The Icon and the Axe: an Interpretative History of Russian Culture*, L – NY (1966) 1970, is stimulating but idiosyncratic. T. Talbot Rice, *A Concise History of Russian Art*, L – NY 1963; G. R. Seaman, *History of Russian Music*, vol. I, Oxford 1967.

SCIENCE: A. Vucinich, *Science in Russian Culture . . .* , 2 vols., Stanford CA 1963, 1970: the first vol. to *c.*1860, the second to 1917. L. R. Graham, *Science in Russia and the Soviet Union: A Short History*, Cambridge 1993.

C. *From the Origins to 1689*

General

G. V. Vernadsky's *A History of Russia*, New Haven CT – L 1944–69, consists of 5 vols., the last in two parts.

RELIGIOUS: Of A. P. Vlasto, *The Entry of the Slavs into Christendom: An Introduction to the Medieval History of the Slavs*, Cambridge 1970, one quarter deals with the Rus' lands. The (posthumously published) work of J. L. I. Fennell, *A History of the Russian Church to 1448*, L 1995, is authoritative. The 2-vol. *Medieval Russian Culture*, ed. respectively H. Birnbaum and M. S. Flier and M. S. Flier and D. Rowland, Berkeley CA – L 1984, 1994, contains interesting essays.

LEGAL: D. H. Kaiser, *The Growth of the Law in Medieval Russia*, Princeton 1980; M. M. Balzer (ed.), *Russian Traditional Culture: Religion, Gender and Customary Law*, Armonk NY 1992.

ECONOMIC: J. Martin, *Treasure of the Land of Darkness: the Fur Trade and its Significance for Medieval Russia*, Cambridge, 1986.

BEFORE KIEVAN RUS': M. Gimbutas, *The Slavs*, L – NY 1971.

KIEVAN RUS': B. A. Rybakov, *Kievan Rus*, Moscow 1984, gives a Soviet view; for a Ukrainian one, see Subtelny (UKRAINE above). D. Obolensky, *Byzantium and the Slavs: Collected Studies*, L 1971, contains 13 essays.

The flavour of the epoch can best be recaptured by reading the chronicles. *The Russian Primary Chronicle*, tr. and ed. S. H. Cross, Cambridge MA 1953, and *The Chronicle of Novgorod, 1016–1471*, tr., ed. R. Mitchell and N. Forbes (1914), repr. Gulf Breeze FL 1970, may be supplemented by S. A. Zenkovsky's ed. of *The Nikonian Chronicle . . . to 1132*, vol. I, Princeton NJ 1984; and, for the Ukrainian lands, G. A. Perfecky's tr. of *The Galician-Volhynian Chronicle*, Munich 1973.

OTHER SOURCES: S. A. Zenkovsky (ed.), *Medieval Russia's Epics, Chronicles and Tales*, NY 1963, brings together works in various genres.

AGRICULTURE: R. E. F. Smith, *The Origins of Farming in Russia*, Paris – The Hague 1959, should not be overlooked.

NOVGOROD: H. Birnbaum, *Lord Novgorod the Great: Essays in the History and Culture of a Medieval City-State*, 2 vols., Columbus OH 1981; M. W. Thompson, *Novgorod the Great*, L 1967.

TATARS AND RUS': C. J. Halperin, *Russia and the Golden Horde: The Mongol Impact on Medieval Russian History*, Bloomington IN 1985, presents an iconoclastic view of the 'Tatar yoke'. In the classic tradition, but relatively free from 'Moscow-centrism': A. E. Presniakov, *The Formation of the Great Russian State: A Study of Russian History in the Thirteenth to Fifteenth Centuries*, tr. A. E. Moorhouse, Chicago 1970.

WEST RUSSIAN LANDS: sadly neglected, but see S. C. Rowell, *Lithuania Ascending: A Pagan Empire Within East Central Europe, 1295–1345*, Oxford 1994.

Growth of Muscovy

Sources: H. W. Dewey (comp., tr., ed.), *Muscovite Judicial Texts, 1488–1556*, Ann Arbor MI 1966; A. Kleimola, *Justice in Medieval Russia . . .*, Philadelphia PA 1975; the two authors have published other works in tandem. S. von Herberstein, *Description of Moscow and Muscovy*, a classic contemporary account first published in 1556, is indifferently ed. B. Picard, tr. J. B. C. Grundy, L 1966.

IVAN III: J. L. I. Fennell, *Ivan the Great of Moscow*, L – NY 1961, is fuller than I. Grey, *Ivan III and the Unification of Russia*, L 1964.

N. S. Kollmann, *Kinship and Politics: The Making of the Muscovite Political System*, Stanford CA 1987, stresses the oligarchical element in the early Russian polity (cf. a forthcoming study, *Honor and Society in Early Modern Russia*); so, too, does G. Alef, *Rulers and Nobles in Fifteenth-Century Muscovy*, L 1983 (collected essays).

IVAN IV: The best short biography is R. G. Skrynnikov, *Ivan the Terrible*, ed., tr. H. F. Graham, Gulf Breeze FL (1974) 1981. A. E. Presniakov, *The Tsardom of Muscovy*, ed., tr. R. F. Price, Gulf Breeze FL 1978, is an essay of 1918. N. Andreyev, *Studies in Muscovy . . .* , L 1970, reprints 14 articles by a leading sixteenth-century specialist; other articles are contained in D. C. Waugh, *Essays in Honor of A. A. Zimin*, Columbus OH 1985. B. Nørretranders, *The Shaping of Czardom under Ivan Groznyj*, Copenhagen 1964. M. Perrie, *The Image of Ivan the Terrible in Russian Folklore*, Cambridge 1987, is stimulating; A. Yanov, *The Origins of Autocracy: Ivan the Terrible in Russian History*, tr. S. Dunn, Berkeley CA – L 1981, is a polemical essay.

FOREIGN ACCOUNTS: L. E. Berry and R. O. Crummey (eds.), *Rude and Barbarous Kingdom: Russia in the Accounts of Sixteenth-Century English Voyagers*, Madison WI – L 1968, contains the writings of Giles Fletcher and Sir Jerome Horsey, *inter alia*. cf. also H. F. Graham's tr. of *The 'Moscovia' of Antonio Possevino SJ*, Pittsburgh PA 1977.

The correspondence between Ivan and Kurbsky and the latter's history of the reign have been tr. and ed. by J. L. I. Fennell, Cambridge 1955, 1965; E. L. Keenan voiced scepticism as to the former's authenticity in *The Kurbsky-Groznyi Apocrypha . . .* , Cambridge MA 1971, but lost out in the ensuing controversy; see N. Rossing and B. Rønne, *Apocryphal – Not Apocryphal? A Critical Analysis . . .* , Copenhagen 1980.

The Domostroi: Rules for Russian Households in the Time of Ivan the Terrible, ed., tr. C. J. Pouncy, Ithaca NY – L 1994, is a prime source on social life in the period.

TERRITORIAL EXPANSION: *to the east*: G. L. Lantzeff and R. A. Pierce, *Eastward to Empire: Exploration and Conquest of the Russian Open Frontier to 1750*, Montreal 1973; J. Pelenski, *Russia and Kazan: Conquest and Imperial Ideology, 1438–1560s*, the Hague – Paris 1974; *to the south:* W. H. McNeill, *Europe's Steppe Frontier, 1550–1800*, Chicago 1964, and works on Ukraine.

Time of Troubles

R. G. Skrynnikov, *The Time of Troubles: Russia in Crisis, 1604–1618*, tr. H. F. Graham, Gulf Breeze FL 1988, is the best survey; J. T. Alexander has translated the pre-revolutionary historian S. F. Platonov's abbreviation of his major work, *The Time of Troubles* ..., Lawrence KS – L 1970. Graham has also translated Platonov's *Boris Godunov, Tsar of Russia*, Gulf Breeze FL 1982, while his essay of 1926, *Moscow and the West*, has been ed. and tr. by J. L. Wieczynski, Gulf Breeze FL 1972.

Several foreign accounts have also been edited and translated into English, esp. works by Isaac Massa and Conrad Bussow, tr., ed. G. E. Orchard, Toronto – L 1982 and Montreal – Kingston 1994 respectively; cf. G. M. Phipps, *Sir John Merrick: English Merchant-Diplomat* ..., Newtonville MA 1983; M. Jansson and N. Rogozhin (eds.), *England and the North: The Russian Embassy of 1613–1614*, tr. P. Bushkovitch, Philadelphia PA 1994.

Seventeenth-century Muscovy

SOURCES: A prime domestic source is *The Muscovite Law Code (Ulozhenie) of 1649*, tr., ed. R. Hellie, pt 1, Irvine CA 1988 (the commentary is forthcoming). Deservedly renowned: *The Travels of Adam Olearius in Seventeenth-Century Russia*, tr., ed. S. H. Baron, Stanford CA 1967. Less reliable is F. de la Neuville, *A Curious and New Account of Muscovy in the Year 1689*, ed. L. A. J. Hughes, tr. J. A. Cutshall, L 1994; cf. *Juraj Križanić (1618–1683), Russophile and Ecumenic Visionary*, ed. T. Eekman and A. Kadić, The Hague – Paris 1976; this eccentric Croat's *Politika*, ed. M. N. Tikhomirov, has been tr. by J. M. Letiche and B. Dmytryshyn, Oxford 1985. For a masterful dissection of all foreigners' accounts: M. Poe, *Foreign Descriptions of Muscovy: An Analytic Bibliography of Primary and Secondary Sources*, Columbus OH 1995.

RULERS: P. Longworth, *Alexis: Tsar of All the Russias*, L 1984, and L. A. J. Hughes, *Sophia: Regent of Russia, 1657–1704*, New Haven CT – L 1990, are both fine biographies. V. O. Klyuchevsky, *The Rise of the Romanovs*, tr. L. Archibald and M. Scholl, L 1970, by Russia's best-known pre-revolutionary historian, is now dated.

SOCIAL AND ECONOMIC: *Readings for Introduction to Russian Civilization: Muscovite Society*, ed. R. Hellie, Chicago 1967, reproduces some basic texts. R. Pipes, *Russia under the Old Regime*, NY 1974, stresses the Russian 'patrimonial' tradition and continues into the nineteenth century, preparing the ground for critical studies of *The Russian Revolution, 1899–1919*, NY – L 1990, and *Russia under the Bolshevik Regime, 1919–1924*, NY – L 1994.

PEASANTS, SERFDOM: to Blum (above) add R. Hellie, *Enserfment and Military Change in Muscovy*, Chicago 1971, and, for documents, R. E. F. Smith, *The Enserfment of the Russian Peasantry*, Cambridge 1968. By the same author: *Peasant Farming in Muscovy*, Cambridge 1977. R. Hellie, *Slavery in Russia, 1450–1725*, Chicago – L 1982, concentrates on the 1580s to 1620s and takes a comparative international approach.

NOBLES: R. O. Crummey, *Aristocrats and Servitors: The Boyar Elite in Russia, 1613–1689*, Princeton NJ 1983.

OF CIALS: two out of fourteen articles in W. McK. Pintner and D. K. Rowney (eds.), *Russian Officialdom: The Bureaucratization of Russian Society from the Seventeenth to the Twentieth Centuries*, Chapel Hill NC 1980, deal with this period.

TOWNSPEOPLE: P. Bushkovitch, *The Merchants of Moscow, 1580–1650*, Cambridge 1980; J. M. Hittle, *The Service City: State and Townsmen in Russia, 1600–1800*, Cambridge MA 1979; S. H. Baron, *Muscovite Russia: Collected Essays*, L 1980.

WOMEN: B. E. Clements *et al.* (eds.), *Russia's Women: Accommodation, Resistance, Transformation*, Berkeley CA – Oxford 1991, has recent studies on this and later periods.

DEMOGRAPHY: H. L. Eaton, *Early Russian Censuses and the Population of Muscovy, 1550–1650*, is a dissertation available in book form.

REVOLTS: P. H. Avrich, *Russian Rebels, 1600–1800*, L 1973, is vividly written and reliable.

RELIGION: W. K. Medlin and C. G. Patrinelis, *Renaissance Influences and Religious Reforms in Russia*, Geneva 1971, needs to be supplemented by P. Meyendorff, *Russia, Ritual and Reform: The Liturgical Reforms of Nikon in the Seventeenth Century*, Crestwood NY 1987, and, from a different viewpoint, P. Bushkovitch, *Religion and Society in Russia: The Sixteenth and Seventeenth Centuries*, NY – Oxford 1992. Some of Nikon's works have been ed. V. A. Tumins and G. V. Vernadsky, The Hague 1982.

EXPANSION TO THE SOUTH: P. Longworth, *The Cossacks*, L 1969; C. B. Stevens, *Soldiers on the Steppe: Army Reform and Social Change in Early Modern Russia*, DeKalb IL 1995.

Still valuable: C. B. O'Brien, *Muscovy and the Ukraine ... 1654–1667*, Berkeley CA 1963; and on Ukrainian politics F. E. Sysyn, *Between Poland and the Ukraine: The Dilemma of Adam Kysil, 1600–1653*, Cambridge MA 1985. G. Le Vasseur, Sieur de Beauplan's contemporary account has been tr., ed. A. B. Pernal and D. F. Essar as *A Description of Ukraine*, 2 vols., Cambridge MA 1993.

EXPANSION TO THE EAST: to works cited above, add M. Mancall, *Russia and China: Their Diplomatic Relations to 1728*, Cambridge MA 1971.

RUSSO-TURKISH RELATIONS await their historian. On the Baltic problem: W. Kirchner, *The Rise of the Baltic Question*, Newark DE 1954; id., *Commercial Relations Between Russia and Europe, 1400–1800*, Bloomington IN 1966 (twelve articles); A. Attman, *The Russian and Polish Markets in International Trade*, Göteborg 1973.

D. *Imperial Russia to 1801*

Peter I

W. Marshall, *Peter the Great*, L – NY 1996, is a useful introductory survey. More thorough: E. V. Anisimov, *The Reforms of Peter the Great: Progress Through Coercion in Russia*, tr. J. T. Alexander, Armonk NY – L 1993; cf. also C. Peterson, *Peter the Great's Administrative and Judicial Reforms . . .*, Stockholm 1979, which considers their Swedish antecedents.

Four biographies of the tsar are: B. H. Sumner, *Peter the Great and the Emergence of Russia*, L 1951; V. O. Klyuchevsky, *Peter the Great*, tr. L. Archibald, L 1958; P. B. Putnam, *Peter the Revolutionary Tsar*, NY 1973; M. S. Anderson, *Peter the Great*, L 1978. The last is the best, but still inferior to the work in German by R. Wittram (1964).

I. T. Pososhkov's treatise of 1724, *The Book of Poverty and Wealth*, has been tr. A. P. Vlasto and ed. with an extensive introduction by L. R. Lewitter, L 1987; M. J. Okenfuss has performed the same service for *The Travel Diary of Peter Tolstoi: A Muscovite in Early Modern Europe*, DeKalb IL 1987.

ECCLESIASTICAL REFORMS: J. Cracraft, *The Church Reform of Peter the Great*, Stanford CA – L 1971; the 'Spiritual Regulation' has been ed., tr. A. V. Muller, Seattle WA 1972.

N. V. Riasanovsky, *The Image of Peter the Great in Russian History and Thought*, Oxford – NY 1985, is best on the early nineteenth century.

Eighteenth century

BIBLIOGRAPHY: P. Clendenning and R. Bartlett, *Eighteenth-Century Russia: A Select Bibliography of Works Published Since 1955*, Newtonville MA 1981; A. G. Cross and G. S. Smith, *Eighteenth-Century Russian Literature, Culture and Thought: A Bibliography of English-Language Scholarship*, Newtonville MA 1984.

RULERS: R. S. Wortman, *Scenarios of Power: Myth and Ceremony in Russian Monarchy*, vol. I: *From Peter the Great to the Death of Nicholas I*, Princeton NJ 1995, takes a highly original approach that stresses the role of ritual. More traditional: W. B. Lincoln, *The Romanovs: Autocrats of All the Russias*, NY 1981.

GOVERNMENT: M. Raeff has pioneered an administrative approach to the study of Imperial Russia that has been widely followed: *Imperial Russia, 1682–1825: The Coming of Age of Modern Russia*, NY 1971; *The Well-Ordered Police State: Social and Institutional Change in the Germanies and Russia, 1600–1800*, New Haven CT 1983; *Understanding Imperial Russia: State and Society in the*

Old Regime, tr. A. Goldhammer, NY 1984; *Political Ideas and Institutions in Imperial Russia* (collected essays), Boulder CO – Oxford 1994. In the same tradition: G. L. Yaney, *The Systematization of Russian Government: Social Evolution in the Domestic Administration of Imperial Russia, 1711–1905*, Urbana IL 1973; J. P. LeDonne, *Ruling Russia: Politics and Administration in the Age of Absolutism, 1762–1796*, Princeton NJ 1984, and *Absolutism and Ruling Class: the Formation of the Russian Political Order*, NY – L 1991; see also Pintner and Rowney (above page 563).

ARMED FORCES: J. L. H. Keep, *Soldiers of the Tsar: Army and Society in Russia, 1462–1874*, Oxford 1985; C. Duffy, *Russia's Military Way to the West: Origins and Nature of Russian Military Power, 1700–1800*, L 1981; W. C. Fuller Jr, *Strategy and Power in Russia, 1600–1914*, NY 1992; P. Longworth, *The Art of Victory: The Life and Achievements of Generalissimo Suvorov*, L 1965.

ECONOMY: A. Kahan's (posthumously published) *The Plow, The Hammer and the Knout: An Economic History of Eighteenth-Century Russia*, ed. R. Hellie, Chicago – L 1985; R. Bartlett (ed.), *Land Commune and Peasant Community in Russia: Communal Forms in Imperial and Early Soviet Society*, L 1990, contains insightful essays on this and later periods.

1725–62

C. S. Leonard, *Reform and Regicide: The Reign of Peter III of Russia*, Bloomington IN 1993, is a revisionist view; the other sovereigns have attracted little scholarly attention.

CATHERINE II: I. de Madariaga, Russia in the Age of Catherine the Great, L 1981, is a classic; more succinct: id., *Catherine the Great: A Short History*, L – New Haven CT 1990. Also rewarding: J. T. Alexander, *Catherine the Great: Life and Legend*, NY – Oxford 1989. Also by this author: *Autocratic Politics in a National Crisis: The Imperial Russian Court and Pugachev's Revolt, 1773–1775*, Bloomington IN 1969; and *Bubonic Plague in Early Modern Russia: Public Health and Urban Disaster*, Baltimore 1980.

SOCIAL AND ECONOMIC: R. P. Bartlett, *Human Capital: The Settlement of Foreigners in Russia, 1762–1804*, Cambridge 1979.

NOBILITY: B. Meehan-Waters, *Autocracy and Aristocracy: The Russian Elite, 1689–1761*, Princeton NJ 1982, stresses continuity with the earlier period. P. Dukes, *Catherine the Great and the Russian Nobility . . .*, Cambridge 1967, should be read in conjunction with R. E. Jones, *The Emancipation of the Russian Nobility, 1762–1785*, Princeton NJ 1973. D. Griffiths and G. E. Munro have tr. and ed. *Catherine II's Charters of 1785 to the Nobility and the Towns*, Bakersfield CA 1991. Nobles in politics: D. L. Ransel, *The Politics of Catherinian Russia: The Panin Party*, New Haven CT – L 1975. Nobles in industry: H. D.

Hudson Jr, *The Rise of the Demidov Family and the Russian Iron Industry in the Eighteenth Century*, Newtonville MA 1986. Cultural life: M. Raeff, *Origins of the Russian Intelligentsia: The Eighteenth-Century Nobility*, NY 1966, a seminal study.

REVOLTS: to Avrich (above) add J. T. Alexander, *Emperor of the Cossacks: Pugachev and the Frontier Jacquerie of 1773–1775*, Lawrence KS 1973.

DAILY LIFE: M. Kochan, *Life in Russia under Catherine the Great*, NY – L 1969.

EIGHTEENTH-CENTURY CULTURE: G. L. Freeze, *The Russian Levites: Parish Clergy in the Eighteenth Century*, Cambridge MA – L 1983, breaks new ground; cf. also R. O. Crummey, *The Old Believers and the World of Antichrist: the Vyg Community and the Russian State, 1694–1855*, Madison WI – L 1970.

The Enlightenment in Russia

J. L. Black, *Citizens for the Fatherland: Education, Educators and Pedagogical Ideals in Eighteenth-Century Russia*, Boulder CO 1979; id., *G.-F. Müller and the Imperial Russian Academy*, Kingston – Montreal 1986. K. A. Papmehl, *Freedom of Expression in Eighteenth-Century Russia*, The Hague 1971, shows the possibilities and limitations. G. Marker, *Publishing, Printing and the Origins of Intellectual Life in Russia, 1700–1800*, Princeton NJ 1985, is informative, while D. Saunders, *The Ukrainian Impact on Russian Culture, 1750–1850*, Edmonton 1985, brings out a frequently neglected aspect. J. Garrard (ed.), *The Eighteenth Century in Russia*, Oxford 1973, and R. Bartlett and J. M. Hartley (eds.), *Russia in the Age of Enlightenment: Essays for Isabel de Madariaga*, L 1990, are two useful collections of articles; cf. also A. G. Cross and G. S. Smith (eds.), *Literature, Lives and Legality in Catherine's Russia*, Nottingham 1994. Cross has also edited a volume on *Great Britain and Russia in the Eighteenth Century: Contacts and Comparisons*, Newtonville MA 1979, and written '*By the Banks of the Thames': Russians in Eighteenth-Century Britain*, Newtonville MA 1980.

INDIVIDUAL WRITERS: M. M. Shcherbatov's *On the Corruption of Morals in Russia* has been tr. and ed. by A. Lentin, Cambridge 1969; on Novikov, see the study by W. G. Jones mentioned in the text; and on Radishchev, D. M. Lang, *The First Russian Radical: Alexander Radishchev*, L 1960, is still the best biography; his *Journey* (1790) has been tr. L. Wiener, ed. R. P. Thaler, Cambridge MA 1959. Catherine II's memoirs are available in several editions, notably that of D. Maroger, L 1955, but need careful handling; the text of her 1766 *Nakaz* has been ed. P. Dukes, Newtonville MA 1977.

Foreign policy

A novel geopolitical approach is taken by J. P. LeDonne, *The Russian Empire and the World, 1700–1917: The Geopolitics of Expansion and Containment*, NY – Oxford 1997.

EXPANSION TO THE EAST: A. S. Donnelly, *The Russian Conquest of Bashkiria, 1552–1740: A Case Study in Imperialism*, New Haven CT – L 1968, is mainly on the 1730s; cf. also C. M. Foust, *Muscovite and Mandarin: Russia's Trade with China and Its Setting, 1727–1805*, Chapel Hill 1969.

EXPANSION TO THE SOUTH: Z. E. Kohut, *Russian Centralism and Ukrainian Autonomy: Imperial Absorption of the Hetmanate, 1760s–1830s*, Cambridge MA 1988; A. W. Fisher, *The Russian Annexation of the Crimea, 1772–1783*, Cambridge 1970; G. F. Jewsbury, *The Russian Annexation of Bessarabia, 1774–1828: A Study of Imperial Expansion*, Boulder CO – Guildford 1976.

EXPANSION TO THE WEST: H. H. Kaplan, *The First Partition of Poland*, NY – L 1962.

ANGLO-RUSSIAN RELATIONS: in addition to Cross (above), see M. S. Anderson, *Britain's Discovery of Russia, 1553–1815*, L 1958, which is mainly concerned with the eighteenth century.

1796–1801

R. E. McGrew, *Tsar Paul I of Russia, 1754–1801*, NY – Oxford 1992, is a fine study; cf. H. Ragsdale (ed.), *Paul I: An Assessment of His Life and Reign*, Pittsburgh 1979, which anticipated this revisionist treatment.

E. Imperial Russia, 1801–1917

General histories

G. H. N. Seton-Watson, *The Russian Empire, 1801–1917*, Oxford 1967; S. Harcave, *Years of the Golden Cockerel: The Last Romanov Tsars, 1814–1917*, NY – L 1968.

Nations and regions

NLAND: D. G. Kirby (ed.), *Finland and Russia, 1808–1920: From Autonomy to Independence: A Selection of Documents*, Basingstoke – L 1975.

POLAND: P. S. Wandycz, *The Lands of Partitioned Poland, 1795–1918*, Seattle 1974; F. W. Thackeray, *Antecedents of Revolution: Alexander I and the Polish Kingdom, 1815–1825*, NY 1980; R. F. Leslie, *Reform and Insurrection in Russian Poland, 1856–1865*, L 1963, Westport CT 1969.

BALTIC LANDS: E. C. Thaden *et al.* (eds.), *Russification in the Baltic Provinces, 1855–1914*, Princeton 1981.

UKRAINE: M. F. Hamm, *Kiev: A Portrait, 1800–1917*, Princeton NJ 1993; and P. Herlihy, *Odessa: A History, 1794–1914*, Cambridge MA 1986, are studies of two cities.

JEWS: H.-D. Löwe, *The Tsars and the Jews: Reform, Reaction and Antisemitism in Imperial Russia, 1772–1917*, Chur 1993 (based on a work in German of 1978); M. Stanislawski, *Tsar Nicholas I and the Jews: The Transformation of Jewish Society in Russia, 1825–1855*, Philadelphia PA 1983; S. Zipperstein, *The Jews of Odessa: A Cultural History, 1794–1881*, Stanford CA 1985; Y. Ro'i, *Jews and Jewish Life in Russia and the Soviet Union*, L 1995, and works cited below.

CAUCASUS: on the Russian advance: M. Gammer, *Muslim Resistance to the Tsar: Shamil and the Conquest of Chechnia and Daghestan*, Portland OR 1994. Georgia: to Suny (Section B, page 558 above) add his edition of essays, *Transcaucasia: Nationalism and Social Change*, Ann Arbor MI 1983; and D. Rayfield, *The Literature of Georgia: A History*, Oxford 1994. T. Swietochowski, *Russia and Azerbaijan: A Borderland in Transition*, NY 1995, is mainly on the twentieth century.

CENTRAL ASIA: E. Allworth (ed.), *Central Asia: 130 Years of Russian Dominance: A Historical Overview*, Durham NC – L 1995 (new ed. of work published in 1967 under another title); R. A. Pierce, *Russian Central Asia, 1867–1917: A Study in Colonial Rule*, Berkeley CA – L 1960.

SIBERIA: G. Diment and Yu. Slezkine (eds.), *Between Heaven and Hell: The Myth of Siberia in Russian Culture*, NY 1993 (nineteenth and twentieth centuries).

1801–25

J. M. Hartley's life of *Alexander I*, L – NY 1994, supersedes A. McConnell, *Tsar Alexander I: Paternalistic Reformer*, NY 1970, and A. Palmer, *Alexander I: Tsar of War and Peace*, L – NY 1974.

STATESMEN: M. Raeff, *Mikhail Speransky: Statesman of Imperial Russia, 1772–1839*, 2nd ed., The Hague 1969; M. Jenkins, *Arakcheev: Grand Vizier of the Russian Empire: A Biography*, L 1969; the former is the more scholarly work. W. Y. Zawadzki, *A Man of Honour: Adam Czartoryski as a Statesman of Russia and Poland*, Oxford 1993.

DECEMBRISTS: P. O'Meary has written biographies of P. I. Pestel' and K. F. Ryleyev, Newtonville MA 1977, and Princeton NJ 1984 respectively.

1825–55

W. B. Lincoln, *Nicholas I: Emperor and Autocrat of All the Russias*, L 1978; A. E. Presniakov, *Emperor Nicholas I of Russia: The Apogee of Autocracy, 1825–1855*, a work of 1923 ed., tr. J. C. Zacek, Gulf Breeze FL 1974.

THIRD DEPARTMENT: P. S. Squire, *The Third Department . . .* , Cambridge 1968; S. Monas, *The Third Section: Police and Society under Nicholas I*, Cambridge MA 1961. Censorship: A. Nikitenko, *The Diary of a Russian Censor*, abridged, ed. H. S. Jacobson, Amherst MA 1975; C. A. Ruud, *Fighting Words: Imperial Censorship and the Russian Press, 1804–1906*, Toronto 1980; see also below.

ARMED FORCES: to Fuller, Keep (above) add J. S. Curtiss, *The Russian Army under Nicholas I, 1825–1855*, Durham NC 1965 and *Russia's Crimean War*, Durham NC 1979; E. K. Wirtschafter, *From Serf to Russian Soldier*, Princeton NJ – Oxford 1990, is a more sociological study.

TRAVELLERS' ACCOUNTS: R. Buss, tr., ed., *Letters from Russia* by the Marquis de Custine, Harmondsworth 1991.

INTELLECTUAL LIFE: N. V. Riasanovsky, *A Parting of Ways: Government and the Educated Public in Russia, 1801–1855*, Oxford 1976, sets the scene. A. Walicki, *History of Russian Thought from the Enlightenment to Marxism*, Oxford 1980, is fundamental; cf. Sir I. Berlin, *Russian Thinkers*, ed. H. Hardy and A. Kelly, L – Toronto 1978.

CHAADAYEV'S WORKS: R. T. McNally (ed.), *The Major Works of Peter Chaadaev*, Notre Dame IN 1969, is preferable to the ed., tr. M.-B. Zeldin, Knoxville TN 1970; cf. McNally, *Chaadaev and His Friends*, Tallahassee FL 1971.

OFFICIAL NATIONALISM: N. V. Riasanovsky, *Nicholas I and Official Nationality in Russia, 1825–1855*, Berkeley CA 1959. A life of the key figure has been written by C. H. Whittaker, *The Origins of Modern Russian Education: An Intellectual Biography of Count Sergei Uvarov, 1786–1855*, DeKalb IL 1984.

SLAVOPHILS: A. Walicki, *The Slavophile Controversy: History of A Conservative Utopia in Nineteenth-Century Russian Thought*, tr. H. Andrews-Rusiecka, Oxford 1975; A. Gleason, *European and Muscovite: Ivan Kireevsky and the Origins of Slavophilism*, Cambridge MA 1972; N. V. Riasanovsky, *Russia and the West in the Teaching of the Slavophiles*, Cambridge MA 1952, retains its value; a more modern study is I. B. Neumann, *Russia and the Idea of Europe: A Study in Identity and International Relations*, L – NY 1995, which starts in the eighteenth century and continues into the twentieth.

WESTERNIZERS: D. Offord, *Portraits of Early Russian Liberals: A Study of the Thought of T. N. Granovsky, V. P. Botkin, P. V. Annenkov, A. V. Druzhinin and K. D. Kavelin*, Cambridge 1985; M. Malia, *Alexander Herzen and the Birth of Russian Socialism, 1812–1855*, L 1961, covers the first part of the subject's life; E. D. J. Acton, *Alexander Herzen and the Role of the Intellectual Revolutionary*, Cambridge 1979. For the Petrashevtsy, see J. H. Seddon, *The Petrashevtsy: A Study of the Russian Revolutionaries of 1848*, Manchester 1985.

Social and economic

PEASANTRY: the work of S. L. Hoch cited in the text is a valuable case-study; cf. also P. Kolchin, *Unfree Labor: American Slavery and Russian Serfdom*, Cambridge MA 1987, which makes some unfamiliar points; D. Moon, *Russian Peasants and Tsarist Legislation on the Eve of Reform: Interaction between Peasants and Officialdom, 1825–1855*, L–NY 1992; E. Kingston-Mann and T. Mixter (eds.), *Peasant Economy, Culture and Politics of European Russia, 1800–1921*, contains an article on the 1825–55 era but is mainly concerned with the post-1861 period.

INDUSTRY AND TRADE: W. L. Blackwell, *The Beginnings of Russian Industrialization, 1800–1860*, Princeton NJ 1968; M. E. Falkus, *The Industrialization of Russia, 1700–1914*, L 1972 (a briefer study); W. M. Pintner, *Russian Economic Policy under Nicholas I*, Ithaca NY – L 1968.

Foreign policy

RUSSIA'S ROLE IN THE NAPOLEONIC WARS: most of the literature is of early vintage, but see C. Duffy's sketch, *Borodino and the War of 1812*, L – NY 1973; A. Palmer, *Napoleon in Russia*, L – NY 1967. On the diplomatic angle: P. K. Grimsted, *The Foreign Ministers of Alexander I . . .* , Berkeley CA 1969, and the work by Zawadzki cited above (page 568).

I. W. Roberts, *Nicholas I and the Russian Intervention in Hungary*, L 1990; D. M. Goldfrank, *The Origins of the Crimean War*, L 1994, are hard on Nicholas. NEAR EAST: M. Atkin, *Russia and Iran, 1780–1828*, Minneapolis MN 1980.

Alexander II and the Reform Era

N. G. O. Pereira, *Tsar-Liberator: Alexander II of Russia*, Newtonville MA 1983, does not quite displace W. E. Mosse, *Alexander II and the Modernization of Russia*, L 1958, repr. 1992, as a handy introduction.

W. B. Lincoln, *The Great Reforms: Autocracy, Bureaucracy and the Politics of Change in Imperial Russia*, DeKalb IL 1990, is fundamental on policy making; Lincoln has also written a life of N. A. Milyutin, Newtonville MA 1977. For the administration generally, see D. Orlovsky, *The Limits of Reform: The Ministry of Internal Affairs in Imperial Russia, 1802–1881*, Cambridge MA – L 1981.

LOCAL GOVERNMENT: S. F. Starr, *Decentralization and Self-Government in*

Russia, 1830–1870, Princeton NJ 1972; T. Emmons and W. S. Vucinich (eds.), *The Zemstvo in Russia: An Experiment in Local Government*, Cambridge 1982, contains useful essays. D. Christian, *Living Water: Vodka and Russian Society on the Eve of Emancipation*, Oxford 1990, deals with an important but generally neglected reform.

SERF EMANCIPATION: T. Emmons, *The Russian Landed Gentry and the Peasant Emancipation of 1861*, Cambridge 1968; D. Field, *The End of Serfdom: Nobility and Bureaucracy in Russia, 1855–1861*, Cambridge MA 1976.

Alexander III and Counter-Reform

There is no Western life of Alexander III, but see the tr. of P. A. Zayonchkovsky, *The Russian Autocracy in Crisis*, Gulf Breeze FL 1979.

ADMINISTRATION: H. W. Whelan, *Alexander III and the State Council: Bureaucracy and Counterreform in Late Imperial Russia*, New Brunswick NJ 1982; T. S. Pearson, *Russian Officialdom in Crisis: Autocracy and Local Self-Government, 1861–1900*, Cambridge – NY 1989; N. B. Weissman, *Reform in Tsarist Russia: The State Bureaucracy and Local Government, 1900–1914*, New Brunswick NJ 1981. R. G. Robbins, *The Tsar's Viceroys: Russian Provincial Governors in the Last Years of the Empire*, Ithaca NY – L 1988. A rare study of problems in a provincial city is R. A. Wade and S. J. Seregny (eds.), *Politics in Provincial Russia: Saratov, 1590–1917*, Columbus OH 1989.

CENSORSHIP: to Ruud (above, page 568) add D. Balmuth, *Censorship in Russia, 1865–1905*, Washington DC 1979.

ARMED FORCES: to Fuller (above, page 565) add B. W. Menning, *Bayonets Before Bullets: The Imperial Russian Army, 1861–1914*, Bloomington IN 1992; P. Gatrell, *Government, Industry and Rearmament in Russia, 1900–1914: The Last Argument of Tsarism*, Cambridge 1994; J. N. Westwood, *Russian Naval Construction, 1905–1945*, Basingstoke – L 1994.

Foreign policy

D. Geyer, *Russian Imperialism: The Interaction of Domestic and Foreign Policy, 1860–1914*, tr. (from German ed., 1977) B. Little, Leamington Spa 1987; *Imperial Russian Foreign Policy*, ed., tr. H. Ragsdale, Cambridge – Washington DC 1993, is a useful vol. of essays. On policy making, see D. McL. McDonald, *United Government and Foreign Policy in Russia, 1900–1914*, Cambridge MA 1992.

G. F. Kennan, *The Decline of Bismarck's World Order: Franco-Russian Relations, 1875–1890*, Princeton NJ 1979, and *The Fateful Alliance: France, Russia and the Coming of the First World War*, NY 1984, are iconoclastic.

MIDDLE AND FAR EAST: F. Kazemzadeh, *Russia and Britain in Persia, 1864–*

1914: A Study in Imperialism, New Haven CT – L 1968; G. A. Lensen, *The Russian Push Towards Japan: Russo-Japanese Relations, 1697–1875*, Princeton NJ 1959; I. H. Nish, *The Origins of the Russo-Japanese War*, L – NY 1985.

The intelligentsia and opposition

THE INTELLIGENTSIA: D. R. Brower, *Training the Nihilists: Education and Radicalism in Tsarist Russia*, Ithaca NY 1975; A. Gleason, *Young Russia: The Genesis of Russian Radicalism in the 1860s*, Chicago – L 1983; E. W. Clowes et al. (eds.), *Between Tsar and People: Educated Society and the Quest for Public Identity in Late Imperial Russia*, Princeton NJ 1991.

'MEN OF THE 1860S': N. G. O. Pereira, *The Thought and Teachings of N. G. Chernyshevsky*, The Hague 1975; A. Kelly, *Mikhail Bakunin: A Study in the Psychology and Politics of Utopianism*, Oxford 1982.

WOMEN RADICALS: R. Stites, *The Women's Liberation Movement in Russia: Feminism, Nihilism and Bolshevism, 1860–1930*, Princeton NJ 1978; B. A. Engel, *Mothers and Daughters: Women of the Intelligentsia in Nineteenth-Century Russia*, Cambridge – NY 1983.

TOLSTOY: Sir I. Berlin, *The Hedgehog and the Fox: An Essay on Tolstoy's View of History*, L – NY 1953.

CONSERVATISM, NATIONALISM: E. C. Thaden, *Conservative Nationalism in Nineteenth-Century Russia*, Seattle 1964. There are lives of Pobedonostsev by R. F. Byrnes, Bloomington – L 1968, of Katkov by K. Durman, NY 1988, of Ivan Aksakov and Leontyev by S. Lukashevich, Cambridge MA 1965 and NY 1967; more recent is W. Dowler, *An Unnecessary Man: The Life of Apollon Grigor'ev*, Toronto 1995.

ANTISEMITISM: J. D. Klier and S. Lambroza (eds.), *Pogroms: Anti-Jewish Violence in Modern Russian History*, Cambridge – NY 1992, downplays the role of the central authorities; cf. E. H. Judge, *Easter in Kishinev: Anatomy of a Pogrom*, NY 1992; H. Rogger, *Jewish Policies and Right-Wing Politics in Imperial Russia*, Berkeley 1986, contains eight essays; see also NATIONS AND REGIONS (above, page 567).

LIBERALISM: G. M. Hamburg, *Boris Chicherin and Early Russian Liberalism, 1828–1866*, Stanford 1992 (first instalment of a major biography); C. Timberlake (ed.), *Essays on Russian Liberalism*, Columbia MO 1972; see WESTERNIZERS (above, page 569), and 1900–1917 (below, page 577).

POPULISM, EARLY MARXISM: The most thorough treatment of the *Narodniki* to 1881 is still F. Venturi, *Roots of Revolution . . .*, tr. F. Haskell, L 1960, but it is uncritical. On individual activists see P. Pomper's lives of P. Lavrov, Chicago – L 1972, and S. Nechaev, New Brunswick NJ 1979; D. Hardy, *Peter Tkachev: the Critic as Jacobin*, Seattle – L 1977; id., *Land and Freedom: The*

Origins of Russian Terrorism, 1876–1879, Westport CT – L 1987. There are two good recent studies of the post-1881 years: D. Offord, *The Russian Revolutionary Movement in the 1880s*, Cambridge 1986; N. M. Naimark, *Terrorists and Social Democrats: The Russian Revolutionary Movement under Alexander III*, Cambridge MA – L 1983. On the Jews' role in Populism, see E. E. Haberer, *Jews and Revolution in Nineteenth-Century Russia*, Cambridge 1995; cf. also R. Brym, *The Jewish Intelligentsia and Russian Marxism*, L 1978. THE EARLY MARXISTS: S. H. Baron, *Plekhanov: Father of Russian Marxism*, Stanford CA 1963; J. Bergman, *Vera Zasulich: A Biography*, Stanford CA 1983; A. Ascher, *Pavel Axelrod and the Development of Menshevism*, Cambridge MA – L 1972. The international background is explored in B. Naarden, *Socialist Europe and Revolutionary Russia: Perception and Prejudice, 1848–1923*, tr. M. Vaughan, Cambridge 1992; cf. M. Donald, *Marxism and Revolution: Karl Kautsky and the Russian Marxists, 1900–1924*, New Haven CT – L 1993. Finally, A. Geifman, *Thou Shalt Kill: Revolutionary Terrorism in Russia, 1894– 1917*, Princeton NJ 1993, deals harshly with the entire left.

Economic and social

DEMOGRAPHY: B. A. Anderson, *Internal Migration during Modernization in Late Nineteenth-Century Russia*, Princeton 1980.
URBANIZATION: J. Bradley, *Muzhik and Muscovite: Urbanization in Late Imperial Russia*, Berkeley CA – L 1985; J. H. Bater, *St Petersburg: Industrialization and Change*, Montreal 1976; D. R. Brower, *The Russian City Between Tradition and Modernity, 1850–1900*, Berkeley CA – L 1990; R. W. Thurston, *Liberal City, Conservative State: Moscow and Russia's Urban Crisis, 1906– 1914*, NY – Oxford 1987.
ENTREPRENEURS: A. J. Rieber, *Merchants and Entrepreneurs in Imperial Russia*, Chapel Hill NC – L 1982; J. A. Ruckman, *The Moscow Business Elite: A Social and Cultural Portrait of Two Generations, 1840–1905*, DeKalb IL 1984; G. Guroff and F. V. Carstensen (eds.), *Entrepreneurship in Imperial Russia and the Soviet Union*, Princeton NJ 1983; J. P. McKay, *Pioneers for Profit: Foreign Entrepreneurship and Russian Industrialization, 1885–1913*, Chicago – L 1970; T. C. Owen, *Capitalism and Politics in Russia: A Social History of the Moscow Merchants, 1855–1905*, Cambridge – NY 1981.
INDUSTRY, NANCE: P. R. Gregory, *Before Command: An Economic History of Russia from Emancipation to the First Five-Year Plan*, Princeton NJ 1994; P. Gatrell, *The Tsarist Economy, 1850–1917*, L – NY 1986; O. Crisp, *Studies on the Russian Economy before 1914*, London 1976. Gregory has also written a close study of *Russian National Income, 1885–1913*, Cambridge 1982.
RAILWAYS: J. N. Westwood, *A History of Russian Railways*, L 1964; S. G.

Marks, *Road to Power: The Trans-Siberian Railroad and the Colonization of Asiatic Russia, 1850–1917*, Ithaca NY – L 1991.

The new ed. of Count S. Witte's *Memoirs* (1921–3) by S. Harcave, Armonk NY – L 1990, says little about economic policy.

LABOUR: R. E. Johnson, *Peasant and Proletarian: The Working Class of Moscow in the Late Nineteenth Century*, New Brunswick NJ – Leicester 1979; V. E. Bonnell, *Roots of Rebellion: Workers' Politics and Organizations in St Petersburg and Moscow, 1900–1914*, Berkeley CA – L 1983; T. H. Friedgut, *Iuzovka and Revolution*, 2 vols., Princeton NJ – Oxford 1989, 1994; C. Wynn, *Workers, Strikes and Pogroms: The Donbas-Dnepr Bend in Late Imperial Russia, 1870–1905*, Princeton NJ – Oxford 1992; L. Engelstein, *Moscow 1905: Working-Class Organization and Political Conflict*, Stanford CA 1982; H. Hogan, *Forging Revolution: Metalworkers, Managers and the State in St Petersburg, 1890–1914*, Bloomington IN 1993. Of wider scope is T. McDaniel, *Autocracy, Capitalism and Revolution in Russia*, Berkeley CA – L 1988.

Peasants, agrarian question

For a pessimistic contemporary view, see *A. N. Engelgardt's Letters from the Country, 1872–1887*, tr., ed. C. A. Frierson, NY – Oxford 1993.

GOVERNMENT POLICY: G. Yaney, *The Urge to Mobilize: Agrarian Reform in Russia, 1861–1930*, Urbana IL – L 1982; D. A. J. Macey, *Government and Peasant in Russia, 1861–1906: The Prehistory of the Stolypin Reforms*, DeKalb IL – L 1987. Landowners: D. C. B. Lieven, *The Aristocracy in Europe, 1815–1914*, Basingstoke – L 1992, takes an interesting comparative approach.

D. Atkinson, *The End of the Russian Land Commune, 1905–1930*, Stanford CA 1983, is admirably thorough; an earlier general survey, still readable, is L. Volin, *A Century of Russian Agriculture: From Alexander II to Khrushchev*, Cambridge MA – L 1970. R. G. Robbins Jr, *Famine in Russia, 1891–2: The Imperial Government Responds to a Crisis*, NY – L 1975, tackles the most tragic moment.

PEASANT CULTURE: S. P. Frank and M. D. Steinberg (eds.), *Cultures in Flux: Lower-Class Values, Practices and Resistance in Late Imperial Russia*, Princeton 1994; and, for the family, C. Worobec, *Peasant Russia: Family and Continuity in the Post-Emancipation Period*, Princeton NJ – L 1991.

Social studies

GENDER PROBLEMS: these loom large in recent research. In addition to Clements *et al.*, Stites (above, page 572), see D. Atkinson *et al.* (eds.), *Women in Russia*, Stanford CA – L 1978 (eighteen essays on the nineteenth and twentieth centuries); L. H. Edmondson, *Feminism in Russia, 1900–1917*,

Stanford CA – L 1984; B. A. Engel, *Between the Fields and the City: Women, Work and Family in Russia, 1861–1914*, Cambridge 1994; R. L. Glickman, *Russian Factory Women: Workplace and Society, 1800–1914*, Berkeley – L 1984; B. Farnsworth and L. Viola (eds.), *Russian Peasant Women*, NY –Oxford 1992; L. Engelstein's controversial *The Keys to Happiness: Sex and the Search for Modernity in Fin-de-siècle Russia*, Ithaca NY – L 1992; L. Bernstein, *Sonia's Daughters: Prostitutes and Their Regulation in Imperial Russia*, Berkeley CA – L 1995, which breaks new ground.

PUBLIC HEALTH: N. M. Frieden, *Russian Physicians in an Era of Reform and Revolution, 1856–1905*, Princeton 1981; J. F. Hutchinson, *Politics and Public Health in Revolutionary Russia, 1890–1918*, Baltimore – L 1990.

CRIME: J. Neuberger, *Hooliganism: Crime, Culture and Power in St Petersburg, 1900–1914*, Berkeley CA – L 1993.

FAMILY: in addition to works on lower-class families (above), J. Tovrov, *The Russian Noble Family: Structure and Change*, NY – L 1987.

CHARITIES: a neglected area before A. Lindenmeyr, *Voluntary Associations and the Russian Autocracy: The Case of Private Charity*, Pittsburgh 1990.

DAILY LIFE: H. Troyat, *Daily Life in Russia under the Last Tsar*, tr. M. Barnes, L – NY 1962, is still readable.

Culture

CHURCHES: G. L. Freeze, *The Parish Clergy in Nineteenth-Century Russia: Crisis, Reform, Counter-Reform*, Princeton NJ – L 1988, continues his work on the eighteenth century. C. E. Timberlake (ed.), *Religious and Secular Forces in Late Tsarist Russia: Essays [for] D. W. Treadgold*, Seattle 1992, supplements an earlier collection, R. L. Nichols and T. G. Stavrou (eds.), *Russian Orthodoxy under the Old Regime*, Minneapolis MN 1978. On the religious revival, N. Zernov, *The Russian Religious Renaissance of the Twentieth Century*, NY 1964; J. W. Cunningham, *A Vanquished Hope: The Movement for Church Renewal in Russia, 1905–6*, Crestwood NY 1981.

EDUCATION: B. Eklof, *Russian Peasant Schools: Officialdom, Village Culture and Popular Pedagogy, 1861–1914*, Berkeley CA 1986; id. (ed.), *School and Society in Tsarist and Soviet Russia*, NY 1993, primarily concerned with elementary education; S. J. Seregny, *Russian Teachers and Peasant Revolution: The Politics of Education in 1905*, Bloomington IN – L 1989. Higher education: J. C. McClelland, *Autocrats and Academics: Education, Culture and Society in Tsarist Russia*, Chicago 1979; D. Kassow, *Students, Professors and the State in Tsarist Russia*, Berkeley CA – L 1989.

POPULAR CULTURE: J. Brooks, *When Russia Learned to Read: Literacy and Popular Literature, 1861–1917*, Princeton NJ – L 1985, is a path-breaking study; cf. C. A. Ruud, *Russian Entrepreneur: Publisher Ivan Sytin of Moscow, 1851–1934*, Kingston (Ont.) 1990.

JOURNALISM: L. McReynolds, *The News under Russia's Old Regime: The Development of a Mass-Circulation Press*, Princeton NJ – L 1991.

ART, ARCHITECTURE: C. Gray, *The Great Experiment: Russian Art, 1863–1922*, NY 1962, is still the best introduction; J. E. Bowlt, *The Silver Age: Russian Art of the Early Twentieth Century and the 'World of Art' Group*, Newtonville MA 1979; B. W. Kean, *French Painters, Russian Collectors: Shchukin, Morozov and Modern French Art, 1890–1914*, L 1995. P. Roosevelt, *Life on the Russian Country Estate: A Social and Cultural History*, New Haven CT – L 1995, is a model study.

R. E. Peterson, *A History of Russian Symbolism*, Amsterdam – Philadelphia PA 1993, is the latest of several such guides to modernism in all the arts.

The 1905 Revolution

Nicholas II: A. M. Verner, *The Crisis of Russian Autocracy: Nicholas II and the 1905 Revolution*, Princeton NJ – L 1990; D. C. B. Lieven, *Nicholas II, Emperor of All the Russias*, L 1993, is more sympathetic to the tsar. Id., *Russia's Rulers under the Old Regime*, New Haven CT – L 1989, is based on an analysis of the State Council. For the reign as a whole: L. Kochan, *Russia in Revolution, 1890–1918*, L 1966.

POLITICS TO 1904: M. Perrie, *The Agrarian Policy of the Russian SR Party . . .*, Cambridge 1976, complements an earlier study of the PSR by O. H. Radkey (mainly concerned with 1917). RSDRP: A. K. Wildman, *The Making of a Workers' Revolution: Russian Social-Democracy, 1891–1903*, Chicago – L 1967; J. L. H. Keep, *The Rise of Social Democracy in Russia*, Oxford 1963. Documents: R. H. McNeal (ed.), *Resolutions and Decisions of the CPSU*, vol. I: *The RSDRP, 1898 – October 1917*, ed. R. C. Elwood, Toronto 1974; N. Harding (ed.), *Marxism in Russia: Key Documents, 1879–1906*, tr. R. Taylor, Cambridge 1983.

LENIN: D. Volkogonov, *Lenin: Life and Legacy*, tr. H. Shukman, L 1994, draws on archival data made available since 1991 and is more critical than R. Service, *Lenin: A Political Life*, vol. I, L 1985, which goes to 1910; his two later volumes are more severe. P. Pomper, *Lenin, Trotsky and Stalin: The Intelligentsia and Power*, NY 1990, is an interesting attempt at psycho-history.

LIBERALS: R. Pipes, *Struve: Liberal on the Left, 1870–1905*, Cambridge MA 1970 (for the sequel, see page 577 below); S. Galai, *The Liberation Movement in Russia, 1900–1905*, Cambridge 1973. There are important articles in O. Crisp and L. Edmondson (eds.), *Civil Rights in Imperial Russia*, Oxford 1989.

THE YEAR 1905: thoroughly treated by A. Ascher, *The Revolution of 1905*, 2 vols., Stanford CA – L 1988, 1992. T. Emmons, *The Formation of Political Parties and the First National Elections in Russia*, Cambridge MA 1983, is an important study.

THE FAR RIGHT: see now D. C. Rawson, *Russian Rightists and the Revolution of 1905*, Cambridge 1995.

REGIONS: R. E. Blobaum, *Rewolucja: Russian Poland, 1904–1907*, Ithaca NY 1995, demonstrates this area's importance; cf. T. Polvinen, *Imperial Borderland: Bobrikov and the Attempted Russification of Finland*, tr. S. Huxley, L 1995.

SOCIAL: to Engelstein's work (above, page 574) add H. Reichman, *Railwaymen and Revolution: Russia 1905*, Berkeley CA – L 1987; T. Shanin, *The Roots of Otherness: Russia's Turn of Century*, 2 vols., L 1985–6; R. Edelman, *Proletarian Peasants: The Revolution of 1905 in Russia's Southwest*, Ithaca NY – L 1987.

ARMED FORCES: J. Bushnell, *Mutiny Amid Repression: Russian Soldiers in the Revolution of 1905–6*, Bloomington IN 1985; W. C. Fuller Jr, *Civil-Military Conflict in Imperial Russia, 1881–1914*, Princeton NJ – L 1985.

Constitutional era

G. A. Hosking, *The Russian Constitutional Experiment: Government and Duma, 1907–1914*, Cambridge 1973.

RIGHT-WING GROUPS: R. T. Manning, *The Crisis of the Old Order in Russia: Gentry and Government*, Princeton NJ 1982; G. M. Hamburg, *Politics of the Russian Nobility, 1881–1905*, New Brunswick NJ 1984; L. H. Haimson (ed.), *The Politics of Rural Russia, 1905–1914*, Columbia MO 1979 (eight essays); R. Edelman, *Gentry Politics on the Eve of the Russian Revolution: The Nationalist Party, 1907–1917*, New Brunswick NJ 1980.

LIBERALS: T. Riha, *A Russian European: Paul Miliukov in Russian Politics*, Notre Dame IN – L 1969, remains the best biography; cf. B.-C. Pinchuk, *The Octobrists in the Third Duma, 1907–1912*, Seattle WA 1974. For the *Vyekhi* controversy: C. Read, *Religion, Revolution and the Russian Intelligentsia, 1900–1912: The Vekhi Debate and Its Intellectual Background*, Totowa NJ 1980; the best translation of these essays, by M. Shatz and J. Zimmermann, appeared in *Canadian-American Slavic Studies*, 1968–70. R. Pipes, *Struve: Liberal on the Right, 1905–1944*, Cambridge MA – L 1980, traces his disenchantment with revolution.

PSR: C. Rice, *Russian Workers and the SR Party through the Revolution of 1905–7*, L – NY 1988; M. Melancon, *'Stormy Petrels': The Socialist-Revolutionaries in Russia's Labour Organization, 1905–1914*, Pittsburgh 1988; id., *The Socialist-Revolutionaries and the Russian Anti-War Movement, 1914–1917*, Columbus OH 1990.

RSDRP: R. C. Elwood, *Russian Social-Democracy in the Underground . . .* , Assen 1974, concentrates on Ukraine; G. Swain, *Russian Social Democracy and the Legal Labour Movement, 1906–1914*, L 1983.

The evolution of Trotsky's views is traced by B. Knei-Paz, *The Social and Political Thought of Leon Trotsky*, Oxford 1978.

THE YOUNG STALIN: R. C. Tucker, *Stalin as Revolutionary, 1879–1929: A Study in History and Personality*, NY 1973 (first of two vols.); cf. also R. McKean, *St Petersburg Between the Revolutions: Workers and Revolutionaries, June 1907–February 1917*, L – New Haven CT 1990. Three Menshevik activists' careers are the subject of L. Haimson *et al.* (eds.), *The Making of Three Russian Revolutionaries: Voices from the Menshevik Past*, Cambridge MA 1987.

Foreign policy and the First World War

The first part of A. I. Solzhenitsyn's epic *The Red Wheel* has been tr. H. T. Willetts, *August 1914*, NY 1989. D. C. B. Lieven, *Russia and the Origins of the First World War*, L 1983, argues that the tsar had little choice. N. Stone, *The Eastern Front, 1914–1917*, L 1975, covers operations; of the many works on internal politics, cf. esp. R. Pearson, *The Russian Moderates and the Crisis of Tsarism, 1914–1917*, NY – L 1977.

W. B. Lincoln's vast trilogy is popular history at its best: *In War's Dark Shadow: The Russians Before the Great War*; *Armageddon: The Russians in War and Revolution, 1914–1918*; *Red Victory: A History of the Russian Civil War*, NY 1983, 1986, 1989.

1917 Revolution

REFERENCE: H. Shukman (ed.), *The Blackwell Encyclopedia of the Russian Revolution*, Oxford 1988; M. Frame (comp.), *The Russian Revolution, 1905–1921: A Bibliographical Guide to Works in English*, Westport CT – L 1995.

FOR AN OVERALL VIEW: O. Figes, *A People's Tragedy: The Russian Revolution, 1891–1924*, L 1996. L. B. Schapiro, *The Russian Revolutions and the Origins of Present-Day Communism*, Harmondsworth 1984, focuses on politics, as does R. Pipes in *The Russian Revolution* (see section C, page 562 above).

FALL OF TSARISM: E. N. Burdzhalov, *Russia's Second Revolution: The February 1917 Uprising in Petrograd*, tr. D. J. Raleigh, Bloomington IN 1987 (Rus. original 1967); T. Hasegawa, *The February Revolution: Petrograd, 1917*, Seattle WA – L 1981.

PROVISIONAL GOVERNMENT: R. P. Browder and A. F. Kerensky (eds.), *The Russian Provisional Government 1917: Documents*, 3 vols., Stanford CA 1961, contains a representative selection of materials. Kerensky has told his story many times; cf. R. Abraham, *Alexander Kerensky: The First Love of the Revolution*, L 1987.

LIBERALS: W. Rosenberg, *Liberals in the Russian Revolution: The Constitutional-Democratic Party, 1917–1921*, Princeton NJ – L 1974, is critical. For the PSR, O. H. Radkey, *The Agrarian Foes of Bolshevism . . .*, NY – L 1958.

RSDRP: Z. Galili, *The Menshevik Leaders in the Russian Revolution . . .*, Princeton NJ – L 1989; I. Getzler, *Martov: A Political Biography of a Russian Social-Democrat*, Cambridge 1967; T. Roobol, *Tsereteli: A Democrat in the Russian Revolution*, The Hague 1976.

ANARCHISTS: P. Avrich, *The Russian Anarchists*, Princeton 1967; id., *The Anarchists in the Russian Revolution*, Ithaca NY – L 1973.

BOLSHEVIKS: A. Rabinowitch, *The Petrograd Bolsheviks and the July Uprising*, Bloomington IN 1968; id., *The Bolsheviks Come to Power*, NY – L 1976; R. V. Daniels, *Red October: The Bolshevik Revolution of 1917*, NY 1967, L 1968; Trotsky's *History of the Russian Revolution* (1932–3) should be approached with caution; S. Lyandres, *The Bolsheviks' 'German Gold' Revisited . . .*, Pittsburg PA 1995.

MASS ORGANIZATIONS: J. L. H. Keep, *The Russian Revolution: A Study in Mass Mobilization*, L 1976, NY 1977; O. Anweiler, *The Soviets: The Russian Workers', Peasants' and Soldiers' Councils, 1905–1921*, tr. R. Hein, NY 1974; R. Wade, *Red Guards and Workers' Militias in the Russian Revolution*, Stanford 1984.

WAR AND PEACE: A. K. Wildman, *The End of the Imperial Army*, 2 vols., Princeton 1980, 1987, is very thorough. L. E. Heenan, *Russian Democracy's Fatal Blunder: The Summer Offensive of 1917*, Westport CT – L 1987; E. Mawdsley, *The Russian Revolution and the Baltic Fleet*, L 1978. J. L. Munck analyses the evidence on Kornilov's intentions in *The Kornilov Revolt . . .*, Aarhus 1987.

Social

There is much Western writing on labour history, some of it explicitly pro-Bolshevik and now dated. The best works are: D. H. Kaiser (ed.), *The Workers' Revolution in Russia, 1917: The View from Below*, Cambridge 1987; D. Koenker, *Moscow Workers and the 1917 Revolution*, Princeton 1981; id. and W. Rosenberg, *Strikes and Revolution in Russia, 1917*, Princeton 1989. On the agrarian movement, Keep (above) and G. Gill, *Peasants and Government in the Russian Revolution*, L 1979; R. Service (ed.), *Society and Politics in the Russian Revolution*, Basingstoke – L 1992.

NATIONAL AND REGIONAL: D. J. Raleigh, *Revolution on the Volga: 1917 in Saratov*, Ithaca NY – L 1986; T. Hunczak (ed.), *The Ukraine, 1917–1921:*

A Study in Revolution, Cambridge MA 1977; R. G. Suny, *The Baku Commune, 1917–1918: Class and Nationality in the Russian Revolution*, Princeton NJ – L 1972; A. Ezergailis, *The 1917 Revolution in Latvia*, Boulder CO 1974. The classic study of the nationalities in 1917–23 is R. Pipes, *Formation of the Soviet Union*, rev. ed., NY 1968.

HISTORICAL CONTROVERSIES: D. Geyer, *The Russian Revolution: Historical Problems and Perspectives*, tr. B. Little (from German ed. 1977), Leamington Spa 1987; S. Fitzpatrick, *The Russian Revolution*, Oxford – NY (1983) 1994; T. Skocpol, *States and Social Revolutions: A Comparative Analysis of France, Russia and China*, Cambridge 1979; E. R. Frankel *et al.* (eds.), *Revolution in Russia: Reassessments of 1917*, Cambridge 1992.

F. *Since 1917*

For reasons of economy, the following list simply gives the full titles of works cited in the text (Chapters 15–24). For bibliography, see Acton, *Russia* (section B above, page 558) and the following manuals: M. Armand *et al.* (eds.), *European Bibliography of Soviet, East European and Slavonic Studies*, Paris, vols. 1–16, 1975–90, in progress; A. Brown *et al.* (eds.), *Cambridge Encyclopedia* (see section A above, page 557); D. L. Jones, *Books in English on the Soviet Union, 1917–1973: A Bibliography*, NY – L 1975 (4,500 titles); J. Vronskaya and V. Chuguyev (eds.), *The Biographical Dictionary of the Former Soviet Union*, L 1992; S. White (ed.), *Political and Economic Encyclopaedia of the Soviet Union and Eastern Europe*, Harlow 1990.

Chapter 15

B. Williams, 'The All-Russian Constituent Assembly, January 5/18, 1918', *Parliaments, Estates and Representation* 5 (1985); R. K. Debo, *Revolution and Survival: The Foreign Policy of Soviet Russia, 1917–1918*, Toronto – L 1979; E. Mawdsley, *The Russian Civil War*, L – Boston 1987; T. C. Fiddick, *Russia's Retreat from Poland, 1920: From Permanent Revolution to Peaceful Coexistence*, Basingstoke – L 1990; M. McAuley, *Bread and Justice: State and Society in Petrograd, 1917–1922*, Oxford 1991; L. T. Lih, *Bread and Authority in Russia, 1914–1921*, Berkeley CA 1990; V. N. Brovkin, *Behind the Front Lines of the Civil War: Political Parties and Social Movements in Russia, 1918–1922*, Princeton NJ – L 1994; I. Getzler, *Kronstadt 1917–1921: The Fate of a Soviet Democracy*, Cambridge 1983; S. Malle, *The Economic Organization of War Communism, 1918–1921*, Berkeley CA – L 1990; R. Service, *The Bolshevik Party in Revolution: A Study in Organizational Change, 1917–1923*, Basingstoke – L 1979.

Chapter 16

A. M. Ball, *And Now My Soul is Hardened: Abandoned Children in Soviet Russia, 1918–1930*, Berkeley CA – L 1994; S. Fitzpatrick *et al.* (eds.), *Russia in the Era of NEP: Explorations in Soviet Society and Culture*, Bloomington IN – L 1991; A. M. Ball, *Russia's Last Capitalists: The NEP men, 1921–1929*, Ann Arbor MI 1986 (also pub. under the title *The NEP men: Private Entrepreneurs in the Soviet Union, 1921–1929*); P. Kenez, *Cinema and Soviet Society*, Cambridge 1992; M. von Hagen, 'The NEP, *Perestroika*, and the Problem of Alternatives', J. E. Tedstrom (ed.), *Socialism, Perestroika, and the Dilemmas of Soviet Economic Reform*, Boulder CO – Oxford 1990; M. Jakobson, *Origins of the Gulag: The Soviet Prison Camp System, 1917–1934*, Lexington KY 1993.

Chapter 17

J. Jacobson, *When the Soviet Union Entered World Politics*, Berkeley CA – L 1994; M. Y. L. Luk, *The Origins of Chinese Bolshevism: An Ideology in the Making, 1920–1928*, Hong Kong – Oxford – NY 1990; K. McDermott, 'Stalin and the Comintern During the "Third Period", 1928–1933', *European History Quarterly* 25 (1995); J. Haslam, *Soviet Foreign Policy, 1930–1933: The Impact of the Depression*, L – NY 1983; id., *The Soviet Union and the Struggle for Collective Security in Europe, 1933–1939*, NY 1984; id., *The Soviet Union and the Threat from the East, 1933–1941: Moscow, Tokyo and the Prelude to the Pacific War*, L – Basingstoke 1992; G. Roberts, *The Soviet Union and the Origins of the Second World War: Russo-German Relations and the Road to War, 1933–1941*, Basingstoke – L 1995; H. Phillips, *Between the Revolution and the West: A Political Biography of M. M. Litvinov*, Boulder CO – L 1992.

Chapter 18

J. Hughes, *Stalin, Siberia and the Crisis of the NEP*, Cambridge 1991; Y. Taniuchi, 'Decision-Making on the Ural–Siberian Method', J. Cooper *et al.* (eds.), *Soviet History 1917–53*, Basingstoke – L 1995; S. Fitzpatrick, *Stalin's Peasants: Resistance and Survival in the Russian Village after Collectivization*, Oxford – NY 1994; R. Conquest, *The Harvest of Sorrow: Soviet Collectivization and the Terror-Famine*, Edmonton – NY 1986; R. W. Davies *et al.* (eds.), *The Economic Transformation of the Soviet Union, 1913–1945*, Cambridge 1994; V. Andrle, *A Social History of Twentieth-Century Russia*, L – NY 1994; D. L. Hoffmann, *Peasant Metropolis: Social Identities in Moscow, 1929–1941*, Ithaca NY – L 1994; S. Fitzpatrick, *The Cultural Front: Power and Culture in Revolutionary Russia*, Ithaca NY – L 1992 (nine essays); J. Hughes, 'Patrimonialism and the Soviet System: The Case of S. I. Syrtsov', *Europe-Asia Studies* 48 (1996); R. C. Tucker, *Stalin in Power: The Revolution from Above,*

1928–1941, NY – L 1990; A. Knight, *Beria: Stalin's First Lieutenant*, Princeton NJ – L 1993; M. Malia, *The Soviet Tragedy: A History of Socialism in Russia, 1917–1991*, NY – Toronto 1994.

Chapter 19

J. L. Wieczynski (ed.), *Operation Barbarossa: The German Attack on the Soviet Union*, Salt Lake City UT 1993; J. Erickson and D. Dilks (eds.), *Barbarosssa: The Axis and the Allies*, Edinburgh 1994; W. Moskoff, *The Bread of Affliction: The Food Supply in the USSR during World War II*, Cambridge 1990; H. Salisbury, *The Siege of Leningrad*, L 1969; H. Shukman (ed.), *Stalin's Generals*, L 1993; T. J. Colton, *Commissars, Commanders and Civilian Authority: The Structure of Soviet Military Politics*, Cambridge MA – L 1979; M. Harrison, *Soviet Planning in Peace and War, 1938–1945*, Cambridge 1985; P. Gatrell and M. Harrison, 'The Russian and Soviet Economies in Two World Wars: A Comparative View', *Economic History Review* 46 (1993); J. Barber and M. Harrison, *The Soviet Home Front, 1941–1945*, L 1991; D. Pospielovsky, *The Russian Church under the Soviet Regime, 1917–1982*, 2 vols., Crestwood NY 1984; L. Dobroszycki and J. S. Gurock (eds.), *The Holocaust in the Soviet Union: Studies and Sources on the Destruction of the Jews in the Nazi-Occupied Territories of the USSR, 1941–1945*, Armonk NY 1993.

Chapter 20

L. E. Razgon, *True Stories: The Memoirs of Lev Razgon*, tr. J. Crowfoot, Dana Point CA 1997 (French ed., Paris 1991, used here; Rus. ed. 1987–8); J. and C. Garrard (eds.), *World War II and the Soviet People: Selected Papers from the Fourth World Congress of Soviet Studies . . .* , NY 1993; S. N. Goncharov *et al.*, *Uncertain Partners: Stalin, Mao and the Korean War*, Stanford CA 1995; G. Roberts, 'Moscow and the Marshall Plan: Politics, Idealogy and the Onset of the Cold War', *Europe-Asia Studies* 46 (1994); M. M. Narinsky, 'Soviet Foreign Policy . . .', G. Gorodetsky (ed.), *Soviet Foreign Policy, 1917–1991: A Retrospective*, L 1994; M. P. Leffler and D. S. Painter, *Origins of the Cold War: An International History*, L – NY 1994.

Chapter 21

B. Dmytryshyn, *USSR: A Concise History*, 3rd ed., NY 1978; L. I. Shelley, *Policing Soviet Society: The Evolution of State Control*, L – NY 1996.

Chapter 23

M. Light (ed.), *Troubled Friendships: Moscow's Third World Ventures*, L 1993; M. Brzoska and T. Ohlson, *Arms Transfers to the Third World, 1971–1985*, Oxford – NY 1987.

Abakumov, V. S., 433, 437
Abalkin, L. I., 537
Abkhazia, 300, 532
Abramov, F. A., 488
Abuladze, T. Ye., 524
Academy of Sciences, 97, 115f., 384, 525
Acmeism, 252, 486
Adashev, A., 33, 35
Adenauer, K., 513
Adrianople, treaty of, 88
Adylov, A., 462
Aehrenthal, A. L. von, 258
Afghanistan: to 1917: 146, 165, 189, 255; 1918–: 502, 512, 542; *see* wars
Africa: 507, 518; east, 508, 511, 542; north, 146, 422, 508f.; south, 508, 510f., 542
agriculture: to 1800: 2, 8, 12, 58, 112; 1801–1917: 140f., 176–82, 184, 239–41, 265; 1918–: 317, 321, 411f., 427, 457, 475–9, 537; collectivization of, 357, 368–75, 390, 440, 446
Ahmed, khan, 24
Aidit, D. N., 501
Aigun, treaty of, 164
Aivazovsky, I. K., 157
Ajubey, A. I., 461
Akayev, A. A., 532
Akhmatova, A. A., 252, 305, 434, 486f.
Aksakov, I. S., 136, 154
Aksakov, K. S., 136
Åland Is., 86
Alaska, 163
Albania, 449, 499
Albazin, 72
alcoholism, *see* vodka

Aleichem, S., 214
Aleutian Is., 163
Alexander I, emperor, 106, 121–32, 139, 426
Alexander II, emperor, 148–51, 154, 158, 160, 167, 170, 172–5, 213
Alexander III, emperor, 175, 202–5, 207, 209f., 216, 223–5
Alexander Nevsky, prince, 16
Alexandra Fedorovna, empress, 264
Alexeyev, M. V., 264, 294
Alexii II (Ridiger), patriarch, 525
Alexis Mikhaylovich, tsar, 56, 66, 71, 76, 79, 95
Alexis Nikolayevich, tsarevich, 243
Alexis Petrovich, tsarevich, 98
Alexis (Simansky), patriarch, 413
Alksnis, V. I., 543
Alliluyeva, N. S., 391
Alliluyeva, S., 437
Almaty (Alma-Ata), 471, 529
Altranstädt, treaty of, 84
Amalrik, A. A., 491
Amanullah, khan, 351
Amin, H., 512
Amur, river, 72, 164, 542
Anarchism, Anarchists, 137, 222, 282, 310, 312, 361
Andrey Bogolyubsky, prince, 10
Andreyeva, N. A., 526
Andropov, Yu. V., 462f., 465, 506, 512, 522, 536
Andrusovo, treaty of, 71
Anna Ivanovna, empress, 108, 119
Antokol'sky, M. M., 214
Antonov, A., 308f.
Antonov, A. I., 419
Antonov-Ovseyenko, V. A., 283, 293

Antonovych, V. B., 170
Aptekman, O. V., 170
Arab lands, Arabs, 437, 446, 508–10
Arakcheyev, A. A., 128f.
Aral Sea, 484f.
Archangel, 66, 81, 115, 189, 295
architecture: to 1917: 7, 30, 75, 97, 114; 1918–: 329, 388, 436, 490
Ardahan, 166
aristocrats, 28f., 31–5, 42, 47, 76–80, 107, 113f., 127, 194; and land, 9, 23, 29, 44, 58, 109, 194
Aristotle da Fioraventi, 30
armaments, 67, 84, 159, 261, 346, 358, 363, 377, 403, 407, 410, 494f., 500, 508, 514–16, 518; see also disarmament
armed forces: to 1700: 8, 15, 33, 48, 68f., 81–3; 1700–1917: 84, 89f., 100, 143, 158f., 168, 230, 241f., 254, 261f.; 1918–41: 285, 289–92, 308, 311, 336f., 370, 394; 1941–: 399, 403, 408–10, 417, 427, 456, 504, 512; disaffection in, 121, 231, 266–8, 273f., 278, 287f.; see also navy
Armed Neutrality league, 102
Armenia, Armenians: to 1917: 63, 88, 212, 223, 280; 1918–: 300f., 471, 531, 536, 543
art: to 1917: 7, 30, 75, 157, 247; 1918– : 326–8, 387f., 434f., 489f.
artisans, see industry
Arzamas, 61
Astrakhan', 34, 85, 88, 115
Atatürk, K., 301, 350
atheism, 317, 326, 370, 413
Augustus II, king, 83, 86
Augustus III, king, 101f.
Auschwitz, 415
Austerlitz, battle of, 123
Austria (-Hungary), Habsburgs: to 1800: 20, 76, 82, 101, 102f., 106; 1801–1917: 122–5, 144–6, 159f., 166f., 169, 208, 225, 245, 254, 258–63, 268, 288, 294; 1918–: 348, 419, 423, 513
autocracy: to 1800: 16, 27, 33, 38, 54,

80, 109; 1801–1917: 122, 132, 149, 155, 161, 197, 204, 209, 233, 236, 267
Avars, 2, 10
Averbakh, L. L., 385
aviation, 346, 351, 377f., 403f., 410, 445, 455, 500, 510
Avraamov, A., 330
Avvakum, archpriest, 74
Axelrod, P. B., 216
Azef, Ye. F., 222, 244
Azerbaijan, Azeris: to 1917: 188, 212, 230, 280; 1918–: 300f., 446, 470, 531
Azov, 70, 81, 87, 101

'bagmen', 305, 319
Baikal, Lake, 72, 189, 296, 484
Bakst, L. S., 252
Baku, 188, 230, 280
Bakunin, M. A., 137, 161, 172
Balakyrev, M. A., 247
Balmont, K. A., 250, 328
Baltic peoples, provinces/states: to 1918: 87, 139, 150, 168, 177, 181, 189, 210, 230, 236, 279; 1918–84: 288, 293, 358, 396, 400f., 415f., 431f., 468–73 passim, 486, 523; 1985–: 527, 529–31, 543, 546; Baltic Germans, 87, 132, 139, 210f., 230
Bandera, S., 431
banks, 65, 112, 181, 192, 480
Baptists, see Protestants
Barclay de Tolly, M. von, 124
Barre, S., 511
Bashkiria (Bashkortostan), Bashkirs, 61, 85, 110, 213, 302, 484, 533
basmachi, 302
Basmanov, F., 37
Batum, 166
Baudelaire, C., 250
Beijing, 164, 226, 542; treaty of, 164
Beilis, M., 242f.
Belarus, Belarusians: to 1917: 12, 103, 167f., 178; 1918–: 297f., 395f., 399, 417, 425, 469, 533, 546
Belgorod, 44

Belgrade, 260, 418, 449; treaty of, 101
Belinsky, V. G., 138f.
Beliy, A. (B. N. Bugayev), 250, 252
Belkin, F., 447
Beloozero, 18
Belov, V., 488
Beneš, E., 424
Benkendorf, A. K., 133, 140
Benois, A. N., 250, 253
Berdyaev, N. A., 251
Berezina, river, 124
Berggol'ts, O. F., 408
Beriya, L. P., 396, 400, 403, 431, 433, 437, 454
Berlin, 102, 343, 401f., 419, 503, 512–15, 517, 540; blockade, 451; congress of, 166; treaty of, 349
Bessarabia, 159, 166, 288, 358, 366, 401, 505
Bezdna, 152
Bierut, B., 447
Bismarck, O. von, 160, 166, 224, 403
'black hundreds', *see* Union of Russian People
black market, 305, 375, 474, 479
Blok, A. A., 250, 331
Blum, L., 360
Blyukher, V. K., 357, 364
Bodrov, S., 547
Bogdanov, A. A., 244, 327, 330
Bogolepov, N. P., 222
Boisdeffre, R. F. C. de, 224
Bokhara, 164, 302
Bolotnikov, I., 50f., 61
Bolsheviks: to 1917: 220, 235, 244f., 271, 273, 276–85; 1918–: *see* CPSU
Bomelius, E., 40
Borodin, A. P., 247
Borodin, M. pseud., 353f.
Borodino, battle of, 124
Borotbisty, 299
Bosnia-Herzegovina, 165f., 258
Boyar Duma, 29, 33, 42, 50, 92f.
Brandt, W., 516f.
Brest-Litovsk, 545; treaty of, 287–90, 402; Union of, 70

Brezhnev, L. I., 383, 458–63, 465, 468, 502, 512, 517; doctrine, 505, 539
Brezhnev, Yu. L., 461
Britain, Great: 1707–1855: 86, 90, 102, 122–6, 143; 1856–1917: 159, 162, 164–6, 183, 187, 191, 226, 254f., 258, 262, 268f., 273; 1918–39: 295f., 298, 300f., 345, 347f., 351, 358–62, 366, 376, 398; 1940–: 401, 420–25, 428
Brodsky, I. A., 487, 524
Bruce, J., 89
Brusilov, A. A., 263
Bryusov, V. Ya., 250, 252
Bucharest, 450, 516
Budenny, S. M., 291, 295
Bug, rivers: southern, 106; western, 297, 366
Bukharin, N. I., 321f., 340, 368, 390, 455, 524
Bukovina, 401, 505
Bulavin, K., 85
Bulgakov, M. A., 327, 385
Bulgakov, S. N., 218, 251
Bulganin, N. A., 454f., 502
Bulgaria: to 1917: 6, 15, 165f., 223f., 258; 1918–: 360, 402, 418, 421, 424, 446, 448
Bulygin, A. I., 233
Bund, Jewish, 218–20, 222
bureaucracy: to 1917: 33, 91f., 127, 133, 138, 154f., 204, 265f.; 1918–: 334, 382f., 456, 459–62, 523
Buryats, 72, 351
Byzantine empire, 3, 5–7, 16, 22, 27–9

Cambodia (Kampuchea), 501, 542
Cadet Corps, 108, 115
Cameron, C., 114
canals, 95, 386
Canton, 353f.
Carpatho-Ukraine, 420
Carter, J., 518
Casimir IV, king, 23
Castro, F., 511, 515, 542
Catherine I, empress, 100

Catherine II, the Great, empress, 57, 100, 102f., 106, 110–20 *passim*, 127f., 132, 436
Catholics: to 1917: 6f., 12, 22, 25, 47f., 74, 77, 103, 136; 1918–: 326, 448, 470, 472, 486, 504, 506, 525
Ceausescu, N., 504, 531
censorship: to 1917: 116f., 121, 126, 134, 137f., 158, 169, 174, 207, 235; 1917–: 285, 387, 434, 456, 524
censuses, 56, 90, 198, 313, 471
Central Asia: to 1917: 88, 157, 162, 164f., 213, 280; 1918–: 302, 379, 468–72, 510, 512, 528, 532
Central Economic Council (VSNKh), 306
Central Political Administration (PUR), 337, 409
Central War Industries Committee, 265
Chaadayev, P. Ya., 136
Chagall, M., 252, 328
Chaliapine (Shalyapin), F. I., 328
Chancellor, R., 39
Charles IX, king, 51
Charles X, king, 71
Charles XII, king, 83f., 86f.
Charykov, N. V., 258
Chayanov, A. V., 179, 385
Chebrikov, V. M., 522, 526
Chechens, Chechnya, 145, 431, 532f., 546f.
Cheka, *see* security police
Chekhov, A. P., 194, 248f.
Chelyabinsk, 294, 372, 377
Chen Duxiu, 354
Cheremis (Mari), 34, 61
Cherkasov, N. K., 435
Chernenko, K. U., 463, 521
Chernigov, 1, 307
Chernobyl, 485, 523, 533, 536
Chernov, V. M., 221, 244, 277
Chernyaev, M. G., 164f.
Chernyshevsky, N. G., 171f.
Chesme, battle of, 105
Chicherin, G. V., 301, 342, 344, 348, 357
China: to 1917: 66, 72, 88, 164, 225f.,

255; 1918–53: 300, 345, 352–4, 363, 444; 1953–: 495, 498–502, 505, 515, 532, 535, 542
Chita, 357
Chuguyev, 129
Chuikov, V. I., 408
Chukotka, 72
Churbanov, Yu. M., 461f.
Churchill, Sir W. S., 401, 407, 421–4
Chuvash, 34, 61
cinema, 254, 329f., 389, 435, 490, 492, 524, 547
Circassians, 145
clergy, 34, 73, 93, 95f., 111, 155
collective security, 358f., 361f.
collectivization, *see* agriculture
colleges (administrative), 89, 92, 127
Comecon, 448
Cominform, 449f., 507
Comintern, 325, 342–5, 349f., 352–4, 422, 449; congresses, 355, 360; Executive Committee, 343f., 356, 363
Commonwealth of Independent States, 545
commune, village, 111, 136, 176, 178f., 197, 221, 239f., 317, 374
Communist parties: China (CCP), 352, 357, 363, 443f.; France (PCF), 360, 398, 449, 452, 507; Germany (KPD), 343–5, 356; Great Britain (CPGB), 398, 422; Italy (PCI), 449, 452, 504, 507; Russian (KPRF), 534, 543, 546
Communist Party of the Soviet Union, 311f., 324f., 331f., 336, 339–41, 453, 455f., 467, 544; cadres, membership, 308, 312, 314, 336f., 433, 459, 469, 472, 523; Central Committee, 393f., 455, 457, 459, 523, 526, 544; congresses: Xth, 312; XVth, 322; XVIIth, 392; XVIIIth, 365; XIXth, 438; XXth, 454; XXIst, 457; XXIInd, 457, 499; XXIIIrd, 459; XXVIth, 459f., XXVIIth, 523; Politburo: to 1953: 312, 343, 346, 369, 371, 390, 393, 431, 435, 437; 1953–: 453–5,

457, 465, 506, 521, 528;
programmes, 457, 523; Secretariat,
apparatus, 312, 339, 383, 390, 460,
507, 521, 527
Congress of People's Deputies, 527
Constantine Nikolayevich, grand
duke, 148, 159
Constantine Pavlovich, grand duke,
106, 130, 144
Constantinople (Byzantium, Istanbul),
3, 5f., 8, 10, 15, 105f., 161, 166,
297; patriarch of, 28, 43, 73
Constituent Assembly, 231, 268, 279,
282, 286f., 293
Constitutional Democrats (Kadets),
235, 237f., 268, 271f., 286
Constitutions: 1906: 236f.; 1918: 285;
1923: 303f.; 1936: 463, 467; 1977:
463, 528; 1993: 546
Constructivism, 329
Contarini, A., 20
Continental Blockade, 123, 142
Cossacks: to 1917: 32; Dnieper, 50,
71, 105; Don. Donets, 47, 53f., 61f.,
70, 85, 105; Kuban, 106, 145;
serving, 68, 102, 123f., 207, 221,
267; Siberia, 34, 72; Terek, 49, 106,
145; Yaik, 110f.; 1918–: 292, 294,
311, 416
Council of Europe, 540, 546
Council of Labour and Defence, 292
Council of Ministers: to 1917: 204,
234, 236, 254; 1946–   : 453
Council of People's Commissars
(1917–46), 284f., 287f., 290, 310f.
Craców, 47, 71, 419
crafts, craftsmen, see industry
Crimea, 6, 105f., 275, 295, 406, 408,
438, 534, 545; see also Tatars,
wars
Cripps, Sir S., 401
CSCE, 540
Cuba, 508, 511f., 515, 542
Cui, C. A., 247
'cult of the individual', 455
Cumans, see Polovtsy
Curzon line, 297, 423
Custine, A. L. L. de., 133

Cyril and Methodius brotherhood,
168f.
Czechoslovakia, Czechs, Slovaks: to
1945: 294, 296, 359, 361f., 365,
419–21, 424; 1945–: 446f., 465,
472, 505–7, 513, 517, 541

Daghestan, 145
Daniel Alexandrovich, prince, 16
Daniel, Yu. M., 465
Danilevsky, N. Ya., 161
Danzig (Gdańsk), 67, 101, 419, 505f.,
514
Darwin, C., 171; social Darwinism,
161
Decembrist revolts, 121, 128–31, 133,
144, 151
De Gaulle, C., 424, 516
Deineka, A. A., 387
De la Gardie, M., 52
Delyanov, I. D., 207f.
Demidov, N. A., 94
Demidov, P. P., 132
'Democratic Centralists', 312
Democratic movement, 463–7
Deng Xiaoping, 535, 537
Denikin, A. I., 295f.
Denmark, Danes: to 1917: 35, 56,
83f., 86, 160, 203, 281; 1918–: 348,
425
denunciation, 36f., 89, 98, 173f., 222,
393, 432
deportations, 23, 214, 371, 396, 399f.,
416, 465
Derzhavin, G. R., 112
Deulino, treaty of, 69
Dezhnev, S., 72
Diaghilev, S. P., 250
Dimitrov, G. M., 360
Dionysius, 30
disarmament, 359, 452, 513f.; arms
control, 452, 492, 515–18, 538f.
Djilas, M., 421
Dmitriy Donskoy, grand prince, 18
Dmitriy Ivanovich, prince, 45
Dnieper, river, 1f., 6, 10–12, 20, 72,
101, 105; Dneprostroy, 377
Dniester, river, 106, 417

Dokuchayev, V. V., 157
Dolgoruky, V. V., 85
Don, river, 2, 95, 294f., 407; *see also* Cossacks
Donets, river, region, 47, 188, 292, 319, 370, 381
Donetsk (Yuzovka, Stalino), 187
Dorosh, Ye. Ya., 488
Dorpat, *see* Tartu
Dostoyevsky, F. M., 157, 245f., 249
Drahomaniw, M. P., 170
Dubček, A., 505
Dubrovin, A. I., 243
Dukhonin, N. N., 288
Duma, State, 127, 198, 233f; Ist, 237; IInd, 238; IIIrd, 241f., 244; IVth, 264, 266–8
Durnovo, P. N., 234
Dvina, rivers: northern, 1, 39; western, 1, 3, 12, 20
Dvinsk, 289
dvoryane, see 'gentry', nobles
Dzerzhinsky, F. E., 311, 338

'Eastern question', 87, 126, 145, 161, 165f., 223f., 255, 258
Eberlein, H., 343
ecology, 473, 484f., 490
education: **to 1917**: 7, 96f., 117, 131f., 140, 153, 156, 165, 198, 208–13 *passim*; **1918–**: 315, 334f., 382f., 389, 448
Eisenhower, D. D., 419
Eisenstein, S. M., 330, 389, 435
Elizabeth I, queen, 40
Elizabetha Petrovna, empress, 87, 102, 115, 119
Elphinstone, J., 105
Enghien, duc d' (A. H. de Bourbon), 123
England, English, 39–41, 45, 52, 66, 82, 137; **1707–**: *see* Britain
Enlightenment in Russia, 98, 114–20, 128, 135
epidemics, 15, 42, 64, 112, 163, 176, 285
Erekle II, king, 106
Erzerum, 263, 296

Estland (later Estonia); **to 1917**: 71, 87, 186, 210f., 230, 279; **1918–**: 296, 298, 366, 418, 469f., 529f.

factory committees, 275–7, 282
Fadeyev, R. A., 161
False Dmitriy I (G. Otrep'ev), 46–50
False Dmitriy II, 51, 53
False Dmitriy III, 53
family: **to 1917**: 31, 141f., 178–80, 193, 199; **1918–**: 313f., 389, 473, 483
famines: **to 1917**: 45f., 112, 176, 285; **1918–**: 313, 325, 372–4, 406, 411f., 432, 441f.
Far East, Russian (Maritime prov.), 164, 357, 364, 395, 411, 500
Fick, H., 99
Filofey, monk, 28
finance: **to 1917**: 8, 66, 112, 142, 149, 151f., 191f., 236f., 276; **1918–**: 440, 535f., 548
Finland, Finns: **to 1917**: 2, 10, 87, 123, 168, 211, 223, 237, 241, 279, 282; **1918–**: 288f., 295, 298, 358, 366, 402; *see* wars
Fletcher, G., 40f.
Florence, Council of, 22
forced labour, 94f., 113, 378; *see also* prison camps, serfdom
Fourier, C., 137
France, French: **to 1789**: 8, 20, 48, 51, 66, 87, 101f.; **1789–1917**: 103, 117, 122–5, 134, 137, 140–6 *passim*, 160, 162, 167, 190, 224f., 248, 254f., 259, 262f., 269, 273; **1918–39**: 295, 297, 348, 358–63, 366; **1940–**: 401, 421, 423f., 516, 528
Franco, F., 360
Frank, S. L., 251
Franz Joseph, emperor, 144
Frederick II, king, 102
freemasonry, 117
Friedland, battle of, 123
Frunze, M. V., 292, 296f., 302, 331f.
Fuchs, K., 439
Futurists, 252, 327f.

Gagarin family, 140–42
Gagarin, Yu. A., 514
Galich, 18
Galich (Ginzburg), A. A., 489
Galicia, 10, 21, 169f., 245, 263, 268, 296
Gamsakhurdia, Z. K., 532
Gapon, G. A., 228f.
Gasprali (Gasprinsky), I., 212
Gastev, A. K., 319
Gel'fman, G., 213
Genoa, conference of, 348
genocide: of Armenians, 471; of Cossacks, 311; of Jews, 414f.
'gentry' (privileged servitors): to 1700: 21, 29, 31, 38, 44, 49–54, 58–62, 68, 93, 105, 107–11, 384; and land, 23, 25, 29–31, 58, 93; 1700–: see nobles
Georgia, Georgians: to 1917: 88, 106, 145, 212, 223, 230, 280; 1918–: 289, 300f., 303, 396, 431, 469, 471, 531f., 543
Gerasimov, A. M., 435
Germans, Germany: to 1917: 8, 66f., 102, 129, 135, 188, 224f., 243, 254–9 passim, 279; 'German suburb', 76–81 passim, 124; Germans in Russia, 34, 40, 76, 97, 99, 115, 191; 1918–45: 342–6, 349, 351, 356–67 passim, 389, 393, 414–17; 1945–: 420, 423–5, 430f., 448, 471, 513, 516f., 540f.; German Democratic Republic (GDR), 450, 503, 505, 513f., 518, 540f.; German Federal Republic (FRG), 451, 503f., 513, 516f., 538, 541; see also Baltic Germans, individual German states
Gershuni, G. A., 222
Gierek, E., 506
Giers, N. K., 224
Gilan, 351, 445
Ginzburg, Ye. S., 489, 524
Gladkov, F. V., 327
glasnost', 158, 521, 523–6
Glazunov, I. S., 489f.
Glinka, M. I., 139

Glinsky family, 32f.
Godunov, B. F., tsar, 43, 45, 47f.
Godunova, I. F., 43, 45
Godunova, X. B., 49
Gogol', N. V., 138f., 168
Gomel', 273
Gomulka, W., 503, 506
Goncharova, N. S., 252
Gorbachev, M. S.: character, 520f.; 394, 463, 491, 521–3, 525–7, 543f.; and culture, 525; and economy, 535–7; and foreign affairs, 495, 519, 522, 535, 538–42; and nationalities, 528–30, 534
Gorbacheva, R. M., 540
Gorchakov, A. M., 160, 162
Gor'ky, M. (A. M. Peshkov), 286, 323, 386
Gottwald, K., 447
government, local, 93, 109, 149, 153f., 205f., 241; municipal, 94, 113, 154, 206
governors, provincial: namestniki, 33; voyevody, 56, 65, 71; (general-) gubernatory, 117, 145, 153, 163, 173
Great Terror, 38, 361, 364, 383, 386, 393–7, 403, 409, 453–5, 465, 467, 489, 499, 520, 524
Greece, Greeks: to 1917: 7, 48, 78, 106, 123, 126, 129, 258f.; 1918–: 348, 396, 418, 424
'Greens': ecologists, 484, 490; rural partisans, 308
Gregory, J.-G., 76
Grigoryev, N., 293, 299
Grodno, 150
Gromyko, A. A., 462, 465, 512, 516f., 522, 538
Grossman, V.S., 524
Grozny, 188
Guards regiments, 81, 90, 92, 100, 108, 121, 128–30, 267
Guchkov, A. I., 264f., 270
GULag, see prison camps
Guomindang (Kuomintang), 352–4, 357, 363, 443f.
Gustavus Adolphus, king, 70

Hallstein, W., 517
Hangö, 86
Hanse, the, 23
Harbin, 225, 357
Hartvig, N. G., 258
Hastings, Lady M., 40
health, public, 153f., 428, 460f., 484;
    see also epidemics
Hegel, G. W. F., 135
Helen Pavlovna, grand duchess, 148
Helphand, A. L., 281
Helsinki (Helsingfors), 400, 516;
    accords, 466, 516, 518; university,
    211
Herberstein, S. von, 20
Herder, J. G. von, 135
Hermogen, patriarch, 52
Herzen, A. I., 137, 171
Hess, R., 402
Himmler, H., 414, 416
Hippius, Z., 250
Hitler, A., 356f., 360, 362, 365–7,
    398, 402, 406f., 419, 493
Hmelnyckyj, B., 71, 471
'Holy Alliance', 125f., 144
Honecker, E., 505
Horsey, Sir J., 40f.
housing, 2, 77, 141, 478, 483
Hughes, J., 187, 190
Human Rights Committee, 466
Hünkâr-Iskelesi, treaty of, 146
Hungary, Hungarians: to 1945: 10,
    87, 144, 342, 418, 420, 424, 436;
    1945–: 446f., 472, 503–6, 535, 541
Huns, 2, 10
Husák, G., 505

ideology, see Marxism-Leninism
Ignatyev, N. P., 162, 166, 202, 258
Igor (Ingvair), prince, 5
Il'minsky, N. I., 212
Imperial . . . Geographical Society,
    148, 170
India, 123, 162, 300, 348, 351, 502,
    508f.
industrialists, industry: artisans, 3, 8,
    14, 25, 63, 110–14 passim, 195f.,
    214, 243; entrepreneurs, factories: to

1917: 94f., 113f., 142f., 149, 168,
    184–9, 195, 261, 265, 275; 1918– :
    306, 318f., 375–8, 404f., 411, 427,
    439, 468, 482f., 535, 544, 548
Ingria, 69, 87
Ingush, Ingushetia, 431, 533
intelligentsia: to 1917: 101, 118, 131,
    134–7, 148, 169, 171, 196–7, 252;
    1918–: 323, 326, 331, 382, 479, 493
Ioffe, A. A., 352
Iran (Persia): to 1917: 39, 88, 106,
    255; 1918–: 351, 402, 421, 445f.,
    508, 510, 512, 531
Irkutsk, 296
Isidore, metropolitan, 22
Islam: to 1917: 6, 12, 15, 88, 106, 145,
    164, 212f., 255, 272, 280; 1918–:
    300–3, 350f., 416, 446, 470–73,
    485, 510, 512, 525, 531f.
Israel, 437, 446, 505, 509f.
Italy, Italians: to 1917: 10, 20, 29f.,
    122, 129, 134, 159f., 258; 1918–:
    348, 363, 402, 407, 421, 490
Itil, 6
Ivan III, the Great, grand prince,
    20–25, 29f.
Ivan IV, 'the Terrible', tsar, 31–41,
    45, 58, 80, 247, 435
Ivan V, tsar, 79
Ivan Kalita, prince, 18, 22, 30
Ivanov, N. I., 267
Ivanov, V. I., 250, 252
Ivanovo-Voznesensk, 143, 182, 200,
    230
Izvol'sky, A. P., 257f.

jadids, 212, 301f.
Japan: to 1917: 88, 164, 188, 225f.,
    255; 1918–39: 352, 354, 357, 363,
    393; 1940–: 402, 425, 430, 442–5,
    500f., 542; see wars
Jaruzelski, W., 506
Jehovah's Witnesses, 431
Jemilev, M., 471
Jena, battle of, 123
Jenkinson, A., 39
Jesuits, 47f., 72, 74
Jews, Judaism: to 1917: 3, 6, 103, 105,

127, 130, 170, 187, 196, 209, 213f.,
230f., 263, 280; 1918–: 327f., 366,
396, 414, 471, 485, 525;
antisemitism, 156, 170, 185, 213f.,
231, 242f., 293, 434, 437f., 448, 473
(*see also* pogroms); 'Judaizers', 27,
73; Zionism, 220, 280, 299, 437; *see
also* genocide
Jiang Jieshi (Chiang Kai-shek), 352f.,
443
Joachim, patriarch, 78
Job, patriarch, 43f.
Joseph II, emperor, 106
Joseph of Volokolamsk, 27, 34

Kabarda, 106
Kadets, *see* Constitutional Democrats
Kaganovich, L. M., 393, 454f.
Kalanta, R., 470
Kalmykia, Kalmyks, 61, 431
Kama, river, 21
Kamchatka, 72, 164
Kamenev, L. B., 281f., 285, 303,
339–41, 390–93
Kamenev, S. S., 295
Kandinsky, V. V., 328
Kankrin, E. F., 143
Kapitsa, P. L., 465
Karachay-Balkars, 431
Karakhan, L. M., 352
Karakozov, D. V., 172
Kardis, treaty of, 71
Karelia, 87, 298, 396, 400
Karimov, I. A., 532
Karmal, B., 512
Kars, 166
Kassim, A., 509
Katayev, V. P., 387
Katkov, M. N., 161, 224
Katyn, 399f., 421f., 525
Kaufman, K. P. von, 164
Kaunas (Kovno), 71, 150, 298, 470
Kazakhs, Kazakhstan: to 1953: 165,
168, 302, 341, 396; 1953–: 455, 466,
471, 476, 485, 528f., 532, 546
Kazan, 19, 36, 63, 111, 294, 302, 346;
khanate of, 20, 24, 33f.; university,
132, 212

Kellogg-Briand pact, 358
Kerch, strait of, 81
Kerensky, A. F., 270–73, 283
Khalkin-Gol, battle of, 364
Khalturin, S. N., 174
Khar'kov, 173, 221, 295, 400, 406f.,
533; university, 132
Khasan, battle of Lake, 364
Khazars, 3, 5f., 12
Kheraskov, M., 115
Khiva, 88, 164, 302
Khlebnikov, V., 252
Khlopko, 46
Khomyakov, A. S., 136f.
Khrushchev, N. S., 392, 394, 441f.,
453–8, 521, 534; and culture, 456,
489–91; and economy, 456, 475–7,
482; and foreign affairs, 494, 498f.,
502, 504, 514f.
Khvorostinin, I. A., 76
Khvylovyj, M., 333
Kiev, 1, 5, 8–10, 72f., 173, 242, 293f.,
294–9 *passim*, 404, 415, 470;
academy, 74; university, 168;
Kievan Rus, 1–11, 16, 491
Kilburger, I., 63
Kipchak ('Golden') Horde, 12, 24
Kireyevsky, I. V., P. V., 136
Kirov, S. M., 340, 391f.
Kiselev, P. D., 140
Kizhi, 63
Knox, Sir A., 295
Koch, E., 414
Kohl, H., 540
Kokand, 302
Kokovtsov, V. N., 242
Kolchak, A. V., 295f.
Kollontay, A. M., 312, 314
Kolomna, 17f., 63
Kolyma, river, 72
kombedy, 307f.
Komsomol, 316, 334f., 382, 472, 492
Komsomol'sk-on-Amur, 379, 411
Kondratyev, N. D., 385
Konev, I. S., 408, 418f.
Königsberg (Kaliningrad), 419f.,
541
Konovalov, A. I., 276

Korea, Koreans, 164, 225f., 396, 444f., 500, 542; *see* wars
Korf, N. A., 156
Kornilov, L. G., 272f., 277, 544
Korolenko, V. G., 323f.
Kosciuszko, T., 103
Kostomarov, N. P., 169
Kostroma, 67, 200, 308
Kosygin, A. N., 459, 482, 502, 517
Kotoshikhin, G., 76
Kovalevskaya, S. V., 158
Krasin, L. B., 327
Krasnitsky, A., 324
Krasnov, P. N., 294
Krasnovodsk, 165, 189
Krasnoyarsk, 275
Kravchuk, L. M., 533
Krivoy Rog, 187
Križanić, J., 161
Kronstadt, 90, 225, 271, 309, 311f.
Krylenko, N. V., 288
Krymov, A. M., 273
Krymov, Yu. S., 387
Kuban', 106, 294
Küçük Kaynarca, treaty of, 105, 146
Kuchum, khan, 34
Kühlmann, R. von, 289f.
Kukryniksy (Kupryanov, Krylov, Sokolov), 435
'kulaks', 307, 318, 322, 369–74
Kulikovo, battle of, 18
Kulish, P. A., 169
Kun, B., 342
Kuprin, A. A., 328
Kurakin family, 112
Kurbsky, A. M., 33, 36, 38
Kurds, 212
Kurile Is., 164, 442
Kurland, 87, 103, 210, 230, 289
Kuropatkin, N. A., 226
Kuropaty, 395, 524
Kursk, 44, 295, 407
Kutuzov, M. I., 124, 413
Kuusinen, O. V., 400
Kuznetsk, 377, 537
Kuznetsov, A. A., 415
Kuznetsov, A. V., 437

Kyrgyz, Kyrgyzstan, 165, 302, 469, 532, 546

Labour party (GB), 345, 348
LaHarpe, C. F. de, 121
Land and Liberty, 173
land captains, 205f.
Landsbergis, V., 530
Lanskoy, S. S., 150
Larionov, M. F., 252
Latvia, Latvians: to 1917: 210f., 223, 230, 279; 1918–: 294, 298, 366, 401, 415, 470, 529f.
Lausanne, convention of, 350
Laval, P., 359
Lavrov, P. L., 172
law: to 1917: 9, 38, 60, 92–4, 100, 110, 117f., 149, 154f., 158, 168, 203, 205, 207, 243; 1918–: 311, 337f., 369, 392f., 438, 454, 466, 524f.; lawyers, 154f., 214, 233, 338f.; *see also* show trials
League of . . . Godless, 326
League of Nations, 359, 400
League of Unions, 233f.
Lebed', A. I., 531
'Legal Marxism', 218
Leikhudes, I., S., 78
Leipzig, battle of, 125
Lena, river, 245
Lend-Lease, 410, 412, 421, 426, 435
Lenin (Ulyanov), V. I.: character, 218–20; to 1917: 216, 235, 237, 244, 266, 279–87; 1918–: 288f., 292, 311, 335, 339, 461, 522, 524; and culture, 314, 328; and economy, 306, 308f., 320–22; and foreign affairs, 288, 297f., 342, 347, 351, 494; and nationalities, 303f.; cult of, 244, 327, 457
Lermontov, M. Yu., 138, 267
Lesczyński, Stanislas, king, 84, 101
Leskov, N. S., 246, 388
Levitin, A., 486
Lewenhaupt, A. L., 85
Liaotung peninsula, 225, 443f.
liberalism, 149, 153, 174, 179, 195, 204f., 215, 223, 232f., 239, 264

Liberation of Labour, 216–18
Liebknecht, K., 343
Ligachev, Ye. K., 522, 526, 536
Likhachev, D. S., 490
literacy, 8, 118, 198, 206, 315, 335
literature: to 1917: 74–6, 115, 137,
    157, 245–7; 1918–: 385–7, 434,
    456f., 463f., 486–9, 523f.
Lithuania, Lithuanians: to 1917: 10,
    12, 16f., 21–5, 29, 32, 167, 170,
    178; 1918–: 289, 298f., 398, 401,
    415, 432, 469f., 472, 529f.
Litvinov, M. M., 357–9, 361, 365f;
    protocol, 357
'Living Church', 324f.
Livonia (Livland), 71, 87, 100, 210,
    230; see wars
Locarno, treaty of, 349
Lodygin, A. N., 157
Łódż, 186
Lominadze, V. V., 390
Lomonosov, M. V., 115f.
London, 348; convention of, 161
Loris-Melikov, M. T., 174, 202
Louis XV, king, 87
Louis-Philippe, king, 144
Lozovsky, S. A., 438
Lublin: government, 418, 423f.;
    Union of, 35
Lumumba, P., 510
Lunacharsky, A. V., 244, 308, 323f.,
    327f., 331
Lurye, A. I., 330
Lüshun, 226f., 443
Luxemburg, R., 343
Lviv (Lwów, Lemberg), 47, 74, 170,
    418, 420
L'vov, G. E., 268, 270, 272
Lyapunov, P. P., 52
Lysenko, T. D., 385, 437, 441, 476,
    491
Lyubech, 9

Macedonia, 259
Magadan, 395
Magnitogorsk, 379, 387
Magnitsky, M. L., 132
Maikop, 407

Makariy, metropolitan, 32
Makhno, N. I., 293
Malenkov, G. M., 434, 437, 453–5
Malevich, K. M., 252, 327
Malinovsky, R. Ya., 418, 442, 450, 455
Malta, 122
Mamontov, K. K., 291
Mamontov, S. I., 250
Manchuria, 225–7, 231, 255, 357,
    364, 442f.
Mandelshtam, N. Ya., 524
Mandelshtam, O. Ye., 252, 386
Maniu, J., 448
Mannerheim, C. G., 298; line, 418
Manstein, C. H., 101
Manstein, F. E. von, 407
Mao Zedong, 301, 354, 363, 443–5,
    449, 498–500, 502
Margeret, J., 48
Maria Theresa, empress, 102
Maring, G., 352
Marselis, P., 67
Marshall Plan, 448
Martov, Yu. O., 217f., 220, 244f.
Marx, K., 135, 216f., 322; Marxism,
    174, 179, 216–20, 235, 321, 335,
    352, 524; -Leninism, 284, 316, 321,
    357, 362, 384, 389f., 420f., 433–6,
    458, 460, 498, 517f., 528, 546
Matveyev, A. S., 77, 80
Mayakovsky, V. V., 252, 327f., 332
Mazepa, I. S., 85f.
Mecklenburg, 86
Medvedev, S., 78
Mekhlis, L. Z., 409
Melnyk, A., 431
Memorial, 524
Mendeleyev, D. I., 157
Mengli-girei, khan, 24
Mensheviks: to 1917: 211, 217, 220,
    235, 245, 265f., 268, 271, 276f., 283,
    286f.; 1918–: 300, 310, 376
Menshikov, A. D., 89, 100
Menshikov, A. S., 146
Menzhinsky, V. R., 338
merchants, 23, 39, 55, 62, 65, 94,
    112f., 163, 170, 184f., 250; see also
    industry

Merezhkovsky, D. S., 250
Merv, 165
Meshchersky, V. P., 203
mestnichestvo, see place-seeking
Metternich, C. W. L. von, 126
Meyerhold, V. E., 327
Michael Alexandrovich, grand duke, 267f.
Michael Fedorovich, tsar, 53–5, 60, 63, 70
Mikhaylov, A. D., 173
Mikhaylovsky, N. K., 220
Mikhoels, S. M., 328, 437f.
Mikoyan, A. I., 443, 504
military colonies, 128f.
militias (levies), 52f., 125
Mill, J. S., 171
Milyukov, P. N., 223, 233, 265, 268, 270
Milyutin, D. A., 159, 202
Milyutin, N. A., 150
Minin, K., 53
mining, 67, 94, 113, 187f., 536f., 548
ministries, 127, 162, 186, 191, 204, 482, 528
Minsk, 221, 275, 418
Mniszech, J., 47
Mniszech, M., 47, 49, 53
Mogilev, 103, 129, 264, 288
Mohyla, P., 73f., 78
Moldavia (Moldova), 87, 101, 288, 431, 442, 528, 531, 543
Molotov, V. M., 355, 365f., 401–4, 413, 424, 437, 448, 454f.
monasteries, 7, 15, 74, 95, 167; and land, 9, 15, 25, 27f., 34, 58f., 107; Novodevichy, 75; Solovetsky, 74, 338; Trinity, 51, 58, 60; Voskresensky, 75; Volokolamsk, 27
Mongolia, Mongols, 10, 12–19, 255, 293, 351, 364, 443, 455, 499
Montenegro, 87, 165, 224, 258
Montgomery, B. L., 422
Mordova, Mordvinians, 61, 466
Morozov family, 185, 253
Morozova, F., 74
Moscow: to 1700: 2, 11f., 16–19, 33,

46, 50–2, 64; 1700–1917: 112, 114, 124, 143, 161, 189, 217, 235, 274; 1918–: 300, 329, 404f., 436, 465; academic life, 78, 116, 132; churches, 388; economic and social, 63–5, 183, 196, 314, 320; Kremlin, 30, 49, 75f., 327, 453, 457; population, 182, 186; theatres, 97, 139, 249
motor transport, 190, 317, 484
Mozhaisk, 17, 19
Mstislavsky family, 43
MTS, 374, 440f., 477
Mukhina, V. I., 388
Müller, G. F., 116
Munich, agreements at, 362, 365
Muradeli, V. I., 435
Muravyov, A. N., M. N., 129f.
Muravyov, M. M., 167f.
Muravyov, N. N., 163
Murmansk, 189, 295, 411
Musavat party, 280, 300
Muscovy Company, 39f.
music, 7, 139, 247f., 330, 388f., 432, 435, 547
musketeers (*streltsy*), 34, 65, 68, 80, 82, 85
Mussolini, B., 355
Mussorgsky, M. I., 43, 157, 247

Nagaya, M., 45, 47
Nagy, I., 503f.
Nakhimov, P. S., 146
Napoleon I, emperor, 122–5
Napoleon III, emperor, 146, 160
Narva, 39, 85; battle of, 84, 123
Naryshkin family, 79f., 82
Naryshkina, N., 79
Nasser, G. A., 509f.
Natanson. A. M., 170
nationalities policy, Soviet, 303, 332f., 433f., 467
NATO, 451, 507, 513, 516–18, 540f., 546
Navarino, battle of, 126
navy: to 1917: 81, 86, 90, 126, 146, 159, 227, 232, 242, 255, 259, 271; 1918–: 309, 485, 501, 511f.

Nazarbayev, N. A., 532
Nazimov, V. I., 150
Near and Middle East, 3, 146, 188,
    300, 348–51, 402, 437, 507–10,
    512, 542
Nekrich, A. M., 491
Neman (Niemen), river, 123f.
Nemirovich-Danchenko, V. I., 249
NEP, 313, 315, 318, 323, 368, 536;
    nepmen, 319f.
Nerchinsk, treaty of, 72, 164
Netherlands, Dutch, 40, 63, 66, 81f.,
    87
Neva, river, 95, 114, 131
Nicholas I, emperor, 130–34, 138,
    143–7, 170, 202
Nicholas II, emperor, 203, 206, 211,
    233f., 241–3, 254, 259, 264, 267,
    270, 311, 524
Nicholas Nikolayevich, grand duke,
    234, 261
Nietzsche, F. W., 249f.
'nihilism', 171
Nikolayev, L., 392
Nikon, patriarch, 74f., 77, 95
Nilus of Sora, 27
Nixon, R. M., 500, 516
Nizhniy Novgorod (Gor'ky), 18f., 53,
    67, 196, 207, 377, 466
NKVD, see security police
Nobel: brothers, 188; prizes, 463,
    488
nobles (dvoryanstvo), 109, 126, 140,
    149–54, 181, 194f., 242; and land,
    93–5, 107–11, 139, 181, 205f.,
    277f.
nomenklatura, 312, 334, 382f., 454,
    459–62, 521f., 526, 548
Norsemen, see Varangians
Noril'sk, 433, 484
Northern Society, 130f.
Norway, 8, 86, 348, 418
Novgorod, 1, 5, 8, 12–16 passim,
    20–4, 37, 40, 52f., 63f., 129, 490
Novikov, N. I., 116f.
Novocherkassk, 481
Novosibirsk, 491
nuclear: energy, 485, 523; weapons,

426, 439, 451f., 456, 492, 494,
    498–500, 513–16, 538, 546
Nystad, treaty of, 86f.

Obruchev, N. N., 224
Ochakov, 101
October manifesto, 234, 236, 241
Octobrists, 241f.
Oder, river, 419; -Neisse line, 423,
    517, 541
Odessa, 106, 114, 213, 217, 232, 415,
    433
Oganovsky, N. P., 179
oil, 188, 300, 306, 318, 351, 378, 406f.,
    510, 536
Oka, river, 2, 10f., 14, 17f.
Okhrana, see security police
Okudzhava, B. Sh., 489
Old Believers: to 1917: 74, 85, 96, 98,
    110, 156, 185, 215; 1918–: 326, 488
Oleg (Helgi), prince, 5
Olesha, Yu. K., 332
Olga (Helga), princess, 5
oprichnina, 37f., 40, 43, 47, 58, 435
Ordyn-Nashchokin, A. L., 77
Ordzhonikidze, G. K., 301, 304, 381
Orekhovo-Zuyevo, 185
Orel, 295
Orenburg, 111, 189
Orlov, Yu. F., 466
Orthodoxy: to 1700: 5–7, 15, 22, 25,
    29f., 38, 44, 54, 70, 73–5;
    1700–1917: 96, 134, 136, 155f.,
    210, 215, 244, 251; 1917–: 324–6,
    370, 413f., 485–8, 528; and secular
    power, 17, 27f., 34, 75, 95, 210,
    243; see also clergy, monasteries,
    Old Believers
Orwell, G., 331, 519, 524
Ostashkov, 400
Ostermann, H. J., 101
Ostrovsky, N. A., 387
Ovechkin, V. V., 488

Pahlen, P. A. von, 126
Pakistan, 502, 512
Pale, Jewish, 170, 196, 213f.
Pamyat', 524, 534

Panferov, F. I., 387
Panin, V. N., 152
Panmunjom, 445
Pan-Slavism, 161, 169
Paris, 125, 128, 253, 388, 500; accords
  (1954), 513; conferences at: (1904),
  223; (1960), 516; (1968–), 500;
  treaty of (1856), 148, 159f.
Pashkevich, I. F., 144
Pasternak, B. L., 252, 463f., 487, 524
Pasternak, L. O., 214
patronage, clientelism, 31, 58, 334,
  339, 383, 461, 526, 547
Pauker, A., 448
Paul I, emperor, 114, 117, 120–23,
  126
Paulus, F. von, 407
Pavlov, D. G., 405
Pavlov, V. S., 543
Pavlovsk, 114
peasants: **to 1700**: 9, 31, 38f., 44–6,
  49, 58–62; **1700–1861**: 93, 99,
  107, 110–13, 125, 139, 152;
  1861–1917: 153, 172, 176–84,
  196–9, 205, 221, 230f., 239–41,
  262; **1918–**: 292, 307f., 315f., 368,
  374f., 440f., 475, 537; *see also*
  commune, state peasants
Pechenegs, 5f.
People's Will, 174f., 218, 221
perestroyka: economic, 536f.; political,
  521f.
Pereyaslavl', treaty of, 71
Perm', 21
Perov, G. V., 247
Pestel', P. I., 130
Peter I, the Great, 57, 69, 74, 77,
  79–99, 114, 136f., 227, 251, 436
Peter II, emperor, 108
Peter III, emperor, 102, 109, 111,
  119f.
Peter, 'tsarevich', 49, 51
Petkov, N., 448
Petlyura, S., 294
Petrashevtsy, 169
Petrunkevich, I. I., 174, 223
Philaret (F. N. Romanov), patriarch,
  46, 51–6 *passim*, 63, 70, 76

Philip, metropolitan, 37
Pietism, 98, 115
Pilnyak, B. A. (Wogau), 331f.
Piłsudski, J., 296f.
Pimen (Izvekov), patriarch, 486
Pisarev, D. I., 172
'place-seeking', 33, 69, 90
planned (command) economy, 322f.,
  376, 380, 439, 474, 482, 523
Platonov, A. P., 385
Platonov, S. F., 384
Plehve, V. K., 222, 226
Plekhanov, G. V., 174, 216–18, 220,
  235, 266
Plevna, battle of, 166
Plisetskaya, M., 465
Pobedonostsev, K. P., 203, 215
Podgorny, N. V., 458
Podolia, 213
pogroms, 196, 213, 230f., 235, 243,
  293, 299
Poincaré, R., 348
Pokrovsky, M. N., 384
Poland, Poles: **to 1569**: 8, 12, 20, 23,
  25; **1569–1795** (Polish-Lithuanian
  Commonwealth): 35, 59, 42, 44–57,
  66, 69–72, 84f., 101–3, 169;
  1795–1918: 124f., 130, 132, 134,
  140, 161, 169f., 197, 242, 255, 263;
  revolts in, 144, 160, 164, 167f., 172,
  211, 230; **1918–38**: 289, 296, 333,
  346f., 349, 357f., 362; **1939–45**:
  396, 399f., 418, 421–5; **1945–**:
  446f., 472, 481, 498, 503–6, 513,
  517, 525, 541
Polish Socialist party (PPS), 223
Polotsk, 1, 35, 103
Polotsky, S., 75f., 78
Polovtsy, 10
Pol Pot, 501
Poltava, 151, 221; battle of, 85f.
Poniatowski, Stanislas, king, 102
Ponomarev, B. N., 512
'popular front', 359–61, 420, 447
population: **to 1917**: 14, 42, 57f.,
  111f., 141, 193, 209, 285; **1918–**:
  304, 313, 427, 472f., 478f., 484, 536;
  see also urbanization

Populism, 167, 170–75, 195, 215f., 220; Neo-, 179, 385

Port Arthur (Dal'nỳ), *see* Lüshun

Portsmouth, N. H., treaty of, 231

Pososhkov, S. T., 89

Potemkin, G. A., 114, 117

Potemkin (battleship), 232, 330

Potsdam conference, 425f

Pozharsky, D. M., 53

Poznań (Posen), 419, 503

Prague, 419, 451, 470; spring (1968), 465, 505

Preobrazhensky, E. A., 322

pretenders, 42, 46, 61, 111

printing and publishing, 75, 97, 116–18, 158, 253, 547

prison camps, colonies, 311, 338, 372, 386, 394–5, 411f., 429–33, 457, 464–6, 489, 524; 'special settlers', 371f., 396, 430

prisoners of war: Axis, 430, 513; Soviet, 416, 429f.

Progressive Bloc, 264

Prokofyev, S. S., 435

Prokshin, A., 524

Proletkul't, 328, 330f.

Protestants: to 1917: 35, 40, 56, 74, 77, 156, 210, 215; 1918–: 326, 448, 464, 486, 525

Provisional government (1917), 268, 270, 278, 280–83

Prussia, 86, 89, 102f., 121–5 *passim*, 144, 160, 356

Pruth, river, 87, 101

Przewalski, N. M., 157

Pskov, 21, 37, 53, 64, 267

Pugachev, Ye., 105, 109–11, 117, 149, 172, 197, 278

purges, *see* Great Terror

Pushkin, A. S., 43, 115, 132, 138, 168, 253, 487

Rachmaninoff, S. V., 328

Radishchev, A. N., 118f.

railways: to 1917: 143, 165, 187, 189f., 233, 254, 258, 265, 276; 1918–: 306, 369, 405, 542; Chinese Eastern, 357, 443f; Trans-Siberian,

182, 189f., 225f., 231, 236, 262, 295

Rákosi, M., 447, 503

Rapallo, treaty of, 348f., 361, 451, 517, 541

Rashidov, Sh. R., 462

Rasputin, G. Ye., 243, 264

Rasputin, V. G., 488

Rastrelli, B., 114

Rathenau, W., 348

Razgon, L. E., 432

Razin, S. T., 61f., 85

Razryad, 33

Reagan, R., 518, 538f.

Reichstadt, treaty of, 166

Repin, I. Ye., 157, 247

Reval, *see* Tallinn

revolution: 1905: 228–36; 1917 (Feb.): 266–80; (Oct.): 245, 280–83

Reza, khan, 351

Ribbentrop, J. von, 366, 401

Riga, 39, 66, 71, 86, 186, 272, 415, 418, 529f.; treaty of, 297, 342, 347

Rimsky-Korsakov, N. A., 157, 247f.

Rokossovsky, K. K., 408, 418f., 447, 504

Romania: to 1917: 123, 146, 223, 259, 263; 1918–45: 288, 358, 362, 365, 401, 407, 417, 424; 1945—: 446, 448, 504, 531

Romanov family, 33, 36, 43, 46, 80, 120, 160, 253

Romanov, G. V., 522

Romany, 414

Romm, M. I., 435

Roosevelt, F. D., 358, 423

Rostopchin, F. V., 131

Rostov-on-Don, 407

Rostov-Suzdal', 10, 16, 20f.

Rostovtsev, Ya. I., 151f.

Rtishchev, F. M., 77

Rubinstein, A. G., N. G., 214, 247

Rublev, A., 15, 490

Rurik (Hrørikr), 5

Russian Liberation Army, 416, 431

Russian national movement, 472f., 488, 490, 547

Russian Nationalist party (1909–), 242

Russian Society of Proletarian
  Writers, 385f.
russification, 168f., 209–15, 434, 468,
  471
Rutskoy, A. V., 543
Ryabushinsky, P. P., 265, 275
Ryangina, S. V., 387f.
Ryazan', 12, 20f., 52, 277f.
Rybakov, A. N., 524
Ryleyev, K. F., 131
Ryutin, M. N., 390f.
Ryzhkov, N. I., 522

Saddat, A., 510
St Petersburg (Petrograd, Leningrad):
  to 1917: 16, 84, 86, 97, 103, 114,
  130, 139, 143, 183f., 217, 252; 1918
  –: 309, 311, 340, 392, 404f., 408,
  437, 545; churches, 139;
  Conservatoire, 247; economic and
  social, 143, 183–6, 217, 265f;
  population, 143, 186, 305; palaces,
  174, 228, 327; Smol'ny, 118, 283;
  theatres, 139, 267; university, 157,
  207
Sajúdis, 530
Sakhalin, 164, 402, 442
Sakharov, A. D., 466, 492, 525f.
Saltykov, S. V., 120
Saltykov-Shchedrin, M. Ye., 246
Samara, 221, 294, 346
Samarkand, 189
samizdat, 464f., 472
Samokhvalov, A. N., 387
Samsonov, A. V., 262
Sanders, L. von, 259
San Stefano, treaty of, 166
Sapieha, J., 51
Sarai, 12, 14, 18
Saratov, 182, 221
Sarkel, 6
Sazonov, S. D., 258, 259
Schulenburg, F. W. von der, 402
science, scientists, 116, 157, 384f.,
  437, 465f., 492
Scotland, Scots, 40, 51, 89, 114
security police: to 1800: 83, 99 (see
  also oprichnina); 1801–1917: 126,

  133f., 173f., 214, 216, 222;
  1917–40: 311, 334, 338, 346, 355,
  361, 371–4, 392–7, 399; 1941–53:
  405, 409, 414, 433, 447; 1954–84:
  454, 457, 462–6, 469, 473, 486,
  491; 1985–: 522f., 525, 530, 534,
  544; see also Great Terror, prison
  camps.
Semenov-Tyan-shansky, P. P., 157
Senate, 92, 100, 126f.
Serbia, 15, 105, 165, 223, 258–60
serfdom, serfs, 16, 38, 44f., 54, 59–61,
  93, 107, 110, 113, 138–42, 375;
  emancipation of, 127, 130, 139, 142,
  148–52, 167, 171, 177f., 194
Sergey (Stragorodsky), patriarch,
  325f., 413
Sergey Alexandrovich, grand duke,
  222
Serov, I. A., 455
'settlers, special', see prison camps
Sevastopol', 147, 406, 546
Seversk, 69, 72
Shakhty, 319, 376
Shalamov, V. T., 489
Shamil, 145
Shanghai, 353, 501
Shatalin, S. S., 537
Shatrov, M. M., 524
Shcharansky, A., 525
Shchekino, 481f.
Shchelokov, N. A., 462
Shcherbakov, A. S., 409
Shcherbitsky, V. V., 470, 533
Shchukin, S. I., 253
Shelepin, A. N., 458, 465
Shelest, P. Ye., 469f., 505
Shelon, battle of, 23
Sheremetev, B. P., 85
Shevardnadze, E. A., 522, 532, 538,
  540, 543
Shevchenko, T. H., 168
Shipov, D. N., 223, 241
Shklovsky, V. B., 305
Shlyapnikov, A. G., 280, 312
shock workers, Stakhanovites, 378,
  381, 412
Sholokhov, M. A., 387

Shostakovich, D. D., 330, 388, 435
show trials, 310, 319, 376, 392f., 448
Shuisky family, 33, 43
Shuisky, Vasiliy, tsar, 45, 47, 49–52, 59, 534
Shumsky, O., 333
Shuvalov, P. I., 167
Shuya, 325
Siberia: to 1917: 34f., 67, 72, 88, 113, 163, 177, 182, 231, 243; 1918–: 293, 368f., 379, 476; exile to, 131, 144, 172, 218
Sigismund III, king, 44, 47, 52
Silvester, 33, 36
Simbirsk, 61
Sinyavsky, A. D., 465
Sipyagin, D. S., 222
Skobelev, M. D., 164f.
Skoropadsky, P. P., 294
Skrypnik, M. A., 333
Slanský, R., 448
slavery, slaves, 9, 37, 44, 46, 49, 60, 93, 142
Slavophils, 97, 136f., 142, 154, 161, 223, 241, 488
Smolensk, 1, 8, 10, 25, 52, 69, 71f., 124, 404, 408
Sniečkus, A., 470
Social Democrats, Finnish, 241, 279
Social Democrats, German, 342, 357, 450
Social Democrats, Russian (RSDRP), 211, 218–23 passim, 235, 244; see Bolsheviks, Mensheviks
socialism, 130, 137, 169–75, 196f., 215
'socialist realism', 386f., 434, 465, 488f.
Socialist Revolutionary party (PSR), 220–22, 231, 239, 244, 268, 271, 277, 286f., 310; Left SRs, 282, 286, 299, 310
social structure, 3, 9, 12, 25, 31, 62, 65, 68, 97, 99, 107, 193f., 196
Sokolovsky, V. D., 451
Solidarity, 506
Solikamsk, 67
Sologub, F., 250

Solovyov, A. K., 173
Solovyov, V. S., 251
Solzhenitsyn, A. I., 136, 262, 432, 456f., 486–8, 524
Sophia Alexeyevna, regent, 57, 74f., 82
Sorge, R., 364
Sovetskaya Gavan', 411
soviets, workers', 230, 235, 277, 309, 311, 457, 527; Central Executive Committee, 271, 277, 283; congresses of, 283, 285, 287, 303; Petrograd, 268, 271, 281–3
space exploration, 514
Spain, Spaniards, 38, 124, 129, 163, 360f., 507
Speransky, M. M., 127, 163
Spiridonova, M. A., 282
sports, leisure, 254, 327, 388f., 492f.
Staden, H. von, 40
Stakhanov, A. G., 381
Stalin, J. V.: character, 341, 391; to 1917: 244, 281; 1917–29: 303f., 321, 327, 336, 338; 1929–53: 80, 310, 390–97, 400, 428, 433, 438; and culture, 388f., 413, 435; and economy, 95, 192, 317, 321, 368–73, 441f; and foreign affairs, 344f., 351–5, 360–67 passim, 398, 402f., 420–27, 442, 446, 448f.; and military, 291, 294, 297, 404–8, 417; cult of, 385, 391, 428, 433, 447, 453; legacy of, 454–7, 463, 465
Stanislavsky, K. S., 249
Starobel'sk, 400
Startsev, O., 75
Stasov, V. V., 247
State Council, 127, 152, 204, 236, 242
State Defence Council, 404, 409
state farms, 321f., 375, 440, 462, 476, 478, 537
state peasants, 107, 140, 178
statistics, 176, 372, 376, 379, 474, 482
Stavropol', 520f.
Stoglav council, 34
Stolypin, P. A., 197, 239–41, 254, 524
Stravinsky, I. F., 328

strikes: **to 1917**: 185f., 197, 229f.,
233–5, 265f., 274f.; **1918–**: 287,
309, 318, 481, 548
Stroganov family, 34, 55, 65
Struve, P. B., 218, 223, 251
Sudebnik, 38
Sultan-Galiev, M., 301, 350
Sumarokov, A. P., 115
Sun Yatsen, 352f.
Supreme Privy Council, 108
Supreme Soviet, 428, 467, 527
Surikov, V. I., 247
Suslov, M. A., 458, 504, 512, 517
Suvorov, A. V., 122, 413
Svanidze, K., 461
Sverdlov, Yu. M., 285
Svyatoslav, prince, 5f.
Sweden, Swedes: **to 1700**: 3, 10, 35,
56, 66, 70, 76, 91, 99; **1700–**: 101,
103, 108, 123, 132, 147, 188, 348,
513; *see* wars
Switzerland, Swiss, 121f., 216, 281,
513
Symbolism, 248–50, 252
Syndicalism, 218, 275, 282, 312
Synod, Holy, 95, 203, 246, 274
Syrtsov, S. I., 390
Sytin, I., 253

Table of Ranks, 90, 93, 109, 127
Taganrog, 130
Taiwan, 444, 499
Tajikistan, Tajiks, 469, 532
Talien (Dairen), 225, 498
Tallinn, 39, 66, 86, 90, 186, 529,
531
Tambov, 140–42, 287, 308f.
Tannenberg, battle of, 262
Taraki, N. M., 512
tariffs, 66, 94, 142, 187, 189–91
Tarkovsky, A. A., 490
Tartu, 132, 210
Tashkent, 164, 189, 302, 502
Tatars, 10–21, 24, 27; of Crimea: **to
1917**: 19f., 24, 35–7, 70–72, 105,
212, 280; **1918–**: 431, 471f., 533; of
Volga, 212f., 302, 350, 533
Tatlin, V. Ye., 252, 329

taxation: **to 1700**: 8f., 14, 18, 55f.,
60–64 *passim*; **1701–1800**: 84, 90f.,
93f., 96, 112; **1801–1917**: 140, 153,
192f., 196, 276; **1918–**: 315, 548
Taylor, F. W., 306
Tbilisi (Tiflis), 211, 280, 532
Tchaikovski, P. I., 248
Tehran, 351, 423
Terek, river, 49, 106
Teutonic Order, 10, 16, 21
Thälmann, E., 356
Thatcher, M., 540
theatre: **to 1917**: 76, 97, 114f., 248f.,
267; **1918–**: 327, 524, 547
Theodore (Fedor) I, 40–45, 51
Third department, *see* security police
'third Rome', 28, 44
Thorez, M., 449
Tikhon (Belavin), patriarch, 324f.
Tilsit, treaty of, 123
Timashuk, L., 438
Timiryazev, K. A., 157; Academy, 383
Timoshenko, S. K., 400
Tito, J. B., 418, 449f., 504
Togliatti, P., 504
Tolbukhin, F. I., 418
Tolstoy, D. A., 156, 172
Tolstoy, L. N., 125, 156f., 215, 245f.,
249, 488
totalitarianism, 397
trade: domestic, 63–5, 94, 112, 305;
foreign, 3, 8, 10, 23, 39, 66, 103,
106, 123, 319, 347, 376; *see also*
black market, merchants
trade unions: **to 1917**: 186, 195, 200,
222, 229, 245, 276; **1918–**: 310, 312,
318f., 378, 457, 481, 537
Tredyakovsky, V. K., 115
Trepov, D. F., 233, 235
Trieste, 450
Trotsky, L. D., 235, 282f., 297, 327,
331, 335f., 339–41, 345, 455, 524;
and economy, 322; and foreign
affairs, 288f., 346; and Red Army,
292, 294, 296; 'Trotskyism', 361,
391, 393
Trubetskoy, D. T., 53
Truman, H. S., 426

Tryapitsin, I. Ya., 430

Tsaritsyn (Stalingrad), 294f., 297, 377, 407, 422

Tsarskoye Selo (Pushkin), 114, 132, 143, 408

Tsereteli, I. G., 276

Tukhachevsky, M. N., 297, 361, 394

Tula, 51, 295, 481

Tupolev, A. N., 377f.

Turgenev, I. S., 157, 245f.

Turkestan, *see* Central Asia

Turkey: to 1700: 15, 22, 28, 35, 50, 56, 70; 1700–1917: 86, 101f., 123, 161f., 212, 255, 259; 1918–: 289, 300–2, 350, 425, 446, 508f., 515, 531; Straits, 161, 224, 254, 258, 268; *see* wars

Turkmenistan, Turcomans, 164f., 302

Turku, 132

Tushino, 51

Tvardovsky, A. T., 456

Tver' (Kalinin), 17, 20f., 153, 316, 400

Ufa, 111, 295

Uglich, 18, 45, 51

Ugra, river, 24

Ukraine, Ukrainians: to 1800: 2, 12, 47, 70–75, 77f., 105f.; 1800–1917: 138, 168–70, 181–7 *passim*, 209, 223, 263, 265, 279f.; 1918–40: 288f., 293–300, 303, 312f., 333, 347, 365, 372f., 396, 399; 1941–52: 406–8, 414f., 417, 420–26, 429, 431–3, 442; 1953–: 464, 468–72, 485, 491, 505, 531, 533f., 544f.

Ulm, battle of, 123

Ulozhenie, 60, 64, 76

Ulyanov, A. I., 216

Uman', 299

Uniate Church, 70, 74, 448, 525

Union of Public Welfare, 129

Union of Russian People, 243, 324f., 524

Union of Salvation, 129

Union of Soviet Writers (USW), 386, 465, 489

United Nations, 425, 464, 466, 507, 510, 530

United States: to 1917: 130, 163, 191, 226, 273, 300, 528; 1918–44: 345, 348, 352, 358, 363, 376f., 410, 421–5, 428; 1945–: 421, 425, 435f., 439, 442–5, 471, 476, 495, 500, 509–19, 538f., 546f.

universities, 116, 132, 156f., 161, 167, 174, 207f., 214, 233, 471

Unkovsky, A. M., 153

Urals, 1, 194, 294, 296, 371; industry in, 67, 94f., 111, 188, 485

urbanization, 179, 182–4, 193, 199f., 313, 379, 441, 479

Uspensky, G. I., 247

Ussuri, river, 164

Ustinov, D. F., 462, 482, 512

Uvarov, S. S., 135

Uzbekistan, Uzbeks, 462, 532

Valdemars, K., 211

Valuyev, P. A., 169

Varangians, 3, 5, 491

Varga, E., 436

Vasilevsky, A. M., 407f.

Vasiliy III, grand prince, 28

Vedrosha, battle of, 25

Vatsetis (Vācetis), I. I., 294

Vavilov, N. I., 385

Vereshchagin, V. V., 247

Versailles, treaty of, 290, 345f., 348, 359

Vertov, D. (D. A. Kaufman), 330

Vienna, 419, 516; congress of, 125

Vietnam, 500–2, 508, 542

Viipuri (Vyborg), 86, 90, 237, 400

Vikzhel, 276

Vilnius, 66, 71, 124, 132, 150, 167f., 298, 401, 418, 529f.

'virgin lands', 476

Vinius, A., 67

Vitebsk, 103

Vladikavkaz, 106

Vladimir, St, grand prince, 6

Vladimir of Staritsa, prince, 35, 37

Vladimir-on-Klyazma, 10, 18f.

Vladimov, G. N., 489

Vladivostok, 164, 225, 262, 295, 357, 445, 542

Vlasov, A. A., 416
vodka, 65, 112, 163, 192f., 232, 473, 536
Voinovich, V. N., 489
Volga, river, region: to 1700: 1f., 10–20 passim, 34, 39, 49, 61f., 66f.; 1700–1917: 95, 105, 178; 1918–: 294–6, 313, 372, 406, 430
Volkhov, river, 3, 37
Voltaire, 116f.
Volynsky, A. P., 88
Voronezh, 44, 81, 173, 199, 406
Vorontsov, M. S., 145
Voroshilov, K. E., 292, 294, 297, 394, 400, 454
Voznesensky, A. A., 464
Voznesensky, N. A., 437
Vvedensky, A., 324
Vyaz'ma, 24
Vyekhi, 251f., 488
Vynnitsa, 524
Vynnychenko, V., 294
Vyshinsky, A. Ya., 393
Vysotsky, V. S., 489

Wałęsa, L., 506
'Wanderers', the, 247
'war communism', 309f., 369
wars: Afghan, 502, 506, 512, 518f., 539, 542; Austrian succession, 102; Crimean, 143, 145–7; Finnish, 298, 364, 400, 403, 418; First World, 181, 187, 189f., 261–5, 272, 287–90, 409; French revolutionary, 122f.; Greek Independence, 126; Japanese, 189, 223, 227, 231, 247, 364; Korean, 445, 513; Livonian, 35, 39f.; Napoleonic, Patriotic, 122–5, 128, 142, 245; Polish, 52f., 56, 70–72, 101, 103, 293, 297; Russian civil, 290–97; Second World, 398–426; Seven Years, 102; Swedish, 16, 44, 50–54, 61, 83–7, 103, 123; Turkish, 69, 72, 81, 83, 87f., 101, 105f., 108, 123, 126, 159, 166
Warsaw, 71, 144, 167, 189, 213, 230, 297, 418, 421, 424; duchy of, 124;

Treaty Organization, 465, 494, 498, 504f., 541
Weber, M., 92, 243
Weiszäcker, R. von, 540
Wielopolski, A., 167
Wilhelm I, emperor, 160
Wilhelm II, emperor, 224, 259
William III, king, 82
Witte, S. Yu., 189, 191f., 204, 221, 226, 234–7
Władysław, king, 52, 70
Wolff, C., 115
women, 193, 199, 274, 314, 479, 492; as revolutionaries, 131; as rulers, 5, 45, 57, 119; education of, 157, 198, 315, 334; in agriculture, 141, 199, 479; in industry, 185, 199f., 265, 314f., 378f., 410; in war, 145, 410
workers, industrial: to 1917: 113f., 142, 172f., 179, 183f., 185, 187f., 254, 265; and revolution, 196, 216f., 228f., 274, 292; 1918–: 305, 315, 318, 334, 378–82, 479–82, 536, 548
Workers' and Peasants' Inspectorate, 339
'workers' control', see Syndicalism
Wrangel (Vrangel'), P. N., 292, 296
Wren, Sir C., 82

Xinjiang (Sinkiang), 255, 363, 444

Yablochkov, P. N., 157
Yagoda, G. G., 392
Yaik, river, 110
Yakovlev, A. N., 430, 522
Yakutia (Sakwa), 163, 533
Yalta, 424f., 443, 450, 503
Yalu, river, 226, 445
Yanushkevich, N. N., 261
Yavlinsky, G. A., 537
Yaroslav I, grand prince, 8f., 22
Yaroslavl', 20f., 115, 132, 428
Yaroslavsky, E. E., 326
Yekaterinburg (Sverdlovsk), 311, 371
Yekaterinoslav, 156, 213
Yeltsin, B. N., 526–8, 530, 534f., 537, 543–6
Yermak, Timofeyevich, 34

Yermolov, A. P., 145
Yesenin, S. A., 332
Yevtushenko, Ye. A., 464, 489, 523f.
Yezhov, N. I., 392–6
Yudenich, N. N., 296
Yugoslavia, 324, 418, 421, 424, 449f., 473, 498f., 503f., 513
Yur'eva-Zakharina, A., 33, 36, 46

Zalygin, S. P., 523
Zamyatin, Ye. I., 305, 331, 386, 524
Zaporozhets, I., 392
Zaslavskaya, T. I., 491
Zarutsky, I., 53
Zasulich, V. I., 173, 216
Zealots of Piety, 73
zemlyachestvo, 183
Zemsky sobor, 38, 42, 45, 50, 52–6, 71, 92f., 136, 202

zemstvo, 153, 156f., 174, 195, 205f., 223, 233, 265, 268; Union, 174
Zhdanov, A. A., 393, 399, 434, 437f., 449
Zhelyabov, A. I., 174
Zhirinovsky, V. V., 534
Zhukov, G. K., 364, 403, 408f., 417, 419, 433, 455
Zimin, A. A., 491
Zimmerwald, 266, 270
Zinoviev, G. E., 282, 309, 339–41, 343, 391–3
Zlatoust, 346
Zoë (Sophia) Palaeologus, 29
Zorndorf, battle of, 102
Zoshchenko, M. M., 434
Zubatov, S. V., 222, 228
Zubov, P. A., 194
Zurabov, A., 238

READ MORE IN PENGUIN

In every corner of the world, on every subject under the sun, Penguin represents quality and variety – the very best in publishing today.

For complete information about books available from Penguin – including Puffins, Penguin Classics and Arkana – and how to order them, write to us at the appropriate address below. Please note that for copyright reasons the selection of books varies from country to country.

In the United Kingdom: Please write to *Dept. EP, Penguin Books Ltd, Bath Road, Harmondsworth, West Drayton, Middlesex UB7 0DA*

In the United States: Please write to *Consumer Sales, Penguin USA, P.O. Box 999, Dept. 17109, Bergenfield, New Jersey 07621-0120.* VISA and MasterCard holders call 1-800-253-6476 to order Penguin titles

In Canada: Please write to *Penguin Books Canada Ltd, 10 Alcorn Avenue, Suite 300, Toronto, Ontario M4V 3B2*

In Australia: Please write to *Penguin Books Australia Ltd, P.O. Box 257, Ringwood, Victoria 3134*

In New Zealand: Please write to *Penguin Books (NZ) Ltd, Private Bag 102902, North Shore Mail Centre, Auckland 10*

In India: Please write to *Penguin Books India Pvt Ltd, 706 Eros Apartments, 56 Nehru Place, New Delhi 110 019*

In the Netherlands: Please write to *Penguin Books Netherlands bv, Postbus 3507, NL-1001 AH Amsterdam*

In Germany: Please write to *Penguin Books Deutschland GmbH, Metzlerstrasse 26, 60594 Frankfurt am Main*

In Spain: Please write to *Penguin Books S. A., Bravo Murillo 19, 1° B, 28015 Madrid*

In Italy: Please write to *Penguin Italia s.r.l., Via Felice Casati 20, I–20124 Milano*

In France: Please write to *Penguin France S. A., 17 rue Lejeune, F–31000 Toulouse*

In Japan: Please write to *Penguin Books Japan, Ishikiribashi Building, 2–5–4, Suido, Bunkyo-ku, Tokyo 112*

In South Africa: Please write to *Longman Penguin Southern Africa (Pty) Ltd, Private Bag X08, Bertsham 2013*

READ MORE IN PENGUIN

A CHOICE OF NON-FICTION

African Nights Kuki Gallmann

Through a tapestry of interwoven true episodes, Kuki Gallmann here evokes the magic that touches all African life. The adventure of a moonlit picnic on a vanishing island; her son's entrancement with chameleons and the mystical visit of a king cobra to his grave; the mysterious compassion of an elephant herd – each event conveys her delight and wonder at the whole fabric of creation.

Far Flung Floyd Keith Floyd

Keith Floyd's culinary odyssey takes him to the far-flung East and the exotic flavours of Malaysia, Hong Kong, Vietnam and Thailand. The irrepressible Floyd as usual spices his recipes with witty stories, wry observation and a generous pinch of gastronomic wisdom.

The Reading Solution Paul Kropp with Wendy Cooling

The Reading Solution makes excellent suggestions for books – both fiction and non-fiction – for readers of all ages that will stimulate a love of reading. Listing hugely enjoyable books from history and humour to thrillers and poetry selections, *The Reading Solution* provides all the help you need to ensure that your child becomes – and stays – a willing, enthusiastic reader.

Lucie Duff Gordon Katherine Frank
A Passage to Egypt

'Lucie Duff Gordon's life is a rich field for a biographer, and Katherine Frank does her justice ... what stays in the mind is a portrait of an exceptional woman, funny, wry, occasionally flamboyant, always generous-spirited, and firmly rooted in the social history of her day' – *The Times Literary Supplement*

The Missing of the Somme Geoff Dyer

'A gentle, patient, loving book. It is about mourning and memory, about how the Great War has been represented – and our sense of it shaped and defined – by different artistic media ... its textures are the very rhythms of memory and consciousness' – *Guardian*

READ MORE IN PENGUIN

A CHOICE OF NON-FICTION

The Pillars of Hercules Paul Theroux

At the gateway to the Mediterranean lie the two Pillars of Hercules. Beginning his journey in Gibraltar, Paul Theroux travels the long way round – through the ravaged developments of the Costa del Sol, into Corsica and Sicily and beyond – to Morocco's southern pillar. 'A terrific book, full of fun as well as anxiety, of vivid characters and curious experiences' – *The Times*

Where the Girls Are Susan J. Douglas

In this brilliantly researched and hugely entertaining examination of women and popular culture, Susan J. Douglas demonstrates the ways in which music, TV, books, advertising, news and film have affected women of her generation. Essential reading for cultural critics, feminists and everyone else who has ever ironed their hair or worn a miniskirt.

Journals: 1954–1958 Allen Ginsberg

These pages open with Ginsberg at the age of twenty-eight, penniless, travelling alone and unknown in California. Yet, by July 1958 he was returning from Paris to New York as the poet who, with Jack Kerouac, led and inspired the Beats . . .

The New Spaniards John Hooper

Spain has become a land of extraordinary paradoxes in which traditional attitudes and contemporary preoccupations exist side by side. The country attracts millions of visitors – yet few see beyond the hotels and resorts of its coastline. John Hooper's fascinating study brings to life the many faces of Spain in the 1990s.

A Tuscan Childhood Kinta Beevor

Kinta Beevor was five when she fell in love with her parents' castle facing the Carrara mountains. 'The descriptions of the harvesting and preparation of food and wine by the locals could not be bettered . . . alive with vivid characters' – *Observer*

READ MORE IN PENGUIN

HISTORY

London: A Social History Roy Porter

'The best and bravest thing he has written. It is important because it makes the whole sweep of London's unique history comprehensible and accessible in a way that no previous writer has ever managed to accomplish. And it is angry because it begins and concludes with a slashing, unanswerable indictment of Thatcherite misrule' – *Independent on Sunday*

Somme Lyn Macdonald

'What the reader will longest remember are the words – heartbroken, blunt, angry – of the men who lived through the bloodbath ... a worthy addition to the literature of the Great War' – *Daily Mail*

Aspects of Aristocracy David Cannadine

'A hugely enjoyable portrait of the upper classes ... It is the perfect history book for the non-historian. Ample in scope but full of human detail, accessible and graceful in its scholarship, witty and opinionated in style' – *Financial Times*

The Penguin History of Greece A. R. Burn

Readable, erudite, enthusiastic and balanced, this one-volume history of Hellas sweeps the reader along from the days of Mycenae and the splendours of Athens to the conquests of Alexander and the final dark decades.

The Laurel and the Ivy Robert Kee

'Parnell continues to haunt the Irish historical imagination a century after his death ... Robert Kee's patient and delicate probing enables him to reconstruct the workings of that elusive mind as persuasively, or at least as plausibly, as seems possible ... This splendid biography, which is as readable as it is rigorous, greatly enhances our understanding of both Parnell, and of the Ireland of his time' – *The Times Literary Supplement*

READ MORE IN PENGUIN

HISTORY

Frauen Alison Owings

Nearly ten years in the making and based on interviews and original research, Alison Owings' remarkable book records the wartime experiences and thoughts of 'ordinary' German women from varying classes and backgrounds.

Byzantium: The Decline and Fall John Julius Norwich

The final volume in the magnificent history of Byzantium. 'As we pass among the spectacularly varied scenes of war, intrigue, theological debate, martial kerfuffle, sacrifice, revenge, blazing ambition and lordly pride, our guide calms our passions with an infinity of curious asides and grace-notes ... Norwich's great trilogy has dispersed none of this magic' – *Independent*

The Anglo-Saxons Edited by James Campbell

'For anyone who wishes to understand the broad sweep of English history, Anglo-Saxon society is an important and fascinating subject. And Campbell's is an important and fascinating book. It is also a finely produced and, at times, a very beautiful book' – *London Review of Books*

Conditions of Liberty Ernest Gellner

'A lucid and brilliant analysis ... he gives excellent reasons for preferring civil society to democracy as the institutional key to modernization ... For Gellner, civil society is a remarkable concept. It is both an inspiring slogan and the reality at the heart of the modern world' – *The Times*

The Habsburgs Andrew Wheatcroft

'Wheatcroft has ... a real feel for the heterogeneous geography of the Habsburg domains – I especially admired his feel for the Spanish Habsburgs. Time and again, he neatly links the monarchs with the specific monuments they constructed for themselves' – *Sunday Telegraph*

READ MORE IN PENGUIN

HISTORY

Citizens Simon Schama

The award-winning chronicle of the French Revolution. 'The most marvellous book I have read about the French Revolution in the last fifty years' – Richard Cobb in *The Times*

The Lure of the Sea Alain Corbin

Alain Corbin's wonderful book explores the dramatic change in Western attitude towards the sea and seaside pleasures that occured between 1750 and 1840. 'A compact and brilliant taxonomy of the shifting meanings of the sea and shore' – *New York Review of Books*

The Tyranny of History W. J. F. Jenner

A fifth of the world's population lives within the boundaries of China, a vast empire barely under the control of the repressive ruling Communist regime. Beneath the economic boom China is in a state of crisis that goes far deeper than the problems of its current leaders to a value system that is rooted in the autocratic traditions of China's past.

The English Bible and the Seventeenth-Century Revolution
Christopher Hill

'What caused the English civil war? What brought Charles I to the scaffold?' Answer to both questions: the Bible. To sustain this provocative thesis, Christopher Hill's new book maps English intellectual history from the Reformation to 1660, showing how scripture dominated every department of thought from sexual relations to political theory ... 'His erudition is staggering' – *Sunday Times*

Fisher's Face Jan Morris

'*Fisher's Face* is funny, touching and informed by wide reading as well as wide travelling' – *New Statesman & Society*. 'A richly beguiling picture of the Victorian Navy, its profound inner security, its glorious assumptions, its extravagant social life and its traditionally eccentric leaders' – *Independent on Sunday*